Introduction to Parallel Computing

Design and Analysis of Algorithms

Vipin Kumar
Ananth Grama
Anshul Gupta
George Karypis

University of Minnesota

The Benjamin/Cummings Publishing Company, Inc.
Redwood City, California ▪ Menlo Park, California
Reading, Massachusetts ▪ New York ▪ Don Mills, Ontario ▪ Wokingham, U.K.
Amsterdam ▪ Bonn ▪ Sydney ▪ Singapore ▪ Tokyo ▪ Madrid ▪ San Juan

Executive editor: *Dan Joraanstad*
Sponsoring editor: *Carter Shanklin*
Editorial assitant: *Melissa Standen*
Production supervisor: *Gwen Larson*
Production management: *Matrix Productions*
Cover design: *Yvo Riezebos Design*

Library of Congress Cataloging-in-Publication Data

Introduction to parallel computing : design and analysis of parallel algorithms
Vipin Kumar... [et al.].
p. cm.
Includes biographical references and index.
ISBN 0-8053-3170-0
1. Parallel processing (Electonic computers) 2. Computer algorithms.
I. Grama, Ananth. II. Gupta, Anshul. III. Karypis, George.
QA76.58.I58 1994
005.2—dc20 93-34230

ISBN 0-8053-3170-0

4 5 6 7 8 9 10-CRW-98 97

The Benjamin/Cummings Publishing Company, Inc.
390 Bridge Parkway
Redwood City, California 94065

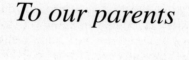

To our parents

Contents

CHAPTER 4

Performance and Scalability of Parallel Systems 117

CHAPTER 5

Dense Matrix Algorithms 151

CHAPTER 9

Dynamic Programming 355

CHAPTER 10

Fast Fourier Transform 377

CHAPTER 11

Solving Sparse Systems of Linear Equations 407

CHAPTER 13

Parallel Programming 525

APPENDIX A

Complexity of Functions and Order Analysis 571

Preface

Parallel computers consisting of thousands of processors are now commercially available. These computers provide many orders of magnitude more raw computing power than traditional supercomputers at much lower cost. They open up new frontiers in the application of computers—many previously unsolvable problems can be solved if the power of these machines is used effectively. The availability of massively parallel computers has created a number of challenges, for example: How should parallel computers be programmed? What algorithms and data structures should be used? How can the quality of the algorithms be analyzed? Which algorithms are suitable for particular parallel computer architectures?

This book attempts to answer these and other questions about parallel computing. It presents a self-contained discussion of the basic concepts of parallel computer architectures and parallel algorithms for a variety of applications. The text is intended for senior undergraduate and graduate-level students, but is advanced enough to serve as a reference for practicing algorithm designers and application programmers. We hope that this book will bring an understanding of parallel processing to a wide range of people interested in solving problems on parallel computers.

Most of the material has been extensively class-tested. The book evolved out of a series of courses on related topics taught by the senior author, Vipin Kumar, over the past ten years. The other three authors have been actively conducting research on parallel computing under the supervision of the senior author. In Fall 1992, they joined him to prepare a comprehensive textbook on the design, analysis, and implementation of parallel algorithms on different parallel architectures. In particular, Ananth Grama took charge of Chapters 1, 2, 8, and 9; Anshul Gupta wrote Chapters 3, 4, 5, 10, and 11; and George Karypis was responsible for Chapters 6, 7, 12, and 13.

It is impossible to cover all the material in this book in a single course. However, a variety of courses can be taught using different chapters. Some suggestions for course contents are:

(1) *Introduction to Parallel Computing*: Chapters 1 and 2, selected parts of Chapters 3, 4, and 13, and a sample of algorithms from the remaining chapters.

(2) *Design and Analysis of Parallel Algorithms*: Chapter 1, portions of Chapters 2, 3, and 4, and selected algorithms from Chapters 5 through 12.

(3) *Parallel Numerical Algorithms* or *Parallel Scientific Computing*: Chapters 1, 5, and 10–12, and parts of Chapters 2–4 and 13.

The senior author has been teaching a two-quarter sequence titled *Introduction to Parallel Computing* in the Computer Science Department at the University of Minnesota using drafts of the book. The first seven chapters are covered in the first quarter, and the remaining six in the second quarter. The senior author also teaches the course *High Performance Computing* for the scientific computing program at the University of Minnesota. This course is taken primarily by graduate students in the sciences and engineering (such as mechanical engineering, chemistry, and biology) who are interested in solving computationally intensive problems on parallel computers. This course covers parts of Chapters 1–5, 11, and 13.

Most chapters of the book include (1) examples and illustrations, (2) problems that supplement the text and test students' understanding of the material, and (3) bibliographic remarks to aid researchers and students interested in learning more about related and advanced topics. The notation used to express the complexity of functions and order analysis is explained in Appendix A. A glossary was originally planned, but was dropped in favor of a comprehensive index. In the index, the number of the page on which a term is explicitly defined appears in boldface type. Furthermore, the term itself appears in bold italics where it is defined. The sections that deal with relatively complicated material are preceded by a '⋆'. An instructors' manual containing slides of the figures and solutions to selected problems is also available from the publisher.

We view this book as a continually evolving resource. Readers are encouraged to send suggestions and information related to the material in the book to the authors, preferably by electronic mail to *book-vk@cs.umn.edu*. We welcome ideas, opinions, critiques, new problems, and programs for the algorithms in the book. Any such input will be added to the information archived in the directory *bc/kumar* at the anonymous FTP site *bc.aw.com* with due credits to the sender(s). On-line errata for the text will be maintained at the same site. In the highly-dynamic field of parallel computing, there is a lot to be gained from a healthy exchange of ideas in this manner.

Acknowledgements

Working on this project has been a source of great pleasure for us. At this juncture, we would like to acknowledge the people who worked with us and helped make this project a reality. We are most indebted to **Tom Nurkkala** and **Daniel Challou**, whose untiring editorial efforts have gone a long way to improve the quality of the text. They read every chapter several times, and gave technical, grammatical, and typesetting comments. Furthermore, their suggestions led to the addition of many new examples and illustrations. Without their contribution, this project would have stretched far longer and the impact of the book would have been diminished. We also express our gratitude to **Michael Heath**, who took great personal interest in the project. His comments were invaluable in improving both the technical content and the quality of the material presented. We appreciate the efforts of Gregory Andrews, Daniel Boley, Shantanu Dutt, Rob Fowler, Joydeep Ghosh, Dirk Grunwald, John Gustafson, Charles Martel, Dan Miranker, Viktor Prasanna, Youcef Saad, and Vikram Saletore in reviewing the manuscript and suggesting improvements. Victor Prasanna used parts of the preliminary drafts of the book for his class and provided valuable feedback. Any remaining errors or omissions in the text are the sole responsibility of the authors.

Many other people contributed to this project in different ways. We thank Jake Aggarwal, Gul Agha, Mani Chandy, Tom Cormen, Tse-Yun Feng, David Fox, Robert Hiromoto, Kai Hwang, Bharat Jairaman, L. V. Kale, Laveen Kanal, Tom Leighton, Babu Narayanan, Lionel Ni, Michael Quinn, Ben Rosen, Sartaj Sahni, Ahmed Sameh, Vineet Singh, Larry Snyder, and N. R. Vempaty for providing valuable input at various stages. We thank the students of the *Introduction to Parallel Computing* course at the University of Minnesota for identifying and working through errors in the drafts. In particular, comments from Minesh Amin, Dan Frankowski, Dave Truckenmiller, and Steve Waldo were very useful. We are thankful to Amy Gaukel for meticulously checking all the references and correcting the errors in them. It was a pleasure to work with the cooperative and helpful staff at Benjamin/Cummings. In particular, we thank John Carter Shanklin, Melissa Standen, Merrill Peterson, Dan Joranstad, and Adam Ray for their effort and cooperation.

We thank our family members, Akash, Chethan, Kalpana, Krista, Renu, Vipasha, and Anshu, for their affectionate support, patience, and encouragement throughout the duration of this project.

The Army Research Office (ARO) and the National Science Foundation provided support to the senior author for parallel computing research over the last decade. In particular, we thank Dr. Jag Chandra and Dr. Ken Clark of the ARO for supporting our research on scalable parallel algorithms at an early stage. Many of the results of this research appear in the book. The Army High Performance Computing Research Center and the Department of Computer Science at the University of Minnesota provided an active and nurturing environment for conducting research. We express our gratitude to the University of Minnesota for the computing facilities used to prepare the manuscript.

Vipin Kumar
Ananth Grama
Anshul Gupta
George Karypis

Minneapolis, Minnesota

CHAPTER 1

Introduction

Ever since conventional serial computers were invented, their speed has steadily increased to match the needs of emerging applications. However, the fundamental physical limitation imposed by the speed of light makes it impossible to achieve further improvements in the speed of such computers indefinitely. Recent trends show that the performance of these computers is beginning to saturate. A natural way to circumvent this saturation is to use an ensemble of processors to solve problems.

A cost-performance comparison of serial computers over the last few decades shows an interesting evolutionary trend. Figure 1.1 represents typical cost-performance curves of serial computers over the past three decades. At the lower end of each curve, performance increases almost linearly (or even faster than linearly) with cost. However, beyond a certain point, each curve starts to saturate, and even small gains in performance come at an exorbitant increase in cost. Furthermore, this transition point has become sharper with the passage of time, primarily as a result of advances in very large scale integration (VLSI)

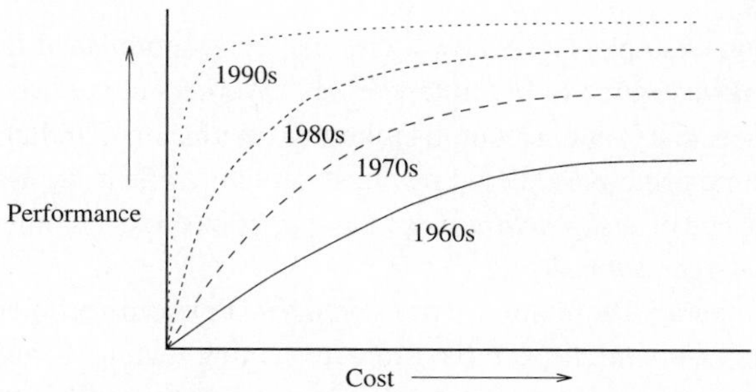

Figure 1.1 Cost versus performance curve and its evolution over the decades.

technology. It is now possible to construct very fast, low-cost processors. This increases the demand for and production of these processors, resulting in lower prices.

Currently, the speed of off-the-shelf microprocessors is within one order of magnitude of the speed of the fastest serial computers. However, microprocessors cost many orders of magnitude less. This implies that, by connecting only a few microprocessors together to form a parallel computer, it is possible to obtain raw computing power comparable to that of the fastest serial computers. Typically, the cost of such a parallel computer is considerably less.

Furthermore, connecting a large number of processors into a parallel computer overcomes the saturation point of the computation rates achievable by serial computers. Thus, parallel computers can provide much higher raw computation rates than the fastest serial computers as long as this power can be translated into high computation rates for actual applications.

1.1 What is Parallel Computing?

This section illustrates some important aspects of parallel computing by drawing an analogy to a real-life scenario.

Consider the problem of stacking (reshelving) a set of library books. A single worker trying to stack all the books in their proper places cannot accomplish the task faster than a certain rate. We can speed up this process, however, by employing more than one worker. Assume that the books are organized into shelves and that the shelves are grouped into bays. One simple way to assign the task to the workers is to divide the books equally among them. Each worker stacks the books one at a time. This division of work may not be the most efficient way to accomplish the task, since the workers must walk all over the library to stack books. An alternate way to divide the work is to assign a fixed and disjoint set of bays to each worker. As before, each worker is assigned an equal number of books arbitrarily. If a worker finds a book that belongs to a bay assigned to him or her, he or she places that book in its assigned spot. Otherwise, he or she passes it on to the worker responsible for the bay it belongs to. The second approach requires less effort from individual workers.

The preceding example shows how a task can be accomplished faster by dividing it into a set of subtasks assigned to multiple workers. Workers cooperate, pass the books to each other when necessary, and accomplish the task in unison. Parallel processing works on precisely the same principles. Dividing a task among workers by assigning them a set of books is an instance of ***task partitioning***. Passing books to each other is an example of ***communication*** between subtasks.

Problems are parallelizable to different degrees. For some problems, assigning partitions to other processors might be more time-consuming than performing the processing locally. Other problems may be completely serial. For example, consider the task of digging a post hole. Although one person can dig a hole in a certain amount of time, employing more people does not reduce this time. Because it is impossible to partition this task, it is poorly suited to parallel processing. Therefore, a problem may have different parallel formulations, which result in varying benefits, and all problems are not equally amenable to parallel processing.

1.2 The Scope of Parallel Computing

Parallel processing is making a tremendous impact on many areas of computer application. With the high raw computing power of parallel computers, it is now possible to address many applications that were until recently beyond the capability of conventional computing techniques.

Many applications, such as weather prediction, biosphere modeling, and pollution monitoring, are modeled by imposing a grid over the domain being modeled. The entities within grid elements are simulated with respect to the influence of other entities and their surroundings. In many cases, this requires solutions to large systems of differential equations. The granularity of the grid determines the accuracy of the model. Since many such systems are evolving with time, time forms an additional dimension for these computations. Even for a small number of grid points, a three-dimensional coordinate system, and a reasonable discretized time step, this modeling process can involve trillions of operations (Example 1.1). Thus, even moderate-sized instances of these problems take an unacceptably long time to solve on serial computers.

Example 1.1 Weather Modeling and Forecasting

Consider the modeling of weather over an area of 3000×3000 miles. The parameters must also be modeled along the vertical plane. Assume that the area is being modeled up to a height of 11 miles. Assume that the $3000 \times 3000 \times 11$ cubic mile domain is partitioned into segments of size $0.1 \times 0.1 \times 0.1$ cubic miles. There are approximately 10^{11} different segments. The weather modeling process involves time as another dimension. Time is quantized and parameters are computed for each segment at regular time intervals.

Let us further assume that we are modeling the weather over a two-day period and the parameters need to be computed once every half hour. (Note that the assumptions are conservative and more accurate modeling requires much higher computation rates.) The computation of parameters inside a segment uses the initial values and the values from neighboring segments. Assume that this computation takes 100 instructions. Therefore, a single updating of the parameters in the entire domain requires $10^{11} \times 100$, or 10^{13} instructions. Since this has to be done approximately 100 times (two days), the total number of operations is 10^{15}. On a serial supercomputer capable of performing one billion instructions per second, this modeling would take approximately 280 hours. Taking 280 hours to predict the weather for the next 48 hours is unreasonable to say the least.

Parallel processing makes it possible to predict the weather not only faster but also more accurately. If we have a parallel computer with a thousand workstation-class processors, we can partition the 10^{11} segments of the domain among these processors. Each processor computes the parameters for 10^8 segments. Processors communicate the value of the parameters in their segments to other processors. Assuming that the computing power of this computer is 100 million instructions per second, and this power is efficiently utilized, the problem can be solved in less than 3 hours. The impact of this reduction in processing time is two-fold. First, parallel computers make it possible to solve a previously unsolvable problem. Second, with the availability of even larger parallel computers, it is possible to model weather using finer grids. This enables more accurate weather prediction. ■

The acquisition and processing of large amounts of data from sources such as satellites and oil wells form another class of computationally expensive problems. Conventional satellites collect billions of bits per second of data relating to parameters such as pollution levels, the thickness of the ozone layer, and weather phenomena. Other applications of satellites that require processing of large amounts of data include remote sensing and telemetry. The computational rates required for handling this data effectively are well beyond the range of conventional serial computers.

Discrete optimization problems include such computationally intensive problems as planning, scheduling, VLSI design, logistics, and control. Discrete optimization problems can be solved by using state-space search techniques. For many of these problems, the size of the state-space increases exponentially with the number of variables. Problems that evaluate trillions of states are fairly commonplace in most such applications. Since processing each state requires a nontrivial amount of computation, finding solutions to large instances of these problems is beyond the scope of conventional sequential computing. Indeed, many practical problems are solved using approximate algorithms that provide suboptimal solutions.

Other applications that can benefit significantly from parallel computing are semiconductor material modeling, ocean modeling, computer tomography, quantum chromodynamics, vehicle design and dynamics, analysis of protein structures, study of chemical phenomena, imaging, ozone layer monitoring, petroleum exploration, natural language understanding, speech recognition, neural network learning, machine vision, database query processing, and automated discovery of concepts and patterns from large databases. Many of the applications mentioned in this section are considered *grand challenge* problems. A ***grand challenge*** is a fundamental problem in science or engineering that has a broad economic and scientific impact, and whose solution could be advanced by applying high-performance computing techniques and resources.

1.3 Issues in Parallel Computing

To use parallel computing effectively, we need to examine the following issues:

Design of Parallel Computers It is important to design parallel computers that can scale up to a large number of processors and are capable of supporting fast communication and data sharing among processors. This is one aspect of parallel computing that has seen the most advances and is the most mature.

Design of Efficient Algorithms A parallel computer is of little use unless efficient parallel algorithms are available. The issues in designing parallel algorithms are very different from those in designing their sequential counterparts. A significant amount of work is being done to develop efficient parallel algorithms for a variety of parallel architectures.

Methods for Evaluating Parallel Algorithms Given a parallel computer and a parallel algorithm running on it, we need to evaluate the performance of the resulting system. Performance analysis allows us to answer questions such as *How fast can a problem be solved using parallel processing?* and *How efficiently are the processors used?*

Parallel Computer Languages Parallel algorithms are implemented on parallel computers using a programming language. This language must be flexible enough to allow efficient implementation and must be easy to program in. New languages and programming paradigms are being developed that try to achieve these goals.

Parallel Programming Tools To facilitate the programming of parallel computers, it is important to develop comprehensive programming environments and tools. These must serve the dual purpose of shielding users from low-level machine characteristics and providing them with design and development tools such as debuggers and simulators.

Portable Parallel Programs Portability is one of the main problems with current parallel computers. Typically, a program written for one parallel computer requires extensive modification to make it run on another parallel computer. This is an important issue that is receiving considerable attention.

Automatic Programming of Parallel Computers Much work is being done on the design of parallelizing compilers, which extract implicit parallelism from programs that have not been parallelized explicitly. Such compilers are expected to allow us to program a parallel computer like a serial computer. We speculate that this approach has limited potential for exploiting the power of large-scale parallel computers.

1.4 Organization and Contents of the Text

This book addresses many of the issues listed in Section 1.3. Architectural models are discussed in Chapter 2, performance metrics are discussed in Chapter 4, parallel algorithms for many numerical and non-numerical problems are discussed in Chapters 5–11, and programming paradigms are discussed in Chapter 13.

Let us now take a closer look at our approach to the design and analysis of parallel algorithms. This text is designed to be a comprehensive and self-contained exposition of problem solving using parallel computers. Although the emphasis of this book is on the design of algorithms, the necessary foundation of hardware principles and programming paradigms is also provided. The algorithms we present are designed and analyzed primarily for hypercube and mesh architectures. The selection of these architectures is based on several criteria which are discussed in detail in Section 2.9. Where appropriate, the PRAM model (which is an idealized model) is used to illustrate the concurrency inherent in an algorithm.

A commonly used approach to parallel algorithm design and analysis is to assume that the number of processors is equal to the number of input elements. However, this assumption is not always useful because for most problems, it is unrealistic to use as many processors as the number of inputs. For example, it is unrealistic to employ a million processors to sort a sequence of one million numbers. Parallel algorithms designed for one input element per processor are often inefficient compared to algorithms that assign multiple input elements to each processor. In this book, we design and analyze algorithms using the latter approach, although the single-element-per-processor case is often used to illustrate the parallelism in a computation.

We design parallel algorithms using a small class of basic communication operations as building blocks. This simplifies the design of algorithms for parallel architectures with diverse interconnection topologies and performance characteristics. Our approach facilitates porting an algorithm between different parallel architectures, as only the basic communication operations need to be reimplemented.

In addition to conventional parallel performance metrics, an important characteristic of a parallel algorithm is its scalability on a parallel architecture. Scalability is the ability of a parallel algorithm to use an increasing number of processors efficiently. We present a performance and scalability analysis for most algorithms in the book. We use the isoefficiency metric for characterizing the scalability of a parallel algorithm-architecture combination.

As Figure 1.2 shows, the book consists of three main focus areas and a few miscellaneous topics. The detailed organization of the book is as follows:

Fundamentals The first four chapters discuss fundamental topics. Chapter 2 introduces an abstract model of computation as well as various architectures and hardware models that form platforms for parallel computing. The properties and costs of different architectures are discussed in detail. The aim of this chapter is to provide the essential background on parallel computer architectures for understanding and analyzing the performance of the algorithms presented in subsequent chapters.

Chapter 3 describes many fundamental data communication operations for different architectures and analyzes their complexity. Most algorithms presented in the book use the basic operations described in this chapter as building blocks.

We present the performance metrics for analyzing parallel algorithms in Chapter 4. We describe the conventional metrics for analyzing the performance of parallel algorithms,

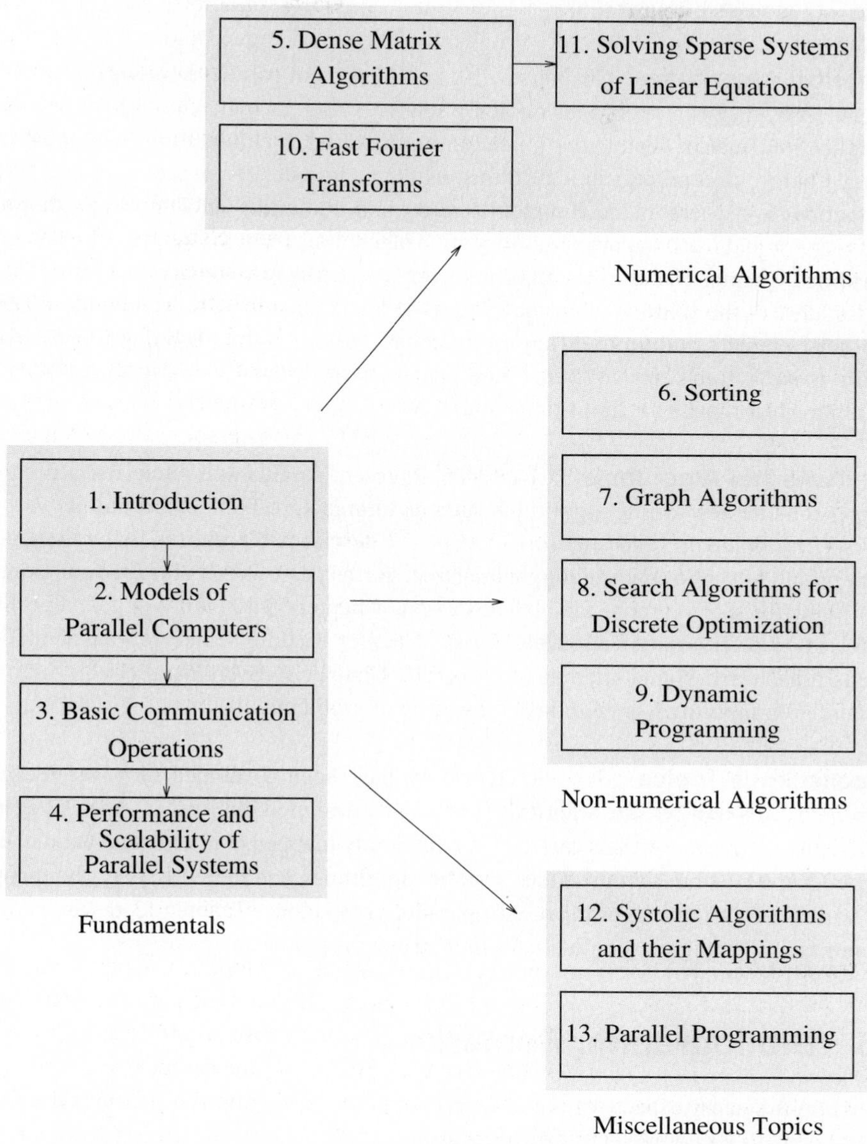

Figure 1.2 Recommended sequence for reading the chapters.

as well as the isoefficiency metric for characterizing the scalability of a parallel algorithm-architecture combination. In Chapter 4, we further motivate our approach of designing and analyzing algorithms while maintaining the input size of a problem and the number of processors as two separate entities.

Numerical Algorithms Chapters 5, 10, and 11 present parallel numerical algorithms. Chapter 5 covers basic operations on dense matrices such as matrix transposition, matrix multiplication, matrix-vector multiplication, and Gaussian elimination. This chapter is included before non-numerical algorithms, as the techniques for partitioning and assigning matrices to processors are common to many non-numerical algorithms. Furthermore, matrix-vector and matrix-matrix multiplication algorithms form the kernels of some graph algorithms. Chapter 10 describes algorithms for computing fast Fourier transforms. Chapter 11 addresses the solution of sparse systems of linear equations, especially those arising from finite element and finite difference methods. Both iterative and direct methods for solving these systems are covered. The chapter also discusses multigrid methods and partitioning techniques for finite element graphs.

Non-numerical Algorithms Chapters 6–9 present parallel non-numerical algorithms. Chapter 6 addresses sorting algorithms such as bitonic sort, bubble sort and its variants, quicksort, sample sort, and shellsort. Chapter 7 describes algorithms for various graph theory problems such as minimum spanning tree, shortest paths, and connected components. Algorithms for sparse graphs are also discussed. Chapters 8 and 9 investigate algorithms for solving discrete optimization problems. Chapter 8 addresses search-based methods such as branch-and-bound and heuristic search. Chapter 9 covers parallel algorithms for dynamic programming formulations of a variety of problems.

Miscellaneous Topics Systolic algorithms have been developed for a variety of applications. Although systolic algorithms are usually designed for problem-specific systolic architectures, these algorithms can often be efficiently mapped onto practical parallel computers. Chapter 12 briefly introduces systolic algorithms, and then discusses the mapping of a variety of systolic algorithms onto parallel computers. Chapter 13 discusses many programming paradigms and illustrates them using programs and examples.

1.5 Bibliographic Remarks

Many books discuss aspects of parallel processing at varying levels of detail. Hardware aspects of parallel computers have been discussed extensively in several textbooks and monographs [AG89, AG94, DeC89, HB84, Hwa93, RF89, Sie85, Sto93, Tab90, Tab91, WF84, Woo86]. A number of texts discuss paradigms and languages for programming parallel computers [And91, AO93, BA82, Bab88, Ble90, Bra89, Con89, CT92, Les93, Per87, Wal91]. Chandy and Misra [CM88] present a methodology for developing provably correct parallel programs by using the UNITY paradigm. Akl [Akl89], Cole [Col89],

Gibbons and Rytter [GR90], Kronsjo [Kro85], Leighton [Lei92], Miller and Stout [MS92], Quinn [Qui87, Qui94], Reif [Rei93], and Smith [Smi93] discuss various aspects of parallel algorithm design and analysis. Jaja [Jaj92] covers parallel algorithms for the PRAM model of computation. Hillis [Hil85, HS86] and Hatcher and Quinn [HQ91] discuss data-parallel programming. Agha [Agh86] discusses a model of concurrent computation based on *actors*. Sharp [Sha85] addresses data-flow computing. Some books provide a general overview of topics in parallel computing [CL93, JGD87, LER92, Mol93, Rei93, SB90, Qui94].

Many books address parallel processing applications in numerical analysis and scientific computing [Car89, DDSvdV91, G$^+$90, GO93, LD90, Mod88, Ort88, Rob90]. Fox et al. [FJL$^+$88] and Angus et al. [AFKW90] provide an application-oriented view of algorithm design for problems in scientific computing. Bertsekas and Tsitsiklis [BT89] discuss parallel algorithms, with emphasis on numerical applications.

Akl and Lyons [AL93] discuss parallel algorithms in computational geometry. Ranka and Sahni [RS90] and Dew, Earnshaw, and Heywood [DEH89] address parallel algorithms for use in computer vision. Green [Gre91] covers parallel algorithms for graphics applications. Many books address the use of parallel processing in artificial intelligence applications [Gup87, HD89, KGK90, KKKS94, Kow88, RZ89, Uhr87].

A useful collection of reviews, bibliographies and indexes has been put together by the Association for Computing Machinery [ACM91]. Messina and Murli [MM91] present a collection of papers on various aspects of the application and potential of parallel computing. The scope of parallel processing and its application to grand challenge problems is discussed by Kaufmann and Smarr [KS93] and in a National Science Foundation report [NSF91]. A report of the Office of Science and Technology Policy [Pre87] defines grand challenge problems, and another report [Pre89] gives a comprehensive list of them.

A number of conferences address various aspects of parallel computing. A few important ones are the ACM Symposium on Parallel Algorithms and Architectures, the Distributed Memory Computing Conference, the International Conference on Parallel Processing, the International Parallel Processing Symposium, the International Conference on Supercomputing, the Symposium on the Frontiers of Massively Parallel Computing, Parallel Computing, the SIAM Conference on Parallel Processing for Scientific Computing, and Supercomputing. Important journals in parallel processing include IEEE Transactions on Parallel and Distributed Systems, International Journal of Parallel Programming, Journal of Parallel and Distributed Computing, Parallel Computing, Parallel Algorithms and Applications, Concurrency: Practice and Experience, and Parallel Processing Letters. These proceedings and journals provide a rich source of information on the state of the art in parallel processing.

Problems

1.1 Consider the problem of adding n numbers. Assume that one person can add two numbers in time t_c. How long will a person take to add n numbers?

Now assume that eight people are available for adding these n numbers and that it is possible to divide the list into eight parts. The eight people have their own pencils and paper (on which to perform additions), are equally skilled, and can add two numbers in time t_c. Furthermore, a person can pass on the result of an addition (in the form of a single number) to the person sitting next to him or her in time t_w. How long will it take to add n numbers in the following scenarios:

(a) All eight people are sitting in a circle.

(b) The eight people are sitting in two rows of four people each.

1.2 Assume the scenario described in Problem 1.1. If you had the liberty of seating the people in any acceptable configuration, how would you seat them so as to minimize the time taken to add the list of numbers? (An acceptable configuration is defined as follows: Assume that the adders are vertices of a graph and that *neighborhood* is defined by the edges between the vertices. Any graph that can be drawn on a piece of paper and that has no intersecting edges represents an acceptable configuration.) What is the time taken by your configuration?

1.3 Consider again the problem of adding n numbers. Assume that one person takes time $t_c(n-1)$ to add these numbers. Is it possible for p people to add this list in time less than $t_c(n-1)/p$? Justify your answer.

1.4 Consider again the scenario of Problem 1.1, but assume that all eight people are adding the numbers standing at a blackboard. Each person can see results from the other person's calculations as they are completed (that is, instantaneously). How long would the eight people take to add the n numbers in this case?

1.5 Answer Problem 1.3 in the context of the scenario presented in Problem 1.4. Is your answer different for this scenario? If so, what specific change resulted in a different answer?

References

[ACM91] ACM. *Resources in Parallel and Concurrent Systems*. ACM Press, New York, NY, 1991.

[AFKW90] I. Angus, G. C. Fox, J. Kim, and D. Walker. *Solving Problems on Concurrent Processors: Software for Concurrent Processors: Volume II*. Prentice-Hall, Englewood Cliffs, NJ, 1990.

[AG89] G. S. Almasi and A. Gottlieb. *Highly Parallel Computing*. Benjamin/Cummings, Redwood City, CA, 1989.

[AG94] G. S. Almasi and A. Gottlieb. *Highly Parallel Computing: Second Edition*. Benjamin/Cummings, Redwood City, CA, 1994.

[Agh86] G. Agha. *Actors: A Model of Concurrent Computation in Distributed Systems*. MIT Press, Cambridge, MA, 1986.

[Akl89] S. G. Akl. *The Design and Analysis of Parallel Algorithms*. Prentice-Hall, Englewood Cliffs, NJ, 1989.

[AL93] S. G. Akl and K. A. Lyons. *Parallel Computational Geometry*. Prentice-Hall, Englewood Cliffs, NJ, 1993.

[And91] G. R. Andrews. *Concurrent Programming: Principles and Practice*. Benjamin/Cummings, Redwood City, CA, 1991.

[AO93] G. R. Andrews and R. A. Olsson. *The SR Programming Language: Concurrency in Practice*. Benjamin/Cummings, Redwood City, CA, 1993.

[BA82] M. Ben-Ari. *Principles of Concurrent Programming*. Prentice-Hall, Englewood Cliffs, NJ, 1982.

[Bab88] R. G. Babb. *Programming Parallel Processors*. Addison-Wesley, Reading, MA, 1988.

[Ble90] G. E. Blelloch. *Vector Models for Data-Parallel Computing*. MIT Press, Cambridge, MA, 1990.

[Bra89] S. Brawer. *Introduction to Parallel Programming*. Academic Press, Boston, MA, 1989.

[BT89] D. P. Bertsekas and J. N. Tsitsiklis. *Parallel and Distributed Computation: Numerical Methods*. Prentice-Hall, Englewood Cliffs, NJ, 1989.

[Car89] G. F. Carey, editor. *Parallel Supercomputing: Methods, Algorithms and Applications*. Wiley, New York, NY, 1989.

[CL93] B. Codenotti and M. Leoncini. *Introduction to Parallel Processing*. Addison-Wesley, Reading, MA, 1993.

[CM88] K. M. Chandy and J. Misra. *Parallel Program Design: A Foundation*. Addison-Wesley, Reading, MA, 1988.

[Col89] M. Cole. *Algorithmic Skeletons: Structured Management of Parallel Computation*. MIT Press, Cambridge, MA, 1989.

[Con89] T. Conlon. *Programming in PARLOG*. Addison-Wesley, Reading, MA, 1989.

[CT92] K. M. Chandy and S. Taylor. *An Introduction to Parallel Programming*. Jones and Bartlett, Austin, TX, 1992.

[DDSvdV91] J. J. Dongarra, I. S. Duff, D. C. Sorensen, and H. A. van der Vorst. *Solving Linear Systems on Vector and Shared Memory Computers*. SIAM, Philadelphia, PA, 1991.

[DeC89] A. L. DeCegama. *The Technology of Parallel Processing: Parallel Processing Architectures and VLSI Hardware: Volume 1*. Prentice-Hall, Englewood Cliffs, NJ, 1989.

[DEH89] P. M. Dew, R. A. Earnshaw, and T. R. Heywood. *Parallel Processing for Computer Vision and Display*. Addison-Wesley, Reading, MA, 1989.

[FJL$^+$88] G. C. Fox, M. Johnson, G. Lyzenga, S. W. Otto, J. Salmon, and D. Walker. *Solving Problems on Concurrent Processors: Volume 1*. Prentice-Hall, Englewood Cliffs, NJ, 1988.

[G$^+$90] K. A. Gallivan et al. *Parallel Algorithms for Matrix Computations*. SIAM, Philadelphia, PA, 1990.

[GO93] G. H. Golub and J. M. Ortega. *Scientific Computing: An Introduction with Parallel Computing*. Academic Press, Boston, MA, 1993.

[GR90] A. Gibbons and W. Rytter. *Efficient Parallel Algorithms*. Cambridge University Press, Cambridge, UK, 1990.

[Gre91] S. Green. *Parallel Processing for Computer Graphics*. MIT Press, Cambridge, MA, 1991.

[Gup87] A. Gupta. *Parallelism in Production Systems.* Morgan Kaufmann, Los Altos, CA, 1987.

[HB84] K. Hwang and F. A. Briggs. *Computer Architecture and Parallel Processing.* McGraw-Hill, New York, NY, 1984.

[HD89] K. Hwang and D. DeGroot. *Parallel Processing for Supercomputers and Artificial Intelligence.* McGraw-Hill, New York, NY, 1989.

[Hil85] W. D. Hillis. *The Connection Machine.* MIT Press, Cambridge, MA, 1985.

[HQ91] P. J. Hatcher and M. J. Quinn. *Data Parallel Programming.* MIT Press, Cambridge, MA, 1991.

[HS86] W. D. Hillis and G. L. Steele. Data parallel algorithms. *Communications of the ACM*, 29(12):1170–1183, 1986.

[Hwa93] K. Hwang. *Advanced Computer Architecture: Parallelism, Scalability, Programmability.* McGraw-Hill, New York, NY, 1993.

[Jaj92] J. Jaja. *An Introduction to Parallel Algorithms.* Addison-Wesley, Reading, MA, 1992.

[JGD87] L. H. Jamieson, D. B. Gannon, and R. J. Douglass, editors. *The Characteristics of Parallel Algorithms.* MIT Press, Cambridge, MA, 1987.

[KGK90] V. Kumar, P. S. Gopalakrishnan, and L. N. Kanal, editors. *Parallel Algorithms for Machine Intelligence and Vision.* Springer-Verlag, New York, NY, 1990.

[KKKS94] L. N. Kanal, V. Kumar, H. Kitano, and C. Suttner, editors. *Parallel Processing for Artificial Intelligence.* North-Holland, Amsterdam, The Netherlands, 1994.

[Kow88] J. S. Kowalik. *Parallel Computation and Computers for Artificial Intelligence.* Kluwer Academic Publishers, Boston, MA, 1988.

[Kro85] L. Kronsjo. *Computational Complexity of Sequential and Parallel Algorithms.* John Wiley and Sons, New York, NY, 1985.

[KS93] W. J. Kaufmann and L. L. Smarr. *Supercomputing and the Transformation of Science.* Scientific American Library, 1993.

[LD90] S. Lakshmivarahan and S. K. Dhall. *Analysis and Design of Parallel Algorithms: Arithmetic and Matrix Problems.* McGraw-Hill, New York, NY, 1990.

[Lei92] F. T. Leighton. *Introduction to Parallel Algorithms and Architectures.* Morgan Kaufmann, San Mateo, CA, 1992.

[LER92] T. G. Lewis and H. El-Rewini. *Introduction to Parallel Computing.* Prentice-Hall, Englewood Cliffs, NJ, 1992.

[Les93] B. P. Lester. *The Art of Parallel Programming.* Prentice-Hall, Englewood Cliffs, NJ, 1993.

[MM91] P. Messina and A. Murli, editors. *Practical Parallel Computing: Status and Prospects.* Wiley, West Sussex, UK, 1991.

[Mod88] J. J. Modi. *Parallel Algorithms and Matrix Computation.* Oxford University Press, Oxford, UK, 1988.

[Mol93] D. I. Moldovan. *Parallel Processing: From Applications to Systems.* Morgan Kaufmann, San Mateo, CA, 1993.

[MS92] R. Miller and Q. F. Stout. *Parallel Algorithms for Regular Architectures.* MIT Press, Cambridge, MA, 1992.

[NSF91] *Grand Challenges: High Performance Computing and Communications*. A Report by the Committee on Physical, Mathematical and Engineering Sciences, NSF/CISE, 1800 G Street NW, Washington, DC, 20550, 1991.

[Ort88] J. M. Ortega. *Introduction to Parallel and Vector Solution of Linear Systems*. Plenum Press, New York, NY, 1988.

[Per87] R. Perrott. *Parallel Programming*. Addison-Wesley, Reading, MA, 1987.

[Pre87] *A Research and Development Strategy for High Performance Computing*. Office of Science and Technology Policy, Executive Office of the President, November 1987.

[Pre89] *The Federal High Performance Computing Program*. Office of Science and Technology Policy, Executive Office of the President, September 1989.

[Qui87] M. J. Quinn. *Designing Efficient Algorithms for Parallel Computers*. McGraw-Hill, New York, NY, 1987.

[Qui94] M. J. Quinn. *Parallel Computing: Theory and Practice*. McGraw-Hill, New York, NY, 1994.

[Rei93] J. H. Reif, editor. *Synthesis of Parallel Algorithms*. Morgan Kaufmann, San Mateo, CA, 1993.

[RF89] D. A. Reed and R. M. Fujimoto. *Multicomputer Networks: Message-Based Parallel Processing*. MIT Press, Cambridge, MA, 1989.

[Rob90] Y. Robert. *The Impact of Vector and Parallel Architectures on Gaussian Elimination*. John Wiley and Sons, New York, NY, 1990.

[RS90] S. Ranka and S. Sahni. *Hypercube Algorithms for Image Processing and Pattern Recognition*. Springer-Verlag, New York, NY, 1990.

[RZ89] M. Reeve and S. E. Zenith, editors. *Parallel Processing and Artificial Intelligence*. Wiley, West Sussex, UK, 1989.

[SB90] R. Suaya and G. Birtwistle, editors. *VLSI and Parallel Computation*. Morgan Kaufmann, San Mateo, CA, 1990.

[Sha85] J. A. Sharp. *Data-Flow Computing*. Ellis Horwood, West Sussex, UK, 1985.

[Sie85] H. J. Siegel. *Interconnection Networks for Large-Scale Parallel Processing*. D. C. Heath, Lexington, MA, 1985.

[Smi93] J. R. Smith. *The Design and Analysis of Parallel Algorithms*. Oxford University Press, Oxford, UK, 1993.

[Sto93] H. S. Stone. *High-Performance Computer Architectures: Third Edition*. Addison-Wesley, Reading, MA, 1993.

[Tab90] D. Tabak. *Multiprocessors*. Prentice-Hall, Englewood Cliffs, NJ, 1990.

[Tab91] D. Tabak. *Advanced Multiprocessors*. McGraw-Hill, New York, NY, 1991.

[Uhr87] L. M. Uhr, editor. *Multi-Computer Architectures for Artificial Intelligence*. Wiley, West Sussex, UK, 1987.

[Wal91] Y. Wallach. *Parallel Processing and Ada*. Prentice-Hall, Englewood Cliffs, NJ, 1991.

[WF84] C. L. Wu and T. Y. Feng. *Interconnection Networks for Parallel and Distributed Processing*. IEEE Computer Society Press, Washington, DC, 1984.

[Woo86] J. V. Woods, editor. *Fifth Generation Computer Architectures*. North-Holland, Amsterdam, The Netherlands, 1986.

CHAPTER 2

Models of Parallel Computers

Traditional sequential computers are based on the model introduced by John von Neumann. As shown in Figure 2.1, this model consists of a central processing unit (CPU) and memory. This computational model takes a single sequence of instructions and operates on a single sequence of data. Computers of this type are often referred to as ***single instruction stream, single data stream*** (SISD) computers.

The speed of an SISD computer is limited by two factors: the execution rate of instructions and the speed at which information is exchanged between memory and the CPU. The latter can be increased by increasing the number of channels on which data can be accessed simultaneously. This is done by dividing memory into a number of banks, each of which is accessed independently (Figure 2.1(b)). This is called ***memory interleaving***.

Another way to increase the rate of information exchange between the CPU and memory is to use a relatively small and very fast memory to act as a buffer to the larger, slower primary memory. This fast memory is called ***cache memory*** (Figure 2.1(c)). It is possible to fetch a block of data from main memory into the cache, from which data can be exchanged with the CPU at much higher transfer rates. Cache memory uses the principle that if a word is accessed from a part of the memory, it is likely that subsequent memory accesses will be to words in the neighborhood of this memory location.

The rate of execution of instructions can also be increased by overlapping the execution of an instruction with the operation of fetching the next instruction to be executed. Thus, while the CPU is busy executing the current instruction, the next instruction is brought from memory into the instruction queue. This technique is called ***instruction pipelining***. In a related technique called ***execution pipelining***, multiple instructions are allowed to be in various stages of execution in functional units such as multipliers and adders (Figure 2.1(d)).

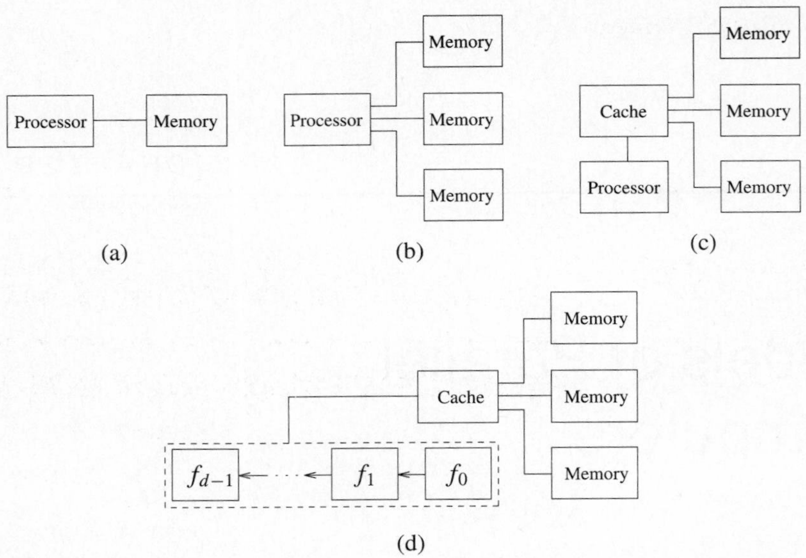

Figure 2.1 The evolution of a typical sequential computer: (a) a simple sequential computer; (b) a sequential computer with memory interleaving; (c) a sequential computer with memory interleaving and cache; and (d) a pipelined processor with d stages.

Memory interleaving, cache memory, and pipelining are now commonly used in high-performance SISD computers; however, they all have limitations. Memory interleaving and, to some extent, pipelining are useful only if a small set of operations is performed on large arrays of data. Cache memories do increase processor-memory bandwidth, but their speed is still limited by hardware technology. An alternate way to speed up the rate of instruction execution is to use multiple CPUs and memory units interconnected in some fashion. The processing rate of such a system grows when the number of CPUs and memory units is increased.

2.1 A Taxonomy of Parallel Architectures

There are many ways in which parallel computers can be constructed. These computers differ along various dimensions such as control mechanism, address-space organization, interconnection network, and granularity of processors.

2.1.1 Control Mechanism

Processing units in parallel computers either operate under the centralized control of a single control unit or work independently. In architectures referred to as ***single instruction***

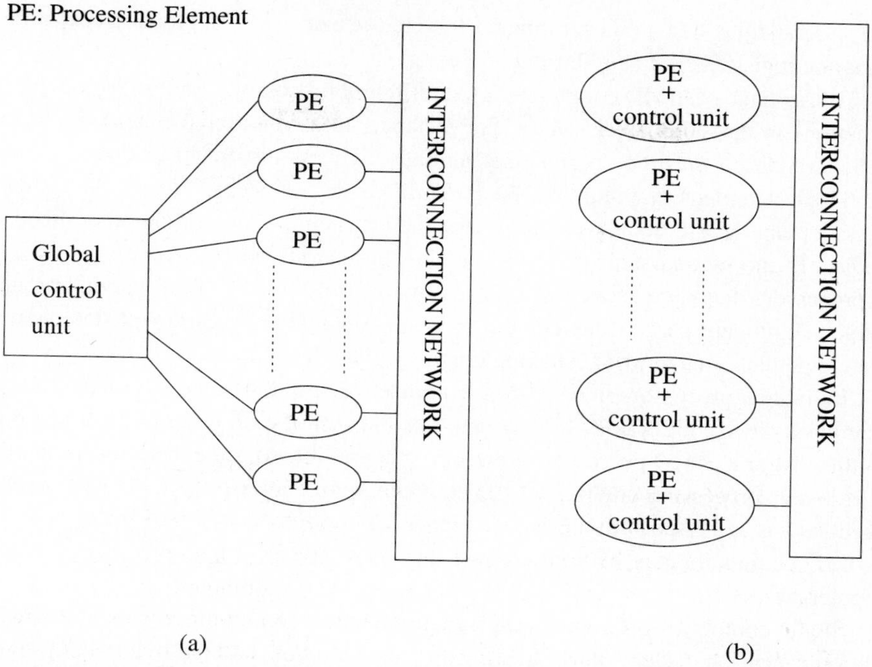

Figure 2.2 A typical SIMD architecture (a) and a typical MIMD architecture (b).

stream, multiple data stream (SIMD), a single control unit dispatches instructions to each processing unit. Figure 2.2(a) illustrates a typical SIMD architecture. In an SIMD parallel computer, the same instruction is executed synchronously by all processing units. Processing units can be selectively switched off during an instruction cycle. Examples of SIMD parallel computers include the Illiac IV, MPP, DAP, CM-2, MasPar MP-1, and MasPar MP-2.

Computers in which each processor is capable of executing a different program independent of the other processors are called ***multiple instruction stream, multiple data stream*** (MIMD) computers. Figure 2.2(b) depicts a typical MIMD computer. Examples of MIMD computers include the Cosmic Cube, nCUBE 2, iPSC, Symmetry, FX-8, FX-2800, TC-2000, CM-5, KSR-1, and Paragon XP/S.

SIMD computers require less hardware than MIMD computers because they have only one global control unit. Furthermore, SIMD computers require less memory because only one copy of the program needs to be stored. In contrast, MIMD computers store the program and operating system at each processor. SIMD computers are naturally suited for ***data-parallel programs***; that is, programs in which the same set of instructions are executed on a large data set. Furthermore, SIMD computers require less startup time (Section 2.7) for communicating with neighboring processors. This is because the communication of a word of data is just like a register transfer (due to the presence of a global clock) with the destination register in the neighboring processor.

A drawback of SIMD computers is that different processors cannot execute different instructions in the same clock cycle. For instance, in a conditional statement, the code for each condition must be executed sequentially. This is illustrated in Figure 2.3. The conditional statement in Figure 2.3(a) is executed in two steps. In the first step, all processors that have B equal to zero execute the instruction $C = A$. All other processors are idle. In the second step, the 'else' part of the instruction ($C = A/B$) is executed. The processors that were active in the first step now become idle. Data-parallel programs in which significant parts of the computation are contained in conditional statements are therefore better suited to MIMD computers than to SIMD computers.

Individual processors in an MIMD computer are more complex, because each processor has its own control unit. It may seem that the cost of each processor must be higher than the cost of a SIMD processor. However, it is possible to use general-purpose microprocessors as processing units in MIMD computers. In contrast, the CPU used in SIMD computers has to be specially designed. Hence, due to the economy of scale, processors in MIMD computers may be both cheaper and more powerful than processors in SIMD computers.

SIMD computers offer automatic synchronization among processors after each instruction execution cycle. Hence, SIMD computers are better suited to parallel programs that require frequent synchronization. Many MIMD computers have extra hardware to provide fast synchronization, which enables them to operate in SIMD mode as well. Examples of such computers are the DADO and CM-5.

2.1.2 Address-Space Organization

Solving a problem on an ensemble of processors requires interaction among processors. The ***message-passing*** and ***shared-address-space*** architectures provide two different means of processor interaction.

Message-Passing Architecture In a message-passing architecture, processors are connected using a message-passing interconnection network. Each processor has its own memory called the ***local*** or ***private memory***, which is accessible only to that processor. Processors can interact only by passing messages. This architecture is also referred to as a ***distributed-memory*** or ***private-memory*** architecture. Figure 2.4 shows the architecture of a typical message-passing architecture. MIMD message-passing computers are commonly referred to as ***multicomputers***. Examples of message-passing parallel computers include the Cosmic Cube, Paragon XP/S, iPSC, CM-5, and nCUBE 2.

Shared-Address-Space Architecture The shared-address-space architecture provides hardware support for read and write access by all processors to a shared address space. Processors interact by modifying data objects stored in the shared address space. MIMD shared-address-space computers are often referred to as ***multiprocessors***.

```
if (B == 0)
        C = A;
else
        C = A/B;
```

(a)

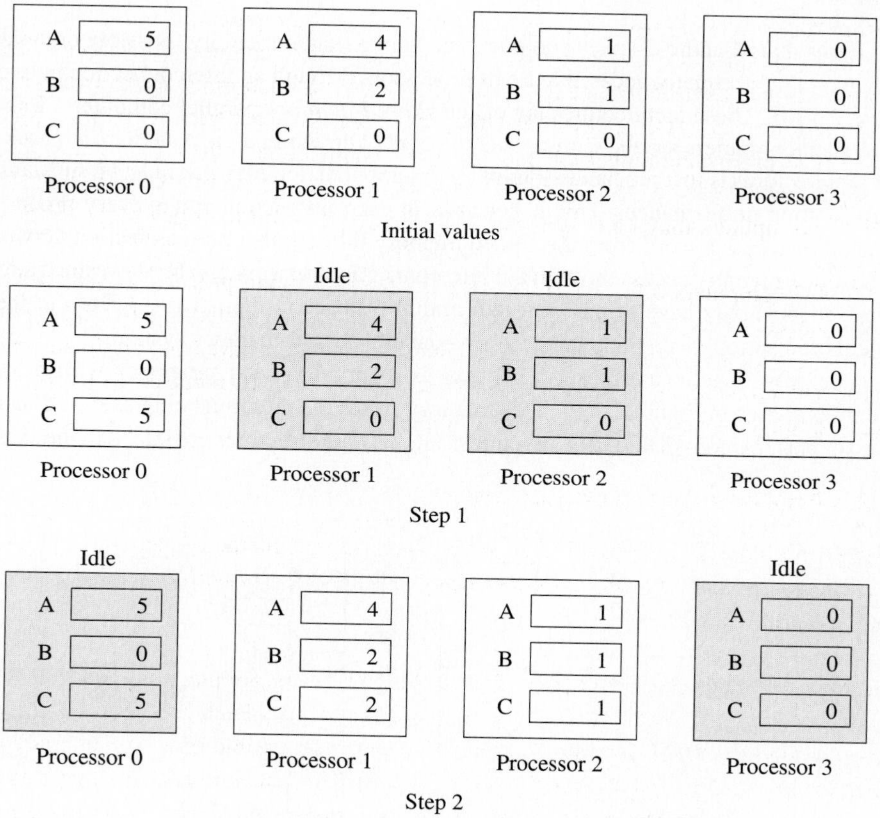

(b)

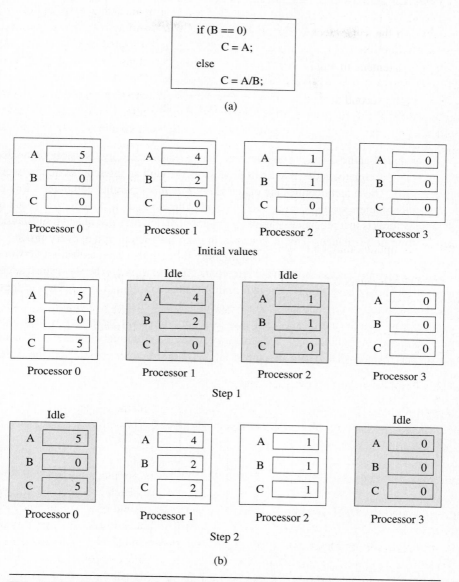

Figure 2.3 Executing a conditional statement on an SIMD computer with four processors: (a) The conditional statement; (b) The execution of the statement in two steps.

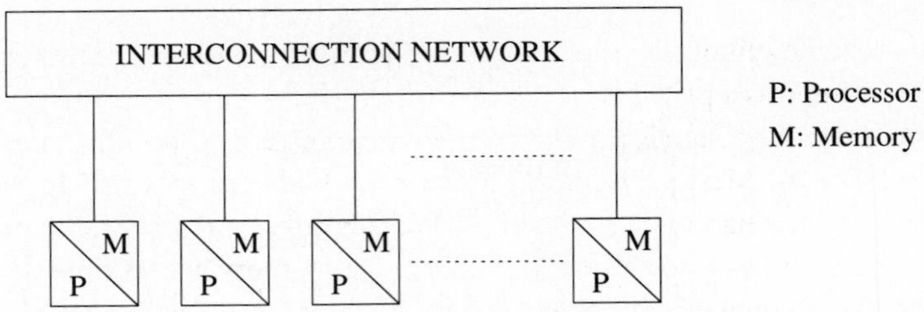

Figure 2.4 A typical message-passing architecture.

Early shared-address-space computers contain a shared memory (possibly organized into banks) that is equally accessible to all processors through an interconnection network (Figure 2.5(a)). These architectures are called ***shared-memory*** parallel computers. Examples of such computers are the C.mmp and the NYU Ultracomputer. A major drawback of these architectures is that the bandwidth of the interconnection network must be substantial to ensure good performance. This is because, in each instruction cycle, every processor may need to access a word from the shared memory through the interconnection network. Furthermore, memory access through the interconnection network can be slow, since a read or write request may have to pass through multiple stages in the network. Both of these problems can seriously degrade the performance of a shared-memory system.

One way to alleviate these drawbacks is to provide each processor with a local memory as shown in Figure 2.5(b). This memory stores the program being executed on the processor and any non-shared data structures. Global data structures are stored in the shared

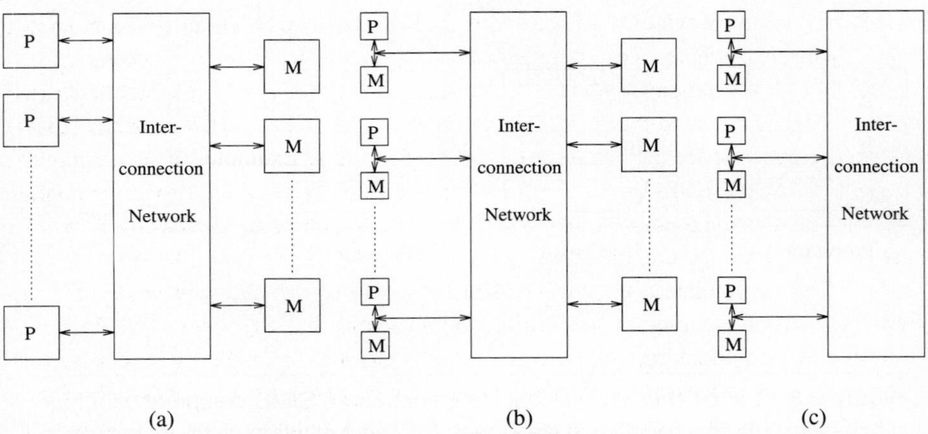

Figure 2.5 Typical shared-address-space architectures: (a) Uniform-memory-access shared-address-space computer; (b) Non-uniform-memory-access shared-address-space computer with local and global memories; (c) Non-uniform-memory-access shared-address-space computer with local memory only.

memory. This scheme eliminates repeated memory references across the interconnection network and thus improves performance.

The local memory concept can be extended to eliminate physically shared memory entirely (Figure 2.5(c)). Memory references to words in other processors' local memories are then mapped by the hardware to the appropriate processors. In such an architecture, local memory access time is much smaller than remote memory access time.

Based on the amount of time a processor takes to access local and global memory, shared-address-space computers are classified into two categories. If the time taken by a processor to access any memory word in the system is identical, the computer is classified as a ***uniform memory access*** (UMA) computer. On the other hand, if the time to access a remote memory bank is longer than the time to access a local one, the computer is called a ***nonuniform memory access*** (NUMA) computer. Figure 2.5(a) represents a UMA computer, whereas Figures 2.5(b) and (c) represent NUMA computers.

Most shared-address-space computers also have a local cache at each processor to increase their effective processor-memory bandwidth. As in sequential computers, a cache provides faster access to the data contained in the local memory. The cache can also be used to provide fast access to remotely-located shared data. Whenever a processor needs data that is located in a non-local memory, it is copied into the local cache. Subsequent access to this data is very fast. The use of a cache introduces the problem of ***cache coherence***. This problem occurs when a processor modifies a shared variable in its cache. After this modification, different processors have different values of the variable, unless copies of the variable in the other caches are simultaneously invalidated or updated. Several mechanisms have been developed for handling the cache coherence problem.

Note that the NUMA architecture is similar to a message-passing architecture—memory is physically distributed in both. The major difference between them is that a NUMA architecture provides hardware support for read and write access to other processors' memories, whereas in a message-passing architecture, remote access must be emulated by explicit message passing. For historical reasons, the NUMA architecture is often referred to as a shared-memory architecture due to its shared address-space. Most recent shared-address-space computers are NUMA computers. Examples of such computers include the TC-2000, KSR-1, and Stanford Dash. In the KSR-1, each processor contains only cache and no local memory. Such an architecture is referred to as ***cache-only memory access*** (COMA) architecture.

It is easy to emulate a message-passing architecture containing p processors on a shared-address-space computer with an identical number of processors. We do this by partitioning the shared address space into p disjoint parts and assigning one such partition exclusively to each processor. A processor sends a message to another processor by writing into the other processor's partition of memory. However, emulating a shared-address-space architecture on a message-passing computer is costly, since accessing another processor's memory requires sending and receiving messages. Hence, shared-address-space computers provide greater flexibility in programming. Furthermore, some problems require rapid access by all processors to large data structures that may be changing dynamically. Such access is better supported by shared-address-space architectures. However, the hardware needed to provide a shared address space tends to be more expensive than that for message passing.

2.1.3 Interconnection Networks

Shared-address-space computers and message-passing computers can be constructed by connecting processors and memory units using a variety of interconnection networks. Interconnection networks can be classified as ***static*** or ***dynamic***. Static networks (Section 2.4) consist of point-to-point communication links among processors and are also referred to as ***direct*** networks. Static networks are typically used to construct message-passing computers. Dynamic networks (Section 2.3) are built using switches and communication links. Communication links are connected to one another dynamically by the switching elements to establish paths among processors and memory banks. Dynamic networks are referred to as ***indirect*** networks and are normally used to construct shared-address-space computers.

2.1.4 Processor Granularity

A parallel computer may be composed of a small number of very powerful processors or a large number of relatively less powerful processors. Processors belonging to the former class are called ***coarse-grain*** computers, and those belonging to the latter are called ***fine-grain*** computers. Machines along the entire spectrum are now commercially available. Coarse grain computers such as the Cray Y-MP offer a small number of processors (8 to 16), each capable of several Gflops (one Gflops equals 10^9 floating-point operations per second). In contrast, fine-grain computers such as the CM-2, MasPar MP-1, and MasPar MP-2 offer a large number of relatively slow processors (for example, the CM-2 contains up to 65,536 one-bit processors, and the MasPar MP-1 contains up to 16,384 four-bit processors). Between these extremes are ***medium-grain*** computers such as the CM-5, nCUBE 2, and Paragon XP/S, containing up to a few thousand processors, each delivering workstation-class performance.

Individual processors in coarse-grain computers are considerably more expensive than those in fine- and medium-grain computers. The reason for this is that the fast processors used in coarse-grain computers are not produced on a large scale. Furthermore, these processors require expensive fabrication techniques. Medium-grain computers, however, are often constructed from inexpensive off-the-shelf hardware.

Different applications are suited to coarse-, medium-, or fine-grain computers to varying degrees. Many applications have only a limited amount of concurrency. Such applications cannot make effective use of a large number of less powerful processors, and are best suited to coarse-grain computers. Fine-grain computers, however, are more cost effective for applications with a high degree of concurrency. Thus, we must make a tradeoff between the cost and the utility of the computer when choosing processor granularity.

The granularity of a parallel computer can be defined as the ratio of the time required for a basic communication operation to the time required for a basic computation. Parallel computers for which this ratio is small are suitable for algorithms requiring frequent communication; that is, algorithms in which the grain size of the computation (before a communication is required) is small. Since such algorithms contain fine-grain parallelism, these parallel computers are often called fine-grain computers. In contrast, parallel computers for which this ratio is large are suited to algorithms that do not require frequent communication. These computers are referred to as coarse-grain computers. According to this criterion, multicomputers such as the nCUBE 2 and Paragon XP/S are coarse-grain computers, whereas multiprocessors such as the C.mmp, TC-2000, and KSR-1 are fine-grain computers.

2.2 An Idealized Parallel Computer

In this section, we define a theoretical model of computation based on shared-memory computers. This model is referred to as a ***parallel random access machine (PRAM)***. Formally, a PRAM consists of p processors and a global memory of unbounded size that is uniformly accessible to all processors. Thus, all processors access the same address space. Processors share a common clock but may execute different instructions in each cycle. PRAM models are therefore synchronous shared-memory MIMD computers. A PRAM model is idealized in the sense that it is a natural extension of the sequential model of computation and provides a means of interaction between processors at no cost.

In any shared-memory parallel computer, more than one processor can try to read from or write into the same memory location simultaneously. The PRAM model can be divided into four subclasses, based on how simultaneous memory accesses are handled.

(1) ***Exclusive-read, exclusive-write (EREW) PRAM.*** In this class, access to a memory location is exclusive. No concurrent read or write operations are allowed. This is the weakest PRAM model, affording minimum concurrency in memory access.

(2) ***Concurrent-read, exclusive-write (CREW) PRAM.*** In this class, multiple read accesses to a memory location are allowed. However, multiple write accesses to a memory location are serialized.

(3) ***Exclusive-read, concurrent-write (ERCW) PRAM.*** Multiple write accesses are allowed to a memory location, but multiple read accesses are serialized.

(4) ***Concurrent-read, concurrent-write (CRCW) PRAM.*** This class allows multiple read and write accesses to a common memory location. This is the most powerful PRAM model. However, it is possible to simulate CRCW on an EREW model (Problem 2.1).

Allowing concurrent read access does not create any semantic discrepancies in the program. However, concurrent write access to a memory location requires arbitration. Several protocols are used to resolve concurrent writes. The most frequently used protocols are as follows:

- ***Common***, in which the concurrent write is allowed if all the values that the processors are attempting to write are identical.
- ***Arbitrary***, in which an arbitrary processor is allowed to proceed with the write operation and the rest fail.
- ***Priority***, in which all processors are organized into a predefined prioritized list, and the processor with the highest priority succeeds and the rest fail.
- ***Sum***, in which the sum of all the quantities is written (the sum-based write conflict resolution model can be extended to any associative operator defined on the quantities being written).

2.3 Dynamic Interconnection Networks

Consider the implementation of an EREW PRAM as a shared-memory computer with p processors and a global memory of m words. The processors are connected to the memory through a set of switching elements. These switching elements determine the memory word being accessed by each processor. In an EREW PRAM, each of the p processors in the ensemble can access any of the memory words, provided that a word is not accessed by more than one processor simultaneously. To ensure such connectivity, the total number of switching elements must be $\Theta(mp)$. For a reasonable memory size, constructing a switching network of this complexity is very expensive. Thus, PRAM models of computation are impossible to realize in practice.

One way to reduce the complexity of the switching network is to reduce the value of m by organizing the memory into banks. A processor switches between banks and not between individual memory words. If the total memory m was organized into b banks, then each of the p processors needs to switch between b banks. This model is only a weak approximation of the EREW PRAM model, because if a processor accesses even one word in a memory bank, no other processor can access any word in the same memory bank.

We now describe some important dynamic interconnection networks used in practical shared-memory architectures.

2.3.1 Crossbar Switching Networks

A simple way to connect p processors to b memory banks is to use a crossbar switch. A crossbar switch employs a grid of switching elements as shown in Figure 2.6. The crossbar switching network is a nonblocking network in the sense that the connection of a processor to a memory bank does not block the connection of any other processor to any other memory bank. Normally, b is greater than or equal to p so that each processor has at least one memory bank to access. If b approaches the size of the memory (that is, each memory bank has one word), then the crossbar simulates an EREW PRAM.

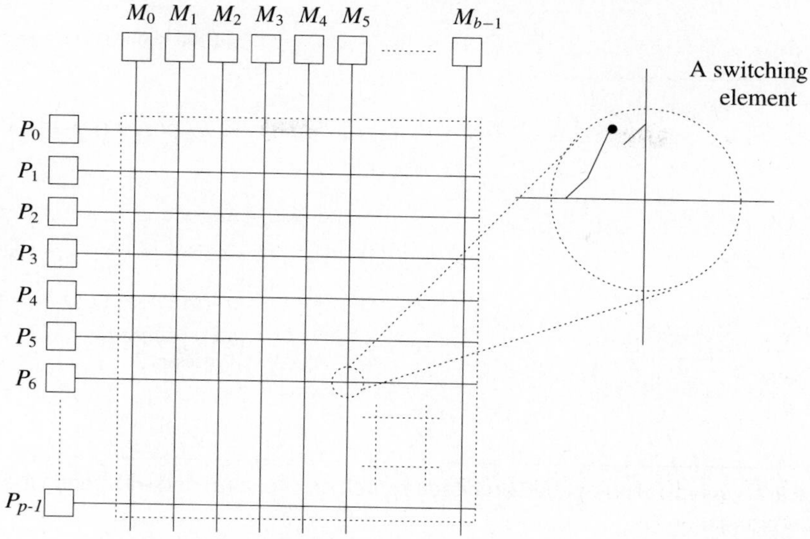

Figure 2.6 A completely nonblocking crossbar switch connecting p processors to b memory banks.

The total number of switching elements required to implement such a network is $\Theta(pb)$. It is reasonable to assume that the number of memory banks b is at least p; otherwise, at any given time, there will be some processors that will be unable to access any memory bank. Therefore, as the value of p is increased, the complexity of the switching network grows as $\Omega(p^2)$. Hence, the switching network becomes practically unrealizable as the number of processors becomes very large. Consequently, crossbar networks are not very scalable in terms of cost.

Several parallel processors based on the crossbar switch have been constructed. The Cray Y-MP and Fujitsu VPP 500 are recent examples of such computers. The VPP 500 uses a 224×224 crossbar network to connect 222 processors and 2 control processors. Implementing a crossbar switch of this magnitude is a task requiring considerable ingenuity.

2.3.2 Bus-Based Networks

In a bus-based network, processors are connected to global memory by means of a common data path called a ***bus***. Such a system is very simple to construct. Figure 2.7(a) illustrates a typical bus architecture. Whenever a processor accesses global memory, that processor generates a request over the bus. The data is then fetched from memory over the same bus.

Given its simplicity of construction and ability to provide uniform access to shared memory, this network appears very attractive. However, the bus can carry only a limited amount of data between the memory and the processors. If we increase the number of processors, each processor spends an increasing amount of time waiting for memory access

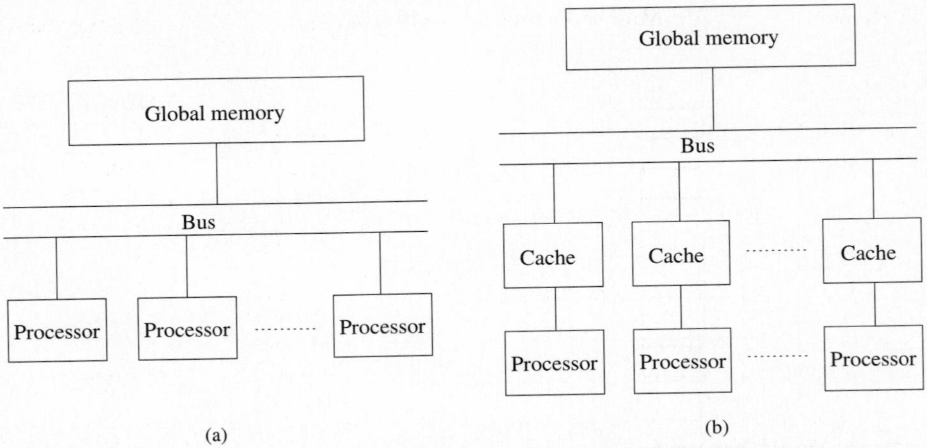

Figure 2.7 A typical bus-based architecture with no cache (a) and with cache memory at each processor (b).

while the bus is in use by other processors. Consequently, the performance of bus-based networks saturates at a small number of processors.

One way to alleviate the bus bottleneck is to provide each processor with a local cache memory, as shown in Figure 2.7(b). In a typical computation, when a reference is made to a memory location, subsequent references are likely to be made to memory locations in the neighborhood of this location. Due to this locality of reference of data and instructions, once a block of data is fetched into a processor's cache memory, subsequent references will likely be to memory words in the cache. In the case of a cache miss (that is, when the word accessed is not in the cache), a block of data containing the required word is brought from the global memory across the shared bus into the local cache.

Local cache memory thus reduces the total number of accesses to global memory. For systems with local cache memory, the bottleneck due to the limited data transmission rate of the bus manifests itself at a higher number of processors. However, replicating data this way leads to the cache coherence problems discussed in Section 2.1.2. Several cache coherence techniques have been developed for bus-based parallel computers containing a small number of processors.

Some of the commercially successful bus-based shared-address-space parallel computers are the Symmetry and Multimax.

2.3.3 Multistage Interconnection Networks

The crossbar interconnection network is scalable in terms of performance but unscalable in terms of cost. Conversely, the shared bus network is scalable in terms of cost but unscalable in terms of performance. An intermediate class of networks called ***multistage interconnection networks*** lies between these two extremes. It is more scalable than the bus in terms of performance and more scalable than the crossbar in terms of cost.

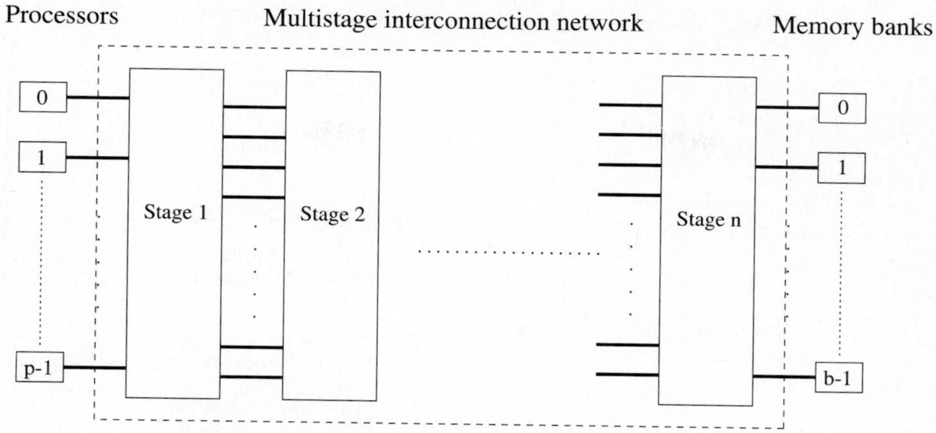

Figure 2.8 The schematic of a typical multistage interconnection network.

Figure 2.9(a) illustrates the cost of crossbar, multistage, and bus-based parallel computers and Figure 2.9(b) illustrates the performance characteristics of these computers in terms of total communication capacity.

The general schematic of a multistage network consisting of p processors and b memory banks is shown in Figure 2.8. A commonly used multistage connection network is the ***omega network***.This network consists of $\log p$ stages (where p is the number of processors and also the number of memory banks). Each stage of the omega network consists of an interconnection pattern that connects p inputs and p outputs; a link exists

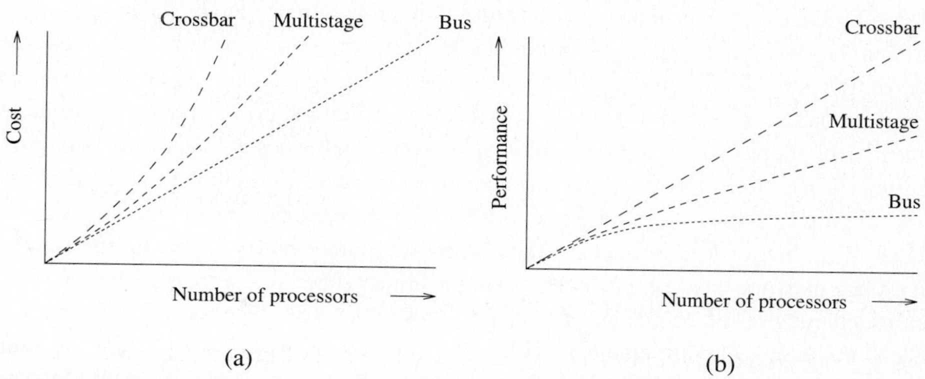

Figure 2.9 (a) Cost versus number of processors for interconnection networks based on bus, multistage, and crossbar connected networks; (b) Performance versus number of processors for the three networks.

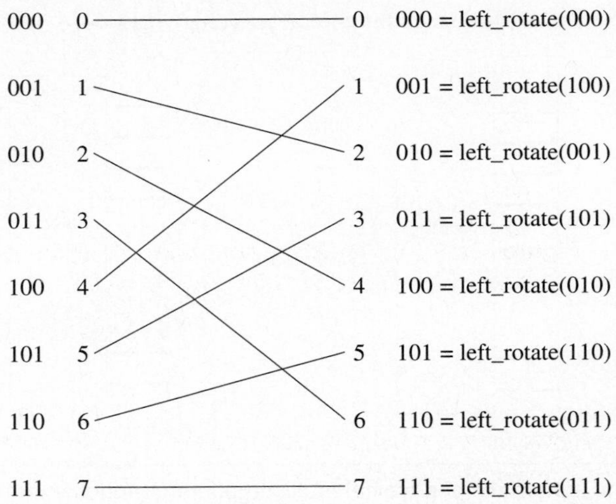

Figure 2.10 A perfect shuffle interconnection for eight inputs and outputs.

between input i and output j if the following is true:

$$j = \begin{cases} 2i, & 0 \leq i \leq p/2 - 1 \\ 2i + 1 - p, & p/2 \leq i \leq p - 1 \end{cases} \tag{2.1}$$

Equation 2.1 represents a left-rotation operation on the binary representation of i to obtain j. This interconnection pattern is called a ***perfect shuffle***. Figure 2.10 shows a perfect shuffle interconnection pattern for eight inputs and outputs. In each stage of an omega network, a perfect shuffle interconnection pattern feeds into a set of $p/2$ switching elements. Each switch is in one of two connection modes. In one mode, the inputs are sent straight through to the outputs, as shown in Figure 2.11(a). This is called the ***pass-through*** connection. In the other mode, the inputs to the switching element are crossed over and then sent out, as shown in Figure 2.11(b). This is called the ***cross-over*** connection. An omega network has $p/2 \times \log p$ switching elements, and the cost of such a network grows as $\Theta(p \log p)$. Note that this cost is less than the $\Theta(p^2)$ cost of a complete crossbar switch.

Figure 2.12 shows an omega network for eight processors. Processors form the input nodes of the network and memory banks form the output nodes. Routing messages in an omega network is accomplished by using a simple scheme. Let s and t be the binary representations of the source and destination of the message. The message traverses the link to the first switching element. If the most significant bits of s and t are the same, then the message is routed in pass-through mode by the switch. If these bits are different, then the message is routed through in crossover mode. This scheme is repeated at the next switching stage using the next most significant bit. Traversing $\log p$ stages uses all $\log p$ bits in the binary representations of s and t.

Figure 2.11 Two switching configurations of the 2×2 switch: (a) Pass-through; (b) Cross-over.

Figure 2.13 shows message routing over an eight-processor omega network from processor two (010) to seven (111) and from processor six (110) to four (100). This figure illustrates an important property of this network. When processor two (010) is communicating with processor seven (111), it blocks the path from processor six (110) to four (100). The communication link AB is used by both communication paths. Thus, in an omega network, access to a memory bank by a processor may disallow access to another memory bank by another processor. Networks with this property are referred to as ***blocking networks***.

Parallel computers based on the omega network include the BBN Butterfly, IBM RP-3, and NYU Ultracomputer.

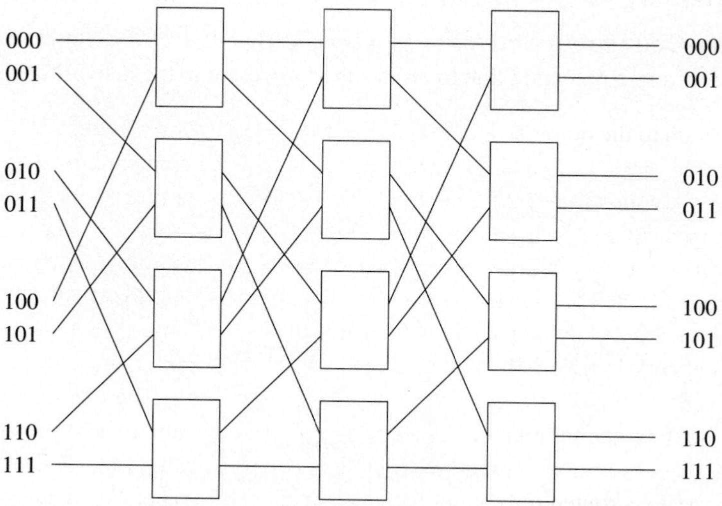

Figure 2.12 A complete omega network connecting eight inputs and eight outputs .

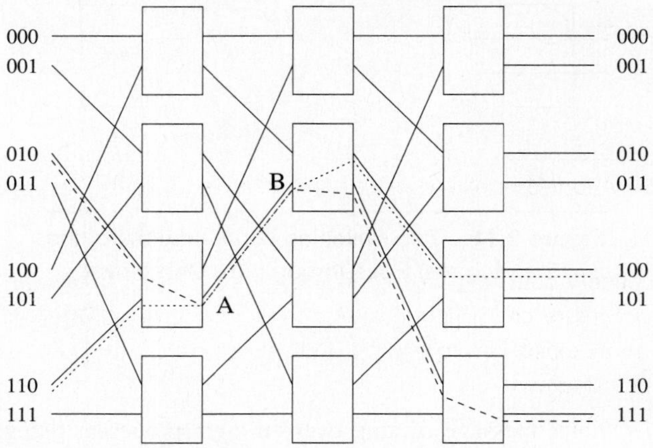

Figure 2.13 An example of blocking in omega network: one of the messages (010 to 111 or 110 to 100) is blocked at link AB.

2.4 Static Interconnection Networks

Message-passing architectures typically use static interconnection networks to connect processors. In this section, we discuss some important static interconnection networks and their properties.

2.4.1 Types of Static Interconnection Networks

Completely-Connected Network In a ***completely-connected network***, each processor has a direct communication link to every other processor in the network. Figure 2.14(a)

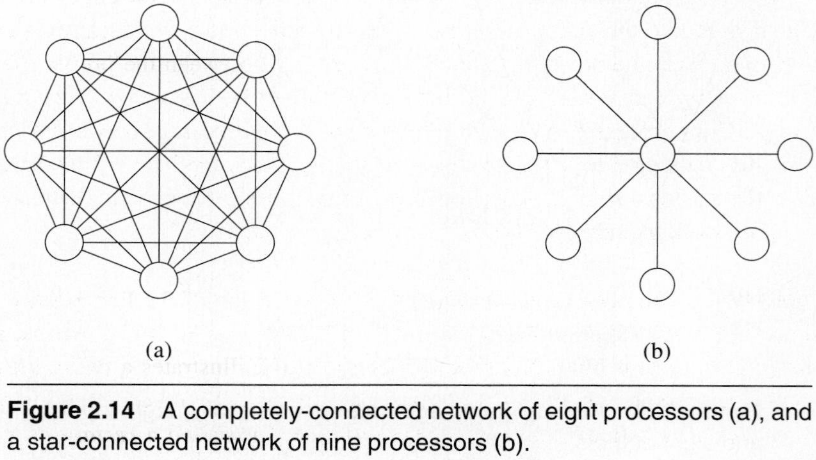

Figure 2.14 A completely-connected network of eight processors (a), and a star-connected network of nine processors (b).

Figure 2.15 A four-processor linear array (a) and a four-processor ring (b).

illustrates a completely-connected network of eight processors. This network is ideal in the sense that a processor can send a message to another processor in a single step, since a communication link exists between them. Completely-connected networks are the static counterparts of crossbar switching networks, since in both networks, the communication between any input/output pair does not block communication between any other pair. However, completely-connected networks can support communications over multiple channels originating at the same processor, whereas crossbar switches cannot.

Star-Connected Network In a ***star-connected network***, one processor acts as the central processor. Every other processor has a communication link connecting it to this processor. Figure 2.14(b) shows a star-connected network of nine processors. The star-connected network is similar to bus-based networks. Communication between any pair of processors is routed through the central processor, just as the shared bus forms the medium for all communication in a bus-based network. The central processor is the bottleneck in the star topology.

A network of workstations connected using an ethernet can be used as a parallel computer. The ethernet forms a common medium for communicating messages between processors. Such a network displays performance characteristics similar to star-connected and bus-based parallel computers.

Linear Array and Ring A simple way to connect processors is illustrated in Figure 2.15(a). Each processor in this network (except the processors at the ends) has a direct communication link to two other processors. Such an interconnection network is called a ***linear array***. A wraparound connection is often provided between the processors at the ends. A linear array with a wraparound connection is referred to as a ***ring***. Figure 2.15(b) shows a ring of four processors. One way of communicating a message between processors is by repeatedly passing it to the processor immediately to the right (or left, depending on which direction yields a shorter path) until it reaches its destination. Parallel computers using a ring network include the ZMOB and CDC Cyberplus.

Mesh Network The ***two-dimensional mesh*** is an extension of the linear array to two dimensions. In a two-dimensional mesh, each processor has a direct communication link connecting it to four other processors. Figure 2.16(a) illustrates a two-dimensional mesh of nine processors. If both dimensions of the mesh contain an equal number of processors, then it is called a ***square mesh***; otherwise it is called a ***rectangular mesh***.

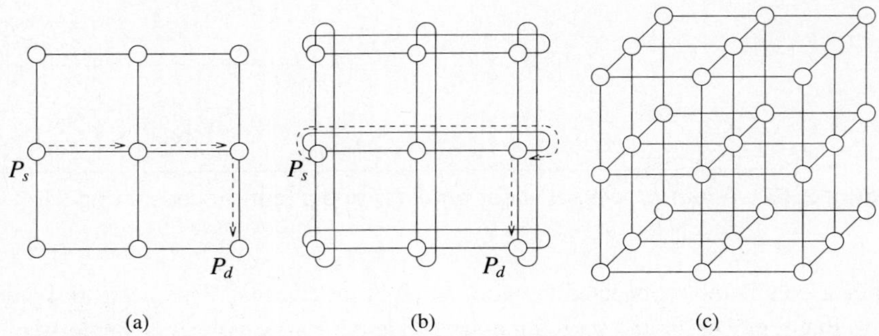

Figure 2.16 (a) A two-dimensional mesh with an illustration of routing a message from processor P_s to processor P_d; (b) a two-dimensional wraparound mesh with an illustration of routing a message from processor P_s to processor P_d; (c) a three-dimensional mesh.

Often, the processors at the periphery are connected by wraparound connections. Such a mesh is called a ***wraparound mesh*** or a ***torus*** (Figure 2.16(b)). A message from one processor to another can be routed in the mesh by first sending it along one dimension and then along the other dimension until it reaches its destination. Figures 2.16(a) and (b) illustrate this routing strategy for communicating a message between two processors. Common extensions of the two-dimensional mesh include the ***three-dimensional mesh*** and the ***three-dimensional wraparound mesh***. Figure 2.16(c) illustrates a three-dimensional mesh. Many commercially available parallel computers are based on the mesh network. These include two-dimensional meshes such as the DAP and Paragon XP/S, and three-dimensional meshes such as the Cray T3D and J-Machine. The Tera computer is based on a sparse three-dimensional mesh network (Figure 3.26).

Tree Network A ***tree network*** is one in which there is only one path between any pair of processors. Both linear arrays and star-connected networks are special cases of

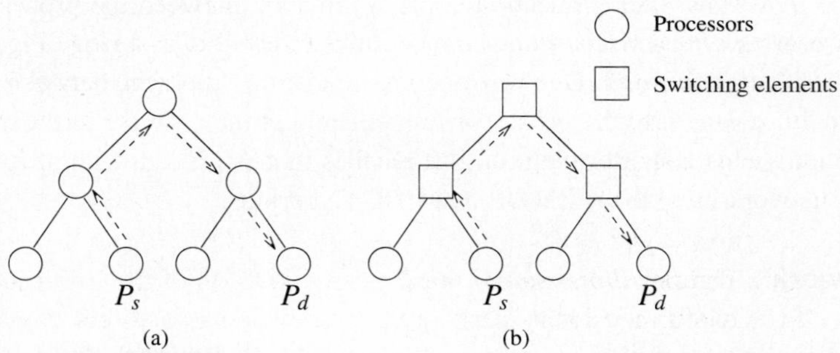

Figure 2.17 Complete binary tree networks and message routing in them.

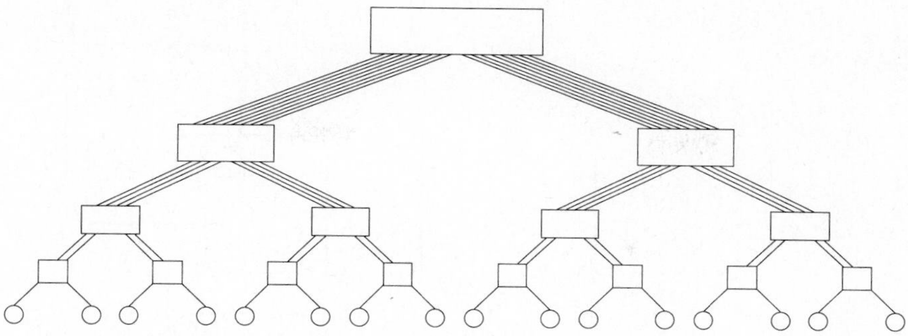

Figure 2.18 A fat tree network of 16 processors.

tree networks. Figure 2.17 shows networks based on complete binary trees. Static tree networks have a processor at each node of the tree (Figure 2.17(a)). Tree networks also have a dynamic counterpart. In a dynamic tree network, nodes at intermediate levels are switching elements and the leaf nodes are processors (Figure 2.17(b)).

To route a message in a tree, the source processor sends the message up the tree until it reaches the processor or the switch at the root of the smallest subtree containing both the source and destination processors. Then the message is sent down the tree toward the destination processor. This is illustrated in Figure 2.17.

Tree networks suffer from a communication bottleneck at higher levels of the tree. For example, when many processors in the left subtree of a node communicate with processors in the right subtree, the root node has to handle all the messages. This problem can be alleviated by increasing the number of communication links between processors that are closer to the root. This network, illustrated in Figure 2.18, is called a ***fat tree***.

The DADO parallel computer uses a static binary tree interconnection network. The CM-5 is based on a dynamic fat-tree network.

Hypercube Network A hypercube is a multidimensional mesh of processors with exactly two processors in each dimension. A d-dimensional hypercube consists of $p = 2^d$ processors. A hypercube can be recursively constructed as follows: a zero-dimensional hypercube is a single processor; a one-dimensional hypercube is constructed by connecting two zero-dimensional hypercubes; in general, a $(d+1)$-dimensional hypercube is constructed by connecting the corresponding processors of two d-dimensional hypercubes.

Figure 2.19 shows hypercubes of dimensions zero to four. This figure also illustrates how we can use the recursive definition of a hypercube to label processors. When a $(d+1)$-dimensional hypercube is constructed by connecting two d-dimensional hypercubes, the labels of the processors of one hypercube are prefixed with a zero and those of the second hypercube are prefixed with a one.

Some of the important properties of a hypercube network are as follows:

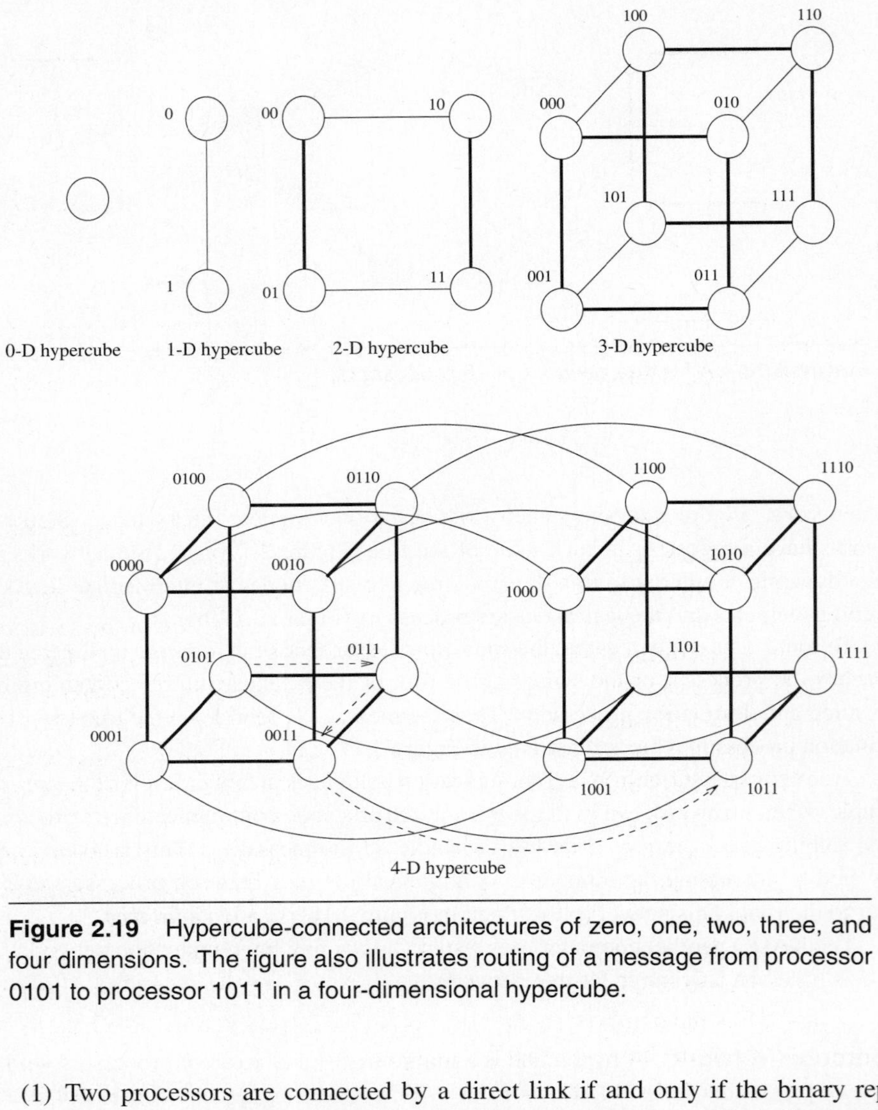

Figure 2.19 Hypercube-connected architectures of zero, one, two, three, and four dimensions. The figure also illustrates routing of a message from processor 0101 to processor 1011 in a four-dimensional hypercube.

(1) Two processors are connected by a direct link if and only if the binary representation of their labels differ at exactly one bit position. This is illustrated in Figure 2.19.

(2) In a d-dimensional hypercube, each processor is directly connected to d other processors.

(3) A d-dimensional hypercube can be partitioned into two $(d - 1)$-dimensional subcubes as follows. Select a bit position and group together all the processors whose labels have a zero at the selected position; all of these processors make up one partition, and the remaining processors comprise the second partition. Since processor labels have d bits, d such partitions exist. This property follows directly from the recursive definition of the hypercube. Figure 2.20 illustrates the three

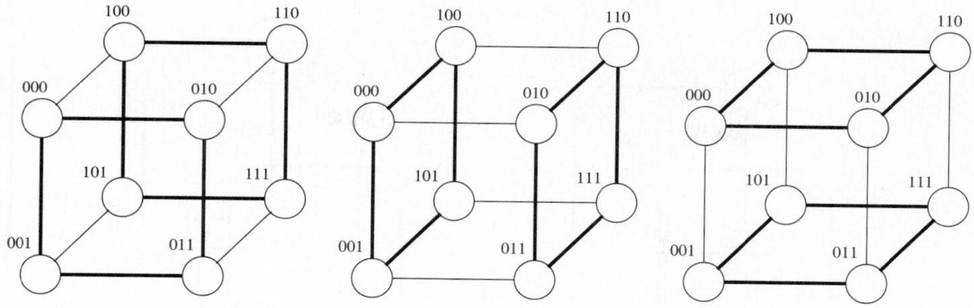

Figure 2.20 Three distinct partitions of a three-dimensional hypercube into two two-dimensional cubes. Links connecting processors within a partition are indicated by bold lines.

partitions of a three-dimensional hypercube. The bold lines in the figure connect the processors that belong to a partition.

(4) The processor labels in a d-dimensional hypercube contain d bits. Fixing any k of these bits, the processors that differ at the remaining $d - k$ bit positions form a $(d - k)$-dimensional subcube composed of $2^{(d-k)}$ processors (Problem 2.7). Since k bits can be fixed in 2^k different ways, there are 2^k such subcubes.
Figure 2.21 illustrates this property. In this figure, $k = 2$ and $d = 4$. The four subcubes (of four processors each) that are formed by fixing the two most significant label bits are shown in Figure 2.21(a). The subcubes formed by fixing the two least significant bits are shown in Figure 2.21(b).

(5) Consider the labels s and t of two processors in a hypercube. The total number of bit positions at which these two labels differ is called the ***Hamming distance*** between them. For example, the Hamming distance between processors labeled 011 and 101 in a three-dimensional hypercube is two. Similarly, the Hamming distance between labels 101 and 010 is three. The Hamming distance between s and t is the number of bits that are one in the binary representation of $s \oplus t$, where $\oplus$ is the bitwise exclusive-or operation.
The number of communication links in the shortest path between two processors is the Hamming distance between their labels. A message can be routed from processor s to processor t by passing the message along dimensions that correspond to bit positions having a one in the binary representation of $s \oplus t$. Figure 2.19 illustrates routing of a message from processor s (labeled 0101) to processor t (labeled 1011). For this example, $s \oplus t$ is 1110. The message is routed along dimensions corresponding to bit positions one, two, and three (assuming the least significant bit is bit position zero). Since the binary representation of $s \oplus t$ can contain at most d ones, the shortest path between any two processors in a hypercube cannot have more than d links.

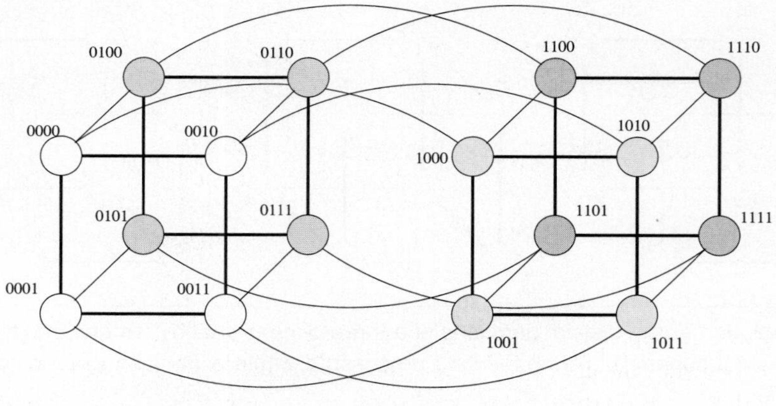

(a)

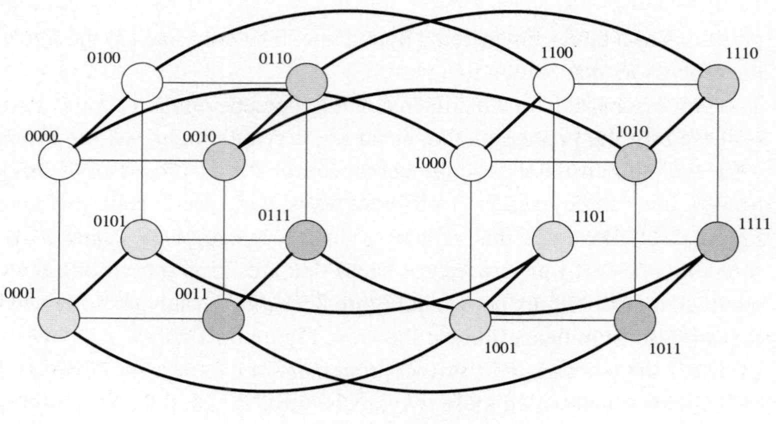

(b)

Figure 2.21 The two-dimensional subcubes of a four-dimensional hypercube formed by fixing the two most significant label bits (a) and the two least significant bits (b). Processors within a subcube are connected by bold lines.

Parallel computers based on the hypercube network include the nCUBE 2, Cosmic Cube, and iPSC.

k-ary d-cube Networks A d-dimensional hypercube, also called a binary d-cube, is a d-dimensional mesh with two processors along each dimension. A ring, in contrast, is a one-dimensional structure with p processors along its only dimension. These topologies define the extremes of a class of topologies called ***k-ary d-cubes***. Here, d is the ***dimension*** of the network and k is the ***radix***, which is defined as the number of processors along each dimension. The number of processors in the network, p, is equal to k^d. A ring of

p processors is a p-ary 1-cube. A two-dimensional wraparound mesh of p processors is a $\sqrt{p}$-ary 2-cube. A k-ary d-cube can be constructed from k k-ary $(d-1)$-cubes by connecting the processors that occupy identical positions in the cubes into rings.

2.4.2 Evaluating Static Interconnection Networks

This section discusses the criteria that characterize the cost and performance of static interconnection networks. We use these criteria to evaluate the networks introduced in the previous subsection.

Diameter The ***diameter*** of a network is the maximum distance between any two processors in the network. The distance between two processors is defined as the shortest path (in terms of number of links) between them. Since distance largely determines communication time, networks with smaller diameters are better. The diameter of a completely-connected network is one, and that of a star-connected network is two. The diameter of a ring network is $\lfloor p/2 \rfloor$. The diameter of a two-dimensional mesh without wraparound connections is $2(\sqrt{p}-1)$ and that of a wraparound mesh is $2\lfloor \sqrt{p}/2 \rfloor$. The diameter of a hypercube-connected network is $\log p$. The diameter of a complete binary tree is $2\log((p+1)/2)$ because the two communicating processors may be in separate subtrees of the root node, and a message might have to travel all the way to the root and then down the other subtree.

Connectivity The ***connectivity*** of a network is a measure of the multiplicity of paths between any two processors. A network with high connectivity is desirable, because it lowers contention for communication resources. One measure of connectivity is the minimum number of arcs that must be removed from the network to break it into two disconnected networks. This is called the ***arc connectivity*** of the network. The arc connectivity is one for linear arrays, as well as tree and star networks. It is two for rings and 2-D meshes without wraparound, four for 2-D wraparound meshes, and d for d-dimensional hypercubes.

Bisection Width and Bisection Bandwidth The ***bisection width*** of a network is defined as the minimum number of communication links that have to be removed to partition the network into two equal halves. The bisection width of a ring is two, since any partition cuts across only two communication links. Similarly, the bisection width of a two-dimensional p-processor mesh without wraparound connections is $\sqrt{p}$ and with wraparound connections is $2\sqrt{p}$. The bisection width of a tree and a star is one, and that of a completely-connected network of p processors is $p^2/4$. The bisection width of a hypercube can be derived from its construction. We construct a d-dimensional hypercube by connecting corresponding links of two $(d-1)$-dimensional hypercubes. Since each of these subcubes contains $2^{(d-1)}$ or $p/2$ processors, at least $p/2$ communication links must cross any partition of a hypercube into two subcubes (Problem 2.9).

The number of bits that can be communicated simultaneously over a link connecting two processors is called the ***channel width***. Channel width is equal to the number of

Table 2.1 A summary of the characteristics of various static network topologies connecting p processors.

Network	Diameter	Bisection Width	Arc Connectivity	Cost (No. of links)
Completely-connected	1	$p^2/4$	$p-1$	$p(p-1)/2$
Star	2	1	1	$p-1$
Complete binary tree	$2\log((p+1)/2)$	1	1	$p-1$
Linear array	$p-1$	1	1	$p-1$
Ring	$\lfloor p/2 \rfloor$	2	2	p
2-D mesh without wraparound	$2(\sqrt{p}-1)$	$\sqrt{p}$	2	$2(p-\sqrt{p})$
2-D wraparound mesh	$2\lfloor \sqrt{p}/2 \rfloor$	$2\sqrt{p}$	4	$2p$
Hypercube	$\log p$	$p/2$	$\log p$	$(p \log p)/2$
Wraparound k-ary d-cube	$d\lfloor k/2 \rfloor$	$2k^{d-1}$	$2d$	dp

physical wires in each communication link. The peak rate at which a single physical wire can deliver bits is called the ***channel rate***. The peak rate at which data can be communicated between the ends of a communication link is called ***channel bandwidth***. Channel bandwidth is the product of channel rate and channel width.

The ***bisection bandwidth*** of a network is defined as the minimum volume of communication allowed between any two halves of the network with an equal number of processors. It is the product of the bisection width and the channel bandwidth.

Cost Many criteria can be used to evaluate the cost of a network. One way of defining the cost of a network is in terms of the number of communication links or the number of wires required by the network. Linear arrays and trees use only $p-1$ links to connect p processors. A d-dimensional wraparound mesh has dp links. A hypercube-connected network has $(p \log p)/2$ links.

The bisection bandwidth of a network can also be used as a measure of its cost, as it provides a lower bound on the area in a two-dimensional packaging or the volume in a three-dimensional packaging. If the bisection width of a network is w, the lower bound on the area in a two-dimensional packaging is $\Theta(w^2)$, and the lower bound on the volume in a three-dimensional packaging is $\Theta(w^{3/2})$. According to this criterion, hypercubes and completely connected networks are more expensive than the other networks.

We summarize the characteristics of various networks in Table 2.1. There is no single network that is superior on the basis of all the criteria. We must make tradeoffs and select a network on the basis of both the system's cost and its intended applications.

2.5 Embedding Other Networks into a Hypercube

Given two graphs, $G(V, E)$ and $G'(V', E')$, embedding graph G into graph G' maps each vertex in the set V onto a vertex (or a set of vertices) in set V' and each edge in the set E onto an edge (or a set of edges) in E'. Let the nodes in a graph correspond to processors and the edges to communication links in an interconnection network. Embedding one graph into another is important because an algorithm may have been designed for a specific interconnection network, and it may be necessary to adapt it to another network.

When mapping graph $G(V, E)$ into $G'(V', E')$, three parameters are important. First, it is possible that more than one edge in E is mapped onto a single edge in E'. This leads to additional traffic on the corresponding communication link. The maximum number of edges mapped onto any edge in E' is called the ***congestion*** of the mapping. Second, an edge in E may be mapped onto multiple contiguous edges in E'. This is significant because traffic on the corresponding communication link must traverse more than one link and will incur longer delays. The maximum number of links in E' that any edge in E is mapped onto is called the ***dilation*** of the mapping. Third, the sets V and V' may contain different numbers of vertices. If so, a processor in V corresponds to more than one processor in V'. The ratio of the number of processors in the set V' to that in set V is called the ***expansion*** of the mapping.

In this section, we discuss embeddings of various interconnection networks into the hypercube. We limit the scope of the discussion to cases in which sets V and V' contain an equal number of processors (an expansion of one). Furthermore, all mappings presented in this section have at most one edge in E that maps onto one edge in E' (a congestion of one).

2.5.1 Embedding a Linear Array into a Hypercube

A linear array (or a ring) composed of 2^d processors (labeled 0 through $2^d - 1$) can be embedded into a d-dimensional hypercube by mapping processor i of the linear array onto processor $G(i, d)$ of the hypercube. The function $G(i, x)$ is defined as follows:

$$\begin{aligned}
G(0, 1) &= 0 \\
G(1, 1) &= 1 \\
G(i, x+1) &= \begin{cases} G(i, x), & i < 2^x \\ 2^x + G(2^{x+1} - 1 - i, x), & i \geq 2^x \end{cases}
\end{aligned}$$

The function G is called the ***binary reflected Gray code*** (RGC). The entry $G(i, d)$ denotes the ith entry in the sequence of Gray codes of d bits. Gray codes of $d + 1$ bits are derived from a table of Gray codes of d bits by reflecting the table and prefixing the reflected entries with a one and the original entries with a zero. This process is illustrated in Figure 2.22(a).

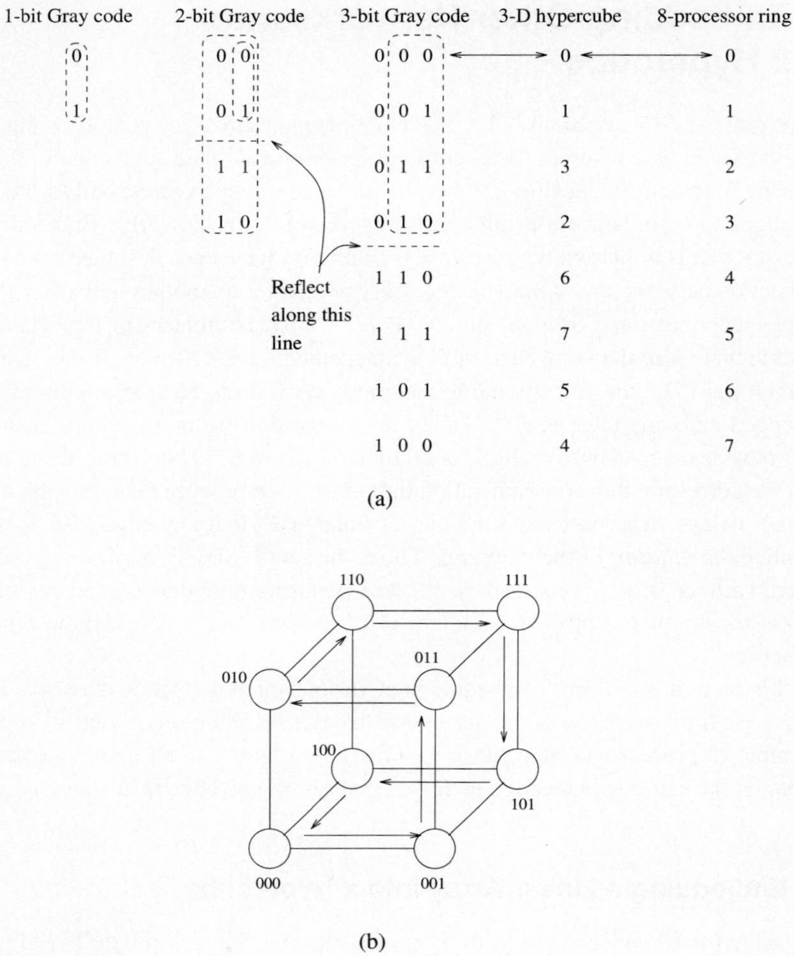

Figure 2.22 A three-bit reflected Gray code ring (a) and its embedding into a three-dimensional hypercube (b).

A careful look at the Gray code table reveals that two adjoining entries ($G(i, d)$ and $G(i + 1, d)$) differ from each other at only one bit position. Since processor i in the linear array is mapped to processor $G(i, d)$, and processor $i + 1$ is mapped to $G(i + 1, d)$, there is a direct link in the hypercube that corresponds to each direct link in the linear array. (Recall that two processors whose labels differ at only one bit position have a direct link in a hypercube.) Therefore, the mapping specified by the function G has a dilation of one and a congestion of one. Figure 2.22(b) illustrates the embedding of an eight-processor ring into a three-dimensional hypercube.

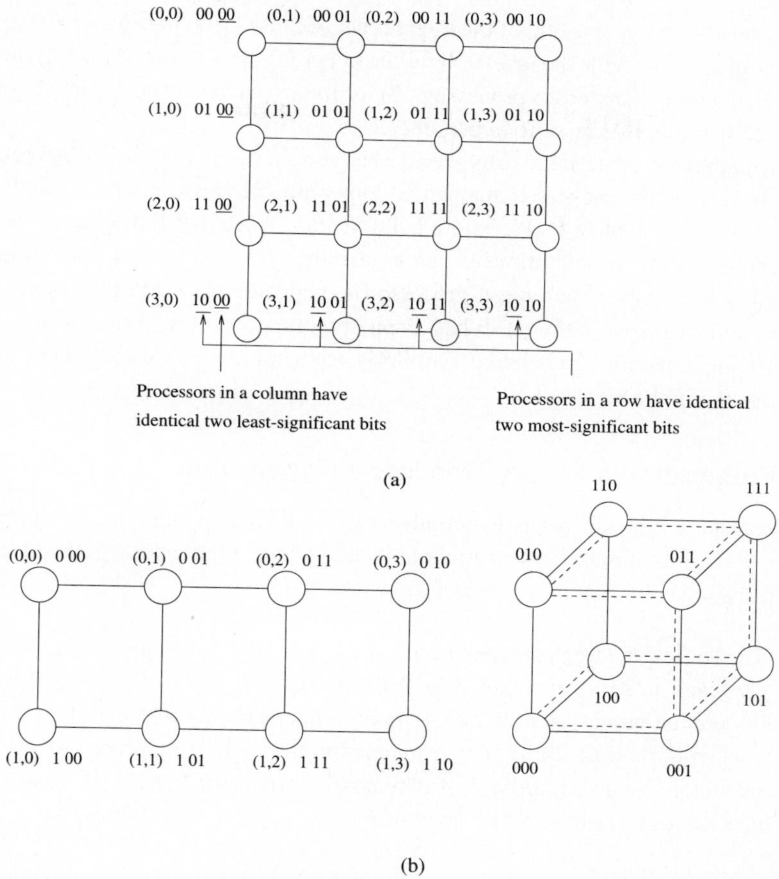

Figure 2.23 (a) A 4×4 mesh illustrating the mapping of mesh processors to processors in a four-dimensional hypercube; and (b) a 2×4 processor mesh embedded into a three-dimensional hypercube.

2.5.2 Embedding a Mesh into a Hypercube

Embedding a mesh into a hypercube is a natural extension of embedding a ring into a hypercube. We can embed a $2^r \times 2^s$ wraparound mesh into a 2^{r+s}-processor hypercube by mapping processor (i, j) of the mesh onto processor $G(i, r) \| G(j, s)$ of the hypercube (where $\|$ denotes concatenation of the two Gray codes). Note that immediate neighbors in the mesh are mapped to hypercube processors whose processor labels differ in exactly one bit position. Therefore, this mapping has a dilation of one and a congestion of one.

For example, consider embedding a 2×4 mesh into an eight-processor hypercube. The values of r and s are one and two, respectively. Processor (i, j) of the mesh is mapped to processor $G(i, 1) \| G(j, 2)$ of the hypercube. Therefore, processor $(0, 0)$ of the mesh is mapped to processor 000 of the hypercube, because $G(0, 1)$ is 0 and $G(0, 2)$ is 00; concatenating the two yields the label 000 for the hypercube processor. Similarly, processor (0, 1) of the mesh is mapped to processor 001 of the hypercube, and so on. Figure 2.23 illustrates embedding meshes into hypercubes.

This mapping of a mesh into a hypercube has certain useful properties. All processors in the same row of the mesh are mapped to hypercube processors whose labels have r identical most significant bits. We know from Section 2.4.1 that fixing any r bits in the processor label of an $(r + s)$-dimensional hypercube yields a subcube of dimension s with 2^s processors. Since each mesh processor is mapped onto a unique processor in the hypercube, and each row in the mesh has 2^s processors, every row in the mesh is mapped to a distinct subcube in the hypercube. Similarly, each column in the mesh is mapped to a distinct subcube in the hypercube.

2.5.3 Embedding a Binary Tree into a Hypercube

Binary trees can be embedded into hypercubes in several ways. Consider a complete binary tree of depth d containing processors only at its leaf nodes. One natural embedding of this tree into a 2^d-processor hypercube is as follows:

(1) The root of the tree is mapped onto any hypercube processor.

(2) For each node m at depth j in the tree, the left child of m is mapped to the hypercube processor to which node m is mapped (say to processor whose label is i), and the right child of m is mapped to the hypercube processor whose label we obtain by inverting bit j of i (that is, to processor $i \oplus 2^{(j-1)}$, where $\oplus$ is the bitwise logical exclusive-or operation).

Figure 2.24 illustrates an eight-processor tree embedded into a three-dimensional hypercube. In the mapping shown in the figure, the root of the tree is mapped onto processor 011 of the hypercube.

Note that this mapping is different from the mapping of a linear array or a mesh into a hypercube. In this mapping, multiple nodes in the tree correspond to a single processor in the hypercube. However, only one processor of the tree is mapped to a single processor in the hypercube. Therefore the expansion of this mapping is one. As we shall see in subsequent chapters, this mapping is very useful for implementing a variety of tree structured communication operations on hypercubes.

2.6 Routing Mechanisms for Static Networks

Efficient algorithms for routing a message to its destination are critical to the performance of parallel computers. A ***routing mechanism*** determines the path a message takes through the network to get from the source to the destination processor. It takes as input a message's

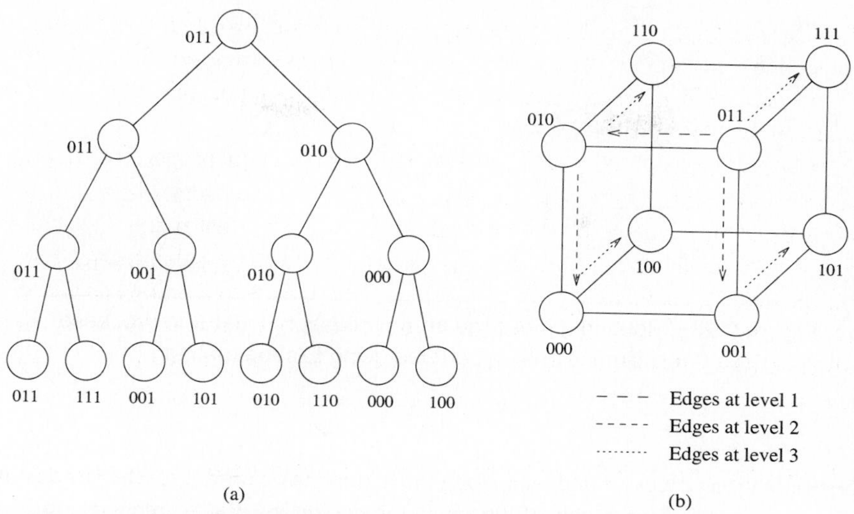

Figure 2.24 A tree rooted at processor 011 (=3) and embedded into a three-dimensional hypercube: (a) the organization of the tree rooted at processor 011, and (b) the tree embedded into a three-dimensional hypercube.

source and destination processors. It may also use information about the state of the network. It returns one or more paths through the network from the source to the destination processor.

Routing mechanisms can be classified as ***minimal*** or ***nonminimal***. A minimal routing mechanism always selects one of the shortest paths between the source and the destination. In a minimal routing scheme, each link brings a message closer to its destination, but the scheme can lead to congestion in parts of the network. A nonminimal routing scheme, in contrast, may route the message along a longer path to avoid network congestion.

Routing mechanisms can also be classified on the basis of how they use information regarding the state of the network. A ***deterministic routing*** scheme determines a unique path for a message, based on its source and destination. It does not use any information regarding the state of the network. Deterministic schemes may result in uneven use of the communication resources in a network. In contrast, an ***adaptive routing*** scheme uses information regarding the current state of the network to determine the path of the message. Adaptive routing detects congestion in the network and routes messages around it.

One commonly used deterministic minimal routing technique is called ***dimension-ordered routing***. Dimension-ordered routing assigns successive channels for traversal by a message based on a numbering scheme determined by the dimension of the channel. The dimension-ordered routing technique for a two-dimensional mesh is called ***XY-routing*** and that for a hypercube is called ***E-cube routing***.

Consider a two-dimensional mesh without wraparound connections. In the XY-routing scheme, a message is sent first along the X dimension until it reaches the column

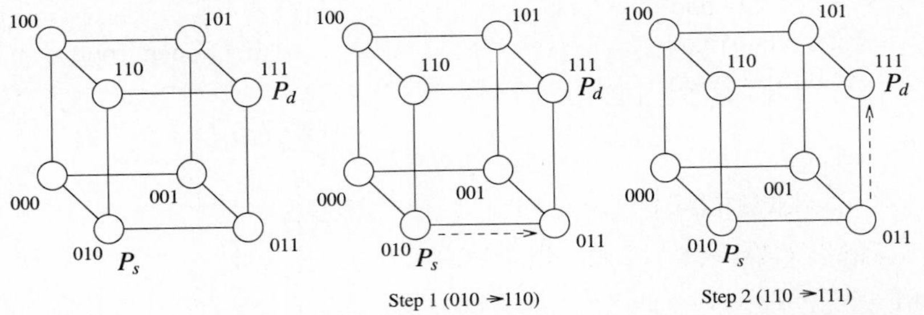

Figure 2.25 Routing a message from processor P_s (010) to processor P_d (111) in a three-dimensional hypercube using E-cube routing.

of the destination processor and then along the Y dimension until it reaches its destination. Let $P_{Sy,Sx}$ represent the position of the source processor and $P_{Dy,Dx}$ represent the position of the destination processor. Any minimal routing scheme should return a path of length $|Sx-Dx|+|Sy-Dy|$. Assume that $Dx \geq Sx$ and $Dy \geq Sy$. In the XY-routing scheme, the message is passed through intermediate processors $P_{Sy,Sx+1}, P_{Sy,Sx+2}, \ldots, P_{Sy,Dx}$ along the X dimension and then through processors $P_{Sy+1,Dx}, P_{Sy+2,Dx}, \ldots, P_{Dy,Dx}$ along the Y dimension to reach the destination. Note that the length of this path is indeed $|Sx - Dx| + |Sy - Dy|$. The routing scheme for meshes discussed in Section 2.4.1 is an example of XY-routing.

E-cube routing for hypercube-connected networks works similarly. Consider a d-dimensional hypercube of p processors. Let P_s and P_d be the labels of the source and destination processors. We know from Section 2.4.1 that the binary representations of these labels are d bits long. Furthermore, the minimum distance between these processors is given by the number of ones in $P_s \oplus P_d$ (where $\oplus$ represents the bitwise exclusive-OR operation). In the E-cube algorithm, processor P_s computes $P_s \oplus P_d$ and sends the message along dimension k, where k is the position of the least significant nonzero bit in $P_s \oplus P_d$. At each intermediate step, processor P_i, which receives the message, computes $P_i \oplus P_d$ and forwards the message along the dimension corresponding to the least significant nonzero bit. This process continues until the message reaches its destination. Example 2.1 illustrates E-cube routing in a three-dimensional hypercube network.

Example 2.1 E-cube Routing in a Hypercube Network

Consider the three-dimensional hypercube shown in Figure 2.25. Let $P_s = 010$ and $P_d = 111$ represent the source and destination processors for a message. Processor P_s computes $010 \oplus 111 = 101$. In the first step, P_s forwards the message along the dimension corresponding to the least significant bit to processor 011. Processor 011 sends the message along the dimension corresponding to the most significant bit $(011 \oplus 111 = 100)$. The message reaches processor 111, which is the destination of the message. ■

In the rest of this book we assume deterministic and minimal message routing for analyzing parallel algorithms. Furthermore, unless otherwise mentioned, routing in hypercubes is assumed to be based on the E-cube algorithm and that in meshes on the XY-routing scheme.

2.7 Communication Costs in Static Interconnection Networks

The time spent communicating information from one processor to another is often a major source of overhead when executing programs on a parallel computer. The time taken to communicate a message between two processors in the network is called ***communication latency***. Communication latency is the sum of the time to prepare a message for transmission and the time taken by the message to traverse the network to its destination. The principal parameters that determine the communication latency are as follows:

(1) ***Startup time*** (t_s): The startup time is the time required to handle a message at the sending processor. This includes the time to prepare the message (adding header, trailer, and error correction information), the time to execute the routing algorithm, and the time to establish an interface between the local processor and the router. This delay is incurred only once for a single message transfer.

(2) ***Per-hop time*** (t_h): After a message leaves a processor, it takes a finite amount of time to reach the next processor in its path. The time taken by the header of a message to travel between two directly-connected processors in the network is called the per-hop time. It is also known as ***node latency***. The per-hop time is directly related to the latency within the routing switch for determining which output buffer or channel the message should be forwarded to.

(3) ***Per-word transfer time*** (t_w): If the channel bandwidth is r words per second, then each word takes time $t_w = 1/r$ to traverse the link. This time is called the per-word transfer time.

Many factors influence the communication latency of a network, such as the topology of the network and the ***switching techniques***. We now discuss two switching techniques that are frequently used in parallel computers. The routing techniques that use them are called store-and-forward routing and cut-through routing.

2.7.1 Store-and-Forward Routing

In store-and-forward routing, when a message is traversing a path with multiple links, each intermediate processor on the path forwards the message to the next processor after it has received and stored the entire message. Figure 2.26(a) shows the communication of a message through a store-and-forward network.

Suppose that a message of size m is being transmitted through such a network. Assume that it traverses l links. At each link, the message incurs a cost t_h for the header and mt_w for the rest of the message to traverse the link. Since there are l such links, the total time is $(t_h + mt_w)l$. Therefore, for store-and-forward routing, the total communication cost for a message of size m words to traverse l communication links is

$$t_{comm} = t_s + (mt_w + t_h)l. \tag{2.2}$$

In current parallel computers, the per-hop time t_h is quite small. For most parallel algorithms, it is less than mt_w even for small values of m and thus can be ignored. For parallel algorithms using store-and-forward routing discussed in this book, we simplify the time given by Equation 2.2 to

$$t_{comm} = t_s + mt_w l.$$

2.7.2 Cut-Through Routing

Store-and-forward routing makes poor use of communication resources. A message is sent from one processor to the next only after the entire message has been received (Figure 2.26(a)). Consider the scenario shown in Figure 2.26(b), in which the original message is broken into two equally sized parts before it is sent. In this case, an intermediate processor waits for only half of the original message to arrive before passing it on. The increased utilization of communication resources and reduced communication time is apparent from Figure 2.26(b). Figure 2.26(c) goes a step further and breaks the message into four parts.

This example demonstrates the underlying principle of ***cut-through routing***, in which a message is advanced from the incoming link to the outgoing link as it arrives. ***Wormhole routing*** is a type of cut-through routing. A message being communicated travels in small units called ***flow-control digits*** or ***flits***. In wormhole routing, flits are pipelined through the communication network. An intermediate processor does not wait for the entire message to arrive before forwarding it. As soon as a flit is received at an intermediate processor, the flit is passed on to the next processor. All flits in a message are routed along the same path. It is no longer necessary to have buffer space at each intermediate processor to store the entire message. Therefore, wormhole routing uses less memory and memory bandwidth at intermediate processors and is faster.

While traversing the network, if a message needs to use a link that is currently in use, then the message is blocked. This may lead to deadlock. Figure 2.27 illustrates deadlock in a wormhole routing network. The destinations of messages 0, 1, 2, and 3 are A, B, C, and D, respectively. A flit from message 0 occupies the link CB (and the associated buffers). However, since link BA is occupied by a flit from message 3, the flit from message 0 is blocked. Similarly, the flit from message 3 is blocked since link AD is in use. We can see that no messages can progress in the network and the network is deadlocked. Deadlocks can be avoided in wormhole networks by using appropriate routing techniques. Both E-cube and XY-routing algorithms are deadlock-free routing schemes.

Consider a message that is traversing such a network. If the message traverses l links, and t_h is the per-hop time, then the header of the message takes lt_h time to reach the

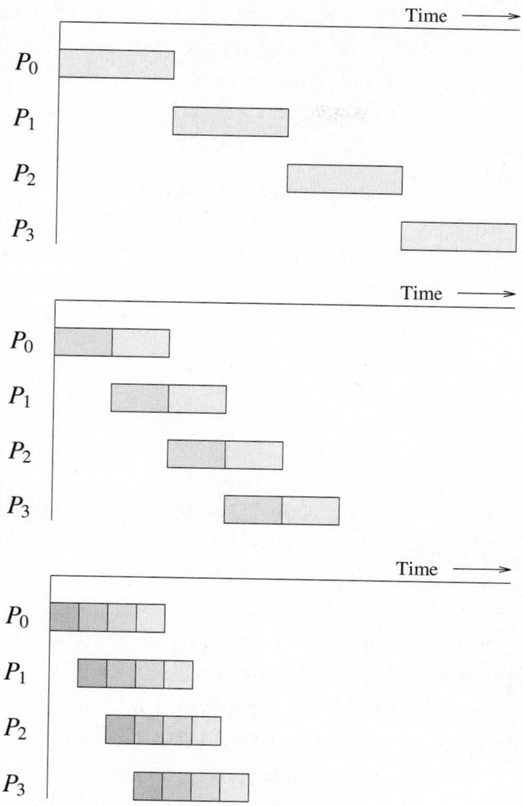

(a) A single message sent over a store-and-forward network

(b) The same message broken into two parts and sent over the network.

(c) The same message broken into four parts and sent over the network.

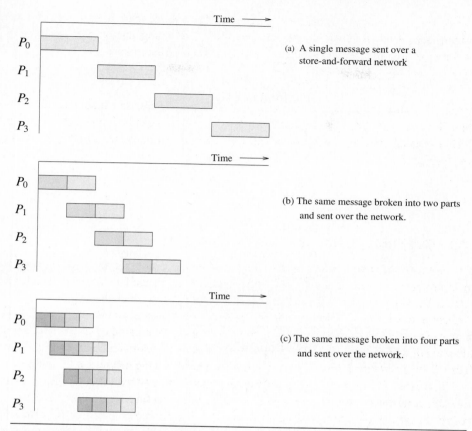

Figure 2.26 Passing a message from processor P_0 to P_3 (a) through a store-and-forward communication network; (b) and (c) extending the concept to cut-through routing. The shaded regions represent the time that the message is in transit. The startup time associated with this message transfer is assumed to be zero.

destination. If the message is m words long, then the entire message will arrive in time mt_w after the arrival of the header of the message. Therefore, the total communication time for cut-through routing is given by

$$t_{comm} = t_s + lt_h + mt_w.$$

This time is an improvement over store-and-forward routing. Disregarding the startup time, the cost to send a message of size m over l hops is only $\Theta(m + l)$ for cut-through routing, whereas in store-and-forward routing, it is $\Theta(ml)$. Note that if the communication is between nearest neighbors (that is, $l = 1$), or if the message size is small, then the communication time is similar for both routing schemes.

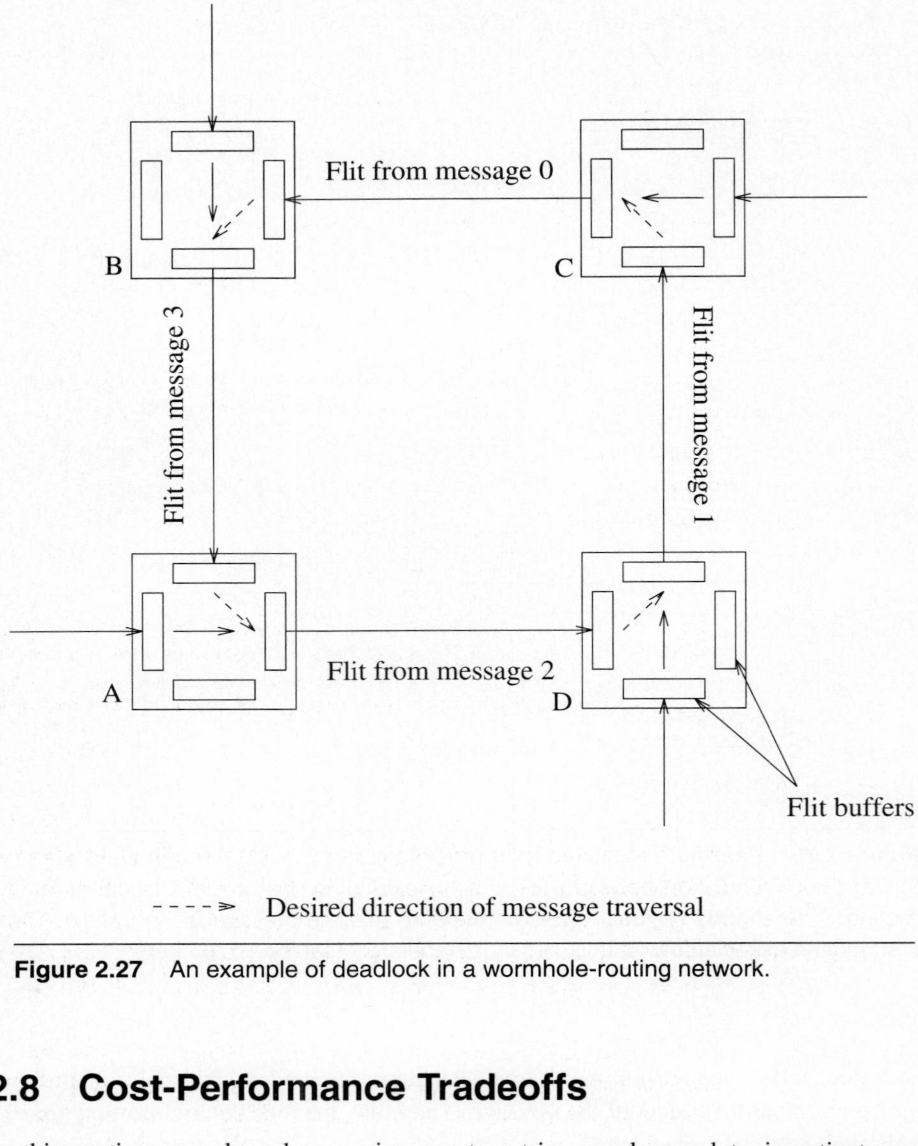

Figure 2.27 An example of deadlock in a wormhole-routing network.

2.8 Cost-Performance Tradeoffs

In this section, we show how various cost metrics can be used to investigate cost-performance tradeoffs in static networks. We illustrate this by analyzing the performance of a mesh and a hypercube network with identical costs.

If the cost of a network is proportional to the number of wires, then a square p-processor wraparound mesh with $(\log p)/4$ wires per channel costs as much as a p-processor hypercube with one wire per channel. Let us compare the average communication latencies of these two networks. The average distance l_{av} between any two processors in a two-dimensional wraparound mesh is $\sqrt{p}/2$ and that in a hypercube is $(\log p)/2$. The time for sending a message of size m between processors that are l_{av} hops apart is given by

$t_s + t_h l_{av} + t_w m$ in networks that use cut-through routing. Since the channel width of the mesh is scaled up by a factor of $(\log p)/4$, the per-word transfer time is reduced by the same factor. Hence, if the per-word transfer time on the hypercube is t_w, then the same time on a mesh with fattened channels is given by $4t_w/(\log p)$. Hence, the average communication latency for a hypercube is given by $t_s + t_h(\log p)/2 + t_w m$ and that for a wraparound mesh of the same cost is $t_s + t_h\sqrt{p}/2 + 4mt_w/(\log p)$.

Let us now investigate the behavior of these expressions. For a fixed number of processors, as the message size is increased, the communication term due to t_w dominates. Comparing t_w for the two networks, we see that the time for a wraparound mesh $(4mt_w/(\log p))$ is less than the time for a hypercube $(t_w m)$ if p is greater than 16 and the message size m is sufficiently large. Under these circumstances, point-to-point communication of large messages between random pairs of processors takes less time on a wraparound mesh with cut-through routing than on a hypercube of the same cost. Furthermore, for algorithms in which communication is suited to a mesh, the extra bandwidth of each channel results in better performance (Problem 3.33). Note that, with store-and-forward routing, the mesh is no longer more cost-efficient than a hypercube. Similar cost-performance tradeoffs can be analyzed for the general case of k-ary d-cubes (Problems 2.19–2.22).

The communication latencies above are computed under light load conditions in the network. As the number of messages increases, there is contention on the network. Contention affects the mesh network more adversely than the hypercube network. Therefore, if the network is heavily loaded, the hypercube will outperform the mesh (Problem 3.33).

If the cost of a network is proportional to its bisection width, then a p-processor wraparound mesh with $\sqrt{p}/4$ wires per channel has a cost equal to a p-processor hypercube with one wire per channel. Let us perform an analysis similar to the one above to investigate cost-performance tradeoffs using this cost metric. Since the mesh channels are wider by a factor of $\sqrt{p}/4$, the per-word transfer time will be lower by an identical factor. Therefore, the communication latencies for the hypercube and the mesh networks of the same cost are given by $t_s + t_h(\log p)/2 + t_w m$ and $t_s + t_h\sqrt{p}/2 + 4mt_w/\sqrt{p}$, respectively. Once again, as the message size m becomes large for a given number of processors, the t_w term dominates. Comparing this term for the two networks, we see that for $p > 16$ and sufficiently large message sizes, a mesh outperforms a hypercube of the same cost. Therefore, for large enough messages, a mesh is always better than a hypercube of the same cost, provided the network is lightly loaded (Problem 3.33). Even when the network is heavily loaded, the performance of a mesh is similar to that of a hypercube of the same cost (Problem 3.33).

2.9 Architectural Models for Parallel Algorithm Design

Different parallel architectures may require different algorithms to solve the same problem efficiently. Is it possible to avoid designing a new algorithm for each architecture? This would be possible if there was a universal abstract model for parallel architectures. Parallel programs designed for this universal model could be ported to specific computers.

The von Neumann model is a universal computational model for sequential computers, enabling the design of portable sequential programs. Although the processor architecture and memory organization of sequential computers differ, they all conform to the same abstract model. Consequently, a program designed for the von Neumann model can be compiled and run relatively efficiently on any sequential computer. In particular, the asymptotic time complexity of an algorithm on different implementations of the von Neumann model is the same. Indeed, the existence of a universal model has played a key role in the impressive growth of the application of sequential computers. If algorithms had to be redesigned for every new sequential architecture, the cost of software development would have been much higher, greatly limiting the cost-effective application of computers.

Universal Models for Parallel Computers A universal model for parallel computers must exhibit two characteristics. First, it must be sufficiently general to capture the salient properties of a large class of parallel computers. Second, programs designed for this abstract model must execute efficiently on actual parallel computers. These characteristics represent conflicting goals. A universal model for parallel computers must make assumptions about the degree of connectivity among the processors. Networks such as linear arrays and meshes have a relatively low degree of connectivity compared to networks such as hypercubes. If the model assumes a low degree of connectivity, algorithms designed for it will be optimal for parallel computers with this characteristic. However, the same algorithms may be sub-optimal for architectures with a high degree of connectivity, because the communication resources of the computer will be under-utilized. On the other hand, if the model assumes a high degree of connectivity among processors, then algorithms designed for the model may be sub-optimal on an architecture such as a mesh, yet optimal on a hypercube. Thus, regardless of the connectivity of the parallel model, it yields sub-optimal performance for some architectures. This argues against the existence of a universal parallel model. No such model is currently known to exist.

Another approach to parallel algorithm design is to design parallel algorithms in terms of basic data communication operations. In this approach, only the implementation of these operations must be optimized for different parallel computers. In practice, a relatively small set of communication operations form the core of many parallel algorithms. Therefore, designing these operations is a relatively simple task. This is the approach to parallel program design that is adopted in the rest of this book.

Role of Data Locality There are two major components of parallel algorithm design. The first one is the identification and specification of the overall problem as a set of tasks that can be performed concurrently. The second is the mapping of these tasks onto different processors so that the overall communication overhead is minimized. The first component specifies ***concurrency***, and the second one specifies ***data locality***. The performance of an algorithm on a parallel architecture depends on both. Concurrency is necessary to keep the processors busy. Locality is important because it minimizes communication overhead. Ideally, a parallel algorithm should have maximum concurrency and locality. However, for most algorithms, there is a tradeoff. An algorithm that has more concurrency often has less locality. As illustrated in Problem 5.36, data locality is important not only in message-passing architectures but also in shared-address-space architectures.

Architectural Models Used in This Book In this book, we discuss parallel algorithms mainly in the context of mesh- and hypercube-connected parallel computers. Although extensive work has been done on PRAM algorithms, we use the PRAM model only to identify concurrency in a problem. The PRAM model captures concurrency in a task; however, it fails to enforce data locality in parallel algorithms. In particular, a PRAM algorithm tells us very little about mapping the computation onto actual processors. This is because communication is free on a PRAM, but is often the most significant overhead on practical parallel computers.

The selection of the mesh topology follows from the following characteristics:

(1) Meshes containing a large number of processors can be constructed relatively inexpensively.
(2) Many applications map naturally onto a mesh network.
(3) Although the mesh network has a high diameter, as message size becomes large, the effect of higher diameter is diminished for networks using cut-through routing. Consequently, many algorithms ported directly from networks with a higher degree of connectivity (such as hypercubes) yield similar performance on mesh architectures. For these algorithms, meshes have a favorable cost-performance ratio.
(4) Several commercially-available parallel computers are based on the mesh network.

The selection of the hypercube was motivated by the following criteria:

(1) For a large class of problems, the fastest hypercube algorithms are asymptotically as fast as the fastest PRAM algorithms. Therefore, hypercubes are able not only to tap maximum concurrency for these applications but also to impose data locality.
(2) For many problems, the best hypercube algorithm is also the best algorithm for other networks such as fat trees, meshes, and multistage networks, provided the algorithm is adapted to them appropriately. Therefore, a hypercube algorithm is often a good starting point for designing algorithms for such architectures.
(3) Hypercubes have an elegant recursive structure that makes them attractive for designing a wide class of algorithms.

2.10 Bibliographic Remarks

Several textbooks discuss parallel architectures and interconnection networks [AG89, DeC89, Hwa93, HB84, Lil92, Sie85, Sto93]. The classification of parallel computers as SISD, SIMD, and MIMD was introduced by Flynn [Fly72]. He also proposed the MISD (multiple instruction stream, single data stream) model. MISD is less natural than the other classes, although it can be viewed as a model for pipelining. Gordon Bell [Bel92] classifies MIMD parallel computers based on the physical and logical memory organization. Ni [Ni91] provides a layered classification of parallel computers based on hardware architecture, address space, communication model, language, programming environment, and applications.

Interconnection networks have been an area of active interest for decades. Feng [Fen81] provides a tutorial on static and dynamic interconnection networks. The perfect shuffle interconnection pattern was introduced by Stone [Sto71]. Omega networks were introduced by Lawrie [Law75]. Other multistage networks have also been proposed. These include the Flip network [Bat76] and the Baseline network [WF80]. Mesh of trees and pyramidal mesh are discussed by Leighton [Lei92]. Leighton [Lei92] provides a detailed discussion of many such networks.

The C.mmp was an early research prototype MIMD shared-address-space parallel computer based on the Crossbar switch [WB72]. The Fujitsu VPP 500 and the Cray Y-MP are more recent examples of crossbar-based parallel computers. Several parallel computers were based on multistage interconnection networks including the BBN Butterfly [BBN89], the NYU Ultracomputer [GGK+83], and the IBM RP-3 [PBG+85]. The Stanford Dash [LLG+92] and the KSR-1 [Ken90] are NUMA shared-address-space computers.

The Cosmic Cube [Sei85] was among the first message-passing parallel computer based on a hypercube-connected network. Commercially available hypercube-based computers include the nCUBE 2 [nCU90], the Intel iPSC-1, iPSC-2, and iPSC/860. Saad and Shultz [SS88, SS89a] derive interesting properties of the hypercube-connected network and a variety of other static networks [SS89b]. Many message-passing computers are based on the mesh network. The Intel Paragon XP/S [Sup91] and the Mosaic C [Sei92] are two-dimensional mesh-based computers. The MIT J-Machine [D+92] is based on a three-dimensional mesh network. The performance of mesh-connected computers can be improved by augmenting the mesh network with broadcast buses [KR87]. The reconfigurable mesh architecture (Figure 2.29) was introduced by Miller et al. [MKRS88].

The DADO parallel computer was based on a tree network [SM86]. It used a complete binary tree of depth ten. Leiserson [Lei85] introduced the fat-tree interconnection network and proved several interesting characteristics of it. He showed that for a given volume of hardware, no network has much better performance than a fat tree. The Thinking Machines CM-5 [Thi91] parallel computer is based on a fat tree interconnection network.

The Illiac IV [Bar68] was among the first SIMD parallel computers. Other SIMD computers include the Goodyear MPP [Bat80], the DAP 610, and more recently the CM-2 [Thi90], MasPar MP-1, and MasPar MP-2 [Nic90]. The CM-5 and DADO incorporate both SIMD and MIMD features. Both are MIMD computers but have extra hardware for fast synchronization, which enables them to operate in SIMD mode. The CM-5 has a control network to augment the data network. The control network provides such functions as broadcasting, reduction, and other global operations.

Leighton [Lei92] and Ranka and Sahni [RS90] discuss embedding one interconnection network into another. Gray codes, used in embedding linear array and mesh topologies, are discussed by Reingold [RND77]. Ranka and Sahni [RS90] discuss the concepts of congestion, dilation, and expansion. Our discussion of embeddings in Section 2.5 is influenced by Ranka and Sahni's discussion [RS90].

A comprehensive survey of cut-through routing techniques is provided by Ni and McKinley [NM93]. The wormhole routing technique was proposed by Dally and Seitz [DS86]. A related technique called ***virtual cut-through***, in which communication buffers are provided at intermediate processors, was described by Kermani and Kleinrock [KK79]. Dally and Seitz [DS87] discuss deadlock-free wormhole routing based on channel dependence graphs. Deterministic routing schemes based on dimension ordering are often used to avoid deadlocks. Cut-through routing has been used in several parallel computers including the nCUBE 2, Paragon XP/S, and J-Machine. Our discussion of wormhole routing is based on the paper by by Ni and McKinley [NM93]. The E-cube routing scheme for hypercubes was proposed by [SB77].

Dally [Dal90b] discusses the cost-performance tradeoffs of networks for message-passing computers. By using the bisection bandwidth of a network as a measure of the cost of the network, he showed that low-dimensional networks (such as two-dimensional meshes) are more cost-effective than high-dimensional networks (such as hypercubes) [Dal87, Dal90b, Dal90a]. Kreeger and Vempaty [KV92] derive the bandwidth equalization factor for a mesh with respect to a hypercube-connected computer for all-to-all personalized communication (Section 3.5). Gupta and Kumar [GK93] analyze the cost-performance tradeoffs of FFT computations on mesh and hypercube networks for two different cost criteria.

The properties of PRAMs have been studied extensively [FW78, KR88, LY86, Sni82, Sni85]. Books by Akl [Akl89], Gibbons [GR90], and Jaja [Jaj92] address PRAM algorithms. Our discussion of PRAM is based upon the book by Jaja [Jaj92]. A number of processor networks have been proposed to simulate PRAM models [AHMP87, HP89, LPP88, LPP89, MV84, Upf84, UW84]. Mehlhorn and Vishkin [MV84] propose the ***module parallel computer*** (MPC) to simulate PRAM models. The MPC is a message-passing parallel computer composed of p processors, each with a fixed amount of memory and connected by a completely-connected network. The MPC is capable of probabilistically simulating T steps of a PRAM in $T \log p$ steps if the total memory is increased by a factor of $\log p$. The main drawback of the MPC model is that a completely-connected network is difficult to construct for a large number of processors. Alt et al. [AHMP87] propose another model called the ***bounded-degree network*** (BDN). In this network, each processor is connected to a fixed number of other processors. Karlin and Upfal [KU86] describe an $O(T \log p)$ time probabilistic simulation of a PRAM on a BDN. Hornick and Preparata [HP89] propose a bipartite network that connects sets of processors and memory pools. They investigate both the message-passing MPC and BDN based on a mesh of trees.

Many modifications of the PRAM model have been proposed that attempt to bring it closer to practical parallel computers. Aggarwal, Chandra, and Snir [ACS89b, ACS89c] propose the LPRAM (local-memory PRAM) model and the BPRAM (block PRAM) model [ACS89b]. They also introduce a hierarchical memory model of computation [ACS89a]. In this model, memory units at different levels are accessed in different times. Parallel algorithms for this model induce locality by bringing data into faster memory units before using them and returning them to the slower memory units. Other PRAM models such as phase PRAM [Gib89], XPRAM [Val90b], and the delay model [PY88] have also been proposed. Many researchers have investigated abstract universal models for parallel computers [C^+93, Sny86, Val90a].

Problems

2.1 As mentioned in Section 2.2, CRCW is the most powerful PRAM model. We also discussed four classes of concurrent write operations for CRCW PRAMs: common CRCW, arbitrary CRCW, priority CRCW, and sum CRCW. It is possible to emulate one CRCW PRAM model on the other PRAM models. Let t be the run time of an algorithm on a priority CRCW PRAM model. Give an upper bound on the run time of this algorithm on the following models:

(a) a common CRCW PRAM

(b) an arbitrary CRCW PRAM

(c) a CREW PRAM

(d) an EREW PRAM

2.2 Consider an EREW PRAM with p processors and m memory locations. We can emulate this model on a p-processor message-passing parallel computer in which each processor has m/p memory locations. Let t be the run time of an algorithm on a p-processor EREW PRAM model. Give an upper bound on the run time of this algorithm on the following architectures:

(a) a p-processor ring

(b) a p-processor mesh

(c) a p-processor hypercube

2.3 [Lei92] The ***butterfly network*** is an interconnection network composed of $\log p$ levels (as the omega network). In a butterfly network, each switching element i at a level l is connected to the identically numbered element at level $l+1$ and to a switching element whose number differs from itself only at the lth most significant bit. Therefore, switching element S_i is connected to element S_j at level l if $j = i$ or $j = i \oplus (2^{\log p - l})$.

Figure 2.28 illustrates an eight-processor butterfly network. Show the equivalence of a butterfly network and an omega network.

Hint: Rearrange the switches of an omega network so that it looks like a butterfly network.

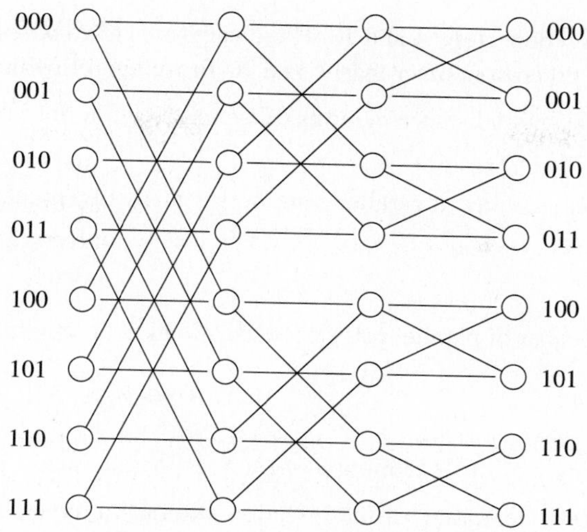

Figure 2.28 An eight-processor butterfly network.

2.4 Consider the omega network described in Section 2.3.3. As shown there, this network is a blocking network (that is, a processor that uses the network to access a memory location might prevent another processor from accessing another memory location). Consider an omega network that connects p processors. Define a function f that maps $P = [0, 1, \ldots, p-1]$ onto a permutation P' of P (that is, $P'[i] = f(P[i])$ and $P'[i] \in P$ for all $0 \le i < p$). Think of this function as mapping communication requests by the processors so that processor $P[i]$ requests communication with processor $P'[i]$.

(a) How many distinct permutation functions exist?

(b) How many of these functions result in non-blocking communication?

(c) What is the probability that an arbitrary function will result in non-blocking communication?

2.5 Given the labeling scheme described in Section 2.4.1, how many distinct labelings exist for a d-dimensional hypercube?

2.6 A cycle in a graph is defined as a path originating and terminating at the same node. The length of a cycle is the number of edges in the cycle. Show that there are no odd-length cycles in a d-dimensional hypercube.

2.7 The labels in a d-dimensional hypercube use d bits. Fixing any k of these bits, show that processors whose labels differ in the remaining $d-k$ bit positions form a $(d-k)$-dimensional subcube composed of $2^{(d-k)}$ processors.

2.8 Let A and B be two processors in a d-dimensional hypercube. Define $H(A, B)$ to be the Hamming distance between A and B, and $P(A, B)$ to be the number of distinct paths connecting A and B. These paths are called ***parallel paths*** and have no common processors other than A and B. Prove the following:

(a) The minimum distance in terms of communication links between A and B is given by $H(A, B)$.

(b) The total number of parallel paths between any two processors is

$$P(A, B) = d.$$

(c) The number of parallel paths between A and B of length $H(A, B)$ is

$$P_{length=H(A,B)}(A, B) = H(A, B).$$

(d) The length of the remaining $d - H(A, B)$ parallel paths is $H(A, B) + 2$.

2.9 In the informal derivation of the bisection width of a hypercube (Section 2.4.2), we used the construction of a hypercube to show that a d-dimensional hypercube is formed from two $(d-1)$-dimensional hypercubes. We argued that because corresponding processors in each of these subcubes have a direct communication link, there are 2^{d-1} links across the partition. However, it is possible to partition a hypercube into two parts such that neither of the partitions is a hypercube. Show that any such partitions will have more than 2^{d-1} direct links between them.

2.10 **[MKRS88]** A $\sqrt{p} \times \sqrt{p}$ ***reconfigurable mesh*** consists of a $\sqrt{p} \times \sqrt{p}$ array of processors connected to a grid-shaped reconfigurable broadcast bus. A 4×4 reconfigurable mesh is shown in Figure 2.29. Each processor has locally-controllable bus switches. The internal connections among the four ports, north (N), east (E), west (W), and south (S), of a processor can be configured during the execution of an algorithm. Note that there are 15 connection patterns. For example, {SW, EN}represents the configuration in which port S is connected to port W and port N is connected to port E. Each bit of the bus carries one of *1-signal* or *0-signal* at any time. The switches allow the broadcast bus to be divided into subbuses, providing smaller reconfigurable meshes. For a given set of switch settings, a ***subbus*** is a maximally-connected subset of the processors. Other than the buses and the switches, the reconfigurable mesh is similar to the standard two-dimensional mesh. Assume that only one processor is allowed to broadcast on a ***subbus*** shared by multiple processors at any time.
Determine the bisection width, the diameter, and the number of switching elements and communication links for a reconfigurable mesh of $\sqrt{p} \times \sqrt{p}$ processors. What are the advantages and disadvantages of a reconfigurable mesh as compared to a wraparound mesh?

2.11 **[Lei92]** A ***mesh of trees*** is a network that imposes a tree interconnection on a grid of processors. A $\sqrt{p} \times \sqrt{p}$ mesh of trees is constructed as follows. Starting with a $\sqrt{p} \times \sqrt{p}$ grid of processors a complete binary tree is imposed on each row of the grid. Then a complete binary tree is imposed on each column of the

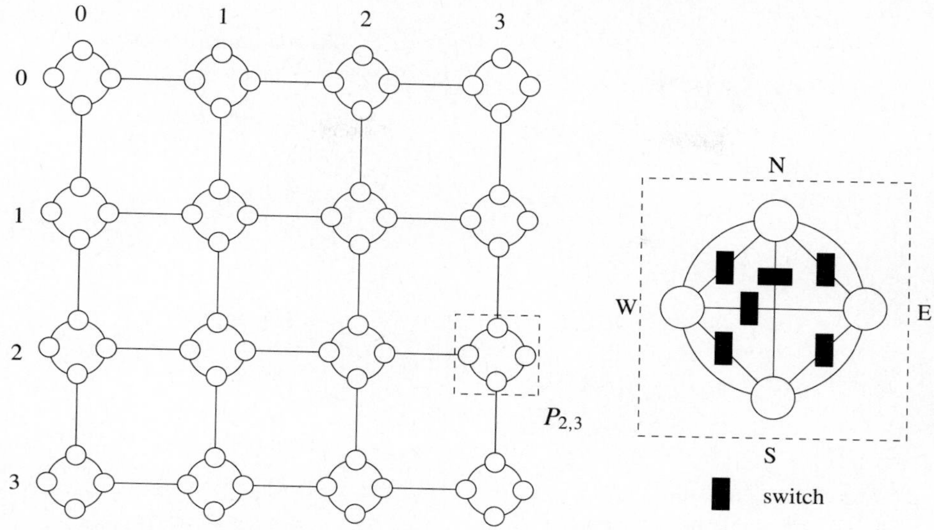

Figure 2.29 Switch connection patterns in reconfigurable mesh.

grid. Figure 2.30 illustrates the construction of a 4×4 mesh of trees. Assume that the nodes at intermediate levels are switching elements. Determine the bisection width, diameter, and total number of switching elements in a $\sqrt{p} \times \sqrt{p}$ mesh of processors.

2.12 **[Lei92]** Extend the two-dimensional mesh of trees (Problem 2.11) to d dimensions to construct a $p^{1/d} \times p^{1/d} \times \cdots \times p^{1/d}$ mesh of trees. We can do this by fixing grid positions in all dimensions to different values and imposing a complete binary tree on the one dimension that is being varied.
Derive the total number of switching elements in a $p^{1/d} \times p^{1/d} \times \cdots \times p^{1/d}$ mesh of trees. Calculate the diameter, bisection width, and wiring cost in terms of the total number of wires. What are the advantages and disadvantages of a mesh of trees as compared to a wraparound mesh?

2.13 **[Lei92]** A network related to the mesh of trees is the d-dimensional ***pyramidal mesh***. A d-dimensional pyramidal mesh imposes a pyramid on the underlying processor grid (as opposed to a complete tree in the mesh of trees). The generalization is as follows. In the mesh of trees, all but one dimension are fixed and a tree is imposed on the remaining dimension. In a pyramid, all but two dimensions are fixed and a pyramid is imposed on the mesh formed by these two dimensions. In a tree, each node i at level k is connected to node $i/2$ at level $k-1$. Similarly, in a pyramid, a node (i, j) at level k is connected to a node $(i/2, j/2)$ at level $k-1$. Furthermore, the nodes at each level are connected in a mesh. A two-dimensional pyramidal mesh is illustrated in Figure 2.31.

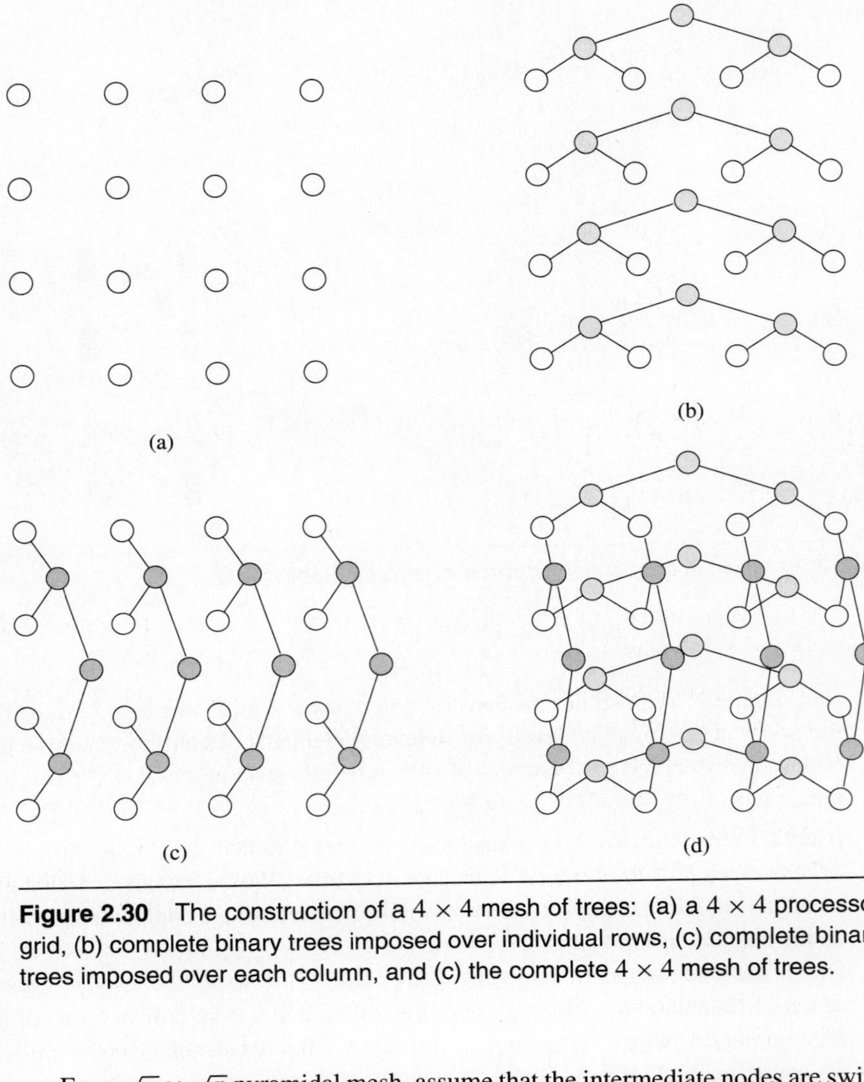

Figure 2.30 The construction of a 4 × 4 mesh of trees: (a) a 4 × 4 processor grid, (b) complete binary trees imposed over individual rows, (c) complete binary trees imposed over each column, and (c) the complete 4 × 4 mesh of trees.

For a $\sqrt{p} \times \sqrt{p}$ pyramidal mesh, assume that the intermediate nodes are switching elements, and derive the diameter, bisection width, arc connectivity, and cost in terms of the number of communication links and switching elements. What are the advantages and disadvantages of a pyramidal mesh as compared to a mesh of trees?

2.14 **[Lei92]** One of the drawbacks of a hypercube-connected network is that different wires in the network are of different lengths. This implies that data takes different times to traverse different communication links. It appears that two-dimensional mesh networks with wraparound connections suffer from this drawback too. However, it is possible to fabricate a two-dimensional wraparound mesh using wires of fixed length. Illustrate this layout by drawing such a 4 × 4 wraparound mesh.

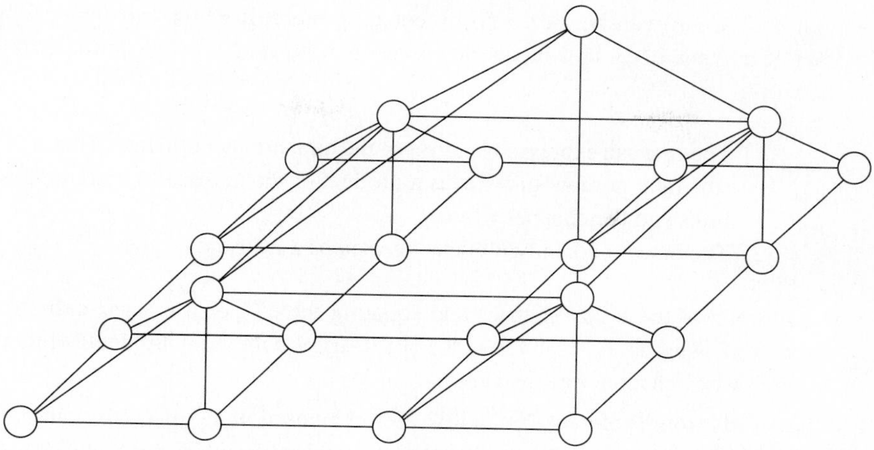

Figure 2.31 A 4×4 pyramidal mesh.

2.15 Show how to embed a p-processor three-dimensional mesh into a p-processor hypercube. What are the allowable values of p for your embedding?

2.16 Show how to embed a p-processor mesh of trees into a p-processor hypercube. Is your embedding different from the mesh embedding discussed in Section 2.5.2?

2.17 Consider a complete binary tree of $2^d - 1$ nodes in which each node is a processor. What is the minimum-dilation mapping of such a tree onto a d-dimensional hypercube?

2.18 The concept of a ***minimum congestion mapping*** is very useful. Consider two parallel computers with different interconnection networks such that a congestion-r mapping of the first into the second exists. Ignoring the dilation of the mapping, if each communication link in the second computer is more than r times faster than the first computer, the second computer is strictly superior to the first.
Now consider mapping a d-dimensional hypercube onto a 2^d-processor mesh. Ignoring the dilation of the mapping, what is the minimum-congestion mapping of the hypercube onto the mesh? Use this result to determine whether a 1024-processor mesh with communication links operating at 25 million bytes per second is strictly better than a 1024-processor hypercube (whose processors are identical to those used in the mesh) with communication links operating at two million bytes per second.

2.19 Derive the diameter, number of links, and bisection width of a k-ary d-cube with p processors. Define l_{av} to be the average distance between any two processors in the network. Derive l_{av} for a k-ary d-cube.

2.20 Consider a hypercube network of p processors. Assume that the channel width of each communication link is one. The channel width of the links in a k-ary d-cube (for $d < \log p$) can be increased by equating the cost of the this network with that of a hypercube. Two distinct measures can be used to evaluate the cost of a network.

(1) The cost can expressed in terms of the total number of wires in the network (the total number of wires is a product of the number of communication links and the channel width).
(2) The bisection bandwidth can be used as a measure of cost.

Using each of these cost metrics and equating the cost of a k-ary d-cube with a hypercube, what is the channel width of a k-ary d-cube with an identical number of processors, channel rate, and cost?

2.21 The results from Problems 2.19 and 2.20 can be used in a cost-performance analysis of static interconnection networks. Consider a k-ary d-cube network of p processors with cut-through routing. Assume a hypercube-connected network of p processors with channel width one. The channel width of other networks in the family is scaled up so that their cost is identical to that of the hypercube. Let s and s' be the scaling factors for the channel width derived by equating the costs specified by the two cost metrics in Problem 2.20.
For each of the two scaling factors s and s', express the average communication time between any two processors as a function of the dimensionality (d) of a k-ary d-cube and the number of processors. Plot the communication time as a function of the dimensionality for $p = 256, 512$, and 1024, message size $m = 512$ bytes, $t_s = 50.0\mu s$, and $t_h = t_w = 0.5\mu s$ (for the hypercube). For these values of p and m, what is the dimensionality of the network that yields the best performance for a given cost?

2.22 Repeat Problem 2.21 for a k-ary d-cube with store-and-forward routing.

References

[ACS89a] A. Aggarwal, A. K. Chandra, and M. Snir. A model for hierarchical memory. Technical Report RC 15118 (No. 67337), IBM T. J. Watson Research Center, Yorktown Heights, NY, 1989.

[ACS89b] A. Aggarwal, A. K. Chandra, and M. Snir. On communication latency in PRAM computations. Technical Report RC 14973 (No. 66882), IBM T. J. Watson Research Center, Yorktown Heights, NY, 1989.

[ACS89c] A. Aggarwal, A. K. Chandra, and M. Snir. Communication complexity of PRAMs. Technical Report RC 14998 (No. 64644), IBM T. J. Watson Research Center, Yorktown Heights, NY, Yorktown Heights, NY, 1989.

[AG89] G. S. Almasi and A. Gottlieb. *Highly Parallel Computing*. Benjamin/Cummings, Redwood City, CA, 1989.

[AHMP87] H. Alt, T. Hagerup, K. Mehlhorn, and F. P. Preparata. Deterministic simulation of idealized parallel computers on more realistic ones. *SIAM Journal of Computing*, 16(5):808–835, October 1987.

[Akl89] S. G. Akl. *The Design and Analysis of Parallel Algorithms*. Prentice-Hall, Englewood Cliffs, NJ, 1989.

[Bar68] G. H. Barnes. The ILLIAC IV computer. *IEEE Transactions on Computers*, C-17(8):746–757, 1968.

[Bat76] K. E. Batcher. The Flip network in STARAN. In *Proceedings of International Conference on Parallel Processing*, 65–71, 1976.

[Bat80] K. E. Batcher. Design of a massively parallel processor. *IEEE Transactions on Computers*, 836–840, September 1980.

[BBN89] BBN Advanced Computers Inc. *TC-2000 Technical Product Summary*. Cambridge, MA. 1989.

[Bel92] C. G. Bell. Ultracomputer: A teraflop before its time. *Communications of the ACM*, 35(8):27–47, 1992.

[C+93] D. Culler et al. LogP: Towards a realistic model of parallel computation. In *Proceedings of the Fourth ACM SIGPLAN Symposium on Principles and Practices of Parallel Programming*, 1–12, 1993. A detailed version is available as Technical Report UCB-CD-93-713, Computer Science Division, University of California, Berkeley, CA.

[D+92] W. J. Dally et al. The message-driven processor. *IEEE Micro*, 12(2):23–39, 1992.

[Dal87] W. J. Dally. *A VLSI Architecture for Concurrent Data Structures*. Kluwer Academic Publishers, Boston, MA, 1987.

[Dal90a] W. J. Dally. Analysis of k-ary n-cube interconnection networks. *IEEE Transactions on Computers*, 39(6), June 1990.

[Dal90b] W. J. Dally. Network and processor architecture for message-driven computers. In R. Sauya and G. Birtwistle, editors, *VLSI and Parallel Computation*. Morgan Kaufmann, San Mateo, CA, 1990.

[DeC89] A. L. DeCegama. *The Technology of Parallel Processing: Parallel Processing Architectures and VLSI Hardware: Volume 1*. Prentice-Hall, Englewood Cliffs, NJ, 1989.

[DS86] W. J. Dally and C. L. Seitz. The torus routing chip. *Journal of Distributed Computing*, 1(3):187–196, 1986.

[DS87] W. J. Dally and C. L. Seitz. Deadlock-free message routing in multiprocessor interconnection networks. *IEEE Transactions on Computers*, C-36(5):547–553, 1987.

[Fen81] T. Y. Feng. A survey of interconnection networks. *IEEE Computer*, 12–27, December 1981.

[Fly72] M. J. Flynn. Some computer organizations and their effectiveness. *IEEE Transactions on Computers*, C-21(9):948–960, 1972.

[FW78] S. Fortune and J. Wyllie. Parallelism in random access machines. In *Proceedings of ACM Symposium on Theory of Computing*, 114–118, 1978.

[GGK+83] A. Gottlieb, R. Grishman, C. P. Kruskal, K. P. McAuliffe, L. Rudolph, and M. Snir. The NYU Ultracomputer—designing a MIMD, shared memory parallel computer. *IEEE Transactions on Computers*, C–32(2):175–189, February 1983.

[Gib89] P. B. Gibbons. A more practical PRAM model. In *Proceedings of the 1989 ACM Symposium on Parallel Algorithms and Architectures*, 158–168, 1989.

[GK93] A. Gupta and V. Kumar. The scalability of FFT on parallel computers. *IEEE Transactions on Parallel and Distributed Systems*, 4(7), July 1993. A detailed version available as Technical Report TR 90-53, Department of Computer Science, University of Minnesota, Minneapolis, MN.

[GR90] A. Gibbons and W. Rytter. *Efficient Parallel Algorithms*. Cambridge University Press, Cambridge, UK, 1990.

[HB84] K. Hwang and F. A. Briggs. *Computer Architecture and Parallel Processing*. McGraw-Hill, New York, NY, 1984.

[HP89] S. W. Hornick and F. P. Preparata. Deterministic PRAM simulation with constant redundancy. In *Proceedings of the 1989 ACM Symposium on Parallel Algorithms and Architectures*, 103–109, 1989.

[Hwa93] K. Hwang. *Advanced Computer Architecture: Parallelism, Scalability, Programmability*. McGraw-Hill, New York, NY, 1993.

[Jaj92] J. Jaja. *An Introduction to Parallel Algorithms*. Addison-Wesley, Reading, MA, 1992.

[Ken90] Kendall Square Research Corporation. *KSR-1 Overview*. Waltham, MA. 1990.

[KK79] P. Kermani and L. Kleinrock. Virtual cut-through: A new communication switching technique. *Computer Networks*, 3(4):267–286, 1979.

[KR87] V. K. P. Kumar and C. S. Raghavendra. Array processor with multiple broadcasting. *Journal of Parallel and Distributed Computing*, 173–190, 1987.

[KR88] R. M. Karp and V. Ramachandran. A survey of complexity of algorithms for shared-memory machines. Technical Report 408, University of California, Berkeley, 1988.

[KU86] A. R. Karlin and E. Upfal. Parallel hashing - an efficient implementation of shared memory. In *Proceedings of 18th ACM Conference on Theory of Computing*, 160–168, 1986.

[KV92] K. Kreeger and N. R. Vempaty. Comparison of meshes vs. hypercubes for data rearrangement. Technical Report UCF-CS-92-28, Department of Computer Science, University of Central Florida, Orlando, FL, 1992.

[Law75] D. H. Lawrie. Access and alignment of data in an array processor. *IEEE Transactions on Computers*, C-24(1):1145–1155, 1975.

[Lei85] C. E. Leiserson. Fat-trees : Universal networks for hardware efficient supercomputing. In *Proceedings of the 1985 International Conference on Parallel Processing*, 393–402, 1985.

[Lei92] F. T. Leighton. *Introduction to Parallel Algorithms and Architectures*. Morgan Kaufmann, San Mateo, CA, 1992.

[Lil92] D. J. Lilja. *Architectural Alternatives for Exploiting Parallelism*. IEEE Computer Society Press, Los Alamitos, CA, 1992.

[LLG+92] D. Lenoski, J. Laudon, K. Gharachorloo, W. D. Weber, A. Gupta, J. L. Hennessy, M. Horowitz, and M. Lam. The stanford dash multiprocessor. *IEEE Computer*, 63–79, March 1992.

[LPP88] F. Luccio, A. Pietracaprina, and G. Pucci. A probabilistic simulation of PRAMs on a bounded degree network. *Information Processing Letters*, 28:141–147, July 1988.

[LPP89] F. Luccio, A. Pietracaprina, and G. Pucci. A new scheme for deterministic simulation of PRAMs in VLSI. *SIAM Journal of Computing*, 1989.

[LY86] M. Li and Y. Yesha. New lower bounds for parallel computations. In *Proceedings of 18th ACM Conference on Theory of Computing*, 177–187, 1986.

[MKRS88] R. Miller, V. K. P. Kumar, D. I. Reisis, and Q. F. Stout. Meshes with reconfigurable buses. In *Proceedings of MIT Conference on Advanced Research in VLSI*, 163–178, 1988.

[MV84] K. Mehlhorn and U. Vishkin. Randomized and deterministic simulations of PRAMs by parallel machines with restricted granularity of parallel memories. *Acta Informatica*, 21(4):339–374, November 1984.

[nCU90] nCUBE Corporation. *nCUBE 6400 Processor Manual*. Beaverton, OR. 1990.

[Ni91] L. M. Ni. A layered classification of parallel computers. In *Proceedings of 1991 International Conference for Young Computer Scientists*, 28–33, 1991.

[Nic90] J. R. Nickolls. The design of the MasPar MP-1: A cost-effective massively parallel computer. In *IEEE Digest of Papers—Comcom*, 25–28. IEEE Computer Society Press, Los Alamitos, CA, 1990.

[NM93] L. M. Ni and McKinley. A survey of wormhole routing techniques in direct connect networks. *IEEE Computer*, 26(2), February 1993.

[PBG+85] G. F. Pfister, W. C. Brantley, D. A. George, S. L. Harvey, W. J. Kleinfelder, K. P. McAuliffe, E. A. Melton, V. A. Norlton, and J. Weiss. The IBM research parallel processor prototype (RP3): Introduction and architecture. In *Proceedings of 1985 International Conference on Parallel Processing*, 764–771, 1985.

[PY88] C. H. Papadimitriou and M. Yannakakis. Towards an architecture independent analysis of parallel algorithms. In *Proceedings of 20th ACM Symposium on Theory of Computing*, 510–513, 1988.

[RND77] E. M. Reingold, J. Nievergelt, and N. Deo. *Combinatorial Algorithms: Theory and Practice*. Prentice-Hall, Englewood Cliffs, NJ, 1977.

[RS90] S. Ranka and S. Sahni. *Hypercube Algorithms for Image Processing and Pattern Recognition*. Springer-Verlag, New York, NY, 1990.

[SB77] H. Sullivan and T. R. Bashkow. A large scale, homogeneous, fully distributed parallel machine. In *Proceedings of Fourth Symposium on Computer Architecture*, 105–124, March 1977.

[Sei85] C. L. Seitz. The cosmic cube. *Communications of the ACM*, 28-1:22–33, 1985.

[Sei92] C. L. Seitz. Mosaic C: An experimental fine-grain multicomputer. Technical report, California Institute of Technology, Pasadena, CA, 1992.

[Sie85] H. J. Siegel. *Interconnection Networks for Large-Scale Parallel Processing*. D. C. Heath, Lexington, MA, 1985.

[SM86] S. J. Stolfo and D. P. Miranker. The DADO production system machine. *Journal of Parallel and Distributed Computing*, 3:269–296, June 1986.

[Sni82] M. Snir. On parallel search. In *Proceedings of Principles of Distributed Computing*, 242–253, 1982.

[Sni85] M. Snir. On parallel searching. *SIAM Journal of Computing*, 14(3):688–708, August 1985.

[Sny86] L. Snyder. Type architectures, shared-memory and the corollary of modest potential. *Annual Review of Computer Science*, 1:289–317, 1986.

[SS88] Y. Saad and M. H. Schultz. Topological properties of hypercubes. *IEEE Transactions on Computers*, 37:867–872, 1988.

[SS89a] Y. Saad and M. H. Schultz. Data communication in hypercubes. *Journal of Parallel and Distributed Computing*, 6:115–135, 1989. Also available as Technical Report YALEU/DCS/RR-428 from the Department of Computer Science, Yale University, New Haven, CT.

[SS89b] Y. Saad and M. H. Schultz. Data communication in parallel architectures. *Parallel Computing*, 11:131–150, 1989.

[Sto71] H. S. Stone. Parallel processing with the perfect shuffle. *IEEE Transactions on Computers*, C-20(2):153–161, 1971.

[Sto93] H. S. Stone. *High-Performance Computer Architecture: Third Edition*. Addison-Wesley, Reading, MA, 1993.

[Sup91] Supercomputer Systems Division, Intel Corporation. *Paragon XP/S Product Overview*. Beaverton, OR. 1991.

[Thi90] Thinking Machines Corporation. *The CM-2 Technical Summary*. Cambridge, MA. 1990.

[Thi91] Thinking Machines Corporation. *The CM-5 Technical Summary*. Cambridge, MA. 1991.

[Upf84] E. Upfal. A probabilistic relation between desirable and feasible models of parallel computation. In *Proceedings of 16th ACM Conference on Theory of Computing*, 258–265, 1984.

[UW84] E. Upfal and A. Widgerson. How to share memory in a distributed system. In *Proceedings of 25th Annual Symposium on the Foundation of Computer Science*, 171–180, 1984.

[Val90a] L. G. Valiant. A bridging model for parallel computation. *Communications of the ACM*, 33(8), 1990.

[Val90b] L. G. Valiant. General purpose parallel architectures. *Handbook of Theoretical Computer Science*, 1990.

[WB72] W. A. Wulf and C. G. Bell. C.mmp—a multimicroprocessor. In *Proceedings of AFIPS Conference*, 765–777, 1972.

[WF80] C. L. Wu and T. Y. Feng. On a class of multistage interconnection networks. *IEEE Transactions on Computers*, 669–702, August 1980.

CHAPTER 3

Basic Communication Operations

In most parallel algorithms, processors need to exchange data. This exchange of data significantly affects the efficiency of parallel programs by introducing communication delays during their execution. There are a few common basic patterns of interprocessor communication that are frequently used as building blocks in a variety of parallel algorithms. Proper implementation of these basic communication operations on various parallel architectures is a key to the efficient execution of the parallel algorithms that use them.

In this chapter, we present efficient algorithms for some basic communication operations on the ring, two-dimensional mesh, and hypercube architectures. For pedagogical reasons we assume that the mesh is a square two-dimensional array of processors with end-to-end wraparound connections in both dimensions. The time taken for any of these operations increases at most by a factor of four in the absence of wraparound connections (Problem 3.14). Although it is unlikely that large scale parallel computers will be based on the ring topology, it is important to understand various communication operations in the context of rings because the rows and columns of wraparound meshes are rings. Parallel algorithms that perform rowwise or columnwise communication on wraparound meshes use ring algorithms. Furthermore, the algorithms for a number of communication operations on a mesh are simple extensions of the corresponding ring algorithms in two dimensions.

We describe the procedures to implement the basic communication operations for both store-and-forward (SF) and cut-through (CT) routing schemes (Section 2.7). We assume that the communication links are bidirectional; that is, two directly-connected processors can send messages of size m to each other simultaneously in time $t_s + t_w m$, where t_s is the message startup time and t_w is the per-word transfer time. We also assume that a processor can send a message on only one of its links at a time. Similarly, it can receive a message on only one link at a time. However, a processor can receive a message while sending another message at the same time on the same or a different link.

In the following sections we describe various communication operations and derive expressions for their time complexity on a variety of parallel architectures. Many of the operations described here have duals and other related operations that we can perform by using procedures very similar to those for the original operations. The ***dual*** of a communication operation is the opposite of the original operation and can be performed by reversing the direction and sequence of messages in the original operation. We will mention such operations wherever applicable.

3.1 Simple Message Transfer between Two Processors

Sending a message from one processor to another is the most basic communication operation. Recall from Section 2.7.1 that, with SF routing, sending a single message containing m words takes $t_s + t_w ml$ time, where l is the number of links traversed by the message. On an ensemble of p processors, l is at most $\lfloor p/2 \rfloor$ for a ring, $2\lfloor \sqrt{p}/2 \rfloor$ for a wraparound square mesh, and $\log p$ for a hypercube (assuming that messages are sent on the shortest path between the source and the destination processors). Thus, with SF routing, the time for a single message transfer on ring, mesh, and hypercube has an upper bound of $t_s + t_w m \lfloor p/2 \rfloor$, $t_s + 2t_w m \lfloor \sqrt{p}/2 \rfloor$, and $t_s + t_w m \log p$, respectively. If CT routing is available, then a message can be sent directly from the source to a destination l links away in time $t_s + t_w m + t_h l$ (Section 2.7.2), where t_h is the per-hop time.

If the size m of the message is very small, the time for a single message transfer is similar in both SF and CT routing schemes. In both cases, it is the sum of a constant and a term proportional to the shortest distance between the processors. On the other hand, if the message is large (that is, $m \gg l$), then the distance between the processors becomes unimportant on a parallel computer using CT routing. For such messages, the time for a single message transfer between any two processors with CT routing is approximately the same as the message transfer time between directly-connected processors on an SF routing network.

3.2 One-to-All Broadcast

Parallel algorithms often require a single processor to send identical data to all other processors or to a subset of them. This operation is known as ***one-to-all broadcast*** or ***single-node broadcast***. Initially, only the source processor has the data of size m that needs to be broadcast. At the termination of the procedure, there are p copies of the initial data—one residing at each processor. Figure 3.1 shows one-to-all broadcast of a message M among p processors. The related problem of ***k-to-all broadcast*** is defined in Problem 3.21.

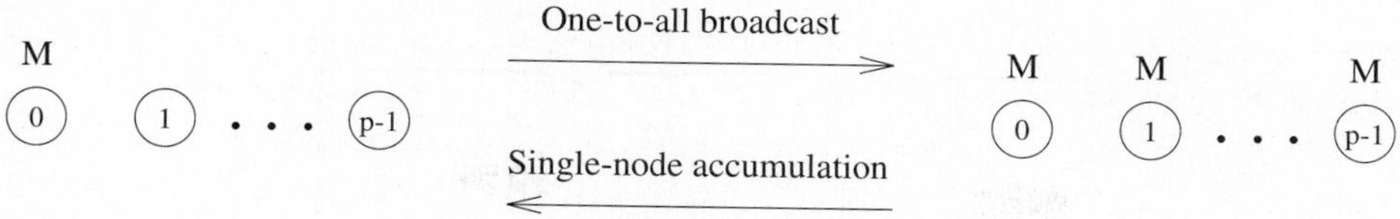

Figure 3.1 One-to-all broadcast and single-node accumulation.

A parallel algorithm may require that a single processor accumulates information from every other processor. This operation is known as ***single-node accumulation***, and is the dual of one-to-all broadcast (Figure 3.1). In single-node accumulation, every processor initially has a message containing m words. The data from all processors are combined through an associative operator, and accumulated at a single destination processor. The total size of the accumulated data remains m after the operation. Thus, single-node accumulation can be used to find the sum, product, maximum, or minimum of a set of numbers, or perform any bitwise operation on elements of the set.

One-to-all broadcast and single-node accumulation are used in several important parallel algorithms including matrix-vector multiplication, Gaussian elimination, shortest paths, and vector inner product. In the following subsections, we consider the implementation of one-to-all broadcast in detail on a variety of architectures using both SF and CT routing schemes.

3.2.1 Store-and-Forward Routing

A naive way to perform one-to-all broadcast is to sequentially send $p - 1$ messages from the source to the other $p - 1$ processors. This is quite wasteful because with SF routing, a message traveling over more than one link is stored on all intermediate processors. We can avoid redundant transmission of the same message if every processor makes a copy of the message upon receiving it, and then forwards it to the next processor. We now present efficient ways to implement one-to-all broadcast with SF routing on the ring, mesh, and hypercube architectures.

Ring

The steps in a one-to-all broadcast on an eight-processor ring are shown in Figure 3.2. The processors are labeled from 0 to 7. Each message transmission step is shown by a numbered, dotted arrow from the source of the message to its destination. Arrows indicating messages sent during the same time step have the same number. As shown in Figure 3.2, the source processor sends the message to its two neighbors in successive steps. Each processor receives a message on one of its links and passes that message to its neighbor on the second link. This process continues until all processors have a copy of the message. The entire procedure requires $\lceil p/2 \rceil$ steps on a p-processor ring. Each of the $\lceil p/2 \rceil$ nearest-neighbor communications takes $t_s + t_w m$ time, so the communication time of one-to-all broadcast

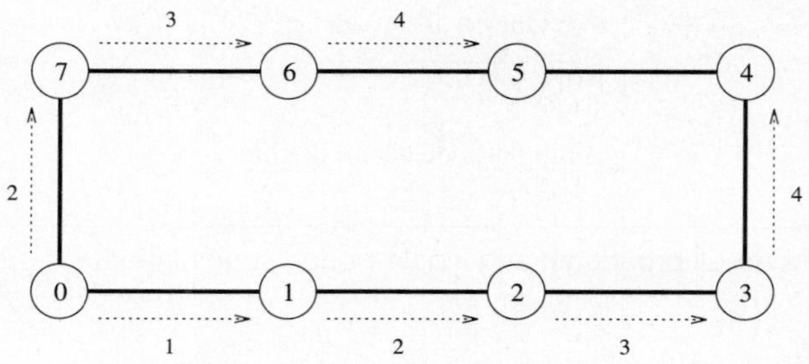

Figure 3.2 One-to-all broadcast on an eight-processor ring with SF routing. Processor 0 is the source of the broadcast. Each message transfer step is shown by a numbered, dotted arrow from the source of the message to its destination. The number on an arrow indicates the time step during which the message is transferred.

on a ring with SF routing is

$$T_{one\_to\_all} = (t_s + t_w m) \left\lceil \frac{p}{2} \right\rceil. \tag{3.1}$$

Example 3.1 Matrix-Vector Multiplication

Consider the problem of multiplying an $n \times n$ matrix with an $n \times 1$ vector on an $n \times n$ mesh of processors. As shown in Figure 3.3, each element of the matrix resides on a different processor, and the vector is distributed among the processors in the topmost row of the mesh. Since all the rows of the matrix must be multiplied with the vector, each processor needs the element of the vector residing in the topmost processor of its column. Hence, before computing the matrix-vector product, each column of processors performs a one-to-all broadcast of the vector elements with the topmost processor of the column as the source. This is done by treating each column of the $n \times n$ mesh as an n-processor ring, and simultaneously applying the ring broadcast procedure described previously to all columns. ∎

Mesh

We can regard each row and column of a square mesh of p processors as a ring of $\sqrt{p}$ processors. So a number of communication algorithms on the mesh are simple extensions of their ring counterparts. Every ring communication operation discussed in this chapter can be performed in two phases on a mesh. In the first phase, the operation is performed along one or all rows by treating the rows as rings. In the second phase, the columns are treated similarly.

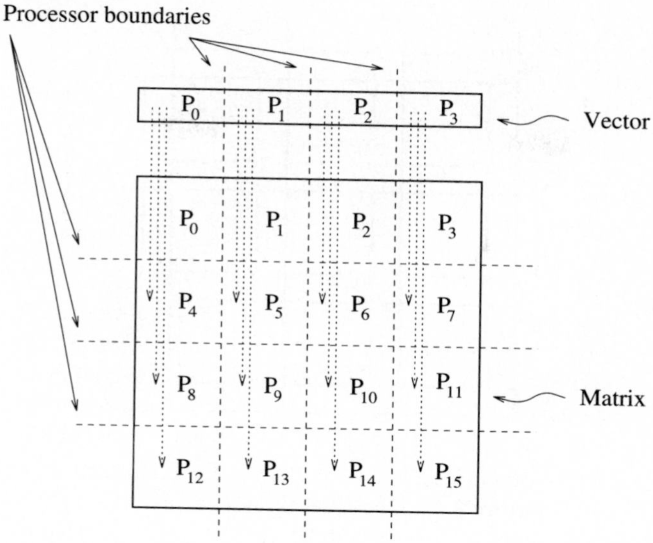

Figure 3.3 One-to-all broadcast in the multiplication of a 4×4 matrix with a 4×1 vector.

Consider the problem of one-to-all broadcast on a two-dimensional square mesh with $\sqrt{p}$ rows and $\sqrt{p}$ columns. First, a one-to-all broadcast is performed from the source to the remaining $(\sqrt{p} - 1)$ processors of the same row. Once all the processors in a row of the mesh have acquired the data, they initiate a one-to-all broadcast in their respective columns. At the end of the second phase, every processor in the mesh has a copy of the initial message. The communication steps for one-to-all broadcast on a mesh are illustrated in Figure 3.4 for $n = 4$, with processor 0 at the bottom-left corner as the source. Steps 1 and 2 correspond to the first phase, and steps 3 and 4 correspond to the second phase.

If the size of the message is m, the row broadcast takes $(t_s + t_w m)\lceil\sqrt{p}/2\rceil$ time. This is the same as the time required for one-to-all broadcast on a ring of $\sqrt{p}$ processors. In the second phase, the one-to-all broadcasts in all the columns are carried out in parallel. Hence, the second phase takes the same amount of time as the first, and the time for the entire broadcast is

$$T_{one\_to\_all} = 2(t_s + t_w m)\left\lceil \frac{\sqrt{p}}{2} \right\rceil. \tag{3.2}$$

We can use a similar procedure for one-to-all broadcast on a three-dimensional mesh as well. In this case, rows of $p^{1/3}$ processors in each of the three dimensions of the mesh are treated as rings. By applying the procedure for the ring in three phases, once along each dimension, the broadcast time is

$$T_{one\_to\_all} = 3(t_s + t_w m)\left\lceil \frac{p^{1/3}}{2} \right\rceil. \tag{3.3}$$

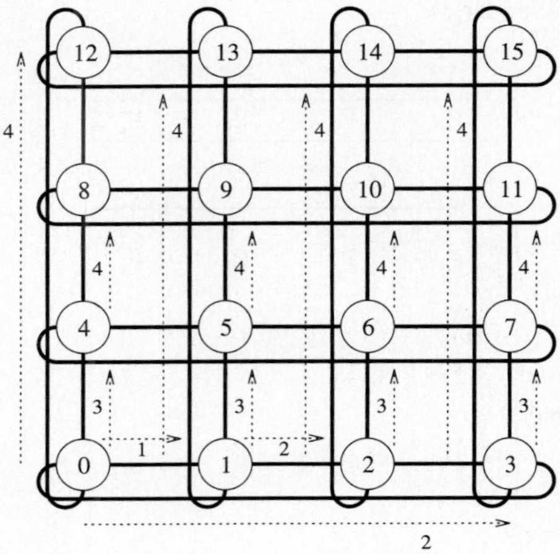

Figure 3.4 One-to-all broadcast on a 16-processor mesh with SF routing.

Hypercube

The previous subsection showed that one-to-all broadcast is performed in two phases on a two-dimensional mesh, with the communication taking place along a different dimension in each phase. Similarly, the process is carried out in three phases on a three-dimensional mesh. A hypercube with 2^d processors can be regarded as a d-dimensional mesh with two processors in each dimension. Hence, the mesh algorithm can be extended for the hypercube, except that the process is now carried out in d steps—one in each dimension.

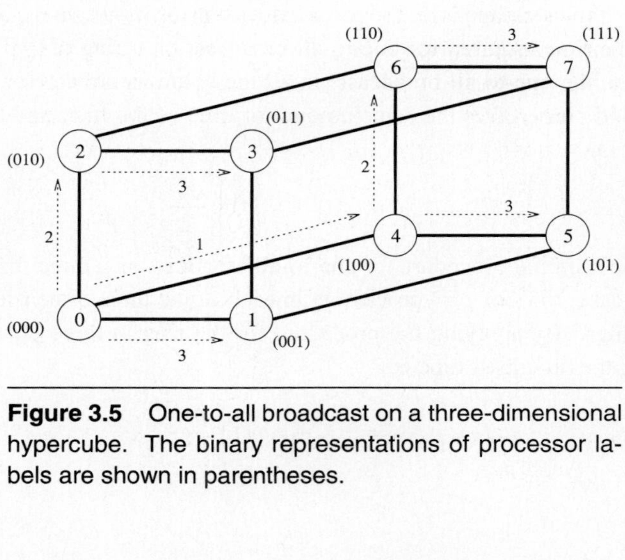

Figure 3.5 One-to-all broadcast on a three-dimensional hypercube. The binary representations of processor labels are shown in parentheses.

```
procedure ONE_TO_ALL_BC(d, my_id, X)
begin
    mask := 2^d - 1;                     /* Set all d bits of mask to 1 */
    for i := d - 1 downto 0 do   /* Outer loop */
    begin
        mask := mask XOR 2^i;   /* Set bit i of mask to 0 */
        if (my_id AND mask) = 0 then
        /* If the lower i bits of my_id are 0 */
            if (my_id AND 2^i) = 0 then
            begin
                msg_destination := my_id XOR 2^i;
                send X to msg_destination;
            endif
            else
            begin
                msg_source := my_id XOR 2^i;
                receive X from msg_source;
            endelse;
    endfor;
end ONE_TO_ALL_BC
```

Program 3.1 One-to-all broadcast of a message X from processor 0 of a d-dimensional hypercube. AND and XOR are bitwise logical-and and exclusive-or operations, respectively.

Each step is a one-to-all broadcast on a two-processor ring, which is the same as a simple message transfer between two directly-connected processors.

Figure 3.5 shows a one-to-all broadcast on an eight-processor hypercube with processor 0 as the source. As the figure shows, there is a total of three communication steps. Note that the order in which the dimensions are chosen for communication does not affect the outcome of the procedure. Figure 3.5 shows only one such order. In this scheme, communication starts along the highest dimension (that is, the dimension specified by the most significant bit of the binary representation of a processor label) and proceeds along successively lower dimensions in subsequent steps. Each of the $\log p$ steps takes $t_s + t_w m$ time for a single message transfer in each dimension. Therefore, the total time taken by the procedure on a p-processor hypercube is

$$T_{one\_to\_all} = (t_s + t_w m) \log p. \qquad (3.4)$$

Example 3.2 A One-to-All Broadcast Procedure for Hypercube

In this example, we describe a procedure ONE_TO_ALL_BC(d, my_id, X) to implement the one-to-all broadcast algorithm on a d-dimensional hypercube. Program 3.1 gives the pseudocode for this procedure when processor 0 is the source of the broadcast. The procedure is executed at all processors concurrently. At any processor, the value of my_id is the label of that processor.

Let X be the message to be broadcast, which initially resides at the source processor 0. The procedure performs d communication steps, one in each dimension of the hypercube. In Program 3.1, communication proceeds from the highest to the lowest dimension (although the order in which dimensions are chosen does not matter). The loop counter i indicates the current dimension of the hypercube in which communication is taking place. Only the processors with zero in the i least significant bits of their labels participate in communication along dimension i. For instance, on the three-dimensional hypercube shown in Figure 3.5, i is equal to 2 in the first time step. Therefore, only processors 0 and 4 communicate, since their two least significant bits are zero. In the next time step, when $i = 1$, all processors (that is, 0, 2, 4, and 6) with zero in their least significant bits participate in communication.

The variable *mask* helps determine which processors communicate in a particular iteration of the loop. The variable *mask* has d (= log p) bits, all of which are initially set to one (line 3). At the beginning of each iteration, the most significant nonzero bit of *mask* is reset to zero (line 6). Line 7 determines which processors communicate in the current iteration of the outer loop. For instance, for the hypercube of Figure 3.5, *mask* is initially set to 111, and it would be 011 during the iteration corresponding to $i = 2$ (the i least significant bits of *mask* are ones). The AND operation on line 7 selects only those processors which have zero in their i least significant bits.

Among the processors selected for communication along dimension i, the processors with a zero in bit position i send the data, and the processors with a one in bit position i receive it. The test to determine the sending and receiving processors is performed on line 8. For example, in Figure 3.5, processor 0 (000) is the sender and processor 4 (100) is the receiver in the iteration corresponding to $i = 2$. Similarly, for $i = 1$, processors 0 (000) and 4 (100) are senders while processors 2 (010) and 6 (110) are receivers.

The procedure terminates after communication has taken place along all dimensions. ∎

Example 3.3 A General One-to-All Broadcast Procedure for Hypercube

Program 3.1 works only if processor 0 is the source of the broadcast. For an arbitrary source, we must relabel the processors of the hypercube by XORing the label of each processor with the label of the source processor before we apply this procedure. A modified one-to-all broadcast procedure that works for any value of $source$ between 0 and $p - 1$ is shown in Program 3.2. By performing the XOR operation at line 3, Program 3.2 relabels the source processor to 0, and relabels the other processors

```
procedure GENERAL_ONE_TO_ALL_BC(d, my_id, source, X)
begin
    my_virtual_id := my_id XOR source;
    mask := 2^d − 1;
    for i := d − 1 downto 0 do      /* Outer loop */
    begin
        mask := mask XOR 2^i;   /* Set bit i of mask to 0 */
        if (my_virtual_id AND mask) = 0 then
            if (my_virtual_id AND 2^i) = 0 then
            begin
                virtual_dest := my_virtual_id XOR 2^i;
                send X to (virtual_dest XOR source);  /* Convert virtual_dest
                                              to the label of the physical destination */
            endif
            else
            begin
                virtual_source := my_virtual_id XOR 2^i;
                receive X from (virtual_source XOR source);
  /* Convert virtual_source to the label of the physical source */
            endelse;
    endfor;
end GENERAL_ONE_TO_ALL_BC
```

Program 3.2 One-to-all broadcast of a message X initiated by $source$ in a d-dimensional hypercube. The AND and XOR operations are bitwise logical operations.

relative to the source. After this relabeling, the algorithm of Program 3.1 can be applied to perform the broadcast. ■

Example 3.4 A Hypercube Procedure for Single-Node Accumulation

Program 3.3 gives a procedure to perform a single-node accumulation on a d-dimensional hypercube such that the final result is accumulated on processor 0. Single node-accumulation is the dual of one-to-all broadcast. We obtain the communication pattern required to implement single-node accumulation by reversing the order and the direction of messages in one-to-all broadcast. Procedure SINGLE_NODE_ACC(d, my_id, m, X, sum) shown in Program 3.3 is very similar to procedure ONE_TO_ALL_BC(d, my_id, X) shown in Program 3.1. One difference is that the communication in single-node accumulation proceeds from the lowest to the highest dimension. This change is reflected in the way that variables *mask* and i are manipulated in Program 3.3. The criterion for determining the source and the destination among a pair of communicating processors is also reversed (line 8).

```
1.  procedure SINGLE_NODE_ACC(d, my_id, m, X, sum)
2.  begin
3.      for j := 0 to m − 1 do sum[j] := X[j];
4.      mask := 0;
5.      for i := 0 to d − 1 do
6.      begin /* Select processors whose lower i bits are 0 */
7.          if (my_id AND mask) = 0 then
8.              if (my_id AND 2^i) ≠ 0 then
9.              begin
10.                 msg_destination := my_id XOR 2^i;
11.                 send sum to msg_destination;
12.             endif
13.             else
14.             begin
15.                 msg_source := my_id XOR 2^i;
16.                 receive X from msg_source;
17.                 for j := 0 to m − 1 do
18.                     sum[j] :=sum[j] + X[j];
19.             endelse;
20.         mask := mask XOR 2^i;   /* Set bit i of mask to 1 */
21.     endfor;
22. end SINGLE_NODE_ACC
```

Program 3.3 Single-node accumulation on a d-dimensional hypercube. Each processor contributes a message X containing m words, and processor 0 is the destination of the sum. The AND and XOR operations are bitwise logical operations.

Apart from these differences, procedure SINGLE_NODE_ACC has extra instructions (lines 17 and 18) to add the contents of the messages received by a processor in each iteration.

Note that any associative operation can be used in place of addition. ■

Among the architectures considered so far, one-to-all broadcast takes the shortest time on a hypercube because a hypercube has a higher connectivity than a ring or a mesh. In Section 3.7.1 we show how we can further reduce the communication time of this procedure by splitting the message into smaller parts and routing each part separately. However, if a message is not routed in parts along separate paths and communication is allowed on only one link of each processor at a time, then one-to-all broadcast cannot be performed in less than $(t_s + t_w m)\log p$ time on any architecture. This can be inferred from two observations regarding the hypercube procedure illustrated in Figure 3.5. First, at any time, each processor that possesses the data is sending that data to a processor that

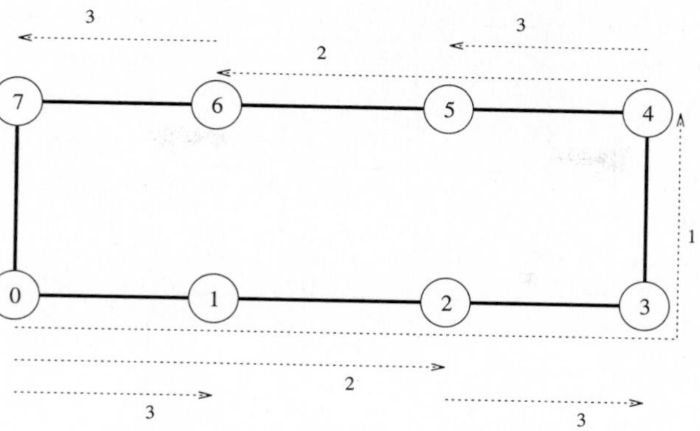

Figure 3.6 One-to-all broadcast with CT routing on an eight-processor ring.

needs it. This is not the case with the ring and the mesh algorithms. For instance, in Figure 3.2, processor 0 does not communicate in steps 3 or 4, although it has the message being broadcast, and there are processors waiting for it. Second, all messages are passed only between directly-connected processors on the hypercube; hence, each communication step is of the minimum possible duration for a message of size m. Thus, on a hypercube, every opportunity to send a message is used and each message transfer is of the smallest possible duration for the given message size. A better-connected architecture cannot send any more messages at a time, or reduce the transfer time for any message (for the same t_s, t_w, and m). Hence, the time $(t_s + t_w m) \log p$ is the best for one-to-all broadcast under the given conditions.

3.2.2 Cut-Through Routing

Of the three architectures considered in Section 3.2.1, one-to-all broadcast with SF routing is fastest on the hypercube. The communication time of one-to-all broadcast on a hypercube does not improve with CT routing due to exclusively nearest-neighbor communication. However, the operation benefits substantially from CT routing on ring and mesh architectures.

Ring

CT routing can be used advantageously for one-to-all broadcast on a ring by mapping the hypercube algorithm onto the ring. In every step, each processor of the ring communicates with the same processor as in the hypercube algorithm. This process is illustrated in Figure 3.6 for an eight-processor ring. Comparing Figure 3.5 with Figure 3.6 shows that, in both cases, communication takes place between the same pair of processors in each step. With CT routing, such a mapping is useful because the complexity of passing a message of size m between processors separated by l links is only $\Theta(m + l)$. As Figure 3.6 illustrates,

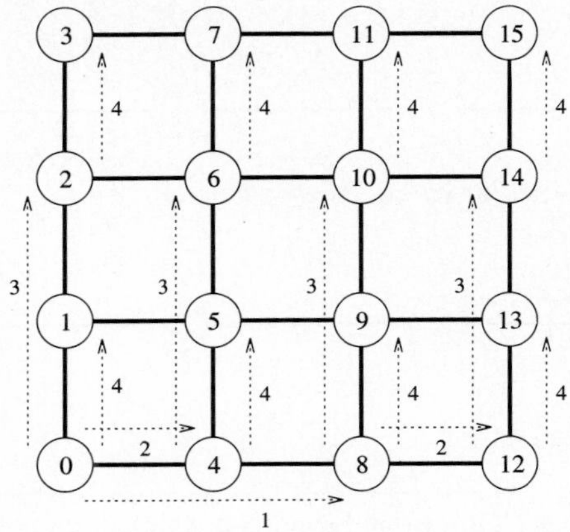

Figure 3.7 One-to-all broadcast on a 16-processor square mesh with CT routing.

in a p-processor ring the source processor first sends the data to a processor at a distance $p/2$. In the second step, both processors that have the data transmit it to processors at a distance of $p/4$ in the same direction. Assuming that p is a power of 2, in the ith step, each processor that has the data sends it to a processor at a distance of $p/2^i$. All messages flow in the same direction. The algorithm concludes after $\log p$ steps.

The communication time in the ith step is $t_s + t_w m + t_h p/2^i$. Hence, the total time for the broadcast with CT routing on a ring of p processors is

$$\begin{aligned} T_{one-to-all} &= \sum_{i=1}^{\log p} (t_s + t_w m + t_h p/2^i) \\ &= t_s \log p + t_w m \log p + t_h(p-1). \end{aligned} \tag{3.5}$$

For sufficiently large values of m, the t_h term is insignificant compared to the others. Thus, CT routing effectively reduces the communication time by a factor of $p/\log p$ over SF routing. For example, if $m = \Omega(p/\log p)$, then a one-to-all broadcast takes $\Theta(p^2/\log p)$ time on ring with SF routing, but only $\Theta(p)$ time with CT routing.

Mesh

On a two-dimensional square mesh with CT routing, one-to-all broadcast is performed in two phases. In each phase the ring procedure is applied in a different dimension of the mesh. The procedure is illustrated in Figure 3.7 for a 16-processor mesh. First, a one-to-all broadcast is initiated by the source processor among the $\sqrt{p}$ processors in its row (call it the source row). Second, a one-to-all broadcast is initiated in each column by its processor in the source row. Each of the two phases takes $(t_s + t_w m) \log \sqrt{p} + t_h(\sqrt{p} - 1)$ time, and

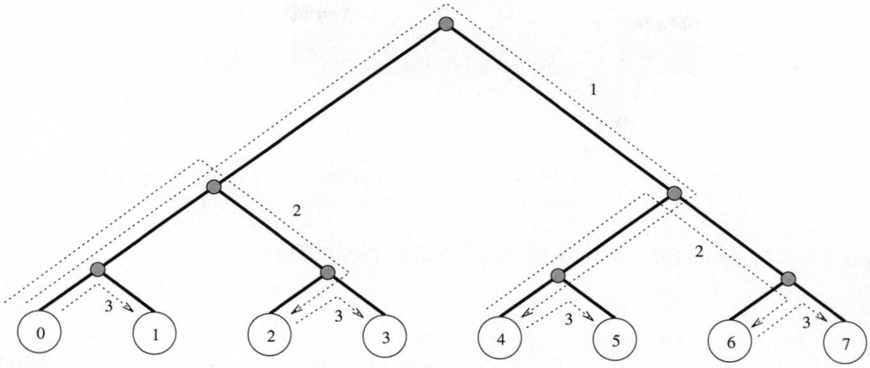

Figure 3.8 One-to-all broadcast on an eight-processor tree.

the time for the entire broadcast is

$$T_{one\_to\_all} = (t_s + t_w m) \log p + 2t_h(\sqrt{p} - 1). \tag{3.6}$$

Every communication step in the 16-processor mesh shown in Figure 3.7 takes place between exactly the same processors as in a 16-processor hypercube. Note that steps 2, 3, and 4 of Figure 3.7 are identical to steps 1, 2, and 3 of Figure 3.5. Like the one-to-all broadcast procedure for a ring with cut-through routing, the mesh procedure is also a direct adaptation of the hypercube procedure given in Programs 3.1 and 3.2.

Balanced Binary Tree

The hypercube algorithm for one-to-all broadcast maps naturally onto a balanced binary tree in which each leaf is a processor and intermediate nodes serve only as switching units. This is illustrated in Figure 3.8 for eight processors. In this figure, the communicating processors have the same labels as in the hypercube algorithm illustrated in Figure 3.5. Figure 3.8 shows that there is no congestion on any of the communication links at any time. The difference between the communication on a hypercube and the tree shown in Figure 3.8 is that there is a different number of switching nodes along different paths on the tree. Assuming that a per-hop time of t_h is associated with each link between two switching nodes or between a processor and a switching node, the time for one-to-all broadcast (Problem 3.1) on the tree is

$$T_{one\_to\_all} = (t_s + t_w m + t_h(\log p + 1)) \log p. \tag{3.7}$$

3.3 All-to-All Broadcast, Reduction, and Prefix Sums

All-to-all broadcast, also known as ***multinode broadcast***, is a generalization of one-to-all broadcast in which all p processors simultaneously initiate a broadcast. A processor

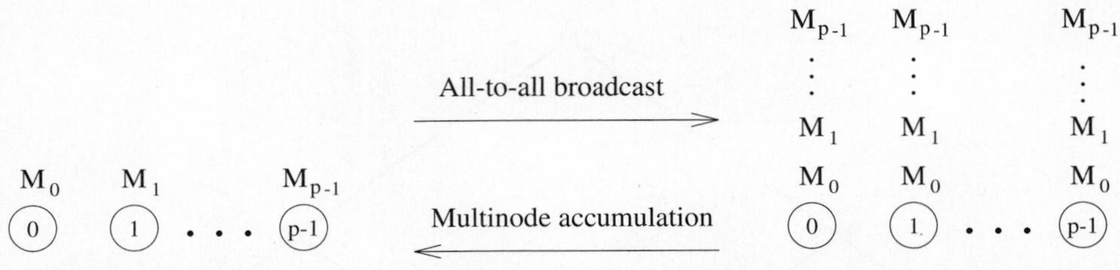

Figure 3.9 All-to-all broadcast and multinode accumulation.

sends the same m-word message to every other processor, but different processors may broadcast different messages. All-to-all broadcast is used in matrix operations, including matrix multiplication and matrix-vector multiplication. The dual of all-to-all broadcast is ***multinode accumulation***, in which every processor is the destination of a single-node accumulation (Problem 3.8). Figure 3.9 illustrates all-to-all broadcast and multinode accumulation.

The communication pattern of all-to-all broadcast can be used to perform some other operations as well, such as, *reduction* and *prefix sums*. Examples 3.7 and 3.8 discuss reduction and prefix sums on a hypercube.

One way to perform an all-to-all broadcast is to perform p one-to-all broadcasts, one starting at each processor. If performed naively, on some architectures this approach may take up to p times as long as a one-to-all broadcast. It is possible to use the communication links in the interconnection network more efficiently by performing all p one-to-all broadcasts simultaneously so that all messages traversing the same path at the same time are concatenated into a single message whose size is the sum of the sizes of individual messages.

The following sections describe all-to-all broadcast on ring, mesh, and hypercube topologies using both SF and CT routings.

3.3.1 Store-and-Forward Routing

Ring

The one-to-all broadcast procedure shown in Figure 3.2 for a ring with SF routing shows that at most two communication links are active during any given time step. For all-to-all broadcast, all channels can be kept busy simultaneously because, unlike one-to-all broadcast, each processor always has some information that it can pass along to its neighbor. Each processor first sends to one of its neighbors the data it needs to broadcast. In subsequent steps, it forwards the data received from one of its neighbors to its other neighbor.

Figure 3.10 illustrates this procedure for an eight-processor ring. As with the previous figures, the integer label of an arrow indicates the time step during which the message is sent. In all-to-all broadcast, p different messages circulate in the p-processor ensemble. In Figure 3.10, each message is identified by its initial source, whose label appears in parentheses along with the time step. For instance, the arc labeled 2 (7) between processors 0

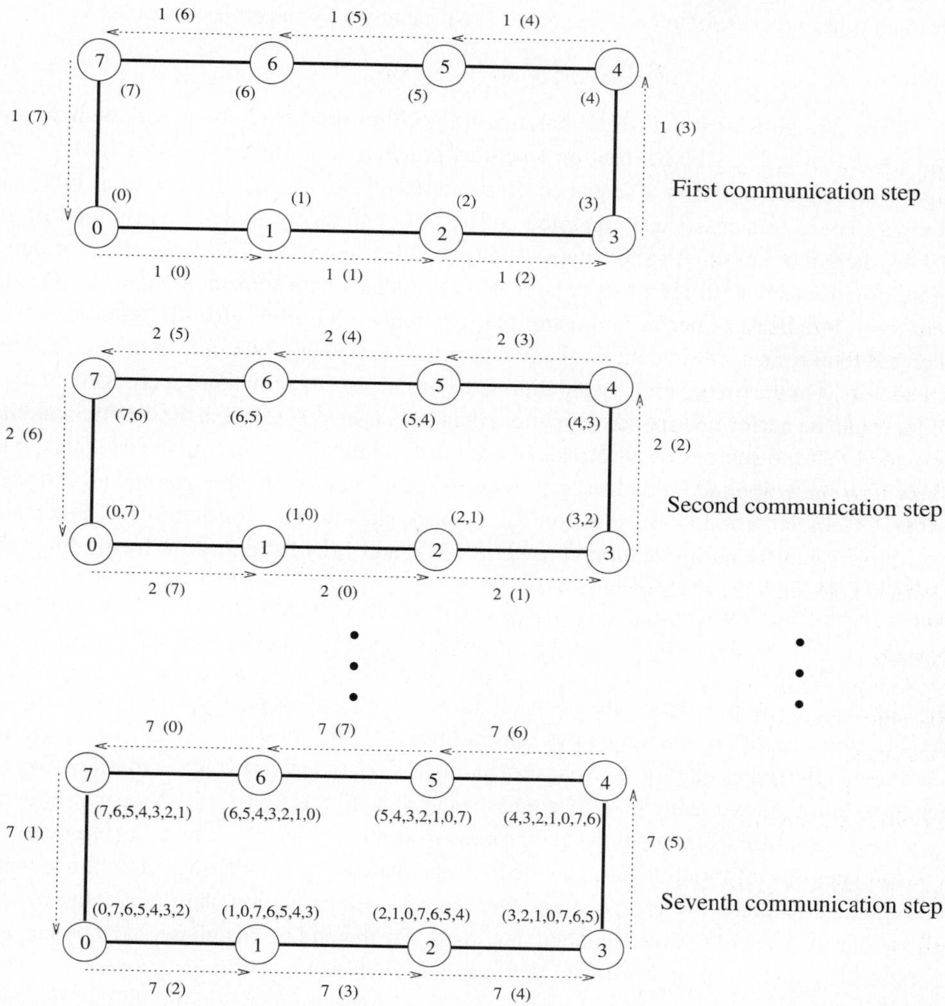

Figure 3.10 All-to-all broadcast on an eight-processor ring with SF routing. In addition to the time step, the label of each arrow has an additional number in parentheses. This number labels a message and indicates the processor from which the message originated in the first step. The number(s) in parentheses next to each processor are the labels of processors from which data has been received prior to the communication step. Only the first, second, and last communication steps are shown.

and 1 represents the data communicated in time step 2 that processor 0 received from processor 7 in the preceding step. As Figure 3.10 shows, if communication is performed circularly in a single direction, then each processor receives all $(p-1)$ pieces of information from all other processors in $(p-1)$ steps. The time taken by the entire operation is

$$T_{all\_to\_all} = (t_s + t_w m)(p-1). \tag{3.8}$$

The straightforward all-to-all broadcast algorithm presented above for a simple architecture like a ring with SF routing has great practical importance. A close look at the algorithm reveals that it is a sequence of p one-to-all broadcasts, each with a different source. These broadcasts are pipelined so that all of them are complete in a total of p nearest-neighbor communication steps. Many parallel algorithms involve a series of one-to-all broadcasts with different sources, often interspersed with some computation. If each one-to-all broadcast is performed using the hypercube algorithm given in Section 3.2.1, then the total time spent in communication is $n(t_s + t_w m)\log p$, where n is the number of broadcasts. On the other hand, by pipelining the broadcasts as shown in Figure 3.10, all the of them can be performed spending no more than $(t_s + t_w m)(p-1)$ time in communication, provided that the sources of all broadcasts are different and $n \le p$. In later chapters, we show how such pipelined broadcast improves the performance of some parallel algorithms such as Gaussian elimination (Section 5.5.1), back substitution (Section 5.5.3), Fox's algorithm for matrix multiplication (Problem 5.23), and Floyd's algorithm for finding the shortest paths in a graph (Section 7.4.3).

Mesh

Just like one-to-all broadcast, the all-to-all broadcast algorithm for the 2-D mesh is based on the ring algorithm, treating rows and columns of the mesh as rings. Once again, communication takes place in two phases. In the first phase, each row of the mesh performs an all-to-all broadcast using the procedure for the ring. In this phase, all processors collect $\sqrt{p}$ messages corresponding to the $\sqrt{p}$ processors of their respective rows. Each processor consolidates this information into a single message of size $m\sqrt{p}$, and proceeds to the second communication phase of the algorithm. The second communication phase is a columnwise all-to-all broadcast of the consolidated messages. By the end of this phase, each processor obtains all p pieces of m-word data that originally resided on different processors. The distribution of data among the processors of a 3×3 mesh at the beginning of the first and the second phases of the algorithm is shown in Figures 3.11(a) and (b), respectively.

The first phase of $\sqrt{p}$ simultaneous all-to-all broadcasts (each among $\sqrt{p}$ processors) concludes in time $(t_s + t_w m)(\sqrt{p}-1)$. The number of processors participating in each all-to-all broadcast in the second phase is also $\sqrt{p}$, but the size of each message is now $m\sqrt{p}$. Therefore, this phase takes $(t_s + t_w m\sqrt{p})(\sqrt{p}-1)$ time to complete. The time for the entire all-to-all broadcast on a p-processor two-dimensional square mesh is the sum of the times spent in the individual phases, which is

$$T_{all\_to\_all} = 2t_s(\sqrt{p}-1) + t_w m(p-1). \tag{3.9}$$

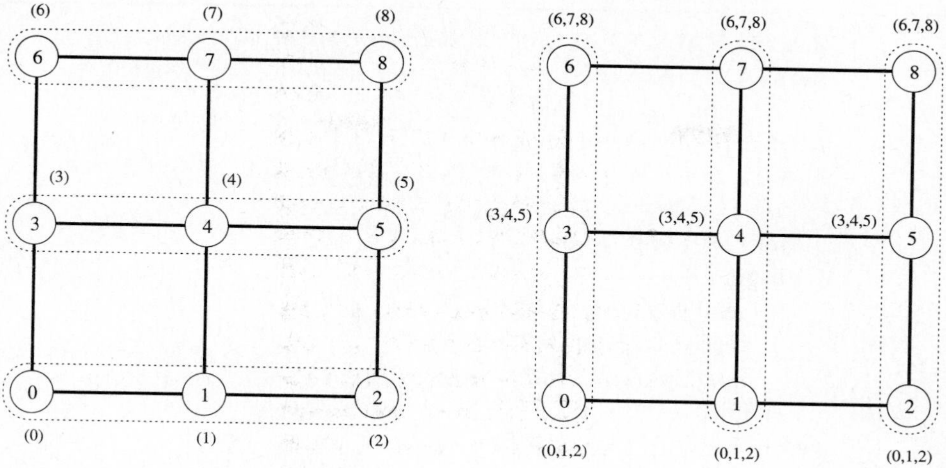

(a) Initial data distribution

(b) Data distribution after rowwise broadcast

Figure 3.11 All-to-all broadcast on a 3×3 mesh. The groups of processors communicating with each other in each phase are enclosed by dotted boundaries. By the end of the second phase, all processors get (0,1,2,3,4,5,6,7) (that is, a message from each processor).

Example 3.5 Procedures for All-to-All Broadcast on Ring and Mesh
Programs 3.4 and 3.5 give procedures for all-to-all broadcast on a p-processor ring and a p-processor mesh, respectively. The initial message to be broadcast is known locally as *my_msg* at each processor. At the end of the procedure, each processor stores the collection of all p messages in *result*. As the programs show, all-to-all broadcast on a mesh applies the ring procedure twice, once along the rows and once along the columns. ■

Hypercube

The hypercube algorithm for all-to-all broadcast is an extension of the mesh algorithm to $\log p$ dimensions. The procedure requires $\log p$ steps. Communication takes place along a different dimension of the p-processor hypercube in each step. In every step, pairs of processors exchange their data and double the size of the message to be transmitted in the next step by concatenating the received message with their current data. Figure 3.12 shows these steps for an eight-processor hypercube with bidirectional communication channels. The size of the messages exchanged in the ith of the $\log p$ steps is $2^{i-1}m$. The time it takes a pair of processors to send and receive messages from each other is $t_s + 2^{i-1}t_w m$. Hence,

```
procedure ALL_TO_ALL_BC_RING(my_id, my_msg, p, result)
begin
    left := (my_id − 1) mod p;
    right := (my_id + 1) mod p;
    result := my_msg;
    msg := result;
    for i := 1 to p − 1 do
    begin
        send msg to right;
        receive msg from left;
        result := result ∪ msg;
    endfor;
end ALL_TO_ALL_BC_RING
```

Program 3.4 All-to-all broadcast on a p-processor ring.

the time it takes to complete the entire procedure is

$$\begin{aligned} T_{all\_to\_all} &= \sum_{i=1}^{\log p} (t_s + 2^{i-1} t_w m) \\ &= t_s \log p + t_w m(p-1). \end{aligned} \tag{3.10}$$

Example 3.6 An All-to-All Broadcast Procedure for Hypercube

Program 3.6 gives a procedure for implementing all-to-all broadcast on a d-dimensional hypercube. Communication starts from the lowest dimension of the hypercube and then proceeds along successively higher dimensions (line 4). In each iteration, processors communicate in pairs so that the labels of the processors communicating with each other in the ith iteration differ in the ith least significant bit of their binary representations (line 6). After an iteration's communication steps, each processor concatenates the data it receives during that iteration with its resident data (line 9). This concatenated message is transmitted in the following iteration. ■

Example 3.7 Reduction on a Hypercube

The communication pattern used in all-to-all broadcast is employed in other hypercube algorithms as well. For example, consider the operation in which every processor of a hypercube starts with one value and needs to know the sum of the values stored at all the processors. This operation is known as ***reduction***. In general, any associative operation (such as logical OR, logical AND, maximum, or minimum) can be used instead of addition. Reduction is often used to implement barrier synchronization (Section 13.4.2) on a message-passing computer. The semantics of the

```
procedure ALL_TO_ALL_BC_MESH(my_id, my_msg, p, result)
begin

/* Communication along rows */
      left := (my_id − 1) mod p;
      right := (my_id + 1) mod p;
      result := my_msg;
      msg := result;
      for i := 1 to √p − 1 do
      begin
          send msg to right;
          receive msg from left;
          result := result ∪ msg;
      endfor;

/* Communication along columns */
      up := (my_id − √p) mod p;
      down := (my_id + √p) mod p;
      msg := result;
      for i := 1 to √p − 1 do
      begin
          send msg to down;
          receive msg from up;
          result := result ∪ msg;
      endfor;
end ALL_TO_ALL_BC_MESH
```

Program 3.5 All-to-all broadcast on a square mesh of p processors.

reduction operation are such that, while executing a parallel program, no processor can finish reduction before each processor has contributed a value.

A naive algorithm for reduction would perform an all-to-all broadcast, gather all the numbers at each processor, and then add them locally on all processors. Since the message size m is one word, the communication time of this procedure is $t_s \log p + t_w(p-1)$. A faster method to perform reduction is to perform a single-node accumulation followed by a one-to-all broadcast. However, there is an even faster way to perform reduction by using the communication pattern of all-to-all broadcast. Figure 3.12 illustrates this algorithm for $p = 8$. Assume that each integer in parentheses in the figure, instead of denoting a message, denotes a number to be added that originally resided at the processor with that integer label. To perform reduction, we follow the communication steps of the all-to-all broadcast

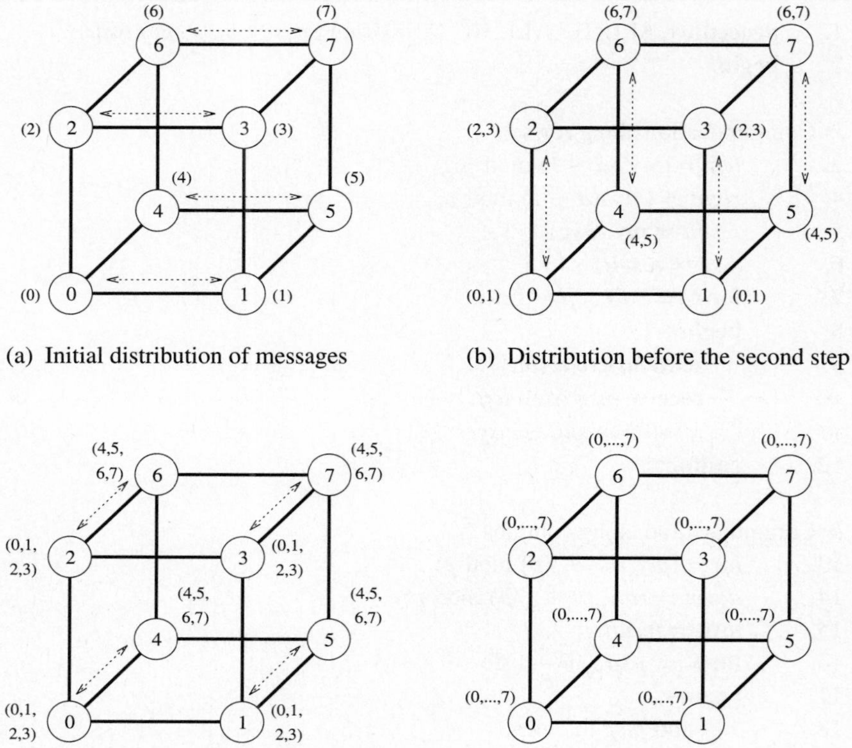

(a) Initial distribution of messages

(b) Distribution before the second step

(c) Distribution before the third step

(d) Final distribution of messages

Figure 3.12 All-to-all broadcast on an eight-processor hypercube.

procedure, but at the end of each step, add two numbers instead of concatenating two messages. At the termination of the reduction procedure, each processor holds the sum $(0 + 1 + 2 + \cdots + 7)$ (rather than eight messages numbered from 0 to 7, as in the case of all-to-all broadcast). Unlike all-to-all broadcast, each message transferred in the reduction operation has only one word. The size of the messages does not double in each step because the numbers are added instead of being concatenated. Therefore, the total communication time for all $\log p$ steps is

$$T_{reduction} = (t_s + t_w) \log p. \tag{3.11}$$

Program 3.6 can be used to perform a sum of p numbers if *my_msg*, *msg* and *result* are numbers (rather than messages), and the union operation ('∪') on line 9 is replaced by addition. ■

```
procedure ALL_TO_ALL_BC_HCUBE(my_id, my_msg, d, result)
begin
   result := my_msg;
   for i := 0 to d − 1 do
   begin
      partner := my_id XOR 2^i;
      send result to partner;
      receive msg from partner;
      result := result ∪ msg;
   endfor;
end ALL_TO_ALL_BC_HCUBE
```

Program 3.6 All-to-all broadcast on a d-dimensional hypercube.

Example 3.8 Prefix Sums on a Hypercube

Finding ***prefix sums*** is another important problem that can be solved by using a communication pattern similar to that used in reduction. Given p numbers $n_0, n_1, \ldots, n_{p-1}$ (one on each processor), the problem is to compute the sums $s_k = \Sigma_{i=0}^{k} n_i$ for all k between 0 and $p - 1$. For example, if the original sequence of numbers is $\langle 0, 1, 2, 3, 4 \rangle$, then the sequence of prefix sums is $\langle 0, 1, 3, 6, 10 \rangle$. Initially, n_k resides on the processor labeled k, and at the end of the procedure, the same processor holds s_k.

Figure 3.13 illustrates the prefix sums procedure for an eight-processor hypercube. This figure is a modification of Figure 3.12. The modification is required to accommodate the fact that in prefix sums the processor with label k uses information from only the k-processor subset of those processors whose labels are less than or equal to k. To accumulate the correct prefix sum, every processor maintains an additional result buffer. This buffer is denoted by square brackets in Figure 3.13. At the end of a communication step, the content of an incoming message is added to the result buffer only if the message comes from a processor with a smaller label than that of the recipient processor. The contents of the outgoing message (denoted by parentheses in the figure) are updated with every incoming message, just as in Example 3.7. For instance, after the first communication step, processors 0, 2, and 4 do not add the data received from processors 1, 3, and 5 to their result buffers. However, the contents of the outgoing messages for the next step are updated.

Since not all of the messages received by a processor contribute to its final result, some of the messages it receives may be redundant. We have omitted these steps of the standard all-to-all broadcast communication pattern from Figure 3.13, although the presence or absence of these messages does not affect the results of the algorithm. Program 3.7 gives a procedure to solve the prefix sums problem on a d-dimensional hypercube. ■

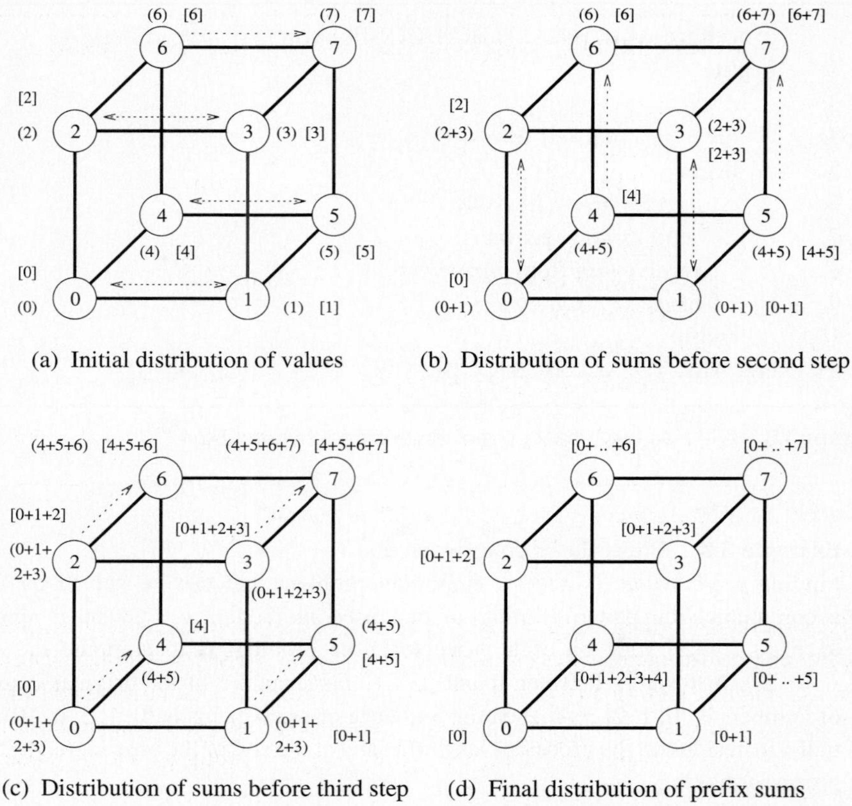

(a) Initial distribution of values

(b) Distribution of sums before second step

(c) Distribution of sums before third step

(d) Final distribution of prefix sums

Figure 3.13 Computing prefix sums on an eight-processor hypercube. At each processor, square brackets show the local prefix sum accumulated in a buffer and parentheses enclose the contents of the outgoing message buffer for the next step.

3.3.2 Cut-Through Routing

For one-to-all broadcast, we obtain better algorithms for the ring and the mesh with CT routing simply by mapping the hypercube algorithm onto them. This strategy does not yield all-to-all broadcast algorithms for ring and mesh that are strictly better with CT routing than with SF routing. The reason is that, unlike one-to-all broadcast, the hypercube procedure for all-to-all broadcast cannot be mapped onto a ring or a mesh because it causes congestion on the communication channels. For instance, Figure 3.14 shows the result of performing the third step (Figure 3.12(c)) of the hypercube all-to-all broadcast procedure on a ring. One of the links of the ring is traversed by all four messages. Hence, passing these messages with CT routing will not be any faster than performing this communication in four steps using SF routing. However, with CT routing the ring and the mesh procedures for all-to-all

```
procedure PREFIX_SUMS_HCUBE(my_id, my_number, d, result)
begin
    result := my_number;
    msg := result;
    for i := 0 to d − 1 do
    begin
        partner := my_id XOR 2^i;
        send msg to partner;
        receive number from partner;
        msg := msg + number;
        if (partner < my_id) then result := result + number;
    endfor;
end PREFIX_SUMS_HCUBE
```

Program 3.7 Prefix sums on a d-dimensional hypercube.

broadcast shown in Figures 3.10 and 3.11 do not require wraparound connections, provided that communication channels are bidirectional. For large messages, the term associated with t_h is comparatively small and can be ignored. In this case, the communication time for all-to-all broadcast with CT routing and bidirectional links is the same on a linear array (mesh without wraparound connections) as with SF routing on a ring (mesh with wraparound connections) (Problem 3.20).

Section 3.3.1 shows that the term associated with t_w in the expressions for the communication time of all-to-all broadcast is $t_w m(p-1)$ for all the architectures. This term also serves as a lower bound for the communication time of all-to-all broadcast for

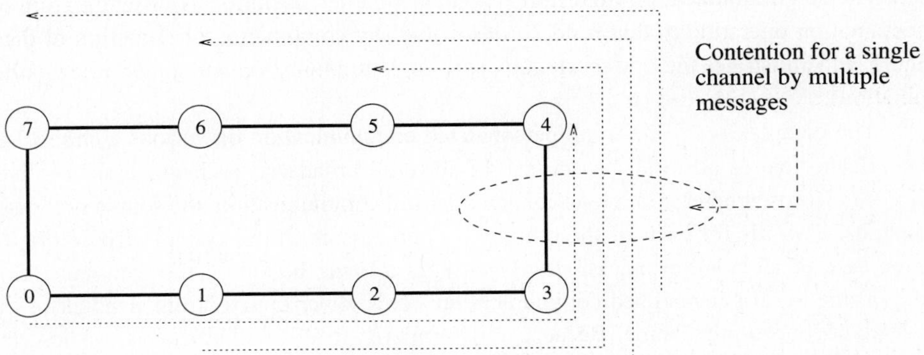

Figure 3.14 Contention for a channel when the communication step of Figure 3.12(c) for the hypercube is mapped onto a ring.

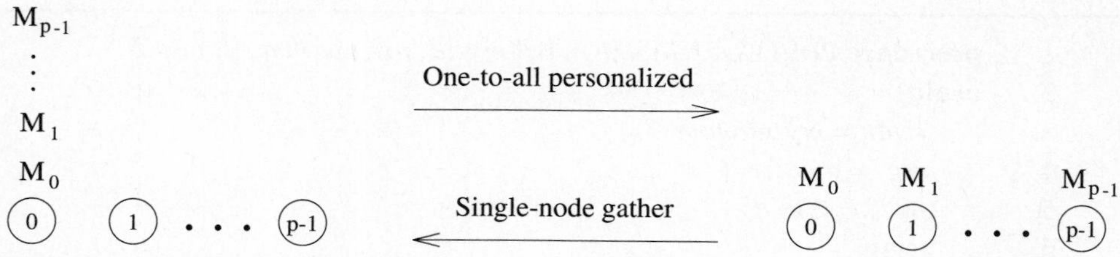

Figure 3.15 One-to-all personalized communication and its dual—single-node gather.

parallel computers on which a processor can communicate on only one of its ports at a time. This is because each processor receives at least $m(p-1)$ words of data, regardless of the architecture or routing scheme.

3.4 One-to-All Personalized Communication

In ***one-to-all personalized communication***, a single processor sends a unique message of size m to every other processor. This operation is also known as ***single-node scatter***. One-to-all personalized communication is different from one-to-all broadcast in that the source processor starts with p unique messages—one destined for each processor. Unlike one-to-all broadcast, one-to-all personalized communication does not involve any duplication of data. The related problem of ***k-to-all personalized communication*** is explored in Problem 3.26. The dual of one-to-all personalized communication is ***single-node gather***, in which a single processor collects a unique message from each other processor. The procedure for single-node gather can be derived for any interconnection topology simply by reversing the direction and sequence of messages in the corresponding one-to-all personalized communication algorithm. Again, a gather operation is different from an accumulation operation in that it does not involve any combination or reduction of data. Figure 3.15 illustrates the one-to-all personalized communication and single-node gather operations.

The complexity of one-to-all personalized communication on various architectures is similar to that of all-to-all broadcast. In all-to-all broadcast, each processor receives $m(p-1)$ words, whereas, in one-to-all personalized communication, the source processor transmits m words for each of the other $p-1$ processors in the system. Therefore, as in the case of all-to-all broadcast, $t_w m(p-1)$ is a lower bound on the communication time of one-to-all personalized communication. This lower bound is independent of the architecture or routing scheme. Because of its similarity to all-to-all broadcast, we describe this operation in detail for only the hypercube architecture. Algorithms for ring and mesh topologies are left as an exercise (Problem 3.6).

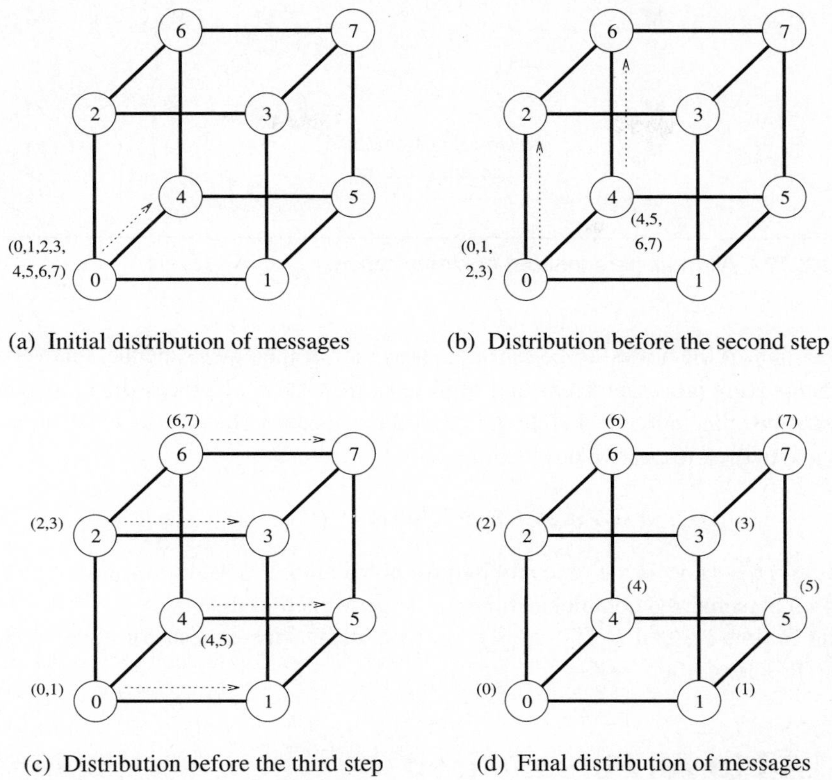

Figure 3.16 One-to-all personalized communication on an eight-processor hypercube.

Hypercube

Figure 3.16 shows the communication steps for one-to-all personalized communication on an eight-processor hypercube. Initially, the source processor (processor 0) contains all the messages. In the figure, messages are identified by the labels of their destination processors. In the first communication step, the source transfers half of the messages to one of its neighbors. In subsequent steps, each processor that has some data transfers half of it to a neighbor that has yet to receive any data. There is a total of $\log p$ communication steps corresponding to the $\log p$ dimensions of the hypercube. Note that the communication pattern of one-to-all broadcast (Figure 3.5) and one-to-all personalized communication (Figure 3.16) are identical. Only the size and the contents of messages are different.

All links of a p-processor hypercube along a certain dimension join two $p/2$-processor subcubes (Section 2.4.1). As Figure 3.16 illustrates, in each communication step of one-to-all personalized communication, data flow from one subcube to another. The data that a processor has before starting communication in a certain dimension are

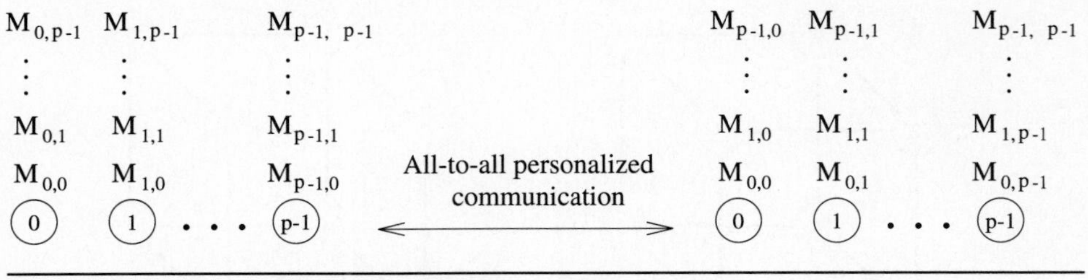

Figure 3.17 All-to-all personalized communication.

such that half of them need to be sent to a processor in the other subcube. In every step, a communicating processor keeps half of its data, meant for the processors in its subcube, and sends the other half to its neighbor in the other subcube. The time in which all data are distributed to their respective destinations is

$$T_{one\_to\_all\_pers} = t_s \log p + t_w m(p - 1). \tag{3.12}$$

This time is the same as the time required for all-to-all broadcast on a similar hypercube. One-to-all personalized communication can be performed in time $(t_s + t_w m)(p - 1)$ on a ring and in time $2t_s(\sqrt{p} - 1) + t_w m(p - 1)$ on a 2-D square mesh for both SF and CT routing (Problem 3.6).

3.5 All-to-All Personalized Communication

In ***all-to-all personalized communication***, also known as ***total exchange***, each processor sends a distinct message of size m to every other processor. Each processor sends different messages to different processors, unlike all-to-all broadcast, in which each processor sends the same message to all other processors. Figure 3.17 illustrates the all-to-all personalized communication operation. This operation is used in parallel fast Fourier transform, matrix transpose, and some parallel database join operations.

We now discuss the implementation of all-to-all personalized communication on parallel computers with ring, mesh, and hypercube interconnection networks. The communication patterns of all-to-all personalized communication are identical to those of all-to-all broadcast on all three architectures. Only the size and the contents of messages are different.

3.5.1 Store-and-Forward Routing

Ring

Figure 3.18 shows the steps in all-to-all personalized communication on a six-processor ring. To perform this operation, every processor sends $p - 1$ pieces of data, each of size m. In the figure, these pieces of data are identified by pairs of integers of the form $\{i, j\}$, where

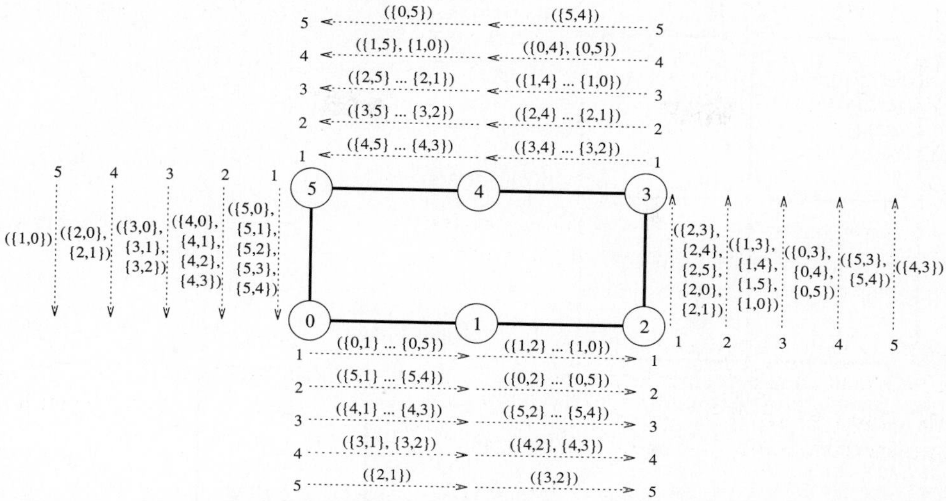

Figure 3.18 All-to-all personalized communication on a six-processor ring. The label of each message is of the form $\{x, y\}$, where x is the label of the processor that originally stored the message, and y is the label of the processor that is the final destination of the message. The label $(\{x_1, y_1\}, \{x_2, y_2\}, \ldots, \{x_n, y_n\})$ indicates a message that is formed by concatenating n individual messages.

i is the source of the message and j is its final destination. First, each processor sends all pieces of data as one consolidated message of size $m(p-1)$ to one of its neighbors (all processors communicate in the same direction). Of the $m(p-1)$ words of data received by a processor in this step, one m-word packet belongs to it. Therefore, each processor extracts the information meant for it from the data received, and forwards the remainder ($p-2$ pieces of size m each) to the next processor. This process continues for $p-1$ steps. The size of the messages being transferred between processors decreases by m words in each successive step. In every step, each processor adds to its collection one m-word packet originating from a different processor. Hence, in $p-1$ steps, every processor receives the information from all other processors in the ensemble. Since the size of the messages transferred in the ith step is $m(p-i)$ on a ring of processors, the total time taken by this operation is

$$
\begin{aligned}
T_{all\_to\_all\_pers} &= \sum_{i=1}^{p-1}(t_s + t_w m(p-i)) \\
&= t_s(p-1) + \sum_{i=1}^{p-1} i t_w m \\
&= (t_s + \frac{1}{2} t_w m p)(p-1). \qquad (3.13)
\end{aligned}
$$

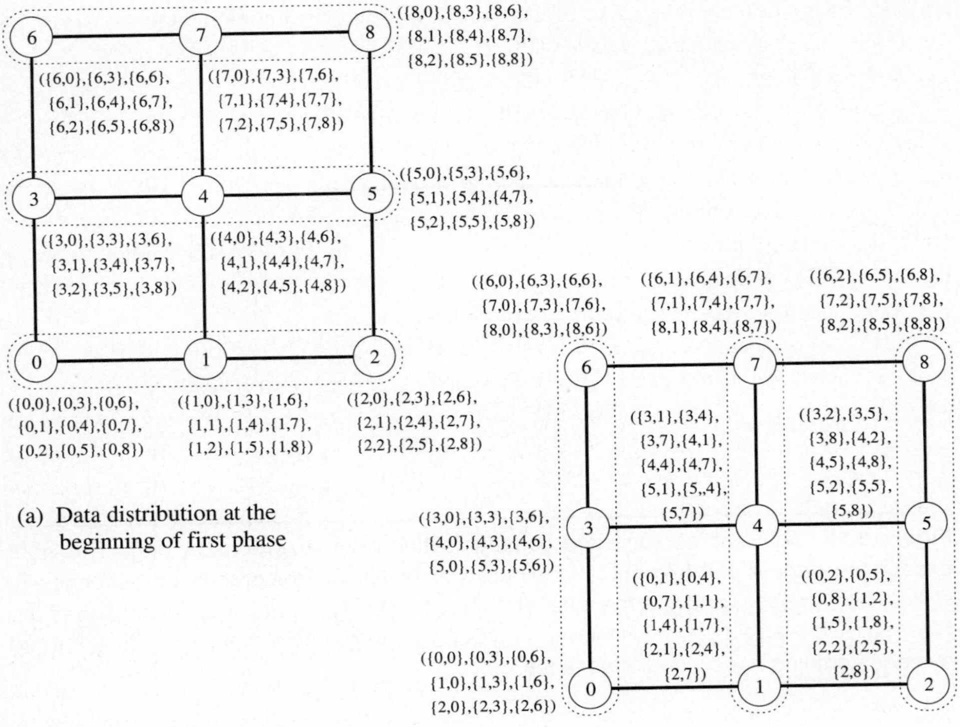

(a) Data distribution at the beginning of first phase

(b) Data distribution at the beginning of second phase

Figure 3.19 The distribution of messages at the beginning of each phase of all-to-all personalized communication on a 3 × 3 mesh. At the end of the second phase, processor i has messages ({0,i}, ..., {8,i}), where $0 \le i \le 8$. The groups of processors communicating together in each phase are enclosed in dotted boundaries.

In the procedure we just described, all messages are sent in the same direction. If half of the messages are sent in one direction and the remaining half are sent in the other direction, then the term associated with t_w can be reduced by a factor of two (Problem 3.3). For the sake of simplicity, we ignore this constant-factor improvement in the remainder of the section.

Mesh

In all-to-all personalized communication on a $\sqrt{p} \times \sqrt{p}$ mesh, each processor first groups its p messages according to the columns of their destination processors. Figure 3.19 shows a 3 × 3 mesh, in which every processor initially has nine m-word messages—one meant for each processor. Each processor assembles its data into three groups of three messages each (in general, $\sqrt{p}$ groups of $\sqrt{p}$ messages each). The first group contains the messages destined for processors labeled 0, 3, and 6; the second group contains the messages for processors labeled 1, 4, and 7; and the last group has messages for processors labeled 2, 5, and 8.

After the messages are grouped, all-to-all personalized communication is performed independently in each row with clustered messages of size $m\sqrt{p}$. One cluster contains the information for all $\sqrt{p}$ processors of a particular column. Figure 3.19(b) shows the distribution of data among the processors at the end of this phase of communication. Assuming a square mesh, we can compute the time spent in this phase by substituting $\sqrt{p}$ for the number of processors, and $m\sqrt{p}$ for the message size in Equation 3.13. The result of this substitution is $(t_s + t_w mp/2)(\sqrt{p} - 1)$.

Before the second communication phase, the messages in each processor are sorted again, this time according to the rows of their destination processors; then communication similar to the first phase takes place in all the columns of the mesh. By the end of this phase, each processor receives a message from every other processor. The time spent in this phase is the same as that in the first phase. Therefore, the total time for all-to-all personalized communication of messages of size m on a p-processor two-dimensional square mesh is

$$T_{all\_to\_all\_pers} = (2t_s + t_w mp)(\sqrt{p} - 1). \tag{3.14}$$

The expression for the communication time of all-to-all personalized communication in Equation 3.14 does not take into account the time required for the local rearrangement of data (that is, sorting the messages by rows or columns). Assuming that initially the data is ready for the first communication phase, the second communication phase requires the rearrangement of mp words of data. If t_r is the time to perform a read and a write operation on a single word of data in a processor's local memory, then the total time spent in data rearrangement by a processor during the entire procedure is $t_r mp$ (Problem 3.27). This time is much smaller than the time spent by each processor in communication.

Hypercube

The all-to-all personalized communication algorithm for a p-processor hypercube with SF routing is simply an extension of the two-dimensional mesh algorithm to $\log p$ dimensions. Figure 3.20 shows the communication steps required to perform this operation on a three-dimensional hypercube. As shown in the figure, communication takes place in $\log p$ steps. Pairs of processors exchange data in a different dimension in each step. Recall that in a p-processor hypercube, a set of $p/2$ links in the same dimension connects two subcubes of $p/2$ processors each (Section 2.4.1). At any stage in all-to-all personalized communication, every processor holds p packets of size m each. While communicating in a particular dimension, every processor sends $p/2$ of these packets (consolidated as one message). The destinations of these packets are the processors of the other subcube connected by the links in current dimension. Thus, $mp/2$ words of data are exchanged along the bidirectional channels in each of the $\log p$ iterations. The resulting total communication time is

$$T_{all\_to\_all\_pers} = (t_s + \frac{1}{2} t_w mp) \log p. \tag{3.15}$$

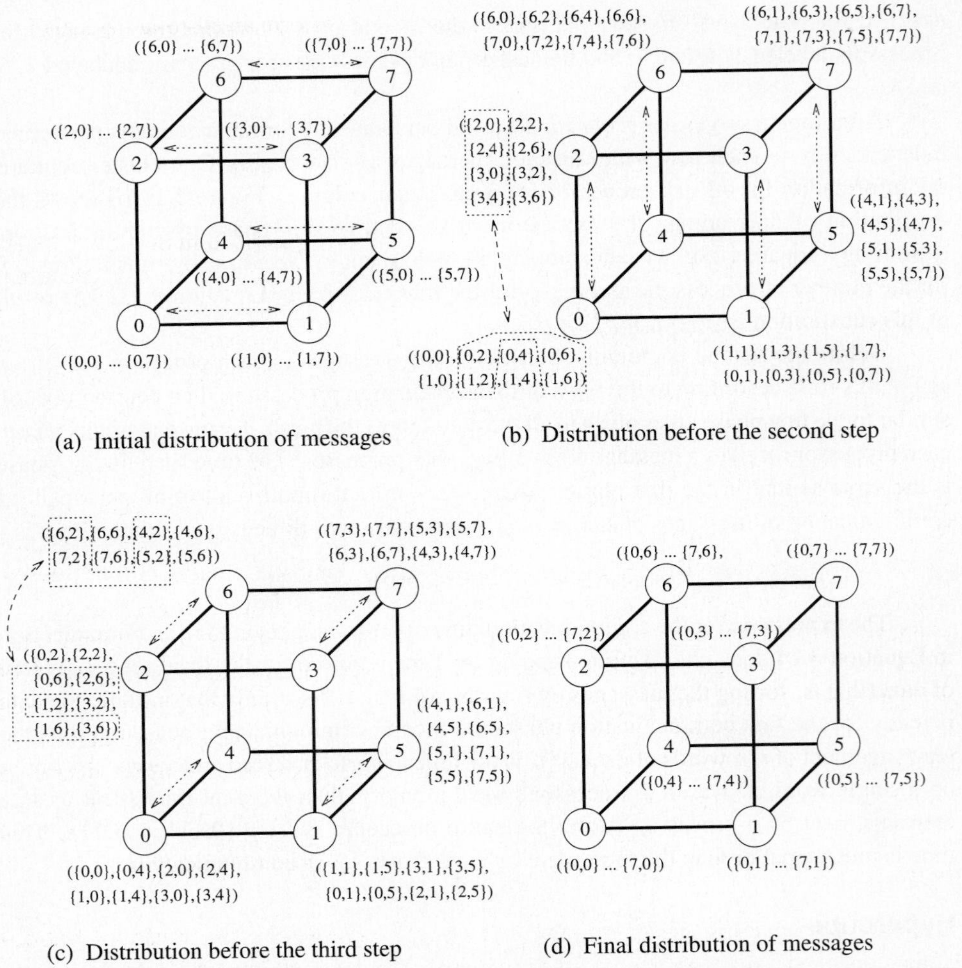

Figure 3.20 All-to-all personalized communication on a three-dimensional hypercube with SF routing.

In the preceding procedure, a processor must rearrange its messages locally before each of the $\log p$ communication steps. This is necessary to make sure that all $p/2$ messages destined for the same processor in a communication step occupy contiguous memory locations so that they can be transmitted as a single consolidated message. Before each of the $\log p$ communication steps, a processor rearranges mp words of data (Problem 3.28). Hence, a total of $t_r mp \log p$ time is spent by each processor in local rearrangement of data during the entire procedure. Here t_r is the time needed to perform a read and a write operation on a single word of data in a processor's local memory. For most practical computers, t_r is much smaller that t_w; hence, the time to perform an all-to-all personalized communication is dominated by the communication time.

3.5.2 Cut-Through Routing

Ring and Mesh

Recall the all-to-all personalized communication procedure described in Section 3.5.1 for a p-processor ring. We know that each processor sends $m(p-1)$ words of data because it has an m-word packet for every other processor. Assume that all messages are sent either clockwise or counterclockwise. The average distance that an m-word packet travels is $(\Sigma_{i=1}^{p-1} i)/(p-1)$, which is equal to $p/2$. Since there are p processors, each performing the same type of communication, the total traffic (the total number of data words transferred between directly-connected processors) on the network is $m(p-1) \times p/2 \times p$. The total number of communication channels in the network to share this load is p. Hence, the communication time for this operation is at least $(t_w \times m(p-1)p^2/2)/p$, which is equal to $t_w m(p-1)p/2$. Ignoring the message startup time t_s, this is exactly the time taken by the ring procedure. Hence, this procedure cannot be improved by using CT routing. Similarly, regardless of the routing mechanism, the mesh procedure of Section 3.5.1 is optimal within a small constant factor (Problem 3.12). However, with CT routing, the ring and mesh procedures for all-to-all personalized communication shown in Figures 3.18 and 3.19 do not require wraparound connections, provided that communication channels are bidirectional. Thus, with CT routing, the times for all-to-all personalized communication on a linear array and a mesh without wraparound are the same as those with SF routing on a ring and a mesh with wraparound, respectively.

Hypercube

Interestingly, using CT (instead of SF) routing does improve the performance of all-to-all personalized communication on a hypercube. The average distance between any two processors on a hypercube is $(\log p)/2$; hence, the total traffic is $m(p-1) \times (\log p)/2 \times p$. Since there is a total of $(p \log p)/2$ links in the hypercube network, the lower bound on the all-to-all personalized communication time is

$$\begin{aligned} T_{all\_to\_all\_pers}^{lower\_bound} &= \frac{t_w m(p-1)(p \log p)/2}{(p \log p)/2} \\ &= t_w m(p-1). \end{aligned}$$

This is smaller than the communication time of $(t_s + t_w mp/2) \log p$ for the hypercube procedure described in Section 3.5.1.

An all-to-all personalized communication effectively results in all pairs of processors exchanging some data. If cut-through routing is available on a hypercube, then the best way to perform this exchange is to have every pair of processors communicate directly with each other. Thus, each processor simply performs $p-1$ communication steps,

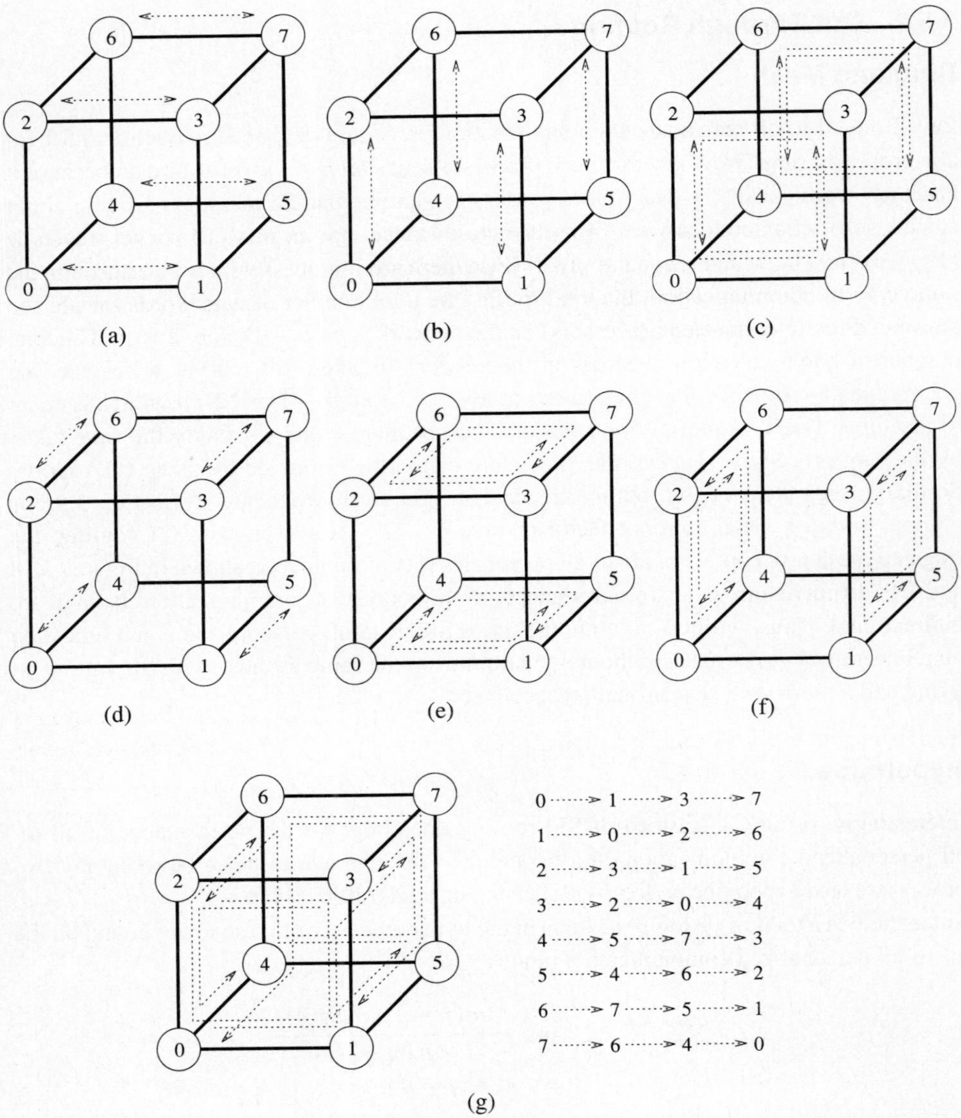

Figure 3.21 Seven steps in all-to-all personalized communication on an eight-processor hypercube with CT routing.

```
procedure ALL_TO_ALL_PERSONAL(d, my_id)
begin
    for i := 1 to 2^d − 1 do
    begin
        partner := my_id XOR i;
        send M_{my_id,partner} to partner;
        receive M_{partner,my_id} from partner;
    endfor;
end ALL_TO_ALL_PERSONAL
```

Program 3.8 A procedure to perform all-to-all personalized communication on a d-dimensional hypercube with CT routing. The message $M_{i,j}$ initially resides on processor i and is destined for processor j.

exchanging m words of data with a different processor in every step. A processor must choose its communication partner in each step so that the hypercube links do not suffer congestion. Figure 3.21 shows one such congestion-free schedule for pairwise exchange of data in a three-dimensional hypercube. As the figure shows, in the jth communication step, processor i exchanges data with processor (i XOR j). For example, in part (a) of the figure (step 1), the labels of communicating partners differ in the least significant bit. In part (g) (step 7), the labels of communicating partners differ in all the bits, as the binary representation of seven is 111. In this figure, all the paths in every communication step are congestion-free, and none of the bidirectional links carry more than one message in the same direction. This is true in general for a hypercube of any dimension. If the messages are routed appropriately, a congestion-free schedule exists for the $p - 1$ communication steps of all-to-all personalized communication on a p-processor hypercube.

Recall from Section 2.4.1 that a message traveling from processor i to processor j on a hypercube must pass through at least l links, where l is the Hamming distance between i and j (that is, the number of nonzero bits in the binary representation of (i XOR j)). A message traveling from processor i to processor j traverses links in l dimensions (corresponding to the nonzero bits in the binary representation of (i XOR j)). Although the message can follow one of the several paths of length l that exist between i and j (assuming $l > 1$), a distinct path is obtained by sorting the dimensions along which the message travels in ascending order. According to this strategy, the first link is chosen in the dimension corresponding to the least significant nonzero bit of (i XOR j), and so on. This routing scheme is known as ***ascending routing*** or ***E-cube routing***. A more detailed description of E-cube routing can be found in Section 2.6. By using E-cube routing, and by choosing communication pairs according to Program 3.8, a communication time of $t_s + t_w m + t_h l$ is guaranteed for a message transfer between processor i and processor j, where l is the Hamming distance between i and j. For a given i, on a p-processor hypercube, the sum of all l for $0 \leq j < p$ is $(p \log p)/2$. The total communication time for the entire operation is

$$T_{all\_to\_all\_pers} = (t_s + t_w m)(p-1) + \frac{1}{2} t_h p \log p. \tag{3.16}$$

A comparison of Equations 3.15 and 3.16 shows the term associated with t_s is higher for the CT routing procedure, while the term associated with t_w is higher for the SF routing procedure by a factor of almost $(\log p)/2$. Furthermore, CT routing obviates the need for local rearrangement of messages required in the SF routing procedure. For small messages, the startup time may dominate, and the procedure of Section 3.5.1 may still be useful.

3.6 Circular Shift

A ***permutation*** is a simultaneous, one-to-one data redistribution operation in which each processor sends a packet of m words to a unique processor. In this section, we discuss a particular type of permutation called circular shift. We define a ***circular q-shift*** as the operation in which processor i sends a data packet to processor $(i + q) \bmod p$ in a p-processor ensemble $(0 < q < p)$. The shift operation finds application in some matrix computations and in string and image pattern matching.

Since the implementation of a circular q-shift is fairly intuitive on a ring (it can be performed by $\min\{q, p - q\}$neighbor-to-neighbor communications in one direction), we discuss this operation in detail only on a mesh and a hypercube.

3.6.1 Store-and-Forward Routing

Mesh

If the processors of the mesh have row-major labels, a circular q-shift can be performed on a p-processor square wraparound mesh in two stages. First, the entire set of data is shifted simultaneously by $(q \bmod \sqrt{p})$ steps along the rows. Then it is shifted by $\lfloor q/\sqrt{p} \rfloor$ steps along the columns. During the circular row shifts, some of the data traverse the wraparound connection from the highest to the lowest labeled processors of the rows. All such data packets must shift an additional step forward along the columns to compensate for the $\sqrt{p}$ distance that they lost while traversing the backward edge in their respective rows.

Figure 3.22 shows a circular 5-shift on a 16-processor mesh. It requires one row shift, a compensatory column shift, and finally one column shift. In practice, we can chose the direction of the shifts in both the rows and the columns to minimize the number of steps in a circular shift. For instance, a 3-shift on a 4×4 mesh can be performed by a single backward row shift. Using this strategy, the number of unit shifts in a direction cannot exceed $\lfloor \sqrt{p}/2 \rfloor$.

Taking into account the compensating column shift for some packets, the total time for any circular q-shift on a p-processor mesh using packets of size m has an upper bound of

$$T_{circular\_shift} = (t_s + t_w m)(2\lfloor \frac{\sqrt{p}}{2} \rfloor + 1).$$

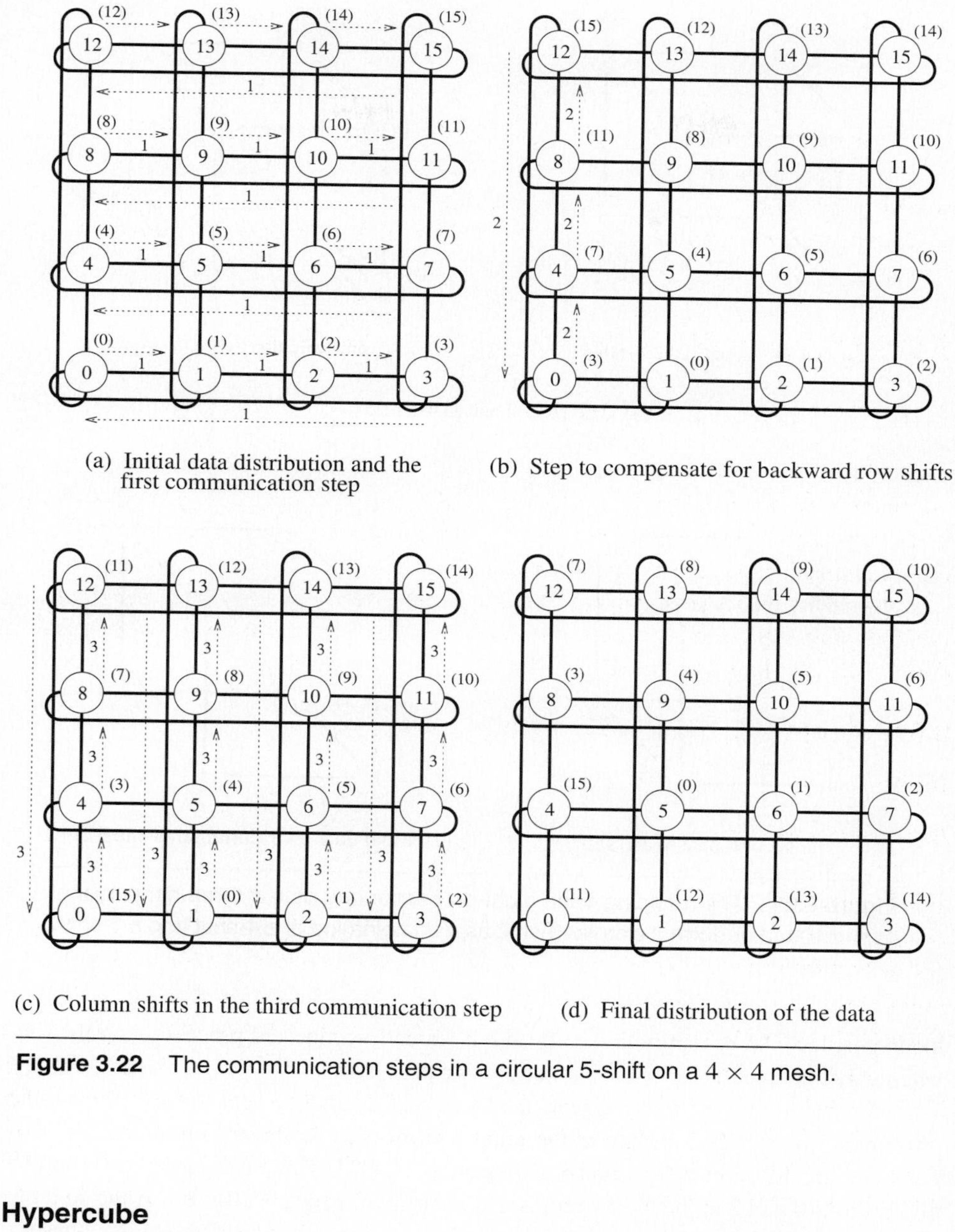

(a) Initial data distribution and the first communication step
(b) Step to compensate for backward row shifts
(c) Column shifts in the third communication step
(d) Final distribution of the data

Figure 3.22 The communication steps in a circular 5-shift on a 4 × 4 mesh.

Hypercube

In developing a hypercube algorithm for the shift operation, we map a ring with 2^d processors onto a d-dimensional hypercube. We do this by assigning processor i of the ring to processor j of the hypercube such that j is the d-bit binary reflected Gray code (RGC) of i. Figure 3.23 illustrates this mapping for eight processors. A property of this mapping is that any two processors at a distance of 2^i on the ring are separated by exactly two links on

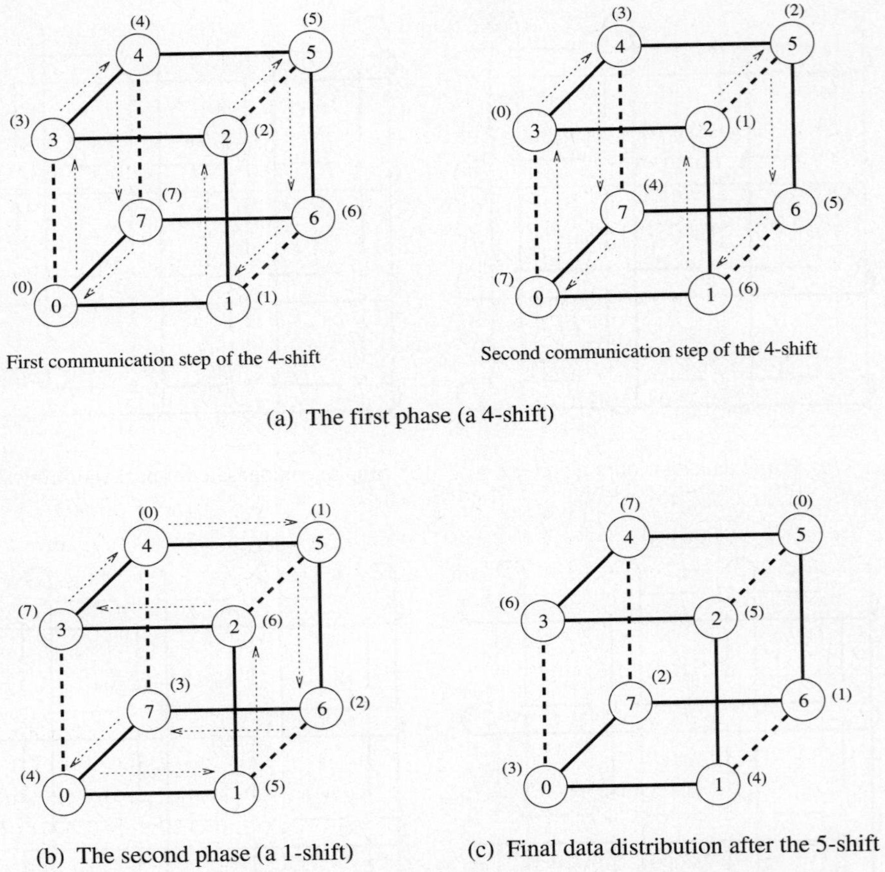

First communication step of the 4-shift
Second communication step of the 4-shift
(a) The first phase (a 4-shift)
(b) The second phase (a 1-shift)
(c) Final data distribution after the 5-shift

Figure 3.23 The mapping of an eight-processor ring onto a three-dimensional hypercube to perform a circular 5-shift as a combination of a 4-shift and a 1-shift.

the hypercube. An exception is $i = 0$ (that is, directly-connected processors on the ring) when only one hypercube link separates the two processors.

To perform a q-shift, we expand q as a sum of distinct powers of two. The number of terms in the sum is the same as the number of ones in the binary representation of q. For example, the number five can be expressed as $2^2 + 2^0$. These two terms correspond to bit positions 0 and 2 in the binary representation of five, which is 101. If q is the sum of s distinct powers of two, then the circular q-shift on a hypercube is performed in s phases.

In each phase of communication, all data packets move closer to their respective destinations by short cutting the ring (mapped onto the hypercube) in leaps of the powers of two. For example, as Figure 3.23 shows, a 5-shift is performed by a 4-shift followed by a 1-shift. The number of communication phases in a q-shift is exactly equal to the number of ones in the binary representation of q. Each phase consists of two communication steps, except the 1-shift, which, if required (that is, if the least significant bit of q is one), consists of a single step. For example, in a 5-shift, the first phase of a 4-shift (Figure 3.23(a)) consists of two steps and the second phase of a 1-shift (Figure 3.23(b)) consists of one step. Thus, the total number of steps for any q in a p-processor hypercube is at most $2 \log p - 1$.

All communications in a given time step are congestion-free. This is ensured by the property of the ring mapping that all processors whose mutual distance on the ring is a power of two are arranged in disjoint subrings on the hypercube. Thus, all processors can freely communicate in a circular fashion in their respective subrings. This is shown in Figure 3.23(a), in which processors labeled 0, 3, 4, and 7 form one subring and processors labeled 1, 2, 5, and 6 form another subring.

The upper bound on the total communication time for any shift of m-word packets on a p-processor hypercube is

$$T_{circular\_shift} = (t_s + t_w m)(2 \log p - 1). \tag{3.17}$$

We can reduce this upper bound to $(t_s + t_w m) \log p$ by performing both forward and backward shifts (Problem 3.29). For example, on eight processors, a 6-shift can be performed by a single backward 2-shift instead of a forward 4-shift followed by a forward 2-shift.

3.6.2 Cut-Through Routing

Cut-through routing does not aid a shift operation on a ring or a mesh due to congestion on communication links. On a hypercube, however, CT routing can improve the time of a shift operation by almost a factor of $\log p$ for large messages. To perform a circular q-shift on hypercube with CT routing, the standard hypercube labeling of processors is used (instead of the RGC labeling used with SF routing). Each processor directly sends the data to be shifted to its destination processor. If the E-cube routing described in Section 3.5.2 is used, then each message has a congestion-free path (Problem 3.30). Figure 3.24 illustrates the non-conflicting paths of all the messages in circular q-shift operations for $1 \leq q < 8$ on an eight-processor hypercube. In a circular q-shift on a p-processor hypercube, the longest path contains $\log p - \gamma(q)$ links, where $\gamma(q)$ is the highest integer j such that q is divisible by 2^j (Problem 3.31). Thus, the total communication time for messages of length m is

$$T_{circular\_shift} = t_s + t_w m + t_h(\log p - \gamma(q)). \tag{3.18}$$

For large messages, this time is approximately equal to $t_s + t_w m$.

3.7 Faster Methods for Some Communication Operations

So far in this chapter, we have derived procedures for various communication operations and their communication times under certain assumptions. We now briefly discuss the impact of relaxing these assumptions on some of the communication operations.

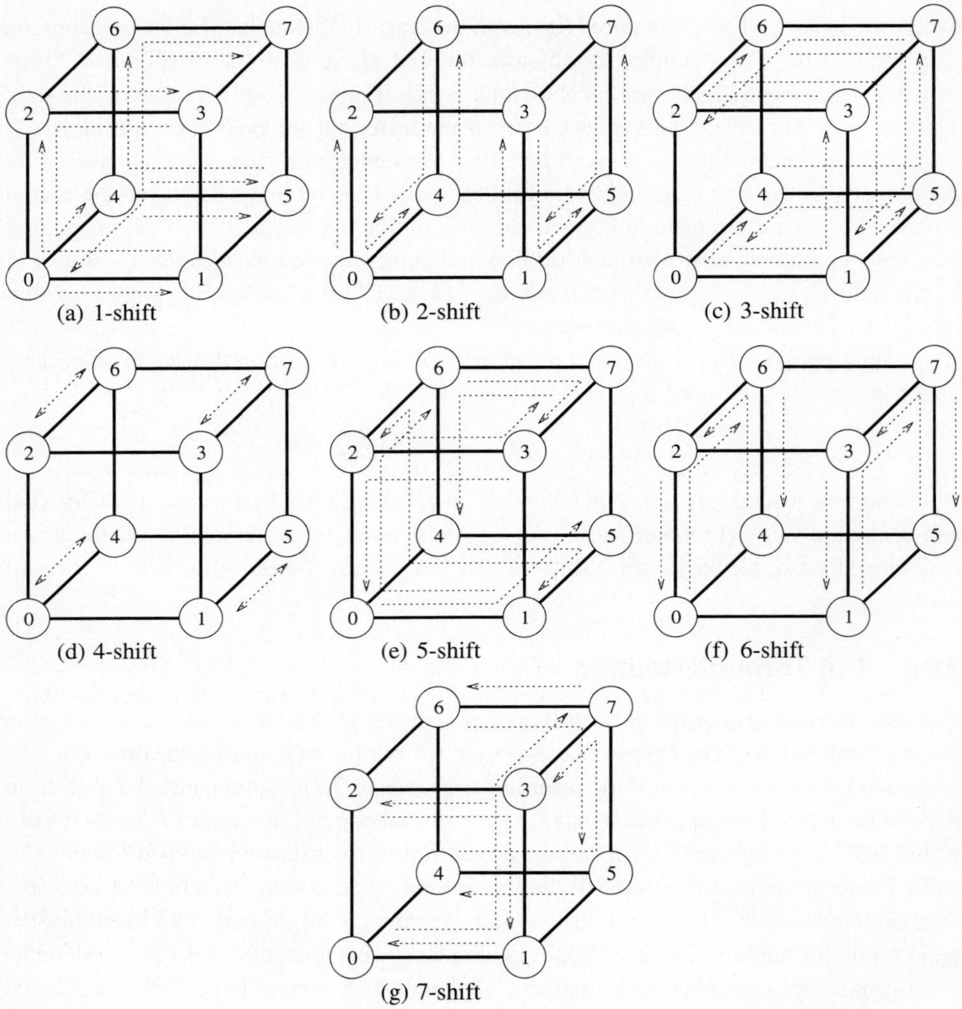

Figure 3.24 Circular q-shifts on an 8-processor hypercube for $1 \leq q < 8$.

★ 3.7.1 Routing Messages in Parts

In the procedures described in Sections 3.1–3.6, we assumed that an entire m-word packet of data travels between the source and the destination processors along the same path. If we split a message into smaller parts and then route these parts through different paths, we may be able to utilize the communication network better. For example, consider the transfer of a message of size m between two processors of a p-processor hypercube. Section 3.1 shows that this communication takes at most $t_s + t_w m \log p$ time with SF routing. One of the properties of a p-processor hypercube is that there are $\log p$ distinct paths between any pair

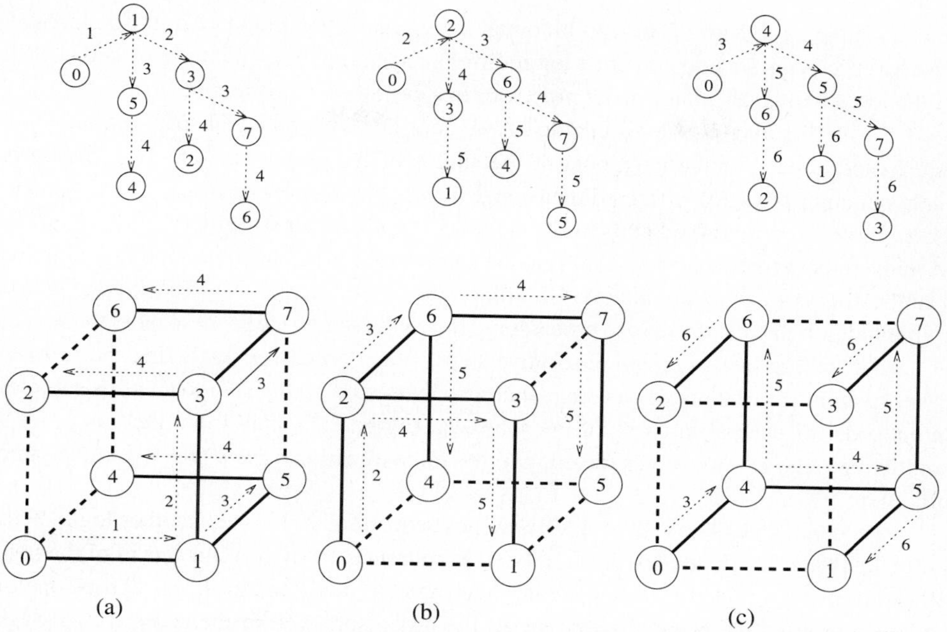

Figure 3.25 The six time-steps in one-to-all broadcast on an eight-processor hypercube with SF routing when the message is split into three parts that are routed separately on three different spanning binomial trees.

of processors. If the labels of two processors differ in l bits, then l of these paths contain l links each, and the remaining $(\log p - l)$ paths contain $l + 2$ links each (Problem 2.8). If the message is split at the source into $\log p$ parts and each part is sent to the destination along a separate path (starting with the longer paths first), then the destination can receive the entire data in at most $2 \log p$ communication steps involving messages of size $m/\log p$. In $\log p$ steps, the source sends the smaller packets out on all the $\log p$ paths. The last packet takes at most $\log p$ steps to reach the destination. That way, the communication time is at most $2(t_s \log p + t_w m)$. This time reflects an improvement by a factor of $\Theta(\log p)$ in the t_w term over the method described in Section 3.1. Although, the t_s term increases by a similar factor, for sufficiently large messages, this method could still be faster than sending the entire message along the same path.

Now consider one-to-all broadcast on a hypercube. We first describe a property of the hypercube network that is useful for performing this operation. A ***spanning tree*** of a graph is defined as a tree whose set of nodes or vertices is identical to that of the graph. A one-node ***binomial tree*** is the node itself. A p-node binomial tree is constructed from two $p/2$-node trees by adding an edge from the root of one tree to the root of the second tree—making the second tree a subtree of the first. It is a property of a p-processor hypercube that a p-node binomial tree can be embedded into it with each node of the tree mapped onto a distinct processor. Thus, this binomial tree is also a spanning tree of the hypercube. Moreover, it is possible to construct $\log p$ different spanning binomial trees rooted at each of the $\log p$ neighbors of any given processor in a p-processor hypercube.

For performing one-to-all broadcast, we consider a hypothetical spanning binomial tree rooted at each of the neighbors of the source of the broadcast. Figure 3.25 shows such spanning trees for a three-dimensional hypercube with processor 0 as the source. These three trees are rooted at the three neighbors of processor 0—processors 1, 2, and 4. Moreover, these trees are oriented so that the source itself is the smallest subtree (ontaining a single node) of each binomial tree. In order to be broadcast, the m-word message is first split into $\log p$ parts at the source processor. The source sends one of these parts to the root of each spanning tree in three consecutive steps. Each processor (including the root) of every spanning tree stores any message that it receives, and sends it out to all of its subtrees in the order of decreasing sizes of the subtrees. Figure 3.25 shows that there is never a conflict between two messages traveling in the same direction on any channel in the same time step.

The source sends out the $\log p$ messages sequentially. It takes another $\log p$ steps for the message sent to the last spanning tree to percolate down to all the leaves of the tree. Since all processors lie on each spanning tree (by definition) and each tree carries one of the $\log p$ parts of the original message, all the processors receive the complete message by the end of the procedure. With individual messages of size $m/\log p$, the time taken to complete all the $2\log p$ steps of the broadcast is

$$\begin{aligned} T_{one\_to\_all} &= (t_s + t_w m/\log p) \times 2\log p \\ &= 2(t_s \log p + t_w m). \end{aligned} \tag{3.19}$$

Note that the t_w term is reduced by a factor of $(\log p)/2$ over the algorithm presented in Section 3.2, but the t_s term has doubled.

In this section, we discussed how the communication time of one-to-all broadcast can be reduced by splitting a message into smaller parts that are routed independently. Another algorithm to perform one-to-all broadcast on a hypercube in time $2(t_s \log p + t_w m)$ is given in Problem 3.24. However, algorithms like the one presented here and in Problem 3.24 are usually difficult to program and incur additional overhead in breaking, routing, queuing, and reassembling the messages. Moreover, the original message must contain at least $\log p$ words for successful splitting. In practice, messages need to be even longer in order to offset the doubled startup cost. Hence, the smarter broadcast algorithms are useful only if the message size if sufficiently large.

3.7.2 All-Port Communication

In a parallel architecture, a single processor may have multiple communication ports with links to other processors in the ensemble. For example, each processor in a two-dimensional wraparound mesh has four ports, and each processor in a d-dimensional hypercube has d ports. In this book, we generally assume what is known as the ***one-port communication*** model. In one-port communication, a processor can send data on only one of its ports at a time. Similarly, a processor can receive data on only one port at a time. However, a processor can send and a receive data simultaneously—either on the same port or on separate ports. In contrast to the one-port model, an ***all-port communication*** model permits simultaneous communication on all the channels connected to a processor.

On a p-processor hypercube with all-port communication, the coefficients of t_w in the expressions for the communication times of one-to-all and all-to-all broadcast and personalized communication are all smaller than their one-port counterparts by a factor of $\log p$. Since the number of channels per processor for a ring or a mesh is constant, all-port communication does not provide any asymptotic improvement in communication time on these architectures.

Despite the apparent speedup, the all-port communication model has certain limitations. For instance, not only is it difficult to program, but it requires that the messages are large enough to be split efficiently among different channels. In several parallel algorithms, an increase in the size of messages means a corresponding increase in the granularity of computation at the processors. When the processors are working with large data sets, the interprocessor communication time is dominated by the computation time if the computational complexity of the algorithm is higher than the communication complexity. For example, in the case of matrix multiplication, there are n^3 computations for n^2 words of data transferred among the processors. If the communication time is a small fraction of the total parallel run time, then improving the communication by using sophisticated techniques is not very advantageous in terms of the overall run time of the parallel algorithm.

Even with today's technology, the one-port communication model is quite relevant. In some state-of-the-art parallel computers such as the CM-5, the all-port model is not applicable at all. The CM-5 can execute most one-port hypercube algorithms without a substantial extra communication penalty. Unlike a real hypercube, each CM-5 processor has only one communication port because its interconnection network is a pseudo fat tree. In any case, even if multiple ports are available, all-port communication can be effective only if data can be fetched and stored in memory at a rate sufficient to sustain all the parallel communication. For example, to utilize all-port communication effectively on a p-processor hypercube, the memory bandwidth must be greater than the communication bandwidth of a single channel by a factor of at least $\log p$; that is, the memory bandwidth must increase with the number of processors to support simultaneous communication on all ports.

3.7.3 Special Hardware for Global Operations

In addition to the standard data network, some parallel computers have a fast control network that can perform certain global operations in a small constant time. One such operation commonly implemented using special hardware is reduction (Example 3.7). A reduction operation starts with a different value on each processor and ends with a single value on each processor. The final value is the result of applying an associative operator

Table 3.1 Summary of communication times of various operations discussed in Sections 3.2–3.5 on different architectures with one-port communication and CT routing. The message size for each operation is m and the number of processors is p. The time for one-to-all broadcast on the hypercube is not optimal, and, as shown in Section 3.7.1 and Problem 3.24, can be improved to $2(t_s \log p + t_w m)$. In the hypercube expression for circular q-shift, $\gamma(q)$ is the highest integer j such that q is divisible by 2^j.

Operation	Ring	2-D Mesh (wraparound, square)	Hypercube
One-to-all broadcast	$(t_s + t_w m) \log p$ $+t_h(p-1)$	$(t_s + t_w m) \log p$ $+2t_h(\sqrt{p}-1)$	$(t_s + t_w m) \log p$
All-to-all broadcast	$(t_s + t_w m)(p-1)$	$2t_s(\sqrt{p}-1) + t_w m(p-1)$	$t_s \log p + t_w m(p-1)$
One-to-all personalized	$(t_s + t_w m)(p-1)$	$2t_s(\sqrt{p}-1) + t_w m(p-1)$	$t_s \log p + t_w m(p-1)$
All-to-all personalized	$(t_s + t_w mp/2)(p-1)$	$(2t_s + t_w mp)(\sqrt{p}-1)$	$(t_s + t_w m)(p-1)$ $+(t_h/2)p \log p$
Circular q-shift	$(t_s + t_w m)\lfloor p/2 \rfloor$	$(t_s + t_w m)(2\lfloor \sqrt{p}/2 \rfloor + 1)$	$t_s + t_w m$ $+t_h(\log p - \gamma(q))$

(such as addition, maximum, minimum, or a logical bitwise operator) on all the starting values.

A fast, (almost) constant time reduction, while providing a natural way to implement accumulation, can also be used to perform broadcasts. If the source starts with a datum to be broadcast, and every other processor starts with a zero, a reduction with addition as the associative operator results in the distribution of the source's datum to all the processors. If t_r is the time to perform one reduction, then the control network provides a fast means to implement one-to-all broadcast of a message of size m in $t_r m$ time, as opposed to $(t_s + t_w m) \log p$ time using the hypercube algorithm described in Section 3.2.

3.8 Summary

Table 3.1 summarizes the communication times for the operations discussed in this chapter on ring, mesh, and hypercube architectures with cut-through routing. Most of the entries in the table are valid for store-and-forward routing as well. The exceptions are: (1) the communication times of one-to-all broadcast on a ring and a mesh with SF routing, which are $(t_s + t_w m)\lceil p/2 \rceil$ and $2(t_s + t_w m)\lceil \sqrt{p}/2 \rceil$, respectively; and (2) the time taken by all-to-all personalized communication operation on a hypercube with SF routing, which is $(t_s + t_w mp/2) \log p$. The time for one-to-all broadcast on the hypercube is not optimal; as we saw in Section 3.7.1, it can be improved to $2(t_s \log p + t_w m)$.

All communication patterns discussed in this chapter are very regular and predictable. Therefore, we have been able to describe their algorithms in terms of discrete time steps, avoiding temporal and spatial (on the channels) overlap of messages. As a result, all the algorithms described here will work as expected on SIMD computers. However, since it is theoretically impossible to impose any synchrony on the processors of an MIMD computer, the communication times may deviate somewhat from their theoretical expressions, especially if communication and computation are interspersed.

3.9 Bibliographic Remarks

In this chapter, we studied a variety of data communication operations for the ring, mesh, and hypercube interconnection topologies. Saad and Schultz [SS89b] discuss implementation issues for these operations on these and other architectures, such as shared-memory and a switch or bus interconnect.

The hypercube algorithm for a certain communication operation is often the best algorithm for other less-connected architectures too, if they support cut-through routing. Due to the versatility of the hypercube architecture and the wide applicability of its algorithms, extensive work has been done on implementing various communication operations on hypercubes [BOS+91, BR90, BT89, FF86, JH89, Joh90, MdV87, RS90, SS89a, SW87]. The properties of a hypercube network that are used in deriving the algorithms for various communication operations on it are described by Saad and Schultz [SS88].

The all-to-all personalized communication problem in particular has been analyzed for the hypercube architecture by Boppana and Raghavendra [BR90], Johnsson and Ho [JH91], Seidel [Sei89], and Take [Tak87]. Ascending or E-cube routing that guarantees congestion-free communication in Program 3.8 for all-to-all personalized communication is described by Nugent [Nug88], and is used in Intel's iPSC/2 hypercube.

The reduction and the prefix sums algorithms of Examples 3.7 and 3.8 are described by Ranka and Sahni [RS90]. Our discussion of the circular shift operation is adapted from Bertsekas and Tsitsiklis [BT89].

The hypercube algorithm for one-to-all broadcast using spanning binomial trees is described by Bertsekas and Tsitsiklis [BT89] and Johnsson and Ho [JH89]. In the spanning tree algorithm described in Section 3.7.1, we split the m-word message to be broadcast into $\log p$ parts of size $m/\log p$ for ease of presenting the algorithm. Johnsson and Ho [JH89] show that the optimal size of the parts is $\lceil (\sqrt{t_s m/t_w \log p}) \rceil$. In this case, the number of messages may be greater than $\log p$. These smaller messages are sent from the root of the spanning binomial tree to its $\log p$ subtrees in a circular fashion. With this strategy, one-to-all broadcast on a p-processor hypercube can be performed in time $t_s \log p + t_w m + 2t_w \lceil (\sqrt{t_s m/t_w \log p}) \rceil \log p$.

Algorithms using the all-port communication model have been described for a variety of communication operations on the hypercube architecture by Bertsekas and Tsitsiklis [BT89], Johnsson and Ho [JH89], Ho and Johnsson [HJ87], Saad and Schultz [SS89a], and Stout and Wagar [SW87]. Johnsson and Ho [JH89] show that on a p-processor hypercube with all-port communication, the coefficients of t_w in the expressions for the communication times of one-to-all and all-to-all broadcast and personalized communication are all smaller than their one-port counterparts by a factor of $\log p$. Gupta and Kumar [GK91] show that all-port communication may not improve the scalability of an algorithm on a parallel architecture over one-port communication.

The network architecture of CM-5 that supports a fast reduction operation is described by Leiserson et al. [L$^+$92]. The same operation is discussed by Stolfo and Miranker [SM86] in the context of the DADO parallel computer. Besides reduction, parallel computers like the CM-5 and DADO also support other related operations such as prefix sums. A generalized form of prefix sums, often referred to as ***scan***, has been used by some researchers as a basic primitive in data-parallel programming. Blelloch [Ble90] define a ***scan vector model***, and describes how a wide variety of parallel programs can be expressed in terms of the scan primitive and its variations.

The elementary operations described in this chapter are not the only ones used in parallel applications. A variety of other useful operations for parallel computers have been described in literature, including selection [Akl89], pointer jumping [HS86, Jaj92], BPC permutations [Joh90, RS90], fetch-and-op [GGK$^+$83], packing [Lev87, Sch80], bit reversal [Loa92], and keyed-scan or multi-prefix [Ble90, Ran89].

Sometimes data communication does not follow any predefined pattern, but is arbitrary, depending on the application. In such cases, a simplistic approach of routing the messages along the shortest data paths between their respective sources and destinations leads to contention and imbalanced communication. Leighton, Maggs, and Rao [LMR88], Valiant [Val82], and Valiant and Brebner [VB81] discuss efficient routing methods for arbitrary permutations of messages.

Problems

3.1 **(One-to-all broadcast on a tree)** Show that one-to-all broadcast of an m-word message can be performed in time $(t_s + t_w m + t_h(\log p + 1)) \log p$ on a balanced binary tree on which each of the p leaves is a processor and each intermediate node is a switching node. Assume that a message takes time $t_s + t_w m + t_h l$ to traverse a path with $l - 1$ switching nodes.

3.2 Consider a linear array (without a wraparound connection) of p processors labeled from 0 to $p - 1$. The average distance (in terms of the number of links) from processor 0 to any of the other $p - 1$ processors is $(\Sigma_{i=1}^{p-1} i)/(p - 1)$, which is equal to $p/2$. Derive an expression for the average distance to any of the (four) corner processors from all the other processors in a $\sqrt{p} \times \sqrt{p}$ mesh without wraparound connections. What is the average distance of a processor in a d-dimensional hypercube from the other processors?

3.3 Describe a procedure for all-to-all personalized communication of m-word messages on a ring of p processors with SF routing such that the procedure takes $t_s(p-1) + t_w mp^2/4$ time if p is even and $t_s(p-1) + t_w m(p^2-1)/4$ time if p is odd.

3.4 **(All-to-all broadcast on a tree)** Given a balanced binary tree as shown in Figure 3.8, describe a procedure to perform all-to-all broadcast that takes $(t_s + t_w mp/2)\log p$ time for m-word messages on p processors. Assume that only the leaves of the tree contain processors, and that an exchange of two m-word messages between any two processors connected by bidirectional channels takes $t_s + t_w mk$ time if the communication channel (or a part of it) is shared by k simultaneous messages.

3.5 Derive an optimal algorithm along the lines of Example 3.7 for adding p numbers on a p-processor mesh and distributing the sum to all the processors. What is its parallel run time? Show that your algorithm is optimal.

3.6 **(One-to-all personalized communication on a ring and a mesh)** Give the procedures and their communication times for one-to-all personalized communication of m-word messages on p processors for the ring and the mesh architectures.
Hint: For the mesh, the algorithm proceeds in two phases as usual and starts with the source distributing pieces of $m\sqrt{p}$ words among the $\sqrt{p}$ processors in its row such that each of these processors receives the data meant for all the $\sqrt{p}$ processors in its column.

3.7 Section 3.2.1 shows informally that the hypercube algorithm described in that section for one-to-all broadcast is optimal if an entire message is routed along the same path. Why can't the same argument be applied to the hypercube algorithm for all-to-all personalized communication described in Section 3.5.1?

3.8 **(Multinode accumulation)** The dual of all-to-all broadcast is multinode accumulation, in which each processor is the destination of a single-node accumulation. For example, consider the scenario where p processors have a vector of p elements each, and the ith processor (for all i such that $0 \leq i < p$) gets the sum of the ith elements of all the vectors. Describe an algorithm to perform multinode accumulation on a hypercube with addition as the associative operator. If each message contains m words and t_{add} is the time to perform one addition, how much time does your algorithm take (in terms of m, p, t_{add}, t_s and t_w)?
Hint: In all-to-all broadcast, each processor starts with a single message and collects p such messages by the end of the operation. In multinode accumulation, each processor starts with a p distinct messages (one meant for each processor) but ends up with a single message.

3.9 Parts (c), (e), and (f) of Figure 3.21 show that for any processor in a three-dimensional hypercube, there are exactly three processors whose shortest distance from the processor is two links. Derive an exact expression for the number of processors (in terms of p and l) whose shortest distance from any given processor in a p-processor hypercube is l.

3.10 Write pseudocode for procedures to perform one-to-all personalized communication, all-to-all personalized communication, and prefix sums on mesh and hypercube architectures with SF routing.

3.11 Give a hypercube algorithm to compute prefix sums of n numbers if p is the number of processors and n/p is an integer greater than 1. Assuming that it takes time t_{add} to add two numbers and time t_s to send a message of unit length between two directly-connected processors, give an exact expression for the total time taken by the algorithm.

3.12 Show that if the message startup time t_s is zero, then the expression $t_w mp(\sqrt{p} - 1)$ for the time taken by all-to-all personalized communication on a $\sqrt{p} \times \sqrt{p}$ mesh is optimal within a small (≤ 4) constant factor.
Hint: Use the result for mesh from Problem 3.2.

3.13 Prove that the hypercube algorithm for all-to-all personalized communication given in Section 3.5.1 is optimal for SF routing.

3.14 Modify the ring and the mesh algorithms in Sections 3.2–3.5 to work without the end-to-end wraparound connections. Compare the new communication times with those of the unmodified procedures. What is the maximum factor by which the time for any of the operations increases on either the ring or the mesh?

3.15 **(3-D mesh)** Give optimal (within a small constant) algorithms for one-to-all and all-to-all broadcasts and personalized communications on a $p^{1/3} \times p^{1/3} \times p^{1/3}$ three-dimensional mesh of p processors with store-and-forward routing. Derive expressions for the total communication times of these procedures.

3.16 **(Sparse 3-D mesh [ACC+90])** Consider the architecture shown in Figure 3.26. It is a regular three-dimensional mesh with no links in alternate rows in two of the three dimensions. What is the total number of links in a regular p-processor sparse 3-D mesh? You can assume that the number of processors in each dimension is even. Derive expressions for communication times of one-to-all (with source in a corner) and all-to-all broadcast and personalized communication on this architecture with store-and-forward routing.

3.17 Assume that the cost of building a parallel computer with p processors is proportional to the total number of communication links within it. Let the cost effectiveness of an architecture be inversely proportional to the product of the cost of a p-processor ensemble of this architecture and the communication time of a certain operation on it. Assuming SF routing and t_s to be zero, which architecture is more cost effective for each of the operations discussed in this chapter—a standard 3-D mesh or a sparse 3-D mesh?

3.18 Repeat Problem 3.17 when t_s is a nonzero constant but $t_w = 0$. Under this model of communication, the message transfer time between two directly-connected pro-

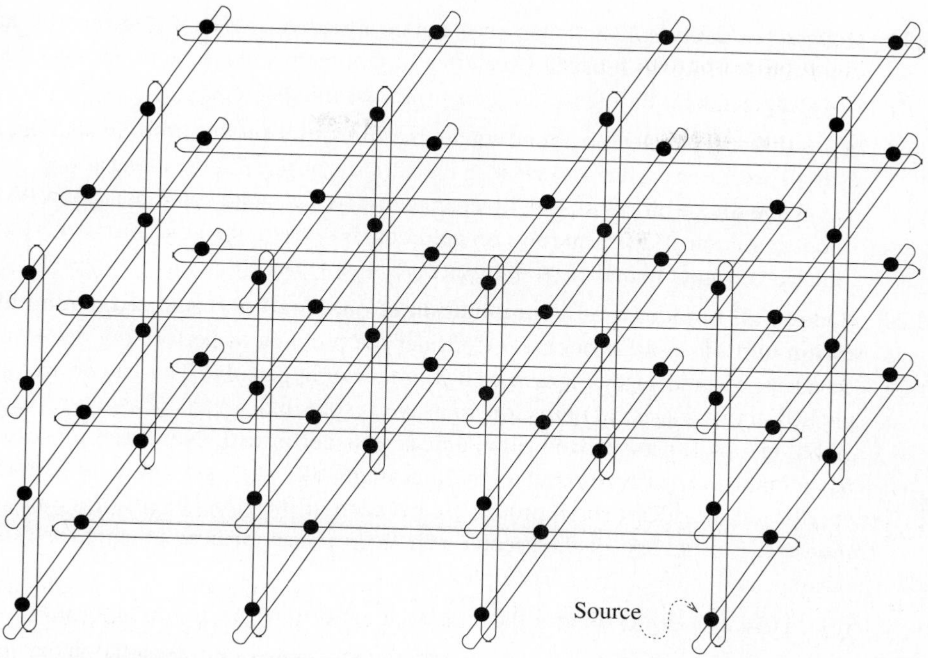

Figure 3.26 A sparse three-dimensional mesh of 64 processors [ACC$^+$90].

cessors is fixed, regardless of the size of the message. Also, if two packets are combined and transmitted as one message, the communication latency is still t_s.

3.19 Consider a parallel computer with p processors that can perform a global reduction in a constant time t_r. The semantics of the reduction operation are described in Example 3.7 and Section 3.7.3. How fast can a one-to-all broadcast be performed on this computer without using regular message passing? If $p = 256$, $t_s = 50$, $t_w = 1$, and $t_r = 10$, then for what message sizes would message passing be faster on a hypercube than when using the fast reduction operation for one-to-all broadcast?

3.20 Show that, with bidirectional communication links and CT routing, an all-to-all broadcast can be performed on a linear array in the same time as on a ring with SF routing. Ignore the term associated with t_h in the communication time for CT routing.

3.21 **(k-to-all broadcast)** Let k-to-all broadcast be an operation in which k processors simultaneously perform a one-to-all broadcast of m-word messages. Give an algorithm for this operation that has a total communication time of $t_s \log p + t_w m(k \log(p/k) + k - 1)$ on a p-processor hypercube. Assume that the m-word messages cannot be split, k is a power of 2, and $1 \leq k \leq p$.

3.22 If messages can be split and their parts can be routed independently, then derive an algorithm for k-to-all broadcast such that its communication time is less than that of the algorithm in Problem 3.21 for a p-processor hypercube.

3.23 Show that, on a 2-D wraparound square mesh of p processors with SF routing, a k-to-all broadcast can be performed in time $2(t_s + t_w m)(\sqrt{p} - 1)$ as long as $k \leq \sqrt{p}$ and all the source processors are in separate rows (or separate columns). Show that, if the restriction of different rows (or columns) is relaxed, then the communication time has an upper bound of $(t_s + t_w m)(2\sqrt{p} + k - 3)$.

3.24 **(One-to-all broadcast as a combination of one-to-all personalized communication and all-to-all broadcast)** Consider the problem of performing one-to-all broadcast of a message of size m on a p-processor hypercube. This can be accomplished in two stages: (1) First, the message is split into p parts of size m/p each and a one-to-all personalized communication is performed. Now each processor has a unique $(1/p)^{\text{th}}$ part of the initial message. (2) The next step is to perform an all-to-all broadcast so all processors get each of the p fragments of the initial message. At the end of the second step, each processor has the entire m-word message and the broadcast is complete.

(a) Derive an expression for the total communication time of this algorithm.

(b) Describe a similar two-stage algorithm for single-node accumulation that has the same communication time.

(c) Although this algorithm is faster than the one presented in Section 3.2 and has the same communication time as the one presented in Section 3.7.1, it has one drawback. Assuming that ease of programming is *not* a consideration, are there any reasons for which you would rather use the algorithm of Section 3.7.1 than this one?

3.25 Show that, if the $m \geq p$, then a single-node accumulation with a message size m can be performed on a p-processor hypercube spending $2(t_s \log p + t_w m)$ time in communication.

Hint: Express single-node accumulation as a combination of multinode accumulation and single-node gather.

3.26 **(k-to-all personalized communication)** In k-to-all personalized communication, k processors simultaneously perform a one-to-all personalized communication ($1 \leq k \leq p$) in a p-processor ensemble with individual packets of size m. Show that, if k is a power of 2, then this operation can be performed on a hypercube with SF routing in time $t_s \log p + t_w m(p - k + (p \log k)/2)$. Also show that, if CT routing is available, the same operation can be performed in time $t_s(\log(p/k) + k - 1) + t_w m(p - 1)$.

3.27 Assuming that it takes t_r time to perform a read and a write operation on a single word of data in a processor's local memory, show that all-to-all personalized communication on a p-processor mesh (Section 3.5.1) spends a total of $t_r mp$ time in internal data movement on the processors, where m is the size of an individual message.

Hint: The internal data movement is equivalent to transposing a $\sqrt{p} \times \sqrt{p}$ array of messages of size m.

3.28 Show that, if m is the size of an individual message and t_r is the time to perform a read and a write operation on a single word of data in a processor's local memory, then the all-to-all personalized communication algorithm for a hypercube with SF routing (Section 3.5.1) requires $t_r mp \log p$ time for internal data movement on the processors.

3.29 **(Circular shift on hypercube [Ozv87])** Show that any circular shift involving m-word messages can be performed in at most $(t_s + t_w m) \log p$ time on a p-processor hypercube with SF routing if both forward and backward shifts are performed.
Hint: Show that any even integer between 0 and p can be expressed as sums and differences of at most $\lfloor \log p/2 \rfloor$ distinct powers of two, and that any odd integer between 0 and p can be expressed as sums and differences of at most $\lceil \log p/2 \rceil$ distinct powers of two.

3.30 Show that in a p-processor hypercube with CT routing, all the p data paths in a circular q-shift are congestion-free if E-cube routing (Section 2.6) is used.
Hint: (1) If $q > p/2$, then a q-shift is isomorphic to a $(p - q)$-shift on a p-processor hypercube. (2) Prove by induction on hypercube dimension. If all paths are congestion-free for a q-shift $(1 \leq q < p)$ on a p-processor hypercube, then all these paths are congestion-free on a $2p$-processor hypercube also.

3.31 Show that the length of the longest path of any message in a circular q-shift on a p-processor hypercube with CT routing is $\log p - \gamma(q)$, where $\gamma(q)$ is the highest integer j such that q is divisible by 2^j.
Hint: (1) If $q = p/2$, then $\gamma(q) = \log p - 1$ on a p-processor hypercube. (2) Prove by induction on hypercube dimension. For a given q, $\gamma(q)$ increases by one each time the number of processors is doubled.

3.32 Derive expression for the parallel run time of the hypercube algorithms for one-to-all broadcast, all-to-all broadcast, one-to-all personalized communication, and all-to-all personalized communication adapted unaltered for a mesh with identical communication links (same channel width and channel rate). Compare the performance of these adaptations with the best mesh algorithms.

3.33 As discussed in Section 2.4.2, two common measures of the cost of a network are (1) the total number of wires in a parallel computer (which is a product of number of communication links and channel width); and (2) the bisection bandwidth. Consider a hypercube in which the channel width of each link is one, that is $t_w = 1$. The channel width of a mesh-connected computer with equal number of processors and identical cost is higher, and is determined by the cost metric used. Let s and s' represent the factors by which the channel width of the mesh is increased in accordance with the two cost metrics. Derive the values of s and s'. Using these, derive the communication time of the following operations on a mesh:

(1) One-to-all broadcast
(2) All-to-all broadcast
(3) One-to-all personalized communication
(4) All-to-all personalized communication

Compare these times with the time taken by the same operations on a hypercube with equal cost.

3.34 Consider a completely-connected network of p processors. For the four communication operations in Problem 3.33 derive an expression for the parallel run time of the hypercube algorithms on the completely-connected network. Comment on whether the added connectivity of the network yields improved performance for these operations.

References

[ACC+90] R. Alverson, D. Callahan, D. Cummings, B. Koblenz, A. Porterfield, and B. Smith. The Tera computer system. In *Proceedings of the 1990 International Conference on Supercomputing*, 1–6, 1990.

[Akl89] S. G. Akl. *The Design and Analysis of Parallel Algorithms*. Prentice-Hall, Englewood Cliffs, NJ, 1989.

[Ble90] G. E. Blelloch. *Vector Models for Data-Parallel Computing*. MIT Press, Cambridge, MA, 1990.

[BOS+91] D. P. Bertsekas, C. Ozveren, G. D. Stamoulis, P. Tseng, and J. N. Tsitsiklis. Optimal communication algorithms for hypercubes. *Journal of Parallel and Distributed Computing*, 11:263–275, 1991.

[BR90] R. Boppana and C. S. Raghavendra. On optimal and practical routing methods for a massive data movement operation on hypercubes. Technical report, University of Southern California, Los Angeles, CA, 1990.

[BT89] D. P. Bertsekas and J. N. Tsitsiklis. *Parallel and Distributed Computation: Numerical Methods*. Prentice-Hall, Englewood Cliffs, NJ, 1989.

[FF86] G. C. Fox and W. Furmanski. Optimal communication algorithms on hypercube. Technical Report CCCP-314, California Institute of Technology, Pasadena, CA, 1986.

[GGK+83] A. Gottlieb, R. Grishman, C. P. Kruskal, K. P. McAuliffe, L. Rudolph, and M. Snir. The NYU Ultracomputer–designing a MIMD, shared-memory parallel machine. *IEEE Transactions on Computers*, C–32(2):175–189, 1983.

[GK91] A. Gupta and V. Kumar. The scalability of matrix multiplication algorithms on parallel computers. Technical Report TR 91-54, Department of Computer Science, University of Minnesota, Minneapolis, MN, 1991. A short version appears in *Proceedings of 1993 International Conference on Parallel Processing*, pages III-115–III-119, 1993.

[HJ87] C.-T. Ho and S. L. Johnsson. Spanning balanced trees in Boolean cubes. Technical Report YALEU/DCS/RR-508, Department of Computer Science, Yale University, New Haven, CT, 1987.

[HS86] W. D. Hillis and G. L. Steele. Data parallel algorithms. *Communications of the ACM*, 29(12):1170–1183, 1986.

[Jaj92] J. Jaja. *An Introduction to Parallel Algorithms*. Addison-Wesley, Reading, MA, 1992.

[JH89] S. L. Johnsson and C.-T. Ho. Optimum broadcasting and personalized communication in hypercubes. *IEEE Transactions on Computers*, 38(9):1249–1268, September 1989.

[JH91] S. L. Johnsson and C.-T. Ho. Optimal all-to-all personalized communication with minimum span on Boolean cubes. In *The Sixth Distributed Memory Computing Conference Proceedings*, 299–304, 1991.

[Joh90] S. L. Johnsson. Communication in network architectures. In R. Suaya and G. Birtwistle, editors, *VLSI and Parallel Computation*, 223–389. Morgan Kaufmann, San Mateo, CA, 1990.

[L+92] C. E. Leiserson et al. The network architecture of the connection machine CM-5. In *Fourth Annual ACM Symposium on Parallel Algorithms and Architectures*, 272–285, 1992.

[Lev87] S. P. Levitan. Measuring communications structures in parallel architectures and algorithms. In L. H. Jamieson, D. B. Gannon, and R. J. Douglass, editors, *The Characteristics of Parallel Algorithms*. MIT Press, Cambridge, MA, 1987.

[LMR88] F. T. Leighton, B. Maggs, and S. K. Rao. Universal packet routing algorithms. In *29th Annual Symposium on Foundations of Computer Science*, 256–271, 1988.

[Loa92] C. V. Loan. *Computational Frameworks for the Fast Fourier Transform*. SIAM, Philadelphia, PA, 1992.

[MdV87] O. A. McBryan and E. F. V. de Velde. Hypercube algorithms and implementations. *SIAM Journal on Scientific and Statistical Computing*, 8(2):s227–s287, March 1987.

[Nug88] S. F. Nugent. The iPSC/2 direct-connect communications technology. In *Proceedings of the Third Conference on Hypercubes, Concurrent Computers, and Applications*, 51–60, 1988.

[Ozv87] C. Ozveren. Communication aspects of parallel processing. Technical Report LIDS-P-1721, Laboratory for Information and Decision Systems, MIT, 1987.

[Ran89] A. G. Ranade. *Fluent Parallel Computation*. Ph.D. thesis, Department of Computer Science, Yale University, New Haven, CT, 1989.

[RS90] S. Ranka and S. Sahni. *Hypercube Algorithms for Image Processing and Pattern Recognition*. Springer-Verlag, New York, NY, 1990.

[Sch80] J. T. Schwartz. Ultracomputers. *ACM Transactions on Programming Languages and Systems*, 2:484–521, October 1980.

[Sei89] S. R. Seidel. Circuit-switched vs. store-and-forward solutions to symmetric communication problems. In *Proceedings of the Fourth Conference on Hypercubes, Concurrent Computers, and Applications*, 253–255, 1989.

[SM86] S. J. Stolfo and D. P. Miranker. The DADO production system machine. *Journal of Parallel and Distributed Computing*, 3:269–296, June 1986.

[SS88] Y. Saad and M. H. Schultz. Topological properties of hypercubes. *IEEE Transactions on Computers*, 37:867–872, 1988.

[SS89a] Y. Saad and M. H. Schultz. Data communication in hypercubes. *Journal of Parallel and Distributed Computing*, 6:115–135, 1989. Also available as Technical Report YALEU/DCS/RR-428 from the Department of Computer Science, Yale University, New Haven, CT.

[SS89b] Y. Saad and M. H. Schultz. Data communication in parallel architectures. *Parallel Computing*, 11:131–150, 1989.

[SW87] Q. F. Stout and B. A. Wagar. Passing messages in link-bound hypercubes. In M. T. Heath, editor, *Hypercube Multiprocessors 1987*, 251–257. SIAM, Philadelphia, PA, 1987.

[Tak87] R. Take. An optimal routing method of all-to-all communication on hypercube networks. In *The 35th Information Processing Society of Japan*, 1987.

[Val82] L. G. Valiant. A scheme for fast parallel communication. *SIAM Journal on Computing*, 11:350–361, 1982.

[VB81] L. G. Valiant and G. J. Brebner. Universal schemes for parallel communication. In *Proceedings of the 13th ACM Symposium on Theory of Computation*, 263–277, 1981.

CHAPTER **4**

Performance and Scalability of Parallel Systems

A sequential algorithm is usually evaluated in terms of its execution time, expressed as a function of the size of its input. The execution time of a parallel algorithm depends not only on input size but also on the architecture of the parallel computer and the number of processors. Hence, a parallel algorithm cannot be evaluated in isolation from a parallel architecture. A ***parallel system*** is the combination of an algorithm and the parallel architecture on which it is implemented. In this chapter, we study various metrics for evaluating the performance of parallel systems. The scalability of a parallel algorithm on an architecture is a measure of its ability to achieve performance proportional to the number of processors. We address scalability in detail and describe a metric to analyze it.

4.1 Performance Metrics for Parallel Systems

In this section, we introduce some metrics that are commonly used to measure the performance of parallel systems.

4.1.1 Run Time

The serial run time of a program is the time elapsed between the beginning and the end of its execution on a sequential computer. The ***parallel run time*** is the time that elapses from the moment that a parallel computation starts to the moment that the last processor finishes execution. We denote the serial run time by T_S and the parallel run time by T_P.

4.1.2 Speedup

When evaluating a parallel system, we are often interested in knowing how much performance gain is achieved by parallelizing a given application over a sequential implementation. Speedup is a measure that captures the relative benefit of solving a problem in parallel. It is defined as the ratio of the time taken to solve a problem on a single processor to the time required to solve the same problem on a parallel computer with p identical processors. We denote speedup by the symbol S.

For a given problem, more than one sequential algorithm may be available, but all of these may not be equally suitable for parallelization. When a serial computer is used, it is natural to use the sequential algorithm that solves the problem in the least amount of time. Given a parallel algorithm, it is fair to judge its performance with respect to the fastest sequential algorithm for solving the same problem on a single processor. Sometimes, the fastest sequential algorithm to solve a problem is not known, or its run time has a large constant that makes it impractical to implement. In such cases, we will take the fastest known algorithm that would be a practical choice for a serial computer to be the best sequential algorithm. We compare the performance of a parallel algorithm to solve a problem with that of the best sequential algorithm to solve the same problem. We formally define the ***speedup*** S as the ratio of the serial run time of the best sequential algorithm for solving a problem to the time taken by the parallel algorithm to solve the same problem on p processors. The p processors used by the parallel algorithm are assumed to be identical to the one used by the sequential algorithm.

Example 4.1 Adding n Numbers on an n-Processor Hypercube

Consider the problem of adding n numbers by using n processors. Initially, each processor is assigned one of the numbers to be added and, at the end of the computation, one of the processors stores the sum of all the numbers. Assuming that n is a power of two, we can perform this on a hypercube or on a shared-memory multiprocessor in $\log n$ steps. Figure 4.1 illustrates the procedure for $n = 16$. The processors are labeled from 0 to 15. Similarly, the 16 numbers to be added are labeled from 0 to 15. The sum of the numbers with consecutive labels from i to j is denoted by Σ_i^j.

Each step shown in Figure 4.1 consists of one addition and the communication of a single word. The processors that communicate with each other are directly connected in a hypercube; that is, their labels differ in only one bit position. Both the addition and communication operations take a constant amount of time. Thus,

$$T_P = \Theta(\log n). \tag{4.1}$$

Since the problem can be solved in $\Theta(n)$ time on a single processor, its speedup is

$$S = \Theta\left(\frac{n}{\log n}\right). \tag{4.2}$$

■

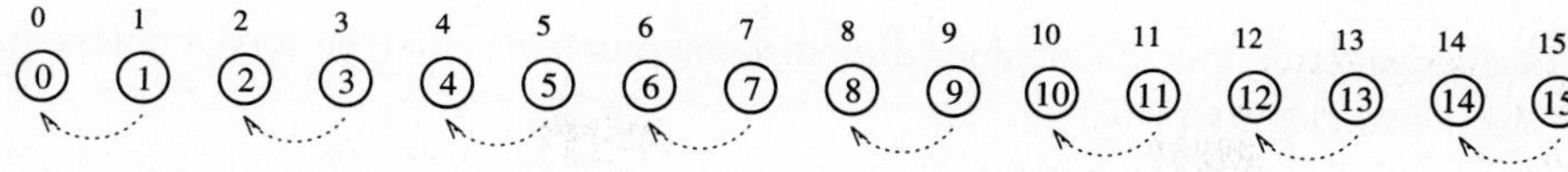

(a) Initial data distribution and the first communication step

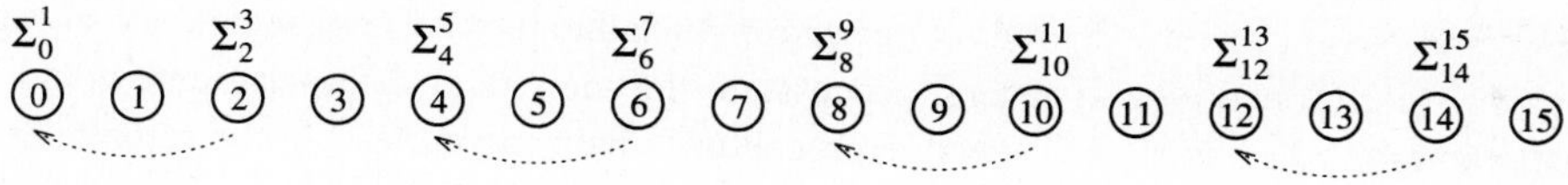

(b) Second communication step

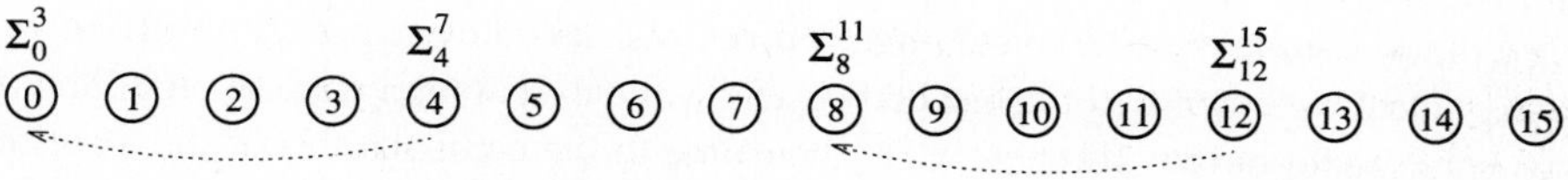

(c) Third communication step

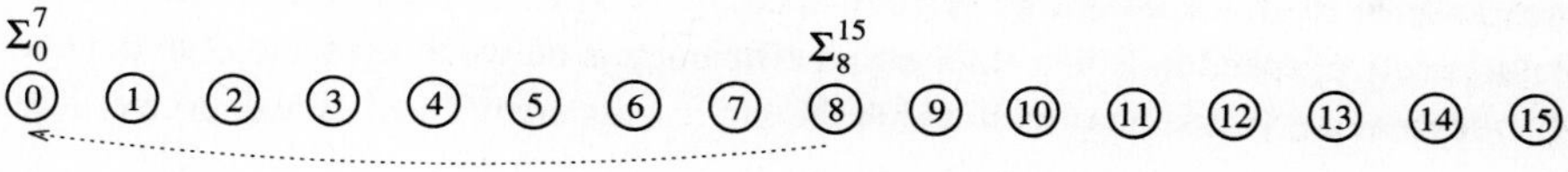

(d) Fourth communication step

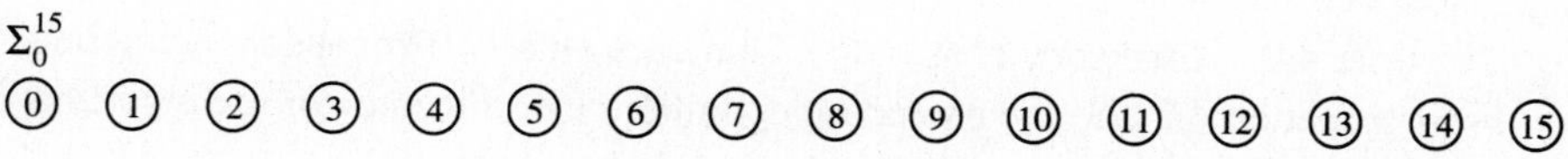

(e) Accumulation of the sum at processor 0 after the final communication

Figure 4.1 Computing the sum of 16 numbers on a 16-processor hypercube. Σ_i^j denotes the sum of numbers with consecutive labels from i to j.

Theoretically, speedup can never exceed the number of processors, p. If the best sequential algorithm takes T_S units of time to solve a given problem on a single processor, then a speedup of p can be obtained on p processors if none of the processors spends more than T_S/p time. A speedup greater than p is possible only if each processor spends less than T_S/p time solving the problem. In that case, a single processor could emulate the p processors and solve the problem in fewer than T_S units of time. This is a contradiction because speedup, by definition, is computed with respect to the best sequential algorithm.

If T_S is the serial run time of that algorithm, then the problem cannot be solved in less than time T_S on a single processor.

In practice, a speedup greater than p is sometimes observed (a phenomenon known as ***superlinear speedup***). This is usually due either to a nonoptimal sequential algorithm (Problem 4.2) or to hardware characteristics that put the sequential algorithm at a disadvantage. For example, the data for a problem might be too large to fit into the main memory of a single processor, thereby degrading its performance due to the use of secondary storage. But when partitioned among several processors, the individual data-partitions would be small enough to fit into their respective processors' main memories. In the remainder of this book, we disregard superlinear speedup due to hierarchical memory.

4.1.3 Efficiency

Only an ideal parallel system containing p processors can deliver a speedup equal to p. In practice, ideal behavior is not achieved because while executing a parallel algorithm, the processors cannot devote 100 percent of their time to the computations of the algorithm. As we saw in Example 4.1, part of the time required by the processors to compute the sum of n numbers is spent in communication. ***Efficiency*** is a measure of the fraction of time for which a processor is usefully employed; it is defined as the ratio of speedup to the number of processors. In an ideal parallel system, speedup is equal to p and efficiency is equal to one. In practice, speedup is less than p and efficiency is between zero and one, depending on the degree of effectiveness with which the processors are utilized. We denote efficiency by the symbol E. Mathematically, it is given by

$$E = \frac{S}{p}. \tag{4.3}$$

Example 4.2 Efficiency of Adding n Numbers on an n-Processor Hypercube

From Equation 4.2 and the preceding definition, the efficiency of the algorithm for adding n numbers on an n-processor hypercube is

$$E = \Theta\left(\frac{1}{\log n}\right). \tag{4.4}$$

■

4.1.4 Cost

We define the ***cost*** of solving a problem on a parallel system as the product of parallel run time and the number of processors used. Cost reflects the sum of the time that each processor spends solving the problem. Efficiency can also be expressed as the ratio of the execution time of the fastest known sequential algorithm for solving a problem to the cost of solving the same problem on p processors.

The cost of solving a problem on a single processor is the execution time of the fastest known sequential algorithm. A parallel system is said to be ***cost-optimal*** if the cost of solving a problem on a parallel computer is proportional to the execution time of the fastest-known sequential algorithm on a single processor. Since efficiency is the ratio of sequential cost to parallel cost, a cost-optimal parallel system has an efficiency of $\Theta(1)$.

Cost is sometimes referred to as ***work*** or ***processor-time product***, and a cost-optimal system is also known as a pT_P-optimal system.

Example 4.3 Cost of Adding n Numbers on an n-Processor Hypercube

The algorithm given in Example 4.1 for adding n numbers on an n-processor hypercube has a processor-time product of $\Theta(n \log n)$. Since the serial run time of this operation is $\Theta(n)$, the parallel system is not cost-optimal. Also, Example 4.2 shows that the efficiency of this parallel system is less than $\Theta(1)$, indicating that the parallel system is not cost-optimal. ■

4.2 The Effect of Granularity and Data Mapping on Performance

Examples 4.1–4.3 examined an algorithm that is not cost-optimal. The algorithm discussed in these examples uses as many processors as the number of inputs, which is excessive in terms of the number of processors. In practice, we assign larger pieces of input data to processors. This corresponds to increasing the granularity of computation on the processors. Using fewer than the maximum possible number of processors to execute a parallel algorithm is called ***scaling down*** a parallel system in terms of the number of processors. A naive way to scale down a parallel system is to design a parallel algorithm for one input element per processor, and then use fewer processors to simulate a large number of processors. If there are n inputs and only p processors ($p < n$), we can use the parallel algorithm designed for n processors by assuming n virtual processors and having each of the p physical processors simulate n/p virtual processors.

As the number of processors decreases by a factor of n/p, the computation at each processor increases by a factor of n/p because each processor now performs the work of n/p processors. If virtual processors are mapped appropriately onto physical processors, the overall communication time does not grow by more than a factor of n/p (Problem 4.5). The total parallel run time increases, at most, by a factor of n/p, and the processor-time product does not increase. Therefore, if a parallel system with n processors is cost-optimal, using p processors (where $p < n$) to simulate n processors preserves cost-optimality.

A drawback of this naive method of increasing computational granularity is that if a parallel system is not cost-optimal to begin with, it may still not be cost-optimal after the granularity of computation increases. This is illustrated by the following example for the problem of adding n numbers.

Example 4.4 Adding n Numbers on a p-Processor Hypercube

Consider the problem of adding n numbers on p processors such that $p < n$ and both n and p are powers of two. We use the same algorithm as in Example 4.1 and

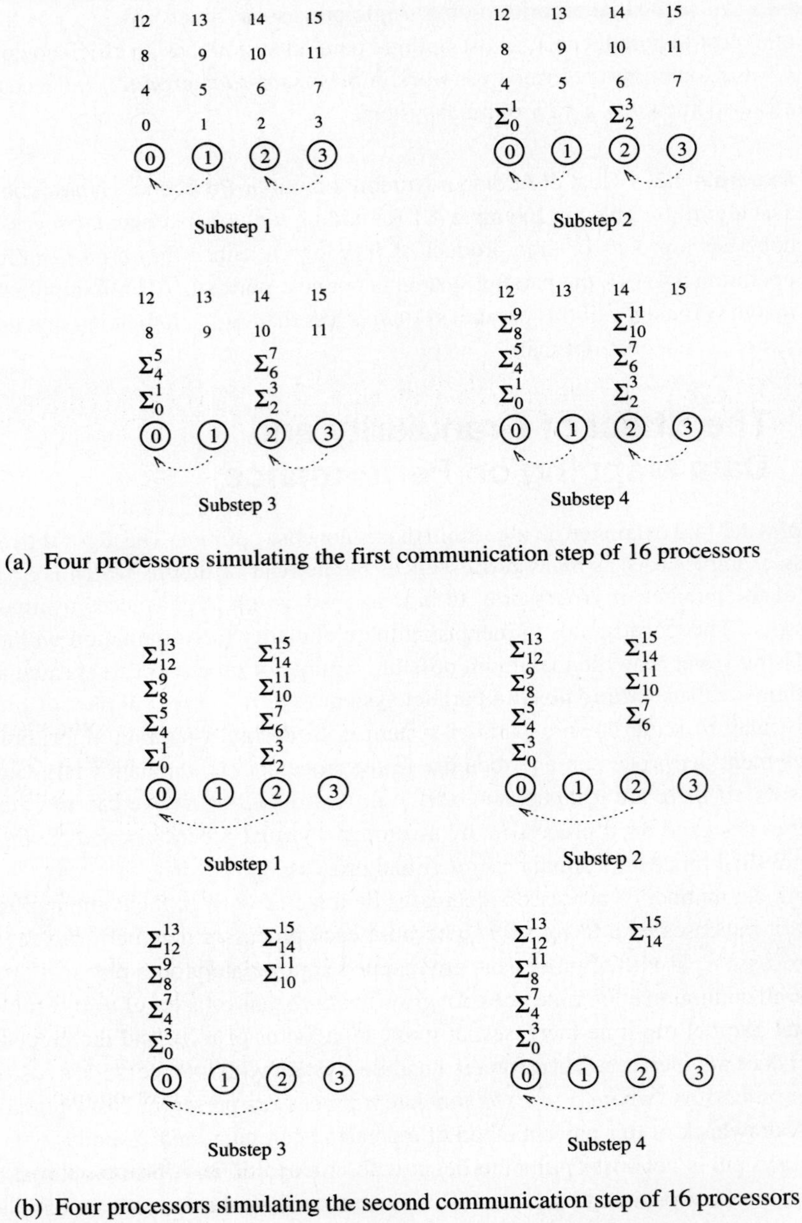

Figure 4.2 Four processors simulating 16 processors to compute the sum of 16 numbers (first two steps). Σ_i^j denotes the sum of numbers with consecutive labels from i to j.

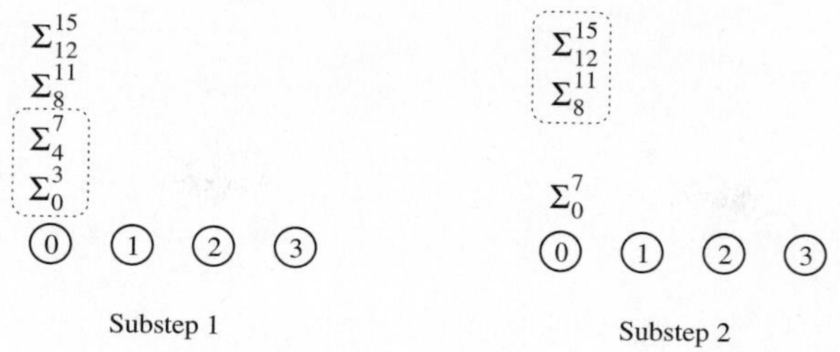

(c) Simulation of the third step in two substeps

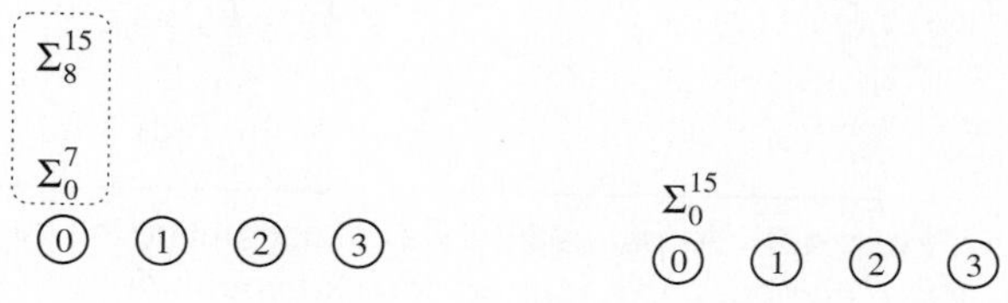

(d) Simulation of the fourth step (e) Final result

Figure 4.2 (cont.) Four processors simulating 16 processors to compute the sum of 16 numbers (last three steps).

simulate n processors on p processors. The steps leading to the solution are shown in Figure 4.2 for $n = 16$ and $p = 4$. Virtual processor i is simulated by the physical processor labeled i mod p; the numbers to be added are distributed similarly. The first $\log p$ of the $\log n$ steps of the original algorithm are simulated in $(n/p)\log p$ steps on p processors. In the remaining steps, no communication is required because the processors that communicate in the original algorithm are simulated by the same processor; hence, the remaining numbers are added locally. The algorithm takes $\Theta((n/p)\log p)$ time in the steps that require communication, after which a single processor is left with n/p numbers to add, taking $\Theta(n/p)$ time. Thus, the overall parallel execution time of this parallel system is $\Theta((n/p)\log p)$. Consequently, its cost is $\Theta(n \log p)$, which is asymptotically higher than the $\Theta(n)$ cost of adding n numbers sequentially. Therefore, the parallel system is not cost-optimal. ■

Example 4.1 showed that n numbers can be added on an n-processor hypercube in $\Theta(\log n)$ time. When using p processors to simulate n processors ($p < n$), the expected parallel run time is $\Theta((n/p)\log n)$ (Problem 4.3). However, in Example 4.4 this task was performed in $\Theta((n/p)\log p)$ time instead. The reason is that every communication step of the original algorithm does not have to be simulated; at times, communication takes place between virtual processors that are simulated by the same physical processor. For example, the simulation of the third and the fourth steps (Figures 4.2(c) and (d)) did not require any

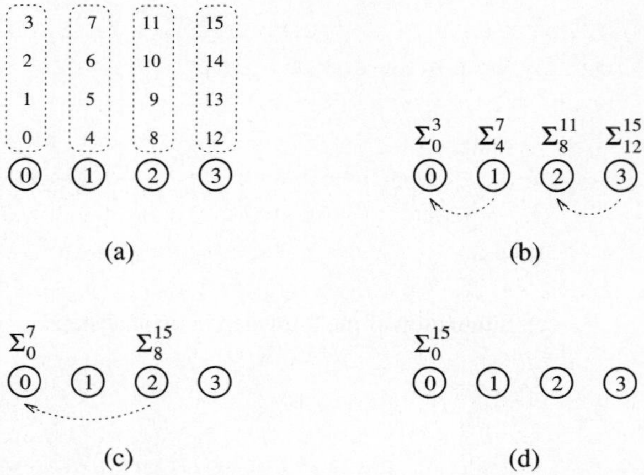

Figure 4.3 A cost-optimal way of computing the sum of 16 numbers on a four-processor hypercube.

communication. However, this reduction in communication was not enough to make the algorithm cost-optimal. Example 4.5 illustrates that the same problem (adding n numbers on a p-processor hypercube) can be performed cost-optimally with a smarter assignment of data to processors.

Example 4.5 Adding n Numbers Cost-Optimally on a Hypercube

An alternate method for adding n numbers by using p processors is illustrated in Figure 4.3 for $n = 16$ and $p = 4$. In the first step of this algorithm, each processor locally adds its n/p numbers in $\Theta(n/p)$ time. Now the problem is reduced to adding the p partial sums on p processors, which can be done in $\Theta(\log p)$ time by the method described in Example 4.1. The parallel run time of this algorithm is $\Theta(n/p + \log p)$ and its cost is $\Theta(n + p \log p)$. As long as $n = \Omega(p \log p)$, the cost is $\Theta(n)$, which is the same as the serial run time. Hence, this parallel system is cost-optimal. ■

These simple examples demonstrate that the manner in which the computation is mapped onto processors may determine whether a parallel system is cost-optimal. Note, however, that we cannot make all non-cost-optimal systems cost-optimal by scaling down the number of processors. An example of such a problem is matrix-vector multiplication involving a random sparse matrix. We discuss this example in detail in Section 11.1.3.

The Role of Mapping Computations onto Processors in Parallel Algorithm Design

Recall that, with proper data mapping, using fewer physical processors to simulate a large number of virtual processors maintains cost-optimality if the parallel system is cost-optimal to begin with. However, if the parallel system is not cost-optimal for a large number of processors, then a simulation does not necessarily result in a cost-optimal system (Example 4.4). Interestingly, even in the first case, despite preserving cost-optimality, the naive approach may result in an inferior parallel formulation in terms of parallel run time.

A naive simulation of many processors by fewer processors may not take into account the fact that there are multiple ways of assigning n virtual processors to p physical processors ($n > p$). The performance of the scaled-down algorithm may be different for different assignments of virtual processors to physical processors. In Example 4.1, the task of dividing n words among n processors was trivial since each processor was assigned only one input element. However, if the n inputs are to be mapped onto p processors, where $n > p$ (that is, n virtual processors are to be simulated by p physical processors), then there is more than one way to assign the inputs to the processors. As Examples 4.4 and 4.5 and Problems 4.4 and 4.3 show, the parallel run time of the same problem is a function of the mapping of virtual processors onto physical processors. This fact will be illustrated in subsequent chapters in which we consider parallel algorithms whose performance critically depends on the data-mapping onto a coarse-grain parallel computer. For example, in Section 5.3 we show that multiplying an $n \times n$ matrix by a vector on a p-processor hypercube is faster if the matrix is divided into p square blocks rather than p slices (or stripes) of n/p rows each. Similarly, in Chapter 10 we present different coarse-grain variations of parallel FFT on a hypercube with cut-through routing. The best choice depends on the relative values of hardware-related constants.

An algorithm requiring W basic computation steps can be mapped onto a maximum of W processors. With this mapping, each processor performs a single step of the sequential algorithm. However, if fewer processors are used, then each processor solves a bigger part of the entire problem. Different sequential algorithms may be available for solving a part of the problem locally at a processor. Sometimes, the choice of the method for performing the local computation affects the asymptotic parallel run time. In fact, the choice of the best algorithm to perform the local computations on each processor may depend on the number of processors. Examples of such parallel systems include some sorting algorithms discussed in Chapter 6, and a matrix multiplication algorithm discussed in Chapter 5. For this matrix multiplication algorithm, two distinct ways to scale down the number of processors yield different expressions for parallel execution time. Either method can be faster depending on the number of processors (Section 5.4.4 and Problem 5.13).

Thus, the optimal parallel algorithm for solving a problem on an arbitrary number of processors cannot be obtained trivially from the most fine-grain parallel algorithm. Moreover, an analysis of a parallel system based on the most fine-grain parallel formulation may obscure the effect of certain hardware features on the performance of the parallel system. For example, the transfer time of a message between two processors is the same with store-and-forward and cut-through routings (Section 2.7) if the message contains only one word. In contrast, cut-through routing often allows much faster transfer of large messages than store-and-forward routing. The performance of many parallel algorithms (Section 3.2.2) is almost identical on a hypercube and a mesh with cut-through routing;

however, their performance is much worse on a mesh with store-and-forward routing. An analysis of the most fine-grain parallel algorithm may not reveal these important facts.

The preceding discussion attempts to illustrate that designing an efficient parallel algorithm involves more than developing an algorithm for one input element or for one computation per processor. Conceiving the finest-grain algorithm is usually easy, and therefore, may serve as a logical first step toward devising a parallel algorithm for a problem. However, the complete design of a parallel algorithm should take into account the mapping of data onto processors and must include a description of its implementation on an arbitrary number of processors. That is why in this book, we keep the input size and the number of processors as two separate variables while designing and analyzing parallel algorithms.

4.3 The Scalability of Parallel Systems

Recall from Section 4.1.2 that the number of processors is an upper bound on the speedup that can be achieved by a parallel system. Speedup is one for a single processor, but if more processors are used, speedup is usually less than the number of processors. The following example illustrates how speedup usually varies with the number of processors.

Example 4.6 Speedup and Efficiency as Functions of the Number of Processors
Consider the problem of adding n numbers on a p-processor hypercube (Example 4.5). Assume that it takes one unit of time both to add two numbers and to communicate a number between two directly-connected processors. Then adding the n/p numbers local to each processor takes $n/p - 1$ time. After the local addition, the p partial sums are added in $\log p$ steps, each consisting of one addition and one communication. Thus, the total parallel run time T_P is $n/p - 1 + 2\log p$. For large values of n and p, this can be approximated by

$$T_P = \frac{n}{p} + 2\log p. \tag{4.5}$$

Since the serial run time is $n - 1$, which can be approximated by n, the expressions for speedup and efficiency are as follows:

$$\begin{aligned} S &= \frac{n}{n/p + 2\log p} \\ &= \frac{np}{n + 2p\log p} \end{aligned} \tag{4.6}$$

$$\begin{aligned} E &= \frac{S}{p} \\ &= \frac{n}{n + 2p\log p} \end{aligned} \tag{4.7}$$

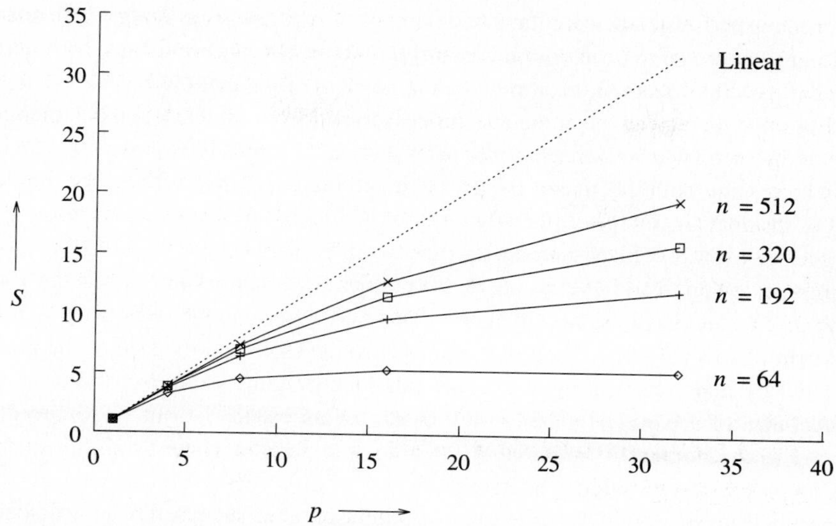

Figure 4.4 Speedup versus the number of processors for adding a list of numbers on a hypercube.

These expressions can be used to calculate the speedup and efficiency for any pair of n and p. Figure 4.4 shows the S versus p curves for a few different values of n and p. Table 4.1 shows the corresponding efficiencies. ■

Figure 4.4 and Table 4.1 illustrate two important facts. First, for a given problem instance, the speedup does not increase linearly as the number of processors increases. The speedup tends to become saturated and the speedup curve flattens. This is a consequence of ***Amdahl's law*** (Problem 4.1). As a consequence of Amdahl's law, the efficiency drops with an increasing number of processors. Second, a larger instance of the same problem yields

Table 4.1 Efficiency as a function of n and p for adding n numbers on p-processor hypercube.

n	$p = 1$	$p = 4$	$p = 8$	$p = 16$	$p = 32$
64	1.0	*.80*	.57	.33	.17
192	1.0	.92	*.80*	.60	.38
320	1.0	.95	.87	.71	.50
512	1.0	.97	.91	*.80*	.62

higher speedup and efficiency for the same number of processors, although both speedup and efficiency continue to drop with increasing p. These two phenomena, shown here for a particular parallel system, are common to a large class of parallel systems.

Given that increasing the number of processors reduces efficiency and that increasing the size of the computation increases efficiency, it should be possible to keep the efficiency fixed by increasing both the size of the problem and the number of processors simultaneously. For instance, in Table 4.1, the efficiency of adding 64 numbers on a hypercube with four processors is 0.80. If the number of processors is increased to 8 and the size of the problem is scaled up to add 192 numbers, the efficiency remains 0.80. Increasing p to 16 and n to 512 results in the same efficiency. This ability to maintain efficiency at a fixed value by simultaneously increasing the number of processors and the size of the problem is exhibited by many parallel systems. We call such systems ***scalable*** parallel systems. The ***scalability*** of a parallel system is a measure of its capacity to increase speedup in proportion to the number of processors. It reflects a parallel system's ability to utilize increasing processing resources effectively.

Recall from Section 4.1.4 that a cost-optimal parallel system has an efficiency of $\Theta(1)$. The scalability and cost-optimality of parallel systems are related. A scalable parallel system can always be made cost-optimal if the number of processors and the size of the computation are chosen appropriately. For instance, Example 4.5 shows that the parallel system for adding n numbers on a p-processor hypercube is cost-optimal when $n = \Omega(p \log p)$. Example 4.7 below shows that the same parallel system is scalable if n is increased in proportion to $\Theta(p \log p)$ as p is increased.

Example 4.7 Scalability of Adding n Numbers on a Hypercube

For the cost-optimal addition of n numbers on a p-processor hypercube, $n = \Omega(p \log p)$. As shown in Table 4.1, the efficiency is 0.80 for $n = 64$ and $p = 4$. At this point, the relation between n and p is $n = 8p \log p$. If the number of processors is increased to eight, then $8p \log p = 192$. Table 4.1 shows that the efficiency is indeed 0.80 with $n = 192$ for eight processors. Similarly, for $p = 16$, the efficiency is 0.80 for $n = 8p \log p = 512$. Thus, this parallel system remains cost-optimal at an efficiency of 0.80 if n is increased as $8p \log p$. ■

4.4 The Isoefficiency Metric of Scalability

A scalable parallel system is one in which the efficiency can be kept fixed as the number of processors is increased, provided that the problem size is also increased. It is useful to determine the rate at which the problem size must increase with respect to the number of processors to keep the efficiency fixed. For different parallel systems, the problem size must increase at different rates in order to maintain a fixed efficiency as the number of processors is increased. This rate determines the degree of scalability of the parallel system. In this section, we formalize the notion of scalability and introduce a metric for quantitatively determining the degree of scalability of a parallel system. However, before we do that, we introduce two important terms: *problem size* and the *overhead function*.

4.4.1 Problem Size

When analyzing parallel systems, we frequently encounter the notion of the size of the problem being solved. So far, we have used the term *problem size* informally, without giving a precise definition. A naive way to express problem size is as a parameter of the input size; for instance, n in case of a matrix operation involving $n \times n$ matrices. A drawback of this definition is that the interpretation of problem size changes from one problem to another. For example, doubling the input size results in an eight-fold increase in the execution time for matrix multiplication and a four-fold increase for matrix addition (assuming that the conventional $\Theta(n^3)$ algorithm is the best matrix multiplication algorithm, and disregarding more complicated algorithms with better asymptotic complexities).

A consistent definition of the size or the magnitude of the problem should be such that, regardless of the problem, doubling the problem size always means performing twice the amount of computation. Therefore, we choose to express problem size in terms of the total number of basic operations required to solve the problem. By this definition, the problem size is $\Theta(n^3)$ for $n \times n$ matrix multiplication (assuming the conventional algorithm) and $\Theta(n^2)$ for $n \times n$ matrix addition. In order to keep it unique for a given problem, we define ***problem size*** as the number of basic computation steps in the best sequential algorithm to solve the problem on a single processor, where the best sequential algorithm is defined as in Section 4.1.2. Because it is defined in terms of sequential time complexity, the problem size is a function of the size of the input. The symbol we use to denote problem size is W.

In the remainder of this chapter, we assume that it takes unit time to perform one basic computation step of an algorithm. This assumption does not affect the analysis of any parallel system because the other hardware-related constants, such as message startup time, per-word transfer time, and per-hop time, can be normalized with respect to the time taken by a basic computation step. With this assumption, the problem size W is equal to the serial run time T_S of the fastest known algorithm to solve the problem on a sequential computer.

4.4.2 The Overhead Function

Real parallel systems do not achieve an efficiency of one or a speedup of p on as many processors. In Examples 4.1 and 4.2, the reason for this was that some of the time was spent on interprocessor communication. In general, besides interprocessor communication, there can be other causes for efficiency loss in parallel systems. All causes of nonoptimal efficiency of a parallel system are collectively referred to as the ***overhead*** due to parallel processing.

We define ***total overhead*** or the ***overhead function*** of a parallel system as the part of its cost (processor-time product) that is not incurred by the fastest known serial algorithm on a sequential computer. It is the total time collectively spent by all the processors in addition to that required by the fastest known sequential algorithm for solving the same problem on a single processor. We denote the overhead function of a parallel system by the symbol T_o. T_o is a function of W and p, and we often write it as $T_o(W, p)$.

The cost of solving a problem of size W on p processors, or the total time spent in solving a problem summed over all processors, is pT_P. W units of this time are spent performing useful work, and the remainder is overhead. Therefore, the relation between cost (pT_P), problem size (W), and the overhead function (T_o) is given by

$$T_o = pT_P - W. \tag{4.8}$$

Example 4.8 Overhead Function for Adding n Numbers on a Hypercube

Consider the problem of adding n numbers on a p-processor hypercube. Under the assumptions of Example 4.6, the parallel execution time is approximately $n/p+2\log p$ (Equation 4.5). The same task can be accomplished sequentially in approximately n time. Thus, out of the $n/p + 2\log p$ time that each processor spends in the parallel execution, approximately n/p is spent performing useful work. The remaining $2\log p$ time per processor leads to a total overhead of

$$\begin{aligned} T_o &\approx p\left(\frac{n}{p} + 2\log p\right) - n \\ &= 2p\log p. \end{aligned} \tag{4.9}$$

■

4.4.3 The Isoefficiency Function

Parallel execution time can be expressed as a function of problem size, overhead function, and the number of processors. Rewriting Equation 4.8, we get the following expressions for parallel run time:

$$T_P = \frac{W + T_o(W, p)}{p} \tag{4.10}$$

The resulting expression for speedup is

$$\begin{aligned} S &= \frac{W}{T_P} \\ &= \frac{Wp}{W + T_o(W, p)}. \end{aligned} \tag{4.11}$$

Finally, we write the expression for efficiency as

$$\begin{aligned} E &= \frac{S}{p} \\ &= \frac{W}{W + T_o(W, p)} \\ &= \frac{1}{1 + T_o(W, p)/W}. \end{aligned} \tag{4.12}$$

In Equation 4.12, if the problem size is kept constant and p is increased, the efficiency decreases because the total overhead T_o increases with p. If W is increased keeping the number of processors fixed, then for scalable parallel systems, the efficiency increases. This is because T_o grows slower than $\Theta(W)$ for a fixed p. For these parallel systems, efficiency can be maintained at a desired value (between 0 and 1) for increasing p, provided W is also increased.

For different parallel systems, W must be increased at different rates with respect to p in order to maintain a fixed efficiency. For instance, in some cases, W might need to grow as an exponential function of p to keep the efficiency from dropping as p increases. Such parallel systems are poorly scalable. The reason is that on these parallel systems it is difficult to obtain good speedups for a large number of processors unless the problem size is enormous. On the other hand, if W needs to grow only linearly with respect to p, then the parallel system is highly scalable. That is because it can easily deliver speedups proportional to the number of processors for reasonable problem sizes.

For scalable parallel systems, efficiency can be maintained at a fixed value (between 0 and 1) if the ratio T_o/W in Equation 4.12 is maintained at a constant value. For a desired value E of efficiency,

$$\begin{aligned} E &= \frac{1}{1 + T_o(W, p)/W}, \\ \frac{T_o(W, p)}{W} &= \frac{1 - E}{E}, \\ W &= \frac{E}{1 - E} T_o(W, p). \end{aligned} \tag{4.13}$$

Let $K = E/(1 - E)$ be a constant depending on the efficiency to be maintained. Since T_o is a function of W and p, Equation 4.13 can be rewritten as

$$W = K T_o(W, p). \tag{4.14}$$

From Equation 4.14, the problem size W can usually be obtained as a function of p by algebraic manipulations. This function dictates the growth rate of W required to keep the efficiency fixed as p increases. We call this function the ***isoefficiency function*** of the parallel system. The isoefficiency function determines the ease with which a parallel system can maintain a constant efficiency and hence achieve speedups increasing in proportion to the number of processors. A small isoefficiency function means that small increments in the problem size are sufficient for the efficient utilization of an increasing number of processors, indicating that the parallel system is highly scalable. However, a large isoefficiency function indicates a poorly scalable parallel system. The isoefficiency function does not exist for unscalable parallel systems, because in such systems the efficiency cannot be kept at any constant value as p increases, no matter how fast the problem size is increased.

Example 4.9 Isoefficiency Function of Adding Numbers on a Hypercube

The overhead function for the problem of adding n numbers on a p-processor hypercube is $2p \log p$, as given by Equation 4.9. Substituting T_o by $2p \log p$ in Equation 4.14, we get

$$W = 2Kp \log p. \tag{4.15}$$

Thus, the asymptotic isoefficiency function for this parallel system is $\Theta(p \log p)$. This means that, if the number of processors is increased from p to p', the problem size (in this case, n) must be increased by a factor of $(p' \log p')/(p \log p)$ to get the same efficiency as on p processors. In other words, increasing the number of processors by a factor of p'/p requires that n be increased by a factor of $(p' \log p')/(p \log p)$ to increase the speedup by a factor of p'/p. ■

In the simple example of adding n numbers, the overhead due to communication (hereafter referred to as the ***communication overhead***) is a function of p only. In general, communication overhead can depend on both the problem size and the number of processors. A typical overhead function can have several distinct terms of different orders of magnitude with respect to p and W. In such a case, it can be cumbersome (or even impossible) to obtain the isoefficiency function as a closed function of p. For example, consider a hypothetical parallel system for which $T_o = p^{3/2} + p^{3/4}W^{3/4}$. For this overhead function, Equation 4.14 can be rewritten as $W = Kp^{3/2} + Kp^{3/4}W^{3/4}$. It is hard to solve this equation for W in terms of p.

Recall that the condition for constant efficiency is that the ratio T_o/W remains fixed. As p and W increase, the efficiency is nondecreasing as long as none of the terms of T_o grows faster than W. If T_o has multiple terms, we balance W against each term of T_o and compute the respective isoefficiency functions for individual terms. The component of T_o that requires the problem size to grow at the highest rate with respect to p determines the overall asymptotic isoefficiency function of the parallel system. Example 4.10 and Section 5.3 further illustrate the technique of isoefficiency analysis in detail.

Example 4.10 Isoefficiency Function of a Parallel System with a Complex Overhead Function

Consider a parallel system for which $T_o = p^{3/2} + p^{3/4}W^{3/4}$. Using only the first term of T_o in Equation 4.14, we get

$$W = Kp^{3/2}. \tag{4.16}$$

Using only the second term, Equation 4.14 yields the following relation between W and p:

$$\begin{aligned} W &= Kp^{3/4}W^{3/4} \\ W^{1/4} &= Kp^{3/4} \\ W &= K^4p^3 \end{aligned} \tag{4.17}$$

To ensure that the efficiency does not decrease as the number of processors increases, the first and second terms of the overhead function require the problem size to grow as $\Theta(p^{3/2})$ and $\Theta(p^3)$, respectively. The asymptotically higher of the two rates, $\Theta(p^3)$, gives the overall asymptotic isoefficiency function of this parallel system, since it subsumes the rate dictated by the other term. ■

In a single expression, the isoefficiency function captures the characteristics of a parallel algorithm as well as the parallel architecture on which it is implemented. After performing the isoefficiency analysis, we can test the performance of a parallel program on a few processors and then predict its performance on a larger number of processors. However, the utility of isoefficiency analysis is not limited to predicting the impact on performance of an increasing number of processors. Section 4.4.6 shows how the isoefficiency function characterizes the amount of parallelism inherent in a parallel algorithm. We will see in later chapters (Chapter 10, for example) that isoefficiency analysis can be used also to study the behavior of a parallel system with respect to changes in hardware parameters such as the speed of processors and communication channels.

4.4.4 Cost-Optimality and the Isoefficiency Function

In Section 4.1.4, we stated that a parallel system is cost-optimal if the product of the number of processors and the parallel execution time is proportional to the execution time of the fastest known sequential algorithm on a single processor. In other words, a parallel system is cost-optimal if and only if

$$pT_P = \Theta(W). \tag{4.18}$$

Substituting the expression for T_P from the right-hand side of Equation 4.10, we get the following:

$$\begin{aligned} W + T_o(W, p) &= \Theta(W) \\ T_o(W, p) &= O(W) && (4.19) \\ W &= \Omega(T_o(W, p)) && (4.20) \end{aligned}$$

Equations 4.19 and 4.20 suggest that a parallel system is cost-optimal if and only if its overhead function does not asymptotically exceed the problem size. This is very similar to the condition given by Equation 4.14 for maintaining a fixed efficiency while increasing the number of processors in a parallel system. If Equation 4.14 yields an isoefficiency function $f(p)$, then it follows from Equation 4.20 that the relation $W = \Omega(f(p))$ must be satisfied to ensure the cost-optimality of a parallel system as it is scaled up. The following example further illustrates the relationship between cost-optimality and the isoefficiency function.

Example 4.11 Relationship Between Cost-Optimality and Isoefficiency Function
Consider the non-cost-optimal parallel system described in Example 4.4. Since the algorithm spends $\Theta((n/p)\log p)$ time in communication, its overhead function is

$\Theta(n \log p)$. The problem size W for adding n numbers is $\Theta(n)$. The isoefficiency function for this parallel system does not exist, because Equation 4.14 cannot be satisfied for any K (hence, any E); T_o is always greater than W. Thus, this parallel system is unscalable.

Now consider the cost-optimal solution to the problem of adding n numbers on a hypercube presented in Example 4.5. For this parallel system, $W \approx n$, and $T_o = \Theta(p \log p)$. From Equation 4.14, its isoefficiency function is $\Theta(p \log p)$; that is, the problem size must increase as $\Theta(p \log p)$ to maintain a constant efficiency. In Example 4.5 we derived the condition for cost-optimality as $W = \Omega(p \log p)$. ■

4.4.5 A Lower Bound on the Isoefficiency Function

We discussed earlier that a smaller isoefficiency function indicates higher scalability. Accordingly, an ideally-scalable parallel system must have the lowest possible isoefficiency function. For a problem consisting of W units of work, no more than W processors can be used cost-optimally; additional processors will be idle. If the problem size grows at a rate slower than $\Theta(p)$ as the number of processors increases, then the number of processors will eventually exceed W. Even for an ideal parallel system with no communication or other overhead, the efficiency will drop because processors added beyond $p = W$ will be idle. Thus, asymptotically, the problem size must increase at least as fast as $\Theta(p)$ to maintain fixed efficiency; hence, $\Omega(p)$ is the asymptotic lower bound on the isoefficiency function. It follows that the isoefficiency function of an ideally scalable parallel system is $\Theta(p)$.

4.4.6 The Degree of Concurrency and the Isoefficiency Function

A lower bound of $\Omega(p)$ is imposed on the isoefficiency function of a parallel system by the number of operations that can be performed concurrently. The maximum number of tasks that can be executed simultaneously at any time in a parallel algorithm is called its ***degree of concurrency***. The degree of concurrency is a measure of the number of operations that an algorithm can perform in parallel for a problem of size W; it is independent of the parallel architecture. If $C(W)$ is the degree of concurrency of a parallel algorithm, then for a problem of size W, no more than $C(W)$ processors can be employed effectively.

Example 4.12 Effect of Concurrency on Isoefficiency Function

Consider solving a system of n equations in n variables by using Gaussian elimination (Section 5.5.1). The total amount of computation is $\Theta(n^3)$. But the n variables must be eliminated one after the other, and eliminating each variable requires $\Theta(n^2)$ computations. Thus, at most $\Theta(n^2)$ processors can be kept busy at any time. Since $W = \Theta(n^3)$ for this problem, the degree of concurrency $C(W)$ is $\Theta(W^{2/3})$ and at most $\Theta(W^{2/3})$ processors can be used efficiently. On the other hand, given p processors, the problem size should be at least $\Omega(p^{3/2})$ to use them all. Thus, the isoefficiency function of this computation due to concurrency is $\Theta(p^{3/2})$. ■

The isoefficiency function due to concurrency is optimal (that is, $\Theta(p)$) only if the degree of concurrency of the parallel algorithm is $\Theta(W)$. If the degree of concurrency of an algorithm is less than $\Theta(W)$, then the isoefficiency function due to concurrency is worse (that is, greater) than $\Theta(p)$. In such cases, the overall isoefficiency function of a parallel system is given by the maximum of the isoefficiency functions due to concurrency, communication, and other overhead.

4.5 Sources of Parallel Overhead

The examples and discussion in this chapter show that the overhead function characterizes a parallel system. Given the overhead function, we can express the parallel run time, speedup, efficiency, and cost of a parallel system in terms of two basic parameters: the problem size W and the number of processors p. This section details the factors that can contribute to the total overhead of a parallel system.

In Section 4.4 we defined the overhead function of a parallel system as the difference between its cost and the serial run time of the fastest known algorithm for solving the same problem. An advantage of defining the overhead function this way is that all the sources of performance degradation in a parallel system are combined in a single expression so that their cumulative effect can be studied. The overhead function encapsulates all the causes of the inefficiencies of a parallel system, whether due to the algorithm, the architecture, or the algorithm-architecture interaction. The major sources of overhead in a parallel system are interprocessor communication, load imbalance, and extra computation.

4.5.1 Interprocessor Communication

Any nontrivial parallel system requires communication among processors. The time to transfer data between processors is usually the most significant source of parallel processing overhead. If each of the p processors spends t_{comm} time performing communication, then interprocessor communication contributes $t_{comm} \times p$ to the overhead function.

4.5.2 Load Imbalance

In many parallel applications (for example, search and optimization), it is impossible (or at least difficult) to predict the size of the subtasks assigned to various processors. Hence, the problem cannot be subdivided statically among the processors while maintaining uniform work load. If different processors have different work loads, some processors may be idle during part of the time that others are working on the problem.

Often some or all processors must synchronize at certain points during the parallel program execution. If all processors are not ready for synchronization at the same time, then the ones that are ready sooner will be idle until all the rest are ready. Whatever the cause of idling, the total idle time of all the processors contributes to the overhead function.

A special case of overhead due to processor idling is the presence of a sequential component in the parallel algorithm. Part of an algorithm may be unparallelizable, allowing only a single processor to work on it. We express the problem size for such an algorithm as the sum of two components: W_S, the work due to the sequential component, and W_P, the work due to the parallelizable component. While one processor is working on W_S, the remaining $p - 1$ are idle. As a result, a serial component of W_S contributes $(p - 1)W_S$ to the overhead function of a p-processor parallel system.

4.5.3 Extra Computation

The fastest known sequential algorithm for a problem may be difficult or impossible to parallelize, forcing us to use a parallel algorithm based on a poorer but easily parallelizable (that is, one with a higher degree of concurrency) sequential algorithm. Let W be the execution time of the fastest known sequential algorithm for a problem and W' be the execution time of a poorer (but more parallelizable) algorithm for the same problem. Then the difference $W' - W$ should be regarded as part of the overhead function because it expresses the amount of extra work performed to solve the problem in parallel. We discuss a few such algorithms in Chapter 6.

A parallel algorithm based on the best serial algorithm may still perform more aggregate computation than the serial algorithm. An example of such an algorithm is fast Fourier transform algorithm discussed in Chapter 10. In its serial version, the results of certain computations can be reused. However, in the parallel version, these results cannot be reused because they are generated by different processors. Therefore, some computations are performed multiple times on different processors. Such extra computations contribute to the overhead function.

4.6 Minimum Execution Time and Minimum Cost-Optimal Execution Time

We are often interested in knowing how fast a problem can be solved, or what the minimum possible execution time of a parallel algorithm is, provided that the number of processors is not a constraint. As we increase the number of processors for a given problem size, either the parallel run time continues to decrease and asymptotically approaches a minimum value, or it starts rising after attaining a minimum value (Problem 4.18). We can determine the minimum parallel run time T_P^{min} for a given W by differentiating the expression for T_P with respect to p and equating the derivative to zero (assuming that the function $T_P(W, p)$ is differentiable with respect to p). The number of processors for which T_P is minimum is determined by the following equation:

$$\frac{\mathrm{d}}{\mathrm{d}p} T_P = 0 \qquad (4.21)$$

Let p_0 be the value of the number of processors that satisfies Equation 4.21. The value of T_P^{min} can be determined by substituting p_0 for p in the expression for T_P. In the following example, we derive the expression for T_P^{min} for the problem of adding n numbers on a hypercube.

Example 4.13 Minimum Execution Time for Adding n Numbers on a Hypercube
Under the assumptions of Example 4.6, the parallel run time for the problem of adding n numbers on a p-processor hypercube can be approximated by

$$T_P = \frac{n}{p} + 2\log p. \tag{4.22}$$

Equating the derivative with respect to p of the right-hand side of the Equation 4.13 to zero we get the solutions for p as follows:

$$\begin{aligned} -\frac{n}{p^2} + \frac{2}{p} &= 0 \\ -n + 2p &= 0 \\ p &= \frac{n}{2} \end{aligned} \tag{4.23}$$

Substituting $p = n/2$ in Equation 4.22, we get

$$T_P^{min} = 2\log n. \tag{4.24}$$

■

In Example 4.13, the processor-time product for $p = p_0$ is $\Theta(n \log n)$, which is higher than the $\Theta(n)$ serial complexity of the problem. Hence, the parallel system is not cost-optimal for the value of p that yields minimum parallel run time. We now derive an important result that gives a lower bound on parallel run time if the problem is solved cost-optimally.

Let $T_P^{cost\_opt}$ be the minimum time in which a problem can be solved by a cost-optimal parallel system. From the discussion regarding the equivalence of cost-optimality and the isoefficiency function in Section 4.4.4, we conclude that if the isoefficiency function of a parallel system is $\Theta(f(p))$, then a problem of size W can be solved cost-optimally if and only if $W = \Omega(f(p))$. In other words, given a problem of size W, a cost-optimal solution requires that $p = O(f^{-1}(W))$. Since the parallel run time is $\Theta(W/p)$ for a cost-optimal parallel system (Equation 4.18), the lower bound on the parallel run time for solving a problem of size W cost-optimally is

$$T_P^{cost\_opt} = \Omega\left(\frac{W}{f^{-1}(W)}\right). \tag{4.25}$$

Example 4.14 Minimum Cost-Optimal Execution Time for Adding n Numbers on a Hypercube
As derived in Example 4.9, the isoefficiency function $f(p)$ of this parallel system is $\Theta(p \log p)$. If $W = n = f(p) = p \log p$, then $\log n = \log p - \log\log p$.

Ignoring the double logarithmic term, $\log n \approx \log p$. If $n = f(p) = p \log p$, then $p = f^{-1}(n) = n/logp \approx n/\log n$. Hence, $f^{-1}(W) = \Theta(n/\log n)$. As a consequence of the relation between cost-optimality and the isoefficiency function, the maximum number of processors that can be used to solve this problem cost-optimally is $\Theta(n/\log n)$. Using $p = n/\log n$ in Equation 4.5, we get

$$\begin{aligned} T_P^{cost\_opt} &= \log n + 2\log\left(\frac{n}{\log n}\right) \\ &= 3\log n - 2\log\log n. \end{aligned} \tag{4.26}$$

■

It is interesting to observe that both T_P^{min} and $T_P^{cost\_opt}$ for adding n numbers on a hypercube are $\Theta(\log n)$ (Equations 4.24 and 4.26). Thus, for this problem, a cost-optimal solution is also the asymptotically fastest solution. The parallel execution time cannot be reduced asymptotically by using a value of p greater than that suggested by the isoefficiency function for a given problem size (due to the equivalence between cost-optimality and the isoefficiency function). This is not true for parallel systems in general, however, and it is quite possible that $T_P^{cost\_opt} > \Theta(T_P^{min})$. The following example illustrates such a parallel system.

Example 4.15 A Parallel Systems with $T_P^{cost\_opt} > \Theta(T_P^{min})$
Consider the hypothetical parallel system of Example 4.10, for which

$$T_o = p^{3/2} + p^{3/4}W^{3/4}. \tag{4.27}$$

From Equation 4.10, the parallel run time for this system is

$$T_P = \frac{W}{p} + p^{1/2} + \frac{W^{3/4}}{p^{1/4}}. \tag{4.28}$$

Using the methodology of Example 4.13,

$$\begin{aligned} \frac{d}{dp}T_P = -\frac{W}{p^2} + \frac{1}{2p^{1/2}} - \frac{W^{3/4}}{4p^{5/4}} &= 0, \\ -W + \frac{1}{2}p^{3/2} - \frac{1}{4}W^{3/4}p^{3/4} &= 0, \\ p^{3/4} &= \frac{1}{4}W^{3/4} \pm (\frac{1}{16}W^{3/2} + 2W)^{1/2} \\ &= \Theta(W^{3/4}), \\ p &= \Theta(W). \end{aligned}$$

From the preceding analysis, $p_0 = \Theta(W)$. Substituting p by the value of p_0 in Equation 4.28, we get

$$T_P^{min} = \Theta(W^{1/2}). \tag{4.29}$$

According to Example 4.10, the overall isoefficiency function for this parallel system is $\Theta(p^3)$, which implies that the maximum number of processors that can be used cost-optimally is $\Theta(W^{1/3})$. Substituting $p = \Theta(W^{1/3})$ in Equation 4.28, we get

$$T_P^{cost\_opt} = \Theta(W^{2/3}). \tag{4.30}$$

A comparison of Equations 4.29 and 4.30 shows that $T_P^{cost\_opt}$ is asymptotically greater than T_P^{min}.

■

In this section, we have seen examples of both types of parallel systems: those for which $T_P^{cost\_opt}$ is asymptotically equal to T_P^{min}, and those for which $T_P^{cost\_opt}$ is asymptotically greater than T_P^{min}. Most parallel systems presented in this book are of the first type. Parallel systems for which the run time can be reduced by an order of magnitude by using an asymptotically higher number of processors than indicated by the isoefficiency function are rare.

While deriving the minimum execution time for any parallel system, it is important to be aware that the maximum number of processors that can be utilized is bounded by the degree of concurrency $C(W)$ of the parallel algorithm. It is quite possible that p_0 is greater than $C(W)$ for a parallel system (Problems 4.19 and 4.20). In such cases, the value of p_0 is meaningless, and T_P^{min} is given by

$$T_P^{min} = \frac{W + T_o(W, C(W))}{C(W)}. \tag{4.31}$$

4.7 Other Scalability Metrics and Bibliographic Remarks

To use today's massively parallel computers effectively, larger problems must be solved as more processors are added. However, when the problem size is fixed, the objective is to attain the best compromise between efficiency and parallel run time. Performance issues for fixed-size problems have been addressed by several researchers [FK89, GK93a, KF90, NW88, TL90, Wor90]. In most situations, additional computing power derived from increasing the number of processors can be used to solve bigger problems. In some situations, however, different ways of increasing the problem size may apply, and a variety of constraints may guide the scaling up of the workload with respect to the number of processors [SHG93].

For many problem domains, it is appropriate to increase the problem size with the number of processors so that the total parallel execution time remains fixed. An example is the domain of weather forecasting, in which the size of the problem can be increased arbitrarily provided that it is solved within a specified time (it does not make sense to take more than 24 hours to forecast the next day's weather). This is known as ***time-constrained scaling*** and has been explored by Gustafson et al. [GMB88, Gus88, Gus92], Sun and Ni [SN90], and Worley [Wor90] (Problem 4.12).

Another method for scaling problem size is to solve the largest problem that fits the available memory. This is called ***memory-constrained scaling*** and has been investigated by Gustafson et al. [GMB88, Gus88], Sun and Ni [SN90, SN93], and Worley [Wor88, Wor90, Wor91]. Since the total memory of a parallel computer increases with the number of processors, it is possible to solve bigger problems on parallel computers with a larger p. Any problem whose memory requirement exceeds the total available memory cannot be solved on the system.

An important scenario is one in which we want to make the most efficient use of the parallel system; in other words, we want the overall performance of the parallel system to increase linearly with p. This is possible only for scalable parallel systems, which are exactly those for which a fixed efficiency can be maintained for arbitrarily large p by simply increasing the problem size. For such systems, it is natural to use the isoefficiency function or related metrics [GGKar, CD87, KR87, KRS88]. Isoefficiency analysis has been found to be very useful in characterizing the scalability of a variety of parallel algorithms [GK91, GK93b, GKS92, Hwa93, KN91, KR87, KR89, KS91, RS90, SKAT91, TL90, WS91a, WS91b]. Gupta and Kumar [GK93a, KG91] have demonstrated the relevance of the isoefficiency function in the fixed time case as well. They have shown that if the isoefficiency function is greater than $\Theta(p)$, then the problem size cannot be increased indefinitely while maintaining a fixed execution time, no matter how many processors are used. A number of other researchers have analyzed the performance of parallel systems with concern for overall efficiency [EZL89, FK89, MS88, NW88, TL90, Zho89, ZRV89].

Kruskal, Rudolph, and Snir [KRS88] define the concept of ***parallel efficient (PE)*** problems. Their definition is related to the concept of isoefficiency function. Problems in the class PE have algorithms with a polynomial isoefficiency function at some efficiency. The class PE makes an important distinction between algorithms with polynomial isoefficiency functions and those with worse isoefficiency functions. Kruskal et al. proved the invariance of the class PE over a variety of parallel computational models and interconnection schemes. An important consequence of this result is that an algorithm with a polynomial isoefficiency on one architecture will have a polynomial isoefficiency on many other architectures as well. There can be exceptions, however; for instance, Gupta and Kumar [GK93b] show that the fast Fourier transform algorithm has a polynomial isoefficiency on a hypercube but an exponential isoefficiency on a mesh.

Vitter and Simons [VS86] define a class of problems called ***PC****. PC* includes problems with efficient parallel algorithms on a PRAM. A problem in class ***P*** (the polynomial-time class) is in PC* if it has a parallel algorithm on a PRAM that can use a polynomial (in terms of input size) number of processors and achieve a minimal efficiency ϵ. Any problem in PC* has at least one parallel algorithm such that, for an efficiency ϵ, its isoefficiency function exists and is a polynomial.

A discussion of various scalability and performance measures can be found in the survey by Kumar and Gupta [KG91]. Besides the ones cited so far, a number of other metrics of performance and scalability of parallel systems have been proposed [BW89, CR89, CR91, Fla90, Hil90, Kun86, Mol87, MR91, NA91, SG91, SR91, VC89].

Flatt and Kennedy [FK89, Fla90] show that if the overhead function satisfies certain mathematical properties, then there exists a unique value p_0 of the number of processors for which T_P is minimum for a given W. A property of T_o on which their analysis depends heavily is that $T_o > \Theta(p)$. Gupta and Kumar [GK93a] show that there exist parallel systems that do not obey this condition, and in such cases the point of peak performance is determined by the degree of concurrency of the algorithm being used.

Marinescu and Rice [MR91] develop a model to describe and analyze a parallel computation on an MIMD computer in terms of the number of threads of control p into which the computation is divided and the number events $g(p)$ as a function of p. They consider the case where each event is of a fixed duration θ and hence $T_o = \theta g(p)$. Under these assumptions on T_o, they conclude that with increasing number of processors, the speedup saturates at some value if $T_o = \Theta(p)$, and it asymptotically approaches zero if $T_o = \Theta(p^m)$, where $m \geq 2$. Gupta and Kumar [GK93a] generalize these results for a wider class of overhead functions. They show that the speedup saturates at some maximum value if $T_o \leq \Theta(p)$, and the speedup attains a maximum value and then drops monotonically with p if $T_o > \Theta(p)$.

Eager et al. [EZL89] and Tang and Li [TL90] have proposed a criterion of optimality of a parallel system so that a balance is struck between efficiency and speedup. They propose that a good choice of operating point on the execution time verses efficiency curve is that where the incremental benefit of adding processors is roughly 1/2 per processor or, in other words, efficiency is 0.5. They conclude that for $T_o = \Theta(p)$, this is also equivalent to operating at a point where the ES product is maximum or $p(T_P)^2$ is minimum. This conclusion is a special case of the more general case presented by Gupta and Kumar [GK93a].

Belkhale and Banerjee [BB90], Leuze et al. [LDP89], Ma and Shea [MS88], and Park and Dowdy [PD89] address the important problem of optimal partitioning of the processors of a parallel computer among several applications of different scalabilities executing simultaneously.

Problems

4.1 **(Amdahl's law [Amd67])** If a problem of size W has a serial component W_S, prove that W/W_S is an upper bound on its speedup, no matter how many processors are used.

4.2 **(Superlinear speedup)** Consider the search tree shown in Figure 4.5(a), in which the dark node represents the solution. (a) If a sequential search of the tree is performed using the standard depth-first search (DFS) algorithm (Section 8.2.1), how much time does take to find the solution if traversing each arc of the tree takes one unit of time? (b) Assume that the tree is partitioned between two processors that are assigned to do the search job, as shown in Figure 4.5(b). If both processors

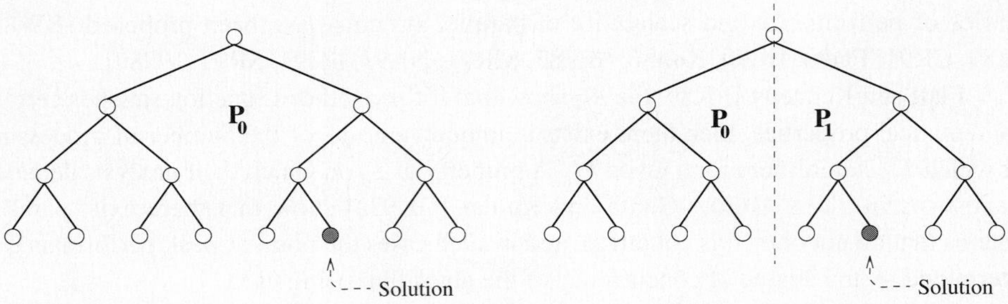

(a) DFS with one processor (b) DFS with two processors

Figure 4.5 Superlinear(?) speedup in parallel depth first search.

perform a DFS on their respective halves of the tree, how much time does take for the solution to be found? What is the speedup? Is there a speedup anomaly? If so, can you explain the anomaly?
Hint: See Section 8.6.

4.3 Assume that it takes unit time to add two numbers and that it takes ten units of time to communicate a number between two directly-connected processors. How much time does it take to add 16 numbers on a four-processor hypercube with the data-mapping shown in Figure 4.6, if the steps shown in Figure 4.1 for 16 processors are simulated on four processors? In general, how much time does it take to simulate the algorithm for adding n numbers on n processors illustrated in Figure 4.1 on a p-processor hypercube ($n > p$) if the ***spiral*** mapping illustrated in Figure 4.6 is used?
Hint: Draw a figure along the lines of Figure 4.2.

4.4 Show that, if n numbers are distributed randomly among p processors of a hypercube ($n > p$), a simulation of the procedure illustrated in Figure 4.1 takes an average of $\Theta((n/p) \log p)$ time.

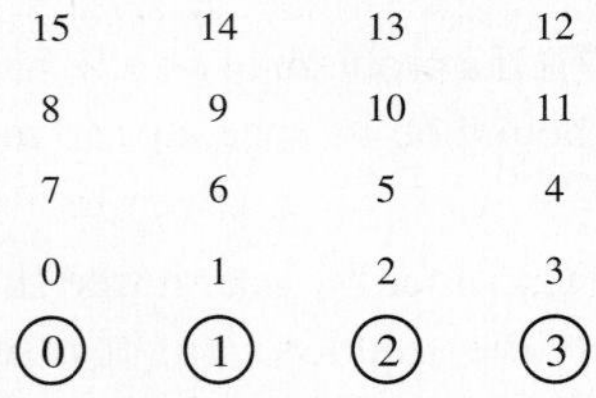

Figure 4.6 A distribution of 16 numbers among four processors.

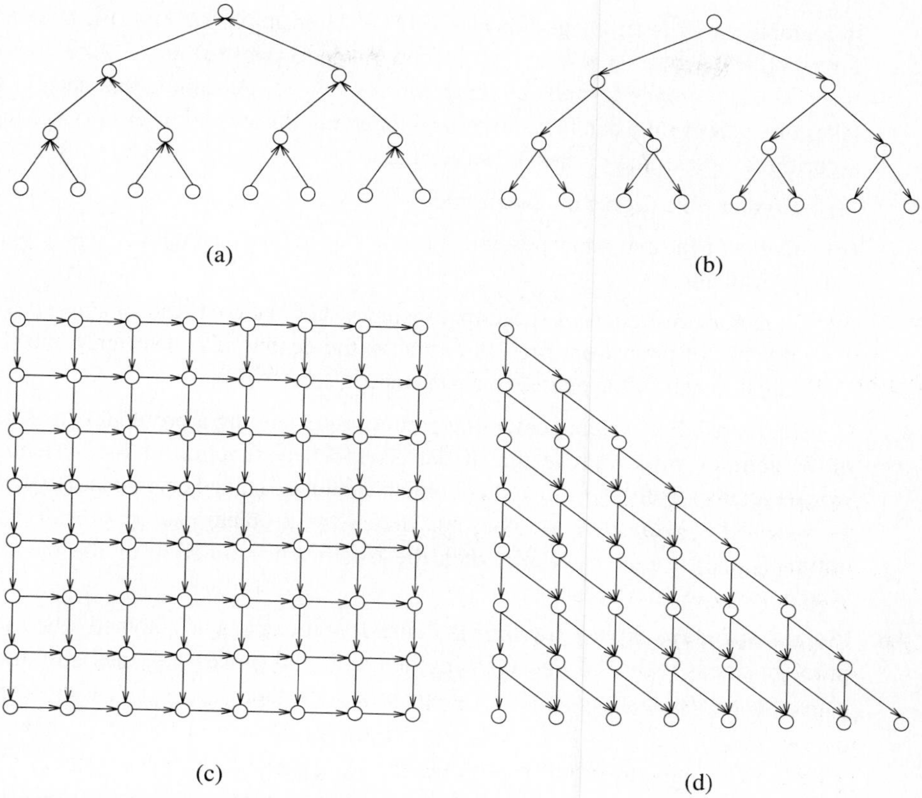

Figure 4.7 Dependency graphs for Problem 4.6.

4.5 Give an example of a parallel system other than the one in Problem 4.4, in which simulating n virtual processors by p physical processors with an inappropriate data-mapping increases the parallel run time by a factor greater than $\Theta(n/p)$.

4.6 **(The DAG model of parallel computation)** Parallel algorithms can often be represented by dependency graphs. If a program can be broken into several tasks, then each node of the graph represents one task. The directed edges of the graph represent the dependencies between the tasks or the order in which they must be performed to yield correct results. A node of the dependency graph can be scheduled for execution as soon as the tasks at all the nodes that have incoming edges to that node have finished execution. For example, in Figure 4.7(b), the nodes on the second level from the root can begin execution only after the task at the root is finished. Any deadlock-free dependency graph must be a ***directed acyclic graph*** (DAG); that is, it is devoid of any cycles. All the nodes that are scheduled for execution can be worked on in parallel provided enough processors are available. Four such dependency graphs are shown in Figure 4.7. If N is the number of nodes in a graph, and n is an integer, then $N = 2^n - 1$ for graphs (a) and (b), $N = n^2$ for graph (c), and $N = n(n+1)/2$ for graph (d) (Graphs (a) and (b) are drawn for $n = 4$ and graphs (c) and (d) are drawn for $n = 8$). Assuming that each task takes one unit of time and that interprocessor communication time is zero, for the algorithms represented by each of these graphs,

(a) Compute the degree of concurrency.

(b) Compute the maximum possible speedup if an unlimited number of processors is available.

(c) Compute the values of speedup, efficiency, and the overhead function if the number of processors is (i) the same as the degree of concurrency and (ii) equal to half of the degree of concurrency.

4.7 Consider a parallel system containing p processors solving a problem consisting of W units of work. Prove that if the isoefficiency function of the system is worse (greater) than $\Theta(p)$, then the problem cannot be solved cost-optimally with $p = \Theta(W)$. Also prove the converse that if the problem can be solved cost-optimally only for $p < \Theta(W)$, then the isoefficiency function of the parallel system is worse than linear.

4.8 **(Scaled speedup)** ***Scaled speedup*** is defined as the speedup obtained when the problem size is increased linearly with the number of processors; that is, if W is chosen as a base problem size for a single processor, then

$$\textit{Scaled speedup} = \frac{pW}{T_P(pW, p)}. \tag{4.32}$$

For the problem of adding n numbers on a p-processor hypercube (Example 4.5), plot the speedup curves, assuming that the base problem for $p = 1$ is that of adding 256 numbers. Use $p = 1, 4, 16, 64$, and 256. Assume that it takes ten time units to communicate a number between two directly-connected processors, and that it takes one unit of time to add two numbers. Now plot the standard speedup curve for the base problem size and compare it with the scaled speedup curve.
Hint: The parallel run time is $(n/p - 1) + 11 \log p$.

4.9 Plot a third speedup curve for Problem 4.8, in which the problem size is scaled up according to the isoefficiency function, which is $\Theta(p \log p)$. Use the same expression for T_P.
Hint: The scaled speedup under this method of scaling is given by the following equation:

$$\textit{Isoefficient scaled speedup} = \frac{pW \log p}{T_P(pW \log p, p)}$$

4.10 Plot the efficiency curves for the problem of adding n numbers on a p-processor hypercube corresponding to the standard speedup curve (Problem 4.8), scaled speedup curve (Problem 4.8), and the speedup curve when the problem size is increased according to the isoefficiency function (Problem 4.9).

4.11 A drawback of increasing the number of processors without increasing the total work load is that the speedup does not increase linearly with the number of processors, and the efficiency drops monotonically. Based on your experience with Problems 4.8 and 4.10, discuss whether or not scaled speedup increases linearly with the number of processors in general. What can you say about the isoefficiency function of a parallel system whose scaled speedup curve matches the speedup curve determined by increasing the problem size according to the isoefficiency function?

4.12 **(Time-constrained scaling)** Using the expression for T_P from Problem 4.8 for p = 1, 4, 16, 64, 256, 1024, and 4096, what is the largest problem that can be solved if the total execution time is not to exceed 512 time units? In general, is it possible to solve an arbitrarily large problem in a fixed amount of time, provided that an unlimited number of processors is available? Why?

4.13 **(Prefix sums on a hypercube)** Consider the problem of computing the prefix sums (Example 3.8) of n numbers on an n-processor hypercube. What is the parallel run time, speedup, and efficiency of this algorithm? Assume that adding two numbers takes one unit of time and that communicating one number between two directly-connected processors takes ten units of time. Is the algorithm cost-optimal?

4.14 Design a cost-optimal version of the prefix sums algorithm (Problem 4.13) for computing all prefix-sums of n numbers on a p-processor hypercube where $p < n$. Assuming that adding two numbers takes one unit of time and that communicating one number between two directly-connected processors takes ten units of time, derive expressions for T_P, S, E, cost, and the isoefficiency function.

4.15 Describe an algorithm for finding the maximum of n numbers on an $\sqrt{n} \times \sqrt{n}$ mesh of processors. Is the algorithm cost-optimal?

4.16 Redesign the algorithm for finding the maximum of n numbers on a mesh (Problem 4.15) to work on fewer than n processors. Assume that a comparison of two numbers can be performed in unit time and that communicating a number between two directly-connected processors takes ten units of time. What is the smallest n (in terms of p) such that the maximum of n numbers can be computed cost-optimally on a p-processor mesh? What is the isoefficiency function of this parallel system?

4.17 Repeat Problems 4.15 and 4.16 when the parallel architecture is a regular 3-D mesh of processors.

4.18 **[GK93a]** Prove that if $T_o \leq \Theta(p)$ for a given problem size, then the parallel execution time will continue to decrease as p is increased and will asymptotically approach a constant value. Also prove that if $T_o > \Theta(p)$, then T_P first decreases and then increases with p; hence, it has a distinct minimum.

4.19 The parallel run time of a parallel implementation of the FFT algorithm on an SIMD hypercube with p processors is given by $T_P = (n/p)\log n + t_w(n/p)\log p$ for an input sequence of length n (Equation 10.4 with $t_s = 0$). The maximum number of processors that the algorithm can use for an n-point FFT is n. What are the values of p_0 (the value of p that satisfies Equation 4.21) and T_P^{min} for $t_w = 10$?

4.20 **[GK93a]** Consider two parallel systems with the same overhead function, but with different digrees of concurrency. Let the overhead function of both parallel systems be $W^{1/3}p^{3/2} + 0.1W^{2/3}p$. Plot T_P versus p curve for $W = 1000,000$, and $1 \leq p \leq 2048$. If the degree of concurrency is $W^{1/3}$ for the first algorithm and $W^{2/3}$ for the second algorithm, compute the values of T_P^{min} for both parallel systems. Also compute the cost and efficiency for both the parallel systems at the point on the T_P versus p curve where their respective minimum run times are achieved.

References

[Amd67] G. M. Amdahl. Validity of the single processor approach to achieving large scale computing capabilities. In *AFIPS Conference Proceedings*, 483–485, 1967.

[BB90] K. P. Belkhale and P. Banerjee. Approximate algorithms for the partitionable independent task scheduling problem. In *Proceedings of the 1990 International Conference on Parallel Processing*, I72–I75, 1990.

[BW89] M. L. Barton and G. R. Withers. Computing performance as a function of the speed, quantity, and the cost of processors. In *Supercomputing '89 Proceedings*, 759–764, 1989.

[CD87] S. Chandran and L. S. Davis. An approach to parallel vision algorithms. In R. Porth, editor, *Parallel Processing*. SIAM, Philadelphia, PA, 1987.

[CR89] E. A. Carmona and M. D. Rice. A model of parallel performance. Technical Report AFWL-TR-89-01, Air Force Weapons Laboratory, 1989.

[CR91] E. A. Carmona and M. D. Rice. Modeling the serial and parallel fractions of a parallel algorithm. *Journal of Parallel and Distributed Computing*, 1991.

[EZL89] D. L. Eager, J. Zahorjan, and E. D. Lazowska. Speedup versus efficiency in parallel systems. *IEEE Transactions on Computers*, 38(3):408–423, 1989.

[FK89] H. P. Flatt and K. Kennedy. Performance of parallel processors. *Parallel Computing*, 12:1–20, 1989.

[Fla90] H. P. Flatt. Further applications of the overhead model for parallel systems. Technical Report G320-3540, IBM Corporation, Palo Alto Scientific Center, Palo Alto, CA, 1990.

[GGKar] A. Grama, A. Gupta, and V. Kumar. Isoefficiency function: A scalability metric for parallel algor ithms and architectures. *IEEE Parallel and Distributed Technology*, 1993 (To Appear). Also available as Technical Report TR 93-24, Department of Computer Science, University of Minnesota, Minneapolis, MN.

[GK91] A. Gupta and V. Kumar. The scalability of matrix multiplication algorithms on parallel computers. Technical Report TR 91-54, Department of Computer Science, University of Minnesota, Minneapolis, MN, 1991. A short version appears in *Proceedings of 1993 International Conference on Parallel Processing*, pages III-115–III-119, 1993.

[GK93a] A. Gupta and V. Kumar. Performance properties of large scale parallel systems. *Journal of Parallel and Distributed Computing*, 19(3), November 1993. Also available as Technical Report 92-32, Department of Computer Science, University of Minnesota, Minneapolis, MN.

[GK93b] A. Gupta and V. Kumar. The scalability of FFT on parallel computers. *IEEE Transactions on Parallel and Distributed Systems*, 4(7), July 1993. A detailed version available as Technical Report TR 90-53, Department of Computer Science, University of Minnesota, Minneapolis, MN.

[GKS92] A. Gupta, V. Kumar, and A. H. Sameh. Performance and scalability of preconditioned conjugate gradient methods on parallel computers. Technical Report TR 92-64, Department of Computer Science, University of Minnesota, Minneapolis, MN, 1992. A short version appears in *Proceedings of the Sixth SIAM Conference on Parallel Processing for Scientific Computing*, pages 664–674, 1993.

[GMB88] J. L. Gustafson, G. R. Montry, and R. E. Benner. Development of parallel methods for a 1024-processor hypercube. *SIAM Journal on Scientific and Statistical Computing*, 9(4):609–638, 1988.

[Gus88] J. L. Gustafson. Reevaluating Amdahl's law. *Communications of the ACM*, 31(5):532–533, 1988.

[Gus92] J. L. Gustafson. The consequences of fixed time performance measurement. In *Proceedings of the 25th Hawaii International Conference on System Sciences: Volume III*, 113–124, 1992.

[Hil90] M. D. Hill. What is scalability? *Computer Architecture News*, 18(4), 1990.

[Hwa93] K. Hwang. *Advanced Computer Architecture: Parallelism, Scalability, Programmability*. McGraw-Hill, New York, NY, 1993.

[KF90] A. H. Karp and H. P. Flatt. Measuring parallel processor performance. *Communications of the ACM*, 33(5):539–543, 1990.

[KG91] V. Kumar and A. Gupta. Analyzing scalability of parallel algorithms and architectures. Technical Report TR 91-18, Department of Computer Science Department, University of Minnesota, Minneapolis, MN, 1991. To appear in *Journal of Parallel and Distributed Computing*, 1994. A shorter version appears in *Proceedings of the 1991 International Conference on Supercomputing*, pages 396-405, 1991.

[KN91] K. Kimura and I. Nobuyuki. Probabilistic analysis of the efficiency of the dynamic load distribution. In *The Sixth Distributed Memory Computing Conference Proceedings*, 1991.

[KR87] V. Kumar and V. N. Rao. Parallel depth-first search, part II: Analysis. *International Journal of Parallel Programming*, 16(6):501–519, 1987.

[KR89] V. Kumar and V. N. Rao. Load balancing on the hypercube architecture. In *Proceedings of the Fourth Conference on Hypercubes, Concurrent Computers, and Applications*, 603–608, 1989.

[KRS88] C. P. Kruskal, L. Rudolph, and M. Snir. A complexity theory of efficient parallel algorithms. Technical Report RC13572, IBM T. J. Watson Research Center, Yorktown Heights, NY, 1988.

[KS91] V. Kumar and V. Singh. Scalability of Parallel Algorithms for the All-Pairs Shortest Path Problem. *Journal of Parallel and Distributed Computing*, 13(2):124–138, October 1991. A short version appears in the *Proceedings of the International Conference on Parallel Processing*, 1990.

[Kun86] H. T. Kung. Memory requirements for balanced computer architectures. In *Proceedings of the 1986 IEEE Symposium on Computer Architecture*, 49–54, 1986.

[LDP89] M. R. Leuze, L. W. Dowdy, and K. H. Park. Multiprogramming a distributed-memory multiprocessor. *Concurrency: Practice and Experience*, 1(1):19–33, September 1989.

[Mol87] C. Moler. Another look at Amdahl's law. Technical Report TN-02-0587-0288, Intel Scientific Computers, 1987.

[MR91] D. C. Marinescu and J. R. Rice. On high level characterization of parallelism. Technical Report CSD-TR-1011, CAPO Report CER-90-32, Computer Science Department, Purdue University, West Lafayette, IN, Revised June 1991. To appear in *Journal of Parallel and Distributed Computing*, 1993.

[MS88] Y. W. E. Ma and D. G. Shea. Downward scalability of parallel architectures. In *Proceedings of the 1988 International Conference on Supercomputing*, 109–120, 1988.

[NA91] D. Nussbaum and A. Agarwal. Scalability of parallel machines. *Communications of the ACM*, 34(3):57–61, 1991.

[NW88] D. M. Nicol and F. H. Willard. Problem size, parallel architecture, and optimal speedup. *Journal of Parallel and Distributed Computing*, 5:404–420, 1988.

[PD89] K. H. Park and L. W. Dowdy. Dynamic partitioning of multiprocessor systems. *International Journal of Parallel Processing*, 18(2):91–120, 1989.

[RS90] S. Ranka and S. Sahni. *Hypercube Algorithms for Image Processing and Pattern Recognition*. Springer-Verlag, New York, NY, 1990.

[SG91] X.-H. Sun and J. L. Gustafson. Toward a better parallel performance metric. *Parallel Computing*, 17:1093–1109, December 1991. Also available as Technical Report IS-5053, UC-32, Ames Laboratory, Iowa State University, Ames, IA.

[SHG93] J. Singh, J. L. Hennessy, and A. Gupta. Scaling parallel programs for multiprocessors: Methodology and examples. *IEEE Computer*, 26(7):42–50, 1993.

[SKAT91] V. Singh, V. Kumar, G. Agha, and C. Tomlinson. Scalability of parallel sorting on mesh multicomputers. *International Journal of Parallel Programming*, 20(2), 1991. A short version appears in *Proceedings of the Fifth International Parallel Processing Symposium*, 1991.

[SN90] X.-H. Sun and L. M. Ni. Another view of parallel speedup. In *Supercomputing '90 Proceedings*, 324–333, 1990.

[SN93] X.-H. Sun and L. M. Ni. Scalable problems and memory-bounded speedup. *Journal of Parallel and Distributed Computing*, 19:27–37, September 1993.

[SR91] X.-H. Sun and D. T. Rover. Scalability of parallel algorithm-machine combinations. Technical Report IS-5057, Ames Laboratory, Iowa State University, Ames, IA, 1991. To appear in *IEEE Transactions on Parallel and Distributed Systems*.

[TL90] Z. Tang and G.-J. Li. Optimal granularity of grid iteration problems. In *Proceedings of the 1990 International Conference on Parallel Processing*, I111–I118, 1990.

[VC89] F. A. Van-Catledge. Towards a general model for evaluating the relative performance of computer systems. *International Journal of Supercomputer Applications*, 3(2):100–108, 1989.

[VS86] J. S. Vitter and R. A. Simons. New classes for parallel complexity: A study of unification and other complete problems for P. *IEEE Transactions on Computers*, May 1986.

[Wor88] P. H. Worley. *Information Requirements and the Implications for Parallel Computation*. Ph.D. thesis, Stanford University, Department of Computer Science, Palo Alto, CA, 1988.

[Wor90] P. H. Worley. The effect of time constraints on scaled speedup. *SIAM Journal on Scientific and Statistical Computing*, 11(5):838–858, 1990.

[Wor91] P. H. Worley. Limits on parallelism in the numerical solution of linear PDEs. *SIAM Journal on Scientific and Statistical Computing*, 12:1–35, January 1991.

[WS91a] J. Woo and S. Sahni. Hypercube computing: Connected components. *Journal of Supercomputing*, 1991. Also available as TR 88-50 from the Department of Computer Science, University of Minnesota, Minneapolis, MN.

[WS91b] J. Woo and S. Sahni. Computing biconnected components on a hypercube. *Journal of Supercomputing*, June 1991. Also available as Technical Report TR 89-7 from the Department of Computer Science, University of Minnesota, Minneapolis, MN.

[Zho89] X. Zhou. Bridging the gap between Amdahl's law and Sandia laboratory's result. *Communications of the ACM*, 32(8):1014–5, 1989.

[ZRV89] J. R. Zorbas, D. J. Reble, and R. E. VanKooten. Measuring the scalability of parallel computer systems. In *Supercomputing '89 Proceedings*, 832–841, 1989.

CHAPTER **5**

Dense Matrix Algorithms

Algorithms involving matrices and vectors are applied in several numerical and non-numerical contexts. We can classify matrices into two broad categories according to the kind of algorithms that are appropriate for them. The first category is ***dense*** or ***full matrices*** with few or no zero entries. The second category is ***sparse matrices***, in which a majority of the elements are zero. More precisely, a matrix is considered sparse if a computation involving it can utilize the number and location of its nonzero elements to reduce the run time over the same computation on a dense matrix of the same size. This chapter discusses some key algorithms for dense matrices. We deal specifically with square matrices for pedagogical reasons, but the algorithms in this chapter, wherever applicable, are readily adaptable for rectangular matrices as well.

5.1 Mapping Matrices onto Processors

In order to processes a matrix in parallel, we must partition it so that the partitions can be assigned to different processors. As we will learn from analyzing the algorithms in this chapter, data partitioning significantly affects the performance of a parallel system. Hence, it is important to determine which data-mapping scheme is the most appropriate one for each algorithm. In the following subsections, we briefly discuss some common ways to partition matrices among processors. We will refer to these as partitioning schemes or mapping schemes.

5.1.1 Striped Partitioning

In the ***striped partitioning*** of a matrix, the matrix is divided into groups of complete rows or columns, and each processor is assigned one such group. The partitioning is uniform if each

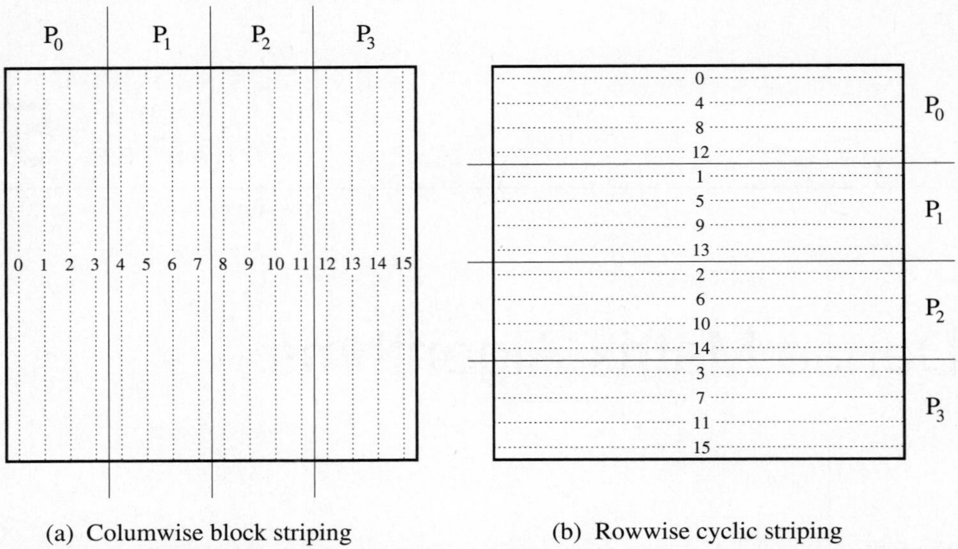

Figure 5.1 Uniform striped partitioning of 16 × 16 matrices on 4 processors.

group contains an equal number of rows or columns. The partitioning is called ***block-striped*** if each processor is assigned contiguous rows or columns, as shown in Figure 5.1(a). In a columnwise block striping of an $n \times n$ matrix on p processors (labeled $P_0, P_1, \ldots, P_{p-1}$), processor P_i contains columns with indices $(n/p)i, (n/p)i + 1, \ldots, (n/p)(i + 1) - 1$. In contrast to block striping, the rows or columns of a matrix can be sequentially distributed among the processors in a wraparound manner. This mapping, shown in Figure 5.1(b) is called ***cyclic-striped*** mapping. In the rowwise cyclic striping of an $n \times n$ matrix on p processors, processor P_i contains rows with indices $i, i + p, i + 2p, \ldots, i + n - p$. We can partition a matrix also by using a mapping that is a hybrid between block and cyclic mappings. In this mapping, called the ***block-cyclic-striped*** mapping, the matrix is striped into blocks of q rows ($q < n/p$) and these blocks are distributed among the processors in a cyclic manner (Problem 5.1).

By using striped partitioning, we can partition an $n \times n$ matrix among a maximum of n processors.

5.1.2 Checkerboard Partitioning

In ***checkerboard partitioning*** shown in Figure 5.2, the matrix is divided into smaller square or rectangular blocks or submatrices that are distributed among processors. In a uniform checkerboard partitioning, all submatrices are of the same size. A checkerboard partitioning splits both the rows and the columns of the matrix, so no processor is assigned any complete row or column. Like striping, checkerboarding can be block (Figure 5.2(a)) or cyclic (Figure 5.2(b)). We can create a cyclic-checkerboard partitioning by mapping

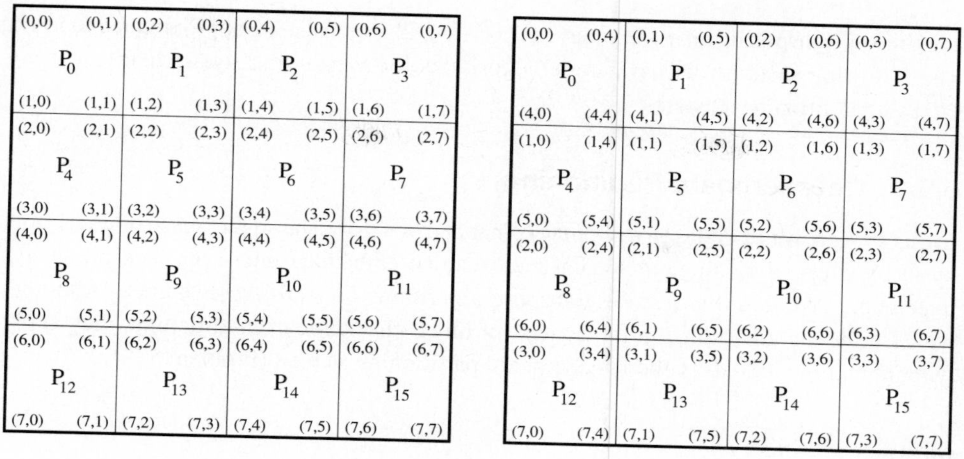

(a) Block-checkerboard partitioning

(b) Cyclic-checkerboard partitioning

Figure 5.2 Checkerboard partitioning of 8 × 8 matrices on 16 processors.

the rows onto the processors in a cyclic manner followed by the columns, or vice versa. Similarly, we can create a hybrid block-cyclic-checkerboard partitioning by dividing the matrix into $q^2 p$ blocks and then mapping these blocks of size $q \times q$ (instead of individual elements) in a cyclic manner.

A checkerboard-partitioned square matrix maps naturally onto a two-dimensional square mesh of processors. For instance, we can map an $n \times n$ matrix onto a p-processor mesh by dividing it into blocks of size $(n/\sqrt{p}) \times (n/\sqrt{p})$. Therefore, for a checkerboard mapping, it is often convenient to visualize the ensemble of processors as a logical two-dimensional mesh. If we need to implement a matrix algorithm using checkerboarding on an architecture other than mesh, then the logical mesh is embedded into the physical interconnection network.

Unlike striping, the lowest level of granularity in checkerboarding is one matrix element per processor. Therefore, checkerboarding can exploit more concurrency than striping (if the parallel algorithm allows it) because the matrix computation can be divided among more processors than in the case of striping. For instance, we can partition an $n \times n$ matrix among a maximum of n^2 processors using checkerboarding, but we cannot use more than n processors with striping.

5.2 Matrix Transposition

The transpose of an $n \times n$ matrix A is a matrix A^T of the same size, such that $A^T[i, j] = A[j, i]$ for $0 \leq i, j < n$. In the process of transposing a matrix, all elements below the principal diagonal move to positions above the principal diagonal and vice versa. If we assume that it takes unit time to exchange a pair of matrix elements, then the sequential run time of transposing an $n \times n$ matrix is $(n^2 - n)/2$, which can be approximated to $n^2/2$. The following sections discuss parallel algorithms for transposing square matrices using different partitioning schemes.

5.2.1 Checkerboard Partitioning

In this section, we consider an $n \times n$ matrix mapped onto a logical square mesh of processors by using checkerboarding. A logical mesh can be embedded into a physical mesh or a hypercube. We describe parallel transpose algorithms for both architectures. Although we describe the algorithms in the context of block-checkerboard partitioning, they apply without modification to cyclic-checkerboard partitioning as well (Problem 5.2).

Mesh

Assume that an $n \times n$ matrix is stored in an $n \times n$ mesh of processors so that one processor holds a single element of the matrix. Figure 5.3 illustrates the transposition procedure for a 4×4 matrix on a 16-processor mesh. Imagine a diagonal running through processors P_0, P_5, P_{10}, and P_{15}. To obtain the transpose, the matrix elements located below this diagonal must move to the corresponding diametrically opposite locations above the diagonal, and vice versa. An element located below the diagonal first moves up to the diagonal, and then to the right to its destination processor. Similarly, an element above the diagonal moves down to the diagonal and then left to its destination processor. Figure 5.3(a) illustrates this communication pattern for transposing a 4×4 matrix on a 16-processor mesh. For example, the matrix element initially on P_8 moves to P_2 through P_4, P_0, and P_1, and the initial element of P_2 moves to P_8 through P_6, P_{10}, and P_9. Figure 5.3(b) shows the final distribution of elements among the processors.

Now we consider the case in which the number of processors p is less that n^2, and the matrix is distributed among the processors by using a uniform block-checkerboard partitioning. The transpose of the entire matrix can be computed in two phases, as shown in Figure 5.4. In the first phase, the square matrix blocks are treated as indivisible units, and the two-dimensional array of blocks is transposed. This step requires interprocessor communication in a pattern identical to that of Figure 5.3(a), except that the $(n/\sqrt{p}) \times (n/\sqrt{p})$ blocks are communicated instead of individual elements. If $p = n^2$, then (as shown earlier), performing these communication steps suffices to compute the transpose of the matrix. However, if $p < n^2$, then all blocks must also be transposed locally within their respective processors. Figure 5.4(b) shows this phase of the algorithm, and this step concludes the process of transposing the entire matrix.

As Figure 5.4(a) shows, the communication paths of the blocks in the same row or column overlap. For example, all the blocks originally in the first column (P_4, P_8, and P_{12}) pass through P_0 to reach their respective destinations in the first row (P_1, P_2 and P_3). Therefore, the various communication steps must be synchronized so that only one message is transmitted along a link at a time. For example, in the first step, P_{12} transmits its block to P_8, P_8 transmits to P_4, and P_4 to P_0.

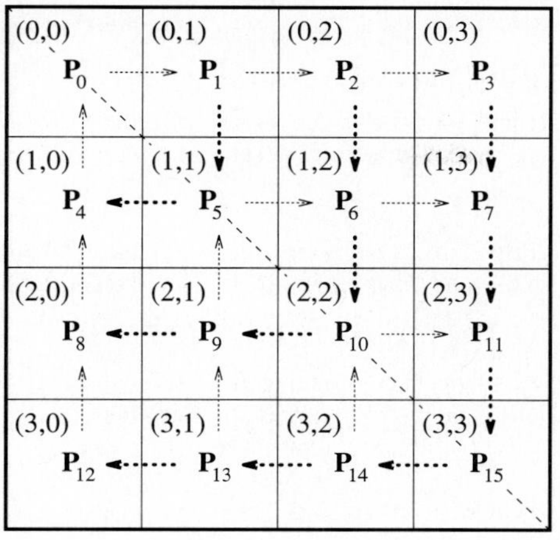

(a) Communication steps

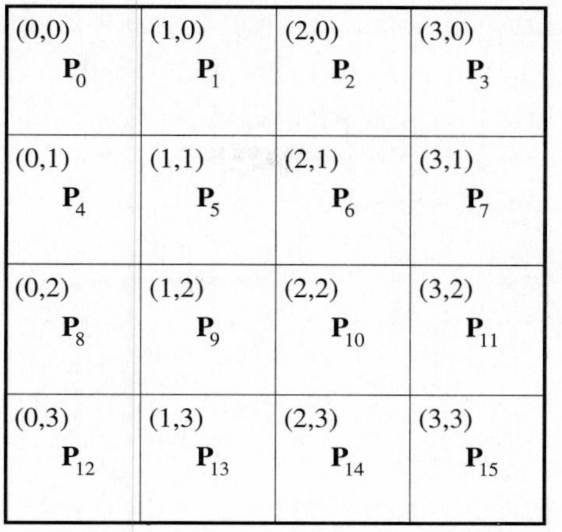

(b) Final configuration

Figure 5.3 Transposing a 4 $\times$ 4 matrix by using checkerboard partitioning on a 16-processor mesh.

During the communication phase, the matrix blocks initially residing on the bottom-left and top-right processors of Figure 5.4(a) cover the longest distances to swap their locations. These paths, covering approximately $2\sqrt{p}$ links each, determine the total time spent in the communication phase. Since a block containing n^2/p elements takes $t_s + t_w n^2/p$ time to move across a single link, it takes a total of $2(t_s + t_w n^2/p)\sqrt{p}$ time for all the blocks to move to their final destinations in the mesh of processors. Assuming that a local exchange of a pair of matrix elements takes unit time, each processor spends approximately $n^2/(2p)$ time units in transposing its $(n/\sqrt{p}) \times (n/\sqrt{p})$ local submatrix. Thus, the total parallel run time of the procedure is

$$T_P = \frac{n^2}{2p} + 2t_s\sqrt{p} + 2t_w\frac{n^2}{\sqrt{p}}. \tag{5.1}$$

The cost or the processor-time product of this parallel system is $n^2/2 + 2t_s p^{3/2} + 2t_w n^2\sqrt{p}$. The term associated with t_w results in a $\Theta(n^2\sqrt{p})$ cost, which is higher than the $\Theta(n^2)$ sequential complexity of transposing an $n \times n$ matrix. Hence, the algorithm is not cost-optimal. The overall communication complexity of this algorithm on a mesh is the same for both store-and-forward and cut-through routing schemes (Problem 5.3).

Hypercube

We have already seen that, if a square matrix is uniformly divided into blocks of equal size, the transpose of the entire matrix can be computed by first transposing the two-dimensional array of blocks and then transposing the elements within each block. Using this property of

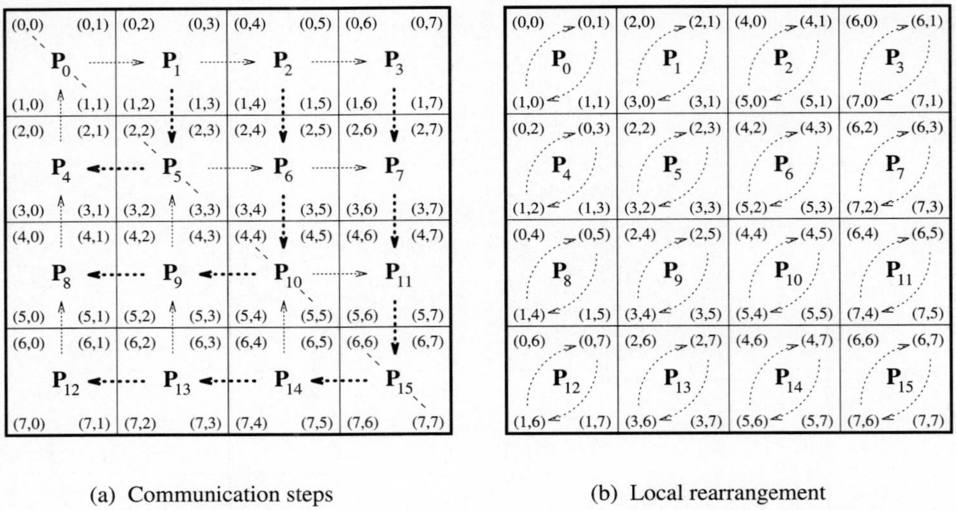

Figure 5.4 The two phases of transposing an 8×8 matrix by using checkerboard partitioning on a 16-processor mesh.

the transposition algorithm, we now develop its recursive formulation, which is suitable for the hypercube architecture. This algorithm, known as the ***recursive transposition algorithm*** (RTA), is illustrated in Figure 5.5 for an 8×8 matrix. If the matrix is checkerboarded into four blocks, the task of transposing the matrix involves exchanging the top-right and bottom-left blocks (Figure 5.5(a)) and then computing the transpose of each of the four blocks internally. We can compute the transforms of these blocks in parallel by further dividing each one of them into four parts (Figure 5.5(b)) and repeating the procedure. The process of subdividing and transposing the blocks is repeated recursively until the entire matrix is transposed (Figures 5.5(c) and (d)).

The RTA maps naturally onto a hypercube. In the first step of the algorithm, we consider a p-processor hypercube to be composed of four subcubes of $p/4$ processors each (assuming that $\sqrt{p}$ is a power of two). Each of the four blocks resulting from the first subdivision of the matrix is mapped onto one of the subcubes. In subsequent steps, a subcube is regarded as a combination of four smaller subcubes. In the final recursive step, the subcubes contain a single processor each. Since each recursive step reduces the size of the subcubes by a factor of four, there is a total of $\log_4 p$ or $(\log p)/2$ steps.

Assume that an $n \times n$ matrix is partitioned among the p processors by using block-checkerboard mapping. The communication steps to implement the RTA are illustrated in Figure 5.6 for $n = 8$ and $p = 16$. This communication pattern uses the property of the hypercube network that every set of corresponding processors of the four subcubes is a 4-processor hypercube (Section 2.4.1). For example, the 16-processor hypercube in Figure 5.6(a) is divided into four subcubes of four processors each. In these subcubes, processors P_0, P_2, P_{10}, and P_8 occupy corresponding positions (the top-left corner) and are

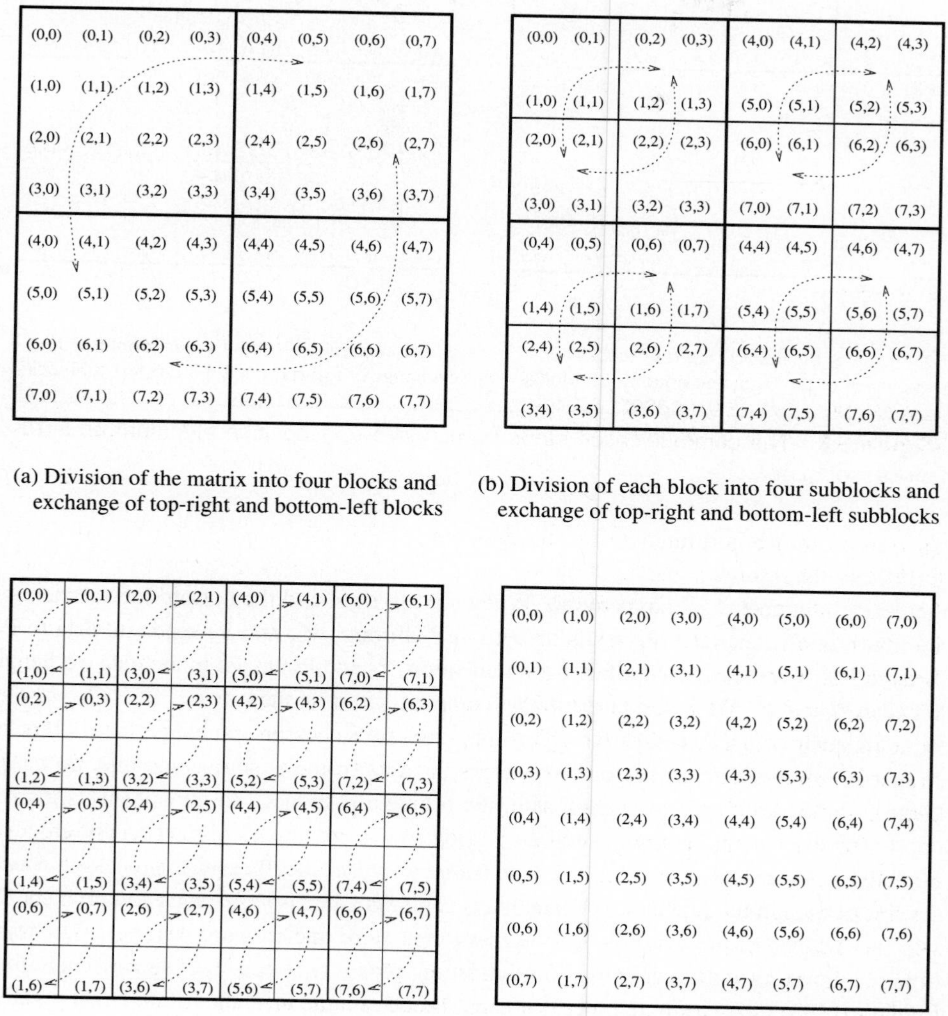

(a) Division of the matrix into four blocks and exchange of top-right and bottom-left blocks

(b) Division of each block into four subblocks and exchange of top-right and bottom-left subblocks

(c) Last subdivision and transposition

(d) Final configuration

Figure 5.5 The recursive transposition algorithm on an 8 × 8 matrix.

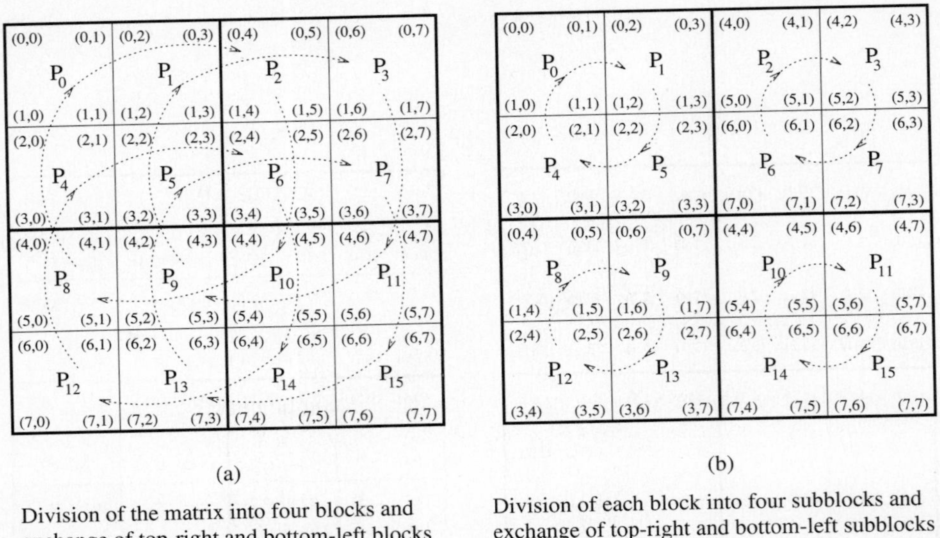
(a)
Division of the matrix into four blocks and exchange of top-right and bottom-left blocks
(b)
Division of each block into four subblocks and exchange of top-right and bottom-left subblocks

Figure 5.6 The communication steps in recursive transposition algorithm on a 16-processor hypercube.

themselves connected in a hypercube. When the top-right and the bottom-left quarters of the matrix are exchanged, P_8 sends its data to P_2 through P_0, and P_2 sends its data to P_8 through P_{10}. Note that, during this communication, P_0 and P_{10} assist in the data exchange between P_0 and P_2 but do not perform any communication of their own.

In each recursive step of the algorithm, pairs of processors exchange matrix blocks so that an intermediate processor first accepts the data from the source and then forwards them to the destination. After each step, the problem is reduced to transposing a matrix one-fourth the size of the original matrix. In $(\log p)/2$ steps, the $n \times n$ matrix is subdivided into blocks of size $(n/\sqrt{p}) \times (n/\sqrt{p})$, which are transposed locally at each processor. Since the size of each individual block of data that is communicated is n^2/p, each communication step takes $2(t_s + t_w n^2/p)$ units of time (assuming store-and-forward routing). The total time spent performing the $(\log p)$ communication steps is $(t_s + t_w n^2/p) \log p$. Accounting for the $n^2/(2p)$ time required to perform transposition on the local blocks, the total parallel run time is

$$T_P = \frac{n^2}{2p} + (t_s + t_w \frac{n^2}{p}) \log p. \tag{5.2}$$

Using a hypercube with cut-through routing improves the communication time of the RTA to $(1/2)(t_s + t_w n^2/p + 2t_h) \log p$. As in the case of a mesh, matrix transposition with checkerboard partitioning is not cost-optimal on the hypercube; its processor-time product is $\Theta(n^2 \log p)$ for both store-and-forward and cut-through routing schemes.

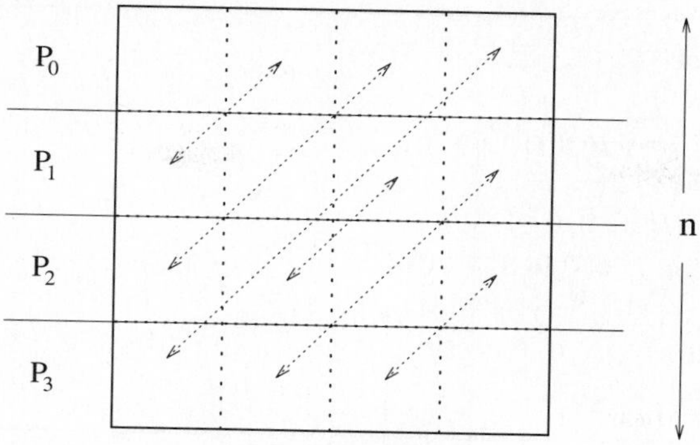

Figure 5.7 All-to-all personalized communication in transposing a 4 × 4 matrix on four processors.

5.2.2 Striped Partitioning

Consider an $n \times n$ matrix mapped onto n processors such that each processor contains one full row of the matrix. With this mapping, processor P_i initially contains the elements of the matrix with indices $[i, 0], [i, 1], \ldots, [i, n-1]$. After the transposition, element $[i, 0]$ belongs to P_0, element $[i, 1]$ belongs to P_1, and so on. In general, element $[i, j]$ initially resides on P_i, but moves to P_j during the transposition. The data-transfer pattern of this procedure is shown in Figure 5.7 for a 4×4 matrix mapped onto four processors by using rowwise striping. Note that in this figure every processor sends a distinct element of the matrix to every other processor. This is an example of all-to-all personalized communication (Section 3.5).

In general, if we use p processors such that $p \leq n$, then each processor initially stores n/p rows (that is, n^2/p elements) of the matrix. Performing the transposition now involves an all-to-all personalized communication of matrix blocks of size $n/p \times n/p$, instead of individual elements. At the end of the communication phase, each processor performs an internal transposition of these blocks. Assuming that each pairwise exchange of elements takes unit time, one such block can be transposed in $n^2/(2p^2)$ time. Since each processor has p such blocks, it spends $n^2/(2p)$ time transposing them. The expressions for the communication time of all-to-all personalized communication on various architectures follow from Table 3.1 when we substitute the message size m by n^2/p^2. The algorithm is cost-optimal only on a hypercube with cut-though routing, on which the communication time is approximately $t_s(p-1) + t_w n^2/p + (1/2)t_h p \log p$. The total parallel run time for matrix transposition on this architecture is

$$T_P = \frac{n^2}{2p} + t_s(p-1) + t_w\frac{n^2}{p} + \frac{1}{2}t_h p \log p. \tag{5.3}$$

```
procedure MAT_VECT (A, x, y)
begin
    for i := 0 to n − 1 do
    begin
        y[i] := 0;
        for j := 0 to n − 1 do
            y[i] := y[i] + A[i, j] × x[j];
    endfor;
end MAT_VECT
```

Program 5.1 A serial algorithm for multiplying an $n \times n$ matrix A with an $n \times 1$ vector x to yield an $n \times 1$ product vector y.

5.3 Matrix-Vector Multiplication

This section addresses the problem of multiplying a dense $n \times n$ matrix A with an $n \times 1$ vector x to yield the $n \times 1$ result vector y. Program 5.1 shows a serial algorithm for this problem. The sequential algorithm requires n^2 multiplications and additions. Assuming that a multiplication and addition pair takes unit time, the sequential run time is

$$W = n^2. \tag{5.4}$$

At least three distinct parallel formulations of matrix-vector multiplication are possible, depending on whether rowwise striping, columnwise striping, or checkerboarding is used.

5.3.1 Rowwise Striping

This section details the parallel algorithm for matrix-vector multiplication using rowwise block striping. The parallel algorithm for columnwise block striping is similar (Problem 5.6) and has a similar expression for parallel run time. Figure 5.8 describes the distribution and movement of data for matrix-vector multiplication with block-striped partitioning.

One Row Per Processor

First, consider the case in which the $n \times n$ matrix is striped among n processors so that each processor stores one complete row of the matrix. The $n \times 1$ vector x is distributed such that each processor stores one of its elements. The initial distribution of the matrix and the vector for rowwise block striping is shown in Figure 5.8(a). Processor P_i initially stores $x[i]$ and $A[i, 0], A[i, 1], \ldots, A[i, n-1]$ and is responsible for computing $y[i]$. Vector x is multiplied with each row of the matrix (Program 5.1); hence, every processor needs the entire vector. Since each processor starts with only one element of x, an all-to-all broadcast is required to distribute all the elements to all the processors. Figure 5.8(b) illustrates this

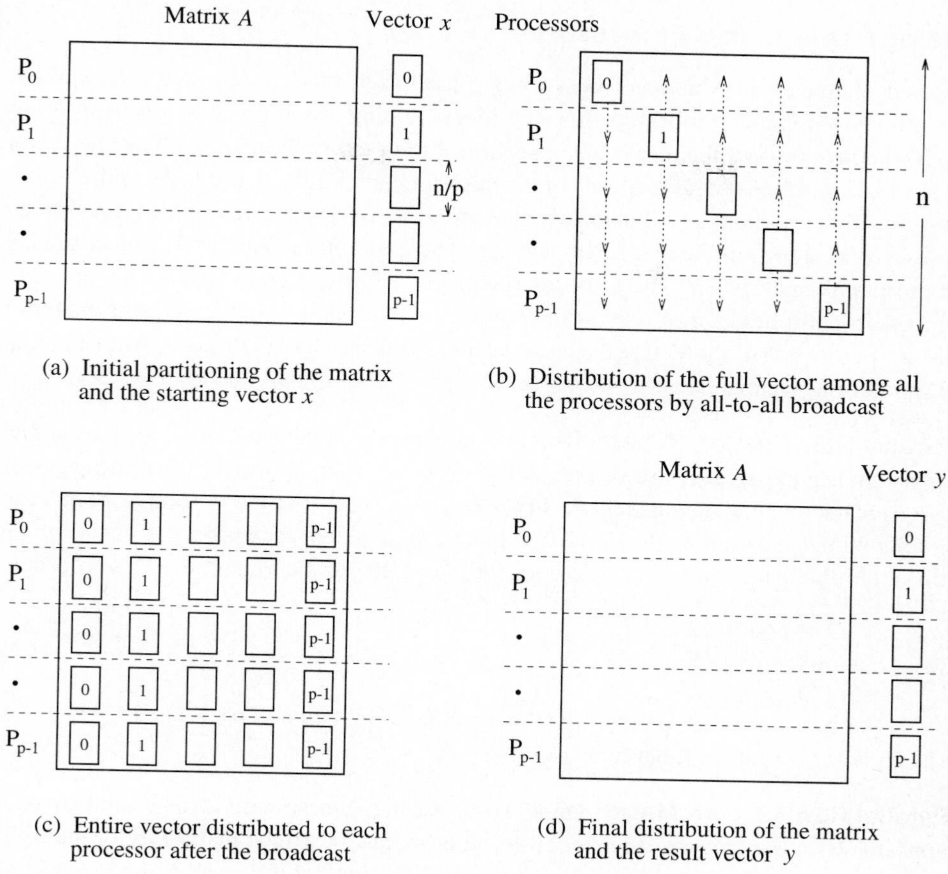

Matrix A
Vector x
Processors
P0
P1
Pp-1
0
1
p-1
n/p
n
(a) Initial partitioning of the matrix and the starting vector x
(b) Distribution of the full vector among all the processors by all-to-all broadcast
Matrix A
Vector y
(c) Entire vector distributed to each processor after the broadcast
(d) Final distribution of the matrix and the result vector y

Figure 5.8 Multiplication of an $n \times n$ matrix with an $n \times 1$ vector using rowwise block-striped partitioning. For the one-row-per-processor case, $p = n$.

communication step. After the vector x is distributed among the processors (Figure 5.8(c)), processor P_i computes $y[i] = \Sigma_{j=0}^{n-1}(A[i, j] \times x[j])$ (lines 7 and 8 of Program 5.1). As Figure 5.8(d) shows, the result vector y is stored exactly the way the starting vector x was stored.

Parallel Run Time Starting with one vector element per processor, the all-to-all broadcast of the vector elements among n processors requires $\Theta(n)$ time on any architecture. The multiplication of a single row of A with x is also performed by each processor in $\Theta(n)$ time. Thus, the entire procedure is completed by n processors in $\Theta(n)$ time, resulting in a processor-time product of $\Theta(n^2)$. The parallel algorithm is cost-optimal because the complexity of the serial algorithm is $\Theta(n^2)$.

Using Fewer than n Processors

Consider the case in which p processors are used such that $p < n$, and the matrix is partitioned among the processors by using block striping. Each processor initially stores n/p complete rows of the matrix and a portion of the vector of size n/p. Since the vector x has to be multiplied with each row of the matrix, every processor needs the entire vector (that is, all the portions residing on separate processors). This again requires an all-to-all broadcast as shown in Figures 5.8(b) and (c). The all-to-all broadcast takes place among p processors and involves messages of size n/p. After this communication step, each processor multiplies its n/p rows with the vector x to produce n/p elements of the result vector. Figure 5.8(d) shows that the result vector y is distributed in the same format as that of the starting vector x.

Parallel Run Time on Hypercube Assume that the architecture used for the parallel algorithm is a hypercube. According to Table 3.1, an all-to-all broadcast of messages of size n/p among p processors takes $t_s \log p + t_w(n/p)(p-1)$ time. For large p, this can be approximated by $t_s \log p + t_w n$. After the communication, each processor spends n^2/p time multiplying its n/p rows with the vector. Thus, the parallel run time of this procedure is

$$T_P = \frac{n^2}{p} + t_s \log p + t_w n. \tag{5.5}$$

The processor-time product for this parallel formulation is $n^2 + t_s p \log p + t_w np$. The algorithm is cost-optimal for $p = O(n)$.

Parallel Run Time on Mesh On a two-dimensional mesh with wrap-around connections, the term associated with t_s for all-to-all broadcast in striped matrix-vector multiplication is $2(\sqrt{p} - 1)$. This is the only change in Equation 5.5 if a mesh is used instead of a hypercube. As we discussed in Chapter 3, the communication time for all-to-all broadcast on a mesh is the same with both store-and-forward and cut-through routing schemes. Hence, irrespective of the routing scheme, the parallel run time is

$$T_P = \frac{n^2}{p} + 2t_s(\sqrt{p} - 1) + t_w n. \tag{5.6}$$

Scalability Analysis We now derive the isoefficiency function for matrix-vector multiplication on a hypercube along the lines of the analysis in Section 4.4 by considering the terms of the overhead function one at a time. Consider the parallel run time given by Equation 5.5 for the hypercube architecture. The relation $T_o = pT_P - W$ gives the following expression for the overhead function of block-striped matrix-vector multiplication on a hypercube:

$$T_o = t_s p \log p + t_w np \tag{5.7}$$

Recall from Chapter 4 that the central relation that determines the isoefficiency function of a parallel system is $W = KT_o$ (Equation 4.14), where $K = E/(1-E)$ and E

is the desired efficiency. Rewriting this relation for matrix-vector multiplication, first with only the t_s term of T_o,

$$W = Kt_s p \log p. \tag{5.8}$$

Equation 5.8 gives the isoefficiency term with respect to message startup time. Similarly, for the t_w term of the overhead function,

$$W = Kt_w np.$$

Since $W = n^2$ (Equation 5.4), we derive an expression for W in terms of p, K, and t_w (that is, the isoefficiency function due to t_w) as follows:

$$\begin{aligned} n^2 &= Kt_w np \\ n &= Kt_w p \\ n^2 &= K^2 t_w^2 p^2 \\ W &= K^2 t_w^2 p^2 \end{aligned} \tag{5.9}$$

Now consider the degree of concurrency of this parallel system. Using striped partitioning, a maximum of n processors can be used to multiply an $n \times n$ matrix with an $n \times 1$ vector. In other words, p is $O(n)$, which yields the following condition:

$$\begin{aligned} n &= \Omega(p) \\ n^2 &= \Omega(p^2) \\ W &= \Omega(p^2) \end{aligned} \tag{5.10}$$

The overall asymptotic isoefficiency function can be determined by comparing Equations 5.8, 5.9, and 5.10. Among the three, Equations 5.9 and 5.10 give the highest asymptotic rate at which the problem size must increase with the number of processors to maintain a fixed efficiency. This rate of $\Theta(p^2)$ is the asymptotic isoefficiency function of matrix-vector multiplication on a hypercube.

We can also perform a similar analysis for the mesh architecture. The isoefficiency function is $\Theta(p^2)$ for meshes with either store-and-forward or cut-through routing schemes (Problem 5.9). Thus, with striped partitioning, matrix-vector multiplication is not any more scalable on a hypercube than on a mesh.

5.3.2 Checkerboard Partitioning

This section discusses parallel matrix-vector multiplication for the case in which the matrix is distributed among the processors by using a block-checkerboard partitioning. Figure 5.9 shows the distribution of the matrix and the distribution and movement of vectors among the processors.

One Element Per Processor

We start with the simple case in which an $n \times n$ matrix is partitioned among n^2 processors such that each processor stores a single element. The $n \times 1$ vector x is distributed only in

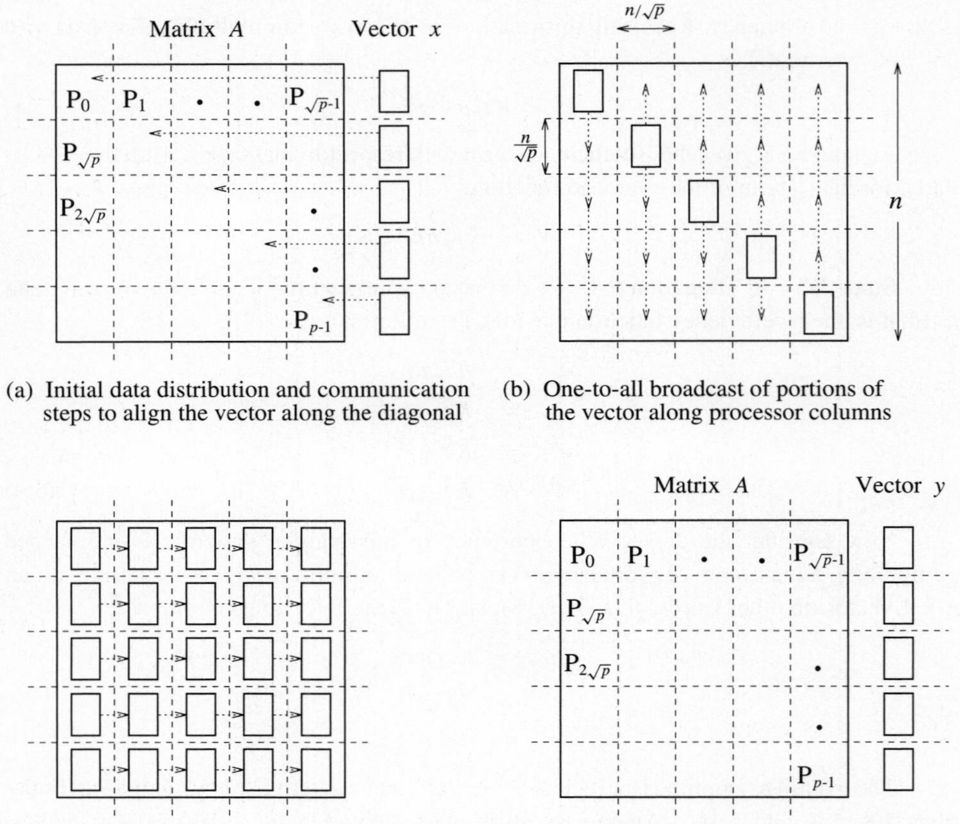

(a) Initial data distribution and communication steps to align the vector along the diagonal

(b) One-to-all broadcast of portions of the vector along processor columns

(c) Single-node accumulation of partial results

(d) Final distribution of the result vector

Figure 5.9 Matrix-vector multiplication with block-checkerboard partitioning. For the one-element-per-processor case, $p = n^2$ if the matrix size is $n \times n$.

the last column of n processors, each of which stores one element of the vector. Since the algorithm multiplies the elements of the vector x with the corresponding elements in each row of the matrix, the vector must be distributed such that the ith element of the vector is available to the ith element of each row of the matrix. The communication steps for this are shown in Figures 5.9(a) and (b). Notice the similarity of Figure 5.9 to Figure 5.8. Before the multiplication, the elements of the matrix and the vector must be in the same relative locations as in Figure 5.8(c). However, the vector communication steps differ between the partitioning strategies. For striping, the elements of the vector cross only the horizontal partition-boundaries (Figure 5.8), but for checkerboarding, the vector elements cross both horizontal and vertical partition-boundaries (Figure 5.9).

As Figure 5.9(a) shows, the first communication step for the checkerboard partitioning aligns the vector x along the principal diagonal of the matrix. Often, the vector is stored along the diagonal instead of the last column, in which case, this step is not required. The second step copies the vector elements from each diagonal processor to all the processors in the corresponding column. As Figure 5.9(b) shows, this step consists of n simultaneous one-to-all broadcast operations, one in each column of processors. After these two communication steps, each processor multiplies its matrix element with the corresponding element of x. To obtain the result vector y, the products computed for each row must be added, leaving the sums in the last column of processors. Figure 5.9(c) shows this step, which requires a single-node accumulation (Section 3.2) in each row with the last processor of the row as the destination. The parallel matrix-vector multiplication is complete after the accumulation step.

Parallel Run Time on Mesh and Hypercube Three basic communication operations are used in this algorithm: one-to-one communication to align the vector along the main diagonal, one-to-all broadcast of each vector element among the n processors of each column, and single-node accumulation in each row. On the mesh architecture, each of these operations takes $\Theta(n)$ time. On a hypercube, each operation takes $\Theta(\log n)$ time. Since each processor performs a single multiplication in constant time, the overall parallel run time of this algorithm is $\Theta(n)$ on an $n \times n$ mesh and $\Theta(\log n)$ on a hypercube with n^2 processors. The cost (processor-time product) is $\Theta(n^3)$ on a mesh and $\Theta(n^2 \log n)$ on a hypercube; hence, the algorithm is not cost-optimal on either architecture.

Using Fewer than n^2 Processors

A cost-optimal parallel implementation of matrix-vector multiplication with block-checkerboard partitioning of the matrix can be obtained if the granularity of computation at each processor is increased by using fewer than n^2 processors.

Consider a two-dimensional mesh of p processors in which each processor stores an $(n/\sqrt{p}) \times (n/\sqrt{p})$ block of the matrix. The vector is distributed in portions of $n/\sqrt{p}$ elements in the last column of processors only. Figure 5.9 also illustrates the initial data-mapping and the various communication steps for this case. The entire vector must be distributed on each row of processors before the multiplication can be performed. First, the vector is aligned along the main diagonal. For this, each processor in the rightmost column sends its $n/\sqrt{p}$ vector elements to the diagonal processor in its row. Then a columnwise one-to-all broadcast of these $n/\sqrt{p}$ elements takes place. Each processor then performs n^2/p multiplications and locally adds the $n/\sqrt{p}$ sets of products. At the end of this step, as shown in Figure 5.9(c), each processor has $n/\sqrt{p}$ partial sums that must be accumulated along each row to obtain the result vector. Hence, the last step of the algorithm is a single-node accumulation of the $n/\sqrt{p}$ values in each row, with the rightmost processor of the row as the destination.

Parallel Run Time on Mesh with Cut-Through Routing Assume that the processors are connected in a two-dimensional $\sqrt{p} \times \sqrt{p}$ cut-through routing mesh. Also assume that the mesh does not have any end-to-end wraparound links. The first step of sending a message of size $n/\sqrt{p}$ from the rightmost processor of a row to the diagonal processor (Figure 5.9(a)) takes the maximum time of $t_s + t_w n/\sqrt{p} + t_h\sqrt{p}$ for the first row of processors in the mesh. We can perform the columnwise one-to-all broadcast in approximately $(t_s + t_w n/\sqrt{p})\log(\sqrt{p}) + t_h\sqrt{p}$ time by using the procedure described in Section 3.2.2 for a ring and linear-array with cut-through routing. Ignoring the time to perform additions, the final rowwise single-node accumulation takes approximately $(t_s + t_w n/\sqrt{p})\log(\sqrt{p}) + t_h\sqrt{p}$ time for communication. Assuming that a multiplication and addition pair takes unit time, each processor spends approximately n^2/p time in computation. Thus, the parallel run time for this procedure is as follows:

$$\begin{aligned} T_P &= \overbrace{n^2/p}^{\text{computation}} + \overbrace{t_s + t_w n/\sqrt{p} + t_h\sqrt{p}}^{\text{aligning the vector along matrix diagonal}} + \\ &\quad \overbrace{(t_s + t_w n/\sqrt{p})\log(\sqrt{p}) + t_h\sqrt{p}}^{\text{columnwise one-to-all broadcast}} + \overbrace{(t_s + t_w n/\sqrt{p})\log(\sqrt{p}) + t_h\sqrt{p}}^{\text{single-node accumulation}} \\ &\approx \frac{n^2}{p} + t_s \log p + t_w \frac{n}{\sqrt{p}} \log p + 3t_h\sqrt{p} \end{aligned} \tag{5.11}$$

Scalability Analysis for Mesh with Cut-Through Routing By using Equations 5.4 and 5.11, and applying the relation $T_o = pT_p - W$ (Equation 4.8), we get the following expression for the overhead function for this parallel system:

$$T_o = t_s p \log p + t_w n\sqrt{p}\log p + 3t_h p^{3/2} \tag{5.12}$$

We now perform an approximate isoefficiency analysis along the lines of Section 4.4 by considering the terms of the overhead function one at a time (see Problem 5.10 for a more precise isoefficiency analysis). For the t_s term of the overhead function, Equation 4.14 yields

$$W = Kt_s p \log p. \tag{5.13}$$

Equation 5.13 gives the isoefficiency term with respect to the message startup time. We can obtain the isoefficiency function due to t_w by balancing the term $t_w n\sqrt{p}\log p$ with the problem size n^2. Using the isoefficiency relation of Equation 4.14, we get the following relations:

$$\begin{aligned} W = n^2 &= Kt_w n\sqrt{p}\log p \\ n &= Kt_w\sqrt{p}\log p \\ n^2 &= K^2t_w^2 p\log^2 p \\ W &= K^2t_w^2 p\log^2 p \end{aligned} \tag{5.14}$$

Substituting the t_h term of the overhead function in the isoefficiency relation of Equation 4.14 yields

$$W = 3Kt_h p^{3/2}. \tag{5.15}$$

Finally, considering that the degree of concurrency of checkerboard partitioning is n^2 (that is, a maximum of n^2 processors can be used), we arrive at the following relation:

$$\begin{aligned} p &= O(n^2) \\ n^2 &= \Omega(p) \\ W &= \Omega(p) \end{aligned} \qquad (5.16)$$

Among Equations 5.13, 5.14, 5.15, and 5.16, the one with the largest right-hand side expression determines the overall isoefficiency function for this parallel system. To simplify the analysis, we ignore the impact of the constants and consider only the asymptotic rate of the growth of problem size that is necessary to maintain constant efficiency. The asymptotic isoefficiency terms due to t_w and t_h (Equations 5.14 and 5.15) clearly dominate the one due to t_s (Equation 5.13). The overall asymptotic isoefficiency function is given by $\Theta(\max\{p^{3/2}, p\log^2 p\})$. Note that $p^{3/2} > p\log^2 p$ only for $p > 65,536$. Depending on the values of the hardware-related constants, either the t_w or the t_h term may determine the overall isoefficiency function. However, for the following cost-optimality analysis, we assume that the overall isoefficiency function is $\Theta(p\log^2 p)$.

The isoefficiency function also determines the criterion for cost-optimality (Section 4.4.4). Assuming an isoefficiency function of $\Theta(p\log^2 p)$, the maximum number of processors that can be used cost-optimally for a given problem size W is determined by the following relations:

$$\begin{aligned} p\log^2 p &= O(n^2) \qquad (5.17) \\ \log p + 2\log\log p &= O(\log n) \end{aligned}$$

Ignoring the lower-order terms,

$$\log p = O(\log n).$$

Substituting $\log n$ for $\log p$ in Equation 5.17,

$$\begin{aligned} p\log^2 n &= O(n^2), \\ p &= O\left(\frac{n^2}{\log^2 n}\right). \end{aligned} \qquad (5.18)$$

The right-hand side of Equation 5.18 gives an asymptotic upper bound on the number of processors that can be used cost-optimally for an $n \times n$ matrix-vector multiplication on a mesh with cut-through routing if a checkerboard partitioning is used.

Parallel Run Time for Mesh with Store-and-Forward Routing The parallel run time for multiplying an $n \times n$ matrix with an $n \times 1$ vector on a p-processor square mesh with store-and-forward routing is approximately $n^2/p + 2t_s\sqrt{p} + 3t_w n$. The resulting isoefficiency function is $\Theta(p^2)$ due to the t_w term. Thus, both the parallel execution time and isoefficiency function are much worse with store-and-forward routing than with

```
1.  procedure MAT_MULT (A, B, C)
2.  begin
3.      for i := 0 to n − 1 do
4.          for j := 0 to n − 1 do
5.              begin
6.                  C[i, j] := 0;
7.                  for k := 0 to n − 1 do
8.                      C[i, j] := C[i, j] + A[i, k] × B[k, j];
9.              endfor;
10. end MAT_MULT
```

Program 5.2 The conventional serial algorithm for multiplication of two $n \times n$ matrices.

cut-through routing. Note that this difference between cut-through and store-and-forward routing is evident only when we analyze this algorithm for multiple elements per processor. In a fine-grain implementation on an $n \times n$ mesh, in which each processor stores a single element of the $n \times n$ matrix, the parallel run time is $\Theta(n)$ for both cut-through and store-and-forward routing.

Comparison of Striped and Checkerboard Partitionings for Matrix-Vector Multiplication

A comparison of Equations 5.6, and 5.11 shows that matrix-vector multiplication is faster with block-checkerboard partitioning of the matrix than with block-striped partitioning for the same number of processors. If the number of processors is greater than n, then striped partitioning cannot be used. However, even if the number of processors is less than or equal to n, the analysis in this section suggests that checkerboard partitioning is preferable. A similar conclusion holds for the hypercube architecture as well.

Among the two partitioning schemes, checkerboard partitioning has a better (smaller) asymptotic isoefficiency function. Thus, matrix-vector multiplication is more scalable with checkerboard partitioning; that is, it can deliver the same efficiency on more processors with checkerboard partitioning than with striped partitioning.

5.4 Matrix Multiplication

This section discusses parallel algorithms for multiplying two $n \times n$ dense, square matrices A and B to yield the product matrix $C = A \times B$. All parallel matrix multiplication algorithms in this chapter are based on the conventional serial algorithm shown in Program 5.2. If we assume that an addition and multiplication pair (line 8) takes unit time, then the sequential run time of this algorithm is n^3. Matrix multiplication algorithms with better asymptotic sequential complexities are available; for example, Strassen's algorithm. However, for the sake of simplicity, in this book we assume that the conventional algorithm

```
1.  procedure BLOCK_MAT_MULT (A, B, C)
2.  begin
3.      for i := 0 to q - 1 do
4.          for j := 0 to q - 1 do
5.              begin
6.                  Initialize all elements of C_{i,j} to zero;
7.                  for k := 0 to q - 1 do
8.                      C_{i,j} := C_{i,j} + A_{i,k} × B_{k,j};
9.              endfor;
10. end BLOCK_MAT_MULT
```

Program 5.3 The block matrix multiplication algorithm for $n \times n$ matrices with a block size of $(n/q) \times (n/q)$.

is the best available serial algorithm. Problem 5.11 explores the performance of parallel matrix multiplication regarding Strassen's method as the base algorithm.

A concept that is useful in a variety of matrix algorithms (including matrix multiplication) is that of block matrix operations. We can often express a matrix computation involving scalar algebraic operations on all its elements in terms of identical matrix algebraic operations on blocks or submatrices of the original matrix. Such algebraic operations on the submatrices are called ***block matrix operations***. For example, an $n \times n$ matrix A can be regarded as a $q \times q$ array of blocks $A_{i,j}$ $(0 \leq i, j < q)$ such that each bock is an $(n/q) \times (n/q)$ submatrix. The matrix multiplication algorithm in Program 5.2 can then be rewritten as Program 5.3, in which the multiplication and addition operations on line 8 are matrix multiplication and matrix addition, respectively. Not only are the final results of Programs 5.2 and 5.3 identical, but so are the total numbers of scalar additions and multiplications performed by each. Program 5.2 performs n^3 additions and multiplications, and Program 5.3 performs q^3 matrix multiplications, each involving $(n/q) \times (n/q)$ matrices and requiring $(n/q)^3$ additions and multiplications. We can use p processors to implement the block version of matrix multiplication in parallel by choosing $q = \sqrt{p}$ and computing a distinct $C_{i,j}$ block at each processor.

In the following sections, we describe a few ways of parallelizing Program 5.3. Each of the following parallel matrix multiplication algorithms use a block-checkerboard partitioning of the matrices.

5.4.1 A Simple Parallel Algorithm

Consider two $n \times n$ matrices A and B partitioned into p blocks $A_{i,j}$ and $B_{i,j}$ $(0 \leq i, j < \sqrt{p})$ of size $(n/\sqrt{p}) \times (n/\sqrt{p})$ each. These blocks are mapped onto a $\sqrt{p} \times \sqrt{p}$ logical mesh of processors. The processors are labeled from $P_{0,0}$ to $P_{\sqrt{p}-1,\sqrt{p}-1}$. Processor $P_{i,j}$ initially stores $A_{i,j}$ and $B_{i,j}$ and computes block $C_{i,j}$ of the result matrix. Computing submatrix $C_{i,j}$ requires all submatrices $A_{i,k}$ and $B_{k,j}$ for $0 \leq k < \sqrt{p}$. To acquire all the required blocks, an all-to-all broadcast of matrix A's blocks is performed in each row of processors, and an all-to-all broadcast of matrix B's blocks is performed in each column. After $P_{i,j}$ acquires $A_{i,0}, A_{i,1}, \ldots, A_{i,\sqrt{p}-1}$ and $B_{0,j}, B_{1,j}, \ldots, B_{\sqrt{p}-1,j}$, it performs the submatrix multiplication and addition step of lines 7 and 8 in Program 5.3.

Performance and Scalability Analysis for Hypercube Assume that the logical mesh of processors is embedded into a p-processor hypercube. The algorithm requires two all-to-all broadcast steps (each consisting of $\sqrt{p}$ concurrent broadcasts in all rows and columns of the processor mesh) among groups of $\sqrt{p}$ processors. The messages consist of submatrices of n^2/p elements. From Table 3.1, the total communication time is $2(t_s \log(\sqrt{p}) + t_w(n^2/p)(\sqrt{p} - 1))$ for the hypercube. After the communication step, each processor computes a submatrix $C_{i,j}$, which requires $\sqrt{p}$ multiplications of $(n/\sqrt{p}) \times (n/\sqrt{p})$ submatrices (lines 7 and 8 of Program 5.3 with $q = \sqrt{p}$). This takes a total of $\sqrt{p} \times (n/\sqrt{p})^3 = n^3/p$ time. Thus, the parallel run time for multiplying two $n \times n$ matrices using this algorithm on a p-processor hypercube is approximately

$$T_P = \frac{n^3}{p} + t_s \log p + 2t_w \frac{n^2}{\sqrt{p}}. \tag{5.19}$$

The processor-time product is $n^3 + t_s p \log p + 2t_w n^2 \sqrt{p}$, and the parallel system is cost-optimal for $p = O(n^2)$.

The isoefficiency functions due to t_s and t_w are $t_s p \log p$ and $8(t_w)^3 p^{3/2}$, respectively. Hence, the overall isoefficiency function due to the communication overhead is $\Theta(p^{3/2})$. This algorithm can use a maximum of n^2 processors; hence, $p \leq n^2$ or $n^3 \geq p^{3/2}$. Therefore, the isoefficiency function due to concurrency is also $\Theta(p^{3/2})$.

A notable drawback of this algorithm is its excessive memory requirements. At the end of the communication phase, every processor has $\sqrt{p}$ blocks of both matrices A and B. Since each block requires $\Theta(n^2/p)$ memory, every processor requires $\Theta(n^2/\sqrt{p})$ memory. The total memory requirement over all the processors is $\Theta(n^2\sqrt{p})$, which is $\sqrt{p}$ times the memory requirement of the sequential algorithm.

Performance on a Mesh If we use a mesh instead of a hypercube, only the term associated with t_s in the parallel run time (Equation 5.19) of this matrix multiplication algorithm is affected. On a wraparound mesh with store-and-forward routing, each all-to-all broadcast among the $\sqrt{p}$ processors of a row or column of the mesh takes approximately $t_s\sqrt{p} + t_w n^2/\sqrt{p}$ time. Thus, the total parallel run time is

$$T_P = \frac{n^3}{p} + 2t_s\sqrt{p} + 2t_w \frac{n^2}{\sqrt{p}}. \tag{5.20}$$

If the messages are large, the parallel execution time is the same on a mesh without wraparound connections that supports cut-through routing and bidirectional communication (Problem 3.20).

5.4.2 Cannon's Algorithm

Cannon's algorithm is a memory-efficient version of the simple algorithm presented in Section 5.4.1. To study this algorithm, we again partition matrices A and B into p square blocks. We label the processors from $P_{0,0}$ to $P_{\sqrt{p}-1,\sqrt{p}-1}$, and initially assign $A_{i,j}$ and $B_{i,j}$ to $P_{i,j}$. Although every processor in the ith row requires all $\sqrt{p}$ submatrices $A_{i,k}$ $(0 \leq k < \sqrt{p})$, it is possible to schedule the computations of the $\sqrt{p}$ processors of the ith row such that, at any given time, each processor is using a different $A_{i,k}$. These blocks can be systematically rotated among the processors after every submatrix multiplication so that every processor gets a fresh $A_{i,k}$ after each rotation. If an identical schedule is applied to the columns, then no processor holds more than one block of each matrix at any time, and the total memory requirement of the algorithm over all the processors is $\Theta(n^2)$. Cannon's algorithm is based on this idea. The scheduling for the multiplication of submatrices on separate processors in Cannon's algorithm is illustrated in Figure 5.10 for 16 processors.

The first communication step of the algorithm aligns the blocks of A and B in such a way that each processor multiplies its local submatrices. As Figure 5.10(a) shows, this alignment is achieved for matrix A by shifting all submatrices $A_{i,j}$ to the left (with wraparound) by i steps. Similarly, as shown in Figure 5.10(b), all submatrices $B_{i,j}$ are shifted up (with wraparound) by j steps. These are circular shift operations (Section 3.6) in each row and column of processors, which leave processor $P_{i,j}$ with submatrices $A_{i,(j+i)\text{mod}\sqrt{p}}$ and $B_{(i+j)\text{mod}\sqrt{p},j}$. Figure 5.10(c) shows the blocks of A and B after the initial alignment, when each processor is ready for the first submatrix multiplication. After a submatrix multiplication step, each block of A moves one step left and each block of B moves one step up (again with wraparound), as shown in Figure 5.10(d). A sequence of $\sqrt{p}$ such submatrix multiplications and single-step shifts pairs up each $A_{i,k}$ and $B_{k,j}$ for k $(0 \leq k < \sqrt{p})$ at $P_{i,j}$. This completes the multiplication of matrices A and B.

Performance on a Hypercube The initial alignment of the two matrices (Figures 5.10 (a) and (b)) involves a rowwise and a columnwise circular shift. In any of these shifts, the maximum distance over which a block shifts is $\sqrt{p}-1$. On a hypercube with cut-through routing, the two shift operations require a total of $2(t_s + t_w n^2/p + t_h \log \sqrt{p})$ time. Each of the $\sqrt{p}$ single-step shifts in the compute-and-shift phase of the algorithm takes $t_s + t_w n^2/p$ time. Thus, the total communication time (for both matrices) during this phase of the algorithm is $2(t_s + t_w n^2/p)\sqrt{p}$. For large enough p, the communication time for the initial alignment can be disregarded in comparison with the time spent in communication during the compute-and-shift phase.

In this algorithm, each processor performs $\sqrt{p}$ multiplications of $(n/\sqrt{p}) \times (n/\sqrt{p})$ submatrices. Assuming that a multiplication and addition pair takes unit time, the total time that each processor spends in computation is n^3/p. Thus, the approximate overall parallel run time of this algorithm is

$$T_P = \frac{n^3}{p} + 2\sqrt{p}t_s + 2t_w\frac{n^2}{\sqrt{p}}. \tag{5.21}$$

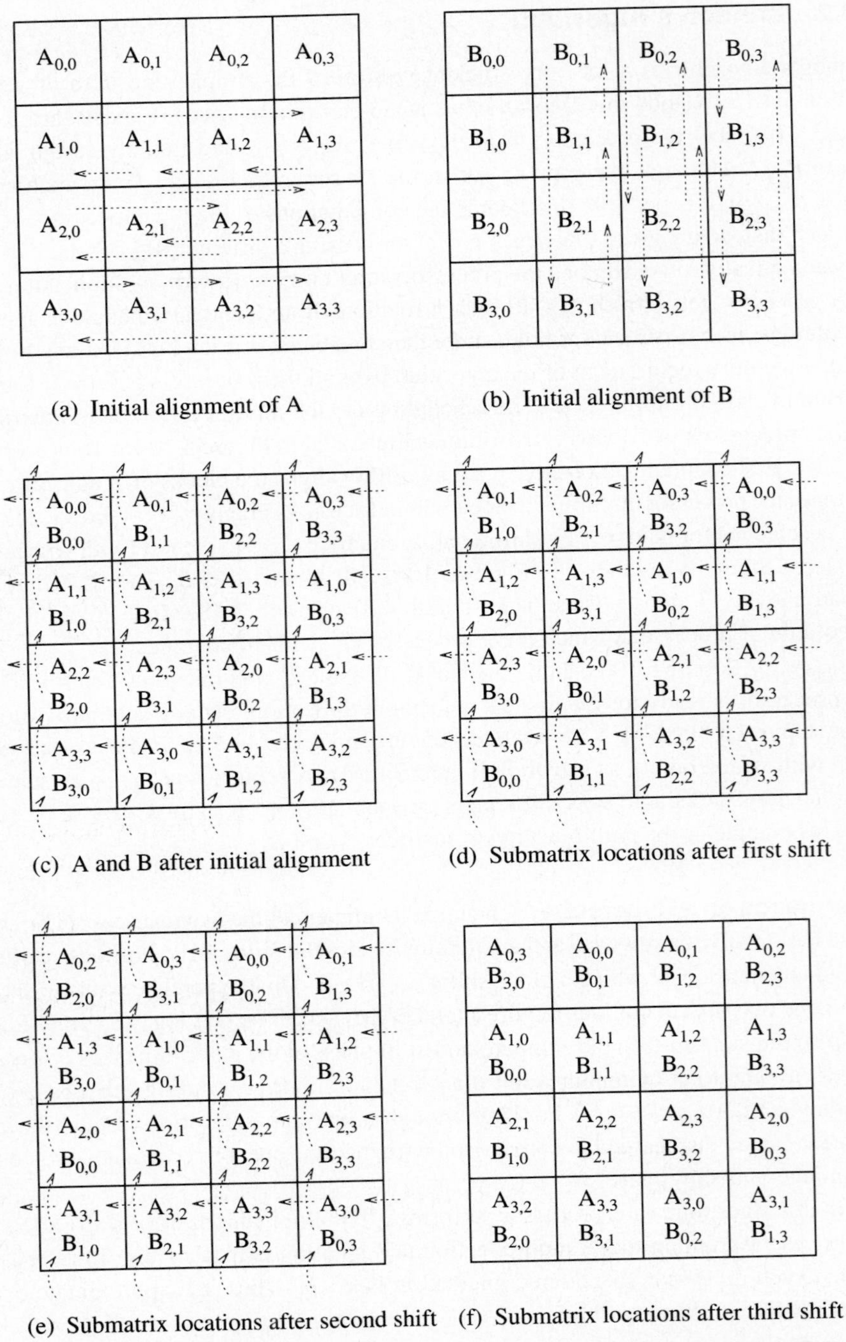

Figure 5.10 The communication steps in Cannon's algorithm on 16 processors.

The cost-optimality condition for Cannon's algorithm on a hypercube is identical to that for the simple algorithm presented in Section 5.4.1. As in the simple algorithm, the isoefficiency function of Cannon's algorithm is $\Theta(p^{3/2})$.

Parallel Run Time on a Mesh If implemented on a mesh, the time required for the initial alignment of matrices is $2(t_s + t_w n^2/p)\sqrt{p}$. This is the same as the communication time of the compute-and-shift phase of the algorithm. Therefore, the total parallel execution time of Cannon's algorithm on a square mesh is

$$T_P = \frac{n^3}{p} + 4\sqrt{p}t_s + 4t_w \frac{n^2}{\sqrt{p}}. \tag{5.22}$$

5.4.3 Fox's Algorithm

This section describes another well-known memory-efficient parallel algorithm for multiplying dense matrices. Again, both $n \times n$ matrices A and B are partitioned among p processors so that each processor initially stores $(n/\sqrt{p}) \times (n/\sqrt{p})$ blocks of each matrix. The algorithm uses one-to-all broadcasts of the blocks of matrix A in processor rows, and single-step circular upward shifts of the blocks of matrix B along processor columns. Initially, each diagonal block $A_{i,i}$ is selected for broadcast. The algorithm performs $\sqrt{p}$ iterations of the following sequence of steps:

(1) Broadcast the selected block of A among the $\sqrt{p}$ processors of the row in which the block lies.
(2) Multiply the block of A received as a result of the broadcast with the resident block of B (the processor initiating the broadcast already has the required block of A and does not have to receive it).
(3) Send the block of B to the processor directly above it (with wraparound) in the processor column, and receive a fresh block of B from the processor below it.
(4) Select the block of A for the next row broadcast. If $A_{i,j}$ was broadcast in the current step, then select $A_{i,(j+1)\bmod\sqrt{p}}$ for the next broadcast.

Parallel Run Time on a Hypercube Figure 5.11 shows the four communication steps for 16 processors. After $\sqrt{p}$ steps, processor $P_{i,j}$ has performed the multiplication $A_{i,k} \times B_{k,j}$ for each k from 0 to $\sqrt{p} - 1$. Each processor spends a total of n^3/p time performing computation. The time for the one-to-all broadcasts of blocks of A dominates the time for single-step shifts of the blocks of B. If the logical mesh of processors is embedded in a hypercube, then each broadcast can be performed in $(t_s + t_w n^2/p)\log\sqrt{p}$ time (Section 3.2.1). Since this operation is repeated $\sqrt{p}$ times, the total communication time is $(1/2)(t_s\sqrt{p} + t_w n^2/\sqrt{p})\log p$ and the parallel run time is

$$T_P = \frac{n^3}{p} + \frac{1}{2}t_s\sqrt{p}\log p + t_w\frac{n^2}{\sqrt{p}}\log p. \tag{5.23}$$

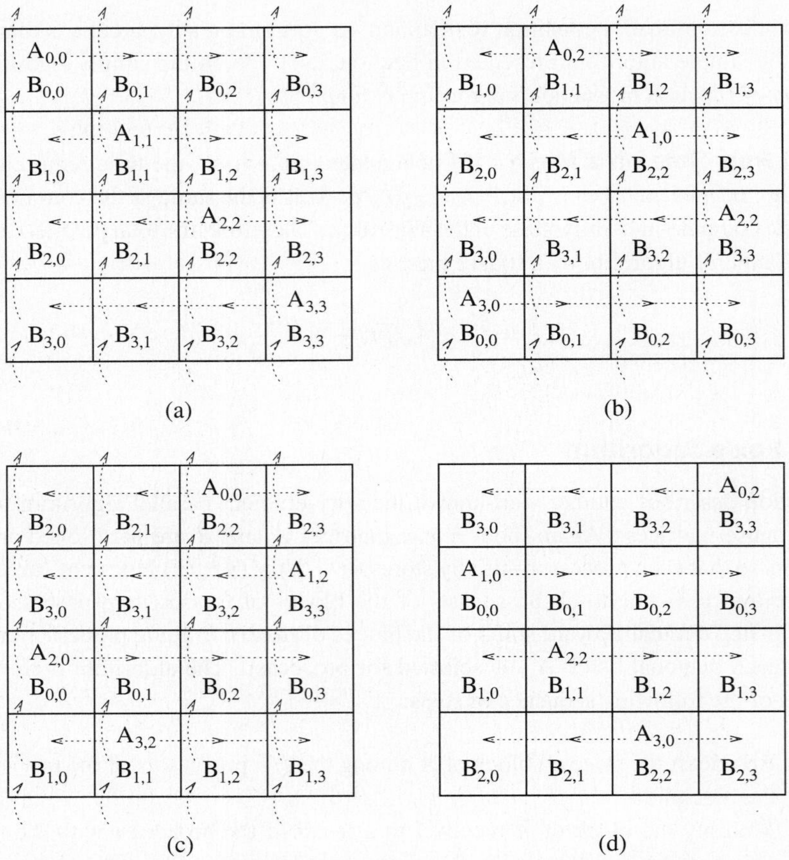

Figure 5.11 The communication steps in Fox's algorithm on 16 processors.

The isoefficiency function of Fox's algorithm on the hypercube is $\Theta(p^{3/2} \log p)$ due to t_s and $\Theta(p^{3/2} (\log p)^3)$ due to t_w. Although the parallel run time and the scalability of this algorithm are inferior to those for both the simple algorithm and Cannon's algorithm, the run time of this algorithm can be improved by interleaving computation and pipelined communication (Problem 5.23).

5.4.4 The DNS Algorithm

The matrix multiplication algorithms presented so far use the block-checkerboard partitioning of matrices and use a maximum of n^2 processors for $n \times n$ matrices. As a result, these algorithms have a parallel run time of $\Omega(n)$ because there are $\Theta(n^3)$ operations in the serial algorithm. We now present a parallel algorithm that can use up to n^3 processors and that performs matrix multiplication in $\Theta(\log n)$ time by using $\Omega(n^3 / \log n)$ processors.

This algorithm is known as the DNS algorithm because it is due to Dekel, Nassimi, and Sahni.

We first describe the algorithm for a CREW PRAM, without concern for any particular interconnection network. Assume that n^3 processors are available for multiplying two $n \times n$ matrices. These processors are arranged in a three-dimensional $n \times n \times n$ logical array. Since the matrix multiplication algorithm performs n^3 scalar multiplications, each of the n^3 processors is assigned a single scalar multiplication. The processors are labeled according to their location in the array, and the multiplication $A[i, k] \times B[k, j]$ is assigned to processor $\text{P}_{i,j,k}$ $(0 \leq i, j, k < n)$. After each processor performs a single multiplication, the contents of $\text{P}_{i,j,0}, \text{P}_{i,j,1}, \ldots, \text{P}_{i,j,n-1}$ are added to obtain $C[i, j]$. The additions for all $C[i, j]$ can be carried out simultaneously in $\log n$ steps. Thus, it takes one step to multiply and $\log n$ steps to add; that is, it takes $\Theta(\log n)$ time to multiply the $n \times n$ matrices on a CREW PRAM.

We now describe a parallel implementation of matrix multiplication based on this idea, using a hypercube-connected parallel computer. Assume that the logical three-dimensional array is mapped onto a hypercube with $n^3 = 2^{3d}$ processors. As Figure 5.12 shows, the processor arrangement can be visualized as n planes of $n \times n$ processors each. Every plane corresponds to a different value of k. Initially, as shown in Figure 5.12(a), the matrices are distributed among the n^2 processors of the plane corresponding to $k = 0$ at the base of the three-dimensional processor array. Processor $\text{P}_{i,j,0}$ initially stores $A[i, j]$ and $B[i, j]$.

In the CREW PRAM algorithm, conceptually, the vertical column of processors $\text{P}_{i,j,*}$ computes the dot product of row $A[i, *]$ and column $B[*, j]$. No data-movement step is necessary because in a CREW PRAM, each processor can access any location in constant time. However, on a hypercube, rows of A and columns of B need to be moved appropriately so that each vertical column of processors $\text{P}_{i,j,*}$ has row $A[i, *]$ and column $B[*, j]$. More precisely, processor $\text{P}_{i,j,k}$ should have $A[i, k]$ and $B[k, j]$.

The communication pattern for distributing the elements of matrix A among the processors is shown in Figures 5.12(a)–(c). First, each column of A moves to a different plane such that the jth column occupies the same position in the plane corresponding to $k = j$ as it initially did in the plane corresponding to $k = 0$. The distribution of A after moving $A[i, j]$ from $\text{P}_{i,j,0}$ to $\text{P}_{i,j,j}$ is shown in Figure 5.12(b). Now all the columns of A are replicated n times in their respective planes by a parallel one-to-all broadcast along the j axis. The result of this step is shown in Figure 5.12(c), in which the n processors $\text{P}_{i,0,j}$, $\text{P}_{i,1,j}, \ldots, \text{P}_{i,n-1,j}$ receive a copy of $A[i, j]$ from $\text{P}_{i,j,j}$. At this point, each vertical column of processors $\text{P}_{i,j,*}$ has row $A[i, *]$. More precisely, processor $\text{P}_{i,j,k}$ has $A[i, k]$.

For matrix B, the communication steps are similar, but the roles of i and j in processor subscripts are switched. In the first one-to-one communication step, $B[i, j]$ is moved from $\text{P}_{i,j,0}$ to $\text{P}_{i,j,i}$. Then it is broadcast from $\text{P}_{i,j,i}$ among $\text{P}_{0,j,i}, \text{P}_{1,j,i}, \ldots, \text{P}_{n-1,j,i}$. The distribution of B after this one-to-all broadcast along the i axis is shown in Figure 5.12(d). At this point, each vertical column of processors $\text{P}_{i,j,*}$ has column $B[*, j]$. Now processor $\text{P}_{i,j,k}$ has $B[k, j]$, in addition to $A[i, k]$.

After these communication steps, $A[i, k]$ and $B[k, j]$ are multiplied at $\text{P}_{i,j,k}$. Now each element $C[i, j]$ of the product matrix is obtained by a single-node accumulation along

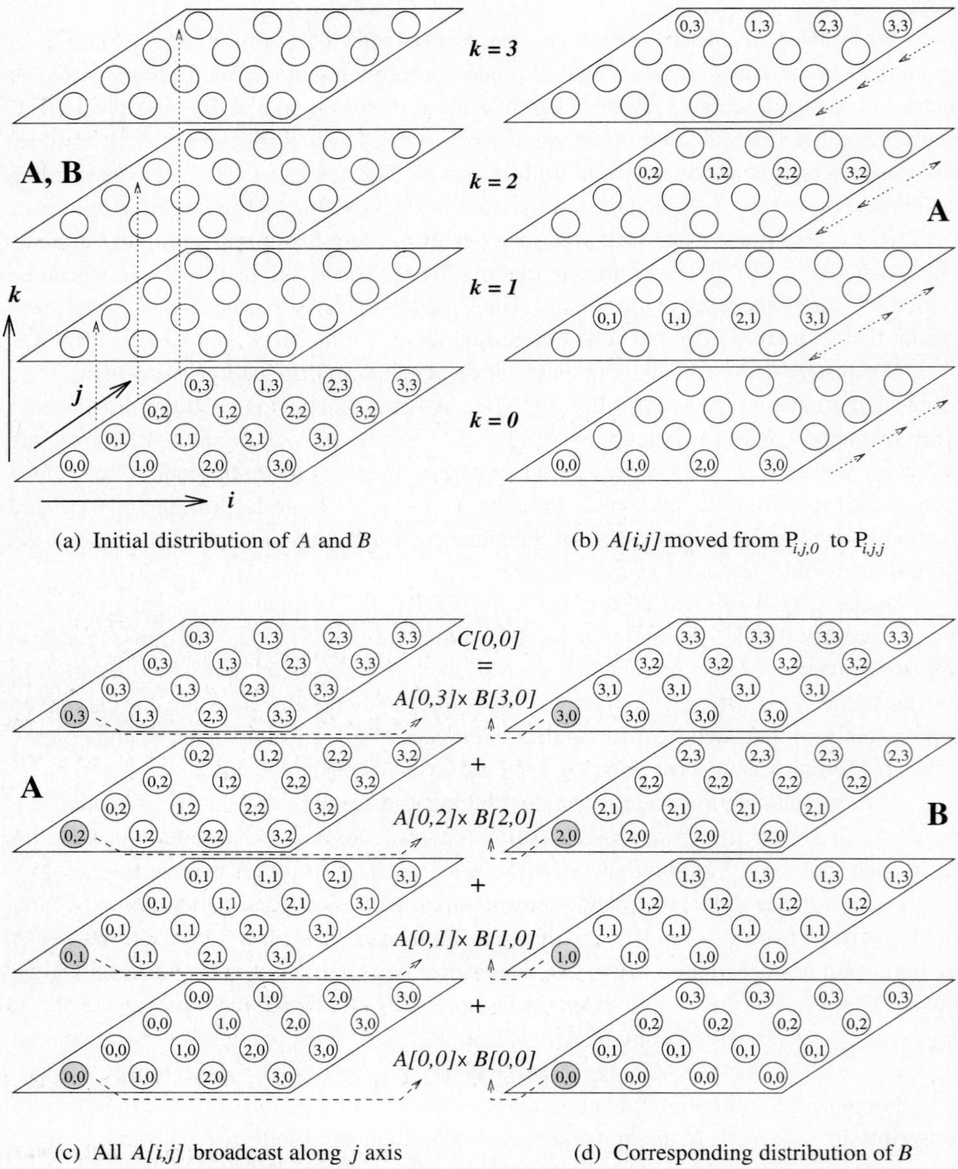

(a) Initial distribution of A and B

(b) $A[i,j]$ moved from $P_{i,j,0}$ to $P_{i,j,j}$

(c) All $A[i,j]$ broadcast along j axis

(d) Corresponding distribution of B

Figure 5.12 The communication steps in the DNS algorithm while multiplying 4 × 4 matrices A and B on 64 processors. The shaded processors in part (c) store elements of the first row of A and the shaded processors in part (d) store elements of the first column of B.

the k axis. During this step, processor $P_{i,j,0}$ accumulates the results of the multiplication from processors $P_{i,j,1}, \ldots, P_{i,j,n-1}$. Figure 5.12 shows this step for $C[0, 0]$.

The DNS algorithm has three main communication steps: (1) moving the columns of A and the rows of B to their respective planes, (2) performing one-to-all broadcast along the j axis for A and along the i axis for B, and (3) single-node accumulation along the k axis. All these operations are performed within subcubes of n hypercube processors and take $\Theta(\log n)$ time. Thus, the parallel run time for multiplying two $n \times n$ matrices using the DNS algorithm on a hypercube with n^3 processors is $\Theta(\log n)$.

DNS Algorithm with Fewer than n³ Processors

The DNS algorithm is not cost-optimal for n^3 processors, since its processor-time product $\Theta(n^3 \log n)$ exceeds the $\Theta(n^3)$ sequential complexity of matrix multiplication. In this subsection, we present a cost-optimal version of this algorithm that uses fewer than n^3 processors. Another variant of the DNS algorithm that uses fewer than n^3 processors is described in Problem 5.13.

Assume that the number of processors p is equal to q^3 for some $q < n$. To implement the DNS algorithm, the two matrices are partitioned into blocks of size $(n/q) \times (n/q)$. Each matrix can thus be regarded as a $q \times q$ two-dimensional square array of blocks. The implementation of this algorithm on q^3 processors is very similar to that on n^3 processors. The only difference is that now we operate on blocks rather than on individual elements. Since $1 \leq q \leq n$, the number of processors can vary between 1 and n^3.

Run Time on a Hypercube with Cut-Through Routing The first one-to-one communication step is performed for both A and B, and takes $t_s + t_w(n/q)^2 + t_h \log q$ time for each matrix on a hypercube with cut-through routing (Section 3.1). The second step of one-to-all broadcast is also performed for both matrices and takes $t_s \log q + t_w(n/q)^2 \log q$ time for each matrix (Section 3.2.1). The final single-node accumulation is performed only once (for matrix C) and takes $t_s \log q + t_w(n/q)^2 \log q$ time (Section 3.2.1). Assuming that each multiplication and addition pair takes unit time, the multiplication of $(n/q) \times (n/q)$ submatrices in each processor takes $(n/q)^3$ time. We can ignore the communication time for the first one-to-one communication step (because it is much smaller than the communication time of one-to-all broadcasts and single-node accumulation) and the computation time for addition in the final accumulation phase (because it is of a smaller order of magnitude than the computation time for multiplying the submatrices). With these assumptions, we get the following approximate expression for the parallel run time of the DNS algorithm on a hypercube with cut-through routing:

$$T_P \approx \left(\frac{n}{q}\right)^3 + 3t_s \log q + 3t_w \left(\frac{n}{q}\right)^2 \log q$$

Since $q = p^{1/3}$, we get

$$T_P = \frac{n^3}{p} + t_s \log p + t_w \frac{n^2}{p^{2/3}} \log p. \tag{5.24}$$

The cost of this parallel system is $n^3 + t_s p \log p + t_w n^2 p^{1/3} \log p$. The isoefficiency function is $\Theta(p \log p)$. The parallel system is cost-optimal for $n^3 = \Omega(p \log p)$, or $p = O(n^3 / \log n)$.

Run Time on a 3-D Mesh with Cut-Through Routing The DNS algorithm is not suitable for a two-dimensional mesh. The reason is that the algorithm naturally maps onto a three-dimensional mesh of processors, and a three-dimensional mesh cannot be embedded into a two-dimensional mesh without excessive congestion and dilation (Section 2.5). On a three-dimensional mesh with cut-through routing, the hypercube algorithm can be implemented without modification. The only change in the parallel run time expression of Equation 5.24 is the addition of a term $3t_h p^{1/3}$ (Problem 5.12).

5.5 Solving a System of Linear Equations

This section discusses the problem of solving a system of linear equations of the form

$$\begin{array}{ccccccccc}
a_{0,0}x_0 & + & a_{0,1}x_1 & + & \cdots & + & a_{0,n-1}x_{n-1} & = & b_0, \\
a_{1,0}x_0 & + & a_{1,1}x_1 & + & \cdots & + & a_{1,n-1}x_{n-1} & = & b_1, \\
\vdots & & \vdots & & & & \vdots & & \vdots \\
a_{n-1,0}x_0 & + & a_{n-1,1}x_1 & + & \cdots & + & a_{n-1,n-1}x_{n-1} & = & b_{n-1}.
\end{array}$$

In matrix notation, this system is written as $Ax = b$. Here A is a dense $n \times n$ matrix of coefficients such that $A[i, j] = a_{i,j}$, b is an $n \times 1$ vector $[b_0, b_1, \ldots, b_{n-1}]^T$, and x is the desired solution vector $[x_0, x_1, \ldots, x_{n-1}]^T$. We will make all subsequent references to $a_{i,j}$ by $A[i, j]$ and x_i by $x[i]$.

A system of equations $Ax = b$ is usually solved in two stages. First, through a series of algebraic manipulations, the original system of equations is reduced to an upper-triangular system of the form

$$\begin{array}{ccccccccccc}
x_0 & + & u_{0,1}x_1 & + & u_{0,2}x_2 & + & \cdots & + & u_{0,n-1}x_{n-1} & = & y_0, \\
 & & x_1 & + & u_{1,2}x_2 & + & \cdots & + & u_{1,n-1}x_{n-1} & = & y_1, \\
 & & & & & & & & \vdots & & \vdots \\
 & & & & & & & & x_{n-1} & = & y_{n-1}.
\end{array}$$

We write this as $Ux = y$, where U is a unit upper-triangular matrix—one in which all subdiagonal entries are zero and all principal diagonal entries are equal to one. Formally, $U[i, j] = 0$ if $i > j$, otherwise $U[i, j] = u_{i,j}$. Furthermore, $U[i, i] = 1$ for $0 \le i < n$. In the second stage of solving a system of linear equations, the upper-triangular system is solved for the variables in reverse order from $x[n-1]$ to $x[0]$ by a procedure known as ***back-substitution*** (Section 5.5.3).

```
1.  procedure GAUSSIAN_ELIMINATION (A, b, y)
2.  begin
3.     for k := 0 to n − 1 do                  /* Outer loop */
4.     begin
5.        for j := k + 1 to n − 1 do
6.           A[k, j] := A[k, j]/A[k, k];  /* Division step */
7.        y[k] := b[k]/A[k, k];
8.        A[k, k] := 1;
9.        for i := k + 1 to n − 1 do
10.       begin
11.          for j := k + 1 to n − 1 do
12.             A[i, j] := A[i, j] − A[i, k] × A[k, j]; /* Elimination step */
13.          b[i] := b[i] − A[i, k] × y[k];
14.          A[i, k] := 0;
15.       endfor;          /* Line 9 */
16.    endfor;             /* Line 3 */
17. end GAUSSIAN_ELIMINATION
```

Program 5.4 A serial Gaussian elimination algorithm that converts the system of linear equations $Ax = b$ to a unit upper-triangular system $Ux = y$. The matrix U occupies the upper-triangular locations of A. This algorithm assumes that $A[k, k] \neq 0$ when it is used as a divisor on lines 6 and 7.

We discuss parallel formulations of the classical Gaussian elimination method for upper-triangularization in Sections 5.5.1 and 5.5.2. In Section 5.5.1, we describe a straightforward Gaussian elimination algorithm assuming that the coefficient matrix is nonsingular, and its rows and columns are permuted in a way that the algorithm is numerically stable. Section 5.5.2 discusses the case in which a numerically stable solution of the system of equations requires permuting the columns of the matrix during the execution of the Gaussian elimination algorithm.

Although we discuss Gaussian elimination in the context of upper-triangularization, a similar procedure can be used to factorize matrix A as the product of a lower-triangular matrix L and a unit upper-triangular matrix U so that $A = L \times U$. This factorization is commonly referred to as ***LU factorization***. Performing LU factorization (rather than upper-triangularization) is particularly useful if multiple systems of equations with the same left-hand side Ax need to be solved.

5.5.1 A Simple Gaussian Elimination Algorithm

The serial Gaussian elimination algorithm has three nested loops. Several variations of the algorithm exist, depending on the order in which the loops are arranged. Program 5.4 shows one variation of Gaussian elimination, which we will adopt for parallel implemen-

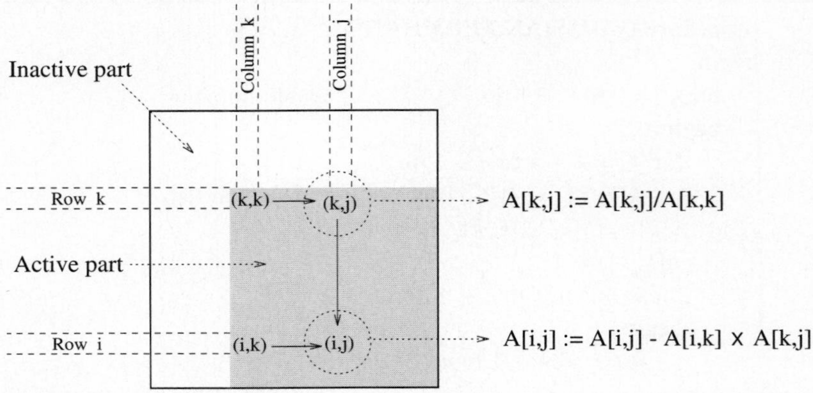

Figure 5.13 A typical computation in Gaussian elimination.

tation in the remainder of this section. This program converts a system of linear equations $Ax = b$ to a unit upper-triangular system $Ux = y$. We assume that the matrix U shares storage with A and overwrites the upper-triangular portion of A. The element $A[k, j]$ computed on line 6 of Program 5.4 is actually $U[k, j]$. Similarly, the element $A[k, k]$ equated to 1 on line 8 is $U[k, k]$. Program 5.4 assumes that $A[k, k] \neq 0$ when it is used as a divisor on lines 6 and 7.

In this section, we will concentrate only on the operations on matrix A in Program 5.4. The operations on vector b on lines 7 and 13 of the program are straightforward to implement. Hence, in the rest of the section, we will ignore these steps. If the steps on lines 7, 8, 13, and 14 are not performed, then Program 5.4 leads to the LU factorization of A as a product $L \times U$. After the termination of the procedure, L is stored in the lower-triangular part of A, and U occupies the locations above the principal diagonal.

For k varying from 0 to $n - 1$, the Gaussian elimination procedure systematically eliminates variable $x[k]$ from equations $k + 1$ to $n - 1$ so that the matrix of coefficients becomes upper-triangular. As shown in Program 5.4, in the kth iteration of the outer loop (starting on line 3), an appropriate multiple of the kth equation is subtracted from each of the equations $k + 1$ to $n - 1$ (loop starting on line 9). The multiples of the kth equation (or the kth row of matrix A) are chosen such that the kth coefficient becomes zero in equations $k+1$ to $n-1$ eliminating $x[k]$ from these equations. A typical computation of the Gaussian elimination procedure in the kth iteration of the outer loop is shown in Figure 5.13. The kth iteration of the outer loop does not involve any computation on rows 1 to $k - 1$ or columns 1 to $k - 1$. Thus, at this stage, only the lower-right $k \times k$ submatrix of A (the shaded portion in Figure 5.13) is computationally active.

Gaussian elimination involves approximately $n^2/2$ divisions (line 6) and approximately $(n^3/3) - (n^2/2)$ subtractions and multiplications (line 12). In this section, we assume that each scalar arithmetic operation takes unit time. With this assumption, the sequential run time of the procedure is approximately $2n^3/3$ (for large n); that is,

$$W = \frac{2}{3}n^3. \tag{5.25}$$

Parallel Implementation with Striped Partitioning

In this subsection, we consider a parallel implementation of Program 5.4, in which the coefficient matrix is rowwise stripe-partitioned among the processors. A parallel implementation of this algorithm with columnwise striping is very similar, and its details can be worked out based on the implementation using rowwise striping (Problems 5.15 and 5.16).

We first consider the case in which one row is assigned to each processor, and the $n \times n$ coefficient matrix A is striped among n processors labeled from P_0 to P_{n-1}. In this mapping, processor P_i initially stores elements $A[i, j]$ for $0 \leq j < n$. Figure 5.14 illustrates this mapping of the matrix onto the processors for $n = 8$. The figure also illustrates the computation and communication that take place in the iteration of the outer loop when $k = 3$.

Program 5.4 and Figure 5.13 show that $A[k, k+1], A[k, k+2], \ldots, A[k, n-1]$ are divided by $A[k, k]$ (line 6) at the beginning of the kth iteration. All matrix elements participating in this operation (shown by the shaded portion of the matrix in Figure 5.14(a)) lie on the same processor. So this step does not require any communication. In the second computation step of the algorithm (the elimination step of line 12), the modified (after division) elements of the kth row are used by all other rows of the active part of the matrix. As Figure 5.14(b) shows, this requires a one-to-all broadcast of the active part of the kth row to the processors storing rows $k+1$ to $n-1$. Finally, the computation $A[i, j] := A[i, j] - A[i, k] \times A[k, j]$ takes place in the remaining active portion of the matrix, which is shown shaded in Figure 5.14(c).

The computation step corresponding to Figure 5.14(a) in the kth iteration requires $n - k - 1$ divisions at processor P_k. Similarly, the computation step of Figure 5.14(c) involves $n - k - 1$ multiplications and subtractions in the kth iteration at all processors P_i, such that $k < i < n$. Assuming a single arithmetic operation takes unit time, the total time spent in computation in the kth iteration is $3(n - k - 1)$. Note that when P_k is performing the divisions, the remaining $p - 1$ processors are idle, and while processors $P_{k+1}, \ldots, P_{n-1}$ are performing the elimination step, processors $P_0, \ldots, P_k$ are idle. Thus, the total time spent during the computation steps shown in Figures 5.14(a) and (c) in this parallel implementation of Gaussian elimination is $3\Sigma_{k=0}^{n-1}(n - k - 1)$, which is equal to $3n(n-1)/2$.

The communication step of Figure 5.14(b) takes $(t_s + t_w(n - k - 1)) \log n$ time (Table 3.1) on a hypercube. Hence, the total communication time over all iterations is $\Sigma_{k=0}^{n-1}(t_s + t_w(n - k - 1)) \log n$, which is equal to $t_s n \log n + t_w(n(n-1)/2) \log n$. The overall parallel run time of this algorithm on a hypercube is

$$T_P = \frac{3}{2}n(n-1) + t_s n \log n + \frac{1}{2}t_w n(n-1) \log n. \tag{5.26}$$

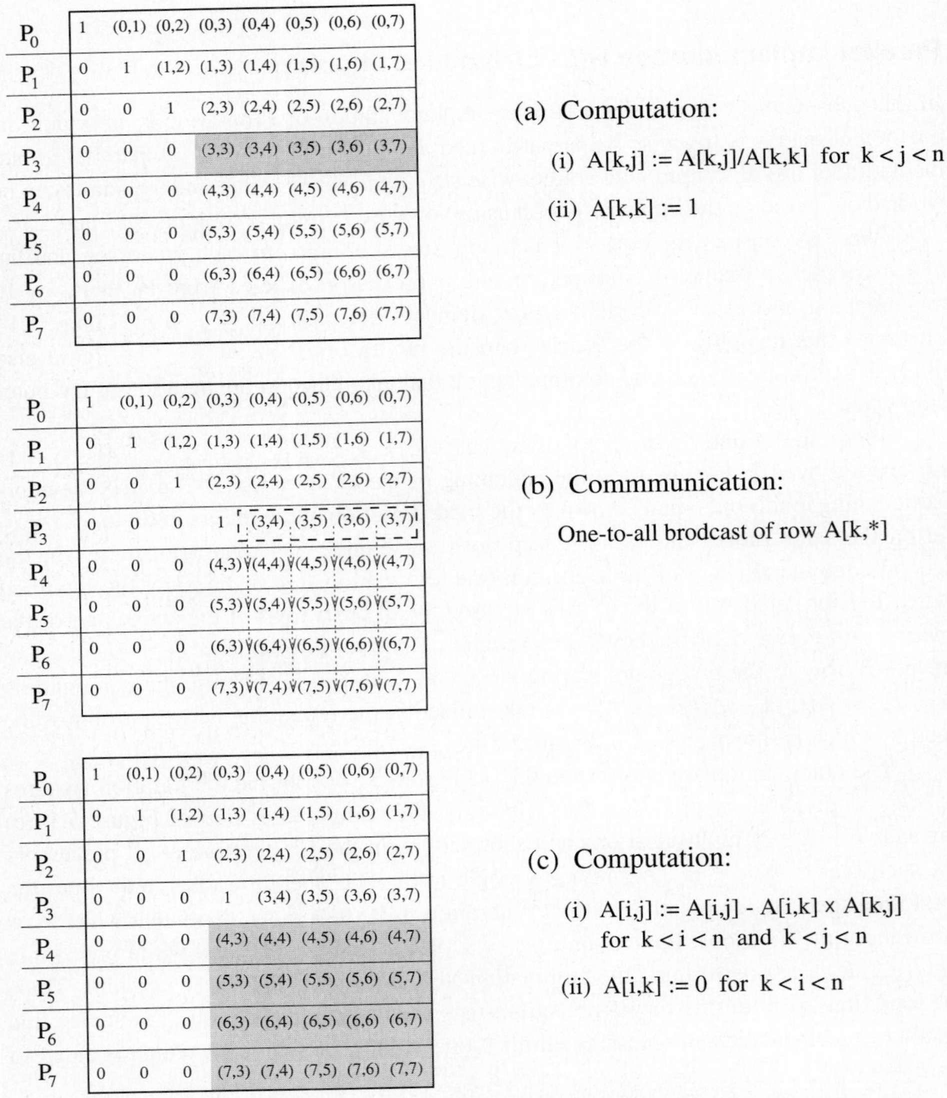

Figure 5.14 Gaussian elimination steps during the iteration corresponding to $k = 3$ for an 8×8 matrix striped rowwise on 8 processors.

Since the number of processors is n, the cost, or the processor-time product, is $\Theta(n^3 \log n)$ (due to the term associated with t_w in Equation 5.26). This cost is asymptotically higher than the sequential run time of this algorithm (Equation 5.25). Hence, the parallel implementation is not cost-optimal.

Pipelined Communication and Computation We now present a parallel implementation of Gaussian elimination that is cost-optimal on an n-processor linear array, mesh, or hypercube for an $n \times n$ coefficient matrix.

In the parallel Gaussian elimination algorithm just presented, the n iterations of the outer loop of Program 5.4 execute sequentially. At any given time, all processors work on the same iteration. The $(k + 1)^{\text{st}}$ iteration starts only after all the computation and communication for the kth iteration is complete. The performance of the algorithm can be improved substantially if the processors work asynchronously; that is, no processor waits for the others to finish an iteration before starting the next one. We call this the ***asynchronous*** or ***pipelined*** version of Gaussian elimination. Figure 5.15 illustrates the pipelined Program 5.4 for a 5×5 matrix striped onto a logical linear array of five processors.

During the kth iteration of Program 5.4, processor P_k broadcasts part of the kth row of the matrix to processors $P_{k+1}, \ldots, P_{n-1}$ (Figure 5.14(b)). Assume that the processors are connected in a linear array, and P_{k+1} is the first processor to receive the kth row from processor P_k. Then processor P_{k+1} must forward this data to P_{k+2}. However, after forwarding the kth row to P_{k+2}, processor P_{k+1} need not wait to perform the elimination step (line 12) until all the processors up to P_{n-1} have received the kth row. Similarly, P_{k+2} can start its computation as soon as it has forwarded the kth row to P_{k+3}, and so on. Meanwhile, after completing the computation for the kth iteration, P_{k+1} can perform the division step (line 6), and start the broadcast of the $(k + 1)^{\text{st}}$ row by sending it to P_{k+2}.

In pipelined Gaussian elimination, each processor independently performs the following sequence of actions repeatedly until all n iterations are complete. For the sake of simplicity, we assume that steps (1) and (2) take the same amount of time (this assumption does not affect the analysis):

(1) If a processor has any data destined for other processors, it sends those data to the appropriate processor.
(2) If the processor can perform some computation using the data it has, it does so.
(3) Otherwise, the processor waits to receive data to be used for one of the above actions.

Figure 5.15 shows the 16 steps in the pipelined parallel execution of Gaussian elimination for a 5×5 matrix striped among five processors. As Figure 5.15(a) shows, the first step is to perform the division on row 0 at processor P_0. The modified row 0 is then sent to P_1 (Figure 5.15(b)), which forwards it to P_2 (Figure 5.15(c)). Now P_1 is free to perform the elimination step using row 0 (Figure 5.15(d)). In the next step (Figure 5.15(e)), P_2 performs the elimination step using row 0. In the same step, P_1, having finished its computation for iteration 0, starts the division step of iteration 1. At any given time, different stages of

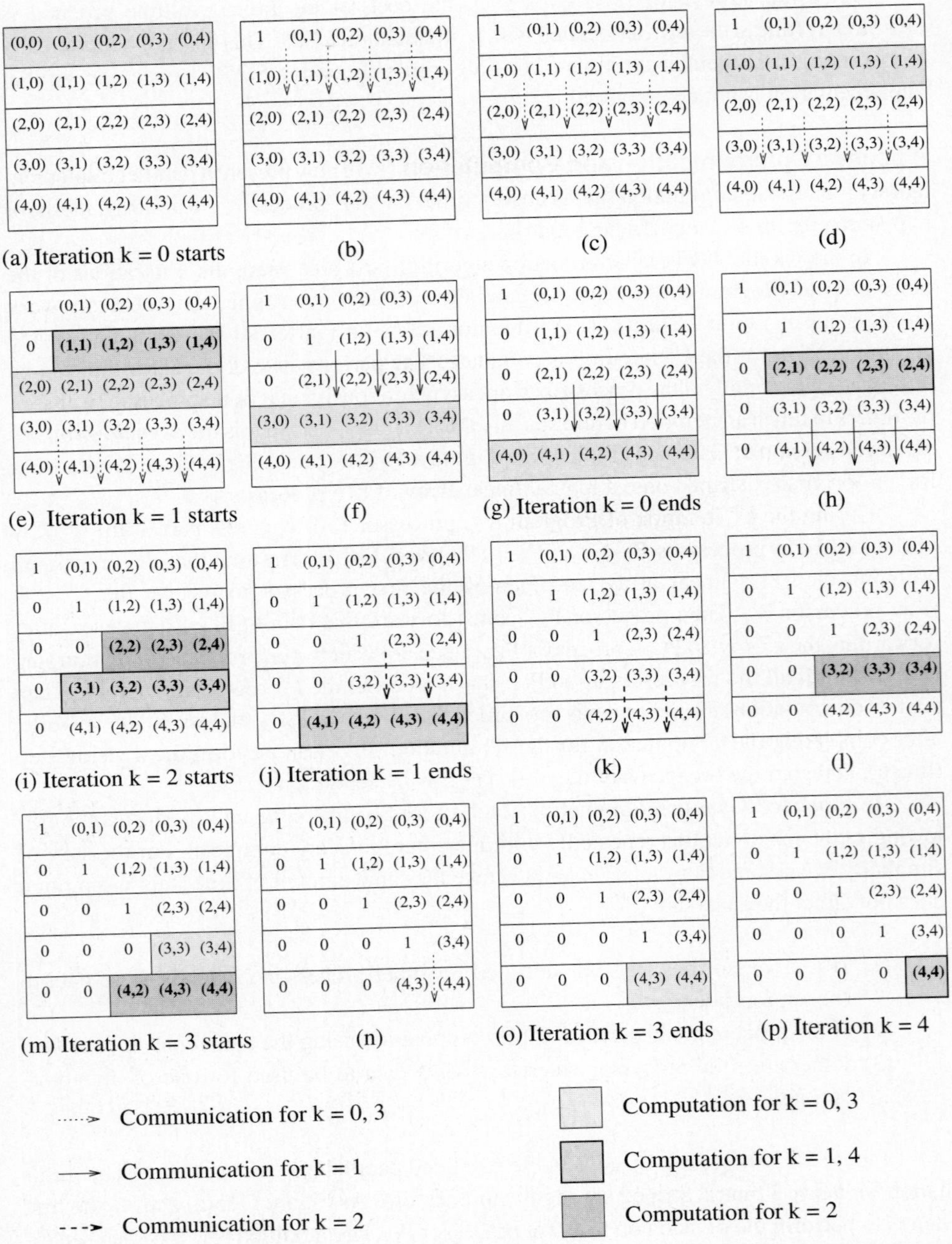

Figure 5.15 Pipelined Gaussian elimination on a 5 × 5 matrix stripe-partitioned with one row per processor.

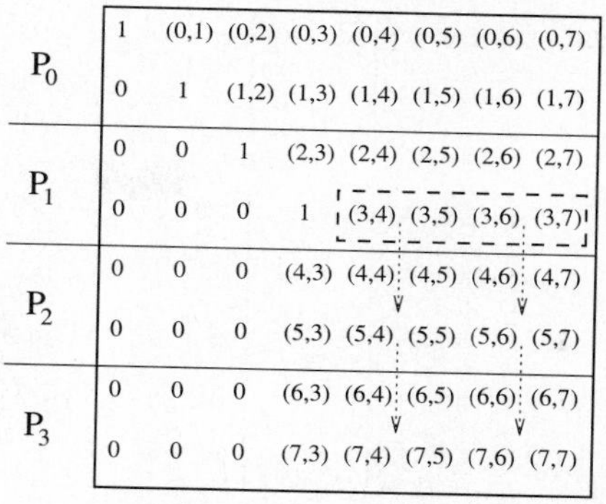

Figure 5.16 The communication in the Gaussian elimination iteration corresponding to $k = 3$ for an 8×8 matrix distributed among four processors using block-checkerboard partitioning.

the same iteration can be active on different processors. For instance, in Figure 5.15(h), processor P_2 performs the elimination step of iteration 1 while processors P_3 and P_4 are engaged in communication for the same iteration. Furthermore, more than one iteration may be active simultaneously on different processors. For instance, in Figure 5.15(i), processor P_2 is performing the division step of iteration 2 while processor P_3 is performing the elimination step of iteration 1.

We now show that, unlike the synchronous algorithm in which all processors work on the same iteration at a time, the pipelined or the asynchronous version of Gaussian elimination is cost-optimal. As Figure 5.15 shows, the initiation of consecutive iterations of the outer loop of Program 5.4 is separated by a constant number of steps. A total of n such iterations are initiated. The last iteration modifies only the bottom-right corner element of the coefficient matrix; hence, it completes in a constant time after its initiation. Thus, the total number of steps in the entire pipelined procedure is $\Theta(n)$ (Problem 5.14). In any step, either $O(n)$ elements are communicated between directly-connected processors, or a division step is performed on $O(n)$ elements of a row, or an elimination step is performed on $O(n)$ elements of a row. Each of these operations take $O(n)$ time. Hence, the entire procedure consists of $\Theta(n)$ steps of $O(n)$ complexity each, and its parallel run time is $O(n^2)$. Since n processors are used, the cost is $O(n^3)$, which is of the same order as the sequential complexity of Gaussian elimination. Hence, the pipelined version of parallel Gaussian elimination with striped partitioning of the coefficient matrix is cost-optimal on a linear array of processors. Since a linear array can be embedded into a mesh or hypercube, the algorithm is cost-optimal on these architectures as well.

Striping with Fewer than n Processors The preceding pipelined implementation of parallel Gaussian elimination can be easily adapted for the case in which $n > p$. Consider

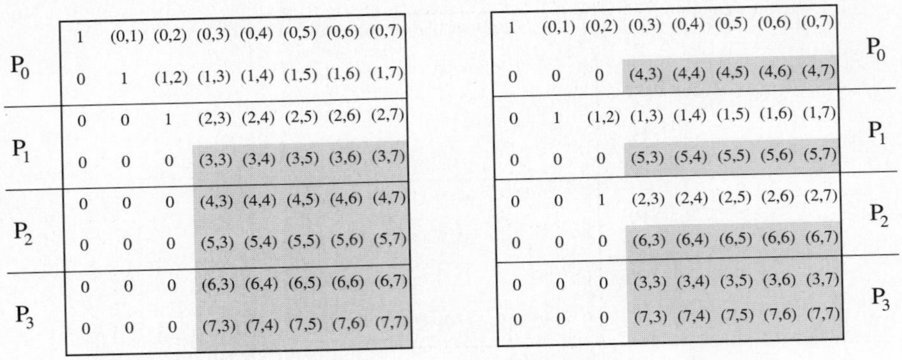

(a) Block-striped mapping (b) Cyclic-striped mapping

Figure 5.17 Computation load on different processors in block and cyclic-striped partitioning of an 8×8 matrix on 4 processors during the Gaussian elimination iteration corresponding to $k = 3$.

an $n \times n$ matrix block-striped among p processors ($p < n$) such that each processor is assigned n/p contiguous rows of the matrix. Figure 5.16 illustrates the communication steps in a typical iteration of Gaussian elimination with such a mapping. As the figure shows, the kth iteration of the algorithm requires that the active part of the kth row be sent to the processors storing rows $k+1, k+2, \ldots, n-1$.

Figure 5.17(a) shows that, with block striping, a processor with all rows belonging to the active part of the matrix performs $(n-k-1)n/p$ multiplications and subtractions during the elimination step of the kth iteration (in the last $(n/p)-1$ iterations, no processor has all active rows, but we ignore this anomaly). If the pipelined version of the algorithm is used, then the number of arithmetic operations on a maximally-loaded processor in the kth iteration ($2(n-k-1)n/p$) is much higher than the number of words communicated ($n-k-1$) by a processor in the same iteration. Thus, for sufficiently large values of n with respect to p, computation dominates communication in each iteration. Assuming that each scalar multiplication and subtraction pair takes unit time, the total parallel run time of this algorithm (ignoring communication overhead) is $2(n/p)\Sigma_{k=0}^{n-1}(n-k-1)$, which is approximately equal to n^3/p.

The processor-time product of this algorithm is n^3, even if the communication costs are ignored. Thus, the cost of the parallel algorithm is higher than the sequential run time (Equation 5.25) by a factor of 3/2. This inefficiency of Gaussian elimination with block striping is due to processor idling resulting from an uneven load distribution. As Figure 5.17(a) shows for an 8×8 matrix and four processors, during the iteration corresponding to $k = 3$ (in the outer loop of Program 5.4), one processor is completely idle, one is partially loaded, and only two processors are fully active. By the time half of the iterations of the outer loop are over, only half the processors are active. The remaining idle processors make the parallel algorithm costlier than the sequential algorithm.

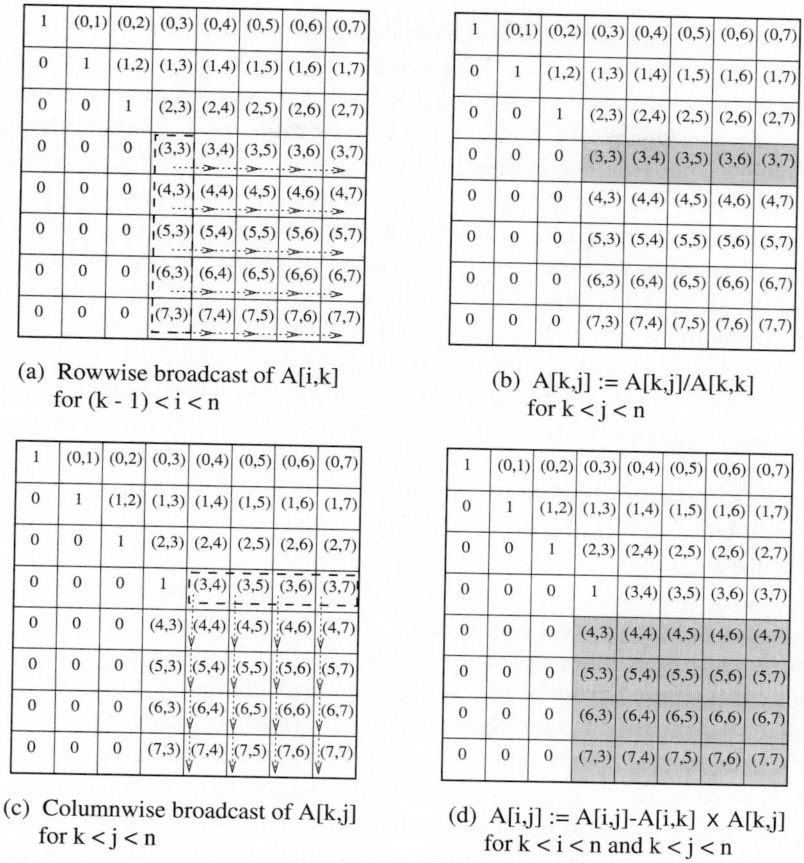

Figure 5.18 Various steps in the Gaussian elimination iteration corresponding to $k = 3$ for an 8×8 matrix on 64 processors of a two-dimensional mesh.

This problem can be alleviated if the matrix is partitioned among the processors by using cyclic-striped mapping as shown in Figure 5.17(b). With the cyclic-striped partitioning, the difference between the computational loads of a maximally loaded processor and the least loaded processor in any iteration is of at most one row (that is, $O(n)$ arithmetic operations). Since there are n iterations, the cumulative overhead due to processor idling is only $O(n^2 p)$ with a cyclic mapping, compared to $\Theta(n^3)$ with a block mapping (Problem 5.19).

Parallel Implementation with Checkerboard Partitioning

We now describe a parallel implementation of Program 5.4 in which the $n \times n$ matrix A is mapped onto an $n \times n$ mesh of processors such that processor $P_{i,j}$ initially stores $A[i, j]$.

The communication and computation steps in the iteration of the outer loop corresponding to $k = 3$ are illustrated in Figure 5.18 for $n = 8$. Program 5.4 and Figures 5.13 and 5.18 show that in the kth iteration of the outer loop, $A[k, k]$ is required by processors $P_{k,k+1}$, $P_{k,k+2}, \ldots, P_{k,n-1}$ to divide $A[k, k+1], A[k, k+2], \ldots, A[k, n-1]$, respectively. After the division on line 6, the modified elements of the kth row are used to perform the elimination step by all the other rows in the active part of the matrix. The modified (after the division on line 6) elements of the kth row are used by all other rows of the active part of the matrix. Similarly, the elements of the kth column are used by all other columns of the active part of the matrix for the elimination step. As Figure 5.18 shows, the communication in the kth iteration requires a one-to-all broadcast of $A[i, k]$ along the ith row (Figure 5.18(a)) for $k \le i < n$, and a one-to-all broadcast of $A[k, j]$ along the jth column (Figure 5.18(c)) for $k < j < n$. As in the case of striped partitioning, a non-cost-optimal parallel formulation results if these broadcasts are performed synchronously on all processors (Problem 5.18).

Pipelined Communication and Computation Based on our experience with Gaussian elimination using striped partitioning of the coefficient matrix, we develop a pipelined version of the algorithm using checkerboard partitioning.

As Figure 5.18 shows, in the kth iteration of the outer loop (lines 3–16 of Program 5.4), $A[k, k]$ is sent to the right from $P_{k,k}$ to $P_{k,k+1}$ to $P_{k,k+2}$, and so on, until it reaches $P_{k,n-1}$. Processor $P_{k,k+1}$ performs the division $A[k, k+1]/A[k, k]$ as soon as it receives $A[k, k]$ from $P_{k,k}$. It does not have to wait for $A[k, k]$ to reach all the way up to $P_{k,n-1}$ before performing its local computation. Similarly, any subsequent processor $P_{k,j}$ of the kth row can perform its division as soon as it receives $A[k, k]$. After performing the division, $A[k, j]$ is ready to be communicated downward in the jth column. As $A[k, j]$ moves down, each processor it passes is free to use it for computation. Processors in the jth column need not wait until $A[k, j]$ reaches the last processor of the column. Thus, $P_{i,j}$ performs the elimination step $A[i, j] := A[i, j] - A[i, k] \times A[k, j]$ as soon as $A[i, k]$ and $A[k, j]$ are available. Since some processors perform the computation for a given iteration earlier than other processors, they start working on subsequent iterations sooner.

The communication and computation can be pipelined in several ways. We present one such scheme in Figure 5.19. In Figure 5.19(a), the iteration of the outer loop for $k = 0$ starts at processor $P_{0,0}$, when $P_{0,0}$ sends $A[0, 0]$ to $P_{0,1}$. Upon receiving $A[0, 0]$, $P_{0,1}$ computes $A[0, 1] := A[0, 1]/A[0, 0]$ (Figure 5.19(b)). Now $P_{0,1}$ forwards $A[0, 0]$ to $P_{0,2}$ and also sends the updated $A[0, 1]$ down to $P_{1,1}$ (Figure 5.19(c)). At the same time, $P_{1,0}$ sends $A[1, 0]$ to $P_{1,1}$. Having received $A[0, 1]$ and $A[1, 0]$, $P_{1,1}$ performs the elimination step $A[1, 1] := A[1, 1] - A[1, 0] \times A[0, 1]$, and having received $A[0, 0]$, $P_{0,2}$ performs the division step $A[0, 2] := A[0, 2]/A[0, 0]$ (Figure 5.19(d)). After this computation step, another set of processors (that is, processors $P_{0,2}$, $P_{1,1}$, and $P_{2,0}$) is ready to initiate communication (Figure 5.19(e)).

All processors performing communication or computation during a particular iteration lie along a diagonal in the bottom-left to top-right direction (for example, $P_{0,2}$, $P_{1,1}$, and $P_{2,0}$ performing communication in Figure 5.19(e) and $P_{0,3}$, $P_{1,2}$, and $P_{2,1}$ performing computation in Figure 5.19(f)). As the parallel algorithm progresses, this diagonal moves

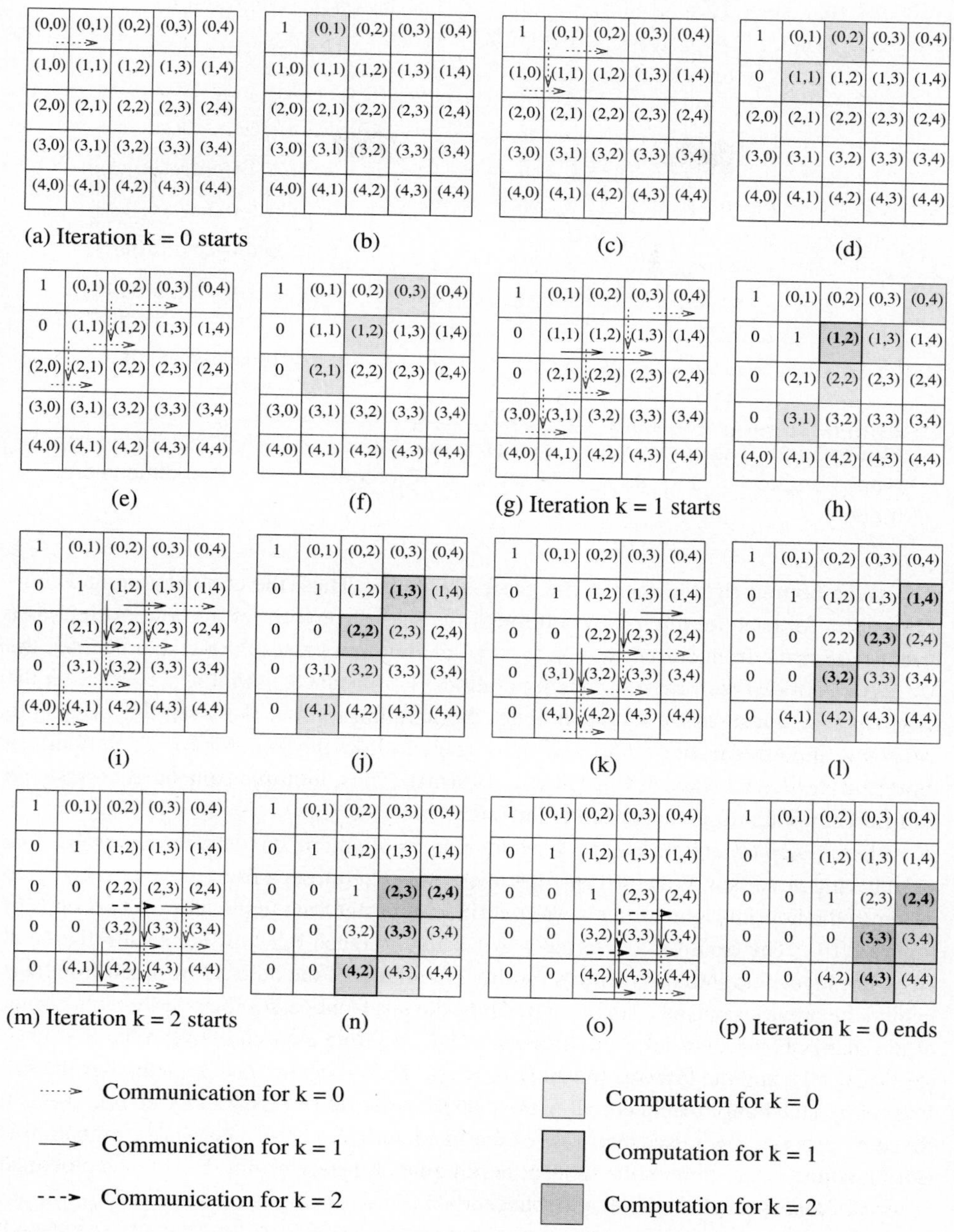

Figure 5.19 Pipelined Gaussian elimination for a 5 × 5 matrix on 25 processors.

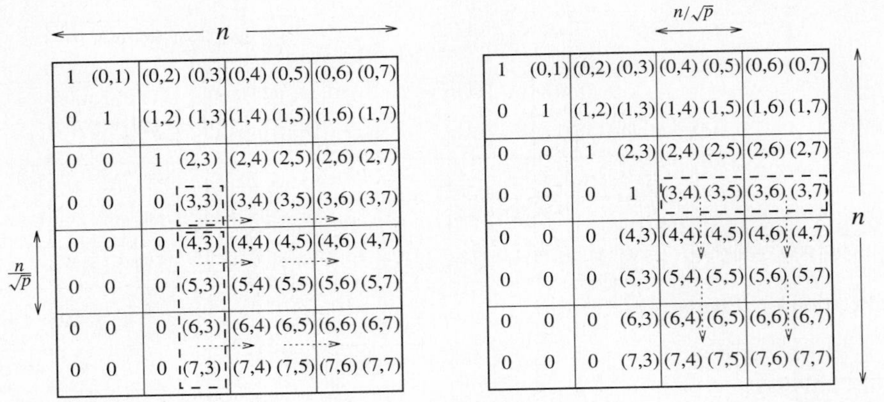

(a) Rowwise broadcast of A[i,k] for i = k to (n - 1)

(b) Columnwise broadcast of A[k,j] for j = (k + 1) to (n - 1)

Figure 5.20 The communication steps in the Gaussian elimination iteration corresponding to $k = 3$ for an 8×8 matrix on 16 processors of a two-dimensional mesh.

toward the bottom-right corner of the processor mesh. Thus, the computation and communication for each iteration moves through the mesh from top-left to bottom-right as a "front." After the front corresponding to a certain iteration passes through a processor, the processor is free to perform subsequent iterations. For instance, in Figure 5.19(g), after the front for $k = 0$ has passed $P_{1,1}$, it initiates the iteration for $k = 1$ by sending $A[1, 1]$ to $P_{1,2}$. This initiates a front for $k = 1$, which closely follows the front for $k = 0$. Similarly, a third front for $k = 2$ starts at $P_{2,2}$ (Figure 5.19(m)). Thus, multiple fronts that correspond to different iterations are active simultaneously.

Every step of an iteration, such as division, elimination, or transmitting a value to a neighboring processor, is a constant-time operation. Therefore, a front moves a single step closer to the bottom-right corner of the matrix in constant time (equivalent to two steps of Figure 5.19). The front for $k = 0$ takes $\Theta(n)$ time to reach $P_{n-1,n-1}$ after its initiation at $P_{0,0}$. The algorithm initiates n fronts for the n iterations of the outer loop. Each front lags behind the previous one by a single step. Thus, the last front passes the bottom-right corner of the matrix $\Theta(n)$ steps after the first one. The total time elapsed between the first front starting at $P_{0,0}$ and the last one finishing is $\Theta(n)$. The procedure is complete after the last front passes the bottom-right corner of the matrix; hence, the total parallel run time is $\Theta(n)$. Since n^2 processor are used, the cost of the pipelined version of Gaussian elimination is $\Theta(n^3)$, which is the same as the sequential run time of the algorithm. Hence, the pipelined version of Gaussian elimination with checkerboard partitioning is cost-optimal.

Checkerboard Partitioning with Fewer than n² Processors Consider the case in which p processors are used so that $p < n^2$ and the matrix is mapped onto a $\sqrt{p} \times \sqrt{p}$ mesh by using block-checkerboard partitioning. Figure 5.20 illustrates that a typical parallel

1	(0,1)	(0,2)	(0,3)	(0,4)	(0,5)	(0,6)	(0,7)
0	1	(1,2)	(1,3)	(1,4)	(1,5)	(1,6)	(1,7)
0	0	1	(2,3)	(2,4)	(2,5)	(2,6)	(2,7)
0	0	0	(3,3)	(3,4)	(3,5)	(3,6)	(3,7)
0	0	0	(4,3)	(4,4)	(4,5)	(4,6)	(4,7)
0	0	0	(5,3)	(5,4)	(5,5)	(5,6)	(5,7)
0	0	0	(6,3)	(6,4)	(6,5)	(6,6)	(6,7)
0	0	0	(7,3)	(7,4)	(7,5)	(7,6)	(7,7)

(a) Block-checkerboard mapping

1	(0,4)	(0,1)	(0,5)	(0,2)	(0,6)	(0,3)	(0,7)
0	(4,4)	0	(4,5)	0	(4,6)	(4,3)	(4,7)
0	(1,4)	1	(1,5)	(1,2)	(1,6)	(1,3)	(1,7)
0	(5,4)	0	(5,5)	0	(5,6)	(5,3)	(5,7)
0	(2,4)	0	(2,5)	1	(2,6)	(2,3)	(2,7)
0	(6,4)	0	(6,5)	0	(6,6)	(6,3)	(6,7)
0	(3,4)	0	(3,5)	0	(3,6)	(3,3)	(3,7)
0	(7,4)	0	(7,5)	0	(7,6)	(7,3)	(7,7)

(b) Cyclic-checkerboard mapping

Figure 5.21 Computational load on different processors in block and cyclic-checkerboard mappings of an 8×8 matrix onto 16 processors during the Gaussian elimination iteration corresponding to $k = 3$.

Gaussian iteration involves a rowwise and a columnwise communication of $n/\sqrt{p}$ values. Figure 5.21(a) illustrates the load distribution in block-checkerboard mapping for $n = 8$ and $p = 16$.

Figures 5.20 and 5.21(a) show that a processor containing a completely active part of the matrix performs n^2/p multiplications and subtractions, and communicates $n/\sqrt{p}$ words along its row and its column (ignoring the fact that in the last $(n/\sqrt{p}) - 1$ iterations, the active part of the matrix becomes smaller than the size of a block, and no processor contains a completely active part of the matrix). If the pipelined version of the algorithm is used, the number of arithmetic operations per processor $(2n^2/p)$ is an order of magnitude higher than the number of words communicated per processor $(n/\sqrt{p})$ in each iteration. Thus, for sufficiently large values of n^2 with respect to p, the communication in each iteration is dominated by computation. Assuming that each scalar arithmetic operation takes unit time, the total parallel run time of this algorithm (ignoring communication cost) is $(2n^2/p) \times n$, which is equal to $2n^3/p$. The processor-time product is $2n^3$, which is three times the cost of the serial algorithm (Equation 5.25). As a result, there is an upper bound of $1/3$ on the efficiency of the parallel algorithm.

As in the case of a block-striped mapping, the inefficiency of Gaussian elimination with a block-checkerboard partitioning of the matrix is due to processor idling resulting from an uneven load distribution. Figure 5.21(a) shows the active part of an 8×8 matrix of coefficients in the iteration of the outer loop for $k = 3$ when the matrix is block-checkerboarded on 16 processors. As shown in the figure, seven out of sixteen processors are fully idle, five are partially loaded, and only four are fully active. By the time half of the iterations of the outer loop have been completed, only one-fourth of the processors are active. The remaining idle processors make the parallel algorithm much costlier than the sequential algorithm.

This problem can be alleviated if the matrix is checkerboarded in a cyclic manner as shown in Figure 5.21(b). With the cyclic-checkerboard partitioning, the maximum difference in computational load between any two processors in any iteration is that of one row and one column update. For example, in Figure 5.21(b), n^2/p matrix elements are active in the bottom-right processor, and $(n-1)^2/p$ elements are active in the top-left processor. The difference in work load between any two processors is at most $\Theta(n/\sqrt{p})$ in any iteration, which contributes $\Theta(n\sqrt{p})$ to the overhead function. Since there are n iterations, the cumulative overhead due to processor idling is only $\Theta(n^2\sqrt{p})$ with cyclic mapping in contrast to $\Theta(n^3)$ with block mapping (Problem 5.19).

From the preceding discussion, we conclude that pipelined parallel Gaussian elimination for an $n \times n$ matrix takes $\Theta(n^3/p)$ time on p processors with both striped and checkerboard partitioning schemes. Checkerboard partitioning can use more processors ($O(n^2)$) than striped partitioning ($O(n)$) for an $n \times n$ coefficient matrix. Hence, an implementation with checkerboard partitioning is more scalable.

5.5.2 Gaussian Elimination with Partial Pivoting

The Gaussian elimination algorithm in Program 5.4 fails if any diagonal entry $A[k, k]$ of the matrix of coefficients is close or equal to zero. To avoid this problem and to ensure the numerical stability of the algorithm, a technique called ***partial pivoting*** is used. At the beginning of the outer loop in the kth iteration, this method selects a column i (called the ***pivot*** column) such that $A[k, i]$ is the largest in magnitude among all $A[k, j]$ such that $k \le j < n$. It then exchanges the kth and the ith columns before starting the iteration. These columns can either be exchanged explicitly by physically moving them into each other's locations, or they can be exchanged implicitly by simply maintaining an $n \times 1$ permutation vector to keep track of the new indices of the columns of A. If partial pivoting is performed with an implicit exchange of column indices, then the factors L and U are not exactly triangular matrices, but columnwise permutations of triangular matrices.

Assuming that columns are exchanged explicitly, the $A[k, k]$ used as the divisor on line 6 of Program 5.4 (after exchanging columns k and i) is greater than or equal to any $A[k, j]$ that it divides in the kth iteration. Partial pivoting in Program 5.4 results in a unit upper-triangular matrix in which all elements above the principal diagonal have an absolute value of less than one.

Striped Partitioning

Performing partial pivoting is straightforward with rowwise striping discussed in Section 5.5.1. Before performing the divide operation in the kth iteration, the processor storing the kth row makes a comparison pass over the active portion of this row, and selects the element with the largest absolute value as the divisor. This element determines the pivot column, and all processors must know the index of this column. This information can be passed on to the rest of the processors along with the modified (after the division) elements of the kth row. The combined pivot-search and division step takes $\Theta(n-k-1)$ time in the

k^{th} iteration, as in case of Gaussian elimination without pivoting. Thus, partial pivoting has no significant effect on the performance of Program 5.4 if the coefficient matrix is striped along the rows.

Now consider a columnwise striping of the coefficient matrix. In the absence of pivoting, parallel implementations of Gaussian elimination with rowwise and columnwise striping are almost identical (Problem 5.16). However, the two are significantly different if partial pivoting is performed.

The first difference is that, unlike rowwise striping, the pivot search is distributed in columnwise striping. If the matrix size is $n \times n$ and the number of processors is p, then the pivot search in columnwise striping involves two steps. During pivot search for the kth iteration, first, each processor determines the maximum of the n/p (or fewer) elements of the kth row that it stores. The next step is to find the maximum of the resulting p (or fewer) values, and to distribute the maximum among all processors. This is very similar to the problem solved in Example 3.7. Assuming a hypercube interconnection network, each pivot search is performed in $\Theta(n/p) + \Theta(\log p)$ time. For sufficiently large values of n with respect to p, this is much less than the $\Theta(n)$ time it takes to perform a pivot search with rowwise striping. This seems to suggest that a columnwise striping is better for partial pivoting that a rowwise striping. However, the following factors favor rowwise striping.

Figure 5.15 shows how communication and computation "fronts" move from top to bottom in the pipelined version of Gaussian elimination with rowwise striping. Similarly, the communication and computation fronts move from left to right in case of columnwise striping. This means that the $(k+1)^{\text{st}}$ row is not ready for pivot search for the $(k+1)^{\text{st}}$ iteration (that is, it is not fully updated) until the front corresponding to the kth iteration reaches the rightmost processor. As a result, the $(k+1)^{\text{st}}$ iteration cannot start until the entire k^{th} iteration is complete. This effectively eliminates pipelining, and we are therefore forced to use the synchronous version with poor efficiency.

While performing partial pivoting, columns of the coefficient matrix may or may not be explicitly exchanged. In either case, the performance of Program 5.4 is adversely affected with columnwise striping. Recall that a cyclic mapping results in a better load balance in Gaussian elimination than a block mapping. A cyclic mapping ensures that the active portion of the matrix is almost uniformly distributed among the processors at every stage of Gaussian elimination. If pivot columns are not exchanged explicitly, then this condition may cease to hold. After a pivot column is used, it no longer stays in the active portion of the matrix. As a result of pivoting without explicit exchange, columns are arbitrarily removed from the different processors' active portions of the matrix. This randomness disturbs the uniform distribution of the active portion. On the other hand, if columns belonging to different processors are exchanged explicitly, then this exchange requires communication between the processors. A rowwise striping neither requires communication for exchanging columns, nor does it lose the load-balance if columns are not exchanged explicitly.

Checkerboard Partitioning

In the case of checkerboard partitioning of the coefficient matrix, partial pivoting seriously restricts pipelining, although it does not completely eliminate it. Recall that in the pipelined version of Gaussian elimination with checkerboard partitioning, fronts corresponding to various iterations move from top-left to bottom-right. The pivot search for the $(k+1)^{st}$ iteration can commence as soon as the front corresponding to the kth iteration has moved past the diagonal of the active matrix joining its top-right and bottom-left corners.

Thus, partial pivoting may lead to considerable performance degradation in parallel Gaussian elimination with checkerboard partitioning. If numerical considerations allow, it may be possible to reduce the performance loss due to partial pivoting. We can restrict the search for the pivot in the kth iteration to a band of q columns (instead of all $n-k$ columns). In this case, the ith column is selected as the pivot in the kth iteration if $A[k, i]$ is the largest element in a band of q elements of the active part of the ith row. This restricted partial pivoting not only reduces the communication cost, but also permits limited pipelining. By restricting the number of columns for pivot search to q, an iteration can start as soon as the previous iteration has updated the first $q+1$ columns.

Another way to get around the loss of pipelining due to partial pivoting in Gaussian elimination with checkerboard partitioning is to use fast algorithms for one-to-all broadcast, such as those described in Section 3.7.1 and Problem 3.24. With checkerboard partitioning of the $n \times n$ coefficient matrix on p processors, a processors spends $\Theta(n/\sqrt{p})$ time in communication in each iteration of the pipelined version of Gaussian elimination. Disregarding the message startup time t_s, a non-pipelined version that performs explicit one-to-all broadcasts using the algorithm of Section 3.2 spends $\Theta((n/\sqrt{p}) \log p)$ time communicating in each iteration. This communication time is higher than that of the pipelined version. The one-to-all broadcast algorithms described in Section 3.7.1 and Problem 3.24 take $\Theta(n/\sqrt{p})$ time in each iteration (disregarding the startup time). This time is asymptotically equal to the per-iteration communication time of the pipelined algorithm. Hence, using a smart algorithm to perform one-to-all broadcast, even non-pipelined parallel Gaussian elimination can attain performance that is at par with that of the pipelined algorithm. However, the one-to-all broadcast algorithms described in Section 3.7.1 and Problem 3.24 split a message into smaller parts and route them separately. For these algorithms to be effective, the sizes of the messages should be large enough; that is, n should be large compared to p.

Although pipelining and pivoting do not go together in Gaussian elimination with checkerboard partitioning, the discussion of checkerboard partitioning in this section is still useful. With some modification, it applies to the Cholesky factorization algorithm (Program 5.6 in Problem 5.22), which does not require pivoting. Cholesky factorization applies only to symmetric, positive definite matrices. A real $n \times n$ matrix A is ***positive definite*** if $x^T Ax > 0$ for any $n \times 1$ nonzero, real vector x. The communication pattern in Cholesky factorization is quite similar to that of Gaussian elimination (Problem 5.22), except that, due to symmetrical lower and upper-triangular halves in the matrix, Cholesky factorization uses only one triangular half of the matrix.

```
1.  procedure BACK_SUBSTITUTION (U, x, y)
2.  begin
3.      for k := n − 1 downto 0 do  /* Main loop */
4.          begin
5.              x[k] := y[k];
6.              for i := k − 1 downto 0 do
7.                  y[i] := y[i] − x[k] × U[i, k];
8.          endfor;
9.  end BACK_SUBSTITUTION
```

Program 5.5 A serial algorithm for back-substitution. U is an upper-triangular matrix with all entries of the principal diagonal equal to one, and all subdiagonal entries equal to zero.

5.5.3 Solving a Triangular System: Back-Substitution

We now briefly discuss the second stage of solving a system of linear equations. After the full matrix A has been reduced to an upper-triangular matrix U with ones along the principal diagonal, we perform back-substitution to determine the vector x. A sequential back-substitution algorithm for solving an upper-triangular system of equations $Ux = y$ is shown in Program 5.5.

Starting with the last equation, each iteration of the main loop (lines 3–8) of Program 5.5 computes the values of a variable and substitutes the variables value back into the remaining equations. The program performs approximately $n^2/2$ multiplications and subtractions. Note that the number of arithmetic operations in back-substitution is less than that in Gaussian elimination by a factor of $\Theta(n)$. Hence, if back-substitution is used in conjunction with Gaussian elimination, it is best to use the matrix partitioning scheme that is the most efficient for parallel Gaussian elimination.

Consider a rowwise block-striped mapping of the $n \times n$ matrix U onto p processors. Let the vector y be distributed uniformly among all the processors. The value of the variable solved in a typical iteration of the main loop (line 3) must be sent to all the processors with equations involving that variable. This communication can be pipelined (Problem 5.29). If so, the time to perform the computations of an iteration dominate the time that a processor spends in communication in an iteration. In every iteration of a pipelined implementation, a processor receives (or generates) the value of a variable and sends that value to another processor. Using the value of the variable solved in the current iteration, a processor also performs up to n/p multiplications and subtractions (lines 6 and 7). Hence, each step of a pipelined implementation requires a constant amount of time for communication and $\Theta(n/p)$ time for computation. The algorithm terminates in $\Theta(n)$ steps (Problem 5.29), and the parallel run time of the entire algorithm is $\Theta(n^2/p)$.

If the matrix is partitioned by using checkerboarding on a $\sqrt{p} \times \sqrt{p}$ logical mesh of processors, and the elements of the vector are distributed along one of the columns of the processor mesh, then only the $\sqrt{p}$ processors containing the vector perform any computation. Using pipelining to communicate the appropriate elements of U to the processor containing the corresponding elements of y for the substitution step (line 7), the algorithm can be executed in $\Theta(n^2/\sqrt{p})$ time (Problem 5.29). Thus, the cost of parallel back-substitution with checkerboard mapping is $\Theta(n^2\sqrt{p})$. The algorithm is not cost-optimal because its sequential cost is only $\Theta(n^2)$. However, the entire process of solving the linear system, including upper-triangularization using Gaussian elimination, is still cost-optimal for $\sqrt{p} = O(n)$ because the sequential complexity of the entire process is $\Theta(n^3)$.

5.5.4 Numerical Considerations in Solving Systems of Linear Equations

A system of linear equations of the form $Ax = b$ can be solved by using a factorization algorithm to express A as the product of a lower-triangular matrix L, and a unit upper-triangular matrix U. The system of equations is then rewritten as $LUx = b$, and is solved in two steps. First, the lower-triangular system $Ly = b$ is solved for y. Second, the upper-triangular system $Ux = y$ is solved for x.

The Gaussian elimination algorithm given in Program 5.4 effectively factorizes A into L and U. However, it also solves the lower-triangular system $Ly = b$ on the fly by means of steps on lines 7 and 13. Program 5.4 gives what is called a ***row-oriented*** Gaussian elimination algorithm. In this algorithm, multiples of rows are subtracted from other rows. The upper-triangular matrix U resulting from this algorithm has all its elements less than or equal to one in magnitude. The lower-triangular matrix L, whether implicit or explicit, may have elements with larger numerical values. While solving the system $Ax = b$, the triangular system $Ly = b$ is solved first. If L contains large elements, then rounding errors can occur while solving for y due to the finite precision of floating-point numbers stored in computer memory. These errors in y are propagated through the solution of $Ux = y$.

An alternate form of Gaussian elimination is the ***column-oriented*** form that can be obtained from Program 5.4 by reversing the roles of rows and columns. In the column-oriented algorithm, multiples of columns are subtracted from other columns, and pivot search is also performed along the columns. All elements of the lower-triangular matrix L generated by the column-oriented algorithm have a magnitude of less than or equal to one. This minimizes numerical error while solving $Ly = b$, and results in a significantly smaller error in the overall solution than the row-oriented algorithm.

From a practical point of view, the column-oriented Gaussian elimination algorithm is more useful than the row-oriented algorithm. We have chosen to present the row-oriented algorithm in detail because it is more intuitive. It is easy to see that the system of linear equations resulting from the subtraction of a multiple of an equation from other equations is equivalent to the original system. The entire discussion on the row-oriented algorithm of Program 5.4 presented in this section applies to the column-oriented algorithm with the roles of rows and columns reversed. For example, columnwise striping is more suitable than rowwise striping for the column-oriented algorithm with partial pivoting.

5.6 Bibliographic Remarks

Matrix transposition with striped partitioning is essentially an all-to-all personalized communication problem [Ede89]. Hence, all the references in Chapter 3 for all-to-all personalized communication apply directly to matrix transposition. The recursive transposition algorithm, popularly known as RTA, was first reported by Eklundh [Ekl72]. Its adaptations for hypercubes have been described by Bertsekas and Tsitsiklis [BT89], Fox and Furmanski [FF86], Johnsson [Joh87], and McBryan and Van de Velde [MdV87] for one-port communication on each processor. Johnsson [Joh87] also discusses parallel RTA for hypercubes that permit simultaneous communication on all channels. Further improvements on the hypercube RTA have been suggested by Ho and Raghunath [HR91], and Johnsson and Ho [JH88], Johnsson [Joh90], Stout and Wagar [SW87].

A number of sources of parallel dense linear algebra algorithms, including those for matrix-vector multiplication and matrix multiplication, are available [CAHH91, GPS90, GL89, Joh87, Mod88, OS85]. Since dense matrix multiplication is highly computationally intensive, there has been a great deal of interest in developing parallel formulations of this algorithm and in testing its performance on various parallel architectures [Akl89, Ber89, CAHH91, Can69, Cha79, CS88, DNS81, dV89, FJL+88, FOH87, GK91, GL89, Hip89, HJE91, Joh87, PV80, Tic88]. Some of the early parallel formulations of matrix multiplication were developed by Cannon [Can69], Dekel, Nassimi, and Sahni [DNS81], and Fox et al. [FOH87]. Variants and improvements of these algorithms have been presented by Berntsen [Ber89], and by Ho, Johnsson, and Edelman [HJE91]. In particular, Berntsen [Ber89] presents an algorithm that has strictly smaller communication overhead than Cannon's algorithm, but has a smaller degree of concurrency. Ho, Johnsson, and Edelman [HJE91] present another variant of Cannon's algorithm for a hypercube that permits communication on all channels simultaneously. This algorithm, while reducing communication, also reduces the degree of concurrency. Gupta and Kumar [GK91] present a detailed scalability analysis of several matrix multiplication algorithms. They present an analysis to determine the best algorithm to multiply two $n \times n$ matrices on a p-processor hypercube for different ranges of n, p and the hardware-related constants. They also show that the improvements suggested by Berntsen and Ho et al. do not improve the overall scalability of matrix multiplication on a hypercube.

Parallel algorithms for LU factorization and solving dense systems of linear equations have been discussed by several researchers [Ber84, BT89, CG87, Cha87, Dav86, DHvdV93, FJL+88, GPS90, Gei85, GH86, GR88, Joh87, LD90, Lei92, Mod88, Mol86, OR88, Ort88, OS86, PR85, Rob90, Saa86, Vav89]. Geist and Heath [GH85, GH86], and Heath [Hea85] specifically concentrate on parallel dense Cholesky factorization. Parallel algorithms for solving triangular systems have also been studied in detail [EHHR88, HR88, LC88, LC89,

RO88, Rom87]. Demmel, Heath, and van der Vorst [DHvdV93] present a comprehensive survey of parallel matrix computations considering numerical implications in detail.

Problems

5.1 In the hybrid block-cyclic striping described in Section 5.1, what are the indices of the rows stored on processor i if the matrix is striped into blocks of q rows ($q < n/p$)?

5.2 Prove that the transposition algorithms presented in Section 5.2.1 for a matrix partitioned in block-checkerboard fashion work without any modification for the cyclic-checkerboard partitioning as well. Similarly, show that the algorithm presented in Section 5.2.2 is applicable for both cyclic-striped and block-striped partitionings.

5.3 Show that, in the mesh algorithm for transposing a matrix described in Section 5.2, the term associated with t_w cannot be made any smaller if cut-through routing is used.

5.4 Write the pseudocode to implement the recursive transposition algorithm presented in Section 5.2.1 for a $\sqrt{p} \times \sqrt{p}$ matrix mapped onto a p-processor hypercube.

5.5 Consider the two algorithms for all-to-all personalized communication in Sections 3.5.1 and 3.5.2. Which method would you use on a 64 processor hypercube with cut-through routing for transposing a 1024×1024 matrix with the striped mapping shown in Figure 5.7 if $t_s = 100\mu$s, $t_w = 1\mu$s, and $t_h = 1\mu$s? Why?

5.6 Describe a parallel formulation of matrix-vector multiplication in which the matrix is block-striped along the columns and the vector is equally partitioned among all the processors. Show that the parallel run time is the same as in case of rowwise striping.
Hint: The basic communication operation used in the case of columnwise striping is multinode accumulation (see Figure 11.11(b) in Section 11.1.3), as opposed to all-to-all broadcast in the case of rowwise striping. Problem 3.8 describes multinode accumulation.

5.7 Section 5.3.2 describes and analyzes matrix-vector multiplication with checkerboard partitioning on a mesh. Show that, if a p-processor hypercube with store-and-forward routing is used, the parallel run time for the same algorithm is approximately $n^2/p + t_s \log p + (3/2)t_w(n/\sqrt{p}) \log p$ for an $n \times n$ matrix. How much improvement in this parallel run time can you obtain by using cut-through routing?

5.8 If $n \gg \sqrt{p}$ in Problem 5.7, then suggest ways of improving the parallel run time to $n^2/p + 2t_s \log p + 3t_w(n/\sqrt{p})$. Is the improved method more scalable than the one used in Problem 5.7?
Hint: See Problems 3.24 and 3.25.

5.9 Derive expressions for the overall asymptotic isoefficiency functions for matrix-vector multiplication on meshes with cut-through and store-and-forward routings when the matrix is partitioned among the processors using rowwise striping.

5.10 The overhead function for multiplying an $n \times n$ checkerboarded matrix with an $n \times 1$ vector on a p-processor mesh with cut-through routing is $t_s p \log p + t_w n \sqrt{p} \log p + 3t_h p^{3/2}$ (Equation 5.12). Substituting this expression in Equation 4.14 yields a quadratic equation in n. Using this equation, determine the precise isoefficiency function for the parallel system and compare it with Equations 5.13, 5.14, and 5.15. Does this comparison alter the conclusion that the term associated with t_w is responsible for the overall isoefficiency function of this parallel system?

5.11 Strassen's method [AHU74, CLR90] for matrix multiplication is an algorithm based on the divide-and-conquer technique. The sequential complexity of multiplying two $n \times n$ matrices using Strassen's algorithm is $\Theta(n^{2.81})$. Consider the simple matrix multiplication algorithm (Section 5.4.1) for multiplying two $n \times n$ matrices on a p-processor hypercube. Assume that the $n/\sqrt{p} \times n/\sqrt{p}$ submatrices are multiplied using Strassen's algorithm at each processor. Derive an expression for the parallel run time of this algorithm. Is the parallel algorithm cost-optimal?

5.12 Derive an expression for the parallel run time of the DNS algorithm for multiplying two $n \times n$ matrices on a $p^{1/3} \times p^{1/3} \times p^{1/3}$ three-dimensional mesh of processors with cut-through routing.

5.13 **(DNS algorithm with fewer than n^3 processors [DNS81])** Section 5.4.4 describes a parallel formulation of the DNS algorithm that uses fewer than n^3 processors. Another variation of this algorithm works with $p = n^2 q$ processors, where $1 \leq q \leq n$. Here the processor arrangement is regarded as a $q \times q \times q$ logical three-dimensional array of "superprocessors," in which each superprocessor is an $(n/q) \times (n/q)$ mesh of processors. This variant can be viewed as identical to the block variant described in Section 5.4.4, except that the role of each processor is now assumed by an $(n/q) \times (n/q)$ logical mesh of processors. This means that each block multiplication of $(n/q) \times (n/q)$ submatrices is performed in parallel by $(n/q)^2$ processors rather than by a single processor. Any of the algorithms described in Sections 5.4.1, 5.4.2, or 5.4.3 can be used to perform this multiplication.

Derive an expression for the parallel run time for this variant of the DNS algorithm in terms of n, p, t_s, and t_w. Compare the expression with Equation 5.24. Discuss the relative merits and drawbacks of the two variations of the DNS algorithm for fewer than n^3 processors.

5.14 Figure 5.15 shows that the pipelined version of Gaussian elimination requires 16 steps for a 5×5 matrix striped rowwise on five processors. Show that, in general, the algorithm illustrated in this figure completes in $4(n-1)$ steps for an $n \times n$ matrix striped rowwise with one row assigned to each processor.

5.15 Describe in detail a parallel implementation of the Gaussian elimination algorithm of Program 5.4 without pivoting if the $n \times n$ coefficient matrix is striped columnwise among p processors. Consider both pipelined and non-pipelined implementations. Also consider the cases $p = n$ and $p < n$.

Hint: The parallel implementation of Gaussian elimination described in Section 5.5.1 shows horizontal and vertical communication on a logical two-dimensional mesh of processors (Figure 5.20). A rowwise striping requires only the vertical part of this communication. Similarly, columnwise striping performs only the horizontal part of this communication.

5.16 Derive expressions for the parallel run times of all the implementations in Problem 5.15. Is the run time of any of these parallel implementations significantly different from the corresponding implementation with rowwise striping?

5.17 Redo Problem 5.16 with partial pivoting. In which implementations are the parallel run times significantly different for rowwise and columnwise partitioning?

5.18 Show that Gaussian elimination on an $n \times n$ matrix checkerboarded on an $n \times n$ mesh of processors is not cost-optimal if the $2n$ one-to-all broadcasts are performed synchronously.

5.19 Show that the cumulative idle time over all the processors in the Gaussian elimination algorithm is $\Theta(n^3)$ for a block mapping, whether the $n \times n$ matrix is striped or checkerboarded. Show that this idle time is reduced to $\Theta(n^2 p)$ for cyclic-striped and $\Theta(n^2 \sqrt{p})$ for cyclic-checkerboard mapping.

5.20 Prove that the isoefficiency function of the asynchronous version of the Gaussian elimination with checkerboard mapping is $\Theta(p^{3/2})$ if pivoting is not performed.

5.21 Derive precise expressions for the parallel run time of Gaussian elimination with and without partial pivoting if the $n \times n$ matrix of coefficients is partitioned among p processors of a square two-dimensional mesh with cut-through routing in the following formats:

(a) Rowwise block striping.
(b) Rowwise cyclic striping.
(c) Columnwise block striping.
(d) Columnwise cyclic striping.

5.22 **(Cholesky factorization)** Program 5.6 describes a row-oriented version of the Cholesky factorization algorithm for factorizing a symmetric positive definite matrix into the form $A = U^T U$. Cholesky factorization does not require pivoting. Describe a pipelined parallel formulation of this algorithm that uses checkerboard partitioning of the matrix on a square mesh of processors with store-and-forward routing. Draw a picture similar to Figure 5.19.

5.23 **(Fox's matrix multiplication algorithm with pipelining)** In Section 5.5.1 we described how pipelining the one-to-all broadcast improved the parallel Gaussian elimination algorithm. Note that Fox's algorithm for matrix multiplication (Section 5.4.3) also involves a one-to-all broadcast. Show that, if the processors within a row do not wait for the completion of the entire broadcast before starting their computations and follow a strategy similar to that in the pipelined version of Gaus-

```
procedure CHOLESKY (A)
begin
    for k := 0 to n − 1 do
        begin
            A[k, k] := √A[k, k];
            for j := k + 1 to n − 1 do
                A[k, j] := A[k, j]/A[k, k];
            for i := k + 1 to n − 1 do
                for j := i to n − 1 do
                    A[i, j] := A[i, j] − A[k, i] × A[k, j];
        endfor;        /* Line 3 */
end CHOLESKY
```

Program 5.6 A row-oriented Cholesky factorization algorithm.

sian elimination, then the $\sqrt{p}$ iterations of the algorithm can be overlapped. Also show that the asymptotic communication complexity of the pipelined version of Fox's algorithm is the same as that of Cannon's algorithm (Section 5.4.2).

5.24 **(Scaled speedup)** Scaled speedup is defined as the speedup obtained when the problem size is increased linearly with the number of processors; that is, if W is chosen as a base problem size for a single processor, then

$$\textit{Scaled Speedup} = \frac{Wp}{T_P(Wp, p)}. \tag{5.27}$$

For the simple matrix multiplication algorithm for the hypercube described in Section 5.4.1, plot the standard and scaled speedup curves for the base problem of multiplying 16 × 16 matrices. Use $p = 1, 4, 16, 64$, and 256. Assume that $t_s = 10$ and $t_w = 1$ in Equation 5.19.

5.25 Plot a third speedup curve for Problem 5.24, in which the problem size is scaled up according to the isoefficiency function, which is $\Theta(p^{3/2})$. Use the same values of t_s and t_w.

Hint: The scaled speedup under this method of scaling is

$$\textit{Isoefficient scaled speedup} = \frac{Wp^{3/2}}{T_P(Wp^{3/2}, p)}.$$

5.26 Plot the efficiency curves for the simple matrix multiplication algorithm on a hypercube corresponding to the standard speedup curve (Problem 5.24), the scaled speedup curve (Problem 5.24), and the speedup curve when the problem size is increased according to the isoefficiency function (Problem 5.25).

5.27 A drawback of increasing the number of processors without increasing the total work load is that the speedup does not increase linearly with the number of processors, and the efficiency drops monotonically. Based on your experience with

```
procedure MAT_MULT_CREW_PRAM (A, B, C, n)
begin
    Organize the n^2 processors into a logical mesh of n × n;
    for each processor P_{i,j} do
    begin
        C[i, j] := 0;
        for k := 0 to n − 1 do
            C[i, j] := C[i, j] + A[i, k] × B[k, j];
    endfor;
end MAT_MULT_CREW_PRAM
```

Program 5.7 An algorithm for multiplying two $n \times n$ matrices A and B on a CREW PRAM, yielding matrix $C = A \times B$.

Problems 5.24 and 5.26, discuss whether using scaled speedup instead of standard speedup solves the problem in general. What can you say about the isoefficiency function of a parallel system whose scaled speedup curve matches the speedup curve determined by increasing the problem size according to the isoefficiency function?

5.28 **(Time-constrained scaling)** Assume that $t_s = 10$ and $t_w = 1$ in the expression of parallel execution time (Equation 5.19) of the hypercube algorithm for matrix multiplication discussed in Section 5.4.1. For $p = 1, 4, 16, 64, 256, 1024$, and 4096, what is the largest problem that can be solved if the total run time is not to exceed 512 time units? In general, is it possible to solve an arbitrarily large problem in a fixed amount of time, provided that an unlimited number of processors is available? Give a brief explanation.

5.29 Describe a pipelined algorithm for performing back-substitution to solve a triangular system of equations of the form $Ux = y$, where the $n \times n$ unit upper-triangular matrix U is checkerboarded onto an $n \times n$ mesh of processors. Give an expression for the parallel run time of the algorithm. Modify the algorithm to work on fewer than n^2 processors, and derive an expression for the parallel execution time of the modified algorithm.

5.30 Consider the parallel algorithm given in Program 5.7 for multiplying two $n \times n$ matrices A and B to obtain the product matrix C. Assume that it takes time t_{local} for a memory read or write operation on a matrix element and time t_c to add and multiply two numbers. Determine the parallel run time for this algorithm on an n^2-processor CREW PRAM. Is this parallel system cost-optimal?

5.31 Assuming that concurrent read accesses to a memory location are serialized on an EREW PRAM, derive the parallel run time of the algorithm given in Program 5.7

```
procedure MAT_MULT_EREW_PRAM (A, B, C, n)
begin
    Organize the n^2 processors into a logical mesh of n × n;
    for each processor P_{i,j} do
    begin
        C[i, j] := 0;
        for k := 0 to n − 1 do
            C[i, j] := C[i, j]+
                    A[i, (i + j + k) mod n] × B[(i + j + k) mod n, j]
    endfor;
end MAT_MULT_EREW_PRAM
```

Program 5.8 An algorithm multiplying of two $n \times n$ matrices A and B on an EREW PRAM, yielding matrix $C = A \times B$.

on an n^2-processor EREW PRAM. Is this algorithm cost-optimal on an EREW PRAM?

5.32 Consider a shared-address-space parallel computer with n^2 processors. Assume that each processor has some local memory, and $A[i, j]$ and $B[i, j]$ are stored in the local memory of processor $P_{i,j}$. Furthermore, processor $P_{i,j}$ computes $C[i, j]$ in its local memory. Assume that it takes $t_{nonlocal}$ to perform a read or write operation on nonlocal memory and t_{local} time on local memory. Note that, in practice, $t_{nonlocal}$ is much higher than t_{local}. Derive an expression for the parallel run time of the algorithm in Program 5.7 on this parallel computer.

5.33 Program 5.7 can be modified so that the parallel run time on an EREW PRAM is less than that in Problem 5.31. The modified program is shown in Program 5.8. What is the parallel run time of Program 5.8 on an EREW PRAM and a shared-address-space parallel computer with memory access times as described in Problems 5.31 and 5.32? Is the algorithm cost-optimal on these architectures?

5.34 Consider an implementation of Program 5.8 on a shared-address-space parallel computer with fewer than n^2 (say, p) processors and with memory access times as described in Problem 5.32. What is the parallel runtime?

5.35 Consider the implementation of the parallel matrix multiplication algorithm presented in Section 5.4.1 on a shared-address-space computer with memory access times as given in Problem 5.32. In this algorithm, each processor first receives all the data it needs into its local memory, and then performs the computation. Derive the parallel run time of this algorithm. Compare the performance of this algorithm with that in Problem 5.34.

5.36 Use the results of Problems 5.30—5.35 to comment on the viability of the PRAM model as a platform for parallel algorithm design. Also comment on the relevance of the message-passing model for shared-address-space computers.

References

[AHU74] A. V. Aho, J. E. Hopcroft, and J. D. Ullman. *The Design and Analysis of Computer Algorithms*. Addison-Wesley, Reading, MA, 1974.

[Akl89] S. G. Akl. *The Design and Analysis of Parallel Algorithms*. Prentice-Hall, Englewood Cliffs, NJ, 1989.

[Ber84] S. Berkowitz. On computing the determinant in small parallel time using a small number of processors. *Information Processing Letters*, 18(3):147–150, March 1984.

[Ber89] J. Berntsen. Communication efficient matrix multiplication on hypercubes. *Parallel Computing*, 12:335–342, 1989.

[BT89] D. P. Bertsekas and J. N. Tsitsiklis. *Parallel and Distributed Computation: Numerical Methods*. Prentice-Hall, Englewood Cliffs, NJ, 1989.

[CAHH91] N. P. Chrisopchoides, M. Aboelaze, E. N. Houstis, and C. E. Houstis. The parallelization of some level 2 and 3 BLAS operations on distributed-memory machines. In *Proceedings of the First International Conference of the Austrian Center of Parallel Computation*. Springer-Verlag Series Lecture Notes in Computer Science, 1991.

[Can69] L. E. Cannon. *A cellular computer to implement the Kalman Filter Algorithm*. Ph.D. thesis, Montana State University, Bozman, MT, 1969.

[CG87] E. Chu and J. A. George. Gaussian elimination with partial pivoting and load balancing on a multiprocessor. *Parallel Computing*, 5:65–74, 1987.

[Cha79] A. K. Chandra. Maximal parallelism in matrix multiplication. Technical Report RC-6193, IBM T. J. Watson Research Center, Yorktown Heights, NY, 1979.

[Cha87] R. Chamberlain. An alternate view of LU factorization on a hypercube multiprocessor. In M. T. Heath, editor, *Hypercube Multiprocessors 1987*, 569–575. SIAM, Philadelphia, PA, 1987.

[CLR90] T. H. Cormen, C. E. Leiserson, and R. L. Rivest. *Introduction to Algorithms*. MIT Press, McGraw-Hill, New York, NY, 1990.

[CS88] V. Cherkassky and R. Smith. Efficient mapping and implementations of matrix algorithms on a hypercube. *The Journal of Supercomputing*, 2:7–27, 1988.

[Dav86] G. J. Davis. Column LU factorization with pivoting on a hypercube multiprocessor. *SIAM Journal on Algebraic and Discrete Methods*, 7:538–550, 1986. Also available as Technical Report ORNL-6219, Oak Ridge National Laboratory, Oak Ridge, TN, 1985.

[DHvdV93] J. W. Demmel, M. T. Heath, and H. A. van der Vorst. Parallel numerical linear algebra. *Acta Numerica*, 111–197, 1993.

[DNS81] E. Dekel, D. Nassimi, and S. Sahni. Parallel matrix and graph algorithms. *SIAM Journal on Computing*, 10:657–673, 1981.

[dV89] E. F. V. de Velde. Multicomputer matrix computations: Theory and practice. In *Proceedings of the Fourth Conference on Hypercubes, Concurrent Computers, and Applications*, 1303–1308, 1989.

[Ede89] A. Edelman. Optimal matrix transposition and bit-reversal on hypercubes: Node address–memory address exchanges. Technical report, Thinking Machines Corporation, Cambridge, MA, 1989.

[EHHR88] S. C. Eisenstat, M. T. Heath, C. S. Henkel, and C. H. Romine. Modified cyclic algorithms for solving triangular systems on distributed-memory multiprocessors. *SIAM Journal on Scientific and Statistical Computing*, 9(3):589–600, 1988.

[Ekl72] J. O. Eklundh. A fast computer method for matrix transposing. *IEEE Transactions on Computers*, 21(7):801–803, 1972.

[FF86] G. C. Fox and W. Furmanski. Optimal communication algorithms on hypercube. Technical Report CCCP-314, California Institute of Technology, Pasadena, CA, 1986.

[FJL$^+$88] G. C. Fox, M. Johnson, G. Lyzenga, S. W. Otto, J. Salmon, and D. Walker. *Solving Problems on Concurrent Processors: Volume 1*. Prentice-Hall, Englewood Cliffs, NJ, 1988.

[FOH87] G. C. Fox, S. W. Otto, and A. J. G. Hey. Matrix algorithms on a hypercube I: Matrix multiplication. *Parallel Computing*, 4:17–31, 1987.

[Gei85] G. A. Geist. Efficient parallel LU factorization with pivoting on a hypercube multiprocessor. Technical Report ORNL-6211, Oak Ridge National Laboratory, Oak Ridge, TN, 1985.

[GH85] G. A. Geist and M. T. Heath. Parallel Cholesky factorization on a hypercube multiprocessor. Technical Report ORNL-6190, Oak Ridge National Laboratory, Oak Ridge, TN, 1985.

[GH86] G. A. Geist and M. T. Heath. Matrix factorization on a hypercube multiprocessor. In M. T. Heath, editor, *Hypercube Multiprocessors 1986*, 161–180. SIAM, Philadelphia, PA, 1986.

[GK91] A. Gupta and V. Kumar. The scalability of matrix multiplication algorithms on parallel computers. Technical Report TR 91-54, Department of Computer Science, University of Minnesota, Minneapolis, MN, 1991. A short version appears in *Proceedings of 1993 International Conference on Parallel Processing*, pages III-115–III-119, 1993.

[GL89] G. H. Golub and C. V. Loan. *Matrix Computations: Second Edition*. The Johns Hopkins University Press, Baltimore, MD, 1989.

[GPS90] K. A. Gallivan, R. J. Plemmons, and A. H. Sameh. Parallel algorithms for dense linear algebra computations. *SIAM Review*, 32(1):54–135, March 1990. Also appears in K. A. Gallivan et al. *Parallel Algorithms for Matrix Computations*. SIAM, Philadelphia, PA, 1990.

[GR88] G. A. Geist and C. H. Romine. LU factorization algorithms on distributed-memory multiprocessor architectures. *SIAM Journal on Scientific and Statistical Computing*, 9(4):639–649, 1988. Also available as Technical Report ORNL/TM-10383, Oak Ridge National Laboratory, Oak Ridge, TN, 1987.

[Hea85] M. T. Heath. Parallel Cholesky factorization in message-passing multiprocessor environments. Technical Report ORNL-6150, Oak Ridge National Laboratory, Oak Ridge, TN, 1985.

[Hip89] P. G. Hipes. Matrix multiplication on the JPL/Caltech Mark IIIfp hypercube. Technical Report C3P 746, Concurrent Computation Program, California Institute of Technology, Pasadena, CA, 1989.

[HJE91] C.-T. Ho, S. L. Johnsson, and A. Edelman. Matrix multiplication on hypercubes using full bandwidth and constant storage. In *Proceedings of the 1991 International Conference on Parallel Processing*, 447–451, 1991.

[HR88] M. T. Heath and C. H. Romine. Parallel solution of triangular systems on distributed-memory multiprocessors. *SIAM Journal on Scientific and Statistical Computing*, 9(3):558–588, 1988.

[HR91] C.-T. Ho and M. T. Raghunath. Efficient communication primitives on circuit-switched hypercubes. In *The Sixth Distributed Memory Computing Conference Proceedings*, 390–397, 1991.

[JH88] S. L. Johnsson and C.-T. Ho. Matrix transposition on Boolean n-cube configured ensemble architectures. *SIAM Journal on Matrix Analysis and Applications*, 9(3):419–454, July 1988.

[Joh87] S. L. Johnsson. Communication efficient basic linear algebra computations on hypercube architectures. *Journal of Parallel and Distributed Computing*, 4(2):133–172, April 1987.

[Joh90] S. L. Johnsson. Communication in network architectures. In R. Suaya and G. Birtwistle, editors, *VLSI and Parallel Computation*, 223–389. Morgan Kaufmann, San Mateo, CA, 1990.

[LC88] G.-J. Li and T. Coleman. A parallel triangular solver for a hypercube multiprocessor. *SIAM Journal on Scientific and Statistical Computing*, 9:485–502, 1988.

[LC89] G.-J. Li and T. Coleman. A new method for solving triangular systems on distributed memory message passing multiprocessors. *SIAM Journal on Scientific and Statistical Computing*, 10:382–396, 1989.

[LD90] S. Lakshmivarahan and S. K. Dhall. *Analysis and Design of Parallel Algorithms: Arithmetic and Matrix Problems*. McGraw-Hill, New York, NY, 1990.

[Lei92] F. T. Leighton. *Introduction to Parallel Algorithms and Architectures*. Morgan Kaufmann, San Mateo, CA, 1992.

[MdV87] O. A. McBryan and E. F. V. de Velde. Hypercube algorithms and implementations. *SIAM Journal on Scientific and Statistical Computing*, 8(2):s227–s287, March 1987.

[Mod88] J. J. Modi. *Parallel Algorithms and Matrix Computation*. Oxford University Press, Oxford, UK, 1988.

[Mol86] C. Moler. Matrix computation on distributed-memory multiprocessors. In M. T. Heath, editor, *Hypercube Multiprocessors 1986*, 181–195. SIAM, Philadelphia, PA, 1986.

[OR88] J. M. Ortega and C. H. Romine. The ijk forms of factorization methods II: Parallel systems. *Parallel Computing*, 7:149–162, 1988.

[Ort88] J. M. Ortega. *Introduction to Parallel and Vector Solution of Linear Systems*. Plenum Press, New York, NY, 1988.

[OS85] D. P. O'Leary and G. W. Stewart. Data-flow algorithms for parallel matrix computations. *Communications of the ACM*, 28:840–853, 1985.

[OS86] D. P. O'Leary and G. W. Stewart. Assignment and scheduling in parallel matrix factorization. *Linear Algebra and its Applications*, 77:275–299, 1986.

[PR85] V. Pan and J. H. Reif. Efficient parallel solution of linear systems. In *17th Annual ACM Symposium on Theory of Computing*, 143–152, 1985.

[PV80] F. P. Preparata and J. Vuillemin. Area-time optimal VLSI networks for matrix multiplication. In *Proceedings of the 14th Princeton Conference on Information Science and Systems*, 300–309, 1980.

[RO88] C. H. Romine and J. M. Ortega. Parallel solution of triangular systems of equations. *Parallel Computing*, 6:109–114, 1988.

[Rob90] Y. Robert. *The Impact of Vector and Parallel Architectures on Gaussian Elimination*. John Wiley and Sons, New York, NY, 1990.

[Rom87] C. H. Romine. The parallel solution of triangular systems on a hypercube. In M. T. Heath, editor, *Hypercube Multiprocessors 1987*, 552–559. SIAM, Philadelphia, PA, 1987.

[Saa86] Y. Saad. Communication complexity of the gaussian elimination algorithm on multiprocessors. *Linear Algebra and its Applications*, 77:315–340, 1986.

[SW87] Q. F. Stout and B. A. Wagar. Passing messages in link-bound hypercubes. In M. T. Heath, editor, *Hypercube Multiprocessors 1987*, 251–257. SIAM, Philadelphia, PA, 1987.

[Tic88] W. F. Tichy. Parallel matrix multiplication on the connection machine. Technical Report RIACS TR 88.41, Research Institute for Advanced Computer Science, NASA Ames Research Center, Moffet Field, CA, 1988.

[Vav89] S. Vavasis. Gaussian elimination with pivoting is P-complete. *SIAM Journal on Discrete Mathematics*, 2:413–423, 1989.

CHAPTER 6

Sorting

Sorting is one of the most common operations performed by a computer. Because sorted data are easier to manipulate than randomly-ordered data, many algorithms require sorted data. Sorting is of additional importance to parallel computing because of its close relation to the task of routing data among processors, which is an essential part of many parallel algorithms. Many parallel sorting algorithms have been investigated for a variety of parallel computer architectures. This chapter presents several parallel sorting algorithms for PRAM, mesh, and hypercube architectures.

Sorting is defined as the task of arranging an unordered collection of elements into monotonically increasing (or decreasing) order. Specifically, let $S = \langle a_1, a_2, \ldots, a_n \rangle$ be a sequence of n elements in arbitrary order; sorting transforms S into a monotonically increasing sequence $S' = \langle a'_1, a'_2, \ldots, a'_n \rangle$ such that $a'_i \leq a'_j$ for $1 \leq i \leq j \leq n$, and S' is a permutation of S.

Sorting algorithms are categorized as ***internal*** or ***external***. In internal sorting, the number of elements to be sorted is small enough to fit into the processor's main memory. In contrast, external sorting algorithms use auxiliary storage (such as tapes and hard disks) for sorting because the number of elements to be sorted is too large to fit into memory. This chapter concentrates on internal sorting algorithms only.

Sorting algorithms can be categorized as ***comparison-based*** and ***noncomparison-based***. A comparison-based algorithm sorts an unordered sequence of elements by repeatedly comparing pairs of elements and, if they are out of order, exchanging them. This fundamental operation of comparison-based sorting is called ***compare-exchange***. The lower bound on the sequential complexity of any comparison-based sorting algorithm is $\Theta(n \log n)$, where n is the number of elements to be sorted. Noncomparison-based algorithms sort by using certain known properties of the elements (such as their binary representation or their distribution). The lower-bound complexity of these algorithms is $\Theta(n)$. We concentrate on comparison-based sorting algorithms in this chapter, although we briefly discuss some noncomparison-based sorting algorithms in Section 6.5.

6.1 Issues in Sorting on Parallel Computers

Parallelizing a sequential sorting algorithm involves distributing the elements to be sorted onto the available processors. This process raises a number of issues that we must address in order to make the presentation of parallel sorting algorithms clearer.

6.1.1 Where the Input and Output Sequences Are Stored

In sequential sorting algorithms, the input and the sorted sequences are stored in the processor's memory. However, in parallel sorting there are two places where these sequences can reside. They may be stored on only one of the processors, or they may be distributed among the processors. The latter approach is particularly useful if sorting is an intermediate step in another algorithm. In this chapter, we assume that the input and sorted sequences are distributed among the processors.

Now consider the precise distribution of the sorted output sequence among the processors. A general method of distribution is to enumerate the processors and use this enumeration to specify a global ordering for the sorted sequence. In other words, the sequence will be sorted with respect to this processor enumeration. For instance, if P_i comes before P_j in the enumeration, all the elements stored in P_i will be smaller than those stored in P_j. We can enumerate the processors in many ways. For certain parallel algorithms and interconnection networks, some enumerations lead to more efficient parallel formulations than others.

Example 6.1 Enumerating Hypercube Processors

As discussed in Section 2.4.1, there are two natural ways to enumerate the processors of a hypercube-connected computer—using each processor's label, and using a Gray-code mapping. Recall that, in the processor-label enumeration, consecutive processors do not necessarily correspond to neighboring hypercube processors, but in the Gray-code enumeration, consecutive processors correspond to neighboring hypercube processors. Consider an algorithm that performs a compare-exchange on elements stored in consecutively enumerated processors. The Gray-code mapping requires less communication than the processor-label enumeration, since all communication is between neighboring processors. ■

6.1.2 How Comparisons Are Performed

A sequential sorting algorithm can easily perform a compare-exchange on two elements because they are stored locally in the processor's memory. In parallel sorting algorithms, this step is not so easy. If the elements reside on the same processor, the comparison can be done easily. But if the elements reside on different processors, the situation becomes more complicated.

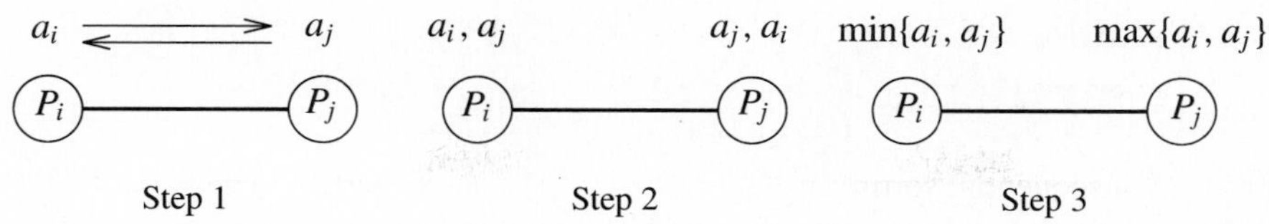

Figure 6.1 A parallel compare-exchange operation. Processors P_i and P_j send their elements to each other. Processor P_i keeps $\min\{a_i, a_j\}$, and P_j keeps $\max\{a_i, a_j\}$.

One Element Per Processor

Consider the case in which each processor holds only one element of the sequence to be sorted. At some point in the execution of the algorithm, a pair of processors (P_i, P_j) may need to compare their elements, a_i and a_j. After the comparison, P_i will hold the smaller and P_j the larger of $\{a_i, a_j\}$. We can perform comparison by having both processors send their elements to each other. Each processor compares the received element with its own and retains the appropriate element. In our example, P_i will keep the smaller and P_j will keep the larger of $\{a_i, a_j\}$. As in the sequential case, we refer to this operation as ***compare-exchange***. As Figure 6.1 illustrates, each compare-exchange operation requires one comparison step and one communication step.

If we assume that processor P_i and P_j are neighbors, and the communication channels are bidirectional, then the communication cost of a compare-exchange step is $(t_s + t_w)$, where t_s and t_w are message-startup time and per-word transfer time, respectively. In commercially available message-passing computers, t_s is significantly larger than t_w, so the communication time is dominated by t_s. Note that in today's parallel computers it takes more time to send an element from one processor to another than it takes to compare the elements. Consequently, any parallel sorting formulation that uses as many processors as elements to be sorted will deliver very poor performance because the overall parallel run time will be dominated by interprocessor communication.

More than One Element Per Processor

A general-purpose parallel sorting algorithm must be able to sort a large sequence with a relatively small number of processors. Let p be the number of processors $P_0, P_1, \ldots, P_{p-1}$, and let n be the number of elements to be sorted. Each processor is assigned a block of n/p elements, and all the processors cooperate to sort the sequence. Let $A_0, A_1, \ldots A_{p-1}$ be the blocks assigned to processors $P_0, P_1, \ldots P_{p-1}$, respectively. We say that $A_i \leq A_j$ if every element of A_i is smaller than every element in A_j. When the sorting algorithm finishes, each processor P_i holds a set A'_i such that $A'_i \leq A'_j$ for $i \leq j$, and $\bigcup_{i=0}^{p-1} A_i = \bigcup_{i=0}^{p-1} A'_i$.

As in the one-element-per-processor case, two processors P_i and P_j may have to redistribute their blocks of n/p elements so that one of them will get the smaller n/p elements and the other will get the larger n/p elements. Let A_i and A_j be the blocks stored in processors P_i and P_j. If the block of n/p elements at each processor is already sorted,

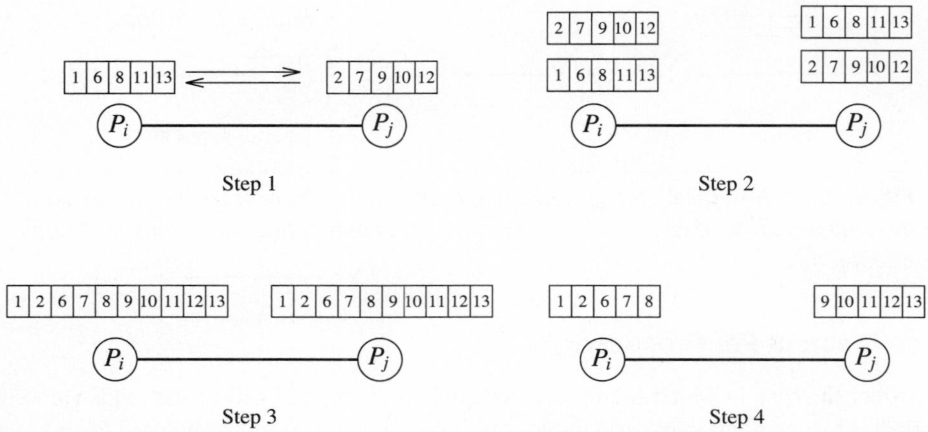

Figure 6.2 A compare-split operation. Each processor sends its block of size n/p to the other processor. Each processor merges the received block with its own block and retains only the appropriate half of the merged block. In this example, processor P_i retains the smaller elements and processor P_j retains the larger elements.

the redistribution can be done efficiently as follows. Each processor sends its block to the other processor. Now each processor merges the two sorted blocks and retains only the appropriate half of the merged block. We refer to this operation of comparing and splitting two sorted blocks as ***compare-split***. The compare-split operation is illustrated in Figure 6.2.

If we assume that processors P_i and P_j are neighbors and that the communication channels are bidirectional, then the communication cost of a compare-split operation is $(t_s + t_w n/p)$. As the block size increases, the significance of t_s decreases, and for sufficiently large blocks it can be ignored. Thus, the time required to merge two sorted blocks of n/p elements is $\Theta(n/p)$.

6.2 Sorting Networks

In the quest for fast sorting methods, a number of networks have been designed that sort n elements in time significantly smaller than $\Theta(n \log n)$. These sorting networks are based on a comparison network model, in which many comparison operations are performed simultaneously.

The key component of these networks is a ***comparator***. A comparator is a device with two inputs x and y and two outputs x' and y'. For an ***increasing comparator***, $x' = \min\{x, y\}$ and $y' = \max\{x, y\}$; for a ***decreasing comparator*** $x' = \max\{x, y\}$ and $y' = \min\{x, y\}$. Figure 6.3 gives the schematic representation of the two types of comparators. As the two elements enter the input wires of the comparator, they are compared and, if necessary, exchanged before they go to the output wires. We denote an increasing comparator by $\oplus$ and a decreasing comparator by $\ominus$. A sorting network is usually made up of a series of

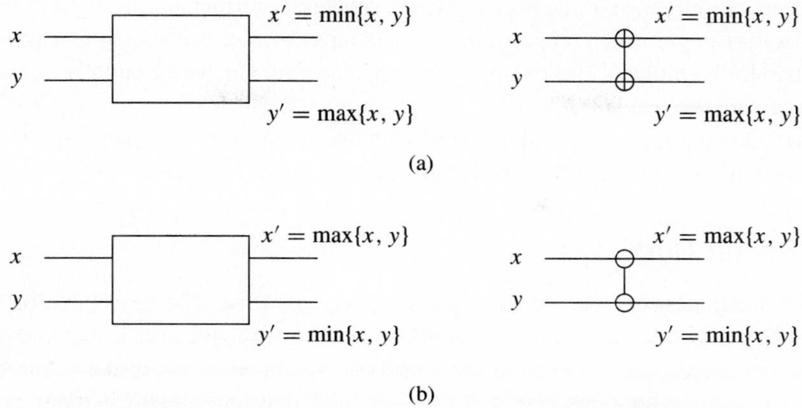

Figure 6.3 A schematic representation of comparators: (a) an increasing comparator, and (b) a decreasing comparator.

columns, and each column contains a number of comparators connected in parallel. Each column of comparators performs a permutation, and the output obtained from the final column is sorted in increasing or decreasing order. Figure 6.4 illustrates a typical sorting network. The ***depth*** of a network is the number of columns it contains. Since the speed of a comparator is a technology-dependent constant, the speed of the network is proportional to its depth.

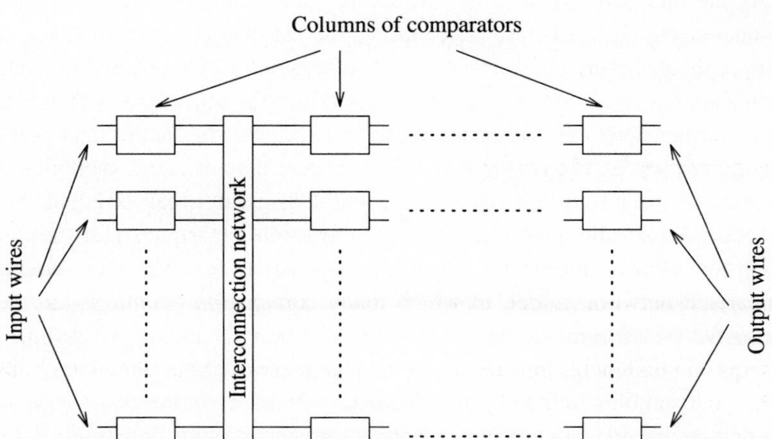

Figure 6.4 A typical sorting network. Every sorting network is made up of a series of columns, and each column contains a number of comparators connected in parallel.

We can convert any sorting network into a sequential sorting algorithm by emulating the comparators in software and performing the comparisons of each column sequentially. The comparator is emulated by a compare-exchange operation, where x and y are compared and, if necessary, exchanged.

The following section describes a sorting network that sorts n elements in $\Theta(\log^2 n)$ time. To simplify the presentation, we assume that n is a power of two.

6.2.1 Bitonic Sort

A bitonic sorting network sorts n elements in $\Theta(\log^2 n)$ time. The key operation of the bitonic sorting network is the rearrangement of a bitonic sequence into a sorted sequence. A ***bitonic sequence*** is a sequence of elements $\langle a_0, a_1, \ldots, a_{n-1}\rangle$ with the property that either (1) there exists an index i, $0 \le i \le n-1$, such that $\langle a_0, \ldots, a_i\rangle$ is monotonically increasing and $\langle a_{i+1}, \ldots, a_{n-1}\rangle$ is monotonically decreasing, or (2) there exists a cyclic shift of indices so that (1) is satisfied. For example, $\langle 1, 2, 4, 7, 6, 0\rangle$ is a bitonic sequence, because it first increases and then decreases. Similarly, $\langle 8, 9, 2, 1, 0, 4\rangle$ is another bitonic sequence, because it is a cyclic shift of $\langle 0, 4, 8, 9, 2, 1\rangle$.

We present a method to rearrange a bitonic sequence to obtain a monotonically increasing sequence. Let $s = \langle a_0, a_1, \ldots, a_{n-1}\rangle$ be a bitonic sequence such that $a_0 \le a_1 \le \ldots \le a_{n/2-1}$ and $a_{n/2} \ge a_{n/2+1} \ge \ldots \ge a_{n-1}$. Consider the following subsequences of s:

$$\begin{aligned} s_1 &= \langle \min\{a_0, a_{n/2}\}, \min\{a_1, a_{n/2+1}\}, \ldots, \min\{a_{n/2-1}, a_{n-1}\}\rangle \\ s_2 &= \langle \max\{a_0, a_{n/2}\}, \max\{a_1, a_{n/2+1}\}, \ldots, \max\{a_{n/2-1}, a_{n-1}\}\rangle \end{aligned} \tag{6.1}$$

In sequence s_1, there is an element $b_i = \min\{a_i, a_{n/2+i}\}$ such that all the elements before b_i are from the increasing part of the original sequence and all the elements after b_i are from the decreasing part. Also, in sequence s_2, the element $b'_i = \max\{a_i, a_{n/2+i}\}$ is such that all the elements before b'_i are from the decreasing part of the original sequence and all the elements after b'_i are from the increasing part. Thus, the sequences s_1 and s_2 are bitonic sequences. Furthermore, every element of the first sequence is smaller than every element of the second sequence. The reason is that b_i is greater than or equal to all elements of s_1, b'_i is less than or equal to all elements of s_2, and b'_i is greater than or equal to b_i. Thus, we have reduced the initial problem of rearranging a bitonic sequence of size n to that of rearranging two smaller bitonic sequences and concatenating the results. We refer to the operation of splitting a bitonic sequence of size n into the two bitonic sequences defined by Equation 6.1 as a ***bitonic split***. Although in obtaining s_1 and s_2 we assumed that the original sequence had increasing and decreasing sequences of the same length, the bitonic split operation also holds for any bitonic sequence (Problem 6.3).

We can recursively obtain shorter bitonic sequences using Equation 6.1 for each of the bitonic subsequences until we obtain subsequences of size one. At that point, the output is sorted in monotonically increasing order. Since after each bitonic split operation the size of the problem is halved, the number of splits required to rearrange the bitonic sequence into a sorted sequence is $\log n$. The procedure of sorting a bitonic sequence using

Original sequence	3	5	8	9	10	12	14	20	95	90	60	40	35	23	18	0
1st Split	3	5	8	9	10	12	14	0	95	90	60	40	35	23	18	20
2nd Split	3	5	8	0	10	12	14	9	35	23	18	20	95	90	60	40
3rd Split	3	0	8	5	10	9	14	12	18	20	35	23	60	40	95	90
4th Split	0	3	5	8	9	10	12	14	18	20	23	35	40	60	90	95

Figure 6.5 Merging a 16-element bitonic sequence through a series of log 16 bitonic splits.

bitonic splits is called ***bitonic merge***. The recursive bitonic merge procedure is illustrated in Figure 6.5.

We now have a method for merging a bitonic sequence into a sorted sequence. This method is easy to implement on a network of comparators. This network of comparators, known as a ***bitonic merging network***, it is illustrated in Figure 6.6. The network contains $\log n$ columns. Each column contains $n/2$ comparators and performs one step of the bitonic merge. This network takes as input the bitonic sequence and outputs the sequence in sorted order. We denote a bitonic merging network with n inputs by $\oplus$BM[n]. If we replace the $\oplus$ comparators in Figure 6.6 by $\ominus$ comparators, the input will be sorted in monotonically decreasing order; such a network is denoted by $\ominus$BM[n].

Armed with the bitonic merging network, consider the task of sorting n unordered elements. This is done by repeatedly merging bitonic sequences of increasing length, as illustrated in Figure 6.7.

Let us now see how this method works. A sequence of two elements x and y forms a bitonic sequence, since either $x \leq y$, in which case the bitonic sequence has x and y in the increasing part and no elements in the decreasing part, or $x \geq y$, in which case the bitonic sequence has x and y in the decreasing part and no elements in the increasing part. Hence, any unsorted sequence of elements is a concatenation of bitonic sequences of size two. Each stage of the network shown in Figure 6.7 merges adjacent bitonic sequences in increasing and decreasing order. According to the definition of a bitonic sequence, the sequence obtained by concatenating the increasing and decreasing sequences is bitonic. Hence, the output of each stage in the network in Figure 6.7 is a concatenation of bitonic sequences that are twice as long as those at the input. By merging larger and larger bitonic sequences, we eventually obtain a bitonic sequence of size n. Merging this sequence sorts the input. We refer to the algorithm embodied in this method as ***bitonic sort*** and the network as a ***bitonic sorting network***. The first three stages of the network in Figure 6.7 are shown explicitly in Figure 6.8. The last stage of Figure 6.7 is shown explicitly in Figure 6.6.

The last stage of an n-element bitonic sorting network contains a bitonic merging network with n inputs. This has a depth of $\log n$. The other stages perform a complete sort of $n/2$ elements. Hence, the depth, $d(n)$, of the network in Figure 6.7 is given by the following recurrence relation:

$$d(n) = d(n/2) + \log n \qquad (6.2)$$

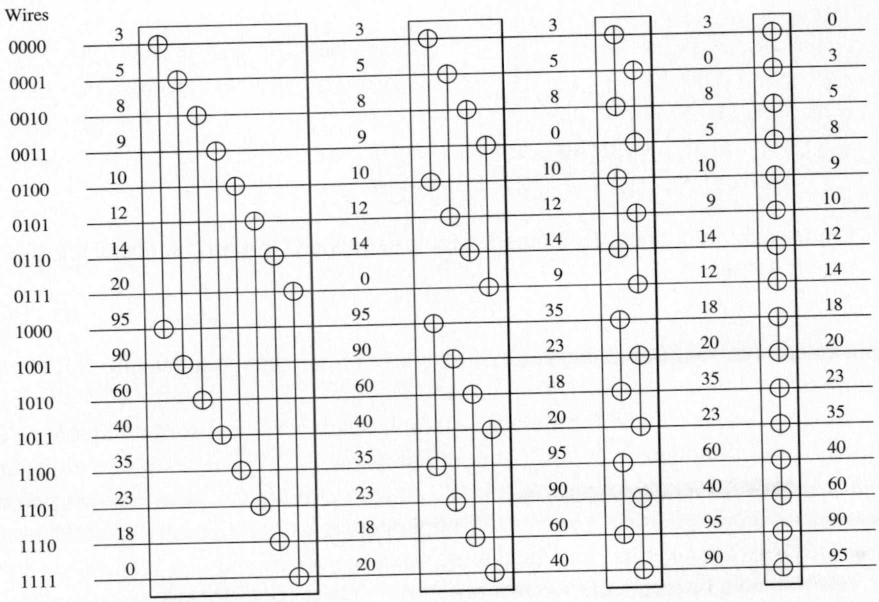

Figure 6.6 A bitonic merging network for $n = 16$. The input wires are numbered $0, 1 \ldots, n-1$, and the binary representation of these numbers is shown. Each column of comparators is drawn separately; the entire figure represents a $\oplus$BM[16] bitonic merging network. The network takes a bitonic sequence and outputs it in sorted order.

Solving Equation 6.2, we obtain $d(n) = \sum_{i=1}^{\log n} i = (\log^2 n + \log n)/2 = \Theta(\log^2 n)$. This network can be implemented on a serial computer, yielding a $\Theta(n \log^2 n)$ sorting algorithm. The bitonic sorting network can also be adapted and used as a sorting algorithm for parallel computers. In the next section, we describe how this can be done for hypercube- and mesh-connected parallel computers.

6.2.2 Mapping Bitonic Sort onto a Hypercube and a Mesh

We discuss two mappings of bitonic sort to hypercube- and mesh-connected computers—one in which each processor holds a single element, and one in which each processor holds a block of elements. The bitonic sorting network for sorting n elements contains $\log n$ stages, and stage i consists of i columns of $n/2$ comparators. As Figures 6.6 and 6.8 show, each column of comparators performs compare-exchange operations on n wires. On a parallel computer, the compare-exchange function is performed by a pair of processors.

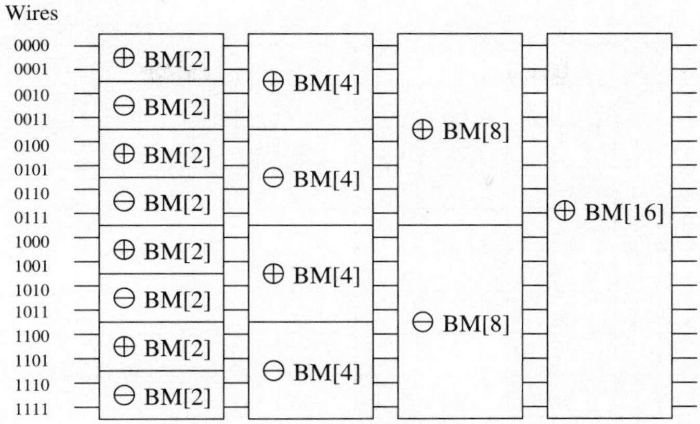

Figure 6.7 A schematic representation of a network that converts an input sequence into a bitonic sequence. In this example, $\oplus$BM[k] and $\ominus$BM[k] denote bitonic merging networks of input size k that use $\oplus$ and $\ominus$ comparators, respectively. The last merging network ($\oplus$BM[16]) sorts the input. In this example, $n = 16$.

One Element Per Processor

In this mapping, each of the n processors contains one element of the input sequence. Graphically, each wire of the bitonic sorting network represents a distinct processor. During each step of the algorithm, the compare-exchange operations performed by a column of comparators are performed by $n/2$ pairs of processors. One important question is how to map processors to wires in order to minimize the distance that the elements travel during a compare-exchange operation. If the mapping is poor, the elements travel a long distance before they can be compared, which will degrade performance. Ideally, wires that perform a compare-exchange should be mapped onto neighboring processors. Then the parallel formulation of bitonic sort will have the best possible performance over all the formulations that require n processors.

To obtain a good mapping, we must further investigate the way that input wires are paired during each stage of bitonic sort. Consider Figures 6.6 and 6.8, which show the full bitonic sorting network for $n = 16$. In each of the $(1 + \log 16)(\log 16)/2 = 10$ comparator columns, certain wires compare-exchange their elements. Focus on the binary representation of the wire labels. In any step, the compare-exchange operation is performed between two wires only if their labels differ in exactly one bit. During each of the four stages, wires whose labels differ in the least-significant bit perform a compare-exchange in the last step of each stage. During the last three stages, wires whose labels differ in the second-least-significant bit perform a compare-exchange in the second-to-last step of each stage. In general, wires whose labels differ in the ith least-significant bit perform

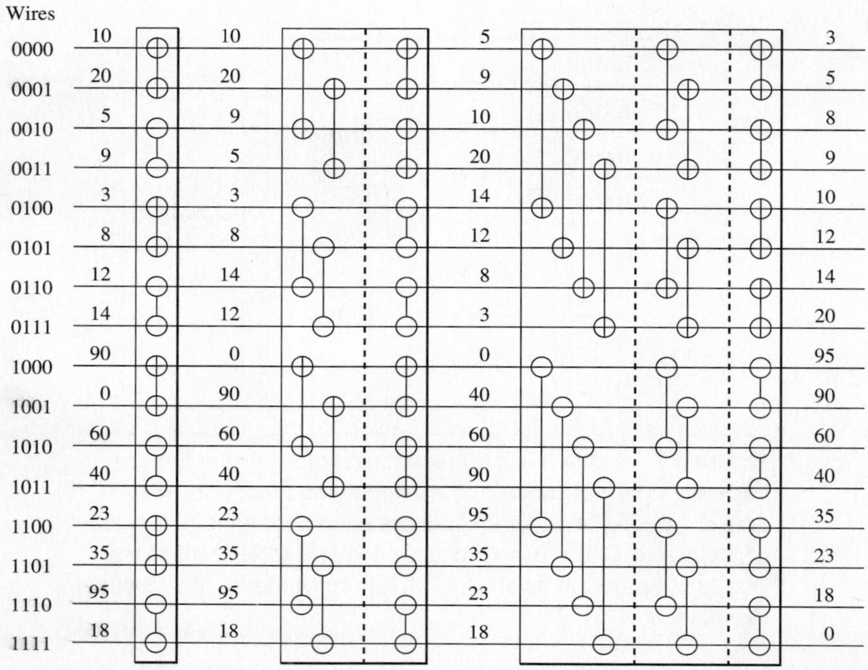

Figure 6.8 The comparator network that transforms an input sequence of 16 unordered numbers into a bitonic sequence. In contrast to Figure 6.6, the columns of comparators in each bitonic merging network are drawn in a single box, separated by a dashed line.

a compare-exchange $(\log n - i + 1)$ times. This observation helps us efficiently map wires onto processors by mapping wires that perform compare-exchange operations more frequently to processors that are close to each other.

Hypercube Mapping wires onto the processors of a hypercube-connected parallel computer is straightforward. Compare-exchange operations take place between wires whose labels differ in only one bit. In a hypercube, processors whose labels differ in only one bit are neighbors (Section 2.4.1). Thus, an optimal mapping of input wires to hypercube processors is the one that maps an input wire with label l to a processor with label l where $l = 0, 1, \ldots, n-1$.

Consider how processors are paired for their compare-exchange steps in a d-dimensional hypercube (that is, $p = 2^d$). In the final stage of bitonic sort, the input has been converted into a bitonic sequence. During the first step of this stage, processors that differ only in the dth bit of the binary representation of their labels (that is, the most significant bit) compare-exchange their elements. Thus, the compare-exchange operation takes place between processors along the dth dimension. Similarly, during the second

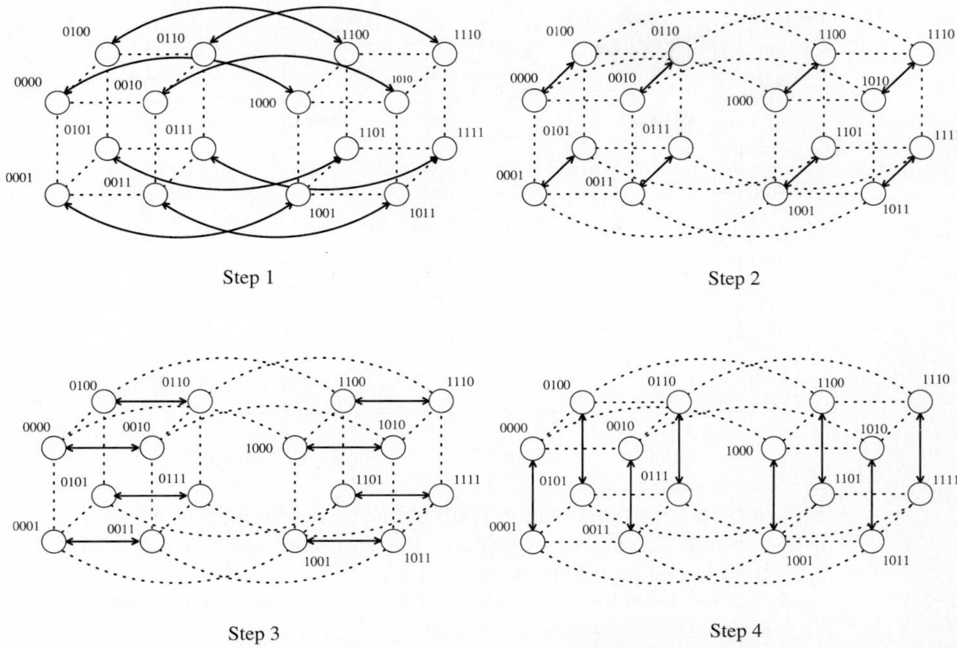

Figure 6.9 Communication during the last stage of bitonic sort. Each wire is mapped to a hypercube processor; each connection represents a compare-exchange between processors.

step of the algorithm, the compare-exchange operation takes place among the processors along the $(d-1)^{\text{st}}$ dimension. In general, during the ith step of the final stage, processors communicate along the $(d-(i-1))^{\text{st}}$ dimension. Figure 6.9 illustrates the communication during the last stage of the bitonic sort algorithm.

A bitonic merge of sequences of size 2^k can be performed on a k-dimensional subcube, with each such sequence assigned to a different subcube (Problem 6.5). Furthermore, during the ith step of this bitonic merge, the processors that compare their elements are neighbors along the $(k-(i-1))^{\text{st}}$ dimension. Figure 6.10 is a modification of Figure 6.7, showing the communication characteristics of the bitonic sort algorithm on a hypercube.

The bitonic sort algorithm for a hypercube is shown in Program 6.1. The algorithm relies on the functions *comp_exchange_max(i)* and *comp_exchange_min(i)*. These functions compare the local element with the element on the nearest processor along the ith dimension and retain either the minimum or the maximum of the two elements. Problem 6.6 explores the correctness of Program 6.1.

During each step of the algorithm, every processor performs a compare-exchange operation. The algorithm performs a total of $(1+\log n)(\log n)/2$ such steps; thus, the

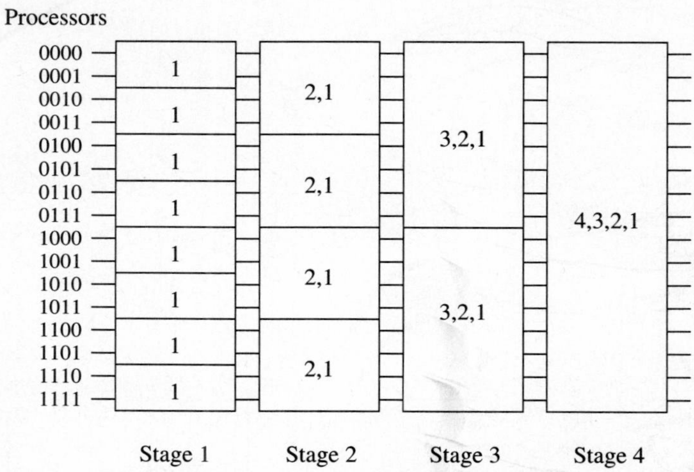

Figure 6.10 Communication characteristics of bitonic sort on a hypercube. During each stage of the algorithm, processors communicate along the dimensions shown.

parallel run time is

$$T_P = \Theta(\log^2 n) \tag{6.3}$$

This parallel formulation of bitonic sort is cost optimal with respect to the sequential implementation of bitonic sort (that is, the processor-time product is $\Theta(n \log^2 n)$), but it is not cost-optimal with respect to an optimal comparison-based sorting algorithm, which has a serial time complexity of $\Theta(n \log n)$.

```
procedure BITONIC_SORT(label, d)
begin
    for i := 0 to d − 1 do
        for j := i downto 0 do
            if (i + 1)st bit of label ≠ jth bit of label then
                comp_exchange_max(j);
            else
                comp_exchange_min(j);
end BITONIC_SORT
```

Program 6.1 Parallel formulation of bitonic sort on a hypercube with $n = 2^d$ processors. In this algorithm, *label* is the processor's label and d is the dimension of the hypercube.

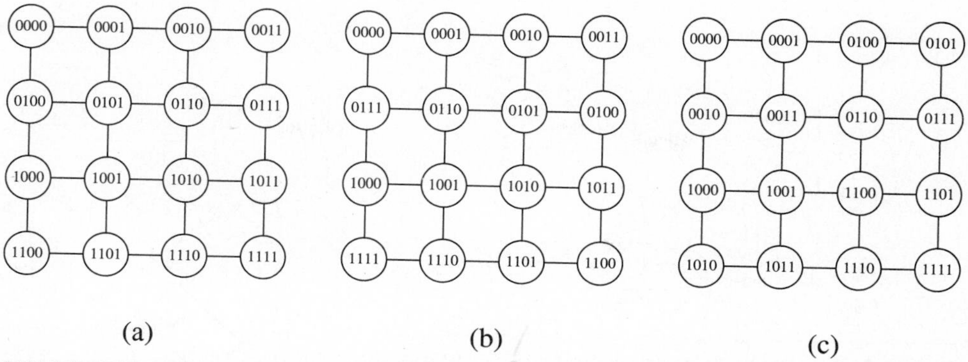

Figure 6.11 Different ways of mapping the input wires of the bitonic sorting network to a mesh of processors: (a) row-major mapping, (b) row-major snakelike mapping, and (c) row-major shuffled mapping.

Mesh Consider how the input wires of the bitonic sorting network can be mapped efficiently onto an n-processor mesh. Unfortunately, the connectivity of a mesh is lower than that of a hypercube, so it is impossible to map wires to processors such that each compare-exchange operation occurs only between neighboring processors. Instead, we map wires such that the most frequent compare-exchange operations occur between neighboring processors.

There are several ways to map the input wires onto the mesh processors. Some of these are illustrated in Figure 6.11. Each processor in this figure is labeled by the wire that is mapped onto it. Of these three mappings, we concentrate on the row-major shuffled mapping, shown in Figure 6.11(c). We leave the other two mappings as exercises (Problem 6.7).

The advantage of row-major shuffled mapping is that processors that perform compare-exchange operations reside on square subsections of the mesh whose size is inversely related to the frequency of compare-exchanges. For example, processors that perform compare-exchange during every stage of bitonic sort (that is, those corresponding to wires that differ in the least-significant bit) are neighbors. In general, wires that differ in the ith least-significant bit are mapped onto mesh processors that are $2^{\lfloor (i-1)/2 \rfloor}$ communication links away. The compare-exchange steps of the last stage of bitonic sort for the row-major shuffled mapping are shown in Figure 6.12. Note that each earlier stage will have only some of these steps.

During the $(1 + \log n)(\log n)/2$ steps of the algorithm, processors that are a certain distance apart compare-exchange their elements. The distance between processors determines the communication overhead of the parallel formulation. The total amount of communication performed by each processor is $\sum_{i=1}^{\log n} \sum_{j=1}^{i} 2^{\lfloor (j-1)/2 \rfloor} \approx 7\sqrt{n}$, which is $\Theta(\sqrt{n})$ (Problem 6.7). During each step of the algorithm, each processor performs at most one comparison; thus, the total computation performed by each processor is $\Theta(\log^2 n)$.

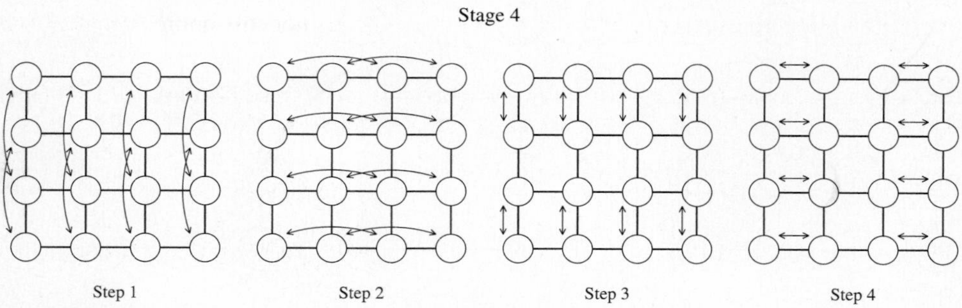

Figure 6.12 The last stage of the bitonic sort algorithm for $n = 16$ on a mesh, using the row-major shuffled mapping. During each step, processor pairs compare-exchange their elements. Arrows indicate the pairs of processors that perform compare-exchange operations.

This yields a parallel run time of

$$T_P = \overbrace{\Theta(\log^2 n)}^{\text{comparisons}} + \overbrace{\Theta(\sqrt{n})}^{\text{communication}}.$$

This is not a cost-optimal formulation, because the processor-time product is $\Theta(n^{1.5})$, but the sequential complexity of sorting is $\Theta(n \log n)$. Although the parallel formulation for a hypercube was optimal with respect to the sequential complexity of bitonic sort, the formulation for mesh is not. Can we do any better? No. When sorting n elements, one per mesh processor, for certain inputs the element stored in the processor at the upper-left corner will end up in the processor at the lower-right corner. For this to happen, this element must travel along $2\sqrt{n} - 1$ communication links before reaching its destination. Thus, the run time of sorting on a mesh is bounded by $\Omega(\sqrt{n})$. Our parallel formulation achieves this lower bound; thus, it is asymptotically optimal for the mesh architecture.

A Block of Elements Per Processor

In the parallel formulations of the bitonic sort algorithm presented so far, we assumed there were as many processors as elements to be sorted. Now we consider the case in which the number of elements to be sorted is greater than the number of processors.

Let p be the number of processors and n be the number of elements to be sorted, such that $p < n$. Each processor is assigned a block of n/p elements and cooperates with the other processors to sort them. One way to obtain a parallel formulation with our new setup is to think of each processor as consisting of n/p smaller processors. In other words, imagine emulating n/p processors by using a single processor. The run time of this formulation will be greater by a factor of n/p because each processor is doing the work of n/p processors. This virtual processor approach (Section 4.2) leads to a poor parallel implementation of bitonic sort. To see this, consider the case of a hypercube with

p processors. Its run time will be $\Theta((n \log^2 n)/p)$, which is not cost-optimal because the processor-time product is $\Theta(n \log^2 n)$.

An alternate way of dealing with blocks of elements is to use the compare-split operation presented in Section 6.1. Think of the (n/p)-element blocks as elements to be sorted using compare-split operations. The problem of sorting the p blocks is identical to that of performing a bitonic sort on the p blocks using compare-split operations instead of compare-exchange operations (Problem 6.8). Since the total number of blocks is p, the bitonic sort algorithm has a total of $(1 + \log p)(\log p)/2$ steps. Because compare-split operations preserve the initial sorted order of the elements in each block, at the end of these steps the n elements will be sorted. The main difference between this formulation and the one that uses virtual processors is that the n/p elements assigned to each processor are initially sorted locally, using a fast sequential sorting algorithm. This initial local sort makes the new formulation more efficient and cost-optimal.

Hypercube The block-based algorithm for a hypercube with p processors is similar to the one-element-per-processor case, but now we have p blocks of size n/p, instead of p elements. Furthermore, the compare-exchange operations are replaced by compare-split operations, each taking $\Theta(n/p)$ computation time and $\Theta(n/p)$ communication time. Initially the processors sort their n/p elements (using merge sort) in $\Theta((n/p)\log(n/p))$ time and then perform $\Theta(\log^2 p)$ compare-split steps. The parallel run time of this formulation is

$$T_P = \overbrace{\Theta\left(\frac{n}{p}\log\frac{n}{p}\right)}^{\text{local sort}} + \overbrace{\Theta\left(\frac{n}{p}\log^2 p\right)}^{\text{comparisons}} + \overbrace{\Theta\left(\frac{n}{p}\log^2 p\right)}^{\text{communication}}.$$

Because the sequential complexity of the best sorting algorithm is $\Theta(n \log n)$, the speedup and efficiency are as follows:

$$\begin{aligned} S &= \frac{\Theta(n \log n)}{\Theta((n/p)\log(n/p)) + \Theta((n/p)\log^2 p)} \\ E &= \frac{1}{1 - \Theta((\log p)/(\log n)) + \Theta((\log^2 p)/(\log n))} \end{aligned} \tag{6.4}$$

From Equation 6.4, for a cost-optimal formulation $(\log^2 p)/(\log n) = O(1)$. Thus, this algorithm can efficiently use up to $p = \Theta(2^{\sqrt{\log n}})$ processors. Also from Equation 6.4, the isoefficiency function due to both communication and extra work is $\Theta(p^{\log p} \log^2 p)$, which is worse than any polynomial isoefficiency function for sufficiently large p. Hence, this parallel formulation of bitonic sort has poor scalability.

Mesh The block-based mesh formulation is also similar to the one-element-per-processor case. The parallel run time, speedup, and efficiency of this formulation are as follows:

$$T_P = \overbrace{\Theta\left(\frac{n}{p}\log\frac{n}{p}\right)}^{\text{local sort}} + \overbrace{\Theta\left(\frac{n}{p}\log^2 p\right)}^{\text{comparisons}} + \overbrace{\Theta\left(\frac{n}{\sqrt{p}}\right)}^{\text{communication}}$$

Table 6.1 The performance of parallel formulations of bitonic sort for n elements on p processors.

Architecture	Maximum Number of Processors for $E = \Theta(1)$	Corresponding Parallel Run Time	Isoefficiency Function
Hypercube	$\Theta(2^{\sqrt{\log n}})$	$\Theta(n/(2^{\sqrt{\log n}}) \log n)$	$\Theta(p^{\log p} \log^2 p)$
Mesh	$\Theta(\log^2 n)$	$\Theta(n/\log n)$	$\Theta(2^{\sqrt{p}}\sqrt{p})$
Ring	$\Theta(\log n)$	$\Theta(n)$	$\Theta(2^p p)$

$$S = \frac{\Theta(n \log n)}{\Theta((n/p)\log(n/p)) + \Theta((n/p)\log^2 p) + \Theta(n/\sqrt{p})}$$

$$E = \frac{1}{1 - \Theta((\log p)/(\log n)) + \Theta((\log^2 p)/(\log n)) + \Theta(\sqrt{p}/\log n)} \quad (6.5)$$

From Equation 6.5, for a cost-optimal formulation $\sqrt{p}/\log n = O(1)$. Thus, this formulation can efficiently use up to $p = \Theta(\log^2 n)$ processors. Also from Equation 6.5, the isoefficiency function $\Theta(2^{\sqrt{p}}\sqrt{p})$. The isoefficiency function of this formulation is exponential, and thus is even worse than that for the hypercube.

From the analysis for hypercube and mesh, we see that parallel formulations of bitonic sort are neither very efficient nor very scalable. This is primarily because the sequential algorithm is suboptimal. Good speedups are possible on large number of processors only if the number of elements to be sorted is very large. In that case, the efficiency of the internal sorting outweighs the inefficiency of the bitonic sort. Table 6.1 summarizes the performance of bitonic sort on hypercube-, mesh-, and ring-connected parallel computer.

6.3 Bubble Sort and Its Variants

The previous section presented a sorting network that could sort n elements in $\Theta(\log^2 n)$ time. We now turn our attention to more traditional sorting algorithms. Since serial algorithms with $\Theta(n \log n)$ time complexity exist, we should be able to use $\Theta(n)$ processors to sort n elements in $\Theta(\log n)$ time. As we will see, this is difficult to achieve. We can, however, easily parallelize sequential sorting algorithms that have $\Theta(n^2)$ complexity. The algorithms we present are based on ***bubble sort***.

The sequential bubble sort algorithm compares and exchanges adjacent elements in the sequence to be sorted. Given a sequence $\langle a_1, a_2, \ldots, a_n \rangle$, the algorithm first performs $n - 1$ compare-exchange operations in the following order: $(a_1, a_2), (a_2, a_3), \ldots, (a_{n-1}, a_n)$. This step moves the largest element to the end of the sequence. The last element in the transformed sequence is then ignored, and the sequence of compare-exchanges is applied to the resulting sequence $\langle a'_1, a'_2, \ldots, a'_{n-1} \rangle$. The sequence is sorted after $n - 1$ iterations. We can improve the performance of bubble sort by terminating when no exchanges take place during an iteration. The bubble sort algorithm is shown in Program 6.2.

```
1.   procedure BUBBLE_SORT(n)
2.   begin
3.       for i := n − 1 downto 1 do
4.           for j := 1 to i do
5.               compare-exchange(a_j, a_{j+1});
6.   end BUBBLE_SORT
```

Program 6.2 Sequential bubble sort algorithm.

An iteration of the inner loop of bubble sort takes $\Theta(n)$ time, and we perform a total of $\Theta(n)$ iterations; thus, the complexity of bubble sort is $\Theta(n^2)$. Bubble sort is difficult to parallelize. To see this, consider how compare-exchange operations are performed during each phase of the algorithm (lines 4 and 5 of Program 6.2). Bubble sort compares all adjacent pairs in order; hence, it is inherently sequential. In the following two sections, we present two variants of bubble sort that are well suited to parallelization.

6.3.1 Odd-Even Transposition

The ***odd-even transposition*** algorithm sorts n elements in n phases (n is even), each of which requires $n/2$ compare-exchange operations. This algorithm alternates between two phases, called the odd and even phases. Let $\langle a_1, a_2, \ldots, a_n \rangle$ be the sequence to be sorted. During the odd phase, elements with odd indices are compared with their right neighbors, and if they are out of sequence they are exchanged; thus, the pairs $(a_1, a_2), (a_3, a_4), \ldots, (a_{n-1}, a_n)$ are compare-exchanged (assuming n is even). Similarly, during the even phase, elements with even indices are compared with their right neighbors, and if they are out of sequence they are exchanged; thus, the pairs $(a_2, a_3), (a_4, a_5), \ldots, (a_{n-2}, a_{n-1})$ are compare-exchanged. After n phases of odd-even exchanges, the sequence is sorted. Each phase of the algorithm (either odd or even) requires $\Theta(n)$ comparisons, and there are a total of n phases; thus, the sequential complexity is $\Theta(n^2)$. The odd-even transposition sort is shown in Program 6.3 and is illustrated in Figure 6.13.

Parallel Formulation

It is easy to parallelize odd-even transposition sort. During each phase of the algorithm, compare-exchange operations on pairs of elements are performed simultaneously. Consider the one-element-per-processor case. Let n be the number of processors (also the number of elements to be sorted). Assume that the processors are connected by a ring interconnection network. Element a_i initially resides on processor P_i for $i = 1, 2, \ldots, n$. During the odd phase, each processor that has an odd label compare-exchanges its element with the element residing on its right neighbor. Similarly, during the even phase, each processor with an even label compare-exchanges its element with the element of its right neighbor. This parallel formulation is presented in Program 6.4.

```
procedure ODD-EVEN(n)
begin
    for i := 1 to n do
    begin
        if i is odd then
            for j := 0 to n/2 − 1 do
                compare-exchange(a_{2j+1}, a_{2j+2});
        if i is even then
            for j := 1 to n/2 − 1 do
                compare-exchange(a_{2j}, a_{2j+1});
    end for
end ODD-EVEN
```

Program 6.3 Sequential odd-even transposition sort algorithm.

During each phase of the algorithm, the odd or even processors perform a compare-exchange step with their right neighbors. As we know from Section 6.1, this requires $\Theta(1)$ time. A total of n such phases are performed; thus, the parallel run time of this formulation is $\Theta(n)$. Since the sequential complexity of the best sorting algorithm for n elements is $\Theta(n \log n)$, this formulation of odd-even transposition sort is not cost-optimal, because its processor-time product is $\Theta(n^2)$.

To obtain a cost-optimal parallel formulation, we use fewer processors. Let p be the number of processors, where $p < n$. Initially, each processor is assigned a block of n/p elements, which it sorts internally (using merge sort or quicksort) in $\Theta((n/p)\log(n/p))$ time. After this, the processors execute p phases ($p/2$ odd and $p/2$ even), performing compare-split operations. At the end of these phases, the list is sorted (Problem 6.10). During each phase, $\Theta(n/p)$ comparisons are performed to merge two blocks, and $\Theta(n/p)$ time is spent communicating. Thus, the parallel run time of the formulation is

$$T_P = \overbrace{\Theta\left(\frac{n}{p}\log\frac{n}{p}\right)}^{\text{local sort}} + \overbrace{\Theta(n)}^{\text{comparisons}} + \overbrace{\Theta(n)}^{\text{communication}}.$$

Since the sequential complexity of sorting is $\Theta(n \log n)$, the speedup and efficiency of this formulation are as follows:

$$\begin{aligned} S &= \frac{\Theta(n \log n)}{\Theta((n/p)\log(n/p)) + \Theta(n)} \\ E &= \frac{1}{1 - \Theta((\log p)/(\log n)) + \Theta(p/\log n)} \end{aligned} \tag{6.6}$$

From Equation 6.6, odd-even transposition sort is cost-optimal when $p = O(\log n)$. The isoefficiency function of this parallel formulation is $\Theta(p\,2^p)$, which is exponential. Thus, it is poorly scalable and is suited to only a small number of processors.

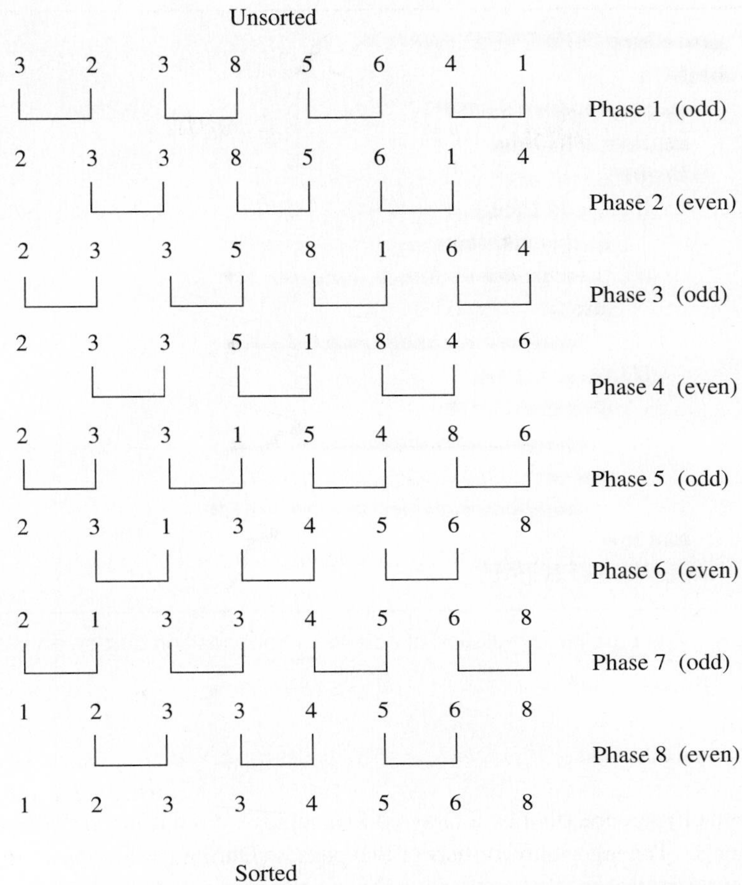

Figure 6.13 Sorting $n = 8$ elements, using the odd-even transposition sort algorithm. During each phase, $n = 8$ elements are compared.

6.3.2 Shellsort

The main limitation of odd-even transposition sort is that it moves elements only one position at a time. If a sequence has just a few elements out of order, and if they are $\Theta(n)$ distance from their proper positions, then the sequential algorithm still requires $\Theta(n^2)$ time to sort the sequence. To make a substantial improvement over odd-even transposition sort, we need an algorithm that moves elements long distances. Shellsort is one such serial sorting algorithm. This section presents a variation of shellsort for a hypercube-connected parallel computer.

Let n be the number of elements to be sorted and $p = 2^d$ be the number of processors in a d-dimensional hypercube. Each processor is assigned a block of n/p elements. A ring,

```
procedure ODD-EVEN_PAR(n)
begin
    id := processor's label
    for i := 1 to n do
    begin
        if i is odd then
            if id is odd then
                compare-exchange_min(id + 1);
            else
                compare-exchange_max(id − 1);
        if i is even then
            if id is even then
                compare-exchange_min(id + 1);
            else
                compare-exchange_max(id − 1);
    end for
end ODD-EVEN_PAR
```

Program 6.4 The parallel formulation of odd-even transposition sort on an n-processor ring.

mapped on the hypercube (that is, a Gray-code mapping), defines the global order of the sorted sequence. The algorithm consists of two phases. During the first phase, processors that are far away from each other in the ring ordering compare-split their elements. Elements thus move long distances to get close to their final destinations in a few steps. During the second phase, the algorithm switches to an odd-even transposition sort similar to the one described in the previous section. The only difference is that the odd and even phases are performed only as long as the blocks on the processors are changing. Because the first phase of the algorithm moves elements close to their final destinations, the number of odd and even phases performed by the second phase may be substantially smaller than p.

Initially, each processor sorts its block of n/p elements internally in $\Theta(n/p \log(n/p))$ time. The first phase consists of d steps. In the first step, each processor performs a compare-split operation with its neighboring processor along the dth dimension. The processor with a 0 in the dth bit position (that is, the most significant bit) in the binary representation of its processor label gets the smallest n/p elements, and the processor with a 1 gets the largest n/p elements. In general, during the ith step, each processor performs a compare-split operation along the $(d - (i - 1))^{\text{st}}$ dimension, and the $(d - (i - 1))^{\text{st}}$ bit position of the binary representation of the processor's label determines which processor gets the smallest and which processor gets the largest n/p elements. The compare-split operations of the first phase are illustrated in Figure 6.14 for $d = 3$. We refer to this algorithm as ***shellsort***.

Note that it is not a direct parallel formulation of the sequential shellsort, but it relies on similar ideas.

In the first phase of the algorithm, each processor performs $d = \log p$ compare-split operations, each requiring $\Theta(n/p)$ time; thus, the complexity of this phase is $\Theta((n \log p)/p)$. In the second phase, l odd and even phases are performed, each requiring $\Theta(n/p)$ time. Thus, the parallel run time of the algorithm is

$$T_P = \overbrace{\Theta\left(\frac{n}{p}\log\frac{n}{p}\right)}^{\text{local sort}} + \overbrace{\Theta\left(\frac{n}{p}\log p\right)}^{\text{first phase}} + \overbrace{\Theta\left(l\frac{n}{p}\right)}^{\text{second phase}}. \quad (6.7)$$

The performance of shellsort depends on the value of l. If l is small, then the algorithm performs significantly better than odd-even transposition sort; if l is $\Theta(p)$, then both algorithms perform similarly. Problem 6.13 investigates the worst-case value of l.

6.4 Quicksort

All the algorithms presented so far have worse sequential complexity than that of the lower bound for comparison-based sorting, $\Theta(n \log n)$. This section examines the ***quicksort*** algorithm, which has an average complexity of $\Theta(n \log n)$. Quicksort is one of the most common sorting algorithms for sequential computers because of its simplicity, low overhead, and optimal average complexity.

Quicksort is a divide-and-conquer algorithm that sorts a sequence by recursively dividing it into smaller subsequences. Assume that the n-element sequence to be sorted is stored in the array $A[1 \dots n]$. Quicksort consists of two steps: divide and conquer. During the divide step, a sequence $A[q \dots r]$ is partitioned (rearranged) into two nonempty subsequences $A[q \dots s]$ and $A[s+1 \dots r]$ such that each element of the first subsequence is smaller than or equal to each element of the second subsequence. During the conquer step, the subsequences are sorted by recursively applying quicksort. Since the subsequences $A[q \dots s]$ and $A[s+1 \dots r]$ are sorted and the first subsequence has smaller elements than the second, the entire sequence is sorted.

How is the sequence $A[q \dots r]$ partitioned into two parts—one with all elements smaller than the other? This is usually accomplished by selecting one element x from $A[q \dots r]$ and using this element to partition the sequence $A[q \dots r]$ into two parts—one with elements less than or equal to x and the other with elements greater than x. Element x is called the ***pivot***. The quicksort algorithm is presented in Program 6.5. This algorithm arbitrarily chooses the first element of the sequence $A[q \dots r]$ as the pivot. The operation of quicksort is illustrated in Figure 6.15.

The complexity of partitioning a sequence of size k is $\Theta(k)$. Quicksort's performance is greatly affected by the way it partitions a sequence. Consider the case in which a sequence of size k is split poorly, into two subsequences of sizes 1 and $k-1$. The run time in this case is given by the recurrence relation $T(n) = T(n-1) + \Theta(n)$, whose solution is $T(n) = \Theta(n^2)$. Alternatively, consider the case in which the sequence is split well, into two roughly equal-size subsequences of $\lfloor k/2 \rfloor$ and $\lceil k/2 \rceil$ elements. In this case, the run time is given by the

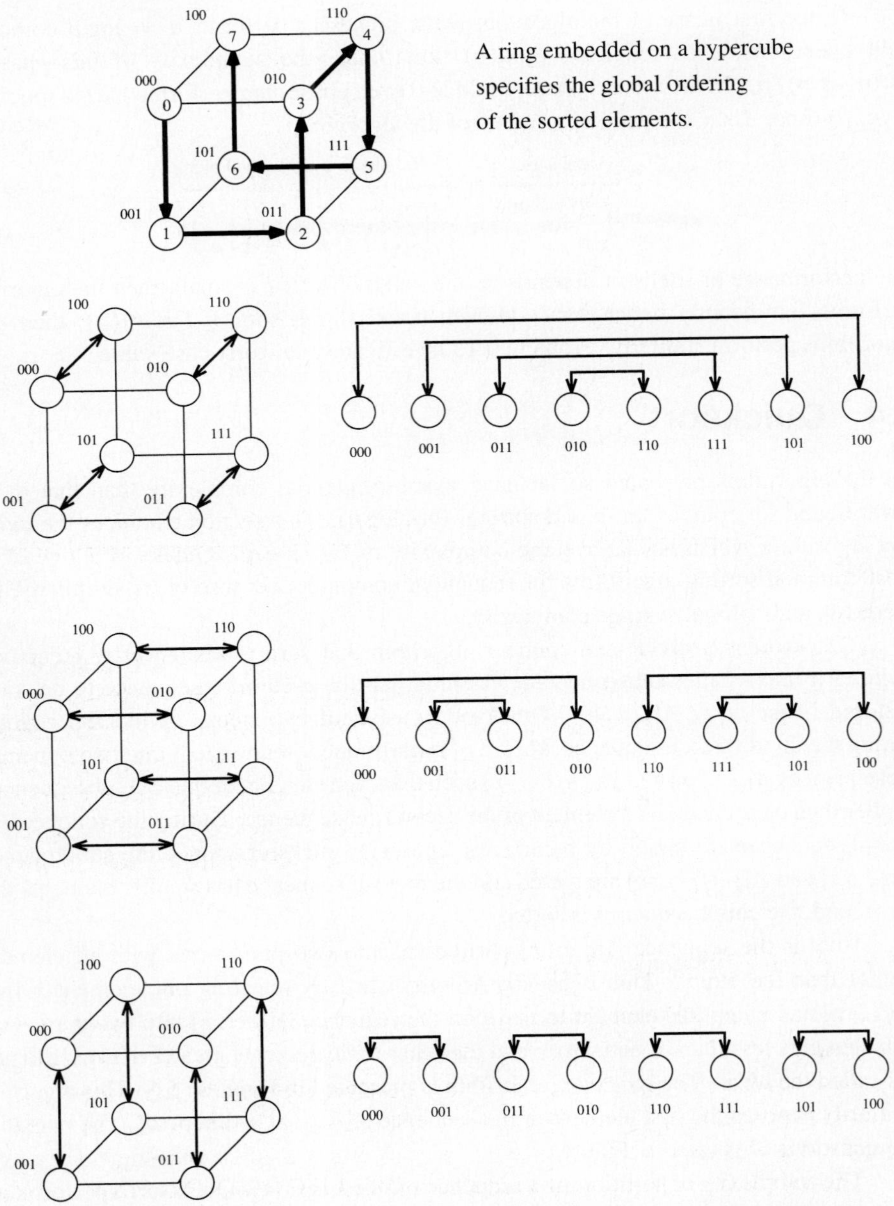

Figure 6.14 An example of the first phase of parallel shellsort on a three-dimensional hypercube.

```
1.  procedure QUICKSORT (A, q, r)
2.  begin
3.      if q < r then
4.      begin
5.          x := A[q];
6.          s := q;
7.          for i := q + 1 to r do
8.              if A[i] ≤ x then
9.              begin
10.                 s := s + 1;
11.                 swap(A[s], A[i]);
12.             end if
13.         swap(A[q], A[s]);
14.         QUICKSORT (A, q, s);
15.         QUICKSORT (A, s + 1, r);
16.     end if
17. end QUICKSORT
```

Program 6.5 The sequential quicksort algorithm.

recurrence relation $T(n) = 2T(n/2) + \Theta(n)$, whose solution is $T(n) = \Theta(n \log n)$. The second split yields an optimal algorithm. Although quicksort can have $O(n^2)$ worst-case complexity, its average complexity is significantly better; the average number of compare-exchange operations needed by quicksort for sorting a randomly-ordered input sequence is $1.4n \log n$, which is asymptotically optimal. There are several ways to select pivots. For example, the pivot can be the median of a small number of elements of the sequence, or it can be an element selected at random. Some pivot selection strategies have advantages over others for certain input sequences.

6.4.1 Parallelizing Quicksort

Quicksort can be parallelized in a variety of ways. First, consider a naive parallel formulation. Lines 14 and 15 of Program 6.5 show that, during each call of QUICKSORT, the array is partitioned into two parts and each part is solved recursively. Sorting the smaller arrays represents two completely independent subproblems that can be solved in parallel. Therefore, one way to parallelize quicksort is to execute it initially on a single processor; then when the algorithm performs its recursive calls (lines 14 and 15), assign one of the subproblems to another processor. Now each of these processors sorts its array by using quicksort and assigns one of its subproblems to other processors. The algorithm terminates when the arrays cannot be further partitioned. Upon termination, each processor holds an element of the array, and the sorted order can be recovered by traversing the processors as we will describe later. This parallel formulation of quicksort uses n processors to sort

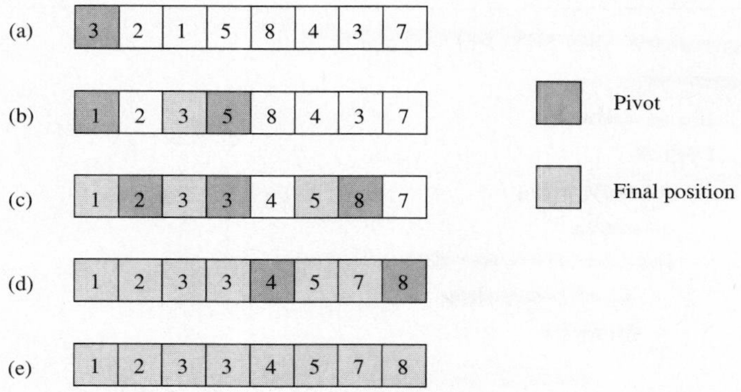

Figure 6.15 Example of the quicksort algorithm sorting a sequence of size $n = 8$.

n elements. Its major drawback is that partitioning the array $A[q \ldots r]$ into two smaller arrays, $A[q \ldots s]$ and $A[s+1 \ldots r]$, is done by a single processor. Since one processor must partition the original array $A[1 \ldots n]$, the run time of this formulation is bounded below by $\Omega(n)$. This formulation is not cost-optimal, because its processor-time product is $\Omega(n^2)$.

The main limitation of the previous parallel formulation is that it performs the partitioning step serially. As we will see in subsequent formulations, performing partitioning in parallel is essential to obtain an efficient parallel quicksort. To see why, consider the recurrence equation $T(n) = 2T(n/2) + \Theta(n)$, which gives the complexity of quicksort for optimal pivot selection. The term $\Theta(n)$ is due to the partitioning of the array. Compare this complexity with the overall complexity of the algorithm, $\Theta(n \log n)$. From these two complexities, we can think of the quicksort algorithm as consisting of $\Theta(\log n)$ steps, each requiring $\Theta(n)$ time—that of splitting the array. Therefore, if the partitioning step is performed in $\Theta(1)$ time, using $\Theta(n)$ processors, it is possible to obtain an overall parallel run time of $\Theta(\log n)$, which leads to a cost-optimal formulation. However, without parallelizing the partitioning step, the best we can do (while maintaining cost-optimality) is to use only $\Theta(\log n)$ processors to sort n elements in $\Theta(n)$ time (Problem 6.14). Hence, parallelizing the partitioning step has the potential to yield a significantly faster parallel formulation.

In the previous paragraph, we hinted that we could partition an array of size n into two smaller arrays in $\Theta(1)$ time by using $\Theta(n)$ processors. However, this is difficult for most parallel computing models. The only known algorithms are for the abstract PRAM models. Because of communication overhead, the partitioning step takes more than $\Theta(1)$ time on mesh-connected and hypercube-connected parallel computers. In the following sections we present three distinct parallel formulations: one for a CRCW PRAM, one for a hypercube, and one for a mesh. Each of these formulations parallelizes quicksort by performing the partitioning step in parallel.

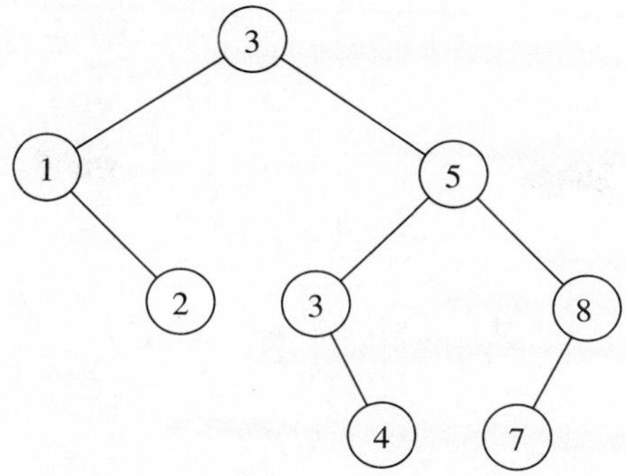

Figure 6.16 A binary tree generated by the execution of the quicksort algorithm. Each level of the tree represents a different array-partitioning iteration. If pivot selection is optimal, then the height of the tree is $\Theta(\log n)$, which is also the number of iterations.

Parallel Formulation for a CRCW PRAM

We will now present a parallel formulation of quicksort for sorting n elements on an n-processor arbitrary CRCW PRAM. Recall from Section 2.2 that an arbitrary CRCW PRAM is a concurrent-read, concurrent-write parallel random-access machine in which write conflicts are resolved arbitrarily. In other words, when more than one processor tries to write to the same memory location, only one arbitrarily chosen processor is allowed to write, and the remaining writes are ignored.

Executing quicksort can be visualized as constructing a binary tree. In this tree, the pivot is the root; elements smaller than or equal to the pivot go to the left subtree, and elements larger than the pivot go to the right subtree. Figure 6.16 illustrates the binary tree constructed by the execution of the quicksort algorithm illustrated in Figure 6.15. We obtain the sorted sequence from this tree by performing an inorder traversal. The PRAM formulation is based on this interpretation of quicksort.

The algorithm starts by selecting a pivot element and partitioning the array into two parts—one with elements smaller than the pivot and the other with elements larger than the pivot. Subsequent pivot elements, one for each new subarray, are then selected in parallel. This formulation does not rearrange elements; instead, since all the processors can read the pivot in constant time, they know which of the two subarrays (smaller or larger) the elements assigned to them belong to. Thus, they can proceed to the next iteration.

The algorithm that constructs the binary tree is shown in Program 6.6. The array to be sorted is stored in $A[1 \dots n]$ and processor i is assigned element $A[i]$. The arrays *leftchild*$[1 \dots n]$ and *rightchild*$[1 \dots n]$ keep track of the children of a given pivot. For each processor, the local variable $parent_i$ stores the label of the processor whose element is the pivot. Initially, all the processors write their processor labels into the variable *root* in line 5.

```
procedure BUILD_TREE (A[1...n])
begin
    for each processor i do
    begin
        root := i;
        parent_i := root;
        leftchild[i] := rightchild[i] := n + 1;
    end for
    repeat for each processor i ≠ root do
    begin
        if (A[i] < A[parent_i]) or
            (A[i] = A[parent_i] and i <parent_i) then
        begin
            leftchild[parent_i] := i;
            if i = leftchild[parent_i] then exit
            else parent_i := leftchild[parent_i];
        end for
        else
        begin
            rightchild[parent_i] := i;
            if i = rightchild[parent_i] then exit
            else parent_i := rightchild[parent_i];
        end else
    end repeat
end BUILD_TREE
```

Program 6.6 The binary tree construction procedure for the CRCW PRAM parallel quicksort formulation.

Because the concurrent write operation is arbitrary, only one of these labels will actually be written into *root*. The value $A[root]$ is used as the first pivot and *root* is copied into $parent_i$ for each processor i. Next, processors that have elements smaller than $A[parent_i]$ write their processor labels into $leftchild[parent_i]$, and those with larger elements write their processor label into $rightchild[parent_i]$. Thus, all processors whose elements belong in the smaller partition have written their labels into $leftchild[parent_i]$, and those with elements in the larger partition have written their labels into $rightchild[parent_i]$. Because of the arbitrary concurrent-write operations, only two values—one for $leftchild[parent_i]$ and one for $rightchild[parent_i]$—are written into these locations. These two values become the labels of the processors that hold the pivot elements for the next iteration, in which two smaller arrays are being partitioned. The algorithm continues until n pivot elements are selected. A processor exits when its element becomes a pivot. The construction of the binary tree is illustrated in Figure 6.17. During each iteration of the algorithm, a level of the tree is constructed in $\Theta(1)$ time. Thus, the average complexity of the binary tree building algorithm is $\Theta(\log n)$ as the average height of the tree is $\Theta(\log n)$ (Problem 6.16).

After building the binary tree, the algorithm determines the position of each element in the sorted array. It traverses the tree and keeps a count of the number of elements in the left and right subtrees of any element. Finally, each element is placed in its proper position in $\Theta(1)$ time, and the array is sorted. The algorithm that traverses the binary tree and computes the position of each element is left as an exercise (Problem 6.15). The average run time of this algorithm is $\Theta(\log n)$ on an n-processor PRAM. Thus, its overall processor-time product is $\Theta(n \log n)$, which is cost-optimal.

Parallel Formulation for a Hypercube

We now turn our attention to a more realistic parallel architecture—the p-processor hypercube-connected parallel computer. The hypercube formulation of quicksort takes advantage of the topological properties of a hypercube. Recall from Section 2.4.1 that a d-dimensional hypercube can be split into two $(d - 1)$-dimensional subcubes so that each processor in one subcube is connected to a processor in the other. This property allows the algorithm to partition the array around a pivot element by simply having corresponding processors—one on each subcube—split their elements. After this split, elements smaller than the pivot will be on one subcube and those larger than the pivot will be on the other.

The quicksort formulation for a hypercube works as follows. Let n be the number of elements to be sorted and $p = 2^d$ be the number of processors in a d-dimensional hypercube. Each processor is assigned a block of n/p elements, and the labels of the processors defines the global order of the sorted sequence. The algorithm starts by selecting a pivot element, which is broadcast to all processors. Each processor, upon receiving the pivot, partitions its local elements into two blocks, one with elements smaller than the pivot and one with elements larger than the pivot. Then the processors connected along the dth communication link exchange appropriate blocks so that one retains elements smaller than the pivot and the other retains elements larger than the pivot. Specifically, each processor with a 0 in the dth bit (the most significant bit) position of the binary representation of its processor label retains the smaller elements, and each processor with a 1 in the dth bit retains the larger elements. After this step, each processor in the $(d - 1)$-dimensional hypercube whose d^{th} label bit is 0 will have elements smaller than the pivot, and each processor in the other $(d - 1)$-dimensional hypercube will have elements larger than the pivot. This procedure is performed recursively in each subcube, splitting the subsequences further. After d such splits—one along each dimension—the sequence is sorted with respect to the global ordering imposed on the processors (Problem 6.17). This does not mean that the elements at each processor are sorted. Therefore, each processor sorts its local elements by using sequential quicksort. This hypercube formulation of quicksort is shown in Program 6.7. The execution of the algorithm is illustrated in Figure 6.18.

(a)

1	2	3	4	5	6	7	8
33	21	13	54	82	33	40	72

(b) root = 4

(c)

	1	2	3	4	5	6	7	8
leftchild				1				
rightchild				5				

(d)

	1	2	3	4	5	6	7	8
leftchild	2			1	8			
rightchild	6			5				

(e)

	1	2	3	4	5	6	7	8
leftchild	2	3		1	8			
rightchild	6			5		7		

(f)

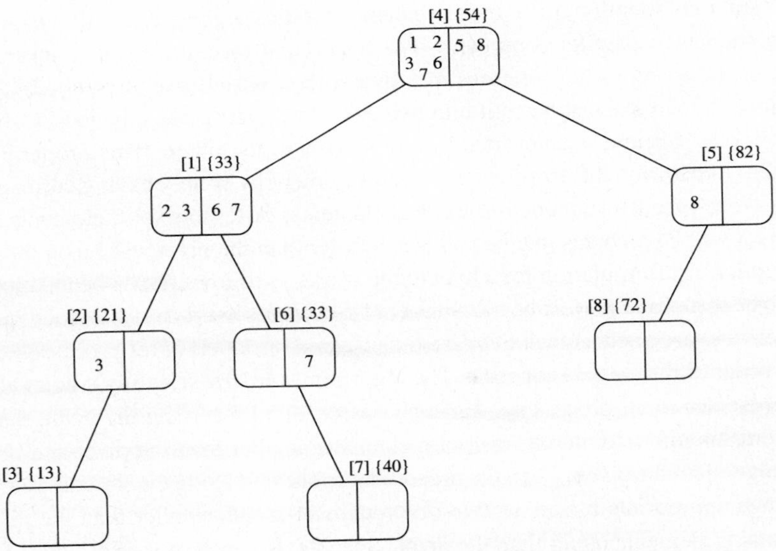

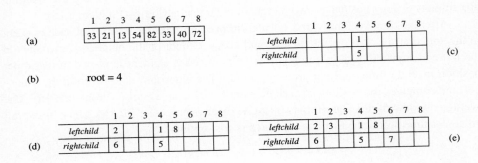

Figure 6.17 The execution of the PRAM algorithm on the array shown in (a). The arrays *leftchild* and *rightchild* are shown in (c), (d), and (e) as the algorithm progresses. Figure (f) shows the binary tree constructed by the algorithm. Each node is labeled by the processor (in square brackets), and the element is stored at that processor (in curly brackets). The element is the pivot. In each node, processors with smaller elements than the pivot are grouped on the left side of the node, and those with larger elements are grouped on the right side. These two groups form the two partitions of the original array. For each partition, a pivot element is selected at random from the two groups that form the children of the node.

```
procedure HYPERCUBE_QUICKSORT (B, n)
begin
    id := processor's label;
    for i := 1 to d do
    begin
        x := pivot;
        partition B into B1 and B2 such that B1 ≤ x < B2;
        if i^th bit is 0 then
        begin
            send B2 to the processor along the i^th communication link;
            C := subsequence received along the i^th communication link;
            B := B1 ∪ C;
        endif
        else
            send B1 to the processor along the i^th communication link;
            C := subsequence received along the i^th communication link;
            B := B2 ∪ C;
        endelse
    endfor
    sort B using sequential quicksort;
end HYPERCUBE_QUICKSORT
```

Program 6.7 A parallel formulation of quicksort on a d-dimensional hypercube. B is the n/p-element subsequence assigned to each processor.

Pivot Selection In the hypercube quicksort algorithm, we glossed over pivot selection. Pivot selection is particularly difficult, and it significantly affects the algorithm's performance. Consider the case in which the first pivot happens to be the largest element in the sequence. In this case, after the first split (along the dth dimension), all the elements will reside on one of the two $(d-1)$-dimensional subcubes—the one that holds the elements smaller than the pivot. The other subcube—the one that holds the elements larger than the pivot—will have no elements. Hence, in the subsequent $(d-1)$ splits, only half the processors will participate in the sorting operation, while the other half will be idle. Although this is a contrived example, it illustrates a significant problem with our hypercube formulation. Ideally, during each split, processors have a sequence of size n/p. However, poorly selected pivots might lead to processors having sequences of significantly different sizes (significantly larger or smaller than n/p). As a result, processors with small sequences will be idle, waiting for processors with large sequences to finish partitioning their sequences. As the difference in sequence length increases, the performance of the parallel formulation decreases.

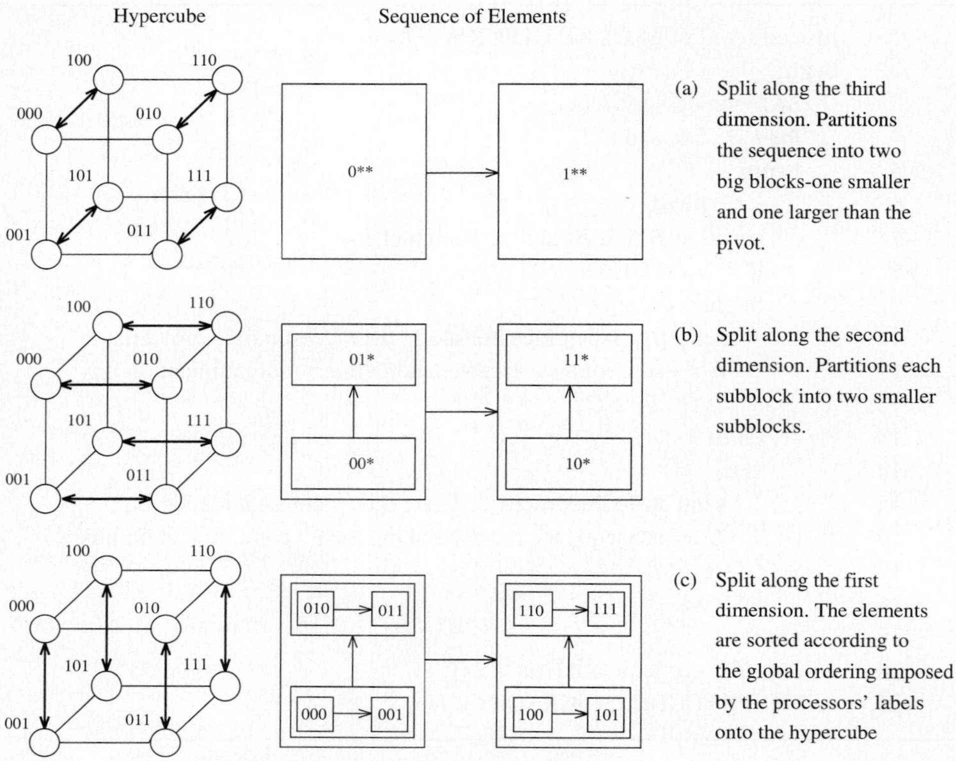

Hypercube
Sequence of Elements
100
110
000
010
101
111
001
011
0**
1**
(a) Split along the third dimension. Partitions the sequence into two big blocks-one smaller and one larger than the pivot.
01*
11*
00*
10*
(b) Split along the second dimension. Partitions each subblock into two smaller subblocks.
010
011
110
111
000
001
100
101
(c) Split along the first dimension. The elements are sorted according to the global ordering imposed by the processors' labels onto the hypercube

Figure 6.18 The execution of the hypercube formulation of quicksort for $d = 3$. The three splits—one along each communication link—are shown in (a), (b), and (c). The second column represents the partitioning of the n-element sequence into subcubes. The arrows between subcubes indicate the movement of larger elements. Each box is marked by the binary representation of the processor labels in that subcube. A $*$ denotes that all the binary combinations are included.

Example 6.2 Importance of Pivot Selection

Assume that, after each of the d splits, the size of the sequence stored in processor P_1 increases by a factor of k where $1 \leq k \leq 2$. That is, after the first split, P_1 has a sequence of size kn/p after the second split, it has a sequence of size k^2n/p and after the last split, it has a sequence of size $k^d n/p$. The time spent by this processor in partitioning its sequence is $\Theta(\sum_{i=o}^{i=d-1} k^i n/p)$, which for $k > 1$ is $\Theta((k^d - 1)n/p)$. Since $p = 2^d$, this expression simplifies to $\Theta((p^{\log k} - 1)n/p)$. If $k = 2$, the time spent by processor P_1 in partitioning is $\Theta(n - n/p)$, and it ends up with a sequence of size $2^d n/p = n$ to sort internally. Hence, using p processors did not improve performance; all the sorting is done by a single processor. However, if $k = 1.1$, then the time spent in partitioning is approximately $\Theta((p^{0.138} - 1)n/p)$ and the local sort involves a sequence of size $n/p^{0.862}$. Ideally, $k = 1$, the partitioning cost is $\Theta((n \log p)/p)$, and the local sort involves a sequence of size n/p. Hence, as k increases, performance decreases. ■

One way to select pivots is to choose them at random as follows. During the ith split, one processor in each of the 2^{i-1} subcubes (of dimension $d - (i - 1)$) randomly selects one of its elements to be the pivot for this subcube. This is analogous to the random pivot selection in the sequential quicksort algorithm. Although this method seems to work for sequential quicksort, it is not well suited to the parallel formulation. To see this, consider the case in which a bad pivot is selected at some point. In sequential quicksort, this leads to a partitioning in which one subsequence is significantly larger than the other. If all subsequent pivot selections are good, one poor pivot will increase the overall work at most an amount equal to the length of the subsequent; thus, it will not significantly degrade the performance of sequential quicksort. In the parallel formulation, however, one poor pivot leads to partitioning a sequence among two subcubes—one with significantly more elements than the other. Even if subsequent pivot choices are good, the load imbalance resulting from one poor pivot will persist and degrade performance in the subsequent steps.

If the initial distribution of elements in each processor is uniform, then a better pivot selection method can be derived. In this case, the n/p elements initially stored at each processor are a representative sample of all n elements. In other words, the median of each n/p-element subsequence is very close to the median of the entire n-element sequence. Recall that during the split along the ith dimension, processors in 2^{d-i} subcubes exchange elements independently. For each such subcube, a processor is chosen arbitrarily, and its median is used as the pivot for the subcube. Why is this a good pivot selection scheme under the assumption of identical initial distributions? Since the distribution of elements on each processor is the same as the overall distribution of the n elements, the median selected to be the pivot during the first step is a good approximation of the overall median. Since the selected pivot is very close to the overall median, roughly half of the elements in each processor are smaller and the other half larger than the pivot. Therefore, the first split retains roughly n/p elements per processor. The elements stored in each processor of the subcube that has elements smaller than the pivot have the same distribution as the $n/2$ smaller elements of the original list. Similarly, the elements stored in each processor of the subcube that has elements larger than the pivot have the same distribution as the $n/2$ larger elements of the original list. Thus, the split not only maintains load balance (roughly n/p elements per processor) but also preserves the assumption of uniform element distribution in each subcube. Therefore, applying the same pivot selection scheme to the subcubes continues to yield good pivot selection.

Can we really assume that the n/p elements in each processor have the same distribution as the overall sequence? The answer depends on the application. In some applications, either the random or the median pivot selection scheme works well, but in others neither scheme delivers good performance. Two additional pivot selection schemes are examined in Problems 6.18 and 6.19.

Analysis We now analyze the complexity of our hypercube quicksort formulation, assuming that pivot selection yields an optimal (or almost optimal) splitting. Consider the case of median pivot selection, discussed in the previous section.

The algorithm performs d iterations (lines 4–19 in Program 6.7). During each iteration it performs the following steps: (1) it selects a pivot, (2) it broadcasts the pivot, and (3) it splits the sequence.

During each pivot selection step, each processor finds the median of its elements. This can be done in $\Theta(1)$ time if the elements in each processor are sorted. Instead of sorting the elements every time a processor needs to find its median, it can presort its n/p elements and maintain them in sorted order in each iteration of the algorithm. To do this, processors merge sorted subsequences as they are exchanged. Maintaining the subsequences in sorted order also eliminates the final sorting step (line 20 in Program 6.7).

After selecting a pivot, the algorithm broadcasts a pivot during the ith iteration in time $\Theta(d - (i - 1))$. Thus, the total time spent broadcasting pivots during all $d = \log p$ iterations is

$$\sum_{i=1}^{d} i = \frac{d(d+1)}{2} = \Theta(\log^2 p)$$

The algorithm performs the third step in three phases. In the first phase, each processor partitions its subsequence into two sequences—one smaller and the other larger than the pivot. Since each processor has $\Theta(n/p)$ elements, and these elements are already sorted, this step requires $\Theta(\log(n/p))$ time. In the second phase, the processors connected along the $(d - (i - 1))^{\text{st}}$ communication link exchange appropriate blocks. Since at most $\Theta(n/p)$ elements are sent between processors, this step requires $\Theta(n/p)$ time. In the third phase, each processor merges its local subsequence with the one received in the second phase to obtain a single sorted subsequence. Since both subsequences are sorted, this step takes $\Theta(n/p)$ time.

Each processor initially sorts its $\Theta(n/p)$ elements by using sequential quicksort in $\Theta((n/p)\log(n/p))$ time. Thus, the parallel run time of this formulation is

$$T_P = \overbrace{\Theta\left(\frac{n}{p}\log\frac{n}{p}\right)}^{\text{local sort}} + \overbrace{\Theta\left(\frac{n}{p}\log p\right)}^{\text{communication}} + \overbrace{\Theta\left(\log^2 p\right)}^{\text{pivot broadcasting}}.$$

Since the sequential complexity of sorting n elements is $\Theta(n \log n)$, the speedup and efficiency are as follows:

$$\begin{aligned} S &= \frac{\Theta(n\log n)}{\Theta((n/p)\log(n/p)) + \Theta((n/p)\log p) + \Theta(\log^2 p)} \\ E &= \frac{1}{1 + \Theta((\log p)/(\log n)) + \Theta((p\log^2 p)/(n\log n))} \end{aligned} \tag{6.8}$$

Equation 6.8 shows that, for a cost-optimal formulation, $(p\log^2 p)/(n\log n) = O(1)$. Thus, this quicksort formulation can use up to $p = \Theta(n/\log n)$ processors efficiently.

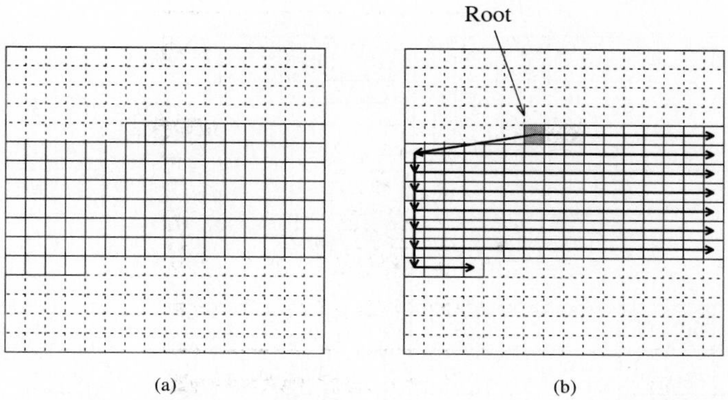

Figure 6.19 (a) An arbitrary portion of a mesh that holds part of the sequence to be sorted at some point during the execution of quicksort, and (b) a binary tree embedded into the same portion of the mesh.

Equation 6.8 also shows that the isoefficiency function due to pivot broadcasting is $\Theta(p \log^2 p)$. This result seems to imply that the quicksort algorithm is very scalable. Like parallel FFT (Section 10.4), the absolute efficiency of this formulation depends upon architectural parameters (Problem 6.21).

Parallel Formulation for a Mesh

We now discuss a parallel formulation of quicksort for a mesh-connected parallel computer. First, consider the case in which one element is assigned to each processor. The recursive partitioning step consists of selecting the pivot and then rearranging the elements in the mesh so that those smaller than the pivot are in one part of the mesh and those larger than the pivot are in the other. We assume that the processors in the mesh are numbered in row-major order. At the end of the quicksort algorithm, elements are sorted with respect to this order.

Consider the partitioning step for an arbitrary subsequence illustrated in Figure 6.19(a). Let k be the length of this sequence, and let $P_m, P_{m+1}, \ldots, P_{m+k}$ be the mesh processors storing it. Partitioning consists of the following four steps:

(1) A pivot is selected at random and sent to processor P_m. Processor P_m broadcasts this pivot to all k processors by using an embedded tree, as shown in Figure 6.19(b). The root (P_m) transmits the pivot toward the leaves. The tree embedding is also used in the following steps.

(2) Information is gathered at each processor and passed up the tree. In particular, each processor counts the number of elements smaller and larger than the pivot in both its left and right subtrees. Each processor knows the pivot value and therefore can determine if its element is smaller or larger. Each processor propagates two

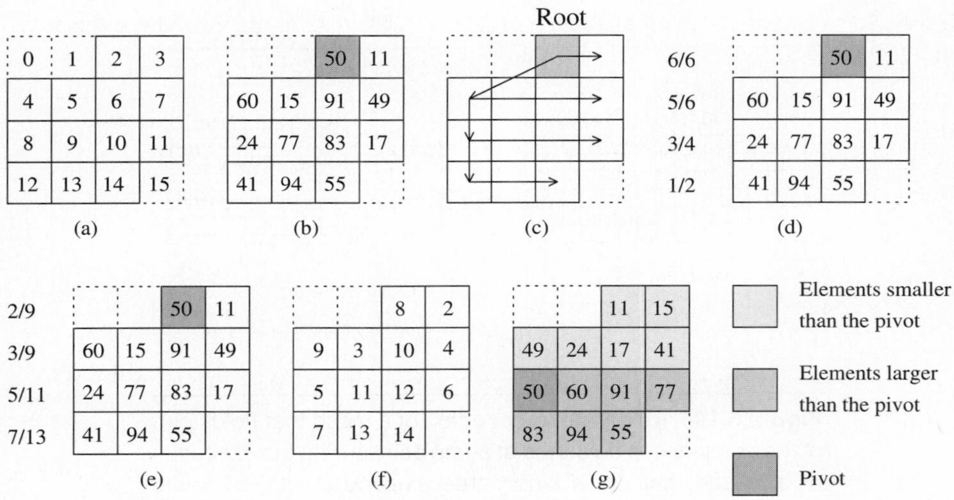

Figure 6.20 Partitioning a sequence of 13 elements on a 4×4 mesh: (a) row-major numbering of the mesh processors, (b) the elements stored in each processor (the shaded element is the pivot), (c) the tree embedded on a portion of the mesh, (d) the number of smaller or larger elements in the processor of the first column after the execution of the second step, (e) the destination of the smaller or larger elements propagated down to the processors in the first column during the third step, (f) the destination of the elements at the end of the third step, and (g) the locations of the elements after one-to-one personalized communication.

values to its parent: the number of elements smaller than the pivot and the number of elements larger than the pivot in the processor's subtree. Because the tree embedded in the mesh is not complete, some nodes will not have left or right subtrees. At the end of this step, processor P_m knows how many of the k elements are smaller and larger than the pivot. If s is the number of the elements smaller than the pivot, then the position of the pivot in the sorted sequence is P_{m+s}.

(3) Information is propagated down the tree to enable each element to be moved to its proper position in the smaller or larger partitions. Each processor in the tree receives from its parent the next empty position in the smaller and larger partitions. Depending on whether the element stored at each processor is smaller or larger than the pivot, the processor propagates the proper information down to its subtrees. Initially, the position for elements smaller than the pivot is P_m and the position for elements larger than the pivot is P_{m+s+1}.

(4) The processors perform a permutation, and each element moves to the proper position in the smaller or larger partition.

This algorithm is illustrated in Figure 6.20. The first three steps of the algorithm traverse the tree embedded on the mesh. Because the longest path from the root to the

Table 6.2 The performance of various parallel formulations of quicksort for n elements on p processors.

Architecture	Maximum Number of Processors for $E = \Theta(1)$	Corresponding Parallel Run Time	Isoefficiency Function
CRCW PRAM	n	$\Theta(\log n)$	$\Theta(n \log n)$
Hypercube			
best case	$\Theta(n/\log n)$	$\Theta(\log^2 n)$	$\Theta(p \log^2 p)$
worst case	$\Theta(\log n)$	$\Theta(n)$	$\Theta(p\, 2^p)$
Mesh	$O(((\log n)/(\log \log n))^2)$		$\Theta(p^{\sqrt{p}} \sqrt{p} \log p)$

leaves is $2\sqrt{n}$, this step requires $O(\sqrt{n})$ time. During the last step of the algorithm, elements are permuted within the mesh in $O(\sqrt{n})$ time. Assuming that pivot selections are good, the algorithm performs $\Theta(\log n)$ iterations. Thus, the parallel run time of this formulation is $O(\sqrt{n} \log n)$. Note that this is not a cost-optimal parallel formulation, because the processor-time product is $O(n^{1.5} \log n)$. We can, however, obtain a cost-optimal formulation by using fewer than n processors (Problem 6.22).

6.4.2 A Comparison of Quicksort Formulations

The previous subsection presented formulations of quicksort for three parallel architectures. The results are summarized in Table 6.2. The PRAM formulation is significantly more scalable than either the hypercube or the mesh formulation. It is also the only one that can use n processors to sort n elements in $\Theta(\log n)$ time. The hypercube formulation depends strongly on the quality of the pivots. If pivot selection is optimal, then its scalability is relatively good. But if pivot selection is poor (leading to large load imbalances), then its isoefficiency function is exponential. The mesh formulation of quicksort has an exponential isoefficiency function and is practical only for small values of p.

6.5 Other Sorting Algorithms

As mentioned in the introduction to this chapter, there are many sorting algorithms, and we cannot explore them all in this chapter. However, in this section we present four additional sorting algorithms that are important both practically and theoretically. Our discussion of these schemes will be brief. Refer to the bibliographic remarks (Section 6.6) for references on these and other algorithms.

6.5.1 Enumeration Sort

All the sorting algorithms presented so far are based on compare-exchange operations. This section considers an algorithm based on ***enumeration sort***, which does not use compare-

```
1.  procedure ENUM_SORT (n)
2.  begin
3.      for each processor P_{1,j} do
4.          C[j] := 0;
5.      for each processor P_{i,j} do
6.          if (A[i] < A[j]) or (A[i] = A[j] and i < j) then
7.              C[j] := 1;
8.          else
9.              C[j] := 0;
10.     for each processor P_{1,j} do
11.         A[C[j]] := A[j];
12. end ENUM_SORT
```

Program 6.8 Enumeration sort on a CRCW PRAM with additive-write conflict resolution.

exchange. The basic idea behind enumeration sort is to determine the rank of each element. The ***rank*** of an element a_i is the number of elements smaller than a_i in the sequence to be sorted. The rank of a_i can be used to place it in its correct position in the sorted sequence. Several parallel algorithms are based on enumeration sort. Here we present one such algorithm that is suited to the CRCW PRAM model. This formulation sorts n elements by using n^2 processors in $\Theta(1)$ time.

Assume that concurrent writes to the same memory location of the CRCW PRAM result in the sum of all the values written being stored at that location (Section 2.2). Consider the n^2 processors as being arranged in a two-dimensional grid. The algorithm consists of two steps. During the first step, each column j of processors computes the number of elements smaller than a_j. During the second step, each processor $P_{1,j}$ of the first row places a_j in its proper position as determined by its rank. The algorithm is shown in Program 6.8. It uses an auxiliary array $C[1 \ldots n]$ to store the rank of each element. The crucial steps of this algorithm are lines 7 and 9. There, each processor $P_{i,j}$, writes 1 in $C[j]$ if the element $A[i]$ is smaller than $A[j]$ and writes 0 otherwise. Because of the additive-write conflict resolution scheme, the effect of these instructions is to count the number of elements smaller than $A[j]$ and thus compute its rank. The run time of this algorithm is $\Theta(1)$. Modifications of this algorithm for various parallel architectures are discussed in Problem 6.23.

6.5.2 Bucket Sort

The algorithm discussed in this section has a lower average run time than the lower bound of $\Omega(n \log n)$ for comparison-based sorting. This is because the algorithm assumes that the n elements to be sorted are uniformly distributed over an interval $[a, b)$. This algorithm is usually called ***bucket sort*** and operates as follows. The interval $[a, b)$ is divided into m equal-sized subintervals referred to as ***buckets***. Each element is placed in the appropriate bucket. Since the n elements are uniformly distributed over the interval $[a, b)$, the number of elements in each bucket is roughly n/m. The algorithm then sorts the elements in each bucket, yielding a sorted sequence. The run time of this algorithm is $\Theta(n \log(n/m))$. For $m = \Theta(n)$, it exhibits linear run time, $\Theta(n)$.

Parallelizing bucket sort is straightforward. Let n be the number of elements to be sorted and p be the number of processors. Initially, each processor is assigned a block of n/p elements, and the number of buckets is selected to be $m = p$. The parallel formulation of bucket sort consists of three steps. In the first step, each processor partitions its block of n/p elements into p subblocks—one for each of the p buckets. This is possible because each processor knows the interval $[a, b)$ and thus the interval for each bucket. In the second step, each processor sends subblocks to the appropriate processors. After this step, each processor has only the elements belonging to the bucket assigned to it. In the third step, each processor sorts its bucket internally by using an optimal sequential sorting algorithm.

We now analyze the complexity of this algorithm on a hypercube-connected computer with cut-through routing. During the first step, a block of size n/p is partitioned into p blocks. This step requires $\Theta(n/p)$ time. The subblock movement of the second step is essentially an all-to-all personalized communication (Section 3.5). If we further assume that the elements in each processor are also uniformly distributed in the range $[a, b)$, then each subblock is of size n/p^2; thus, this step requires $\Theta(n/p) + \Theta(p \log p)$ time. Finally, the third step internally sorts a block of $\Theta(n/p)$ elements and requires $\Theta(n/p)$ time using bucket sort. Therefore, the run time of this algorithm is

$$T_P = \overbrace{\Theta\left(\frac{n}{p}\right)}^{\text{block partitioning}} + \overbrace{\Theta\left(\frac{n}{p}\right) + \Theta(p \log p)}^{\text{all-to-all personalized broadcast}} + \overbrace{\Theta\left(\frac{n}{p}\right)}^{\text{local sort}}. \qquad (6.9)$$

Analyzing the scalability of this algorithm is left as an exercise (Problem 6.24).

From Equation 6.9 we see that the performance of bucket sort is better than most of the algorithms presented earlier. Thus, bucket sort is a good choice if input elements are uniformly distributed over a known interval.

6.5.3 Sample Sort

The bucket sort algorithm presented in the previous subsection requires the input to be uniformly distributed over an interval $[a, b)$. However, in many cases the input may not have such a distribution or its distribution may be unknown. Thus, using bucket sort may result in buckets that have a significantly different number of elements, thereby degrading performance. In such situations an algorithm called ***sample sort*** will yield significantly better performance. The idea behind sample sort is simple. A sample of size s is selected from the n-element sequence, and the range of the buckets is determined by sorting the sample and choosing $m - 1$ elements from the result. These elements (called ***splitters***) divide the sample into m equal-sized buckets. After defining the buckets, the algorithm proceeds in the same way as bucket sort. The performance of sample sort depends on the sample size s and the way it is selected from the n-element sequence.

Consider a splitter selection scheme that guarantees that the number of elements ending up in each bucket is roughly the same for all buckets. Let n be the number of elements to be sorted and m be the number of buckets. The scheme works as follows. It divides the n elements into m blocks of size n/m each, and sorts each block by using quicksort. From each sorted block it chooses $m-1$ evenly spaced elements. The $m(m-1)$ elements selected from all the blocks represent the sample used to determine the buckets. This scheme guarantees that the number of elements ending up in each bucket is less than $2n/m$ (Problem 6.25).

How can we parallelize the splitter selection scheme? Let p be the number of processors. As in bucket sort, set $m = p$; thus, at the end of the algorithm, each processor contains only the elements belonging to a single bucket. Each processor is assigned a block of n/p elements, which it sorts sequentially. It then chooses $p-1$ evenly spaced elements from the sorted block. Each processor sends its $p-1$ sample elements to one processor—say P_0. Processor P_0 then sequentially sorts the $p(p-1)$ sample elements and selects the $p-1$ splitters. Finally, processor P_0 broadcasts the $p-1$ splitters to all the other processors. Now the algorithm proceeds in a manner identical to that of bucket sort.

Consider a formulation of sample sort on a hypercube-connected parallel computer with cut-through routing. The internal sort of n/p elements requires $\Theta((n/p)\log(n/p))$ time, and the selection of $p-1$ sample elements requires $\Theta(p)$ time. Sending $p-1$ elements to processor P_0 is similar to a single-node gather operation (Section 3.4); the time required is $\Theta(p^2)$. The time to internally sort the $p(p-1)$ sample elements at P_0 is $\Theta(p^2 \log p)$, and the time to select $p-1$ splitters is $\Theta(p)$. The $p-1$ splitters are sent to all the other processors by using one-to-all broadcast (Section 3.2), which requires $\Theta(p \log p)$ time. Each processor can *insert* these $p-1$ splitters in its local sorted block of size n/p by performing $p-1$ binary searches. Each processor thus partitions its block into p subblocks—one for each bucket. The time required for this partitioning is $\Theta(p \log(n/p))$. Each processor then sends subblocks to the appropriate processors (that is, buckets). The communication time for this step is difficult to compute precisely, as it depends on the size of the subblocks to be communicated. These subblocks can vary arbitrarily between 0 and n/p. Thus, the upper bound on the communication time is $O(n) + O(p \log p)$.

If we assume that the elements stored in each processor are uniformly distributed, then each subblock has roughly $\Theta(n/p^2)$ elements. In this case, the parallel run time is

$$T_P = \overbrace{\Theta\left(\frac{n}{p}\log\frac{n}{p}\right)}^{\text{local sort}} + \overbrace{\Theta\left(p^2 \log p\right)}^{\text{sort sample}} + \overbrace{\Theta\left(p \log \frac{n}{p}\right)}^{\text{block partition}} + \overbrace{\Theta(n/p) + O(p \log p)}^{\text{communication}}. \quad (6.10)$$

In this case, the isoefficiency function is $\Theta(p^3 \log p)$. If bitonic sort is used to sort the $p(p-1)$ sample elements, then the time for sorting the sample would be $\Theta(p \log p)$, and the isoefficiency will be reduced to $\Theta(p^2 \log p)$ (Problem 6.27).

6.5.4 Radix Sort

The ***radix sort*** algorithm relies on the binary representation of the elements to be sorted. Let b be the number of bits in the binary representation of an element. The radix sort algorithm examines the elements to be sorted r bits at a time, where $r < b$. Radix sort requires b/r iterations. During iteration i, it sorts the elements according to their i^{th} least significant block of r bits. For radix sort to work properly, each of the b/r sorts must be stable. A sorting algorithm is ***stable*** if its output preserves the order of input elements with the same value. Radix sort is stable if it preserves the input order of any two r-bit blocks when these blocks are equal. The most common implementation of the intermediate b/r radix-2^r sorts uses enumeration sort (Section 6.5.1) because the range of possible values $[0 \dots 2^r - 1]$ is small. For such cases, enumeration sort significantly outperforms any comparison-based sorting algorithm.

Consider a parallel formulation of radix sort for n elements on an n-processor hypercube. The parallel radix sort algorithm is shown in Program 6.9. The main loop of the algorithm (lines 3–17) performs the b/r enumeration sorts of the r-bit blocks. The enumeration sort is performed by using the *prefix_sum()* and *parallel_sum()* functions. These functions are similar to those described in Examples 3.7 and 3.8. During each iteration of the inner loop (lines 6–15), radix sort determines the position of the elements with an r-bit value of j. It does this by summing all the elements with the same value and then assigning them to processors. The variable *rank* holds the position of each element. At the end of the loop (line 16), each processor sends its element to the appropriate processor. Processor labels determine the global order of sorted elements.

As shown in Examples 3.7 and 3.8, the complexity of both the *parallel_sum()* and *prefix_sum()* operations is $\Theta(\log n)$ on an n-processor hypercube. The complexity of the communication step on line 16 is $\Theta(n)$. Thus, the parallel run time of this algorithm is

$$T_P = \frac{b}{r} 2^r (\Theta(\log n) + \Theta(n))$$

6.6 Bibliographic Remarks

Knuth [Knu73] discusses sorting networks and their history. The question of whether a sorting network could sort n elements in $O(\log n)$ time remained open for a long time. In 1983, Ajtai, Komlos, and Szemeredi [AKS83] discovered a sorting network that could sort n elements in $O(\log n)$ time by using $O(n \log n)$ comparators. Unfortunately, the constant of their sorting network is quite large (many thousands), and thus is not practical. The bitonic sorting network was discovered by Batcher [Bat68], who also discovered the network for odd-even sort. These were the first networks capable of sorting n elements in $O(\log^2 n)$ time. Stone [Sto71] maps the bitonic sort onto a perfect-shuffle interconnection network, sorting n elements by using n processors in $O(\log^2 n)$ time. Siegel [Sie77] shows that bitonic sort can also be performed on the hypercube in $O(\log^2 n)$ time. The block-based hypercube formulation of bitonic sort is discussed in Johnsson [Joh84] and Fox

```
procedure RADIX_SORT(A, r)
begin
    for i := 0 to b/r do
    begin
        offset := 0;
        for j := 0 to 2^r − 1 do
        begin
            flag := 0;
            if the i^th least significant r-bit block of A[P_k] = j then
                flag := 1;
            index := prefix_sum(flag)
            if flag = 1 then
                rank := offset + index;
            offset := parallel_sum(flag);
        endfor
        each processor P_k send its element A[P_k] to processor P_rank;
    endfor
end RADIX_SORT
```

Program 6.9 A parallel radix sort algorithm, in which each element of the array $A[1 \ldots n]$ to be sorted is assigned to one processor. The function *prefix_sum()* computes the prefix sum of the *flag* variable, and the function *parallel_sum()* returns the total sum of the *flag* variable.

et al. [FJL+88]. Program 6.1 is adopted from [FJL+88]. The shuffled row-major indexing formulation of bitonic sort on a mesh-connected computer is presented by Thompson and Kung [TK77]. They also show how the odd-even merge sort can be used with snakelike row-major indexing. Nassimi and Sahni [NS79] present a row-major indexed bitonic sort formulation for a mesh with the same performance as shuffled row-major indexing. An improved version of the mesh odd-even merge is proposed by Kumar and Hirschberg [KH83]. The compare-split operation can be implemented in many ways. Baudet and Stevenson [BS78] describe one way to perform this operation. An alternative way of performing a compare-split operation based on a bitonic sort (Problem 6.1) that requires no additional memory was discovered by Hsiao and Menon [HM80].

The odd-even transposition sort is described by Knuth [Knu73]. Several early references to parallel sorting by odd-even transposition are given by Knuth [Knu73] and Kung [Kun80]. The block-based extension of the algorithm is due to Baudet and Stevenson [BS78]. Another variation of block-based odd-even transposition sort that uses bitonic merge-split is described by DeWitt, Friedland, Hsiao, and Menon [DFHM82]. Their algorithm uses p processors and runs in $O(n + n \log(n/p))$ time. In contrast to the algorithm of Baudet and Stevenson [BS78], which is faster but requires $4n/p$ storage locations in each processor, the algorithm of DeWitt et al. requires only $n/p + 1$ storage locations to perform the compare-split operation.

The shellsort algorithm described in Section 6.3.2 is due to Fox et al. [FJL$^+$88]. They show that, as n increases, the probability that the final odd-even transposition will exhibit worst-case performance (in other words, will require p phases) diminishes. A different shellsort algorithm based on the original sequential algorithm [She59] is described by Quinn [Qui88].

The sequential quicksort algorithm is due to Hoare [Hoa62]. Sedgewick [Sed78] provides a good reference on the details of the implementation and how they affect its performance. The random pivot-selection scheme is described and analyzed by Robin [Rob75]. The algorithm for sequence partitioning on a single processor was suggested by Sedgewick [Sed78] and used in parallel formulations by Raskin [Ras78], Deminet [Dem82], and Quinn [Qui88]. The CRCW PRAM algorithm (Section 6.4.1) is due to Chlebus and Vrto [CV91]. Many other quicksort-based algorithms for PRAM and shared-memory parallel computers have been developed that can sort n elements in $\Theta(\log n)$ time by using $\Theta(n)$ processors. Martel and Gusfield [MG89] developed a quicksort algorithm for a CRCW PRAM that requires $O(n^3)$ space on the average. An algorithm suited to shared-memory parallel computers with fetch-and-add capabilities was discovered by Heidelberger, Norton, and Robinson [HNR90]. Their algorithm runs in $\Theta(\log n)$ time on the average and can be adapted for commercially available shared-memory computers. The hypercube formulation of quicksort described in Section 6.4.1 is due to Wagar [Wag87]. His hyperquicksort algorithm uses the median-based pivot-selection scheme and assumes that the elements in each processor have the same distribution. His experimental results show that hyperquicksort is faster than bitonic sort on a hypercube. An alternate pivot-selection scheme (Problem 6.18) was implemented by Fox et al. [FJL$^+$88]. This scheme significantly improves the performance of hyperquicksort when the elements are not evenly distributed in each processor. Plaxton [Pla89] describes a quicksort algorithm on a p-processor hypercube that sorts n elements in $O((n \log n)/p + (n \log^{3/2} p)/p + \log^3 p \log(n/p))$ time. This algorithm uses an $O((n/p) \log \log p + \log^2 p \log(n/p))$ time parallel selection algorithm to determine the perfect pivot selection. The mesh formulation of quicksort (Section 6.4.1) is due to Singh, Kumar, Agha, and Tomlinson [SKAT91]. They also describe a modification to the algorithm that reduces the complexity of each step by a factor of $\Theta(\log p)$.

The sequential bucket sort algorithm was first proposed by Isaac and Singleton in 1956. Hirschberg [Hir78] proposed a bucket sort algorithm for the EREW PRAM model. This algorithm sorts n elements in the range $[0 \ldots n-1]$ in $\Theta(\log n)$ time by using n processors. A side effect of this algorithm is that duplicate elements are eliminated. Their algorithm requires $\Theta(n^2)$ space. Hirschberg [Hir78] generalizes this algorithm so that duplicate elements remain in the sorted array. The generalized algorithm sorts n elements in $\Theta(k \log n)$ time by using $n^{1+1/k}$ processors, where k is an arbitrary integer.

The sequential sample sort algorithm was discovered by Frazer and McKellar [FM70]. The parallel sample sort algorithm (Section 6.5.3) was discovered by Shi and Schaeffer [SS90]. Several parallel formulations of sample sort for different parallel architectures have been proposed. Abali, Ozguner, and Bataineh [AOB93] presented a splitter selection scheme that guarantees the number of element ending up in each bucket is n/p. Their algorithm requires $O((n \log n)/p + p \log^2 n)$ time, on average, to sort n elements on a p-processor hypercube. Reif and Valiant [RV87] present a sample sort algorithm that sorts n elements on an n-processor hypercube-connected computer in $O(\log n)$ time with high probability. Won and Sahni [WS88] and Seidel and George [SG88] present parallel formulations of a variation of sample sort called ***bin sort*** [FKO86].

Many other parallel sorting algorithms have been proposed. Various parallel sorting algorithms can be efficiently implemented on a PRAM model or on shared-memory computers. Akl [Akl85], Borodin and Hopcroft [BH82], Shiloach and Vishkin [SV81], and Bitton, DeWitt, Hsiao, and Menon [BDHM84] provide a good survey of the subject. Valiant [Val75] proposed a sorting algorithm for a shared-memory SIMD computer that sorts by merging. It sorts n elements in $O(\log n \log\log n)$ time by using $n/2$ processors. Reischuk [Rei81] was the first to develop an algorithm that sorted n elements in $\Theta(\log n)$ time for an n-processor PRAM. Cole [Col88] developed a parallel merge-sort algorithm that sorts n elements in $\Theta(\log n)$ time on an EREW PRAM. Natvig [Nat90] has shown that the constants hidden behind the asymptotic notation are very large. In fact, the $\Theta(\log^2 n)$ bitonic sort outperforms the $\Theta(\log n)$ merge sort as long as n is smaller than 7.6×10^{22}! Plaxton [Pla89] has developed a hypercube sorting algorithm, called ***smoothsort***, that runs asymptotically faster than any previously known algorithm for that architecture. Leighton [Lei85] proposed a sorting algorithm, called ***columnsort***, that consists of a sequence of sorts followed by elementary matrix operations. Columnsort is a generalization of Batcher's odd-even sort. Nigam and Sahni [NS93] presented an algorithm based on Leighton's columnsort for reconfigurable meshes with buses that sorts n elements on an n^2-processor mesh in $O(1)$ time.

Problems

6.1 Consider the following technique for performing the compare-split operation. Let $x_1, x_2, \ldots, x_k$ be the elements stored at processor P_i in increasing order, and let $y_1, y_2, \ldots, y_k$ be the elements stored at processor P_j in decreasing order. Processor P_i sends x_1 to P_j. Processor P_j compares x_1 with y_1 and then sends the larger element back to processor P_i and keeps the smaller element for itself. The same procedure is repeated for pairs $(x_2, y_2), (x_3, y_3), \ldots, (x_k, y_k)$. If for any pair (x_l, y_l) for $1 \leq l \leq k$, $x_l \geq y_l$, then no more exchanges are needed. Finally, each processor sorts its elements. Show that this method correctly performs a compare-split operation. Analyze its run time, and compare the relative merits of this method to those of the method presented in the text. Is this method better suited for MIMD or SIMD parallel computers?

6.2 Show that the $\leq$ relation, as defined in Section 6.1 for blocks of elements, is a partial ordering relation.
Hint: A relation is a ***partial ordering*** if it is reflexive, antisymmetric, and transitive.

6.3 Consider the following sequence $s = \{a_0, a_1, \ldots, a_{n-1}\}$, where n is a power of 2. In the following cases, prove that the sequences s_1 and s_2 obtained by performing the bitonic split operation described in Section 6.2.1, on the sequence s, satisfies the properties that (1) s_1 and s_2 are bitonic sequences, and (2) the elements of s_1 are smaller than the elements of s_2.

(a) s is a bitonic sequence such that $a_0 \leq a_1 \leq \cdots \leq a_{n/2-1}$ and $a_{n/2} \geq a_{n/2+1} \geq \cdots \geq a_{n-1}$.

(b) s is a bitonic sequence such that $a_0 \leq a_1 \leq \cdots \leq a_i$ and $a_{i+1} \geq a_{i+2} \geq \cdots \geq a_{n-1}$ for some i, $0 \leq i \leq n-1$.

(c) s is a bitonic sequence that becomes increasing-decreasing after shifting its elements.

6.4 In the parallel formulations of bitonic sort, we assumed that we had n processors available to sort n items. Show how the algorithm needs to be modified when only $n/2$ processors are available.

6.5 Show that, in the hypercube formulation of bitonic sort, each bitonic merge of sequences of size 2^k is performed on a k-dimensional hypercube and each sequence is assigned to a separate hypercube.

6.6 Show that the parallel formulation of bitonic sort shown in Program 6.1 is correct. In particular, show that the algorithm correctly compare-exchanges elements and that the elements end up in the appropriate processors.

6.7 Consider the parallel formulation of bitonic sort for a mesh-connected parallel computer. Compute the exact parallel run time of the following formulations:

(a) One that uses the row-major mapping shown in Figure 6.11(a) for a mesh with store-and-forward routing

(b) One that uses the row-major snakelike mapping shown in Figure 6.11(b) for a mesh with store-and-forward routing

(c) One that uses the row-major shuffled mapping shown in Figure 6.11(c) for a mesh with store-and-forward routing

Also, determine how the above run times change when cut-through routing is used.

6.8 Show that the block-based bitonic sort algorithm that uses compare-split operations is correct.

6.9 Consider a ring-connected parallel computer with n processors. Show how to map the input wires of the bitonic sorting network onto the ring so that the communication cost is minimized. Analyze the performance of your mapping. Consider the case in which only p processors are available. Analyze the performance of your parallel formulation for this case. What is the largest number of processors that can be used while maintaining a cost-optimal parallel formulation? What is the isoefficiency function of your scheme?

6.10 Prove that the block-based odd-even transposition sort yields a correct algorithm.

Hint: This problem is similar to Problem 6.8.

6.11 Show how to apply the idea of the shellsort algorithm (Section 6.3.2) to a p-processor mesh-connected computer. Your algorithm does not need to be an exact copy of the hypercube formulation.

6.12 Show how to parallelize the sequential shellsort algorithm for a p-processor hypercube. Note that the shellsort algorithm presented in Section 6.3.2 is not an exact parallelization of the sequential algorithm.

6.13 Consider the shellsort algorithm presented in Section 6.3.2. Its performance depends on the value of l, which is the number of odd and even phases performed during the second phase of the algorithm. Describe a worst-case initial key distribution that will require $l = \Theta(p)$ phases. What is the probability of this worst-case scenario?

6.14 In Section 6.4.1 we discussed a parallel formulation of quicksort for a CREW PRAM that is based on assigning each subproblem to a separate processor. This formulation uses n processors to sort n elements. Based on this approach, derive a parallel formulation that uses p processors, where $(p < n)$. Derive expressions for the parallel run time, efficiency, and isoefficiency function. What is the maximum number of processors that your parallel formulation can use and still remain cost-optimal?

6.15 Derive an algorithm that traverses the binary search tree constructed by the algorithm in Program 6.6 and determines the position of each element in the sorted array. Your algorithm should use n processors and solve the problem in $\Theta(\log n)$ time on an arbitrary CRCW PRAM.

6.16 Consider the PRAM formulation of the quicksort algorithm (Section 6.4.1). Compute the average height of the binary tree generated by the algorithm.

6.17 Consider the parallel formulation of quicksort for a d-dimensional hypercube described in Section 6.4.1. Show that after d splits—one along each communication link—the elements are sorted according to the global order defined by the processor's labels.

6.18 An alternative way of selecting pivots in the parallel formulation of quicksort for a d-dimensional hypercube (Section 6.4.1) is to select all the $2^d - 1$ pivots at once as follows:

(a) Each processor picks a sample of l elements at random.

(b) All processors together sort the sample of $l \times 2^d$ items by using the shellsort algorithm (Section 6.3.2).

(c) Choose $2^d - 1$ equally distanced pivots from this list.

(d) Broadcast pivots so that all the processors know the pivots.

How does the quality of this pivot selection scheme depend on l? Do you think l should be a function of n? Under what assumptions will this scheme select good pivots? Do you think this scheme works when the elements are not identically distributed on each processor? Analyze the complexity of this scheme.

6.19 Another pivot selection scheme for parallel quicksort for hypercube (Section 6.4.1) is as follows. During the split along the ith dimension, 2^{i-1} pairs of processors exchange elements. The pivot is selected in two steps. In the first step, each of the 2^{i-1} pairs of processors compute the median of their combined sequences. In the second step, the median of the 2^{i-1} medians is computed. This median of medians becomes the pivot for the split along the ith communication link. Subsequent pivots are selected in the same way among the participating subcubes. Under what assumptions will this scheme yield good pivot selections? Is this better than the median scheme described in the text? Analyze the complexity of selecting the pivot.

Hint: If A and B are two sorted sequences, each having n elements, then we can find the median of $A \cup B$ in $\Theta(\log n)$ time.

6.20 In our hypercube formulation of quicksort (Section 6.4.1) each iteration is followed by a barrier synchronization. Is barrier synchronization necessary to ensure the correctness of the algorithm? If not, then how does the performance change in the absence of barrier synchronization.

6.21 Consider the quicksort formulation for the hypercube presented in Section 6.4.1. Compute the exact (that is, using t_s, t_w, and t_c) parallel run time and efficiency of the algorithm under the assumption of perfect pivots. Compute the various components of the isoefficiency function of your formulation when

(a) $t_c = 1, t_w = 1, t_s = 1$

(b) $t_c = 1, t_w = 1, t_s = 10$

(c) $t_c = 1, t_w = 10, t_s = 100$

for cases in which the desired efficiency is 0.50, 0.75, and 0.95. Does the scalability of this formulation depend on the desired efficiency and the architectural characteristics of the machine?

6.22 Consider the quicksort formulation for a mesh described in Section 6.4.1. Describe a scaled-down formulation that uses $p < n$ processors. Analyze its parallel run time, speedup, and isoefficiency function.

6.23 Consider the enumeration sort algorithm presented in Section 6.5.1. Show how the algorithm can be implemented on each of the following:

(a) a CREW PRAM

(b) a EREW PRAM

(c) a hypercube-connected parallel computer

(d) a mesh-connected parallel computer

Analyze the performance of your formulations. Furthermore, show how you can extend this enumeration sort to a hypercube to sort n elements using p processors.

6.24 Derive expressions for the speedup, efficiency, and isoefficiency function of the bucket sort parallel formulation presented in Section 6.5.2. Compare these expressions with the expressions for the other sorting algorithms presented in this chapter. Which parallel formulations perform better than bucket sort, and which perform worse?

6.25 Show that the splitter selection scheme described in Section 6.5.3 guarantees that the number of elements in each of the m buckets is less than $2n/m$.

6.26 Derive expressions for the speedup, efficiency, and isoefficiency function of the sample sort parallel formulation presented in Section 6.5.3. Derive these metrics under each of the following conditions: (1) the p subblocks at each processor are of equal size, and (2) the size of the p subblocks at each processor can vary by a factor of $\log p$.

6.27 In the sample sort algorithm presented in Section 6.5.3, all processors send $p-1$ elements to processor P_0, who sorts the $p(p-1)$ elements, and distributes splitters to all the processors. Modify the algorithm so that the processors sort the $p(p-1)$ elements in parallel using bitonic sort. How will you choose the splitters? Compute the parallel run time, speedup, and efficiency of your formulation.

6.28 How does the performance of radix sort (Section 6.5.4) depend on the value of r? Compute the value of r that minimizes the run time of the algorithm.

6.29 Extend the radix sort algorithm presented in Section 6.5.4 to the case in which p processors ($p < n$) are used to sort n elements. Derive expressions for the speedup, efficiency, and isoefficiency function for this parallel formulation. Can you devise a better ranking mechanism?

References

[Akl85] S. G. Akl. *Parallel Sorting Algorithms*. Academic Press, San Diego, CA, 1985.

[AKS83] M. Ajtai, J. Komlos, and E. Szemeredi. An $O(n \log n)$ sorting network. In *Proceedings of the 15th Annual ACM Symposium on Theory of Computing*, 1–9, 1983.

[AOB93] B. Abali, F. Ozguner, and A. Bataineh. Balanced parallel sort on hypercube multiprocessors. *IEEE Transactions on Parallel and Distributed Systems*, 4(5):572–581, May 1993.

[Bat68] K. E. Batcher. Sorting networks and their applications. In *Proceedings of the 1968 Spring Joint Computer Conference*, 307–314, 1968.

[BDHM84] D. Bitton, D. J. DeWitt, D. K. Hsiao, and M. J. Menon. A taxonomy of parallel sorting. *Computing Surveys*, 16(3):287–318, September 1984.

[BH82] A. Borodin and J. E. Hopcroft. Routing merging and sorting on parallel models of computation. In *Proceedings of the 14th Annual ACM Symposium on Theory of Computing*, 338–344, May 1982.

[BS78] G. M. Baudet and D. Stevenson. Optimal sorting algorithms for parallel computers. *IEEE Transactions on Computers*, C–27(1):84–87, January 1978.

[Col88] R. Cole. Parallel merge sort. *SIAM Journal on Computing*, 17(4):770–785, August 1988.

[CV91] B. Chlebus and I. Vrto. Parallel quick sort. *Journal of Parallel and Distributed Computing*, 11:332–337, 1991.

[Dem82] J. Deminet. Experiences with multiprocessor algorithms. *IEEE Transactions on Computers*, C-31(4):278–288, 1982.

[DFHM82] D. J. DeWitt, D. B. Friedland, D. K. Hsiao, and M. J. Menon. A taxonomy of parallel sorting algorithms. Technical Report TR-482, Computer Sciences Department, University of Wisconsin, Madison, WI, 1982.

[FJL+88] G. C. Fox, M. Johnson, G. Lyzenga, S. W. Otto, J. Salmon, and D. Walker. *Solving Problems on Concurrent Processors: Vol. 1*. Prentice Hall, Englewood Cliffs, NJ, 1988.

[FKO86] E. Felten, S. Karlin, and S. W. Otto. Sorting on a hypercube. *Caltech/JPL*, 1986. Hm 244.

[FM70] W. D. Frazer and A. C. McKellar. Samplesort: A sampling approach to minimal storage tree sorting. *Journal of the ACM*, 17(3):496–507, July 1970.

[Hir78] D. S. Hirschberg. Fast parallel sorting algorithms. *Communications of ACM*, 21(8):657–666, August 1978.

[HM80] D. K. Hsiao and M. J. Menon. Parallel record-sorting methods for hardware realization. Osu-cisrc-tr-80-7, Computer Science Information Department, Ohio State University, Columbus, OH, 1980.

[HNR90] P. Heidelberger, A. Norton, and J. T. Robinson. Parallel quicksort using fetch-and-add. *IEEE Transactions on Computers*, C-39(1):133–138, January 1990.

[Hoa62] C. A. R. Hoare. Quicksort. *Computer Journal*, 5:10–15, 1962.

[Joh84] S. L. Johnsson. Combining parallel and sequential sorting on a boolean n-cube. In *Proceedings of International Conference on Parallel Processing*, 1984.

[KH83] M. Kumar and D. S. Hirschberg. An efficient implementation of Batcher's odd-even merge algorithm and its application in parallel sorting schemes. *IEEE Transactions on Computers*, C–32, March 1983.

[Knu73] D. E. Knuth. *The Art of Computer Programming: Sorting and Searching*. Addison-Wesley, Reading, MA, 1973.

[Kun80] J. T. Kung. The structure of parallel algorithms. In M. Yovits, editor, *Advances in Computing*, 73–74. Academic Press, San Diego, CA, 1980.

[Lei85] F. T. Leighton. Tight bounds on the complexity of parallel sorting. *IEEE Transactions on Computers*, C–34(4):344–354, April 1985.

[MG89] C. U. Martel and D. Q. Gusfield. A fast parallel quicksort algorithm. *Information Processing Letters*, 30:97–102, 1989.

[Nat90] L. Natvig. Investigating the practical value of Cole's $O(\log n)$ time crew pram merge sort algorithm. In *5th International Symposium on Computing and Information Sciences*, October 1990.

[NS79] D. Nassimi and S. Sahni. Bitonic sort on a mesh connected parallel computer. *IEEE Transactions on Computers*, C–28(1), January 1979.

[NS93] M. Nigam and S. Sahni. Sorting n numbers on $n \times n$ reconfigurable meshes with buses. In *7th International Parallel Processing Symposium*, 174–181, 1993.

[Pla89] C. C. Plaxton. Load balancing, selection and sorting on the hypercube. In *Proceedings 1989 ACM Symposium on Parallel Algorithms and Architectures*, 64–73, 1989.

[Qui88] M. J. Quinn. Parallel sorting algorithms for tightly coupled multiprocessors. *Parallel Computing*, 6:349–357, 1988.

[Ras78] L. Raskin. *Performance Evaluation of Multiple Processor Systems*. Ph.D. thesis, Carnegie-Mellon University, Pittsburgh, PA, 1978.

[Rei81] R. Reischuk. Probabilistic algorithms for sorting and selection. *SIAM Journal of Computing*, 396–409, 1981.

[Rob75] M. O. Robin. Probabilistic algorithms. In J. Traub, editor, *Algorithms and Complexity: New Directions and Recent Results*, 21–39. Academic Press, San Diego, CA, 1975.

[RV87] J. H. Reif and L. G. Valiant. A logarithmic time sort for linear size networks. *Journal of the ACM*, 34(1):60–76, January 1987.

[Sed78] R. Sedgewick. Implementing quicksort programs. *Communications of the ACM*, 21(10):847–857, 1978.

[SG88] S. R. Seidel and W. L. George. Binsorting on hypercube with d-port communication. In *Proceedings of the Third Conference on Hypercube Concurrent Computers*, 1455–1461, January 1988.

[She59] D. L. Shell. A high-speed sorting procedure. *Communication of ACM*, 2(7):30–32, July 1959.

[Sie77] H. J. Siegel. The universality of various types of SIMD machine interconnection networks. In *Proceedings of the 4th Annual Symposium on Computer Architecture*, 23–25, 1977.

[SKAT91] V. Singh, V. Kumar, G. Agha, and C. Tomlinson. Efficient algorithms for parallel sorting on mesh multicomputers. *International Journal of Parallel Programming*, 20(2):95–131, 1991. Shorter version in proceedings of the 1991 International Parallel Processing Symposium.

[SS90] H. Shi and J. Schaeffer. Parallel sorting by regular sampling. *Journal of Parallel and Distributed Computing*, (14):361–372, 1990.

[Sto71] H. S. Stone. Parallel processing with the perfect shuffle. *IEEE Transactions on Computers*, C-20:153–161, 1971.

[SV81] Y. Shiloach and U. Vishkin. Finding the maximum, merging and sorting in a parallel computation model. *Journal of Algorithms*, 88–102, 1981.

[TK77] C. D. Thompson and H. T. Kung. Sorting on a mesh-connected parallel computer. *Communications of the ACM*, 20(4):263–271, April 1977.

[Val75] L. G. Valiant. Parallelism in comparison problems. *SIAM Journal of Computing*, 4(3):348–355, September 1975.

[Wag87] B. A. Wagar. Hyperquicksort: A fast sorting algorithm for hypercubes. In *Proceedings of the Second Conference on Hypercube Multiprocessors*, 292–299, 1987.

[WS88] Y. Won and S. Sahni. A balanced bin sort for hypercube multiprocessors. *Journal of Supercomputing*, (2):435–448, 1988.

CHAPTER 7

Graph Algorithms

Graph theory plays an important role in computer science because it provides an easy and systematic way to model many problems. Many problems can be expressed in terms of graphs, and can be solved using standard graph algorithms. This chapter presents parallel formulations of some important and fundamental graph algorithms.

7.1 Definitions and Representation

An ***undirected graph*** G is a pair (V, E), where V is a finite set of points called ***vertices*** and E is a finite set of ***edges***. An edge $e \in E$ is an unordered pair (u, v), where $u, v \in V$. An edge (u, v) indicates that vertices u and v are connected. Similarly, a ***directed graph*** G, is a pair (V, E), where V is the set of vertices as we just defined, but an edge $(u, v) \in E$ is an ordered pair; that is, it indicates that there is a connection from u to v. Figure 7.1 illustrates an undirected and a directed graph. We use the term ***graph*** to refer to both directed and undirected graphs.

Many definitions are common to directed and undirected graphs, although certain terms have slightly different meanings for each. If (u, v) is an edge in an undirected graph, (u, v) is ***incident on*** vertices u and v. However, if a graph is directed, then edge (u, v) is ***incident from*** vertex u and is ***incident to*** vertex v. For example, in Figure 7.1(a), edge e is incident on vertices 5 and 4, but in Figure 7.1(b), edge f is incident from vertex 5 and incident to vertex 2. If (u, v) is an edge in a undirected graph $G = (V, E)$, vertices u and v are said to be ***adjacent***. If the graph is directed, vertex v is said to be ***adjacent to*** vertex u.

A ***path*** from a vertex v to a vertex u is a sequence $\langle v_0, v_1, v_2, \ldots, v_k \rangle$ of vertices where $v_0 = v$, $v_k = u$, and $(v_i, v_{i+1}) \in E$ for $i = 0, 2, \ldots, k - 1$. The length of a path is defined as the number of edges in the path. If there exists a path from v to u, then u is ***reachable*** from v. A path is ***simple*** if all of its vertices are distinct. A path forms a ***cycle*** if its starting and ending vertices are the same—that is, $v_0 = v_k$. A graph with no cycles is called ***acyclic***. A cycle is ***simple*** if all the intermediate vertices are distinct.

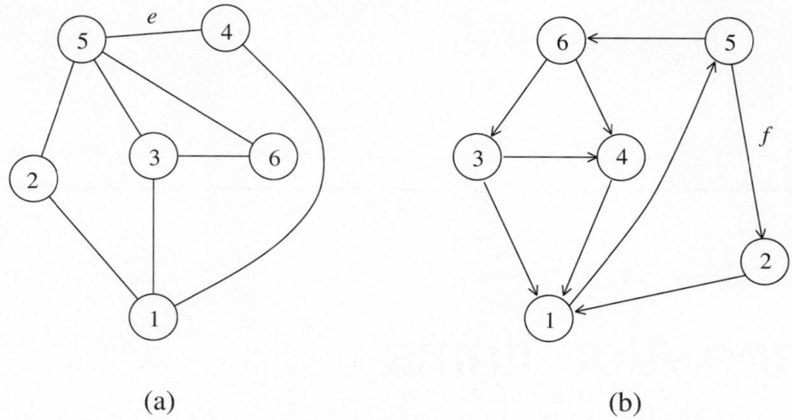

Figure 7.1 (a) An undirected graph and (b) a directed graph.

For example, in Figure 7.1(a), the sequence $\langle 3, 6, 5, 4 \rangle$ is a path from vertex 3 to vertex 4, and in Figure 7.1(b) there is a directed simple cycle $\langle 1, 5, 6, 4, 1 \rangle$. Additionally, in Figure 7.1(a), the sequence $\langle 1, 2, 5, 3, 6, 5, 4, 1 \rangle$ is an undirected cycle that is not simple because it contains the loop $\langle 5, 3, 6, 5 \rangle$.

An undirected graph is ***connected*** if every pair of vertices is connected by a path. We say that a graph $G' = (V', E')$ is a ***subgraph*** of $G = (V, E)$ if $V' \subseteq V$ and $E' \subseteq E$. Given a set $V' \subseteq V$, the subgraph of G ***induced*** by V' is the graph $G' = (V', E')$, where $E' = \{(u, v) \in E | u, v \in V'\}$. A ***complete graph*** is a graph in which each pair of vertices is adjacent. A ***forest*** is an acyclic graph, and a ***tree*** is a connected acyclic graph. Note that if $G = (V, E)$ is a tree, then $|E| = |V| - 1$.

Sometimes weights are associated with each edge in E. Weights are usually real numbers representing the cost or benefit of traversing the associated edge. For example, in an electronic circuit a resistor can be represented by an edge whose weight is its resistance. A graph that has weights associated with each edge is called a ***weighted graph*** and is denoted by $G = (V, E, w)$, where V and E are as we just defined and $w : E \rightarrow \Re$ is a real-valued function defined on E. The weight of a graph is defined as the sum of the weights of its edges. The weight of a path is the sum of the weights of its edges.

There are two standard methods for representing a graph in a computer program. The first method is to use a matrix, and the second method is to use a linked list.

Consider a graph $G = (V, E)$ with n vertices numbered $1, 2, \ldots, n$. The ***adjacency matrix*** of this graph is an $n \times n$ array $A = (a_{i,j})$, which is defined as follows:

$$a_{i,j} = \begin{cases} 1 & \text{if } (v_i, v_j) \in E \\ 0 & \text{otherwise} \end{cases}$$

Figure 7.2 illustrates an adjacency matrix representation of an undirected graph. Note that the adjacency matrix of an undirected graph is symmetric. The adjacency matrix

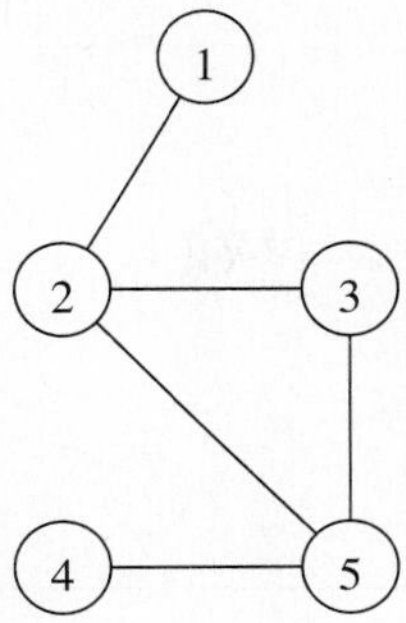

$$A = \begin{bmatrix} 0 & 1 & 0 & 0 & 0 \\ 1 & 0 & 1 & 0 & 1 \\ 0 & 1 & 0 & 0 & 1 \\ 0 & 0 & 0 & 0 & 1 \\ 0 & 1 & 1 & 1 & 0 \end{bmatrix}$$

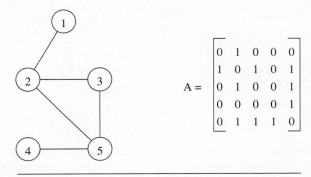

Figure 7.2 An undirected graph and its adjacency matrix representation.

representation can be modified to facilitate weighted graphs. In this case, $A = (a_{i,j})$ is defined as follows:

$$a_{i,j} = \begin{cases} w(v_i, v_j) & \text{if } (v_i, v_j) \in E \\ 0 & \text{if } i = j \\ \infty & \text{otherwise} \end{cases}$$

We refer to this modified adjacency matrix as the ***weighted adjacency matrix***. The space required to store the adjacency matrix of a graph with n vertices is $\Theta(n^2)$.

The ***adjacency list*** representation of a graph $G = (V, E)$ consists of an array $Adj[1..|V|]$ of lists. For each $v \in V$, $Adj[v]$ is a linked list of all vertices u such that G contains an edge $(v, u) \in E$. In other words, $Adj[v]$ is a list of all vertices adjacent to v. Figure 7.3 shows an example of the adjacency list representation. The adjacency list representation can be modified to accommodate weighted graphs by storing the weight of each edge $(v, u) \in E$ in the adjacency list of vertex v. The space required to store the adjacency list is $\Theta(|E|)$.

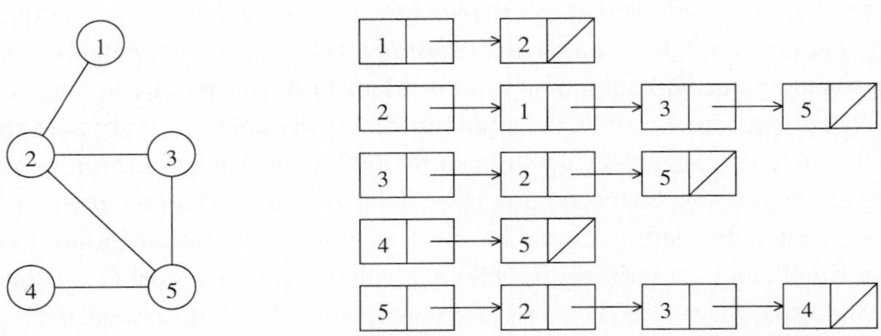

Figure 7.3 An undirected graph and its adjacency list representation.

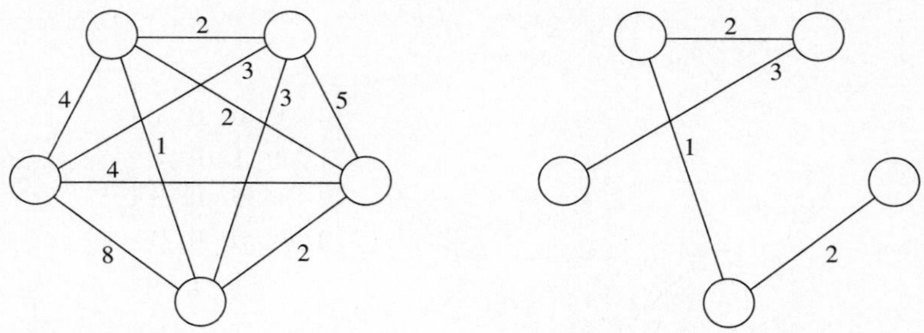

Figure 7.4 An undirected graph and its minimum spanning tree.

The nature of the graph determines which representation should be used. A graph $G = (V, E)$ is ***sparse*** if $|E|$ is much smaller than $O(|V|^2)$; otherwise it is ***dense***. The adjacency matrix representation is useful for dense graphs, and the adjacency list representation is good for sparse graphs. Note that the sequential run time of an algorithm using an adjacency matrix is bounded below by $\Omega(|V|^2)$ because the entire array must be accessed. However, if the adjacency list representation is used, the run time is bounded below by $\Omega(|V| + |E|)$ for the same reason. Thus, if the graph is sparse ($|E|$ is much smaller than $|V|^2$), the adjacency list representation is better than the adjacency matrix representation.

The rest of this chapter presents several graph algorithms. The first four sections present algorithms for dense graphs, and the last section discusses algorithms for sparse graphs. We assume that dense graphs are represented by an adjacency matrix, and sparse graphs by an adjacency list. Throughout this chapter, n denotes the number of vertices in the graph.

7.2 Minimum Spanning Tree: Prim's Algorithm

A ***spanning tree*** of an undirected graph G is a subgraph of G that is a tree containing all the vertices of G. In a weighted graph, the weight of a subgraph is the sum of the weights of the edges in the subgraph. A ***minimum spanning tree*** (MST) for a weighted undirected graph is a spanning tree with minimum weight. Many problems require finding an MST of an undirected graph. For example, the minimum length of cable necessary to connect a set of computers in a network can be determined by finding the MST of the undirected graph containing all the possible connections. Figure 7.4 shows an MST of an undirected graph.

If G is not connected, it cannot have a spanning tree. Instead, it has a ***spanning forest***. For simplicity in describing the MST algorithm, we assume that G is connected. If G is not connected, we can find its connected components (Section 7.6) and apply the MST algorithm on them. Alternatively, we can modify the MST algorithm to output a minimum spanning forest.

```
1.   procedure PRIM_MST(V, E, w, r)
2.   begin
3.       V_T := {r};
4.       d[r] := 0;
5.       for all v ∈ (V − V_T) do
6.           if edge (r, v) exists set d[v] := w(r, v);
7.           else set d[v] := ∞;
8.       while V_T ≠ V do
9.       begin
10.          find a vertex u such that d[u] = min{d[v]|v ∈ (V − V_T)};
11.          V_T := V_T ∪ {u};
12.          for all v ∈ (V − V_T) do
13.              d[v] = min{d[v], w(u, v)};
14.      endwhile
15.  end PRIM_MST
```

Program 7.1 Prim's sequential minimum spanning tree algorithm.

Prim's algorithm for finding an MST is a greedy algorithm. The algorithm begins by selecting an arbitrary starting vertex. It then grows the minimum spanning tree by choosing a new vertex and edge that are guaranteed to be in the minimum spanning tree. The algorithm continues until all the vertices have been selected.

Let $G = (V, E, w)$ be the weighted undirected graph for which the minimum spanning tree is to be found, and let $A = (a_{i,j})$ be its weighted adjacency matrix. Prim's algorithm is shown in Program 7.1. The algorithm uses the set V_T to hold the vertices of the minimum spanning tree during its construction. It also uses an array $d[1..n]$ in which, for each vertex $v \in (V - V_T)$, $d[v]$ holds the weight of the edge with the least weight from any vertex in V_T to vertex v. Initially, V_T contains an arbitrary vertex r that becomes the root of the MST. Furthermore, $d[r] = 0$, and for all v such that $v \in (V - V_T)$, $d[v] = w(r, v)$ if such an edge exists; otherwise $d[v] = \infty$. During each iteration of the algorithm, a new vertex u is added to V_T such that $d[u] = \min\{d[v] | v \in (V - V_T)\}$. After this vertex is added, all values of $d[v]$ such that $v \in (V - V_T)$ are updated because there may now be an edge with a smaller weight between vertex v and the newly added vertex u. The algorithm terminates when $V_T = V$. Figure 7.5 illustrates the algorithm. Upon termination of Prim's algorithm, the cost of the minimum spanning tree is $\sum_{v \in V} d[v]$. Program 7.1 can be easily modified to store the edges that belong in the minimum spanning tree.

In Program 7.1, the body of the **while** loop (lines 10–13) is executed $n-1$ times. Both the computation of $\min\{d[v] | v \in (V - V_T)\}$ (line 10), and the **for** loop (lines 12 and 13) execute in $O(n)$ steps. Thus, the overall complexity of Prim's algorithm is $\Theta(n^2)$.

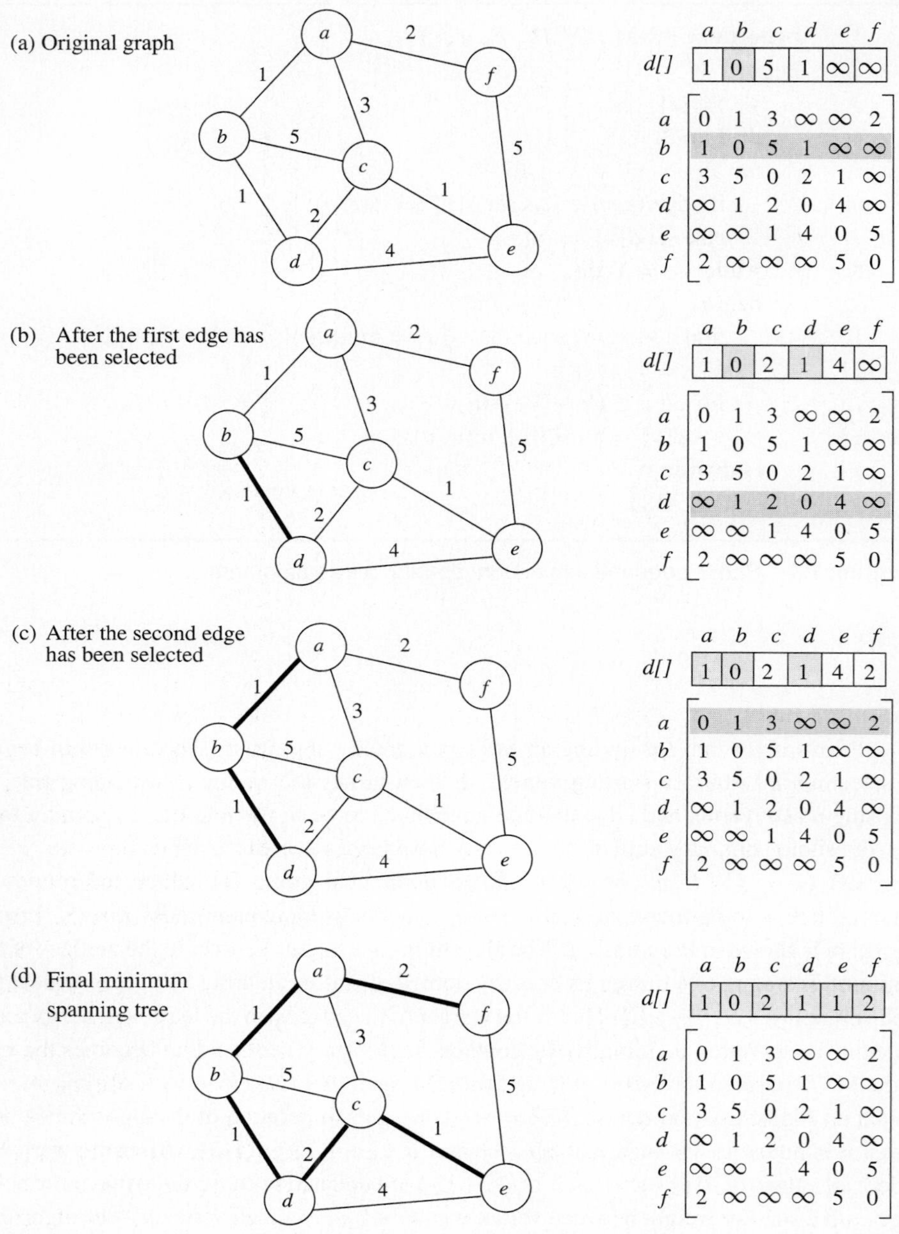

Figure 7.5 Prim's minimum spanning tree algorithm. The MST is rooted at vertex b. During each iteration, the minimum cost edge connecting a vertex in V_T to a vertex in $V - V_T$ is selected and the corresponding vertex is added to V_T (shown shaded in the distance array d). The $d[v]$ values of the vertices in $V - V_T$ are then updated.

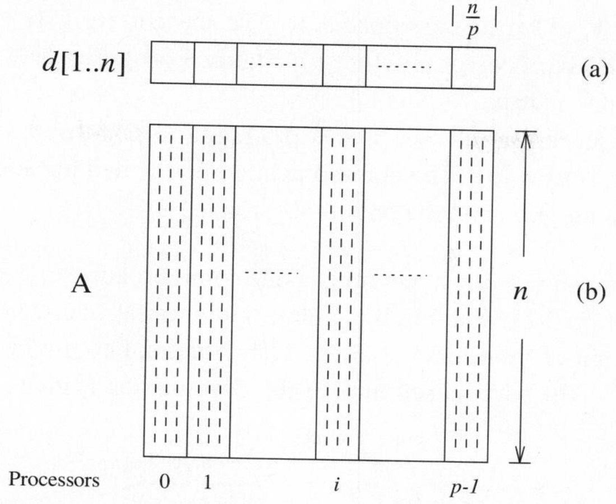

Figure 7.6 The partitioning of the distance array d and the adjacency matrix A among p processors.

Parallel Formulation

Prim's algorithm is iterative. Each iteration adds a new vertex to the minimum spanning tree. Since the value of $d[v]$ for a vertex v may change every time a new vertex u is added in V_T, it is impossible to select more than one vertex to include in the minimum spanning tree. For example, in the graph of Figure 7.5, after selecting vertex b, if both vertices d and c are selected, the MST will not be found. That is because, after selecting vertex d, the value of $d[c]$ is updated from 5 to 2. Thus, different iterations of the **while** loop cannot be performed in parallel. However, each iteration can be performed in parallel as follows.

Let p be the number of processors, and let n be the number of vertices in the graph. The set V is partitioned into p subsets using the block-striped partitioning (Section 5.1.1). Each subset has n/p consecutive vertices, and the work associated with each subset is assigned to a different processor. Let V_i be the subset of vertices assigned to processor P_i for $i = 0, 1, \ldots, p-1$. Each processor P_i stores the part of the array d that corresponds to V_i (that is, processor P_i stores $d[v]$ such that $v \in V_i$). Figure 7.6(a) illustrates the partitioning. Each processor P_i computes $d_i[u] = \min\{d_i[v] | v \in (V - V_T) \cap V_i\}$ during each iteration of the **while** loop. The global minimum is then obtained over all $d_i[u]$ by using the single-node accumulation operation (Section 3.2) and is stored in processor P_0. Processor P_0 now holds the new vertex u, which will be inserted into V_T. Processor P_0 broadcasts u to all processors by using one-to-all broadcast (Section 3.2). The processor P_i responsible for vertex u marks u as belonging to set V_T. Finally, each processor updates the values of $d[v]$ for its local vertices.

When a new vertex u is inserted into V_T, the values of $d[v]$ for $v \in (V - V_T)$ must be updated. The processor responsible for v must know the weight of the edge (u, v). Hence, each processor P_i needs to store the columns of the weighted adjacency matrix corresponding to set V_i of vertices assigned to it. The space to store the required part of the adjacency matrix at each processor is $\Theta(n^2/p)$. Figure 7.6(b) illustrates the partitioning of the weighted adjacency matrix.

The computation performed by a processor to minimize and update the values of $d[v]$ during each iteration is $\Theta(n/p)$. The communication performed in each iteration is due to the single-node accumulation and the one-to-all broadcast.

Hypercube For a p-processor hypercube, a one-to-all broadcast of one word takes time $(t_s + t_w) \log p$ (Section 3.2). Finding the global minimum of one word at each processor takes the same amount of time (Section 3.2). Thus, the total communication cost of each iteration is $\Theta(\log p)$. The parallel run time of this formulation is given by

$$T_P = \overbrace{\Theta\left(\frac{n^2}{p}\right)}^{\text{computation}} + \overbrace{\Theta(n \log p)}^{\text{communication}}.$$

Since the sequential run time is $W = \Theta(n^2)$, the speedup and efficiency are as follows:

$$\begin{aligned} S &= \frac{\Theta(n^2)}{\Theta(n^2/p) + \Theta(n \log p)} \\ E &= \frac{1}{1 + \Theta((p \log p)/n)} \end{aligned} \tag{7.1}$$

From Equation 7.1 we see that for a cost-optimal parallel formulation $(p \log p)/n = O(1)$. Thus, the hypercube formulation of Prim's algorithm can use only $p = O(n/\log n)$ processors. Furthermore, from Equation 7.1, the isoefficiency function due to communication is $\Theta(p^2 \log^2 p)$. Since n must grow at least as fast as p in this formulation, the isoefficiency function due to concurrency is $\Theta(p^2)$. Thus, the overall isoefficiency of this formulation is $\Theta(p^2 \log^2 p)$.

Mesh For a p-processor mesh, finding a global minimum and performing a one-to-all broadcast each take $\Theta(\sqrt{p})$ time. Therefore, the parallel run time of Prim's algorithm is

$$T_P = \overbrace{\Theta\left(\frac{n^2}{p}\right)}^{\text{computation}} + \overbrace{\Theta(n\sqrt{p})}^{\text{communication}}. \tag{7.2}$$

Since the sequential run time is $W = \Theta(n^2)$, the speedup and efficiency are as follows:

$$\begin{aligned} S &= \frac{\Theta(n^2)}{\Theta(n^2/p) + \Theta(n\sqrt{p})} \\ E &= \frac{1}{1 + \Theta(p^{1.5}/n)} \end{aligned} \tag{7.3}$$

From Equation 7.3 we see that for a cost-optimal algorithm, $p^{1.5}/n = O(1)$. Therefore, only $O(n^{0.66})$ processors can be used efficiently. Also from Equation 7.3, the isoefficiency function due to communication is $\Theta(p^3)$. This is the overall isoefficiency function as well.

```
procedure DIJKSTRA_SINGLE_SOURCE_SP(V, E, w, s)
begin
    V_T := {s};
    for all v ∈ (V − V_T) do
        if (s, v) exists set l[v] := w(s, v);
        else set l[v] = ∞;
    while V_T ≠ V do
    begin
        find a vertex u such that l[u] = min{l[v] | v ∈ (V − V_T)};
        V_T := V_T ∪ {u};
        for all v ∈ (V − V_T) do
            l[v] = min{l[v], l[u] + w(u, v)};
    endwhile
end DIJKSTRA_SINGLE_SOURCE_SP
```

Program 7.2 Dijkstra's sequential single-source shortest paths algorithm.

7.3 Single-Source Shortest Paths: Dijkstra's Algorithm

For a weighted graph $G = (V, E, w)$, the ***single-source shortest paths*** problem is to find the shortest paths from a vertex $v \in V$ to all other vertices in V. A ***shortest path*** from u to v is a minimum-weight path. Depending on the application, edge weights may represent time, cost, penalty, loss, or any other quantity that accumulates additively along a path to be minimized. In the following section, we present Dijkstra's algorithm, which solves the single-source shortest-paths problem on directed graphs with non-negative weights.

Dijkstra's algorithm, which finds the shortest paths from a single vertex s, is similar to Prim's minimum spanning tree algorithm. Like Prim's algorithm, it incrementally finds the shortest paths from s to the other vertices of G. It is also greedy; that is, it always chooses an edge to a vertex that appears closest. Program 7.2 shows Dijkstra's algorithm. Comparing this algorithm with Prim's minimum spanning tree algorithm, we see that the two are almost identical. The main difference is that, for each vertex $u \in (V - V_T)$, Dijkstra's algorithm stores $l[u]$, the minimum cost to reach vertex u from vertex s by means of vertices in V_T; Prim's algorithm stores $d[u]$, the cost of the minimum-cost edge connecting a vertex in V_T to u. The run time of Dijkstra's algorithm is $\Theta(n^2)$.

Parallel Formulation

The parallel formulation of Dijkstra's single-source shortest paths algorithm is very similar to the parallel formulation of Prim's algorithm for minimum spanning trees (Section 7.2). The weighted adjacency matrix is partitioned using the block-striped mapping (Section 5.1.1). Each of the p processors is assigned n/p consecutive columns of the

Table 7.1 The performance of Prim's and Dijkstra's algorithms on different architectures.

Architecture	Maximum Number of Processors for $E = \Theta(1)$	Corresponding Parallel Run Time	Isoefficiency Function
Ring	$\Theta(\sqrt{n})$	$\Theta(n^{1.5})$	$\Theta(p^4)$
Mesh	$\Theta(n^{0.66})$	$\Theta(n^{1.33})$	$\Theta(p^3)$
Hypercube	$\Theta(n/\log n)$	$\Theta(n \log n)$	$\Theta(p^2 \log^2 p)$

weighted adjacency matrix, and computes n/p values of the array l. During each iteration, all processors perform computation and communication similar to that performed by the parallel formulation of Prim's algorithm.

Table 7.1 shows performance metrics for both Prim's and Dijkstra's algorithms on ring-, mesh-, and hypercube-connected computers. In all cases, the parallel run time for a cost-optimal formulation is also the minimum parallel run time that can be achieved on each architecture in asymptotic terms (Problem 7.1).

7.4 All-Pairs Shortest Paths

Instead of finding the shortest paths from a single vertex v to every other vertex, we are sometimes interested in finding the shortest paths between all pairs of vertices. Formally, given a weighted graph $G(V, E, w)$, the ***all-pairs shortest paths*** problem is to find the shortest paths between all pairs of vertices $v_i, v_j \in V$ such that $i \neq j$. For a graph with n vertices, the output of an all-pairs shortest paths algorithm is an $n \times n$ matrix $D = (d_{i,j})$ such that $d_{i,j}$ is the cost of the shortest path from vertex v_i to vertex v_j.

The following sections present three algorithms to solve the all-pairs shortest paths problem. The first algorithm uses matrix multiplication, the second uses Dijkstra's single-source shortest paths algorithm, and the third uses Floyd's algorithm. Dijkstra's algorithm requires non-negative edge weights (Problem 7.4). The other two algorithms work with graphs having negative-weight edges provided they contain no negative-weight cycles.

7.4.1 Matrix-Multiplication Based Algorithm

Consider a weighted graph $G = (V, E, w)$ with no negative-weight cycles, whose weighted adjacency matrix is $A = (a_{i,j})$. Let $p_{i,j}^{(k)}$ be the minimum-weight path from vertex v_i to vertex v_j containing at most k edges, and let $d_{i,j}^{(k)}$ be the weight of $p_{i,j}^{(k)}$. If vertices v_i and v_j are distinct (that is, $i \neq j$), and if there is a vertex v_m such that the edge (v_m, v_j) belongs to $p_{i,j}^{(k)}$, then we can decompose the path $p_{i,j}^{(k)}$ into a path from vertex v_i to vertex v_m and the edge (v_m, v_j). Since the path $p_{i,j}^{(k)}$ has at most k edges, the path from vertex v_i to vertex v_m has at most $(k-1)$ edges. Thus, $p_{i,j}^{(k)} = p_{i,m}^{(k-1)} + (v_m, v_j)$. Therefore, $d_{i,j}^{(k)}$ is the minimum of $d_{i,j}^{(k-1)}$ (that is, the weight of the shortest path from vertex v_i to vertex v_j) and the minimum of any path from vertex v_i to vertex v_j containing at most k edges, obtained by considering all possible predecessors v_m of vertex v_j. Hence, $d_{i,j}^{(k)}$ is recursively defined as

$$d_{i,j}^{(k)} = \min\left\{d_{i,j}^{(k-1)}, \min_{1\le m\le n}\{d_{i,m}^{(k-1)} + w(v_m, v_j)\}\right\}.$$

Since $w(v_j, v_j) = 0$, the above equation simplifies to

$$d_{i,j}^{(k)} = \min_{1\le m\le n}\{d_{i,m}^{(k-1)} + w(v_m, v_j)\}. \tag{7.4}$$

where $d_{i,j}^{(1)} = a_{i,j}$. Let $D^{(k)} = (d_{i,j}^{(k)})$ be the matrix that stores the weights of the shortest paths between any two vertices containing at most k edges. Since a shortest path between any pair of vertices has at most $(n-1)$ edges, the matrix $D^{(n-1)}$ contains the weights of the shortest paths between all pairs of vertices in G.

Matrix $D^{(k)}$ is computed from matrix $D^{(k-1)}$ by using Equation 7.4, and the weighted adjacency matrix A by using a modified matrix-multiplication algorithm. The modified algorithm uses addition and minimization instead of multiplication and addition. Specifically, when we multiply $C = A \times B$ using standard matrix multiplication, $c_{i,j} = \sum_{k=1}^{k=n} a_{i,k} \times b_{k,j}$, whereas when using addition and minimization, $c_{i,j} = \min_{k=1}^{k=n}(a_{i,k} + b_{k,j})$. This modified matrix multiplication computes $D^{(k)}$ by multiplying matrices $D^{(k-1)}$ and A for $2 \le k \le n-1$. Since $D^{(1)} = A$, it follows that $D^{(k)} = A^k$ (that is, the kth power of A). The matrix $D^{(n-1)}$ is computed by computing $A^2, A^4, A^8, \ldots, A^{n-1}$. This requires only $\lceil\log(n-1)\rceil$ modified multiplications. Figure 7.7 illustrates the computation steps of the algorithm.

Using the standard $\Theta(n^3)$ algorithm for matrix multiplication, the complexity of the all-pairs shortest paths algorithm is $\Theta(n^3 \log n)$. Since the complexity of the best-known sequential all-pairs shortest paths algorithm is $\Theta(n^3)$, this algorithm is not optimal. However, this algorithm has a high degree of parallelism.

Parallel Formulation

Parallelizing the preceding algorithm is straightforward. Each of the $\lceil\log(n-1)\rceil$ steps of the algorithm requires a matrix multiplication. The parallel formulations of matrix multiplication presented in Section 5.4 can perform each step. To simplify the presentation, we assume that $n-1$ is a power of 2, but the analysis applies to any value of n (Problem 7.5).

Consider a hypercube-connected parallel computer with n^3 processors. Multiplying two $n \times n$ matrices takes time $\Theta(\log n)$ using the DNS algorithm (Section 5.4.4). Thus, the time to perform $\log n$ modified matrix multiplications is $\Theta(\log^2 n)$. For the all-pairs shortest paths problem, the best-known sequential algorithm has a complexity of $\Theta(n^3)$; thus, the speedup and efficiency are as follows:

$$S = \frac{\Theta(n^3)}{\Theta(\log^2 n)}$$

$$E = \frac{1}{\Theta(\log^2 n)}$$

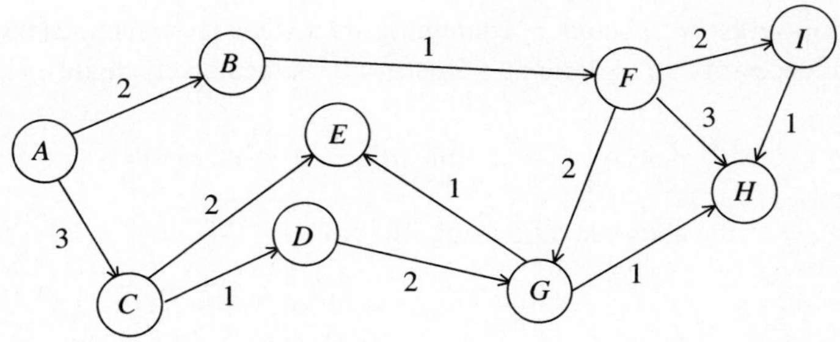

$$A^1 = \begin{pmatrix} 0 & 2 & 3 & \infty & \infty & \infty & \infty & \infty & \infty \\ \infty & 0 & \infty & \infty & \infty & 1 & \infty & \infty & \infty \\ \infty & \infty & 0 & 1 & 2 & \infty & \infty & \infty & \infty \\ \infty & \infty & \infty & 0 & \infty & \infty & 2 & \infty & \infty \\ \infty & \infty & \infty & \infty & 0 & \infty & \infty & \infty & \infty \\ \infty & \infty & \infty & \infty & \infty & 0 & 2 & 3 & 2 \\ \infty & \infty & \infty & \infty & 1 & \infty & 0 & 1 & \infty \\ \infty & \infty & \infty & \infty & \infty & \infty & \infty & 0 & \infty \\ \infty & \infty & \infty & \infty & \infty & \infty & \infty & 1 & 0 \end{pmatrix} \quad A^2 = \begin{pmatrix} 0 & 2 & 3 & 4 & 5 & 3 & \infty & \infty & \infty \\ \infty & 0 & \infty & \infty & \infty & 1 & 3 & 4 & 3 \\ \infty & \infty & 0 & 1 & 2 & \infty & 3 & \infty & \infty \\ \infty & \infty & \infty & 0 & 3 & \infty & 2 & 3 & \infty \\ \infty & \infty & \infty & \infty & 0 & \infty & \infty & \infty & \infty \\ \infty & \infty & \infty & \infty & 3 & 0 & 2 & 3 & 2 \\ \infty & \infty & \infty & \infty & 1 & \infty & 0 & 1 & \infty \\ \infty & \infty & \infty & \infty & \infty & \infty & \infty & 0 & \infty \\ \infty & \infty & \infty & \infty & \infty & \infty & \infty & 1 & 0 \end{pmatrix}$$

$$A^4 = \begin{pmatrix} 0 & 2 & 3 & 4 & 5 & 3 & 5 & 6 & 5 \\ \infty & 0 & \infty & \infty & 4 & 1 & 3 & 4 & 3 \\ \infty & \infty & 0 & 1 & 2 & \infty & 3 & 4 & \infty \\ \infty & \infty & \infty & 0 & 3 & \infty & 2 & 3 & \infty \\ \infty & \infty & \infty & \infty & 0 & \infty & \infty & \infty & \infty \\ \infty & \infty & \infty & \infty & 3 & 0 & 2 & 3 & 2 \\ \infty & \infty & \infty & \infty & 1 & \infty & 0 & 1 & \infty \\ \infty & \infty & \infty & \infty & \infty & \infty & \infty & 0 & \infty \\ \infty & \infty & \infty & \infty & \infty & \infty & \infty & 1 & 0 \end{pmatrix} \quad A^8 = \begin{pmatrix} 0 & 2 & 3 & 4 & 5 & 3 & 5 & 6 & 5 \\ \infty & 0 & \infty & \infty & 4 & 1 & 3 & 4 & 3 \\ \infty & \infty & 0 & 1 & 2 & \infty & 3 & 4 & \infty \\ \infty & \infty & \infty & 0 & 3 & \infty & 2 & 3 & \infty \\ \infty & \infty & \infty & \infty & 0 & \infty & \infty & \infty & \infty \\ \infty & \infty & \infty & \infty & 3 & 0 & 2 & 3 & 2 \\ \infty & \infty & \infty & \infty & 1 & \infty & 0 & 1 & \infty \\ \infty & \infty & \infty & \infty & \infty & \infty & \infty & 0 & \infty \\ \infty & \infty & \infty & \infty & \infty & \infty & \infty & 1 & 0 \end{pmatrix}$$

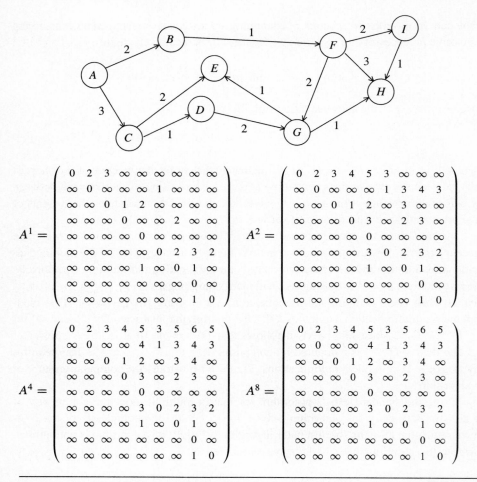

Figure 7.7 An example of the matrix-multiplication-based all-pairs shortest paths algorithm.

We can improve the efficiency of this formulation to $\Theta(1/\log n)$ if we use $\Theta(n^3/\log n)$ processors in the DNS matrix-multiplication algorithm. Still, it remains an unscalable parallel formulation. However, it is the fastest-known parallel algorithm for solving this problem. In the next sections we present some parallel algorithms that are not as fast, but are cost optimal.

7.4.2 Dijkstra's Algorithm

In Section 7.3 we presented Dijkstra's algorithm for finding the shortest paths from a vertex v to all the other vertices in a graph. This algorithm can also be used to solve the all-pairs shortest paths problem by executing the single-source algorithm on each processor, for each vertex v. We refer to this algorithm as Dijkstra's all-pairs shortest paths algorithm. Since the complexity of Dijkstra's single-source algorithm is $\Theta(n^2)$, the complexity of the all-pairs algorithm is $\Theta(n^3)$.

Parallel Formulations

Dijkstra's all-pairs shortest paths problem can be parallelized in two distinct ways. One approach partitions the vertices among different processors and has each processor compute the single-source shortest paths for all vertices assigned to it. We refer to this approach as the ***source-partitioned formulation***. Another approach assigns each vertex to a set of processors and uses the parallel formulation of the single-source algorithm (Section 7.3) to solve the problem on each set of processors. We refer to this approach as the ***source-parallel formulation***. The following sections discuss and analyze these two approaches.

Source-Partitioned Formulation The source-partitioned parallel formulation of Dijkstra's algorithm uses n processors. Each processor P_i finds the shortest paths from vertex v_i to all other vertices by executing Dijkstra's sequential single-source shortest paths algorithm. It requires no interprocessor communication. Thus, the parallel run time of this formulation is given by

$$T_P = \Theta(n^2).$$

Since the sequential run time is $W = \Theta(n^3)$, the speedup and efficiency are as follows:

$$\begin{aligned} S &= \frac{\Theta(n^3)}{\Theta(n^2)} \\ E &= \Theta(1) \end{aligned} \tag{7.5}$$

It might seem that, due to the absence of communication, this is an excellent parallel formulation. However, that is not entirely true. The algorithm can use at most n processors. Therefore, the isoefficiency function due to concurrency is $\Theta(p^3)$, which is the overall isoefficiency function of the algorithm. If the number of processors available for solving the problem is small (that is, $n = \Theta(p)$), then this algorithm has good performance. However, if the number of processors is greater than n, other algorithms will eventually outperform this algorithm because of its poor scalability.

Source-Parallel Formulation The major problem with the source-partitioned parallel formulation is that it can keep only n processors busy doing useful work. Performance can be improved if the parallel formulation of Dijkstra's single-source algorithm (Section 7.3) is used to solve the problem for each vertex v. The source-parallel formulation is similar to the source-partitioned formulation, except that the single-source algorithm runs on disjoint subsets of processors.

Specifically, p processors are divided into n partitions, each with p/n processors (this formulation is of interest only if $p > n$). Each of the n single-source shortest paths problems is solved by one of the n partitions. In other words, we first parallelize the

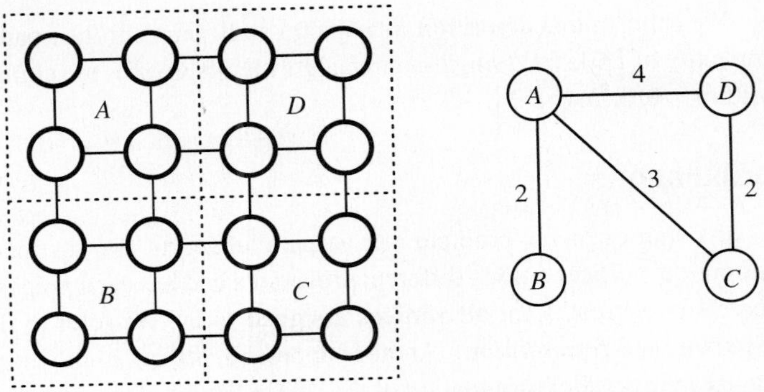

Figure 7.8 Partitioning a $\sqrt{p} \times \sqrt{p}$ mesh into n submeshes, each of size $\sqrt{p/n} \times \sqrt{p/n}$. In this example, $p = 16$ and $n = 4$. Each of the $\sqrt{p/n} \times \sqrt{p/n} = 2 \times 2$ meshes solves the single-source shortest paths problem for a given source vertex. In this example, each submesh is marked by the source vertex of its single-source algorithm.

all-pairs shortest paths problem by assigning each vertex to a separate set of processors, and then parallelize the single-source algorithm by using the set of p/n processors to solve it. The total number of processors that can be used efficiently by this formulation is $O(n^2)$.

The analysis presented in Section 7.3 can be used to derive the performance of this formulation of Dijkstra's all-pairs algorithm. Assume that we have a p-processor mesh such that $\sqrt{p}$ is a multiple of $\sqrt{n}$. The $\sqrt{p} \times \sqrt{p}$ mesh is partitioned into n submeshes of size $\sqrt{p/n} \times \sqrt{p/n}$ each. Figure 7.8 illustrates this partitioning. If the single-source algorithm is executed on each submesh, the parallel run time is

$$T_P = \overbrace{\Theta\left(\frac{n^3}{p}\right)}^{\text{computation}} + \overbrace{\Theta(\sqrt{np})}^{\text{communication}}. \tag{7.6}$$

Notice the similarities between Equation 7.6 and 7.2. These similarities are not surprising because each set of p/n processors forms a mesh and carries out the computation independently. Thus, the time required by each set of p/n processors to solve the single-source problem determines the overall run time. Since the sequential run time is $W = \Theta(n^3)$, the speedup and efficiency are as follows:

$$\begin{aligned} S &= \frac{\Theta(n^3)}{\Theta(n^3/p) + \Theta(\sqrt{np})} \\ E &= \frac{1}{1 + \Theta(p^{1.5}/n^{2.5})} \end{aligned} \tag{7.7}$$

From Equation 7.7 we see that for a cost-optimal formulation $p^{1.5}/n^{2.5} = O(1)$. Hence, this formulation can use up to $O(n^{1.66})$ processors efficiently. Equation 7.7 also shows that the isoefficiency function due to communication is $\Theta(p^{1.8})$. The isoefficiency function due to concurrency is $\Theta(p^{1.5})$. Thus, the overall isoefficiency function is $\Theta(p^{1.8})$.

Comparing the two parallel formulations of Dijkstra's all-pairs algorithm, we see that the source-partitioned formulation performs no communication, can use no more than n processors, and solves the problem in $\Theta(n^2)$ time. In contrast, the source-parallel formulation uses up to $n^{1.66}$ processors, has some communication overhead, and solves the problem in $\Theta(n^{1.33})$ time when $n^{1.66}$ processors are used. Thus, the source-parallel formulation exploits more parallelism than does the source-partitioned formulation.

7.4.3 Floyd's Algorithm

Floyd's algorithm for solving the all-pairs shortest paths problem is based on the following observation. Let $G = (V, E, w)$ be the weighted graph, and let $V = \{v_1, v_2, \ldots, v_n\}$ be the vertices of G. Consider a subset $\{v_1, v_2, \ldots, v_k\}$ of vertices for some k where $k \leq n$. For any pair of vertices $v_i, v_j \in V$, consider all paths from v_i to v_j whose intermediate vertices belong to the set $\{v_1, v_2, \ldots, v_k\}$. Let $p_{i,j}^{(k)}$ be the minimum-weight path among them, and let $d_{i,j}^{(k)}$ be the weight of $p_{i,j}^{(k)}$. If vertex v_k is not in the shortest path from v_i to v_j, then $p_{i,j}^{(k)}$ is the same as $p_{i,j}^{(k-1)}$. However, if v_k is in $p_{i,j}^{(k)}$, then we can break $p_{i,j}^{(k)}$ into two paths—one from v_i to v_k and one from v_k to v_j. Each of these paths uses vertices from $\{v_1, v_2, \ldots, v_{k-1}\}$. Thus, $d_{i,j}^{(k)} = d_{i,k}^{(k-1)} + d_{k,j}^{(k-1)}$. These observations are expressed in the following recurrence equation:

$$d_{i,j}^{(k)} = \begin{cases} w(v_i, v_j) & \text{if } k = 0 \\ \min\left\{d_{i,j}^{(k-1)}, d_{i,k}^{(k-1)} + d_{k,j}^{(k-1)}\right\} & \text{if } k \geq 1 \end{cases} \qquad (7.8)$$

The length of the shortest path from v_i to v_j is given by $d_{i,j}^{(n)}$. In general, the solution is a matrix $D^{(n)} = (d_{i,j}^{(n)})$.

Floyd's algorithm solves Equation 7.8 bottom-up in the order of increasing values of k. Program 7.3 shows Floyd's all-pairs algorithm. The run time of Floyd's algorithm is determined by the triple-nested **for** loops in lines 4–7. Each execution of line 7 takes $\Theta(1)$ time; thus, the complexity of the algorithm is $\Theta(n^3)$. Program 7.3 seems to imply that we must store n matrices of size $n \times n$. However, when computing matrix $D^{(k)}$, only matrix $D^{(k-1)}$ is needed. Consequently, at most two $n \times n$ matrices must be stored. Therefore, the overall space complexity is $\Theta(n^2)$. Furthermore, the algorithm works correctly even when only one copy of D is used (Problem 7.8).

Parallel Formulation

A generic parallel formulation of Floyd's algorithm assigns the task of computing matrix $D^{(k)}$ for each value of k to a set of processors. Let p be the number of processors available. Matrix $D^{(k)}$ is partitioned into p parts, and each part is assigned to a processor. Each

```
procedure FLOYD_ALL_PAIRS_SP(A)
begin
    D^(0) = A;
    for k = 1 to n do
        for i = 1 to n do
            for j = 1 to n do
                d^(k)_{i,j} := min( d^(k-1)_{i,j}, d^(k-1)_{i,k} + d^(k-1)_{k,j} );
end FLOYD_ALL_PAIRS_SP
```

Program 7.3 Floyd's all-pairs shortest paths algorithm. This program computes the all-pairs shortest paths of the graph $G = (V, E)$ with adjacency matrix A.

processor computes the $D^{(k)}$ values of its partition. To accomplish this, a processor must access the corresponding segments of the kth row and column of matrix $D^{(k-1)}$. The following section describes one technique for partitioning matrix $D^{(k)}$. Another technique is considered in Problem 7.10.

Block-Checkerboard Mapping One way to partition matrix $D^{(k)}$ is to use the block-checkerboard mapping (Section 5.1.2). Specifically, matrix $D^{(k)}$ is divided into p squares of size $(n/\sqrt{p}) \times (n/\sqrt{p})$, and each square is assigned to one of the p processors. It is helpful to think of the p processors as arranged in a logical grid of size $\sqrt{p} \times \sqrt{p}$. Note that this is only a conceptual layout and does not necessarily reflect the actual processor interconnection network. We refer to the processor on the ith row and j^{th} column as $P_{i,j}$. Processor $P_{i,j}$ is assigned a square subblock of $D^{(k)}$ whose upper-left corner is

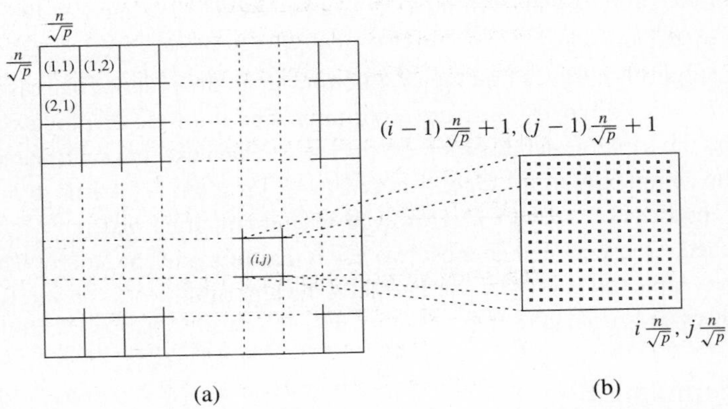

Figure 7.9 (a) Matrix $D^{(k)}$ partitioned by block checkerboarding into $\sqrt{p} \times \sqrt{p}$ subblocks, and (b) the square subblock of $D^{(k)}$ assigned to processor $P_{i,j}$.

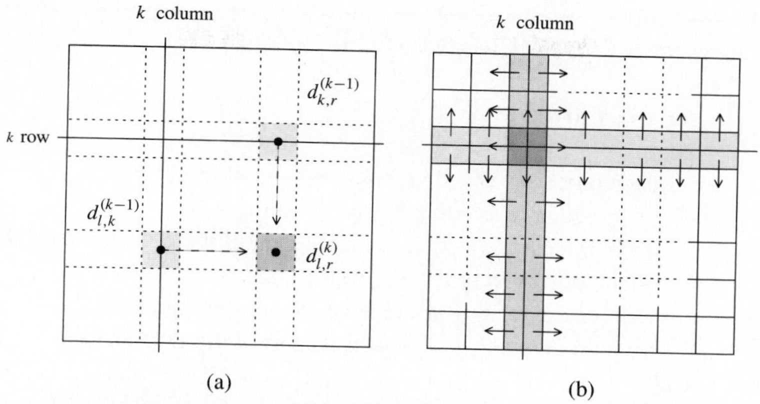

Figure 7.10 (a) Communication patterns used in the block-checkerboard partitioning. When computing $d_{i,j}^{(k)}$, information must be sent to the highlighted processor from two other processors along the same row and column. (b) The row and column of $\sqrt{p}$ processors that contain the kth row and column send them along processor columns and rows.

$((i-1)n/\sqrt{p}+1, (j-1)n/\sqrt{p}+1)$ and whose lower-right corner is $(in/\sqrt{p}, jn/\sqrt{p})$. Each processor updates its part of the matrix during each iteration. Figure 7.9(a) illustrates the block-checkerboard partitioning technique.

During the kth iteration of the algorithm, each processor $P_{i,j}$ needs certain segments of the kth row and k^{th} column of the $D^{(k-1)}$ matrix. For example, to compute $d_{l,r}^{(k)}$ it must get $d_{l,k}^{(k-1)}$ and $d_{k,r}^{(k-1)}$. As Figure 7.10 illustrates, $d_{l,k}^{(k-1)}$ resides on a processor along the same row, and element $d_{k,r}^{(k-1)}$ resides on a processor along the same column as $P_{i,j}$. Segments are transferred as follows. During the kth iteration of the algorithm, each of the $\sqrt{p}$ processors containing part of the kth row send it to the $\sqrt{p}-1$ processors in the same column. Similarly, each of the $\sqrt{p}$ processors containing part of the kth column send it to the $\sqrt{p}-1$ processors in the same row.

Program 7.4 shows the parallel formulation of Floyd's algorithm using the block-checkerboard partitioning. We analyze the performance of this algorithm on a p-processor hypercube with cut-through routing. As discussed in Section 2.5, a $\sqrt{p} \times \sqrt{p}$ virtual mesh can be mapped to a p-processor hypercube. Recall that each row and column of this virtual mesh is a hypercube of $\sqrt{p}$ processors. During each iteration of the algorithm, the kth row and k^{th} column of processors perform a one-to-all broadcast along a row or a column of $\sqrt{p}$ processors. Each such processor has $n/\sqrt{p}$ elements of the kth row or column, so it sends $n/\sqrt{p}$ elements. This broadcast requires $\Theta((n \log p)/\sqrt{p})$ time. The synchronization step on line 7 requires $\Theta(\log p)$ time. Since each processor is assigned n^2/p elements of the $D^{(k)}$ matrix, the time to compute corresponding $D^{(k)}$ values is $\Theta(n^2/p)$. Therefore, the

```
1.  procedure FLOYD_CHECKERBOARD(D^(0))
2.  begin
3.      for k = 1 to n do
4.      begin
5.          each processor P_{i,j} that has a segment of the k^th row of D^(k-1);
                broadcasts it to the P_{*,j} processors;
6.          each processor P_{i,j} that has a segment of the k^th column of D^(k-1);
                broadcasts it to the P_{i,*} processors;
7.          each processor waits to receive the needed segments;
8.          each processor P_{i,j} computes its part of the D^(k) matrix;
9.      end
10. end FLOYD_CHECKERBOARD
```

Program 7.4 Floyd's parallel formulation using the block-checkerboard partitioning. $P_{*,j}$ denotes all the processors in the jth column, and $P_{i,*}$ denotes all the processors in the ith row. The matrix $D^{(0)}$ is the adjacency matrix.

parallel run time of the block-checkerboard formulation of Floyd's algorithm is

$$T_P = \overbrace{\Theta\left(\frac{n^3}{p}\right)}^{\text{computation}} + \overbrace{\Theta\left(\frac{n^2}{\sqrt{p}}\log p\right)}^{\text{communication}}.$$

Since the sequential run time is $W = \Theta(n^3)$, the speedup and efficiency are as follows:

$$S = \frac{\Theta(n^3)}{\Theta(n^3/p) + \Theta((n^2 \log p)/\sqrt{p})}$$

$$E = \frac{1}{1 + \Theta((\sqrt{p}\log p)/n)} \tag{7.9}$$

From Equation 7.9 we see that for a cost-optimal formulation $(\sqrt{p}\log p)/n = O(1)$; thus, block checkerboarding can efficiently use up to $O(n^2/\log^2 n)$ hypercube processors. Equation 7.9 can also be used to derive the isoefficiency function due to communication, which is $\Theta(p^{1.5}\log^3 p)$. The isoefficiency function due to concurrency is $\Theta(p^{1.5})$. Thus, the overall isoefficiency function is $\Theta(p^{1.5}\log^3 p)$. The parallel run time, the speedup, and the isoefficiency function for a mesh can be determined similarly (Table 7.2).

Speeding Things Up In the block-checkerboard formulation of Floyd's algorithm, a synchronization step ensures that all processors have the appropriate segments of matrix $D^{(k-1)}$ before computing elements of matrix $D^{(k)}$ (line 7 in Program 7.4). In other words, the kth iteration starts only when the $(k-1)^{\text{st}}$ iteration has completed and the relevant parts of matrix $D^{(k-1)}$ have been transmitted to all processors. The synchronization step can be removed without affecting the correctness of the algorithm. To accomplish this, a processor starts working on the kth iteration as soon as it has computed the $(k-1)^{st}$ iteration and has the relevant parts of the $D^{(k-1)}$ matrix. This formulation is called ***pipelined block checkerboarding***. A similar technique is used in Section 5.5 to improve the performance of Gaussian elimination.

Consider a p-processor mesh. Assume that processor $P_{i,j}$ starts working on the kth iteration as soon as it has finished the $(k-1)^{st}$ iteration and has received the relevant parts of the $D^{(k-1)}$ matrix. When processor $P_{i,j}$ has elements of the kth row and has finished the $(k-1)^{st}$ iteration, it sends the part of matrix $D^{(k-1)}$ stored locally to processors $P_{i,j-1}$ and $P_{i,j+1}$. It does this because that part of the $D^{(k-1)}$ matrix is used to compute the $D^{(k)}$ matrix. Similarly, when processor $P_{i,j}$ has elements of the kth column and has finished the $(k-1)^{st}$ iteration, it sends the part of matrix $D^{(k-1)}$ stored locally to processors $P_{i-1,j}$ and $P_{i+1,j}$. When processor $P_{i,j}$ receives elements of matrix $D^{(k)}$ from a processor along its row in the logical mesh, it stores them locally and forwards them to the processor on the side opposite of where it received them. The columns follow a similar communication protocol. Elements of matrix $D^{(k)}$ are not forwarded when they reach a mesh boundary. Figure 7.11 illustrates this communication and termination protocol for processors within a row (or a column).

Consider the movement of values in the first iteration. In each step, $n/\sqrt{p}$ elements of the first row are sent from processor $P_{i,j}$ to $P_{i+1,j}$. Similarly, elements of the first column are sent from processor $P_{i,j}$ to processor $P_{i,j+1}$. Each such step takes $\Theta(n/\sqrt{p})$ time. After $\Theta(\sqrt{p})$ steps, processor $P_{\sqrt{p},\sqrt{p}}$ gets the relevant elements of the first row and first column in time $\Theta(n)$. The values of successive rows and columns follow after $\Theta(n^2/p)$ time in a pipelined mode. Hence, processor $P_{\sqrt{p},\sqrt{p}}$ finishes its share of the shortest path computation in time $\Theta(n^3/p) + \Theta(n)$. When processor $P_{\sqrt{p},\sqrt{p}}$ has finished the $(n-1)^{st}$ iteration, it sends the relevant values of the nth row and column to the other processors. These values reach processor $P_{1,1}$ in time $\Theta(n)$. The overall parallel run time of this formulation is

$$T_P = \overbrace{\Theta\left(\frac{n^3}{p}\right)}^{\text{computation}} + \overbrace{\Theta(n)}^{\text{communication}}.$$

Since the sequential run time is $W = \Theta(n^3)$, the speedup and efficiency are as follows:

$$\begin{aligned} S &= \frac{\Theta(n^3)}{\Theta(n^3/p) + \Theta(n)} \\ E &= \frac{1}{1 + \Theta(p/n^2)} \end{aligned} \tag{7.10}$$

From Equation 7.10 we see that for a cost-optimal formulation $p/n^2 = O(1)$. Thus, the pipelined formulation of Floyd's algorithm uses up to $O(n^2)$ processors efficiently. Also from Equation 7.10, we can derive the isoefficiency function due to communication, which is $\Theta(p^{1.5})$. This is the overall isoefficiency function as well. Comparing the pipelined formulation to the synchronized block-checkerboard formulation, we see that the former is significantly faster.

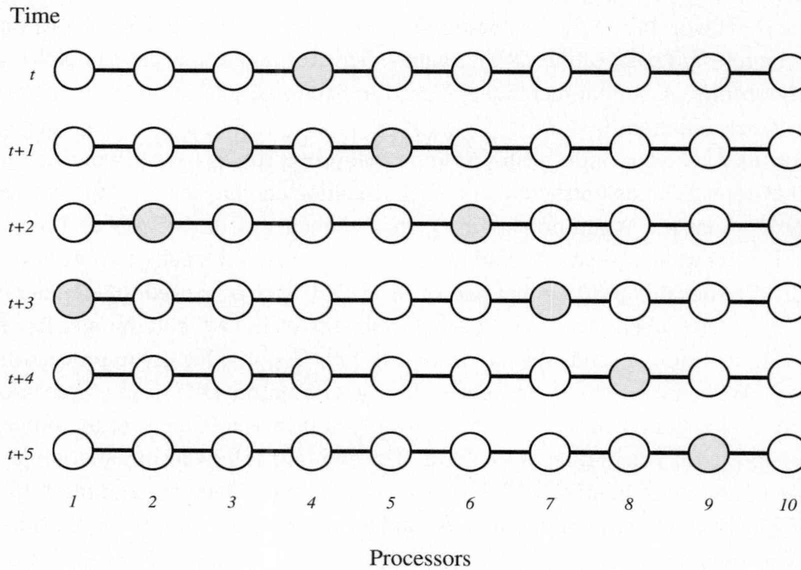

Figure 7.11 Communication protocol followed in the pipelined block checkerboarding formulation of Floyd's algorithm. Assume that processor 4 at time t has just computed a segment of the kth column of the $D^{(k-1)}$ matrix. It sends the segment to processors 3 and 5. These processors receive the segment at time $t+1$ (where the time unit is the time it takes for a matrix segment to travel over the communication link between adjacent processors). Similarly, processors farther away from processor 4 receive the segment later. Processor 1 (at the boundary) does not forward the segment after receiving it.

7.4.4 Performance Comparisons

The performance of the all-pairs shortest paths algorithms previously presented is summarized in Table 7.2 for a variety of architectures. Floyd's pipelined formulation is the most scalable and can use up to $\Theta(n^2)$ processors to solve the problem in $\Theta(n)$ time. This parallel formulation performs equally well on a mesh- or hypercube-connected computer. Furthermore, its performance is independent of the type of routing (store-and-forward or cut-through).

7.5 Transitive Closure

In many applications we wish to determine if any two vertices in a graph are connected. This is usually done by finding the transitive closure of a graph. Formally, if $G = (V, E)$ is a graph, then the ***transitive closure*** of G is defined as the graph $G^* = (V, E^*)$, where $E^* = \{(v_i, v_j) |$ there is a path from v_i to v_j in $G\}$. We compute the transitive closure of a

Table 7.2 The performance and scalability of the all-pairs shortest paths algorithms on various architectures.

	Maximum Number of Processors for $E = \Theta(1)$	Corresponding Parallel Run Time	Isoefficiency Function
Dijkstra source-partitioned			
Hypercube	$\Theta(n)$	$\Theta(n^2)$	$\Theta(p^3)$
Mesh	$\Theta(n)$	$\Theta(n^2)$	$\Theta(p^3)$
Dijkstra source-parallel			
Hypercube	$\Theta(n^2/\log n)$	$\Theta(n \log n)$	$\Theta((p \log p)^{1.5})$
Mesh	$\Theta(n^{1.67})$	$\Theta(n^{1.33})$	$\Theta(p^{1.8})$
Floyd block-striped mapping			
Hypercube	$\Theta(n/\log n)$	$\Theta(n^2 \log n)$	$\Theta((p \log p)^3)$
Mesh (SF)	$\Theta(n^{0.22})$	$\Theta(n^{2.78})$	$\Theta(p^{4.5})$
Mesh (CT)	$\Theta(n/\log n)$	$\Theta(n^2 \log n)$	$\Theta((p \log p)^3)$
Floyd block-checkerboard mapping			
Hypercube	$\Theta(n^2/\log^2 n)$	$\Theta(n \log^2 n)$	$\Theta(p^{1.5} \log^3 p)$
Mesh (SF)	$\Theta(n)$	$\Theta(n^2)$	$\Theta(p^3)$
Mesh (CT)	$\Theta(n^{1.33})$	$\Theta(n^{1.67})$	$\Theta(p^{2.25})$
Floyd pipelined block checkerboarding			
Hypercube	$\Theta(n^2)$	$\Theta(n)$	$\Theta(p^{1.5})$
Mesh	$\Theta(n^2)$	$\Theta(n)$	$\Theta(p^{1.5})$

graph by computing the connectivity matrix A^*. The ***connectivity matrix*** of G is a matrix $A^* = (a^*_{i,j})$ such that $a^*_{i,j} = 1$ if there is a path from v_i to v_j or $i = j$, and $a^*_{i,j} = \infty$ otherwise.

To compute A^* we assign a weight of 1 to each edge of E and use any of the all-pairs shortest paths algorithms on this weighted graph. Matrix A^* can be obtained from matrix D, where D is the solution to the all-pairs shortest paths problem, as follows:

$$a^*_{i,j} = \begin{cases} \infty & \text{if } d_{i,j} = \infty \\ 1 & \text{if } d_{i,j} > 0 \text{ or } i = j \end{cases}$$

Another method for computing A^* is to use Floyd's algorithm on the adjacency matrix of G, replacing the *min* and $+$ operations in line 7 of Program 7.3 by logical **or** and logical **and** operations. In this case, we initially set $a_{i,j} = 1$ if $i = j$ or $(v_i, v_j) \in E$, and $a_{i,j} = 0$ otherwise. Matrix A^* is obtained by setting $a^*_{i,j} = \infty$ if $d_{i,j} = 0$ and $a^*_{i,j} = 1$ otherwise. The complexity of computing the transitive closure is $\Theta(n^3)$.

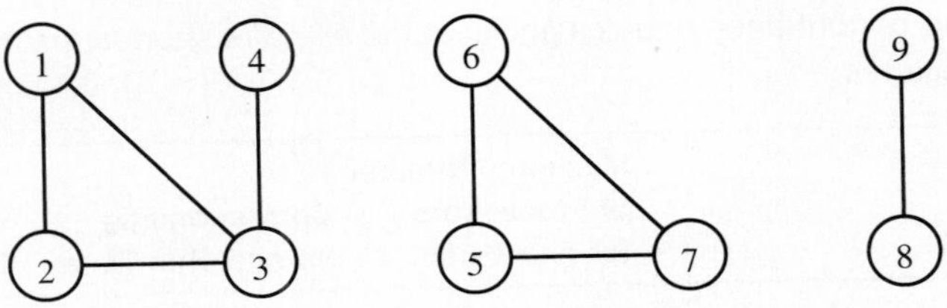

Figure 7.12 A graph with three connected components: $\{1, 2, 3, 4\}$, $\{5, 6, 7\}$, and $\{8, 9\}$.

7.6 Connected Components

The ***connected components*** of an undirected graph $G = (V, E)$ are the maximal disjoint sets $C_1, C_2, \ldots, C_k$ such that $V = C_1 \cup C_2 \cup \ldots \cup C_k$, and $u, v \in C_i$ if and only if u is reachable from v and v is reachable from u. The connected components of an undirected graph are the equivalence classes of vertices under the "is reachable from" relation. For example, Figure 7.12 shows a graph with three connected components.

7.6.1 A Depth-First Search Based Algorithm

We can find the connected components of a graph by performing a depth-first traversal on the graph. The outcome of this depth-first traversal is a forest of depth-first trees. Each tree in the forest contains vertices that belong to a different connected component. Figure 7.13 illustrates this algorithm. The correctness of this algorithm follows directly from the definition of a spanning tree (that is, a depth-first tree is also a spanning tree of a graph induced by the set of vertices in the depth-first tree) and from the fact that G is undirected. The run time of this algorithm is $\Theta(|E|)$ because the depth-first traversal algorithm traverses all the edges in G.

Parallel Formulation

The connected-component algorithm can be parallelized by partitioning the adjacency matrix of G into p parts and assigning each part to one of p processors. Each processor P_i has a subgraph G_i of G, where $G_i = (V, E_i)$ and E_i are the edges that correspond to the portion of the adjacency matrix assigned to this processor. In the first step of this parallel formulation, each processor P_i computes the depth-first spanning forest of the graph G_i. At the end of this step, p spanning forests have been constructed. During the second step, spanning forests are merged pairwise until only one spanning forest remains. The remaining spanning forest has the property that two vertices are in the same connected component of G if they are in the same tree. Figure 7.14 illustrates this algorithm.

To efficiently merge pairs of spanning forests, the algorithm uses disjoint sets of edges. Assume that each tree in the spanning forest of a subgraph of G is represented by a set. The sets for different trees are pairwise disjoint. The following operations are defined on the disjoint sets:

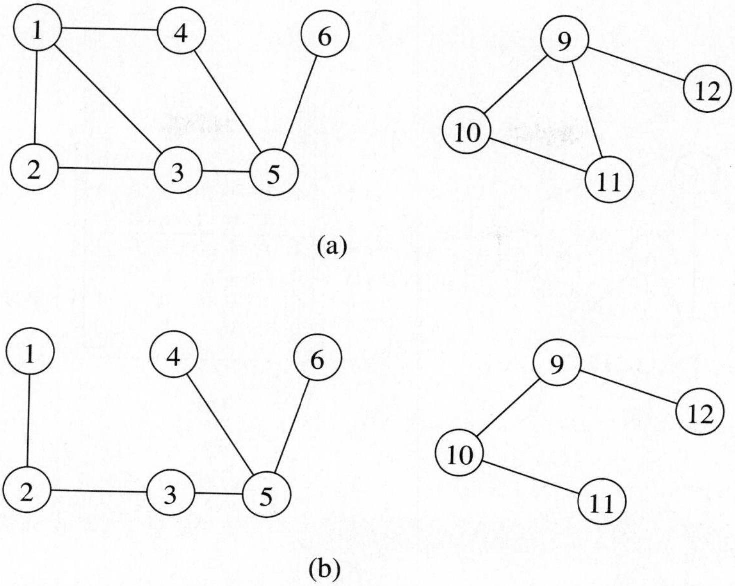

Figure 7.13 Part (b) is a depth-first forest obtained from depth-first traversal of the graph in part (a). Each of these trees is a connected component of the graph in part (a).

find(x) returns a pointer to the representative element of the set containing x. Each set has its own unique representative.

union(x, y) unites the sets containing the elements x and y. The two sets are assumed to be disjoint prior to the operation.

The spanning forests are merged as follows. Let A and B be the two spanning forests to be merged. At most $n - 1$ edges (since A and B are forests) of one are merged with the edges of the other. Suppose we want to merge forest A into forest B. For each edge (u, v) of A, a find operation is performed for each vertex to determine if the two vertices are already in the same tree of B. If not, then the two trees (sets) of B containing u and v are united by a union operation. Otherwise, no union operation is necessary. Hence, merging A and B requires at most $2(n - 1)$ find operations and $(n - 1)$ union operations. We can implement the disjoint-set data structure by using disjoint-set forests with ranking and path compression. Using this implementation, the cost to perform $2(n - 1)$ finds and $(n - 1)$ unions is $O(n)$. A detailed description of the disjoint-set forest is beyond the scope of this book. Refer to the bibliographic remarks (Section 7.8) for references.

Having discussed how to efficiently merge two spanning trees, we now concentrate on how to partition the adjacency matrix of G and distribute it among p processors. The next section discusses a formulation that uses block-striped partitioning. An alternative partitioning scheme is discussed in Problem 7.14.

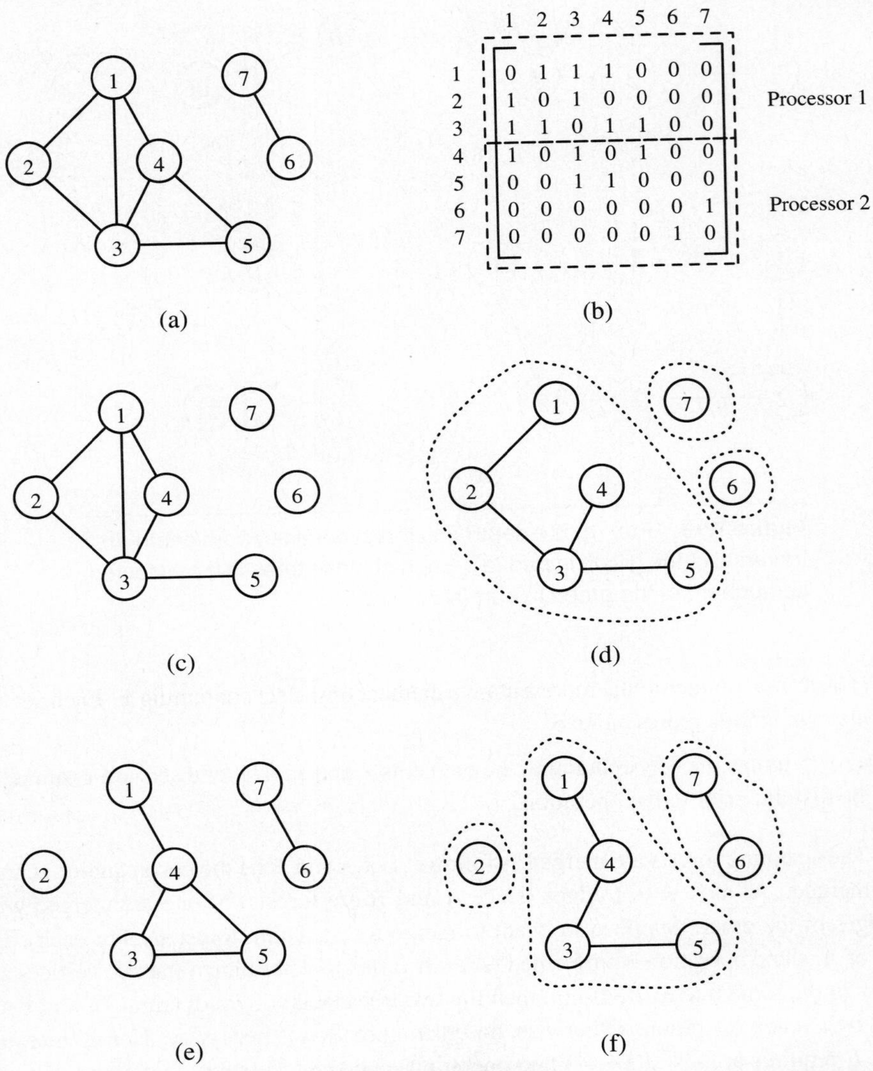

Figure 7.14 Computing connected components in parallel. The adjacency matrix of the graph G in (a) is partitioned into two parts as shown in (b). Next, each processor gets a subgraph of G as shown in (c) and (e). Each processor then computes the spanning forest of the subgraph, as shown in (d) and (f). Finally, the two spanning trees are merged to form the solution.

Block-Striped Mapping The $n \times n$ adjacency matrix is partitioned into p stripes (Section 5.1.1). Each stripe is composed of n/p consecutive rows and is assigned to one of the p processors. To compute the connected components, each processor first computes a spanning forest for the n-vertex graph represented by the n/p rows of the adjacency matrix assigned to it.

Consider a p-processor hypercube. Computing the spanning forest based on the $(n/p) \times n$ adjacency matrix assigned to each processor requires $\Theta(n^2/p)$ time. The second step of the algorithm—the pairwise merging of spanning forests—is performed by embedding a virtual tree in the hypercube. There are $\log p$ merging stages, and each takes $\Theta(n)$ time. Thus, the cost due to merging is $\Theta(n \log p)$. Finally, during each merging stage, spanning forests are sent between nearest neighbors. Recall that $\Theta(n)$ edges of the spanning forest are transmitted. Thus, the communication cost is $\Theta(n \log p)$. The parallel run time of the connected-component algorithm is

$$T_P = \overbrace{\Theta\left(\frac{n^2}{p}\right)}^{\text{local computation}} + \overbrace{\Theta(n \log p)}^{\text{forest merging}}.$$

Since the sequential complexity is $W = \Theta(n^2)$, the speedup and efficiency are as follows:

$$\begin{aligned} S &= \frac{\Theta(n^2)}{\Theta(n^2/p) + \Theta(n \log p)} \\ E &= \frac{1}{1 + \Theta((p \log p)/n)} \end{aligned} \tag{7.11}$$

From Equation 7.11 we see that for a cost-optimal formulation $p = O(n/\log n)$. Also from Equation 7.11, we derive the isoefficiency function, which is $\Theta(p^2 \log^2 p)$. This is the isoefficiency function due to communication and due to the extra computations performed in the merging stage. The isoefficiency function due to concurrency is $\Theta(p^2)$; thus, the overall isoefficiency function is $\Theta(p^2 \log^2 p)$. The performance of this parallel formulation is similar to that of Prim's minimum spanning tree algorithm and Dijkstra's single-source shortest paths algorithm on a hypercube. The performance of this algorithm on a mesh can be computed similarly (Problem 7.13).

7.7 Algorithms for Sparse Graphs

The parallel algorithms in the previous sections are based on the best-known algorithms for dense-graph problems. However, we have yet to address parallel algorithms for sparse graphs. Recall that a graph $G = (V, E)$ is sparse if $|E|$ is much smaller than $|V|^2$. Figure 7.15 shows some examples of sparse graphs.

Any dense-graph algorithm works correctly on sparse graphs also. However, if the sparseness of the graph is taken into account, it is usually possible to obtain significantly better performance. For example, the run time of Prim's minimum spanning tree algorithm

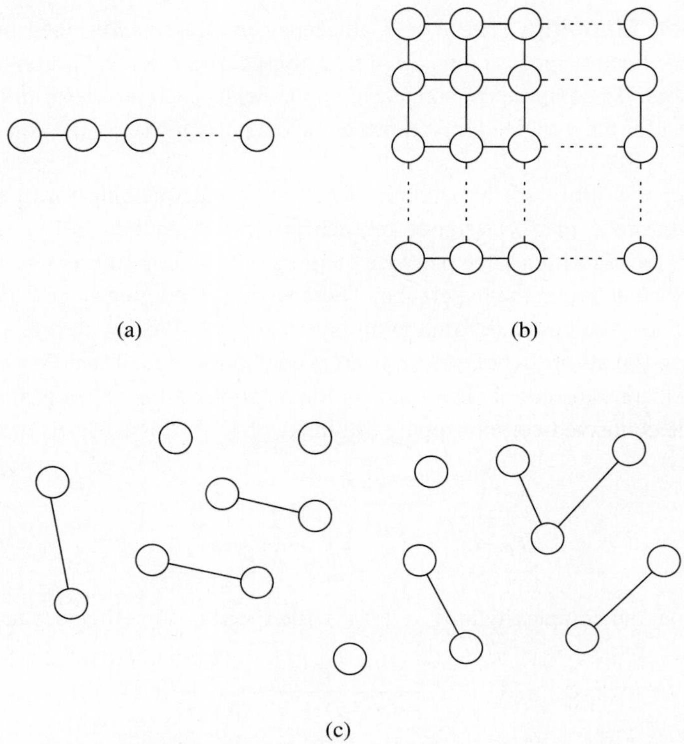

Figure 7.15 Examples of sparse graphs: (a) a linear graph, in which each vertex has two incident edges; (b) a grid graph, in which each vertex has four incident vertices; and (c) a random sparse graph.

(Section 7.2) is $\Theta(n^2)$ regardless of the number of edges in the graph. By modifying Prim's algorithm to use adjacency lists and a binary heap, the complexity of the algorithm decreases to $\Theta(|E| \log n)$. This modified algorithm outperforms the original algorithm as long as $|E| = O(n^2/\log n)$. An important step in developing sparse-graph algorithms is to use an adjacency list instead of an adjacency matrix. This change in representation is crucial, since the complexity of adjacency-matrix-based algorithms is usually $\Omega(n^2)$, independent of the number of edges. Conversely, the complexity of adjacency-list-based algorithms is usually $\Omega(n + |E|)$, which depends on the sparseness of the graph.

In the parallel formulations of sequential algorithms for dense graphs, we obtained good performance by partitioning the adjacency matrix of a graph so that each processor performed roughly an equal amount of work and communication was localized. We were able to achieve this largely because the graph was dense. For example, consider Floyd's all-pairs shortest paths algorithm. By assigning equal-sized blocks from the adjacency

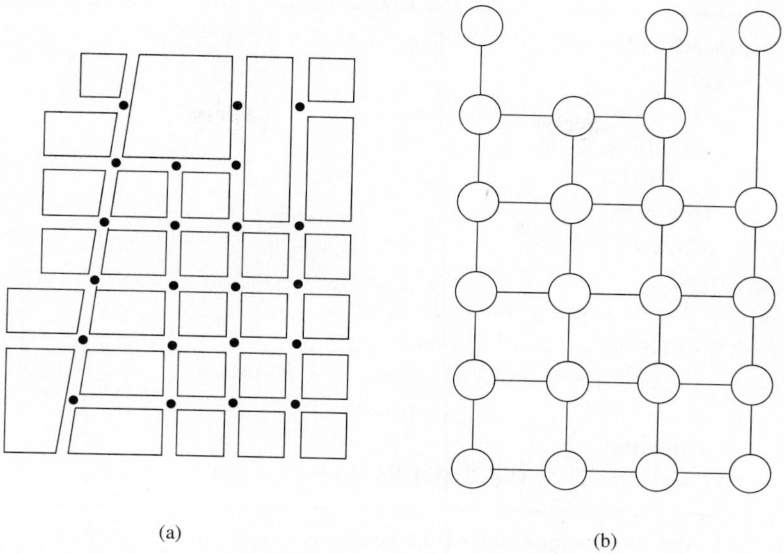

Figure 7.16 A street map (a) can be represented by a graph (b). In the graph shown in (b), each street intersection is a vertex and each edge is a street segment. The vertices of (b) are the intersections of (a) marked by dots.

matrix to all processors, the work was uniformly distributed. Moreover, since each block consisted of consecutive rows and columns, communication overhead was limited.

However, it is difficult to achieve even work distribution and low communication overhead for sparse graphs. Consider the problem of partitioning the adjacency list of a graph. One possible partition assigns an equal number of vertices and their adjacency lists to each processor. However, the number of edges incident on a given vertex is essentially random. Hence, some processors may be assigned a large number of edges while others receive very few, leading to a significant work imbalance among the processors. Alternatively, we can assign an equal number of edges to each processor. This may require splitting the adjacency list of a vertex among processors. As a result, the time spent communicating information among processors that store separate parts of the adjacency list may increase dramatically. Thus, it is hard to derive efficient parallel formulations for general sparse graphs (Problems 7.16 and 7.17). However, we can often derive efficient parallel formulations if the sparse graph has certain structure. For example, consider the street map shown in Figure 7.16. The graph corresponding to the map is sparse: the number of edges incident on any vertex is at most four. We refer to such graphs as ***grid graphs***. The next section presents efficient algorithms to compute single-source shortest paths for such graphs.

```
procedure JOHNSON_SINGLE_SOURCE_SP(V, E, s)
begin
    Q := V;
    for all v ∈ Q do
        l[v] := ∞;
    l[s] := 0;
    while Q ≠ ∅ do
    begin
        u := extract_min(Q);
        for each v ∈ Adj[u] do
            if v ∈ Q and l[u] + w(u, v) < l[v] then
                l[v] := l[u] + w(u, v);
    endwhile
end JOHNSON_SINGLE_SOURCE_SP
```

Program 7.5 Johnson's sequential single-source shortest paths algorithm.

7.7.1 Single-Source Shortest Paths

It is easy to modify Dijkstra's single-source shortest paths algorithm so that it finds the shortest paths for sparse graphs efficiently. The modified algorithm is known as Johnson's algorithm. Recall that Dijkstra's algorithm performs the following two steps in each iteration. First, it extracts a vertex $u \in (V - V_T)$ such that $l[u] = \min\{l[v] | v \in (V - V_T)\}$ and inserts it into set V_T. Second, for each vertex $v \in (V - V_T)$, it computes $l[v] = \min\{l[v], l[u] + w(u, v)\}$. Note that, during the second step, only the vertices in the adjacency list of vertex u need to be considered. Since the graph is sparse, the number of vertices adjacent to vertex u is considerably smaller than $\Theta(n)$; thus, using the adjacency-list representation improves performance.

Johnson's algorithm uses a priority queue Q to store the value $l[v]$ for each vertex $v \in (V - V_T)$. The priority queue is constructed so that the vertex with the smallest value in l is always at the front of the queue. A common way to implement a priority queue is as a binary min-heap. A binary min-heap allows us to update the value $l[v]$ for each vertex v in $O(\log n)$ time. Program 7.5 shows Johnson's algorithm. Initially, for each vertex v other than the source, it inserts $l[v] = \infty$ in the priority queue. For the source vertex s it inserts $l[s] = 0$. At each step of the algorithm, the vertex $u \in (V - V_T)$ with the minimum value in l is removed from the priority queue. The adjacency list for u is traversed, and for each edge (u, v) the distance $l[v]$ to vertex v is updated in the heap. Updating vertices in the heap dominates the overall run time of the algorithm. The total number of updates is equal to the number of edges; thus, the overall complexity of Johnson's algorithm is $\Theta(|E| \log n)$.

Parallel Formulation

An efficient parallel formulation of Johnson's algorithm must maintain the priority queue Q efficiently. One strategy is for a single processor to maintain Q. All other processors compute new values of $l[v]$ for $v \in (V - V_T)$. Since in each iteration the algorithm updates roughly $|E|/|V|$ vertices, no more than $|E|/|V|$ processors can be kept busy on the average. Furthermore, every processor sends the value of l that it computes to the processor with the priority queue. This processor updates the priority queue upon receiving new values of $l[v]$ for $v \in (V - V_T)$. Since each queue access takes $O(\log n)$ time, the parallel run time is $O(|E| \log n)$. Note that this is the same as the sequential run time. The main limitation of this scheme is the centralized priority queue. One way to alleviate this limitation is to distribute the priority queue. In the remainder of this section, we describe one approach to accomplish this distribution. Problem 7.15 discusses another approach.

Let p be the number of processors, and let $G = (V, E)$ be a sparse graph. We partition the set of vertices V into p disjoint sets $V_1, V_2, \ldots, V_p$, and assign each set of vertices and its associated adjacency lists to one of the p processors. Each processor maintains a priority queue for the vertices assigned to it, and computes the shortest paths from the source to these vertices. Thus, the priority queue Q is partitioned into p disjoint priority queues $Q_1, Q_2, \ldots, Q_p$, each assigned to a separate processor. In addition to the priority queue, each processor P_i also maintains an array sp such that $sp[v]$ stores the cost of the shortest path from the source vertex to v for each vertex $v \in V_i$. The cost $sp[v]$ is updated to $l[v]$ each time vertex v is extracted from the priority queue. Initially, $sp[v] = \infty$ for every vertex v other than the source, and we insert $l[s]$ into the appropriate priority queue for the source vertex s. Each processor executes Johnson's algorithm on its local priority queue. At the end of the algorithm, $sp[v]$ stores the length of the shortest path from source to vertex v.

When processor P_i extracts the vertex $u \in V_i$ with the smallest value $l[u]$ from Q_i, the l values of vertices assigned to processors other than P_i may need to be updated. Processor P_i sends a message to processors with relevant vertices, notifying them of the new values. Upon receiving these values, processors update the values of l. For example, assume that there is an edge (u, v) such that $u \in V_i$ and $v \in V_j$, and that processor P_i has just extracted vertex u from its priority queue. Processor P_i then sends a message to P_j containing the potential new value of $l[v]$, which is $l[u] + w(u, v)$. Processor P_j, upon receiving this message, sets the value of $l[v]$ stored in its priority queue to $\min\{l[v], l[u] + w(u, v)\}$.

Since both processors P_i and P_j execute Johnson's algorithm, it is possible that processor P_j has already extracted vertex v from its priority queue. This means that processor P_j might have already computed the shortest path $sp[v]$ from the source to vertex v. Then there are two possible cases: either $sp[v] \leq l[u] + w(u, v)$, or $sp[v] > l[u] + w(u, v)$. The first case means that there is a longer path to vertex v passing through vertex u, and the second case means that there is a shorter path to vertex v passing through vertex u. For the first case, processor P_j needs to do nothing, since the shortest path to v does not change. For the second case, processor P_j must update the cost of the shortest path to vertex v. This is done by inserting the vertex v back into the priority queue with

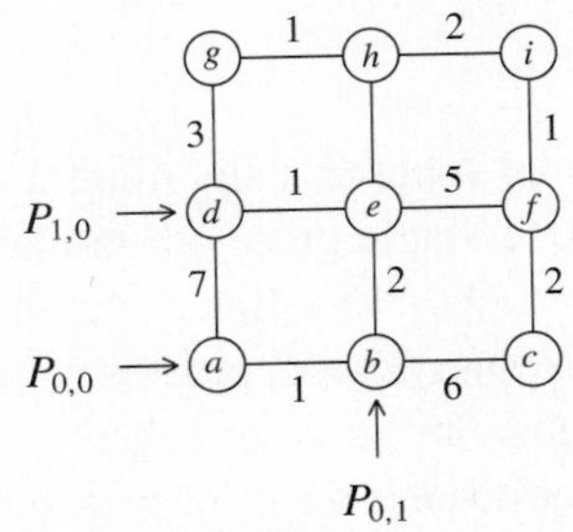

Figure 7.17 A grid graph.

$l[v] = l[u] + w(u, v)$ and disregarding the value of $sp[v]$. Since a vertex v can be reinserted into the priority queue, the algorithm terminates only when all the queues become empty.

It is possible that while processor P_i is extracting a vertex v from Q_i, another processor P_j might have already extracted a vertex u from Q_j such that $l[v] < l[u]$. As a result, if there is a path from vertex v to vertex u, the cost of the shortest path to vertex u might decrease after extracting vertex v. If there is only a single priority queue, vertex v would have been extracted earlier than vertex u. Thus, the distributed algorithm does not extract vertices in a nondecreasing order of l values. As a result, it performs computations that must be redone. These intermediate computations are extra work done by the parallel formulation compared to the sequential algorithm. Depending on the graph, the amount of extra work might be significant.

Example 7.1 Problems with Distributed Management of the Priority Queue
Consider the grid graph shown in Figure 7.17. Each vertex of this graph is assigned to a separate processor, and vertex a is the source for the shortest paths. Processor $P_{0,0}$ extracts vertex a from its local queue and sends the values $l[a] + w(a, b)$ and $l[a] + w(a, d)$ to processors $P_{0,1}$ and $P_{1,0}$, respectively. These processors insert the values into their priority queues and then perform computations. Consider processor $P_{1,0}$. Since $l[d]$ is the only value stored in its priority queue, this processor extracts vertex d from it, assuming that the path $\langle a, d\rangle$ is the shortest path from vertex a to vertex d. But the path $\langle a, d\rangle$ is not the shortest path from vertex a to d. The shortest path is $\langle a, b, e, d\rangle$. Thus, at a later time, processor $P_{0.0}$, receives a smaller value for $l[d]$ corresponding to the actual shortest path, and it will have to redo some of the computations it has already performed. Therefore, distributed management of the priority queue can lead to extra computations. ■

Initially, only the priority queue of the processor with the source vertex is non empty. After that, the priority queues of other processors become populated as messages containing new l values are created and sent to adjacent processors. When processors receive new l values, they insert them into their priority queues and perform computations. Consider the problem of computing the single-source shortest paths in a grid graph where the source

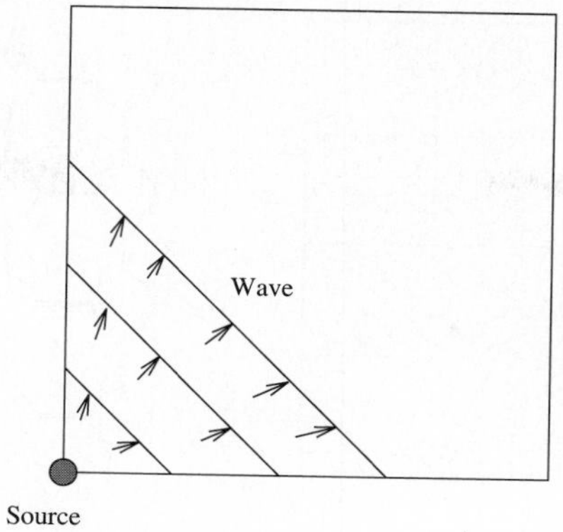

Figure 7.18 The wave of activity in the priority queues.

is located at the bottom-left corner. The computations propagate across the grid graph in the form of a wave. A processor is idle before the wave arrives, and becomes idle again after the wave has passed. This process is illustrated in Figure 7.18. At any time during the execution of the algorithm, only the processors along the wave are busy. The other processors have either finished their computations or have not yet started them. The next sections discuss three mappings of grid graphs onto a p-processor mesh.

Block-Checkerboard Mapping One way to map an $n \times n$ grid graph onto p processors is to use the block-checkerboard mapping (Section 5.1.2). Specifically, we can view the p processors as a logical mesh and assign a different block of $n/\sqrt{p} \times n/\sqrt{p}$ vertices to each processor. Figure 7.19 illustrates this mapping.

At any time, the number of busy processors is equal to the number of processors intersected by the wave. Since the wave moves diagonally, no more than $O(\sqrt{p})$ processors are busy at any time. Let W be the overall work performed by the sequential algorithm. If we assume that, at any time, $\sqrt{p}$ processors are performing computations, and if we ignore the overhead due to interprocessor communication and extra work, then the maximum speedup and efficiency are as follows:

$$S = \frac{W}{W/\sqrt{p}} = \sqrt{p}$$

$$E = \frac{1}{\sqrt{p}}$$

The efficiency of this mapping is poor and becomes worse as the number of processors increases.

Cyclic-Checkerboard Mapping The main limitation of the block-checkerboard mapping is that each processor is responsible for only a small, confined area of the grid.

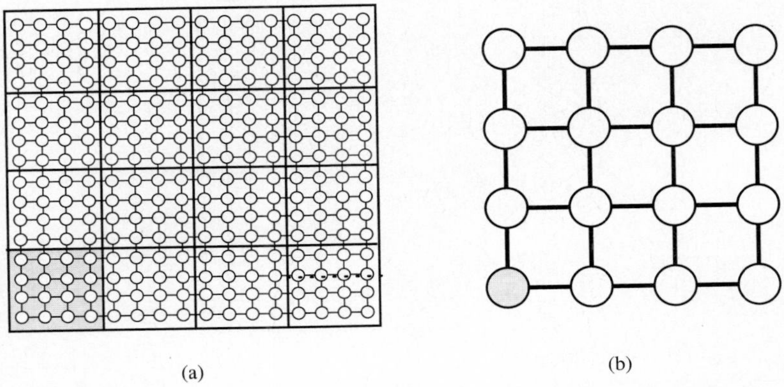

Figure 7.19 Mapping the grid graph (a) onto a mesh (b) by using the block-checkerboard mapping. In this example, $n = 16$ and $\sqrt{p} = 4$. The shaded vertices are mapped onto the shaded processor.

Alternatively, we can make each processor responsible for scattered areas of the grid by using the cyclic-checkerboard mapping (Section 5.1.2). This increases the time during which a processor stays busy. In cyclic-checkerboard mapping, the $n \times n$ grid graph is divided into n^2/p blocks, each of size $\sqrt{p} \times \sqrt{p}$. Each block is mapped onto the $\sqrt{p} \times \sqrt{p}$ processor mesh. Figure 7.20 illustrates this mapping. Each processor contains a block of n^2/p vertices. These vertices belong to diagonals of the graph that are $\sqrt{p}$ vertices apart. Each processor is assigned roughly $2n/\sqrt{p}$ such diagonals.

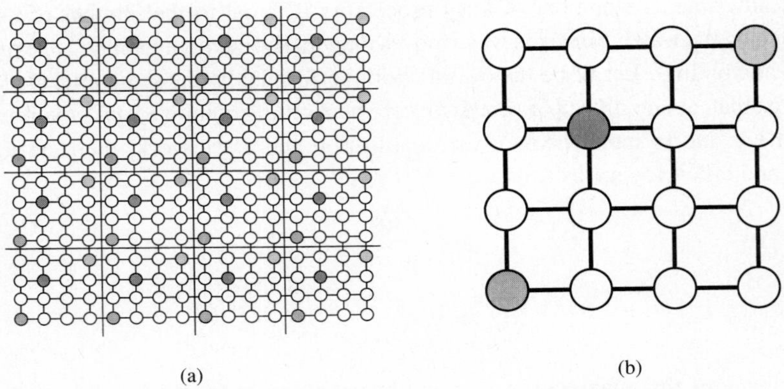

Figure 7.20 Mapping the grid graph (a) onto a mesh (b) by using the cyclic-checkerboard mapping. In this example, $n = 16$ and $\sqrt{p} = 4$. The shaded graph vertices are mapped onto the correspondingly shaded mesh processors.

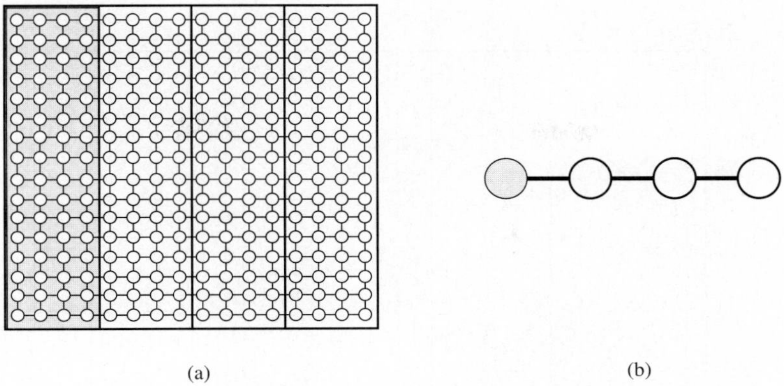

Figure 7.21 Mapping the grid graph (a) onto a linear array of processors (b). In this example, $n = 16$ and $p = 4$. The shaded vertices are mapped onto the shaded processor.

Now each processor is responsible for vertices that belong to different parts of the grid graph. As the wave propagates through the graph, the wave intersects some of the vertices on each processor. Thus, processors remain busy for most of the algorithm. The cyclic-checkerboard mapping, though, incurs a higher communication overhead than does the block-checkerboard mapping. Since adjacent vertices reside on separate processors, every time a processor extracts a vertex u from its priority queue it must notify other processors of the new value of $l[u]$. The analysis of this mapping is left as an exercise (Problem 7.18).

Block-Striped Mapping The two mappings discussed so far have limitations. The block-checkerboard mapping fails to keep more than $O(\sqrt{p})$ processors busy at any time, and the cyclic-checkerboard mapping has high communication overhead. Another mapping treats the p processors as a linear array and assigns n/p stripes of the grid graph to each processor by using the block-striped mapping. Figure 7.21 illustrates this mapping.

Initially, the wave intersects only one processor. As computation progresses, the wave spills over to the second processor so that two processors are busy. As the algorithm continues, the wave intersects more processors, which become busy. This process continues until all p processors are busy (that is, until they all have been intersected by the wave). After this point, the number of busy processors decreases. Figure 7.22 illustrates the propagation of the wave. If we assume that the wave propagates at a constant rate, then $p/2$ processors (on the average) are busy. Ignoring any overhead, the speedup and efficiency of this mapping are as follows:

$$S = \frac{W}{W/(p/2)} = \frac{p}{2}$$

$$E = \frac{1}{2}$$

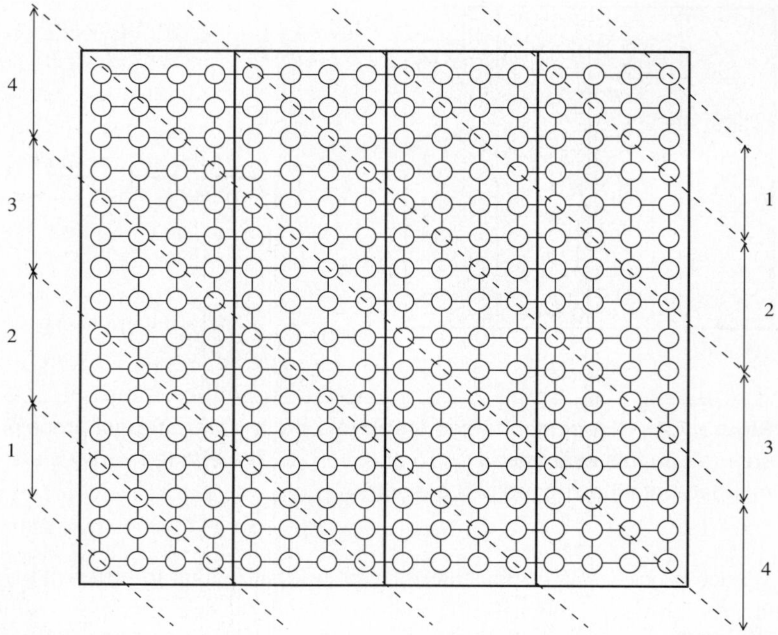

Figure 7.22 The number of busy processors as the computational wave propagates across the grid graph.

Thus, the efficiency of this mapping is at most 50 percent. The block-striped mapping is substantially better than the block-checkerboard mapping but cannot use more than $O(n)$ processors.

7.8 Bibliographic Remarks

Detailed discussions of graph theory and graph algorithms can be found in numerous texts. Gibbons [Gib85] provides a good reference to the algorithms presented in this chapter. Aho, Hopcroft, and Ullman [AHU74], and Cormen, Leiserson, and Rivest [CLR89] provide a detailed description of various graph algorithms and issues related to their efficient implementation on sequential computers.

The sequential minimum spanning tree algorithm described in Section 7.2 is due to Prim [Pri57]. Bentley [Ben80] and Deo and Yoo [DY81] present parallel formulations of Prim's MST algorithm. Deo and Yoo's algorithm is suited to a shared-address-space computer. It finds the MST in $\Theta(n^{1.5})$ using $\Theta(n^{0.5})$ processors. Bentley's algorithm works on a tree-connected systolic array and finds the MST in $\Theta(n \log n)$ time using $n/\log n$ processors. The hypercube formulation of Prim's MST algorithm in Section 7.2 is similar to Bentley's algorithm.

The MST of a graph can be also computed by using either Kruskal's [Kru56] or Sollin's [Sol77] sequential algorithms. The complexity of Sollin's algorithm (Problem 7.22) is $\Theta(n^2 \log n)$. Savage and JaJa [SJ81] have developed a formulation of Sollin's algorithm for the CREW PRAM. Their algorithm uses n^2 processors and solves the problem in $\Theta(\log^2 n)$ time. Chin, Lam, and Chen [CLC82] have developed a formulation of Sollin's algorithm for a CREW PRAM that uses $n\lceil n/\log n\rceil$ processors and finds the MST in $\Theta(\log^2 n)$ time. Awerbuch and Shiloach [AS87] present a formulation of Sollin's algorithm for the shuffle-exchange network that uses $\Theta(n^2)$ processors and runs in $\Theta(\log^2 n)$ time. Doshi and Varman [DV87] present a $\Theta(n^2/p)$ time algorithm for a p-processor ring-connected computer for Sollin's algorithm. Leighton [Lei83] and Nath, Maheshwari, and Bhatt [NMB83] present parallel formulations of Sollin's algorithm for a mesh of trees network. The first algorithm runs in $\Theta(\log^2 n)$, and the second algorithm runs in $\Theta(\log^4 n)$ time for an $n \times n$ mesh of trees. Huang [Hua85] describes a formulation of Sollin's algorithm that runs in $\Theta(n^2/p)$ on a $\sqrt{p} \times \sqrt{p}$ mesh of trees.

The single-source shortest paths algorithm in Section 7.3 was discovered by Dijkstra [Dij59]. Due to the similarity between Dijkstra's algorithm and Prim's MST algorithm, all the parallel formulations of Prim's algorithm discussed in the previous paragraph can also be applied to the single-source shortest paths problem. Bellman [Bel58] and Ford [FR62] independently developed a single-source shortest paths algorithm that operates on graphs with negative weights but without negative-weight cycles. The Bellman-Ford single-source algorithm has a sequential complexity of $O(|V||E|)$. Paige and Kruskal [PK89] present parallel formulations of both the Dijkstra and Bellman-Ford single-source shortest paths algorithm. Their formulation of Dijkstra's algorithm runs on an EREW PRAM of $\Theta(n)$ processors and runs in $\Theta(n \log n)$ time. Their formulation of Bellman-Ford's algorithm runs in $\Theta(n|E|/p + n \log p)$ time on a p-processor EREW PRAM where $p \le |E|$. They also present algorithms for the CRCW PRAM [PK89].

Significant work has been done on the all-pairs shortest paths problem. Dekel, Nassimi, and Sahni [DNS81] present a matrix multiplication algorithm (the DNS algorithm discussed in Section 5.4.4) for a hypercube-connected parallel computer that computes the all-pairs shortest paths in $\Theta(\log^2 n)$ using n^3 processors. Savage [Sav77] presents a matrix multiplication–based algorithm for the CREW PRAM that uses $n^3/\log n$ processors and runs in $\Theta(\log^2 n)$ time. For the matrix multiplication problem, the best-known algorithm uses $O(n^{2.376})$ operations and is due to Coppersmith and Winograd [CW90]. The source-partitioning formulation of Dijkstra's all-pairs shortest paths is discussed by Jenq and Sahni [JS87] and Kumar and Singh [KS91]. The source parallel formulation of Dijkstra's all-pairs shortest paths algorithm is discussed by Paige and Kruskal [PK89] and Kumar and Singh [KS91]. The Floyd's all-pairs shortest paths algorithm discussed in Section 7.4.3 is due to Floyd [Flo62]. The block-checkerboard and block-striped mappings (Problem 7.10) are presented by Jenq and Sahni [JS87], and the pipelined version of Floyd's algorithm is presented by Bertsekas and Tsitsiklis [BT89] and Kumar and Singh [KS91]. Kumar and Singh [KS91] present, isoefficiency analysis and performance comparison of different parallel formulations for the all-pairs shortest paths on hypercube- and mesh-connected computers. The discussion in Section 7.4.4 is based upon the work of Kumar and Singh [KS91] and of Jenq and Sahni [JS87]. In particular, Program 7.4 is adopted from the paper by Jenq and Sahni [JS87]. Levitt and Kautz [LK72] present a formulation of Floyd's algorithm for two-dimensional cellular arrays, that uses n^2 processors and runs in $\Theta(n)$ time. Deo, Pank, and Lord have developed a parallel formulation of Floyd's algorithm for the CREW PRAM model that has complexity $\Theta(n)$ on n^2 processors. Chandy and Misra [CM82] present a distributed all-pairs shortest-path algorithm based on diffusing computation.

The connected-components algorithm discussed in Section 7.6 was discovered by Woo and Sahni [WS89]. Cormen, Leiserson, and Rivest [CLR89] discusses ways to efficiently implement disjoint-set data structures with ranking and path compression. Several algorithms exist for computing the connected components; many of them are based on the technique of vertex collapsing, similar to Sollin's algorithm for the minimum spanning tree. Most of the parallel formulations of Sollin's algorithm can also find the connected components. Hirschberg [Hir76] and Hirschberg, Chandra, and Sarwate [HCS79] developed formulations of the connected-components algorithm based on vertex collapsing. The former has a complexity of $\Theta(\log^2 n)$ on a CREW PRAM with n^2 processors, and the latter has similar complexity and uses $n\lceil n/\log n\rceil$ processors. Chin, Lam, and Chen [CLC81] made the vertex collapse algorithm more efficient by reducing the number of processors to $n\lceil n/\log^2 n\rceil$ for a CREW PRAM, while keeping the run time at $\Theta(\log^2 n)$. Nassimi and Sahni [NS80] used the vertex collapsing technique to develop a formulation for a mesh-connected computer that finds the connected components in time $\Theta(n)$ by using n^2 processors.

The single-source shortest paths algorithm for sparse graphs, discussed in Section 7.7.1, was discovered by Johnson [Joh77]. Paige and Kruskal [PK89] discuss the possibility of maintaining the queue Q in parallel. Rao and Kumar [RK88] presented techniques to perform concurrent insertions and deletions in a priority queue. The block checkerboarding, cyclic checkerboarding, and block striping formulation of Johnson's algorithm (Section 7.7.1) are due to Wada and Ichiyoshi [WI89]. They also presented theoretical and experimental evaluation of these schemes on a mesh-connected parallel computer.

Other parallel graph algorithms have been proposed. Shiloach and Vishkin [SV82] presented an algorithm for finding the maximum flow in a directed flow network with n vertices that runs in time $O(n^2 \log n)$ on a n-processor EREW PRAM. Goldberg and Tarjan [GT88] presented a different maximum-flow algorithm that runs in time $O(n^2 \log n)$ on a n-processor EREW PRAM but requires less space. Atallah and Kosaraju [AK84] proposed a number of algorithms for a mesh-connected parallel computer. The algorithms they considered are: finding the bridges and articulation points of an undirected graph, finding the length of the shortest cycle, finding a MST, finding the cyclic index, and testing if a graph is bipartite, Tarjan and Vishkin [TV85] presented algorithms for computing the biconnected components of a graph. Their CRCW PRAM formulation runs in time $\Theta(\log n)$ by using $\Theta(|E| + |V|)$ processors, and their CREW PRAM formulation runs in time $\Theta(\log^2 n)$ by using $\Theta(n^2/\log^2 n)$ processors.

Problems

7.1 In the parallel formulation of Prim's minimum spanning tree algorithm (Section 7.2), the maximum number of processors that can be used efficiently on a hypercube is $\Theta(n/\log n)$. By using $\Theta(n/\log n)$ processors the run time is $\Theta(n \log n)$. What is the run time if you use $\Theta(n)$ processors? What is the minimum parallel run time that can be obtained on a hypercube? How does this time compare with the run time obtained when you use $\Theta(n/\log n)$ processors?

7.2 Show how Dijkstra's single-source algorithm and its parallel formulation (Section 7.3) need to be modified in order to output the shortest paths instead of the cost. Analyze the run time of your sequential and parallel formulations.

7.3 Given a graph $G = (V, E)$, the breadth-first ranking of vertices of G are the values assigned to the vertices of V in a breadth-first traversal of G from a node v. Show how the breadth-first ranking of vertices of G can be performed on a p-processor mesh.

7.4 Dijkstra's single-source shortest paths algorithm (Section 7.3) requires non-negative edge weights. Show how Dijkstra's algorithm can be modified to work on graphs with negative weights but no negative cycles in $\Theta(|E||V|)$ time. Analyze the performance of the parallel formulation of the modified algorithm on a p-processor hypercube.

7.5 Modify the algorithm presented in Section 7.4.1 for computing the cost of the shortest paths between all pairs of vertices when n is not a power of 2. What is its sequential run time?

7.6 Modify the algorithm presented in Section 7.4.1 so that it also records the paths in addition to their costs. Use any required additional data structures.

7.7 Compute the total amount of memory required by the different parallel formulations of the all-pairs shortest paths problem described in Section 7.4.

7.8 Show that Floyd's algorithm in Section 7.4.3 is correct if we replace line 7 of Program 7.3 by the following line:

$$d_{i,j} = \min\{d_{i,j}, (d_{i,k} + d_{k,j})\}$$

7.9 Compute the parallel run time, speedup, and efficiency of Floyd's all-pairs shortest paths algorithm using block-checkerboard partitioning on a p-processor mesh with store-and-forward routing and a p-processor mesh with cut-through routing.

7.10 An alternative way of partitioning the matrix $D^{(k)}$ in Floyd's all-pairs shortest paths algorithm is to use the block-striped partitioning (Section 5.1.1). Each of the p processors is assigned n/p consecutive columns of the $D^{(k)}$ matrix.

(a) Compute the parallel run time, speedup, and efficiency of block-striped partitioning on a hypercube-connected parallel computer. What are the advantages and disadvantages of this partitioning over the block-checkerboard partitioning presented in Section 7.4.3?

(b) Compute the parallel run time, speedup, and efficiency of block-striped partitioning on a p-processor mesh with store-and-forward routing, a p-processor mesh with cut-through routing, and a p-processor ring.

7.11 Describe and analyze the performance of a parallel formulation of Floyd's algorithm that uses block-striped partitioning and the pipelining technique described in Section 7.4.3.

7.12 Compute the exact parallel run time, speedup, and efficiency of Floyd's pipelined formulation (Section 7.4.3).

7.13 Compute the parallel run time, the speedup, and the efficiency of the parallel formulation of the connected-component algorithm presented in Section 7.6 for a p-processor mesh with store-and-forward routing and with cut-through routing. Comment on the difference in the performance of the two architectures.

7.14 The parallel formulation for the connected-component problem presented in Section 7.6 uses block-striped partitioning to partition the matrix among processors. Consider an alternative parallel formulation in which block-checkerboard partitioning is used instead. Describe this formulation and analyze its performance and scalability on a hypercube, a mesh with SF-routing, and a mesh with CT-routing. How does this scheme compare with block-striped partitioning?

7.15 Consider the problem of parallelizing Johnson's single-source shortest paths algorithm for sparse graphs (Section 7.7.1). One way of parallelizing it is to use p_1 processors to maintain the priority queue and p_2 processors to perform the computations of the new l values. How many processors can be efficiently used to maintain the priority queue (in other words, what is the maximum value for p_1)? How many processors can be used to update the l values? Is the parallel formulation that is obtained by using the $p_1 + p_2$ processors cost-optimal? Describe an algorithm that uses p_1 processors to maintain the priority queue.

7.16 Consider Dijkstra's single-source shortest paths algorithm for sparse graphs (Section 7.7). We can parallelize this algorithm on a p-processor hypercube by splitting the n adjacency lists among the processors horizontally; that is, each processor gets n/p lists. What is the parallel run time of this formulation? Alternatively, we can partition the adjacency list vertically among the processors; that is, each processor gets a fraction of each adjacency list. If an adjacency list contains m elements, then each processor contains a sublist of m/p elements. The last element in each sublist has a pointer to the element in the next processor. What is the parallel run time and speedup of this formulation? What is the maximum number of processors that it can use?

7.17 Repeat Problem 7.16 for Floyd's all-pairs shortest paths algorithm.

7.18 Compute the parallel run time, speedup, and efficiency of the cyclic-checkerboard mapping of the sparse graph single-source shortest paths algorithm (Section 7.7.1) for a mesh-connected computer. You may ignore the overhead due to extra work, but you should take into account the overhead due to communication.

7.19 Analyze the performance of the single-source shortest paths algorithm for sparse graphs (Section 7.7.1) when the block-cyclic-checkerboard mapping is used (Section 5.1.2). Compare it with the performance of the cyclic-checkerboard mapping computed in Problem 7.18. As in Problem 7.18, ignore extra computation but include communication overhead.

7.20 Consider the block-cyclic-striped mapping described in Section 5.1.1. Describe how you will apply this mapping to the single-source shortest paths problem for sparse graphs. Compute the parallel run time, speedup, and efficiency of this mapping. In your analysis, include the communication overhead but not the overhead due to extra work.

7.21 Of the mapping schemes presented in Section 7.7.1 and in Problems 7.19 and 7.20, which one has the smallest overhead due to extra computation?

7.22 Sollin's algorithm (Section 7.8) starts with a forest of n isolated vertices. In each iteration, the algorithm simultaneously determines, for each tree in the forest, the smallest edge joining any vertex in that tree to a vertex in another tree. All such edges are added to the forest. Furthermore, two trees are never joined by more than one edge. This process continues until there is only one tree in the forest—the minimum spanning tree. Since the number of trees is reduced by a factor of at least two in each iteration, Sollin's algorithm requires at most $\log n$ iterations to find the MST. Each iteration requires at most $O(n^2)$ comparisons to find the smallest edge incident on each vertex; thus, the sequential complexity of Sollin's algorithm is $\Theta(n^2 \log n)$.

Develop a parallel formulation of Sollin's algorithm on an n-processor hypercube-connected parallel computer. What is the run time of your formulation? Is it cost optimal?

References

[AHU74] A. V. Aho, J. E. Hopcroft, and J. D. Ullman. *The Design and Analysis of Computer Algorithms*. Addison-Wesley, Reading, MA, 1974.

[AK84] M. J. Atallah and S. R. Kosaraju. Graph problems on a mesh-connected processor array. *Journal of ACM*, 31(3):649–667, July 1984.

[AS87] B. Awerbuch and Y. Shiloach. New connectivity and MSF algorithms for shuffle-exchange network and PRAM. *IEEE Transactions on Computers*, C–36(10):1258–1263, October 1987.

[Bel58] R. Bellman. On a routing problem. *Quarterly of Applied Mathematics*, 16(1):87–90, 1958.

[Ben80] J. L. Bentley. A parallel algorithm for constructing minimum spanning trees. *Journal of the ACM*, 27(1):51–59, March 1980.

[BT89] D. P. Bertsekas and J. N. Tsitsiklis. *Parallel and Distributed Computation: Numerical Methods*. Prentice Hall, Englewood Cliffs, NJ, 1989.

[CLC81] F. Y. Chin, J. Lam, and I. Chen. Optimal parallel algorithms for the connected component problem. In *Proceedings of the 1981 International Conference on Parallel Processing*, 170–175, 1981.

[CLC82] F. Y. Chin, J. Lam, and I. Chen. Efficient parallel algorithms for some graph problems. *Communication of the ACM*, 25(9):659–665, September 1982.

[CLR89] T. H. Cormen, C. E. Leiserson, and R. L. Rivest. *Introduction to Algorithms*. MIT Press, McGraw-Hill, Cambridge, MA, 1989.

[CM82] K. M. Chandy and J. Misra. Distributed computation on graphs: Shortest path algorithms. *Communication of the ACM*, 25(11):833–837, November 1982.

[CW90] D. Coppersmith and S. Winograd. Matrix multiplication via arithmetic progressions. *Journal of Symbolic Computations*, 9(3):251–280, September 1990.

[Dij59] E. W. Dijkstra. A note on two problems in connection with graphs. *Numerische Mathematik*, 1:269–271, 1959.

[DNS81] E. Dekel, D. Nassimi, and S. Sahni. Parallel matrix and graph algorithms. *SIAM Journal of Computing*, 10(4):657–75, November 1981.

[DV87] K. A. Doshi and P. J. Varman. Optimal graph algorithms on a fixed-size linear array. *IEEE Transactions on Computers*, C–36(4):460–470, April 1987.

[DY81] N. Deo and Y. B. Yoo. Parallel algorithms for the minimum spanning tree problem. In *Proceedings of the 1981 International Conference on Parallel Processing*, 188–189, 1981.

[Flo62] R. W. Floyd. Algorithm 97: Shortest path. *Communications of the ACM*, 5(6):345, June 1962.

[FR62] L. R. Ford and R. L. Rivest. *Flows in Networks*. Princeton University Press, Princeton, NJ, 1962.

[Gib85] A. Gibbons. *Algorithmic Graph Theory*. Cambridge University Press, Cambridge, MA, 1985.

[GT88] A. V. Goldberg and R. E. Tarjan. A new approach to the maximum-flow problem. *Journal of the ACM*, 35(4):921–940, October 1988.

[HCS79] D. S. Hirschberg, A. K. Chandra, and D. V. Sarwate. Computing connected components on parallel computers. *Communications of the ACM*, 22(8):461–464, August 1979.

[Hir76] D. S. Hirschberg. Parallel algorithms for the transitive closure and connected component problem. In *Proceedings of the 8th Annual ACM Symposium on the Theory of Computing*, 55–57, 1976.

[Hua85] M. A. Huang. Solving some graph problems with optimal or near-optimal speedup on mesh-of-trees networks. In *Proceedings of the 26th Annual IEEE Symposium on Foundations of Computer Science*, 232–340, 1985.

[Joh77] D. B. Johnson. Efficient algorithms for shortest paths in sparse networks. *Journal of the ACM*, 24(1):1–13, March 1977.

[JS87] J. Jenq and S. Sahni. All pairs shortest paths on a hypercube multiprocessor. In *International Conference of Parallel Processing*, 713–716, 1987.

[Kru56] J. B. Kruskal. On the shortest spanning subtree of a graph and the traveling salesman problem. In *Proceedings of the AMS*, volume 7, 48–50, 1956.

[KS91] V. Kumar and V. Singh. Scalability of parallel algorithms for all-pairs shortest-path problem. *Journal of Parallel and Distributed Computing*, 13:124–138, 1991.

[Lei83] F. T. Leighton. Parallel computations using meshes of trees. In *Proceedings of 1983 International Workshop of Graph Theoretic Computer Science*, 1983.

[LK72] K. N. Levitt and W. T. Kautz. Cellular arrays for the solution of graph problems. *Communications of the ACM*, 15(9):789–801, September 1972.

[NMB83] D. Nath, S. N. Maheshwari, and P. C. P. Bhatt. Efficient VLSI networks for parallel processing based on orthogonal trees. *IEEE Transactions on Computers*, C–32:21–23, June 1983.

[NS80] D. Nassimi and S. Sahni. Finding connected components and connected ones on a mesh-connected computer. *SIAM Journal of Computing*, 9(4):744–757, November 1980.

[PK89] R. C. Paige and C. P. Kruskal. Parallel algorithms for shortest path problems. In *Proceedings of 1989 International Conference on Parallel Processing*, 14–19, 1989.

[Pri57] R. C. Prim. Shortest connection network and some generalizations. *Bell Systems Technical Journal*, 36:1389–1401, 1957.

[RK88] V. N. Rao and V. Kumar. Concurrent access of priority queues. *IEEE Transactions on Computers*, C–37 (12), 1988.

[Sav77] C. Savage. *Parallel Algorithms for Graph Theoretic Problems*. Ph.D. thesis, Mathematics Department, University of Illinois, Urbana, IL, 1977.

[SJ81] C. Savage and J. Jaja. Fast, efficient parallel algorithms for some graph problems. *SIAM Journal of Computing*, 10(4):682–690, November 1981.

[Sol77] M. Sollin. An algorithm attributed to Sollin. In S. Goodman and S. Hedetniemi, editors, *Introduction to The Design and Analysis of Algorithms*, chapter 5.5. McGraw-Hill, Cambridge, MA, 1977.

[SV82] Y. Shiloach and U. Vishkin. An $O(n^2 \log n)$ parallel max-flow algorithm. *Journal of Algorithms*, 3:128–146, 1982.

[TV85] R. E. Tarjan and U. Vishkin. An efficient parallel biconnectivity algorithm. *SIAM Journal on Computing*, 14(4):862–874, November 1985.

[WI89] K. Wada and N. Ichiyoshi. A distributed shortest path algorithm and its mapping on the Multi-PSI. In *Proceedings of International Conference of Parallel Processing*, 1989.

[WS89] J. Woo and S. Sahni. Hypercube computing: Connected components. *Journal of Supercomputing*, 3:209–234, 1989.

CHAPTER 8

Search Algorithms for Discrete Optimization Problems

Search algorithms can be used to solve discrete optimization problems (DOPs), a class of computationally expensive problems with significant theoretical and practical interest. Search algorithms solve DOPs by evaluating candidate solutions from a finite or countably infinite set of possible solutions to find one that satisfies a problem-specific criterion. DOPs are also referred to as combinatorial problems.

8.1 Definitions and Examples

A ***discrete optimization problem*** can be expressed as a tuple (S, f). The set S is a finite or countably infinite set of all solutions that satisfy specified constraints. This set is called the set of ***feasible solutions***. The function f is the cost function that maps each element in set S onto the set of real numbers R.

$$f : S \rightarrow R$$

The objective of a DOP is to find a feasible solution x_{opt}, such that $f(x_{opt}) \leq f(x)$ for all $x \in S$.

Problems from various domains can be formulated as DOPs. Some examples are planning and scheduling, the optimal layout of VLSI chips, robot motion planning, test-pattern generation for digital circuits, and logistics and control.

Example 8.1 The 0/1 Integer-Linear-Programming Problem

In the 0/1 integer-linear-programming problem, we are given an $m \times n$ matrix A, an

$m \times 1$ vector b, and an $n \times 1$ vector c. The objective is to determine an $n \times 1$ vector $\overline{x}$ whose elements can take on only the value 0 or 1. The vector must satisfy the constraint

$$A\overline{x} \geq b$$

and the function

$$f(\overline{x}) = c^T\overline{x}$$

must be minimized. For this problem, the set S is the set of all values of the vector $\overline{x}$ that satisfy the equation $A\overline{x} \geq b$. ∎

Example 8.2 The 8-Puzzle Problem

The 8-puzzle problem consists of a 3×3 grid containing eight tiles, numbered one through eight. One of the grid segments (called the "blank") is empty. A tile can be moved into the blank position from a position adjacent to it, thus creating a blank in the tile's original position. Depending on the configuration of the grid, up to four moves are possible: up, down, left, and right. The initial and final configurations of the tiles are specified. The objective is to determine a shortest sequence of moves that transforms the initial configuration to the final configuration. Figure 8.1 illustrates sample initial and final configurations and a sequence of moves leading from the initial configuration to the final configuration.

The set S for this problem is the set of all sequences of moves that lead from the initial to the final configurations. The cost function f of an element in S is defined as the number of moves in the sequence. ∎

In most problems of practical interest, the solution set S is quite large. Consequently, it is not feasible to exhaustively enumerate the elements in S to determine the optimal element x_{opt}. Instead, a DOP can be reformulated as the problem of finding a minimum-cost path in a graph from a designated initial node to one of several possible goal nodes. Each element x in S can be viewed as a path from the initial node to one of the goal nodes. There is a cost associated with each edge of the graph, and a cost function f is defined in terms of these edge costs. For many problems, the cost of a path is the sum of the edge costs. Such a graph is called a ***state space***, and the nodes of the graph are called ***states***. A ***terminal node*** is one that has no successors. All other nodes are called ***nonterminal nodes***. The 8-puzzle problem can be naturally formulated as a graph search problem. In particular, the initial configuration is the initial node, and the final configuration is the goal node. Example 8.3 illustrates the process of reformulating the 0/1 Integer-Linear-Programming Problem as a graph search problem.

Example 8.3 The 0/1 Integer-Linear-Programming Problem Revisited

Consider an instance of the 0/1 integer-linear-programming problem defined in Ex-

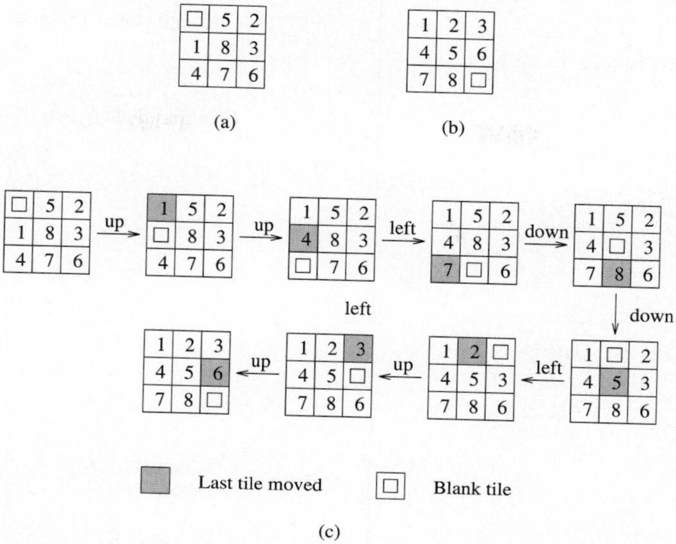

Figure 8.1 An 8-puzzle problem instance: (a) initial configuration; (b) final configuration; and (c) a sequence of moves leading from the initial to the final configuration.

ample 8.1. Let the values of A, b, and c be given by

$$A = \begin{bmatrix} 5 & 2 & 1 & 2 \\ 1 & -1 & -1 & 2 \\ 3 & 1 & 1 & 3 \end{bmatrix}, \; b = \begin{bmatrix} 8 \\ 2 \\ 5 \end{bmatrix}, \; c = \begin{bmatrix} 2 \\ 1 \\ -1 \\ -2 \end{bmatrix}.$$

The constraints corresponding to A, b, and c are as follows:

$$\begin{aligned} 5x_1 + 2x_2 + x_3 + 2x_4 &\geq 8 \\ x_1 - x_2 - x_3 + 2x_4 &\geq 2 \\ 3x_1 + x_2 + x_3 + 3x_4 &\geq 5 \end{aligned}$$

and the function $f(x)$ to be minimized is

$$f(x) = 2x_1 + x_2 - x_3 - 2x_4.$$

Each of the four elements of vector $\overline{x}$ can take the value 0 or 1. There are $2^4 = 16$ possible values for x. However, many of these values do not satisfy the problem's constraints.

The problem can be reformulated as a graph-search problem. The initial node represents the state in which none of the elements of vector x have been assigned

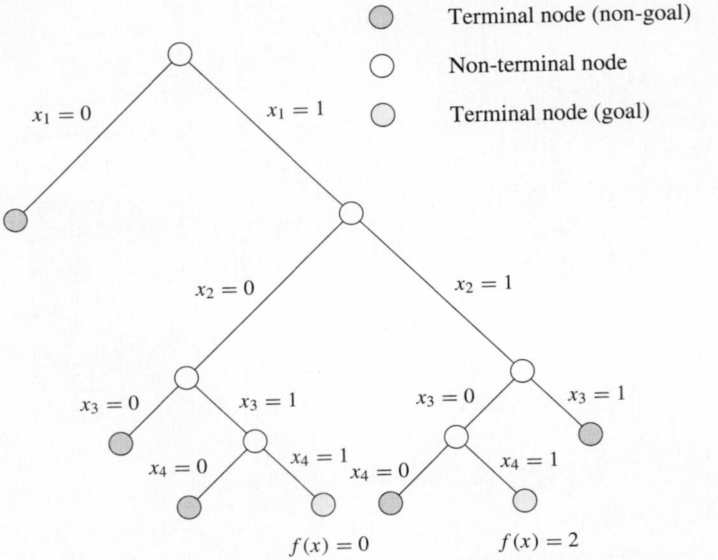

Figure 8.2 The graph corresponding to the 0/1 integer-linear-programming problem.

values. In this example, we assign values to vector elements in subscript order; that is, first x_1, then x_2, and so on. The initial node generates two nodes corresponding to $x_1 = 0$ and $x_1 = 1$. After a variable x_i has been assigned a value, it is called a ***fixed variable***. All variables that are not fixed are called ***free variables***.

After instantiating a variable to 0 or 1, it is possible to check whether an instantiation of the remaining free variables can lead to a feasible solution. We do this by using the following condition:

$$\sum_{x_j \text{is free}} \max\{A[i, j], 0\} + \sum_{x_j \text{is fixed}} A[i, j]x_j \geq b_i, \quad i = 1, \ldots, m \tag{8.1}$$

The left side of Equation 8.1 is the maximum value of $\sum_{k=1}^{n} A[i, k]x_k$ that can be obtained by instantiating the free variables to either 0 or 1. If this value is greater than or equal to b_i, for $i = 1, 2, \ldots, m$, then the node may lead to a feasible solution.

For each of the nodes corresponding to $x_1 = 0$ and $x_1 = 1$, the next variable (x_2) is selected and assigned a value. The nodes are then checked for feasibility. This process continues until all the variables have been assigned and the feasible set has been generated. Figure 8.2 illustrates this process.

Function $f(x)$ is evaluated for each of the feasible solutions; the solution with the minimum value is the desired solution. Note that it is unnecessary to generate the entire feasible set to determine the solution. Several search algorithms can determine an optimal solution by searching only a portion of the graph. ■

For some problems, it is possible to estimate the cost to reach the goal state from an intermediate state. This cost is called a ***heuristic estimate***. Let $h(x)$ denote the heuristic estimate of reaching the goal state from state x and $g(x)$ denote the cost of reaching state x from initial state s along the current path. The function h is called a ***heuristic function***. If $h(x)$ is a lower bound on the cost of reaching the goal state from state x for all x, then h is called ***admissible***. We define function $l(x)$ as the sum $h(x) + g(x)$. If h is admissible, then $l(x)$ is a lower bound on the cost of the path to a goal state that can be obtained by extending the current path between s and x. In subsequent examples we will see how an admissible heuristic can be used to determine the least-cost sequence of moves from the initial state to a goal state.

Example 8.4 An Admissible Heuristic Function for the 8-Puzzle

Assume that each position in the 8-puzzle grid is represented as a pair. The pair $(1, 1)$ represents the top-left grid position and the pair $(3, 3)$ represents the bottom-right position. The distance between positions (i, j) and (k, l) is defined as $|i-k|+|j-l|$. This distance is called the ***Manhattan distance***. The sum of the Manhattan distances between the initial and final positions of all tiles is an estimate of the number of moves required to transform the current configuration into the final configuration. This estimate is called the ***Manhattan heuristic***. Note that if $h(x)$ is the Manhattan distance between configuration x and the final configuration, then $h(x)$ is also a lower bound on the number of moves from configuration x to the final configuration. Hence the Manhattan heuristic is admissible.

■

Once a DOP has been formulated as a graph search problem, it can be solved by algorithms such as branch-and-bound search and heuristic search. These techniques use heuristics and the structure of the search space to solve DOPs without searching the set S exhaustively.

DOPs belong to the class of NP-hard problems. One may argue that it is pointless to apply parallel processing to these problems, since we can never reduce their worst-case run time to a polynomial without using exponentially many processors. However, the average-time complexity of heuristic search algorithms for many problems is polynomial. Furthermore, there are heuristic search algorithms that find suboptimal solutions for specific problems in polynomial time. In such cases, bigger problem instances can be solved using parallel computers. Many DOPs (such as, robot motion planning, speech understanding, and task scheduling) require real-time solutions. For these applications, parallel processing may be the only way to obtain acceptable performance. Other problems, for which optimal solutions are highly desirable, can be solved for moderate-sized instances in a reasonable amount of time by using parallel search techniques (for example, VLSI floor-plan optimization, and computer-aided design).

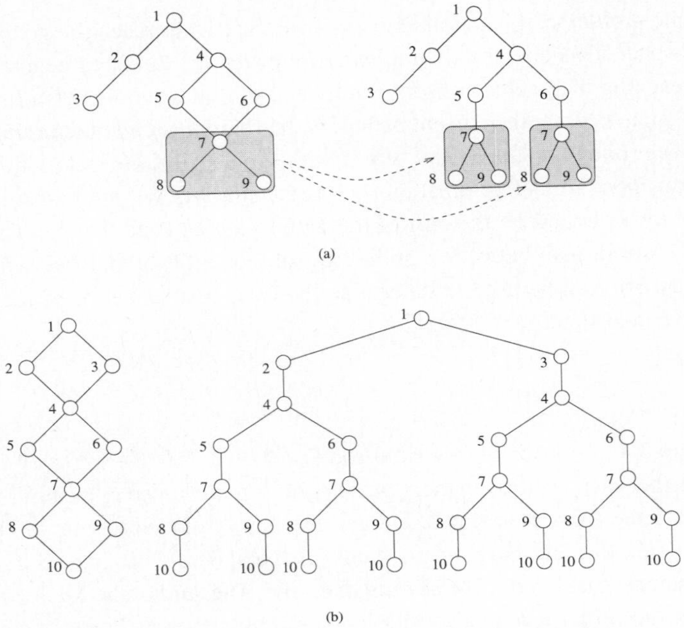

Figure 8.3 Two examples of unfolding a graph into a tree.

8.2 Sequential Search Algorithms

The most suitable sequential search algorithm to apply to a state space depends on whether the space forms a graph or a tree. In a tree, each new successor leads to an unexplored part of the search space. An example of this is the 0/1 integer-programming problem. In a graph, however, a state can be reached along multiple paths. An example of such a problem is the 8-puzzle. For such problems, whenever a state is generated, it is necessary to check if the state has already been generated. If this check is not performed, then effectively the search graph is unfolded into a tree in which a state is repeated for every path that leads to it (Figure 8.3).

For many problems, unfolding increases the size of the search space by a small factor (for example, the 8-puzzle). For some problems, however, unfolded graphs are much larger than the original graphs. Figure 8.3(b) illustrates a graph whose corresponding tree has exponentially higher number of states. In this section, we present an overview of various sequential algorithms used to solve DOPs that are formulated as tree or graph search problems.

8.2.1 Depth-First Search Algorithms

Depth-first search (DFS) algorithms solve DOPs that can be formulated as tree-search problems. DFS begins by expanding the initial node and generating its successors. In each subsequent step, DFS expands one of the most recently generated nodes. If this node has no successors (or cannot lead to any solutions), then DFS backtracks and expands a different node. In some DFS algorithms, successors of a node are expanded in an order determined by their heuristic values. A major advantage of DFS is that its storage requirement is linear in the depth of the state space being searched. The following sections discuss three algorithms based on depth-first search.

Simple Backtracking

Simple backtracking is a depth-first search method that terminates upon finding the first solution. Thus, it is not guaranteed to find a minimum-cost solution. Simple backtracking uses no heuristic information to order the successors of an expanded node. A variant, ***ordered backtracking***, does use heuristics to order the successors of an expanded node.

Depth-First Branch-and-Bound

Depth-first branch-and-bound (DFBB) exhaustively searches the state space; that is, it continues to search even after finding a solution path. Whenever it finds a new solution path, it updates the current best solution path. DFBB discards inferior partial solution paths (that is, partial solution paths whose extensions are guaranteed to be worse than the current best solution path). Upon termination, the current best solution is a globally optimal solution.

Iterative Deepening A*

Trees corresponding to DOPs can be very deep. Thus, a DFS algorithm may get stuck searching a deep part of the search space when a solution exists higher up on another branch. For such trees, we impose a bound on the depth to which the DFS algorithm searches. If the node to be expanded is beyond the depth bound, then the node is not expanded and the algorithm backtracks. If a solution is not found, then the entire state space is searched again using a larger depth bound. This technique is called ***iterative deepening depth-first search*** (ID-DFS). Note that this method is guaranteed to find a solution path with the fewest edges. However, it is not guaranteed to find a least-cost path.

Iterative deepening A* (IDA*) is a variant of ID-DFS. IDA* uses the l-values of nodes to bound depth (recall from Section 8.1, that for node x, $l(x) = g(x) + h(x)$). IDA* repeatedly performs cost-bounded DFS over the search space. In each iteration, IDA* expands nodes depth-first. If the l-value of the node to be expanded is greater than the cost bound, then IDA* backtracks. If a solution is not found within the current cost bound, then IDA* repeats the entire depth-first search using a higher cost bound. In the first iteration, the cost bound is set to the l-value of the initial state s. Note that since $g(s)$ is zero, $l(s)$ is equal to $h(s)$. In each subsequent iteration, the cost bound is increased. The new cost bound is equal to the minimum l-value of the nodes that were generated but could not be expanded in the previous iteration. The algorithm terminates when a goal node is expanded. IDA* is guaranteed to find an optimal solution if the heuristic function is admissible. It

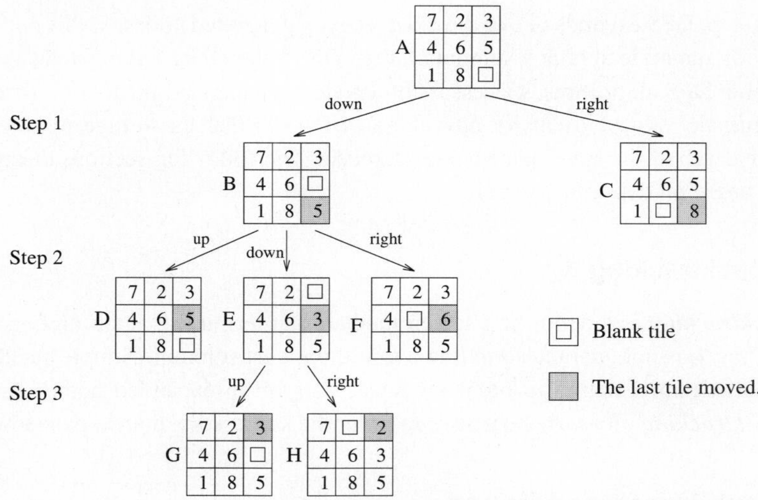

Figure 8.4 States resulting from the first three steps of depth-first search applied to an instance of the 8-puzzle.

may appear that IDA* performs a lot of redundant work across iterations. However, for many problems the redundant work performed by IDA* is minimal, because most of the work is done deep in the search space.

Example 8.5 Depth-First Search: The 8-Puzzle

Figure 8.4 shows the execution of depth-first search for solving the 8-puzzle problem. The search starts at the initial configuration. Successors of this state are generated by applying possible moves. During each step of the search algorithm a new state is selected, and its successors are generated. The DFS algorithm expands the deepest node in the tree. In step 1, the initial state A generates states B and C. One of these is selected according to a predetermined criterion. In the example, we order successors by applicable moves as follows: up, down, left, and right. In step 2, the DFS algorithm selects state B and generates states D, E, and F. Note that the state D can be discarded, as it is a duplicate of the parent of B. In step 3, state E is expanded to generate states G and H. Again G can be discarded because it is a duplicate of B. The search proceeds in this way until the algorithm backtracks or the final configuration is generated. ■

In each step of the DFS algorithm, untried alternatives must be stored. For example, in the 8-puzzle problem, up to three untried alternatives are stored at each step. In general, if m is the amount of storage required to store a state, and d is the maximum depth, then the total space requirement of the DFS algorithm is $\Theta(md)$. The state-space tree searched by parallel DFS can be efficiently represented as a stack. Since the depth of the stack increases

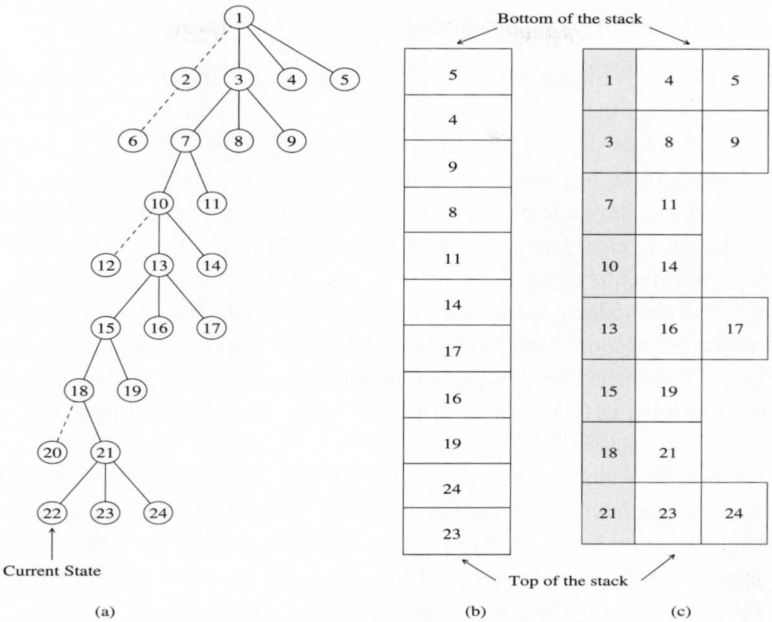

Figure 8.5 Representing a DFS tree: (a) the DFS tree; Successor nodes shown with dashed lines have already been explored; (b) the stack storing untried alternatives only; and (c) the stack storing untried alternatives along with their parent. The shaded blocks represent the parent state and the block to the right represents successor states that have not been explored.

linearly with the depth of the tree, the memory requirements of a stack representation are low.

There are two ways of storing untried alternatives using a stack. In the first representation, untried alternates are pushed on the stack at each step. The ancestors of a state are not represented on the stack. Figure 8.5(b) illustrates this representation for the tree shown in Figure 8.5(a). In the second representation, shown in Figure 8.5(c), untried alternatives are stored along with their parent state. It is necessary to use the second representation if the sequence of transformations from the initial state to the goal state is required as a part of the solution. Furthermore, if the state space is a graph in which it is possible to generate an ancestor state by applying a sequence of transformations to the current state, then it is desirable to use the second representation, because it allows us to check for duplication of ancestor states and thus remove any cycles from the state-space graph. The second representation is useful for problems such as the 8-puzzle. In Example 8.5, using the second representation allows the algorithm to detect that nodes D and G should be discarded.

8.2.2 Best-First Search Algorithms

Best-first search (BFS) algorithms can search both graphs and trees. These algorithms use heuristics to direct the search to portions of the search space likely to yield solutions. Smaller heuristic values are assigned to more promising nodes. BFS maintains two lists: *open* and *closed*. At the beginning, the initial node is placed on the *open* list. This list is sorted according to a heuristic evaluation function that measures how likely each node is to yield a solution. In each step of the search, the most promising node from the *open* list is removed. If this node is a goal node, then the algorithm terminates. Otherwise, the node is expanded. The expanded node is placed on the *closed* list. The successors of the newly expanded node are placed on the *open* list under one of the following circumstances: (1) the successor is not already on the *open* or *closed* lists, and (2) the successor is already on the *open* or *closed* list but has a lower heuristic value. In the second case, the node with the higher heuristic value is deleted.

A common BFS technique is the ***A* algorithm***. The A* algorithm uses the lower bound function l as a heuristic evaluation function. Recall from Section 8.1 that for each node x, $l(x)$ is the sum of $g(x)$ and $h(x)$. Nodes in the *open* list are ordered according to the value of the l function. At each step, the node with the smallest l-value (that is, the best node) is removed from the *open* list and expanded. Its successors are inserted into the *open* list at the proper positions and the node itself is inserted into the *closed* list. For an admissible heuristic function, A* finds an optimal solution.

The main drawback of any BFS algorithm is that its memory requirement is linear in the size of the search space explored. For many problems, the size of the search space is exponential in the depth of the tree expanded. For problems with large search spaces, memory becomes a limitation.

Example 8.6 Best-First Search: The 8-Puzzle

Consider the 8-puzzle problem from Examples 8.2 and 8.4. Figure 8.6 illustrates four steps of best-first search on the 8-puzzle. At each step, a state x with the minimum l-value ($l(x) = g(x) + h(x)$) is selected for expansion. Ties are broken arbitrarily. BFS can check for a duplicate nodes, since all previously generated nodes are kept on either the *open* or *closed* list. ■

8.3 Search Overhead Factor

Parallel search algorithms incur overhead from several sources. These include communication overhead, idle time due to load imbalance, and contention for shared data structures. Thus, if both the sequential and parallel formulations of an algorithm do the same amount of work, the speedup of parallel search on p processors is less than p. However, the amount of work done by a parallel formulation is often different from that done by the corresponding sequential formulation because they may explore different parts of the search space.

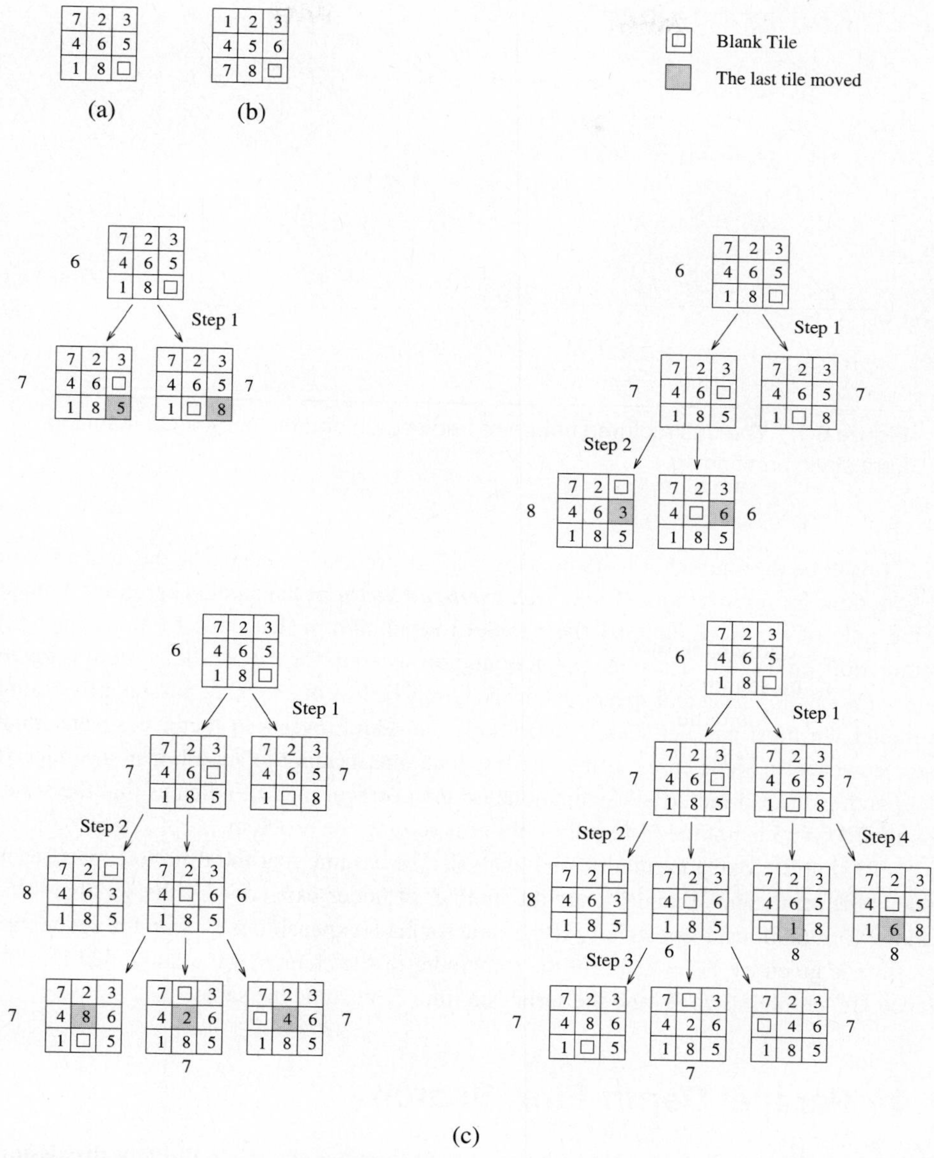

Figure 8.6 Applying best-first search to the 8-puzzle: (a) initial configuration; (b) final configuration; and (c) states resulting from the first four steps of best-first search. Each state is labeled with its h-value (that is, the Manhattan distance from the state to the final state).

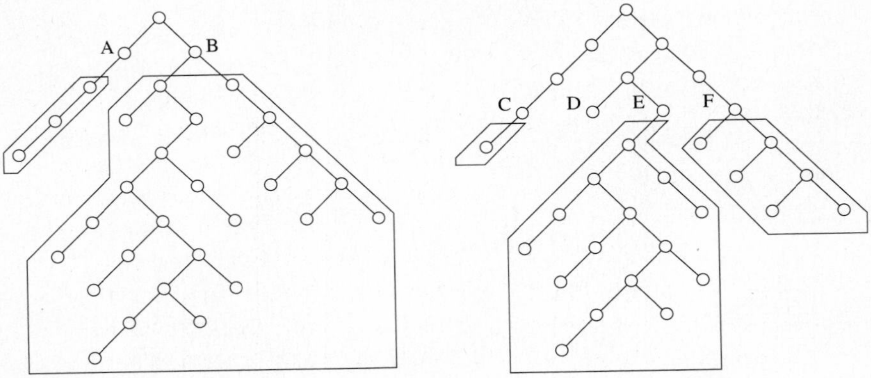

Figure 8.7 The unstructured nature of tree search and the imbalance resulting from static partitioning.

Let W be the amount of work done by a single processor, and W_p be the total amount of work done by p processors. The ***search overhead factor*** of the parallel system is defined as the ratio of the work done by the parallel formulation to that done by the sequential formulation, or W_p/W. Thus, the upper bound on speedup for the parallel system is given by $p \times (W/W_p)$. The actual speedup, however, may be less due to other parallel processing overhead. In most parallel search algorithms, the search overhead factor is greater than one. However, in some cases, it may be less than one, leading to superlinear speedup. If the search overhead factor is less than one on the average, then it indicates that the serial search algorithm is not the fastest algorithm for solving the problem.

To simplify our presentation and analysis, we assume that the time to expand each node is the same, and W and W_p are the number of nodes expanded by the serial and the parallel formulations, respectively. If the time for each expansion is t_c, then the sequential run time is given by $T_S = t_c W$. In the remainder of the chapter, we assume that $t_c = 1$. Hence, the problem size W and the serial run time T_s become the same.

8.4 Parallel Depth-First Search

This section discusses parallel algorithms for depth-first search. To simplify the discussion, we focus on the case of simple backtracking. Parallel formulations of depth-first branch-and-bound and IDA* are similar and are discussed in Sections 8.4.7 and 8.4.8.

The critical issue in such algorithms is the distribution of the search space among the processors. Consider the tree shown in Figure 8.7. Note that the left subtree (rooted at node A) can be searched in parallel with the right subtree (rooted at node B). By statically assigning a node in the tree to a processor, it is possible to expand the whole subtree rooted at that node without communicating with another processor. Thus, it seems that such a static allocation yields a good parallel search algorithm.

Let us see what happens if we try to apply this approach to the tree in Figure 8.7. Assume that we have two processors. The root node is expanded to generate two nodes (A and B), and each of these nodes is assigned to one of the processors. Each processor now searches the subtrees rooted at its assigned node independently. At this point, the problem with static node assignment becomes apparent. The processor exploring the subtree rooted at node A expands considerably fewer nodes than does the other processor. Due to this imbalance in the work load, one processor is idle for a significant amount of time, reducing efficiency. Using more processors worsens the imbalance. Consider the partitioning of the tree for four processors. Nodes A and B are expanded to generate nodes C, D, E, and F. Assume that each of these nodes is assigned to one of the four processors. Now the processor searching the subtree rooted at node E does most of the work, and those searching the subtrees rooted at nodes C and D spend most of their time idle. The static partitioning of unstructured trees yields poor performance because of substantial variation in the size of partitions of the search space rooted at different nodes. Furthermore, since the search space is usually generated dynamically, it is difficult to get a good estimate of the size of the search space beforehand. Therefore, it is necessary to balance the search space among processors dynamically.

In ***dynamic load balancing***, when a processor runs out of work, it gets more work from another processor that has work. Consider the two-processor partitioning of the tree in Figure 8.7(a). Assume that nodes A and B are assigned to the two processors as we just described. In this case when the processor searching the subtree rooted at node A runs out of work, it requests work from the other processor. Although the dynamic distribution of work results in communication overhead for work requests and work transfers, it reduces load imbalance among processors. This section explores several schemes for dynamically balancing the load between processors.

A parallel formulation of DFS based on dynamic load balancing is as follows. Each processor performs DFS on a disjoint part of the search space. After a processor finishes searching its part of the search space, it requests an unsearched part from other processors. Whenever any processor finds a goal node, all the processors terminate. If the search space is finite and has no solutions, then all the processors eventually run out of work, and the algorithm terminates.

Since each processor searches the state space depth-first, unexplored states can be conveniently stored as a stack. Each processor maintains its own local stack on which it executes DFS. When a processor's local stack is empty, it requests untried alternatives from another processor's stack. In the beginning, the entire search space is assigned to one processor, and other processors are assigned null search spaces (that is, empty stacks). The search space is distributed among the processors as they request work. We refer to the processor that sends work as the ***donor*** processor and to the processor that requests and receives work as the ***recipient*** processor.

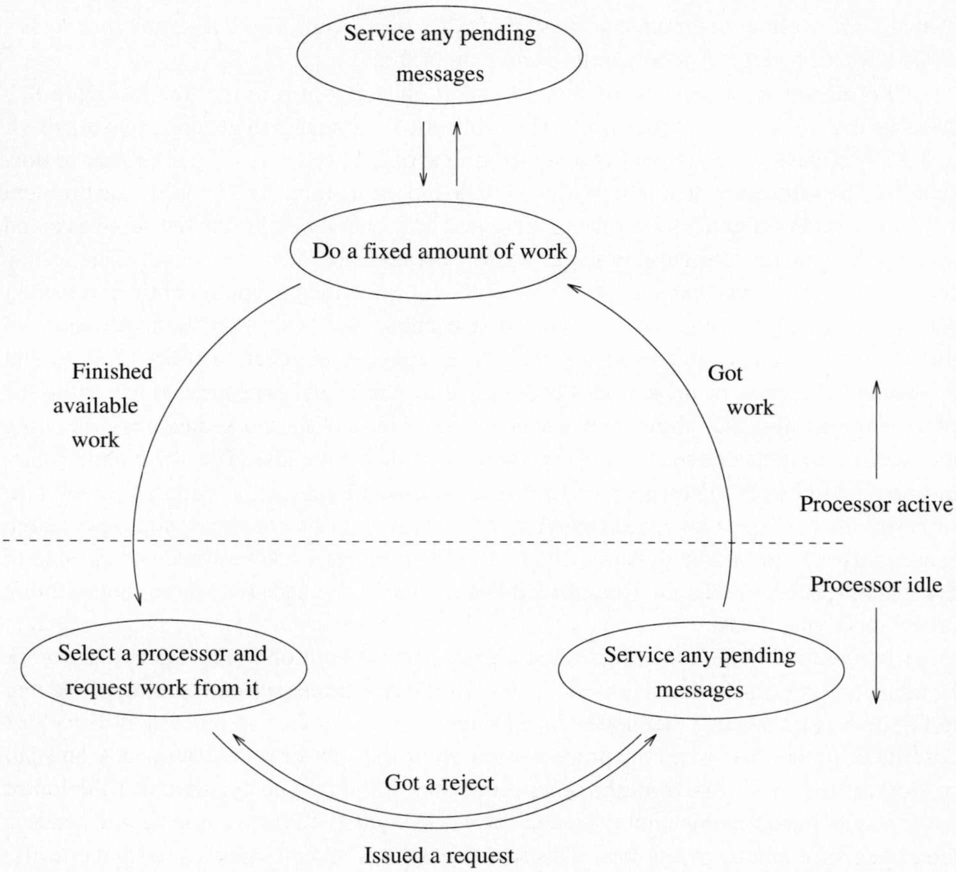

Figure 8.8 A generic scheme for dynamic load balancing.

As illustrated in Figure 8.8, each processor can be in one of two states: *active* (that is, it has work) or *idle* (that is, it is trying to get work). An idle processor selects a donor processor and sends it a work request. If the idle processor receives work (part of the state space to be searched) from the donor processor, it becomes active. If it receives a *reject* message (because the donor has no work), it selects another donor and sends a work request to that donor. This process repeats until the processor gets work or all the processors become idle. When a processor is idle and it receives a work request, that processor returns a *reject* message.

In the active state, a processor does a fixed amount of work (expands a fixed number of nodes) and then checks for pending work requests. When a work request is received, the processor partitions its work into two parts and sends one part to the requesting processor. When a processor has exhausted its own search space, it becomes idle. This process continues until a solution is found or until the entire space has been searched. If a solution is found, a message is broadcast to all processors to stop searching. A termination detection algorithm is used to detect whether all processors have become idle without finding a solution (Section 8.4.5).

8.4.1 Important Parameters of Parallel DFS

Two characteristics of parallel DFS are critical to determining its performance. First is the method for splitting work at a processor, and the second is the scheme to determine the donor processor when a processor becomes idle.

Work-Splitting Strategies

When work is transferred, the donor's stack is split into two stacks, one of which is sent to the recipient. In other words, some of the nodes (that is, alternatives) are removed from the donor's stack and added to the recipient's stack. If too little work is sent, the recipient quickly becomes idle; if too much, the donor becomes idle. Ideally, the stack is split into two equal pieces such that the size of the search space represented by each stack is the same. Such a split is called a ***half-split***. It is difficult to get a good estimate of the size of the tree rooted at an unexpanded alternative in the stack. However, the alternatives near the bottom of the stack (that is, close to the initial node) tend to have bigger trees rooted at them, and alternatives near the top of the stack tend to have small trees rooted at them. To avoid sending very small amounts of work, nodes beyond a specified stack depth are not given away. This depth is called the ***cutoff depth***.

Some possible strategies for splitting the search space are (1) send nodes near the bottom of the stack, (2) send nodes near the cutoff depth, and (3) send half the nodes between the bottom of the stack and the cutoff depth. The suitability of a splitting strategy depends on the nature of the search space. If the search space is uniform, both strategies 1 and 3 work well. If the search space is highly irregular, strategy 3 usually works well. If a strong heuristic is available (to order successors so that goal nodes move to the left of the state-space tree), strategy 2 is likely to perform better, since it tries to distribute those parts of the search space likely to contain a solution. The cost of splitting also becomes important if the stacks are deep. For such stacks, strategy 1 has lower cost than strategies 2 and 3.

Figure 8.9 shows the partitioning of the DFS tree of Figure 8.5(a) into two subtrees using strategy 3. Note that the states beyond the cutoff depth are not partitioned. Figure 8.9 also shows the representation of the stack corresponding to the two subtrees. The stack representation used in the figure stores only the unexplored alternatives.

Load-Balancing Schemes

This section discusses three dynamic load-balancing schemes: asynchronous round robin, global round robin, and random polling.

Asynchronous Round Robin In asynchronous round robin (ARR), each processor maintains an independent variable, *target*. Whenever a processor runs out of work, it uses

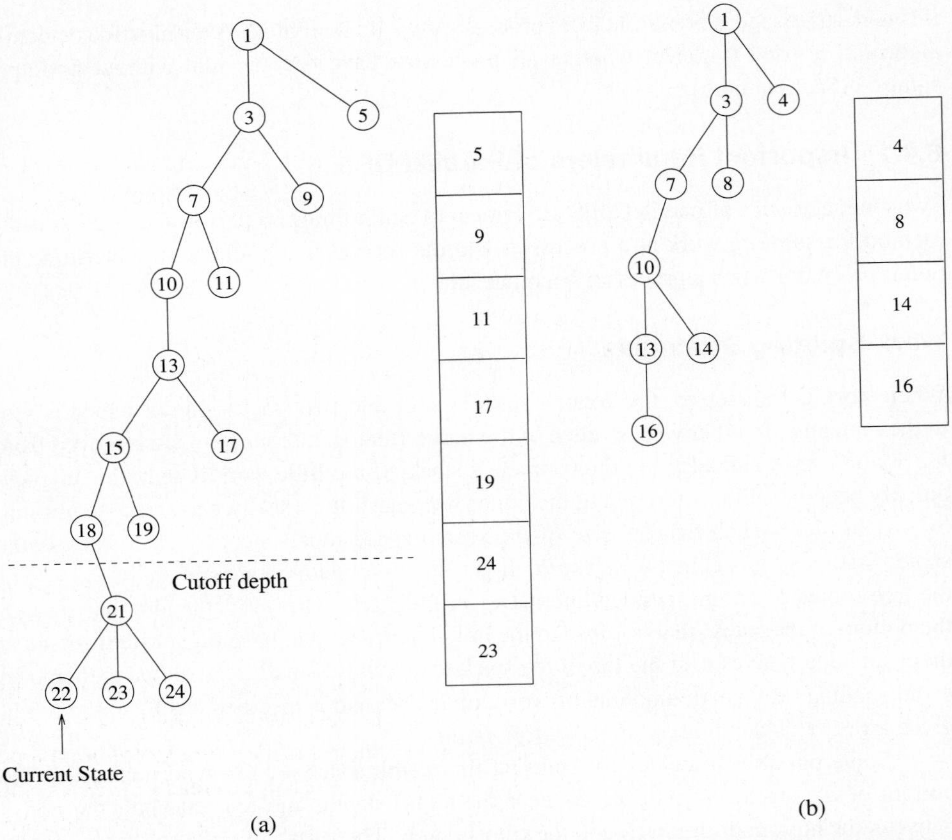

Figure 8.9 Splitting the DFS tree in Figure 8.5. The two subtrees along with their stack representations are shown in (a) and (b).

target as the label of a donor processor and sends it a work request. The value of the *target* is incremented (modulo p) each time a work request is sent. The initial value of *target* at each processor is set to $((label + 1) \text{ modulo } p)$ where *label* is the local processor label. Note that work requests are generated independently by each processor. However, it is possible for two or more processors to request work from the same donor at nearly the same time.

Global Round Robin Global round robin (GRR) uses a single global variable called *target*, stored at processor P_0. Whenever a processor needs work, it requests and receives the value of *target* from P_0; then P_0 increments *target* (modulo p) before responding to another request. The recipient processor then sends a request to the donor whose label is the value of *target* received from processor P_0. GRR ensures that successive work requests are distributed evenly over all processors. A drawback of this scheme is the contention at processor P_0 for access to *target*.

Random Polling Random polling (RP) is the simplest load-balancing scheme. When a processor becomes idle, it randomly selects a donor. Each processor is selected as a donor with equal probability, ensuring that work requests are evenly distributed.

8.4.2 A General Framework for Analysis of Parallel DFS

To analyze the performance and scalability of parallel DFS algorithms for any load-balancing scheme, we must compute the overhead T_o of the algorithm. Overhead in any load-balancing scheme is due to communication (requesting and sending work), idle time (waiting for work), termination detection, and contention for shared resources. If the search overhead factor is greater than one (that is, if parallel search does more work than serial search), this will add another term to T_o. In this section we assume that the search overhead factor is one. We analyze the case in which the search overhead factor is other than one in Section 8.6.1.

For the load-balancing schemes discussed in Section 8.4.1, idle time is subsumed by communication overhead due to work requests and transfers. When a processor becomes idle, it immediately selects a donor processor and sends it a work request. The total time that the processor remains idle is equal to the time for the request to reach the donor and for the reply to arrive. At that point, the idle processor either becomes busy or generates another work request. Therefore, the time spent in communication subsumes the time that a processor is idle. Since communication overhead is the dominant overhead in parallel DFS, we next consider a method to compute the communication overhead for each load-balancing scheme.

It is difficult to derive a precise expression for the communication overhead of the load-balancing schemes for DFS because they are dynamic. This section describes a technique that provides an upper bound on this overhead. We make the following assumptions in the analysis.

(1) The work at any processor can be partitioned into independent pieces as long as its size exceeds a threshold ϵ.

(2) A reasonable work-splitting mechanism is available. Assume that work w at one processor is partitioned into two parts: ψw and $(1 - \psi)w$ for $0 \leq \psi \leq 1$. Then there exists an arbitrarily small constant α ($0 < \alpha \leq 0.5$), such that $\psi w > \alpha w$ and $(1 - \psi)w > \alpha w$. We call such a splitting mechanism ***α-splitting***. The constant α sets a lower bound on the load imbalance that results from work splitting: both partitions of w have at least αw work.

The first assumption is satisfied by most depth-first search algorithms. The third work-splitting strategy described in Section 8.4.1 results in α-splitting even for highly irregular search spaces.

In the load-balancing schemes to be analyzed, the total work is dynamically partitioned among the processors. Processors work on disjoint parts of the search space independently. An idle processor polls for work. When it finds a donor processor with work, the work is split and a part of it is transferred to the idle processor. If the donor has work w_i, and it is split into two pieces of size w_j and w_k, then assumption 2 states that there is a constant α such that $w_j > \alpha w_i$ and $w_k > \alpha w_i$. Note that α is less than 0.5. Therefore, after a work transfer, neither processor (donor and recipient) has more than $(1 - \alpha)w_i$ work. Suppose there are p pieces of work whose sizes are $w_0, w_1, \ldots, w_{p-1}$. Assume that the size of the largest piece is w. If all of these pieces are split, the splitting strategy yields $2p$ pieces of work whose sizes are given by $\psi_0 w_0, \psi_1 w_1, \ldots, \psi_{p-1} w_{p-1}, (1-\psi_0)w_0, (1-\psi_1)w_1, \ldots, (1-\psi_{p-1})w_{p-1}$. Among them, the size of the largest piece is given by $(1 - \alpha)w$.

Assume that there are p processors and a single piece of work is assigned to each processor. If every processor receives a work request at least once, then each of these p pieces has been split at least once. Thus, the maximum work at any of the processors has been reduced by a factor of $(1 - \alpha)$. We define $V(p)$ such that, after every $V(p)$ work requests, each processor receives at least one work request. Note that $V(p) \geq p$. In general, $V(p)$ depends on the load-balancing algorithm. Initially, processor P_0 has W units of work, and all other processors have no work. After $V(p)$ requests, the maximum work remaining at any processor is less than $(1-\alpha)W$; after $2V(p)$ requests, the maximum work remaining at any processor is less than $(1 - \alpha)^2 W$. Similarly, after $(\log_{1/(1-\alpha)}(W/\epsilon))V(p)$ requests, the maximum work remaining at any processor is below a threshold value ϵ. Hence, the total number of work requests is $O(V(p) \log W)$.

Communication overhead is caused by work requests and work transfers. The total number of work transfers cannot exceed the total number of work requests. Therefore, the total number of work requests, weighted by the total communication cost of one work request and a corresponding work transfer, gives an upper bound on the total communication overhead. For simplicity, we assume the message size of the work request and work transfer to be constant. In general, the size of the stack should grow logarithmically with respect to the size of the search space. The analysis for this case can be done similarly (Problem 8.4).

If t_{comm} is the time required to send a piece of work, then the communication overhead T_o is given by

$$T_o = t_{comm} V(p) \log W \tag{8.2}$$

The corresponding efficiency E is given by

$$E = \frac{1}{1 + T_o/W}$$

$$= \frac{1}{1 + (t_{comm} V(p) \log W)/W}$$

Our goal is to derive isoefficiency functions for each load-balancing scheme on different parallel architectures (we focus on the hypercube and network of workstations). In Section 4.4 we showed that the isoefficiency function can be derived by balancing the problem size W and the overhead function T_o. As shown by Equation 8.2, T_o depends on two values: t_{comm} and $V(p)$. The value of t_{comm} is determined by the parallel architecture, and the function $V(p)$ is determined by the load-balancing scheme. In the following subsections, we derive $V(p)$ for each scheme introduced in Section 8.4.1. Then in Sections 8.4.3 and 8.4.4 we apply these results to hypercubes and networks of workstations respectively.

Computation of V(p) for Various Load-Balancing Schemes

Equation 8.2 shows that $V(p)$ is an important component of the total communication overhead. In this section, we compute the value of $V(p)$ for different load-balancing schemes.

Asynchronous Round Robin The worst case value of $V(p)$ for ARR occurs when all processors send work requests at the same time to the same processor. This case is illustrated in the following scenario. Assume that processor $p-1$ had all the work and that the local counters of all the other processors (0 to $p-2$) were pointing to processor zero. In this case, for processor $p-1$ to receive a work request, one processor must send $p-1$ requests while each of the remaining $p-2$ processors generate up to $p-2$ work requests (to all processors except processor $p-1$ and itself). Thus, $V(p)$ has an upper bound of $(p-1)+(p-2)(p-2)$; that is, $V(p) = O(p^2)$. Note that the actual value of $V(p)$ is between p and p^2.

Global Round Robin In GRR, all processors receive requests in sequence. After p requests, each processor has received one request. Therefore, $V(p)$ is p.

Random Polling For RR, the worst-case value of $V(p)$ is unbounded. Hence, we compute the average-case value of $V(p)$.

Consider a collection of p boxes. In each trial, a box is chosen at random and marked. We are interested in the mean number of trials required to mark all the boxes. In our algorithm, each trial corresponds to a processor sending another randomly selected processor a request for work.

Let $F(i, p)$ represent a state in which i of the p boxes have been marked, and $p-i$ boxes have not been marked. Since the next box to be marked is picked at random, there is i/p probability that it will be a marked box and $(p-i)/p$ probability that it will be an unmarked box. Hence the system remains in state $F(i, p)$ with a probability of i/p and transits to state $F(i+1, p)$ with a probability of $(p-i)/p$. Let $f(i, p)$ denote the average number of trials needed to change from state $F(i, p)$ to $F(p, p)$. Then, $V(p) = f(0, p)$.

We have

$$\begin{aligned} f(i,p) &= \frac{i}{p}(1+f(i,p)) + \frac{p-i}{p}(1+f(i+1,p)), \\ \frac{p-i}{p} f(i,p) &= 1 + \frac{p-i}{p} f(i+1,p), \\ f(i,p) &= \frac{p}{p-i} + f(i+1,p). \end{aligned}$$

Hence,

$$\begin{aligned} f(0,p) &= p \times \sum_{i=0}^{p-1} \frac{1}{p-i}, \\ &= p \times \sum_{i=1}^{p} \frac{1}{i}, \\ &= p \times H_p, \end{aligned}$$

where H_p is a harmonic number. It can be shown that, as p becomes large, $H_p \simeq 1.69 \ln p$ (where $\ln p$ denotes the natural logarithm of p). Thus, $V(p) = \Theta(p \log p)$.

8.4.3 Analysis of Load-Balancing Schemes for Hypercubes

This section analyzes the performance of the load-balancing schemes introduced in Section 8.4.1 on hypercube-connected parallel computers. We assume that work is transferred in fixed-size messages (the effect of relaxing this assumption is explored in Problem 8.4). For a hypercube, the average distance between any randomly chosen pair of processors is $\Theta(\log p)$. Therefore, the asymptotic value of $t_{comm} = \Theta(\log p)$. The communication overhead T_o (Equation 8.2) reduces to

$$T_o = O(V(p) \log p \log W). \tag{8.3}$$

We balance this overhead with problem size W for each load-balancing scheme to derive the isoefficiency function due to communication.

Asynchronous Round Robin

As discussed in Section 8.4.2, $V(p)$ for ARR is $O(p^2)$. Substituting into Equation 8.3, communication overhead T_o is given by $O(p^2 \log p \log W)$. Balancing communication overhead against problem size W, we have

$$W = O(p^2 \log p \log W).$$

Substituting W into the right-hand side of the same equation and simplifying

$$\begin{aligned} W &= O(p^2 \log p \log(p^2 \log p \log W)), \\ &= O(p^2 \log p \log p + p^2 \log p \log\log p + p^2 \log p \log\log W). \end{aligned}$$

The double-log terms ($\log \log p$ and $\log \log W$) are asymptotically smaller than the first term and can be ignored. The isoefficiency function for this scheme is therefore given by $O(p^2 \log^2 p)$.

Global Round Robin

From Section 8.4.2, $V(p) = \Theta(p)$ for GRR. Substituting into Equation 8.3, this yields a communication overhead T_o of $O(p \log p \log W)$. Simplifying as for ARR, the isoefficiency function for this scheme due to communication overhead is $O(p \log^2 p)$.

In this scheme, however, the global variable *target* is accessed repeatedly, possibly causing contention. The number of times this variable is accessed is equal to the total number of work requests, $O(p \log W)$. If the processors are used efficiently, the total execution time is $\Theta(W/p)$. Assume that there is no contention for *target* while solving a problem of size W on p processors. Then, W/p is larger than the total time during which the shared variable is accessed. As the number of processors increases, the execution time (W/p) decreases, but the number of times the shared variable is accessed increases. Thus, there is a crossover point beyond which the shared variable becomes a bottleneck, prohibiting further reduction in run time. This bottleneck can be eliminated by increasing W at a rate such that the ratio between W/p and $O(p \log W)$ remains constant. This requires W to grow with respect to p as follows:

$$\frac{W}{p} = O(p \log W) \tag{8.4}$$

We can simplify Equation 8.4 to express W in terms of p. This yields an isoefficiency term of $O(p^2 \log p)$.

Since the isoefficiency function due to contention asymptotically dominates the isoefficiency function due to communication, the overall isoefficiency function is given by $O(p^2 \log p)$. Note that although it is difficult to estimate the actual overhead due to contention for the shared variable, we are able to determine the resulting isoefficiency function.

Random Polling

We saw in Section 8.4.2 that $V(p) = \Theta(p \log p)$ for RP. Substituting this value into Equation 8.3, the communication overhead T_o is $O(p \log^2 p \log W)$. Equating T_o with the problem size W and simplifying as before, we derive the isoefficiency function due to communication overhead as $O(p \log^3 p)$. Since there is no contention in RP, this function also gives its overall isoefficiency function.

The Effect of Machine Characteristics on the Isoefficiency Function

For the processors available in current parallel computers, asymptotic communication costs can differ from actual communication costs. In such cases, we use a more precise expression for communication cost.

In the preceding analysis, we had assumed $t_{comm} = \Theta(\log p)$. On a hypercube with cut-through routing, the time to communicate a message of m words between a pair of processors $\log p$ hops apart is given by $t_s + mt_w + t_h \log p$ (Section 2.7.2). Since we assume fixed-size messages, the communication time is $k + t_h \log p$, where k is a constant. Although asymptotically $(k + t_h \log p)$ is $\Theta(\log p)$, for practical values of t_s and message size m, in many cases, $t_s + mt_w$ dominates $t_h \log p$. Consequently, the approximate message transfer time is $t_s + mt_w$, which is a constant assuming a constant message size m. For practical configurations of such a machine, t_{comm} is thus $\Theta(1)$ rather than $\Theta(\log p)$ for ARR, GRR, and RP.

For both RP and ARR, the dominant isoefficiency term is due to communication; thus, reducing t_{comm} to $\Theta(1)$ decreases the isoefficiency functions of both schemes by a log factor. The isoefficiency functions of RP and ARR are thus $O(p \log^2 p)$ and $O(p^2 \log p)$, respectively. However, the dominant isoefficiency term in GRR is due to contention, which is not affected by this machine characteristic, so its isoefficiency function remains $O(p^2 \log p)$.

8.4.4 Analysis of Load-Balancing Schemes for a Network of Workstations

In this section, we analyze the scalability of the load-balancing schemes on a network of workstations. We assume that the workstations are connected by an Ethernet; that is, the time to deliver a fixed-size message between any pair of processors is constant. The limited bandwidth of the Ethernet imposes an upper bound on the number of messages that can be handled in a given period of time. As the number of processors increases, the total traffic on the network also increases, causing contention over the Ethernet.

Since message delivery time is constant, t_{comm} is given by $\Theta(1)$. Substituting into Equation 8.2, the communication overhead is given by

$$T_o = O(V(p) \log W) \tag{8.5}$$

We use this equation to derive the isoefficiency term, resulting from the communication, for each load-balancing scheme. The contention over the shared bus cannot be expressed in a closed form, so we use the isoefficiency function to characterize the overhead due to bus contention.

Asynchronous Round Robin From Section 8.4.2, $V(p) = O(p^2)$ for ARR. Substituting $V(p)$ into Equation 8.5, the communication overhead T_o is $O(p^2 \log W)$. Equating communication overhead with problem size W and simplifying as before, the isoefficiency term due to communication for ARR is $O(p^2 \log p)$.

For the isoefficiency term due to bus contention, we use an analysis similar to that for analyzing the contention for the *target* variable in GRR on the hypercube. The total number of messages on the bus over the entire execution is given by $O(V(p) \log W)$. If the processors are utilized efficiently, the total execution time is $\Theta(W/p)$. Thus, W must grow at least at a rate such that the ratio of $O(V(p) \log W)$ and $\Theta(W/p)$ remains constant.

Substituting for $V(p)$ and equating these two terms yields an isoefficiency term due to contention of $O(p^3 \log p)$.

Since the isoefficiency term resulting from bus contention dominates that due to communication, the overall isoefficiency function of ARR is $O(p^3 \log p)$.

Global Round Robin For GRR, Section 8.4.2 showed that $V(p) = \Theta(p)$. Substituting $V(p)$ into Equation 8.5 the communication overhead T_o is $O(p \log W)$. Equating communication overhead with problem size and simplifying as before, the isoefficiency term due to communication for GRR is $O(p \log p)$.

Consider the isoefficiency term resulting from contention at processor P_0. This processor handles $V(p) \log W$ requests for the value of *target*, in $\Theta(W/p)$ time. Equating the time $\Theta(W/p)$ with the number of messages $\Theta(p \log W)$ and simplifying yields an isoefficiency term of $O(p^2 \log p)$. Using a similar analysis, the isoefficiency term resulting from bus contention is also $O(p^2 \log p)$. Thus, the overall isoefficiency function of GRR is $O(p^2 \log p)$.

Random Polling The value of $V(p)$ for RP is $\Theta(p \log p)$ (Section 8.4.2). Substituting $V(p)$ into Equation 8.5, RP has a communication overhead T_o of $O(p \log p \log W)$ and a corresponding isoefficiency term of $O(p \log^2 p)$.

For isoefficiency term resulting from bus contention, we equate the total number of messages with the parallel run time. The total number of messages is $O(V(p) \log W)$, and the time (assuming good efficiency) is $\Theta(W/p)$. Substituting for $V(p)$ and equating these two terms yields the isoefficiency term resulting from contention, $O(p^2 \log^2 p)$. Since the isoefficiency term resulting from contention asymptotically dominates the isoefficiency term due to communication, the overall isoefficiency function is $O(p^2 \log^2 p)$.

Table 8.1 presents isoefficiency terms for communication and contention, and overall isoefficiency functions for a network of workstations and a hypercube. The isoefficiency analysis of ARR, GRR, and RP can be done for ring and mesh similarly. Table 8.2 gives the isoefficiency functions of three schemes for various architectures.

8.4.5 Termination Detection

One aspect of parallel DFS that has not been addressed so far is termination detection. In this section, we present two schemes for termination detection that can be used with the load-balancing algorithms discussed in Section 8.4.1.

Dijkstra's Token Termination Detection Algorithm

Consider a simplified scenario in which once a processor goes idle, it never receives more work. Visualize the p processors as being connected in a ring (note that it is possible to embed a ring into a large class of networks such as mesh and hypercube as shown in Section 2.5). Processor P_0 initiates a token when it becomes idle. This token is sent to the next processor in the ring, P_1. At any stage in the computation, if a processor receives a token, the token is held at the processor until the computation assigned to the processor is complete. On completion, the token is passed to the next processor in the ring. If the processor was already idle, the token is passed to the next processor. Note that if at any time the token is passed to processor P_i, then all processors $P_0, \ldots, P_{i-1}$ have completed their computation. Processor P_{p-1} passes its token to processor P_0; when it receives the token, processor P_0 knows that all processors have completed their computation and the algorithm can terminate.

Such a simple scheme cannot be applied to the search algorithms described in this chapter, because after a processor goes idle, it may receive more work from other processors. The token termination detection scheme thus must be modified.

In the modified scheme, the processors are also organized into a ring. A processor can be in one of two states: *black* or *white*. Initially, all processors are in state *white*. As before, the token travels in the sequence $P_0, P_1, \ldots, P_{p-1}, P_0$. If the only work transfers allowed in the system are from processor P_i to P_j such that $i < j$, then the simple termination scheme is still adequate. However, if processor P_j sends work to processor P_i, the token must traverse the ring again. In this case processor P_j is marked *black* since it causes the token to go around the ring again. Processor P_0 must be able to tell by looking at the token it receives whether it should be propagated around the ring again. Therefore the token itself is of two types. A *white* (or valid) token, which when received by processor P_0 implies termination; and a *black* (or invalid) token, which implies that the token must traverse the ring again. The modified termination algorithm works as follows:

(1) When it becomes idle, processor P_0 initiates termination detection by making itself *white* and sending a *white* token to processor P_1.
(2) If processor P_i sends work to processor P_j and $i > j$ then processor P_i becomes *black*.

Table 8.1 Various overheads for load-balancing over a network of workstations (WS) and a hypercube, and their corresponding isoefficiency terms.

		Isoefficiency terms			
Architecture	**Scheme**	**Communication**	**Contention (shared data)**	**Contention (bus)**	**Isoefficiency function**
	ARR	$O(p^2 \log p)$		$O(p^3 \log p)$	$O(p^3 \log p)$
WS	GRR	$O(p \log p)$	$O(p^2 \log p)$	$O(p^2 \log p)$	$O(p^2 \log p)$
	RP	$O(p \log^2 p)$		$O(p^2 \log^2 p)$	$O(p^2 \log^2 p)$
	ARR	$O(p^2 \log^2 p)$			$O(p^2 \log^2 p)$
Hypercube	GRR	$O(p \log^2 p)$	$O(p^2 \log p)$		$O(p^2 \log p)$
	RP	$O(p \log^3 p)$			$O(p \log^3 p)$

Table 8.2 The isoefficiency function of load-balancing schemes for a hypercube, a ring, a mesh, and a network of workstations (WS).

	Scheme		
Architecture	**ARR**	**GRR**	**RP**
Hypercube	$O(p^2 \log^2 p)$	$O(p^2 \log p)$	$O(p \log^3 p)$
Ring	$O(p^3 \log p)$	$O(p^2 \log p)$	$O(p^2 \log^2 p)$
Mesh	$O(p^{2.5} \log p)$	$O(p^2 \log p)$	$O(p^{1.5} \log^2 p)$
WS	$O(p^3 \log p)$	$O(p^2 \log p)$	$O(p^2 \log^2 p)$

(3) If processor P_i has the token and P_i is idle, then it passes the token to P_{i+1}. If P_i is *black*, then the color of the token is set to *black* before it is sent to P_{i+1}. If P_i is *white*, the token is passed unchanged.
(4) After P_i passes the token to P_{i+1}, P_i becomes *white*.

The algorithm terminates when processor P_0 receives a *white* token. The algorithm correctly detects termination by accounting for the possibility of a processor receiving work after already having been accounted for by the token.

The run time of this algorithm is $O(P)$ with a small constant. For a small number of processors, this scheme can be used without a significant impact on the overall performance. For a large number of processors, this algorithm can cause the overall isoefficiency function of the load-balancing scheme to be at least $O(p^2)$ (Problem 8.5).

Tree-Based Termination Detection

Tree-based termination detection associates weights with individual work pieces. Initially processor P_0 has all the work and a weight of one is associated with it. When its work is partitioned and sent to another processor, processor P_0 retains half of the weight and gives half of it to the processor receiving the work. If P_i is the recipient processor and w_i is the weight at processor P_i, then after the first work transfer, both w_0 and w_i are 0.5. Each time the work at a processor is partitioned, the weight is halved. When a processor completes its computation, it returns its weight to the processor from which it received work. Termination is signaled when the weight w_0 at processor P_0 becomes one and processor P_0 has finished its work.

Example 8.7 Tree-based Termination Detection
Figure 8.10 illustrates tree based termination detection for four processors. Initially, processor P_0 has all the weight ($w_0 = 1$), and the weight at the remaining processors is 0 ($w_1 = w_2 = w_3 = 0$). In step 1, processor P_0 partitions its work and gives part of it to processor P_1. After this step, w_0 and w_1 are 0.5 and w_2 and w_3 are 0. In step

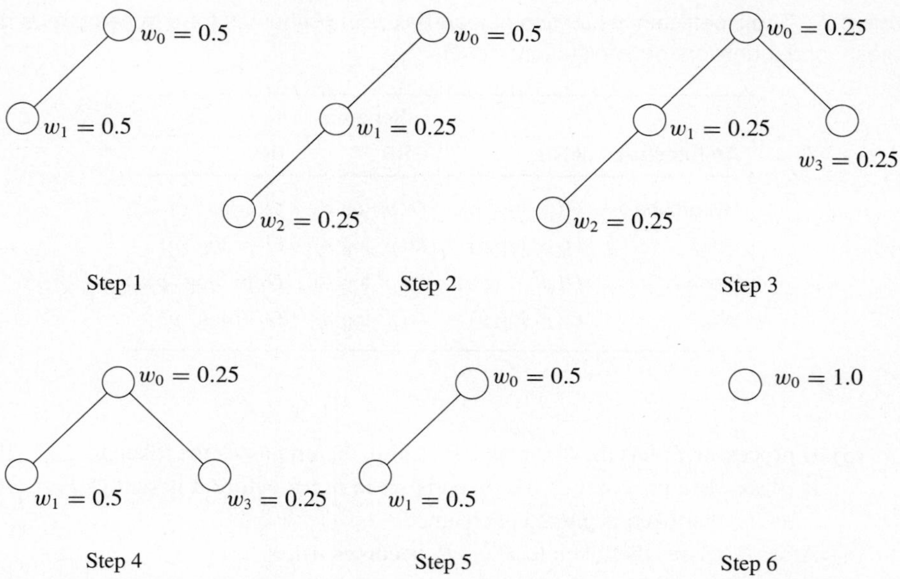

Figure 8.10 Tree based terminations detection. Steps 1–6 illustrate the weights at various processors after each work transfer.

2, processor P_1 gives half of its work to processor P_2. The weights w_1 and w_2 after this work transfer are 0.25 and the weights w_0 and w_3 remain unchanged. In step 3, processor P_3 gets work from processor P_1 and the weights of all processors become 0.25. In step 4, processor P_2 completes its work and sends its weight to processor P_1. The weight w_1 of processor P_1 becomes 0.5. As processors complete their work, weights are propagated up the tree until the weight w_0 at processor P_0 becomes 1. At this point, all work has been completed and termination can be signaled. ■

This termination detection algorithm has a significant drawback. Due to the finite precision of computers, recursive halving of the weight may make the weight so small that it becomes 0. In this case, weight will be lost and termination will never be signaled. This condition can be alleviated by using the inverse of the weights. If processor P_i has weight w_i, instead of manipulating the weight itself, it manipulates $1/w_i$. The details of this algorithm are considered in Problem 8.6.

The tree-based termination detection algorithm does not change the overall isoefficiency function of any of the search schemes we have considered. This follows from the fact that there are exactly two weight transfers associated with each work transfer. Therefore, the algorithm has the effect of increasing the communication overhead by a constant factor. In asymptotic terms, this change does not alter the isoefficiency function.

Table 8.3 Average Speedups for various load-balancing schemes.

	Number of processors							
Scheme	8	16	32	64	128	256	512	1024
ARR	7.506	14.936	29.664	57.721	103.738	178.92	259.372	284.425
GRR	7.384	14.734	29.291	57.729	110.754	184.828	155.051	
RP	7.524	15.000	29.814	58.857	114.645	218.255	397.585	660.582

8.4.6 Experimental Results

In this section, we demonstrate the validity of scalability analysis for various parallel DFS algorithms. The satisfiability problem tests the validity of boolean formulae. Such problems arise in areas such as VLSI design and theorem proving. The ***satisfiability problem*** can be stated as follows: given a boolean formula containing binary variables in conjunctive normal form, determine if it is unsatisfiable. A boolean formula is unsatisfiable if there exists no assignment of truth values to variables for which the formula is true.

The Davis-Putnam algorithm is a fast and efficient way to solve this problem. The algorithm works by performing a depth-first search of the binary tree formed by true or false assignments to the literals in the boolean expression. Let n be the number of literals. Then the maximum depth of the tree cannot exceed n. If, after a partial assignment of values to literals, the formula becomes false, then the algorithm backtracks. The formula is unsatisfiable, if depth-first search fails to find an assignment to variables for which the formula is true.

Even if a formula is unsatisfiable, only a small subset of the 2^n possible combinations will actually be explored. For example, for a 65-variable problem, the total number of possible combinations is 2^{65} (approximately 3.7×10^{19}), but only about 10^7 nodes are actually expanded in a specific problem instance. The search tree for this problem is pruned in a highly nonuniform fashion and any attempt to partition the tree statically results in an extremely poor load balance.

The satisfiability problem is used to test the load-balancing schemes on the nCUBE 2 parallel computer for up to 1024 processors. Recall from Chapter 2 that the nCUBE 2 is a MIMD parallel computer with a hypercube interconnection network. We implemented the Davis-Putnam algorithm, and incorporated the load-balancing algorithms discussed in Section 8.4.1. This program was run on several unsatisfiable formulae. By choosing unsatisfiable instances, we ensured that the number of nodes expanded by the parallel formulation is the same as the number expanded by the sequential one; any speedup loss was due only to the overhead of load balancing.

In the problem instances on which the program was tested, the total number of nodes in the tree varied between approximately 100 thousand and 10 million. The depth of the trees (which is equal to the number of variables in the formula) varied between 35 and 65.

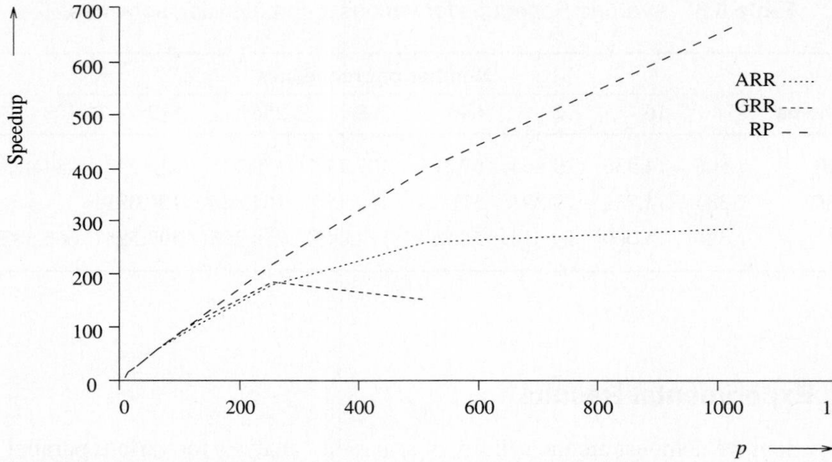

Figure 8.11 Speedups of parallel DFS using ARR, GRR and RP load-balancing schemes.

Speedup was calculated with respect to the optimum sequential execution time for the same problem. Average speedup was calculated by taking the ratio of the cumulative time to solve all the problems in parallel using a given number of processors to the corresponding cumulative sequential time. On a given number of processors, the speedup and efficiency were largely determined by the tree size (which is roughly proportional to the sequential run time). Thus, speedup on similar-sized problems were quite similar.

All schemes were tested on a sample set of five problem instances. Table 8.3 shows the average speedup obtained by parallel algorithms using different load-balancing techniques. Figure 8.11 is a graph of the speedups obtained. Table 8.4 presents the total number of work requests made by RP and GRR for one problem instance. Figure 8.12 shows the corresponding graph and compares the number of messages generated with the expected values $O(p \log^2 p)$ and $O(p \log p)$ for RP and GRR, respectively.

The isoefficiency function of GRR is $O(p^2 \log p)$ which is much worse than the isoefficiency function of RP. This is reflected in the performance of our implementation. From Figure 8.11, we see that the performance of GRR deteriorates very rapidly for more

Table 8.4 Number of requests generated for GRR and RP.

	Number of processors							
Scheme	8	16	32	64	128	256	512	1024
GRR	260	661	1572	3445	8557	17088	41382	72874
RP	562	2013	5106	15060	46056	136457	382695	885872

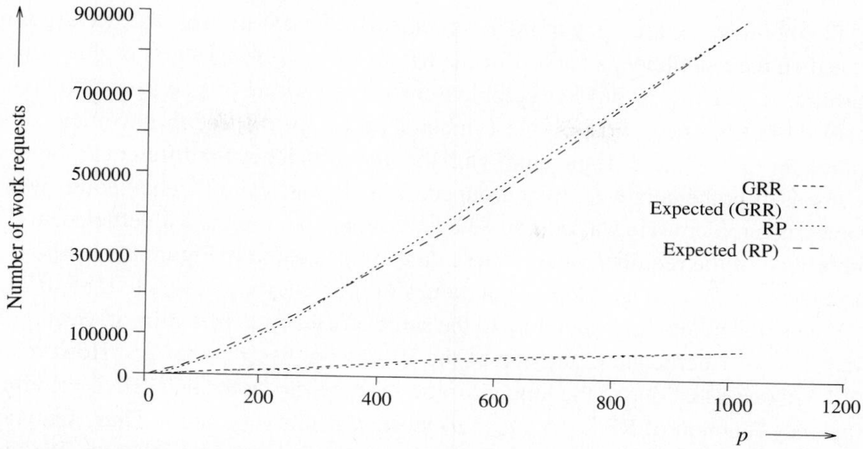

Figure 8.12 Number of work requests generated for RP and GRR and their expected values ($O(p \log p)$ and $O(p \log^2 p)$ respectively).

than 256 processors. Good speedups can be obtained for $p > 256$ only for very large problem instances. Experimental results also show that ARR is more scalable than GRR, but significantly less scalable than RP. Although the isoefficiency function of ARR is $O(p^2 \log^2 p)$ and that of GRR is $O(p^2 \log p)$, ARR performs better than GRR. The reason for this is that $p^2 \log^2 p$ is an upper bound, derived using $V(p) = O(p^2)$. This value of $V(p)$ is only a loose upper bound for ARR. In contrast, the value of $V(p)$ used for GRR ($\Theta(p)$) is a tight bound.

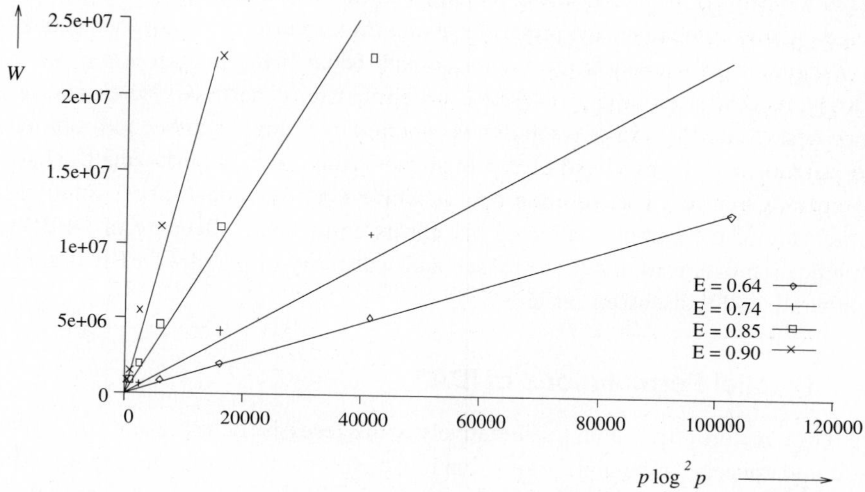

Figure 8.13 Experimental isoefficiency curves for RP for different efficiencies.

To determine the accuracy of the isoefficiency functions in Table 8.2, we experimentally verified the isoefficiency curves for the RP technique (the selection of this technique was arbitrary). We ran 30 different problem instances varying in size from 100 thousand nodes to 10 million nodes on a varying number of processors. Speedup and efficiency were computed for each of these. Data points with the same efficiency for different problem sizes and number of processors were then grouped. Where identical efficiency points were not available, the problem size was computed by averaging over points with efficiencies in the neighborhood of the required value. These data are presented in Figure 8.13, which plots the problem size W against $p \log^2 p$ for values of efficiency equal to 0.9, 0.85, 0.74, and 0.64. We expect points corresponding to the same efficiency to be collinear. Section 8.4.2 showed that the isoefficiency function of the RP scheme is $O(p \log^3 p)$. However, Section 8.4.3 showed that due to the long message startup time on the nCUBE 2, the effective isoefficiency function of RP is $O(p \log^2 p)$ when p is not very large. Thus, analytically, the points corresponding to the same efficiency on the graph must be collinear. We can see from Figure 8.13 that the points are reasonably collinear, which shows that the experimental isoefficiency function of RP is close to the theoretically derived isoefficiency function.

8.4.7 Parallel Formulations of Depth-First Branch-and-Bound Search

Parallel formulations of depth-first branch-and-bound search (DFBB) are similar to those of DFS. The preceding formulations of DFS can be applied to DFBB with one minor modification: all processors are kept informed of the current best solution path. The current best solution path for many problems can be represented by a small data structure. For shared-address-space computers, this data structure can be stored in a globally accessible memory. Each time a processor finds a solution, its cost is compared to that of the current best solution path. If the cost is lower, then the current best solution path is replaced. On a message-passing computer, each processor maintains the current best solution path known to it. Whenever a processor finds a solution path better than the current best known, it broadcasts its cost to all other processors, which update (if necessary) their current best solution cost. Since the cost of a solution is captured by a single number and solutions are found infrequently, the overhead of communicating this value is fairly small. Note that, if a processor's current best solution path is worse than the globally best solution path, the efficiency of the search is affected but not its correctness. Because of DFBB's low communication overhead, the performance and scalability of parallel DFBB is similar to that of parallel DFS discussed earlier.

8.4.8 Parallel Formulations of IDA*

Since IDA* explores the search tree iteratively with successively increasing cost bounds, it is natural to conceive a parallel formulation in which separate processors explore separate parts of the search space independently. Processors may be exploring the tree using different cost bounds. This approach suffers from two drawbacks.

(1) It is unclear how to select a threshold for a particular processor. If the threshold chosen for a processor happens to be higher than the global minimum threshold, then the processor will explore portions of the tree that are not explored by sequential IDA*.
(2) This approach may not find an optimal solution. A solution found by one processor in a particular iteration is not provably optimal until all the other processors have also exhausted the search space associated with thresholds lower than the cost of the solution found.

A more effective approach executes each iteration of IDA* by using parallel DFS (Section 8.4). All processors use the same cost bound; each processor stores the bound locally and performs DFS on its own search space. After each iteration of parallel IDA*, a designated processor determines the cost bound for the next iteration and restarts parallel DFS with the new bound. The search terminates when a processor finds a goal node and informs all the other processors. The performance and scalability of this parallel formulation of IDA* are similar to those of the parallel DFS algorithm.

8.4.9 Parallel DFS on SIMD Computers

The algorithms discussed in previous chapters are equally applicable to SIMD and MIMD computers. However, parallel DFS algorithms on SIMD computers pose two problems. First, since all processors execute identical instructions on an SIMD computer, they must all be in the same stage of node expansion. Expanding different nodes in a graph requires different amounts of computation. Furthermore, it is possible that some processors may be backtracking while others are expanding nodes. These differing activities are implemented on an SIMD computer using conditional statements as shown in Figure 2.3. Since only a subset of processors are busy for each condition, the overall execution rate on an SIMD computer is smaller than that on an MIMD computer. Second, due to the architectural constraints of SIMD computers, load balancing must be performed globally. This is in contrast to MIMD computers which can balance load among a small subset of processors while others are busy doing work. Thus, the load-balancing schemes developed for MIMD computers usually perform poorly on SIMD computers. In the following discussion, we address load-balancing schemes that are suited to SIMD computers.

At any time during the execution of DFS on an SIMD computer, all the processors are in either a ***search phase*** or a ***load-balancing phase***. In the search phase, processors perform DFS on disjoint parts of the search space, expanding nodes synchronously with other processors. When a processor finishes searching its part of the search space, it stays idle until it receives work during the next load-balancing phase. In the load-balancing phase, busy processors split their work and share it with idle processors. When a goal node is found, all processors quit. Thus, the critical components of parallel DFS on an SIMD computer are: (1) a triggering mechanism that determines when load balancing is appropriate, and (2) the load balancing mechanism itself.

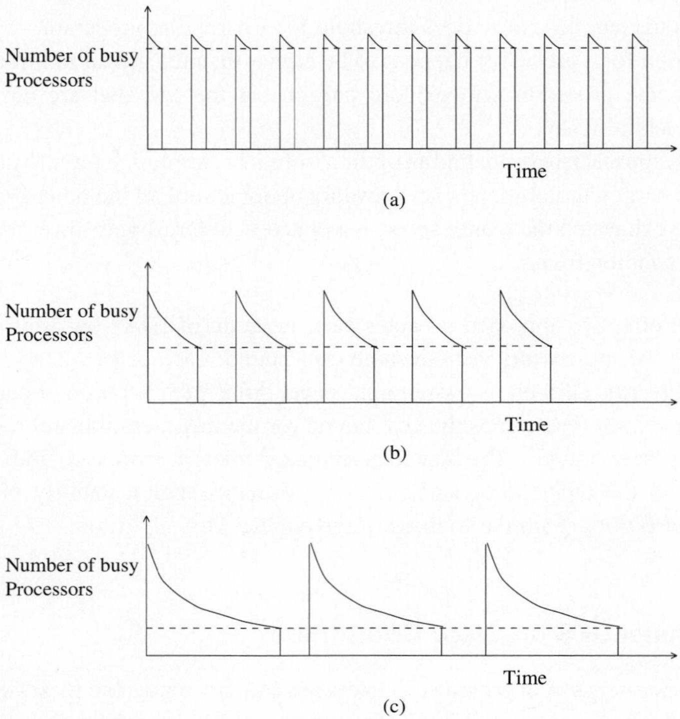

Figure 8.14 Three different triggering mechanisms: (a) a high triggering frequency leads to high load-balancing cost, (b) the optimal frequency yields good performance, and (c) a low frequency leads to high idle times.

All processors switch from the search phase to the load-balancing phase when a triggering condition is satisfied. The ***triggering frequency*** is critical to the performance of the parallel algorithm. If the triggering frequency is high, a significant fraction of the time is spent load balancing. (Figure 8.14(a)). If the frequency is low, however, the idle time becomes large (Figure 8.14(c)). In either case the performance is poor. Figure 8.14(b) illustrates a better triggering frequency for this example. A triggering mechanism may be ***static*** or ***dynamic***. Static triggering maintains a uniform criterion for entering the load-balancing phase throughout execution. An example of such a scheme is one in which the ratio of active to idle processors triggers load balancing. Whenever this ratio falls below a preset threshold, all the processors enter the load-balancing phase.

Dynamic triggering uses a trigger value that changes dynamically, adapting to the characteristics of the problem. An example of dynamic triggering is one that balances the idle time with the time spent doing load balancing. Let w_{idle} be the total idle time of all the processors since the beginning of the current search phase and t_L be the total time spent by each processor in the next load-balancing phase. Then, the cost of the next load-balancing

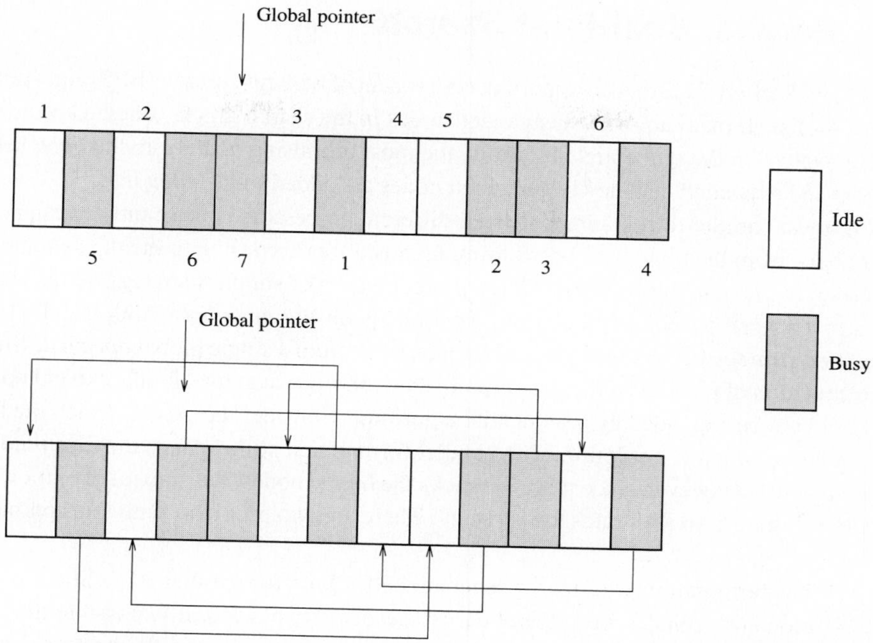

Figure 8.15 Mapping idle and busy processors with the use of a global pointer.

phase is $t_L \times p$. The condition that triggers load balancing is

$$w_{idle} \geq t_L \times p \tag{8.6}$$

Note that, if triggering takes place earlier, the load-balancing overhead will be higher than the overhead due to idling. If triggering takes place later, then idling overhead begins to dominate. Thus, this triggering scheme balances the total idle time during the search phase with the cost of the next load-balancing phase.

When a load-balancing phase begins, each idle processor must be paired with a donor processor that has work. The donor splits its work and sends part of it to the idle processor. A simple method for pairing processors enumerates those without work and those with work, and then establishes a mapping between the two sets of processors. A global pointer is maintained that points to the last processor that donated work during the previous load-balancing phase. During the load-balancing phase, busy processors are paired with idle processors, starting from the first busy processor following the one indicated by the global pointer. When the pointer reaches the last processor, it starts again from the first. This matching scheme is illustrated in Figure 8.15.

The scalability of these schemes can be analyzed by using a framework similar to that for MIMD computers. Furthermore, formulations with scalability identical to MIMD computers can be devised for SIMD computers (Problem 8.11).

8.5 Parallel Best-First Search

Recall from Section 8.2.2 that an important component of best-first search (BFS) algorithms is the *open* list. It maintains the unexpanded nodes in the search graph, ordered according to their l-value. In the sequential algorithm, the most promising node from the *open* list is removed and expanded, and newly generated nodes are added to the *open* list.

In most parallel formulations of BFS, different processors concurrently expand different nodes from the *open* list. These formulations differ according to the data structures they use to implement the *open* list. Given p processors, the simplest strategy assigns each processor to work on one of the current best nodes on the *open* list. This is called the ***centralized strategy*** because each processor gets work from a single global *open* list. Since this formulation of parallel BFS expands more than one node at a time, it may expand nodes that would not be expanded by a sequential algorithm. Consider the case in which the first node on the *open* list is a solution. The parallel formulation still expands the first p nodes on the *open* list. However, since it always picks the best p nodes, the amount of extra work is limited. Figure 8.16 illustrates this strategy. There are two problems with this approach:

(1) The termination criterion of sequential BFS fails for parallel BFS. Since at any moment, p nodes from the *open* list are being expanded, it is possible that one of the nodes may be a solution that does not correspond to the best goal node (or the path found is not the shortest path). This is because the remaining $p-1$ nodes may lead to search spaces containing better goal nodes. Therefore, if the cost of a solution found by a processor is c, then this solution is not guaranteed to correspond to the best goal node until the cost of nodes being searched at other processors is known to be at least c. The termination criterion must be modified to ensure that termination occurs only after the best solution has been found.

(2) Since the *open* list is accessed for each node expansion, it must be easily accessible to all processors. This can severely limit performance on message-passing architectures, because a message is exchanged for each node expansion. Even on shared-address-space architectures, contention for the *open* list limits speedup. Let t_{exp} be the average time to expand a single node, and t_{access} be the average time to access the *open* list for a single-node expansion. If there are n nodes to be expanded by both the sequential and parallel formulations (assuming that they do an equal amount of work), then the sequential run time is given by $n(t_{access} + t_{exp})$. Assume that it is impossible to parallelize the expansion of individual nodes. Then the parallel run time will be at least nt_{access}, because the *open* list has to be accessed at least once for each node expanded. Hence, an upper bound on the speedup is $(t_{access} + t_{exp})/t_{access}$.

One way to avoid the contention due to a centralized *open* list is to let each processor have a local *open* list. Initially, the search space is statically divided among the processors by expanding some nodes and distributing them to the local *open* lists of various processors. All the processors then select and expand nodes simultaneously. Consider a scenario where

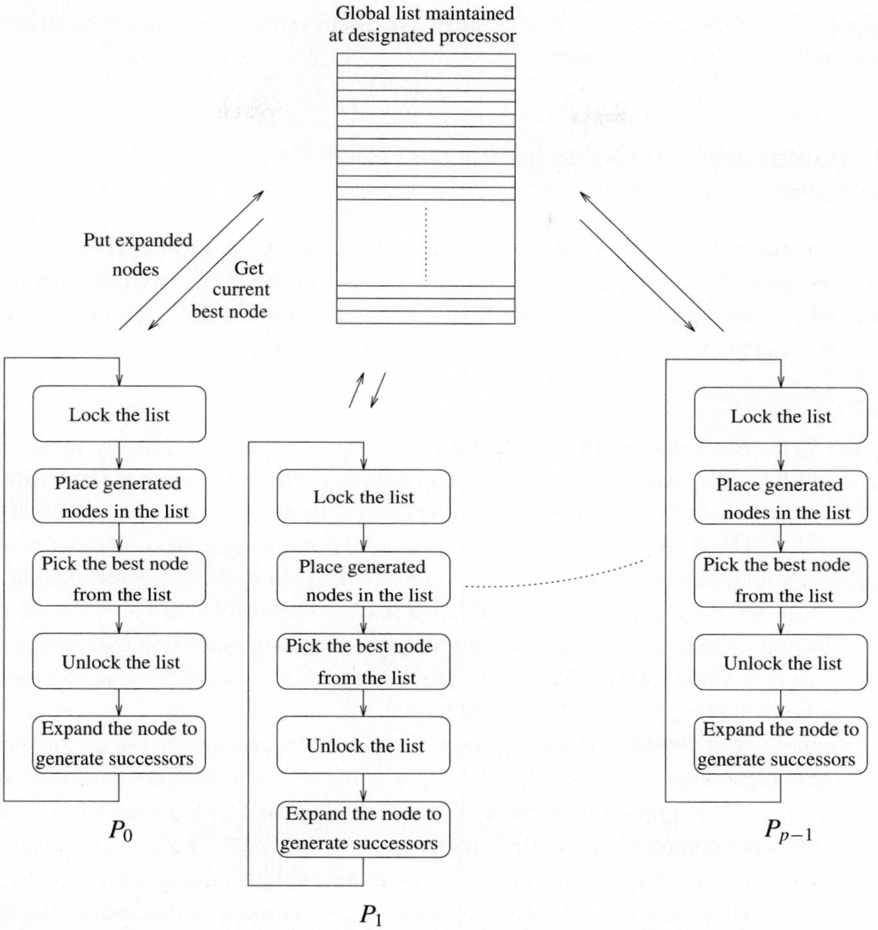

Figure 8.16 A general schematic for parallel best-first search using a centralized strategy. The locking operation is used here to serialize queue access by various processors.

processors do not communicate with each other. In this case, some processors might explore parts of the search space that would not be explored by the sequential algorithm. This leads to a high search overhead factor and poor speedup. Consequently, the processors must communicate among themselves to minimize unnecessary search. The use of a distributed *open* list trades-off communication and computation: decreasing communication between distributed *open* lists increases search overhead factor, and decreasing search overhead factor with increased communication increases communication overhead.

The best choice of communication strategy for parallel BFS depends on whether the search space is a tree or a graph. Searching a graph incurs the additional overhead of checking for duplicate nodes on the closed list. We discuss some communication strategies for tree and graph search separately.

Communication Strategies for Parallel Best-First Tree Search

A communication strategy allows state-space nodes to be exchanged between *open* lists on different processors. The objective of a communication strategy is to ensure that nodes with good l-values are distributed evenly among processors. In this section we discuss three such strategies:

(1) In the ***random communication strategy***, each processor periodically sends some of its best nodes to the *open* list of a randomly selected processor. This strategy ensures that, if a processor stores a good part of the search space, the others get part of it. The strategy can be implemented easily on message-passing systems with low diameter (such as a hypercube) and shared-address-space parallel computers. If nodes are transferred frequently, the search overhead factor can be made very small; otherwise it can become quite large. The communication cost determines the best node transfer frequency. If the communication cost is low, it is best to communicate after every node expansion.

(2) In the ***ring communication strategy***, the processors are mapped in a virtual ring. Each processor periodically exchanges some of its best nodes with the *open* lists of its neighbors in the ring. This strategy is well suited even for message-passing computers with high diameter (such as the ring). Of course, it can also be implemented on low-diameter message-passing architectures and shared-address-space architectures. As before, the cost of communication determines the node transfer frequency. Figure 8.17 illustrates the ring communication strategy.

Unless the search space is highly uniform, the search overhead factor of this scheme is very high. The reason is that this scheme takes a long time to distribute good nodes from one processor to all other processors.

(3) In the ***blackboard communication strategy***, there is a shared blackboard through which nodes are switched among processors as follows. After selecting the best node from its local *open* list, a processor expands the node only if its l-value is within a tolerable limit of the best node on the blackboard. If the selected node is much better than the best node on the blackboard, the processor sends some of its best nodes to the blackboard before expanding the current node. If the selected node is much worse than the best node on the blackboard, the processor retrieves some good nodes from the blackboard and reselects a node for expansion. Figure 8.18 illustrates the blackboard communication strategy. The blackboard strategy is suited only to shared-address-space computers, because the value of the best node in the blackboard has to be checked after each node expansion.

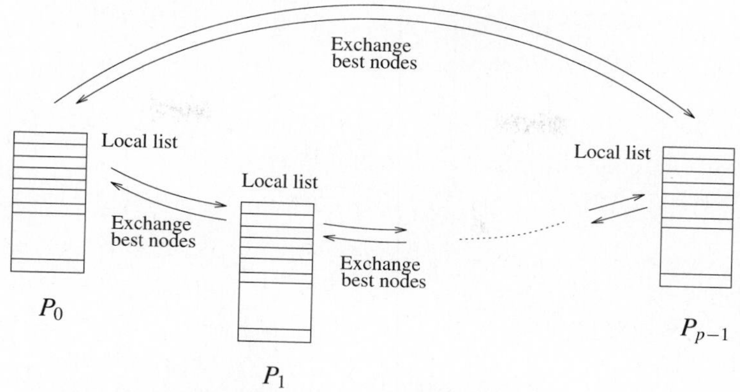

Figure 8.17 A message-passing implementation of parallel best-first search using the ring communication strategy.

Communication Strategies for Parallel Best-First Graph Search

While searching graphs, an algorithm must check for node replication. This task is distributed among processors. One way to check for replication is to map each node to a specific processor. Subsequently, whenever a node is generated, it is mapped to the same processor, which checks for replication locally. This technique can be implemented using a hash function that takes a node as input and returns a processor label. When a node is generated, it is sent to the processor whose label is returned by the hash function for that node. Upon receiving the node, a processor checks whether it already exists in the local *open* or *closed* lists. If not, the node is inserted in the *open* list. If the node already exists,

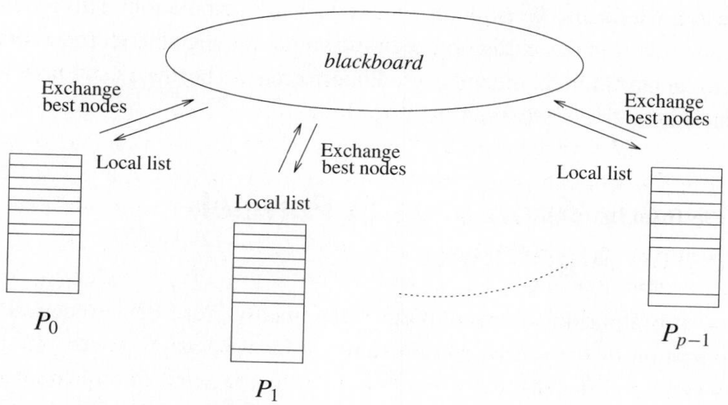

Figure 8.18 An implementation of parallel best-first search using the blackboard communication strategy.

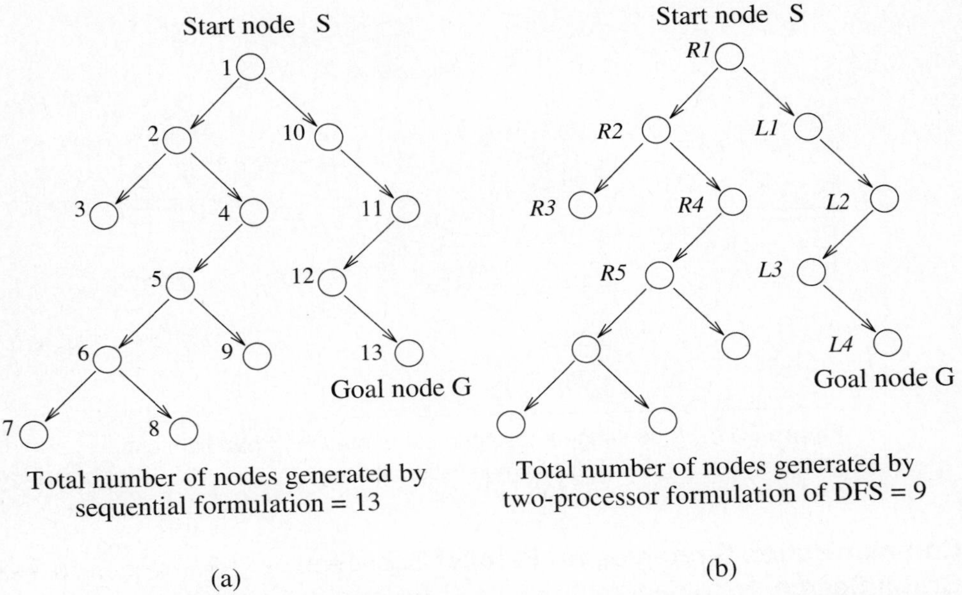

Figure 8.19 The difference in number of nodes searched by sequential and parallel formulations of DFS. For this example, parallel DFS reaches a goal node after searching fewer nodes than sequential DFS.

and if the new node has a better cost associated with it, then the previous version of the node is replaced by the new node on the *open* list.

For a random hash function, the load-balancing property of this distribution strategy is similar to the random-distribution technique discussed in the previous section. This result follows from the fact that each processor is equally likely to be assigned a part of the search space that would also be explored by a sequential formulation. This method ensures an even distribution of nodes with good heuristic values among all the processors (Problem 8.12). However, hashing techniques degrade performance because each node generation results in communication (Problem 8.13).

8.6 Speedup Anomalies in Parallel Search Algorithms

In parallel search algorithms, speedup can vary greatly from one execution to another because the portion of the search space examined by various processors are determined dynamically and can differ for each execution. Consider the case of sequential and parallel DFS performed on the tree illustrated in Figure 8.19. Figure 8.19(a) illustrates sequential DFS search. The order of node expansions is indicated by node labels. The sequential formulation generates 13 nodes before reaching the goal node G.

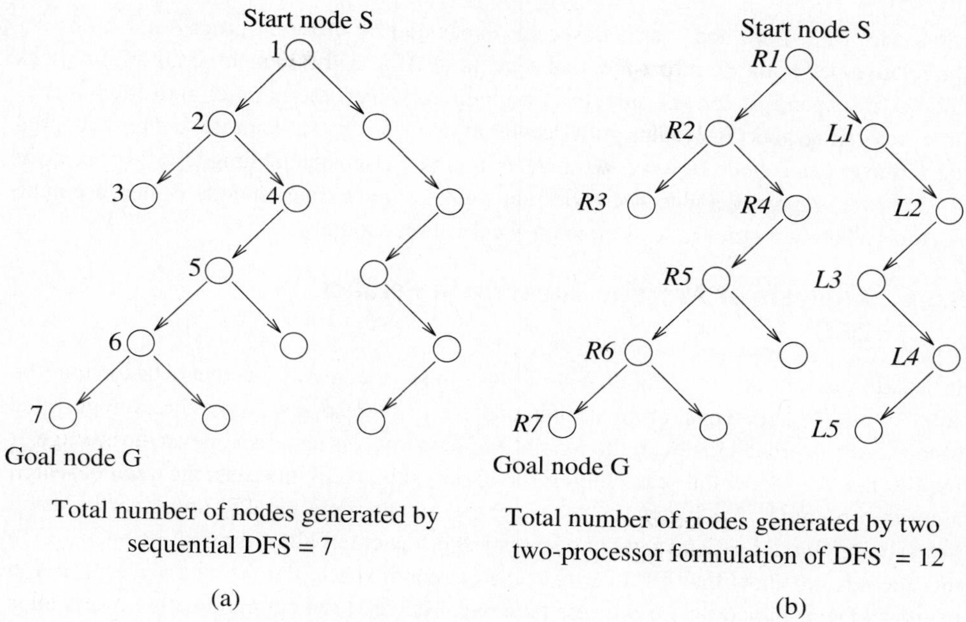

Figure 8.20 A parallel DFS formulation that searches more nodes than its sequential counterpart.

Now consider the parallel formulation of DFS illustrated for the same tree in Figure 8.19(b) for two processors. The nodes expanded by the processors are labeled R and L. The parallel formulation reaches the goal node after generating only nine nodes. That is, the parallel formulation arrives at the goal node after searching fewer nodes than its sequential counterpart. In this case, the search overhead factor is $9/13$ (less than one), and if communication overhead is not too large, the speedup will be superlinear.

Finally, consider the situation in Figure 8.20. The sequential formulation (Figure 8.20(a)) generates seven nodes before reaching the goal node, but the parallel formulation generates twelve nodes. In this case, the search overhead factor is greater than one, resulting in sublinear speedup.

In summary, for some executions, the parallel version finds a solution after generating fewer nodes than the sequential version, making it possible to obtain superlinear speedup. For other executions, the parallel version finds a solution after generating more nodes, resulting in sublinear speedup. Executions yielding speedups greater than p by using p processors are referred to as ***acceleration anomalies***. Speedups of less than p using p processors are called ***deceleration anomalies***.

Speedup anomalies also manifest themselves in best-first search algorithms. Here, anomalies are caused by nodes on the *open* list that have identical heuristic values but require vastly different amounts of search to detect a solution. Assume that two such nodes exist; node A leads rapidly to the goal node, and node B leads nowhere after extensive work.

In parallel BFS, both nodes are chosen for expansion by different processors. Consider the relative performance of parallel and sequential BFS. If the sequential algorithm picks node A to expand, it arrives quickly at a goal. However, the parallel algorithm wastes time expanding node B, leading to a deceleration anomaly. In contrast, if the sequential algorithm expands node B, it wastes substantial time before abandoning it in favor of node A. However, the parallel algorithm does not waste as much time on node B, because node A yields a solution quickly, leading to an acceleration anomaly.

★ 8.6.1 Analysis of Average Speedup in Parallel DFS

In isolated executions of parallel search algorithms, the search overhead factor may be equal to one, less than one, or greater than one. It is interesting to know the average value of the search overhead factor. If the search overhead factor is less than one on the average, it implies that the sequential search algorithm is not optimal. In this case, the parallel search algorithm running on a sequential processor (by emulating a parallel processor by using time-slicing) would expand fewer nodes than the sequential algorithm on the average. In this section, we show that for a certain type of search space, the average value of search overhead factor in parallel DFS is less than one. Hence, if the communication overhead is not too large, then on the average, parallel DFS will provide superlinear speedup for this type of search space.

Assumptions

We make the following assumptions for analyzing speedup anomalies:

(1) The state-space tree has M leaf nodes. Solutions occur only at leaf nodes. The amount of computation needed to generate each leaf node is the same. The number of nodes generated in the tree is proportional to the number of leaf nodes generated. This is a reasonable assumption for search trees in which each node has more than one successor on the average.

(2) Both sequential and parallel DFS stop after finding one solution.

(3) In parallel DFS, the state-space tree is equally partitioned among p processors; thus, each processor gets a subtree with M/p leaf nodes.

(4) There is at least one solution in the entire tree. (Otherwise, both parallel search and sequential search generate the entire tree without finding a solution, resulting in linear speedup.)

(5) There is no information to order the search of the state-space tree; hence, the density of solutions across the unexplored nodes is independent of the order of the search.

(6) The solution density ρ is defined as the probability of the leaf node being a solution. We assume a Bernoulli distribution of solutions; that is, the event of a leaf node being a solution is independent of any other leaf node being a solution. We also assume that $\rho \ll 1$.

(7) The total number of nodes generated by p processors before one of the processors finds a solution is denoted by W_p. The average number of leaf nodes generated by sequential DFS before a solution is found is given by W. Both W and W_p are less than or equal to M.

Analysis of the Search Overhead Factor

Consider the scenario in which the M leaf nodes are statically divided into p regions, each with $K = M/p$ leaves. Let the density of solutions among the leaves in the ith region be ρ_i. In the parallel algorithm, each processor P_i searches region i independently until a processor finds a solution. In the sequential algorithm, the regions are searched in random order.

Theorem 8.6.1: Let ρ be the solution density in a region; and assume that the number of leaves K in the region is large. Then, if $\rho > 0$, the mean number of leaves generated by a single processor searching the region is $1/\rho$.

Proof: Since we have a Bernoulli distribution, the mean number of trials is given by

$$\begin{aligned}\rho + 2\rho(1-\rho) + \cdots + K\rho(1-\rho)^{K-1} &= \frac{1-(1-\rho)^{K+1}}{\rho} - (K+1)(1-\rho)^K, \\ &= \frac{1}{\rho} - (1-\rho)^K(\frac{1}{\rho} + K). \qquad (8.7)\end{aligned}$$

For a fixed value of ρ and a large value of K, the second term in Equation 8.7 becomes small; hence, the mean number of trials is approximately equal to $1/\rho$. □

Sequential DFS selects any one of the p regions with probability $1/p$ and searches it to find a solution. Hence, the average number of leaf nodes expanded by sequential DFS is

$$W \simeq \frac{1}{p}(\frac{1}{\rho_1} + \frac{1}{\rho_2} + \cdots + \frac{1}{\rho_p}).$$

This expression assumes that a solution is always found in the selected region; thus, only one region must be searched. However, the probability of region i not having any solutions is $(1-\rho_i)^K$. In this case, another region must be searched. Taking this into account makes the expression for W more precise and increases the average value of W somewhat. The overall results of the analysis will not change.

In each step of parallel DFS, one node from each of the p regions is explored simultaneously. Hence the probability of success in a step of the parallel algorithm is $1 - \prod_{i=1}^{p}(1-\rho_i)$. This is approximately $\rho_1 + \rho_2 + \cdots + \rho_p$ (neglecting the second-order terms, since each ρ_i are assumed to be small). Hence,

$$W_p \simeq \frac{p}{\rho_1 + \rho_2 + \cdots + \rho_p}.$$

Inspecting the above equations, we see that $W = 1/HM$ and $W_p = 1/AM$, where HM is the harmonic mean of $\rho_1, \rho_2, \ldots, \rho_p$; and AM is their arithmetic mean. Since the arithmetic mean (AM) and the harmonic mean (HM) satisfy the relation $AM \geq HM$, we have $W \geq W_p$. In particular,

- when $\rho_1 = \rho_2 = \cdots = \rho_p$, $AM = HM$, therefore $W \simeq W_p$. When solutions are uniformly distributed, the average search overhead factor for parallel DFS is one.
- when each ρ_i is different, $AM > HM$, therefore $W > W_p$. When solution densities in various regions are nonuniform, the average search overhead factor for parallel DFS is less than one, making it possible to obtain superlinear speedups.

The assumption that each node can be a solution independent of the other nodes being solutions is false for most practical problems. Still, the preceding analysis suggests that parallel DFS obtains higher efficiency than sequential DFS provided that the solutions are not distributed uniformly in the search space and that no information about solution density in various regions is available. This characteristic applies to a variety of problem spaces searched by simple backtracking. The result that the search overhead factor for parallel DFS is at least one on the average is important, since DFS is currently the best known and most practical sequential algorithm used to solve many important problems.

8.7 Bibliographic Remarks

Extensive literature is available on search algorithms for discrete optimization techniques such as branch-and-bound and heuristic search [KK88a, LW66, Pea84]. The relationship between branch-and-bound search, dynamic programming, and heuristic search techniques in artificial intelligence is explored by Kumar and Kanal [KK83, KK88b]. The average time complexity of heuristic search algorithms for many problems is shown to be polynomial by Smith [Smi84] and Wilf [Wil86]. Extensive work has been done on parallel formulations of search algorithms. We briefly outline some of these contributions.

Parallel Depth-First Search Algorithms

Many parallel algorithms for DFS have been formulated [AJM88, FM87, KK92, KGR91, KR87, MV87, Ran91, Rao90, SK90, SK89, Vor87b]. Load balancing is the central issue in parallel DFS. In this chapter, distribution of work in parallel DFS was done using stack splitting [KGR91, KR87]. An alternative scheme for work-distribution is node splitting, in which only a single node is given out [FK88, FTI90, Ran91]

This chapter discussed formulations of state-space search in which a processor requests work when it goes idle. Such load-balancing schemes are called ***receiver-initiated*** schemes. In other load-balancing schemes, a processor that has work gives away part of its work to another processor (with or without receiving a request). These schemes are called ***sender-initiated*** schemes.

Several researchers have used receiver-initiated load-balancing schemes in parallel DFS [FM87, KR87, KGR91]. Kumar et al. [KGR91] analyze these load-balancing schemes including global round robin, random polling, asynchronous round robin, and nearest neighbor. The description and analysis of these schemes in Section 8.4 is based on the papers by Kumar et al. [KGR91, KR87].

Parallel DFS using sender-initiated load balancing has been proposed by some researchers [FK88, FTI90, PFK90, Ran91, SK89]. Furuichi et al. propose the single-level and multilevel sender-based schemes [FTI90]. Kimura and Nobuyuki [KN91] presented the scalability analysis of these schemes. Ferguson and Korf [FK88, PFK90] present a load-balancing scheme called ***distributed tree search*** (DTS).

Other techniques using randomized allocation have been presented for parallel DFS of state-space trees [KP92, Ran91, SK89, SK90]. Issues relating to granularity control in parallel DFS have also been explored [RK87, SK89].

Saletore and Kale [SK90] present a formulation of parallel DFS in which nodes are assigned priorities and are expanded accordingly. They show that the search overhead factor of this prioritized DFS formulation is very close to one, allowing it to yield consistently increasing speedups with an increasing number of processors for sufficiently large problems.

In some parallel formulations of depth-first search, the state space is searched independently in a random order by different processors [JAM87, JAM88]. Challou et al. [CGK93] and Ertel [Ert92] show that such methods are useful for solving robot motion planning and theorem proving problems, respectively.

Most generic DFS formulations apply to depth-first branch-and-bound and IDA*. Some researchers have specifically studied parallel formulations of depth-first branch-and-bound [AKR89, AKR90, EDH80]. Many parallel formulations of IDA* have been proposed [RK87, RKR87, KS91, PKF92, MD92].

Most of the parallel DFS formulations are suited only for MIMD computers. Due to the nature of the search problem, SIMD computers were considered inherently unsuitable for parallel search. However, work by Frye and Myczkowski [FM92], Powley et al. [PKF92], and Mahanti and Daniels [MD92] showed that parallel depth-first search techniques can be developed even for SIMD computers. Karypis and Kumar [KK92] presented load-balancing schemes for parallel DFS for SIMD computers that are as scalable as the schemes for MIMD computers. The discussion in Section 8.4.9 is based upon [KK92].

Several researchers have experimentally evaluated parallel DFS. Finkel and Manber [FM87] present performance results for problems such as the traveling salesman problem and the knight's tour for the Crystal multicomputer developed at the University of Wisconsin. Monien and Vornberger [MV87] show linear speedups on a network of transputers for a variety of combinatorial problems. Kumar et al. [AKR89, AKR90, AKRS91, KGR91] show linear speedups for problems such as the 15-puzzle, tautology verification, and automatic test pattern generation for various architectures such as a 128-processor BBN Butterfly, a 128-processor Intel iPSC, a 1024-processor nCUBE 2, and a 128-processor Symult 2010. Kumar, Grama, and Rao [GKR91, KGR91, KR87, RK87] have investigated the scalability and performance of many of these schemes for hypercubes, meshes, and networks of workstations. Experimental results in Section 8.4.6 are taken from the paper by Kumar, Grama, and Rao [KGR91].

Many researchers have proposed termination detection algorithms for use in parallel search. Dijkstra [DSG83] proposed the ring termination detection algorithm. The termination detection algorithm based on weights, discussed in Section 8.4.5, is similar to the one proposed by Rokusawa et al. [RICN88]. Dutt and Mahapatra [DM93] discuss the termination detection algorithm based on minimum spanning trees.

Parallel Formulations of Alpha-Beta Search

Alpha-beta search is essentially a depth-first branch-and-bound search technique that finds an optimal solution tree of an AND/OR graph [KK83, KK88b]. Many researchers have developed parallel formulations of alpha-beta search [ABJ82, Bau78, FK88, FF82, HB88, Lin83, MC82, MFMV90, MP85, PFK90]. Some of these methods have shown reasonable speedups on dozens of processors [FK88, MFMV90, PFK90]. However, the speedup in most parallel formulations of alpha-beta search saturate beyond a small number of processors. The reason is that the degree of interaction among different subtrees is much higher in alpha-beta search than in DFS on state-space trees.

Parallel Best-First Search

Many researchers have investigated parallel formulations of A* and branch-and-bound algorithms [KK84, KRR88, LK85, MV87, Qui89, HD89, Vor86, WM84, Rao90, GKP92, AM88, CJP83, KB57, LP92, Rou87, PC89, PR89, PR90, PRV88, Ten90, MRSR92, Vor87a, Moh83, MV85, HD87]. All these formulations use different data structures to store the *open* list. Some formulations use the centralized strategy [Moh83, HD87]; some use distributed strategies such as the random communication strategy [Vor87c, Dal87, KRR88]; the ring communication strategy [Vor86, WM84]; and the blackboard communication strategy [KRR88]. Kumar et al. [KRR88] experimentally evaluated the centralized strategy and some distributed strategies in the context of the traveling salesman problem, the vertex cover problem and the 15-puzzle. Dutt and Mahapatra [DM93, MD93] have proposed and evaluated a number of other communication strategies.

Manzini analyzed the hashing technique for distributing nodes in parallel graph search [MS90]. Evett et al. [EHMN90] proposed parallel retracting A* (PRA*), which operates under limited-memory conditions. In this formulation, each node is hashed to a unique processor. If a processor receives more nodes than it can store locally, it retracts nodes with poorer heuristic values. These retracted nodes are reexpanded when more promising nodes fail to yield a solution.

Karp and Zhang [KZ88] analyze the performance of parallel best-first branch-and-bound (that is, A*) by using a random distribution of nodes for a specific model of search trees. Renolet et al. [RDK89] use Monte Carlo simulations to model the performance of parallel best-first search. Wah and Yu [WY85] present stochastic models to analyze the performance of parallel formulations of depth-first branch-and-bound and best-first branch-and-bound search.

Bixby [Bix91] presents a parallel branch-and-cut algorithm to solve the symmetric traveling salesman problem. He also presents solutions of the LP relaxations of airline crew-scheduling models. Miller et al. [Mil91] present parallel formulations of the best-first branch-and-bound technique for solving the asymmetric traveling salesman problem on heterogeneous network computer architectures. Roucairol [Rou91] presents parallel best-first branch-and-bound formulations for shared-address-space computers and uses them to solve the multiknapsack and quadratic-assignment problems.

Speedup Anomalies in Parallel Formulations of Search Algorithms

Many researchers have analyzed speedup anomalies in parallel search algorithms [IYF79, LS84, Kor81, LW86, MVS86, RKR87]. Lai and Sahni [LS84] present early work quantifying speedup anomalies in best-first search. Lai and Sprague [LS86] present enhancements and extensions to this work. Lai and Sprague [LS85] also present an analytical model and derive characteristics of the lower-bound function for which anomalies are guaranteed not to occur as the number of processors is increased. Li and Wah [LW84, LW86] and Wah et al. [WLY84] investigate dominance relations and heuristic functions and their effect on detrimental (speedup of < 1 using p processors) and acceleration anomalies. Quinn and Deo [QD86] derive an upper bound on the speedup attainable by any parallel formulation of the branch-and-bound algorithm using the best-bound search strategy. Rao and Kumar [RK88, RK93] analyze the average speedup in parallel DFS for two separate models with and without heuristic ordering information. They show that the search overhead factor in these cases is at most one. Section 8.6.1 is based on the results of Rao and Kumar [RK93].

Finally, many programming environments have been developed for implementing parallel search. Some examples are DIB [FM87], Chare-Kernel [SK89], MANIP [WM84], and PICOS [RDK89].

Problems

8.1 **[KR87]** Consider a parallel formulation of DFS using a nearest neighbor search-space distribution. This technique works as follows: when a processor runs out of work, it sends a work request to its immediate neighbors in a round-robin fashion. For example, on a hypercube, a processor sends requests only to its $\log p$ neighbors. For networks in which the distance between all pairs of processors is the same, this scheme is identical to the asynchronous round robin scheme. The nearest neighbor scheme ensures the locality of communication for both work requests and actual work transfers. A potential drawback of the scheme is that any localized concentration of work takes longer to be distributed to distant processors.

Analyze the performance and scalability of this parallel formulation for a hypercube, a mesh, and a ring.

8.2 **[KGR91]** In Section 8.4.1, we identified access to the global pointer, *target*, as a bottleneck in the GRR load-balancing scheme. Consider a modification of this scheme in which it is augmented with message combining. This scheme works as

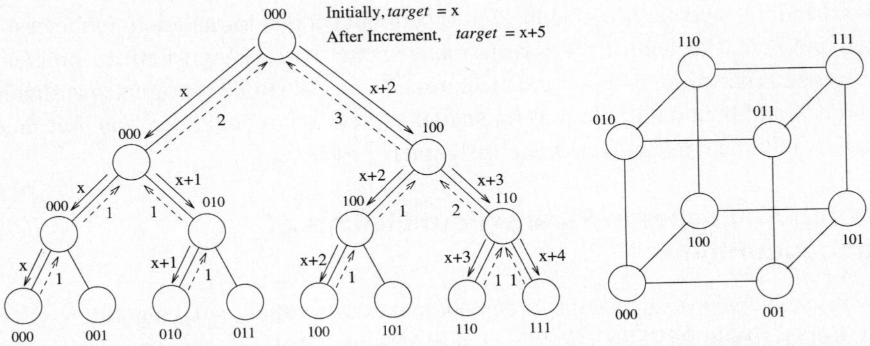

Figure 8.21 Message combining on an eight-processor hypercube.

follows: All the requests to read the value of the global pointer *target* at processor zero are combined at intermediate processors. Thus, the total number of requests handled by processor zero is greatly reduced. This technique is essentially a software implementation of the fetch-and-add operation. This scheme is called GRR-M (GRR with message combining).

The implementation of this scheme on a hypercube is illustrated in Figure 8.21. A spanning tree rooted at processor zero is embedded into the hypercube (Section 2.5). Every processor is at a leaf of the spanning tree. When a processor wants to atomically read and increment *target*, it sends a request up the spanning tree toward processor zero. An internal node of the spanning tree holds a request from one of its children for at most time δ, then forwards the message to its parent. If a request comes from the node's other child within time δ, the two requests are combined and sent up as a single request. If i is the total number of increment requests that have been combined, the resulting increment of *target* is i.

The returned value at each processor is equal to what it would have been if all the requests to *target* had been serialized. This is done as follows: each combined message is stored in a table at each processor until the request is granted. When the value of *target* is sent back to an internal node, two values are sent down to the left and right children if both requested a value of *target*. The two values are determined from the entries in the table corresponding to increment requests by the two children. A similar implementation can be formulated for other architectures.

The scheme is illustrated by Figure 8.21, in which the original value of *target* is x, and processors P_0, P_2, P_4, P_6 and P_7 issue requests. The total requested increment is five. After the messages are combined and processed, the value of *target* received at these processors is x, $x+1$, $x+2$, $x+3$ and $x+4$, respectively.

Analyze the performance and scalability of this scheme for a hypercube and a mesh.

8.3 **[Lin92]** Consider another load-balancing strategy. Assume that each processor maintains a variable called *counter*. Initially, each processor initializes its local copy of *counter* to zero. Whenever a processor goes idle, it searches for two processors P_i and P_{i+1} in a ring embedded into any architecture, such that the value of *counter* at P_i is greater than that at P_{i+1}. The idle processor then sends a work request to processor P_{i+1}. If no such pair of processors exists, the request is sent to processor zero. On receiving a work request, a processor increments its local value of *counter*.

Devise algorithms to detect the pairs P_i and P_{i+1}. Analyze the scalability of this load-balancing scheme based on your algorithm to detect the pairs P_i and P_{i+1} for a hypercube, a mesh, and a network of workstations.

Hint: The upper bound on the number of work transfers for this scheme is similar to that for GRR.

8.4 In the analysis of various load-balancing schemes presented in Section 8.4.2, we assumed that the cost of transferring work is independent of the amount of work transferred. However, there are problems for which the work-transfer cost is a function of the amount of work transferred. Examples of such problems are found in tree-search applications for domains in which strong heuristics are available. For such applications, the size of the stack used to represent the search tree can vary significantly with the number of nodes in the search tree.

(a) Consider a case in which the size of the stack for representing a search space of w nodes varies as $\sqrt{w}$. Assume that the load-balancing scheme used is GRR. Analyze the performance of this scheme for the hypercube and a network of workstations.

(b) Consider a case in which the size of the stack for representing a search space of w nodes varies as $\log w$. Analyze the performance of the GRR and GRR-M schemes on a hypercube and a network of workstations.

8.5 Consider Dijkstra's token termination detection scheme described in Section 8.4.5. Show that the contribution of termination detection using this scheme to the overall isoefficiency function is $\Theta(p^2)$. Comment on the value of the constants associated with this isoefficiency term.

8.6 Consider the tree-based termination detection scheme in Section 8.4.5. In this algorithm, the weights may become very small and may eventually become zero due to the finite precision of computers. In such cases, termination is never signaled. The algorithm can be modified by manipulating the reciprocal of the weight instead of the weight itself. Write the modified termination algorithm and show that it is capable of detecting termination correctly.

8.7 **[DM93]** Consider a termination detection algorithm in which a spanning tree of minimum diameter is mapped onto the architecture of the given parallel computer. The ***center*** of such a tree is a vertex with the minimum distance to the vertex farthest from it. The center of a spanning tree is considered to be its root. For example, a spanning tree of depth $\log p$ rooted at processor 0 can be mapped onto the hypercube.

While executing parallel search, a processor can be either *idle* or *busy*. The termination detection algorithm requires all work transfers in the system to be acknowledged by an *ack* message. A processor is busy if it has work, or if it has sent work to another processor and the corresponding *ack* message has not been received; otherwise the processor is idle. Processors at the leaves of the spanning tree send *stop* messages to their parent when they become idle. Processors at intermediate levels in the tree pass the *stop* message on to their parents when they have received *stop* messages from all their children and they themselves become idle. When the root processor receives *stop* messages from all its children and becomes idle, termination is signaled.

Since it is possible for a processor to receive work after it has sent a *stop* message to its parent, a processor signals that it has received work by sending a *resume* message to its parent. The *resume* message moves up the tree until it meets the previously issued *stop* message. On meeting the *stop* message, the *resume* message nullifies the *stop* message. An *ack* message is then sent to the processor that transferred part of its work.

Show using examples that this termination detection technique correctly signals termination. Determine the isoefficiency term due to this termination detection scheme for a hypercube and a linear array.

8.8 **[FTI90, KN91]** Consider the single-level load-balancing scheme which works as follows: a designated processor called *manager* generates many subtasks and gives them one-by-one to the requesting processors on demand. The *manager* traverses the search tree depth-first to a predetermined cutoff depth and distributes nodes at that depth as subtasks. Increasing the cutoff depth increases the number of subtasks, but makes them smaller. The processors request another subtask from the manager only after finishing the previous one. Hence, if a processor gets subtasks corresponding to large subtrees, it will send fewer requests to the *manager*. If the cutoff depth is large enough, this scheme results in good load balance among the processors. However, if the cutoff depth is too large, the subtasks given out to the processors become small and the processors send more frequent requests to the *manager*. In this case, the *manager* becomes a bottleneck. Hence, this scheme has a poor scalability. Figure 8.22 illustrates the single-level work-distribution scheme.

Assume that the cost of communicating a piece of work between any two processors is negligible. Derive analytical expressions for the scalability of the single-level load-balancing scheme.

8.9 **[FTI90, KN91]** Consider the multilevel work-distribution scheme that circumvents the subtask generation bottleneck of the single-level scheme through multiple-level subtask generation. In this scheme, processors are arranged in an m-ary tree of depth d. The task of top-level subtask generation is given to the root processor. It divides the task into super-subtasks and distributes them to its successor processors on demand. These processors subdivide the super-subtasks into subtasks and

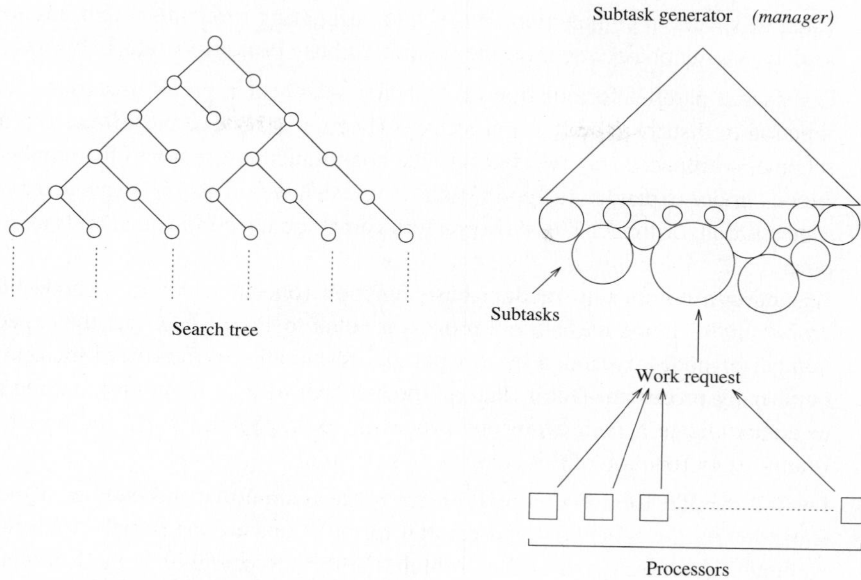

Figure 8.22 The single-level work-distribution scheme for tree search.

distribute them to successor processors on request. The leaf processors repeatedly request work from their parents as soon as they have finished their previous work. A leaf processor is allocated to another subtask generator when its designated subtask generator runs out of work. For $d = 1$, the multi- and single-level schemes are identical. Comment on the performance and scalability of this scheme.

8.10 **[FK88]** Consider the ***distributed tree search*** scheme in which processors are allocated to separate parts of the search tree dynamically. Initially, all the processors are assigned to the root. When the root node is expanded (by one of the processors assigned to it), disjoint subsets of processors at the root is assigned to each successor, in accordance with a selected processor-allocation strategy. One possible processor-allocation strategy is to equally divide the processors among ancestor nodes. This process continues until there is only one processor assigned to a node. At this time, the processor searches the tree rooted at the node sequentially. If a processor finishes searching the search tree rooted at the node, it is reassigned to its parent node. If the parent node has other successor nodes still being explored, then this processor is allocated to one of them. Otherwise, the processor is assigned to its parent. This process continues until the entire tree is searched. Comment on the performance and scalability of this scheme.

8.11 Consider the SIMD implementation of parallel DFS presented in Section 8.4.9. Assume that the work is split by using an α-splitting technique (Section 8.4.2). For the global pointer scheme presented in Section 8.4.9, derive the scalability when it is used in conjunction with a static triggering mechanism that initiates a load-balancing phase whenever the fraction of busy processors falls below 0.5.

8.12 Consider a parallel formulation of best-first search of a graph that uses a hash function to distribute nodes to processors (Section 8.5). The performance of this scheme is influenced by two factors: the communication cost and the number of "good" nodes expanded (a "good" node is one that would also be expanded by the sequential algorithm). These two factors can be analyzed independently of each other.

Assuming a completely random hash function (one in which each node has a probability of being hashed to a processor equal to $1/p$), show that the expected number of nodes expanded by this parallel formulation differs from the optimal number by a constant factor (that is, independent of p). Assuming that the cost to communicate a node from one processor to another is $\Theta(1)$, and derive the isoefficiency function of this scheme.

8.13 For the parallel formulation in Problem 8.12, assume that the number of nodes expanded by the sequential and parallel formulations are the same. Analyze the communication overhead of this formulation for a hypercube. Is the formulation scalable? If so, what is the isoefficiency function? If not, for what interconnection network would the formulation be scalable?

References

[ABJ82] S. G. Akl, D. T. Bernard, and R. J. Jordan. Design and implementation of a parallel tree search algorithm. *IEEE Transactions on Pattern Analysis and Machine Intelligence*, PAMI-4:192–203, 1982.

[AJM88] D. P. Agrawal, V. K. Janakiram, and R. Mehrotra. A randomized parallel branch-and-bound algorithm. In *Proceedings of the 1988 International Conference on Parallel Processing*, 1988.

[AKR89] S. Arvindam, V. Kumar, and V. N. Rao. Floorplan optimization on multiprocessors. In *Proceedings of the 1989 International Conference on Computer Design*, 1989. Also published as Technical Report ACT-OODS-241-89, Microelectronics and Computer Corporation, Austin, TX.

[AKR90] S. Arvindam, V. Kumar, and V. N. Rao. Efficient parallel algorithms for search problems: Applications in VLSI CAD. In *Proceedings of the Third Symposium on the Frontiers of Massively Parallel Computation*, 1990.

[AKRS91] S. Arvindam, V. Kumar, V. N. Rao, and V. Singh. Automatic test pattern generation on multiprocessors. *Parallel Computing*, 17(12):1323–1342, December 1991.

[AM88] T. S. Abdelrahman and T. N. Mudge. Parallel branch-and-bound algorithms on hypercube multiprocessors. In *Proceedings of the Third Conference on Hypercubes, Concurrent Computers, and Applications*, 1492–1499, New York, NY, 1988. ACM Press.

[Bau78] G. M. Baudet. *The Design and Analysis of Algorithms for Asynchronous Multiprocessors*. Ph.D. thesis, Carnegie-Mellon University, Pittsburgh, PA, 1978.

[Bix91] R. Bixby. Two applications of linear programming. In *Proceedings of the Workshop on Parallel Computing of Discrete Optimization Problems*, 1991.

[CGK93] D. Challou, M. Gini, and V. Kumar. Parallel search algorithms for robot motion planning. In *Proceedings of the IEEE Conference on Robotics and Automation*, 46–51, 1993.

[CJP83] H. Crowder, E. L. Johnson, and M. Padberg. Solving large-scale zero-one linear programming problem. *Operations Research*, 2:803–834, 1983.

[Dal87] W. J. Dally. *A VLSI Architecture for Concurrent Data Structures*. Kluwer Academic Publishers, Boston, MA, 1987.

[DM93] S. Dutt and N. R. Mahapatra. Parallel a* algorithms and their performance on hypercube multiprocessors. In *Proceedings of the Seventh International Parallel Processing Symposium*, 797–803, 1993.

[DSG83] E. W. Dijkstra, W. H. Seijen, and A. J. M. V. Gasteren. Derivation of a termination detection algorithm for a distributed computation. *Information Processing Letters*, 16–5:217–219, 1983.

[EDH80] O. I. El-Dessouki and W. H. Huen. Distributed enumeration on network computers. *IEEE Transactions on Computers*, C-29:818–825, September 1980.

[EHMN90] M. Evett, J. Hendler, A. Mahanti, and D. Nau. PRA*: A memory-limited heuristic search procedure for the connection machine. In *Proceedings of the Third Symposium on the Frontiers of Massively Parallel Computation*, 145–149, 1990.

[Ert92] W. Ertel. OR—parallel theorem proving with random competition. In A. Voronokov, editor, *LPAR '92: Logic Programming and Automated Reasoning*, 226–237. Springer-Verlag, New York, NY, 1992.

[FF82] R. A. Finkel and J. P. Fishburn. Parallelism in alpha-beta search. *Artificial Intelligence*, 19:89–106, 1982.

[FK88] C. Ferguson and R. Korf. Distributed tree search and its application to alpha-beta pruning. In *Proceedings of the 1988 National Conference on Artificial Intelligence*, 1988.

[FM87] R. A. Finkel and U. Manber. DIB—a distributed implementation of backtracking. *ACM Transactions on Programming Languages and Systems*, 9(2):235–256, April 1987.

[FM92] R. Frye and J. Myczkowski. Load balancing algorithms on the connection machine and their use in monte-carlo methods. In *Proceedings of the Unstructured Scientific Computation on Multipr ocessors Conference*, 1992.

[FTI90] M. Furuichi, K. Taki, and N. Ichiyoshi. A multi-level load balancing scheme for OR-parallel exhaustive search programs on the Multi-PSI. In *Proceedings of the Second ACM SIGPLAN Symposium on Principles and Practice of Parallel Programming*, 50–59, 1990.

[GKP92] A. Grama, V. Kumar, and P. M. Pardalos. Parallel processing of discrete optimization problems. In *Encyclopaedia of Microcomputers*, 129–157. Marcel Dekker Inc., New York, NY, 1992.

[GKR91] A. Grama, V. Kumar, and V. N. Rao. Experimental evaluation of load balancing techniques for the hypercube. In *Proceedings of the Parallel Computing '91 Conference*, 497–514, 1991.

[HB88] M. M. Huntbach and F. W. Burton. Alpha-beta search on virtual tree machines. *Information Science*, 44:3–17, 1988.

[HD87] S.-R. Huang and L. S. Davis. A tight upper bound for the speedup of parallel best-first branch-and-bound algorithms. Technical report, Center for Automation Research, University of Maryland, College Park, MD, 1987.

[HD89] S.-R. Huang and L. S. Davis. Parallel iterative A* search: An admissible distributed heuristic search algorithm. In *Proceedings of the International Joint Conference on Artificial Intelligence*, 23–29, 1989.

[IYF79] M. Imai, Y. Yoshida, and T. Fukumura. A parallel searching scheme for multiprocessor systems and its application to combinatorial problems. In *Proceedings of the International Joint Conference on Artificial Intelligence*, 416–418, 1979.

[JAM87] V. K. Janakiram, D. P. Agrawal, and R. Mehrotra. Randomized parallel algorithms for prolog programs and backtracking applications. In *Proceedings of the 1987 International Conference on Parallel Processing*, 278–281, 1987.

[JAM88] V. K. Janakiram, D. P. Agrawal, and R. Mehrotra. A randomized parallel backtracking algorithm. *IEEE Transactions on Computers*, C-37 (12), 1988.

[KB57] T. C. Koopmans and M. J. Beckmann. Assignment problems and the location of economic activities. *Econometrica*, 25:53–76, 1957.

[KGR91] V. Kumar, A. Grama, and V. N. Rao. Scalable load balancing techniques for parallel computers. Technical Report 91-55, Computer Science Department, University of Minnesota, 1991. To appear in *Journal of Distributed and Parallel Computing*, 1994.

[KK83] V. Kumar and L. N. Kanal. A general branch-and-bound formulations for understanding and synthesizing and/or tree search procedures. *Artificial Intelligence*, 21:179–198, 1983.

[KK84] V. Kumar and L. N. Kanal. Parallel branch-and-bound formulations for and/or tree search. *IEEE Transactions on Pattern Analysis and Machine Intelligence*, PAMI–6:768–778, 1984.

[KK88a] L. N. Kanal and V. Kumar. *Search in Artificial Intelligence*. Springer-Verlag, New York, NY, 1988.

[KK88b] V. Kumar and L. N. Kanal. The CDP: A unifying formulation for heuristic search, dynamic programming, and branch-and-bound. In L. N. Kanal and V. Kumar, editors, *Search in Artificial Intelligence*, 1–27. Springer-Verlag, New York, NY, 1988.

[KK92] G. Karypis and V. Kumar. Unstructured Tree Search on SIMD Parallel Computers. Technical Report 92–21, Computer Science Department, University of Minnesota, 1992. A short version appears in *Supercomputing '92 Proceedings*, pages 453–462, 1992.

[KN91] K. Kimura and I. Nobuyuki. Probabilistic analysis of the efficiency of the dynamic load distribution. In *The Sixth Distributed Memory Computing Conference Proceedings*, 1991.

[Kor81] W. Kornfeld. The use of parallelism to implement a heuristic search. In *Proceedings of the International Joint Conference on Artifi cial Intelligence*, 575–580, 1981.

[KP92] C. Kaklamanis and G. Persiano. Branch-and-bound and backtrack search on mesh-connected arrays of processors. In *Proceedings of Fourth Annual Symposium on Parallel Algorithms and Architectures*, 118–126, 1992.

[KR87] V. Kumar and V. N. Rao. Parallel depth-first search, part II: Analysis. *International Journal of Parallel Programming*, 16(6):501–519, 1987.

[KRR88] V. Kumar, K. Ramesh, and V. N. Rao. Parallel best-first search of state-space graphs: A summary of results. In *Proceedings of the 1988 National Conference on Artificial Intelligence*, 122–126, 1988.

[KS91] L. V. Kale and V. Saletore. Efficient parallel execution of IDA* on shared and distributed-memory multiprocessors. In *The Sixth Distributed Memory Computing Conference Proceedings*, 1991.

[KZ88] R. M. Karp and Y. Zhang. A randomized parallel branch-and-bound procedure. In *Proceedings of the ACM Annual Symposium on Theory of Computing*, 290–300, 1988.

[Lin83] G. Lindstrom. The key node method: A highly parallel alpha-beta algorithm. Technical Report 83-101, Computer Science Department, University of Utah, Salt Lake City, UT, 1983.

[Lin92] Z. Lin. A distributed fair polling scheme applied to or-parallel logic programming. *International Journal of Parallel Programming*, 20(4), August 1992.

[LK85] D. B. Leifker and L. N. Kanal. A hybrid SSS*/alpha-beta algorithm for parallel search of game trees. In *Proceedings of the International Joint Conference on Artificial Intelligence*, 1044–1046, 1985.

[LP92] Y. Li and P. M. Pardalos. Parallel algorithms for the quadratic assignment problem. In P. M. Pardalos, editor, *Advances in Optimization and Parallel Computing*, 177–189. North-Holland, Amersterdam, The Netherlands, 1992.

[LS84] T. H. Lai and S. Sahni. Anomalies in parallel branch and bound algorithms. *Communications of the ACM*, 594–602, 1984.

[LS85] T. H. Lai and A. Sprague. Performance of parallel branch-and-bound algorithms. *IEEE Transactions on Computers*, C-34(10), October 1985.

[LS86] T. H. Lai and A. Sprague. A note on anomalies in parallel branch-and-bound algorithms with one-to-one bounding functions. *Information Processing Letters*, 23:119–122, October 1986.

[LW66] E. L. Lawler and D. Woods. Branch-and-bound methods: A survey. *Operations Research*, 14, 1966.

[LW84] G.-J. Li and B. W. Wah. Computational efficiency of parallel approximate branch-and-bound algorithms. In *Proceedings of the 1984 International Conference on Parallel Processing*, 473–480, 1984.

[LW86] G.-J. Li and B. W. Wah. Coping with anomalies in parallel branch-and-bound algorithms. *IEEE Transactions on Computers*, C-35, June 1986.

[MC82] T. A. Marsland and M. Campbell. Parallel search of strongly ordered game trees. *Computing Surveys*, 14:533–551, 1982.

[MD92] A. Mahanti and C. Daniels. SIMD parallel heuristic search. *Artificial Intelligence*, 1992.

[MD93] N. R. Mahapatra and S. Dutt. Scalable duplicate pruning strategies for parallel a* graph search. In *Proceedings of the Fifth IEEE Symposium on Parallel and Distributed Processing*, 1993.

[MFMV90] B. Monien, R. Feldmann, P. Mysliwietz, and O. Vornberger. Parallel game tree search by dynamic tree decomposition. In V. Kumar, P. S. Gopalakrishnan, and L. N. Kanal, editors, *Parallel Algorithms for Machine Intelligence and Vision*. Springer-Verlag, New York, NY, 1990.

[Mil91] D. Miller. Exact distributed algorithms for travelling salesman problem. In *Proceedings of the Workshop On Parallel Computing of Discrete Optimization Problems*, 1991.

[Moh83] J. Mohan. Experience with two parallel programs solving the traveling salesman problem. In *Proceedings of the 1983 International Conference on Parallel Processing*, 191–193, 1983.

[MP85] T. A. Marsland and F. Popowich. Parallel game tree search. *IEEE Transactions on Pattern Analysis and Machine Intelligence*, PAMI-7(4):442–452, July 1985.

[MRSR92] G. P. McKeown, V. J. Rayward-Smith, and S. A. Rush. *Parallel Branch-and-Bound*, chapter 5, 111–150. Advanced Topics in Computer Science. Blackwell Scientific Publications, Oxford, UK, 1992.

[MS90] G. Manzini and M. Somalvico. Probabilistic performance analysis of heuristic search using parallel hash tables. In *Proceedings of the International Symposium on Artificial Intelligence and Mathematics*, 1990.

[MV85] B. Monien and O. Vornberger. The ring machine. Technical report, University of Paderborn, FRG, 1985. Also in *Computers and Artificial Intelligence*, 3(1987).

[MV87] B. Monien and O. Vornberger. Parallel processing of combinatorial search trees. In *Proceedings of International Workshop on Parallel Algorithms and Architectures*, 1987.

[MVS86] B. Monien, O. Vornberger, and E. Spekenmeyer. Superlinear speedup for parallel backtracking. Technical Report 30, University of Paderborn, FRG, 1986.

[PC89] P. M. Pardalos and J. Crouse. A parallel algorithm for the quadratic assignment problem. In *Supercomputing '89 Proceedings*, 351–360. ACM Press, New York, NY, 1989.

[Pea84] J. Pearl. *Heuristics—Intelligent Search Strategies for Computer Problem Solving*. Addison-Wesley, Reading, MA, 1984.

[PFK90] C. Powley, C. Ferguson, and R. Korf. Parallel heuristic search: Two approaches. In V. Kumar, P. S. Gopalakrishnan, and L. N. Kanal, editors, *Parallel Algorithms for Machine Intelligence and Vision*. Springer-Verlag, New York, NY, 1990.

[PKF92] C. Powley, R. Korf, and C. Ferguson. IDA* on the connection machine. *Artificial Intelligence*, 1992.

[PR89] P. M. Pardalos and G. P. Rodgers. Parallel branch-and-bound algorithms for unconstrainted quadratic zero-one programming. In R. Sharda et al., editors, *Impacts of Recent Computer Advances on Operations Research*, 131–143. North-Holland, Amersterdam, The Netherlands, 1989.

[PR90] P. M. Pardalos and G. P. Rodgers. Parallel branch-and-bound algorithms for quadratic zero-one programming on a hypercube architecture. *Annals of Operations Research*, 22:271–292, 1990.

[PRV88] G. Plateau, C. Roucairol, and I. Valabregue. Algorithm PR2 for the parallel size reduction of the 0/1 multiknapsack problem. In *INRIA Rapports de Recherche*, number 811, 1988.

[QD86] M. J. Quinn and N. Deo. An upper bound for the speedup of parallel branch-and-bound algorithms. *BIT*, 26(1), March 1986.

[Qui89] M. J. Quinn. Analysis and implementation of branch-and-bound algorithms on a hypercube multicomputer. *IEEE Transactions on Computers*, 1989.

[Ran91] A. G. Ranade. Optimal speedup for backtrack search on a butterfly network. In *Proceedings of the Third ACM Symposium on Parallel Algorithms and Architectures*, 1991.

[Rao90] V. N. Rao. *Parallel Processing of Heuristic Search*. Ph.D. thesis, University of Texas, Austin, TX, 1990.

[RDK89] C. Renolet, M. Diamond, and J. Kimbel. Analytical and heuristic modeling of distributed algorithms. Technical Report E3646, FMC Corporation, Advanced Systems Center, Minneapolis, MN, 1989.

[RICN88] K. Rokusawa, N. Ichiyoshi, T. Chikayama, and H. Nakashima. An efficient termination detection and abortion algorithm for distributed processing systems. In *Proceedings of 1988 International Conference on Parallel Processing: Vol I*, 18–22, 1988.

[RK87] V. N. Rao and V. Kumar. Parallel depth-first search, part I: Implementation. *International Journal of Parallel Programming*, 16(6):479–499, 1987.

[RK88] V. N. Rao and V. Kumar. Superlinear speedup in state-space search. In *Proceedings of the 1988 Foundation of Software Technology and Theoretical Computer Science*, number 338, 161–174. Springer-Verlag Series Lecture Notes in Computer Science, 1988.

[RK93] V. N. Rao and V. Kumar. On the efficicency of parallel backtracking. *IEEE Transactions on Parallel and Distributed Systems*, 4(4):427–437, April 1993. Also available as Technical Report TR 90-55, Department of Computer Science, University of Minnesota, Minneapolis, MN.

[RKR87] V. N. Rao, V. Kumar, and K. Ramesh. A parallel implementation of iterative-deepening-A*. In *Proceedings of the National Conference on Artificial Intelligence (AAAI-87)*, 878–882, 1987.

[Rou87] C. Roucairol. A parallel branch-and-bound algorithm for the quadratic assignment problem. *Discrete Applied Mathematics*, 18:211–225, 1987.

[Rou91] C. Roucairol. Parallel branch-and-bound on shared-memory multiprocessors. In *Proceedings of the Workshop On Parallel Computing of Discrete Optimization Problems*, 1991.

[SK89] W. Shu and L. V. Kale. A dynamic scheduling strategy for the chare-kernel system. In *Proceedings of Supercomputing Conference*, 389–398, 1989.

[SK90] V. Saletore and L. V. Kale. Consistent linear speedup to a first solution in parallel state-space search. In *Proceedings of the 1990 National Conference on Artificial Intelligence*, 227–233, 1990.

[Smi84] D. R. Smith. Random trees and the analysis of branch and bound procedures. *Journal of the ACM*, 31(1), 1984.

[Ten90] S. Teng. Adaptive parallel algorithms for integral knapsack problems. *Journal of Parallel and Distributed Computing*, 8:400–406, 1990.

[Vor86] O. Vornberger. Implementing branch-and-bound in a ring of processors. Technical Report 29, University of Paderborn, FRG, 1986.

[Vor87a] O. Vornberger. Load balancing in a network of transputers. In *Proceedings of Second International Workshop on Distributed Algorithms*, 1987.

[Vor87b] O. Vornberger. The personal supercomputer: A network of transputers. In *Proceedings of the 1987 International Conference on Supercomputing*, 1987.

[Vor87c] O. Vornberger. Load balancing in a network of transputers. In *Proceedings of the Second International Workshop on Distributed Parallel Algorithms*, 1987.

[Wil86] H. S. Wilf. *Algorithms and Complexity*. Prentice-Hall, Englewood Cliffs, NJ, 1986.

[WLY84] B. W. Wah, G.-J. Li, and C. F. Yu. The status of MANIP—a multicomputer architecture for solving combinatorial extremum-search problems. In *Proceedings of 11th Annual International Symposium on Computer Architecture*, 56–63, 1984.

[WM84] B. W. Wah and Y. W. E. Ma. MANIP—a multicomputer architecture for solving combinatorial extremum-search problems. *IEEE Transactions on Computers*, C–33, May 1984.

[WY85] B. W. Wah and C. F. Yu. Stochastic modeling of branch-and-bound algorithms with best-first search. *IEEE Transactions on Software Engineering*, SE-11, September 1985.

CHAPTER 9

Dynamic Programming

Dynamic programming (DP) is a commonly used technique for solving a wide variety of discrete optimization problems such as scheduling, string-editing, packaging, and inventory management. DP views a problem as a set of interdependent subproblems. It solves subproblems and uses the results to solve larger subproblems until the entire problem is solved. The solution to a subproblem is expressed as a function of solutions to one or more subproblems at the preceding levels.

Consider a DP formulation for the problem of finding a shortest (least-cost) path between a pair of vertices in an acyclic graph. (Refer to Section 7.1 for an introduction to graph terminology.) An edge connecting node i to node j has cost $c(i, j)$. If two vertices i and j are not connected then $c(i, j) = \infty$. The graph contains n nodes numbered $0, 1, \ldots, n-1$, and has an edge from node i to node j only if $i < j$. The shortest-path problem is to find a least-cost path between nodes 0 and $n-1$. Let $f(x)$ denote the cost of the least-cost path from node 0 to node x. Thus, $f(0)$ is zero, and finding $f(n-1)$ solves the problem. The DP formulation for this problem yields the following recursive equations for $f(x)$:

$$f(x) = \begin{cases} 0 & x = 0 \\ \min_{0 \le j < x} \{f(j) + c(j, x)\} & 1 \le x \le n-1 \end{cases} \tag{9.1}$$

Example 9.1 The Shortest-Path Problem

Consider the five-node acyclic graph shown in Figure 9.1. The problem is to find $f(4)$. It can be computed given $f(3)$ and $f(2)$. More precisely,

$$f(4) = \min\{f(3) + c(3, 4), f(2) + c(2, 4)\}.$$

Therefore, $f(2)$ and $f(3)$ are elements of the set of subproblems on which $f(4)$ depends. Similarly, $f(3)$ depends on $f(1)$ and $f(2)$, and $f(1)$ and $f(2)$ depend on

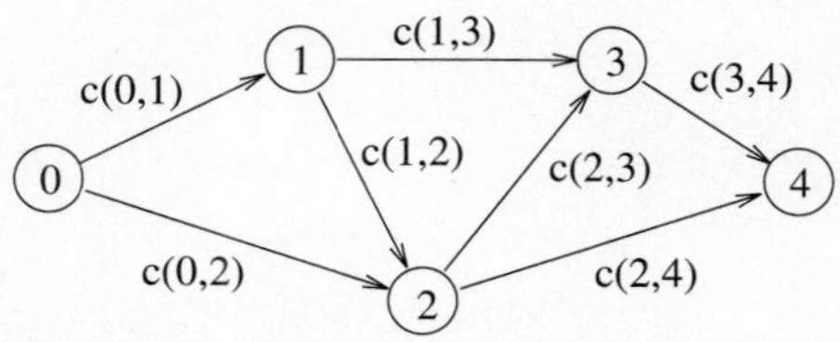

Figure 9.1 A graph for which the shortest path between nodes 0 and 4 is to be computed.

$f(0)$. Since $f(0)$ is known, it is used to solve $f(1)$ and $f(2)$, which are used to solve $f(3)$. ■

In general, the solution to a DP problem is expressed as a minimum (or maximum) of possible alternative solutions. Each of these alternative solutions is constructed by composing one or more subproblems. If r represents the cost of a solution composed of subproblems $x_1, x_2, \ldots, x_l$, then r can be written as

$$r = g(f(x_1), f(x_2), \ldots, f(x_l)).$$

The function g is called the ***composition function***, and its nature depends on the problem. If the optimal solution to each problem is determined by composing optimal solutions to the subproblems and selecting the minimum (or maximum), the formulation is said to be a DP formulation. Figure 9.2 illustrates an instance of composition and minimization of solutions. The solution to problem x_8 is the minimum of the three possible solutions having costs r_1, r_2, and r_3. The cost of the first solution is determined by composing solutions to subproblems x_1 and x_3, the second solution by composing solutions to subproblems x_4 and x_5, and the third solution by composing solutions to subproblems x_2, x_6, and x_7.

DP represents the solution to an optimization problem as a recursive equation whose left side is an unknown quantity and whose right side is a minimization (or maximization) expression. Such an equation is called a ***functional equation*** or an ***optimization equation***. In Equation 9.1, the composition function g is given by $f(j) + c(j, x)$. This function is additive, since it is the sum of two terms. In a general DP formulation, the cost function need not be additive. A functional equation that contains a single recursive term (for example, $f(j)$) yields a ***monadic*** DP formulation. For an arbitrary DP formulation, the cost function may contain multiple recursive terms. DP formulations whose cost function contains multiple recursive terms are called ***polyadic*** formulations.

The dependencies between subproblems in a DP formulation can be represented by a directed graph. Each node in the graph represents a subproblem. A directed edge from node i to node j indicates that the solution to the subproblem represented by node i is used to compute the solution to the subproblem represented by node j. If the graph is acyclic, then the nodes of the graph can be organized into levels such that subproblems at a particular

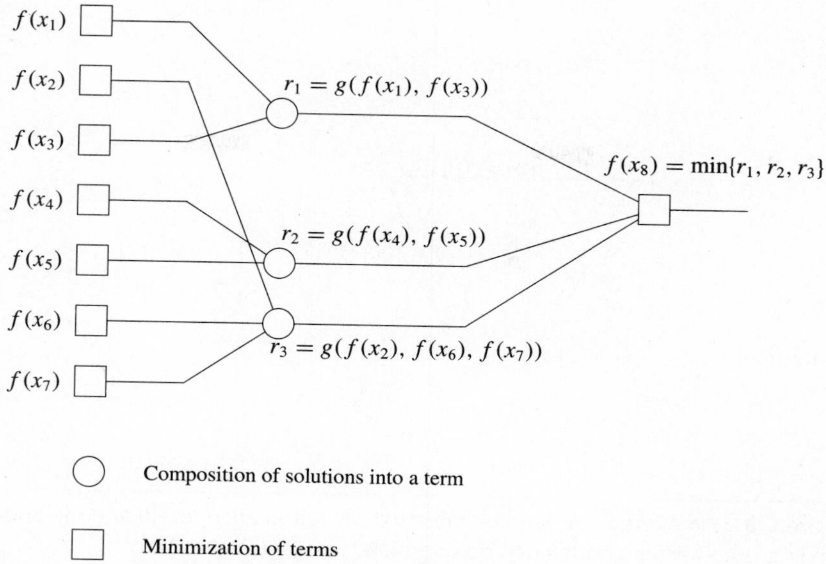

Figure 9.2 The computation and composition of subproblem solutions to solve problem $f(x_8)$.

level depend only on subproblems at previous levels. In this case, the DP formulation can be categorized as follows. If subproblems at all levels depend only on the results at the immediately preceding levels, the formulation is called a ***serial*** DP formulation; otherwise, it is called a ***nonserial*** DP formulation.

Based on the preceding classification criteria, we define four classes of DP formulations: ***serial monadic***, ***serial polyadic***, ***nonserial monadic***, and ***nonserial polyadic***. These classes, however, are not exhaustive; some DP formulations cannot be classified into any of these categories.

Due to the wide variety of problems solved using DP, it is difficult to develop generic parallel algorithms for them. However, parallel formulations of the problems in each of the four DP categories have certain similarities. In this chapter, we discuss parallel DP formulations for sample problems in each class. These samples suggest parallel algorithms for other problems in the same class. Note, however, that not all DP problems can be parallelized as illustrated in these examples.

9.1 Serial Monadic DP Formulations

We can solve many problems by using serial monadic DP formulations. This section discusses the shortest-path problem for a multistage graph and the 0/1 knapsack problem. We present parallel algorithms for both and point out the specific properties that influence the parallel formulations.

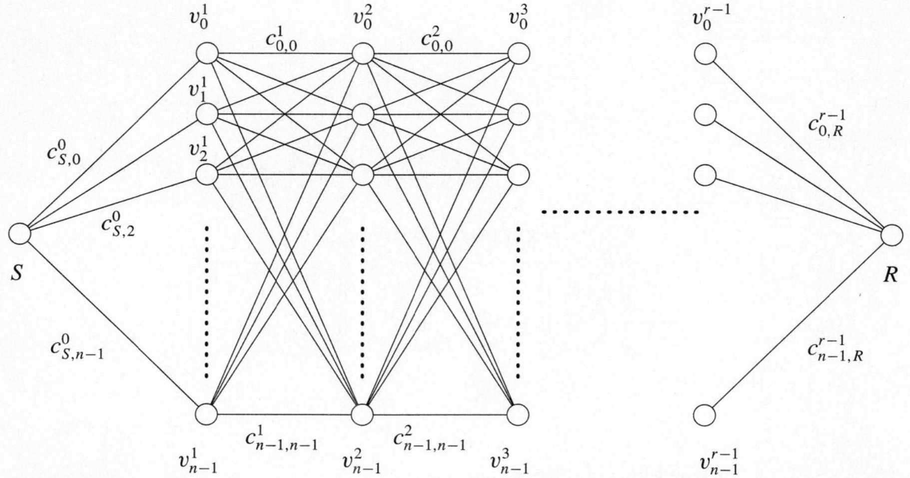

Figure 9.3 An example of a serial monadic DP formulation for finding the shortest path in a graph whose nodes can be organized into levels.

9.1.1 The Shortest-Path Problem

Consider a weighted multistage graph of $r + 1$ levels, as shown in Figure 9.3. Each node at level i is connected to every node at level $i + 1$. Levels zero and r contain only one node, and every other level contains n nodes. We refer to the node at level zero as the starting node S and the node at level r as the terminating node R. The objective of this problem is to find the shortest path from S to R. The ith node at level l in the graph is labeled v_i^l. The cost of an edge connecting v_i^l to node v_j^{l+1} is labeled $c_{i,j}^l$. The cost of reaching the goal node R from any node v_i^l is represented by C_i^l. If there are n nodes at level l, the vector $[C_0^l, C_1^l, \ldots, C_{n-1}^l]^T$ is referred to as $\mathcal{C}^l$. The shortest-path problem reduces to computing $\mathcal{C}^0$. Since the graph has only one starting node, $\mathcal{C}^0 = [C_0^0]$. The structure of the graph is such that any path from v_i^l to R includes a node v_j^{l+1} $(0 \leq j \leq n-1)$. The cost of any such path is the sum of the cost of the path between v_i^l and v_j^{l+1} and the cost of the shortest path between v_j^{l+1} and R (which is given by C_j^{l+1}). Thus, C_i^l, the cost of the shortest path between v_i^l and R, is equal to the minimum cost over all paths through each node in level $l + 1$. Therefore,

$$C_i^l = \min \left\{ (c_{i,j}^l + C_j^{l+1}) | j \text{ is a node at level } l+1 \right\}. \tag{9.2}$$

Since all nodes v_j^{r-1} have only one edge connecting them to the goal node R at level r, the cost C_j^{r-1} is equal to $c_{j,R}^{r-1}$. Hence,

$$\mathcal{C}^{r-1} = [c_{0,R}^{r-1}, c_{1,R}^{r-1}, \ldots, c_{n-1,R}^{r-1}]. \tag{9.3}$$

Because Equation 9.2 contains only one recursive term in its right-hand side, it is a monadic formulation. Note that the solution to a subproblem requires solutions to subproblems only at the immediately preceding level. Consequently, this is a serial monadic formulation.

Using this recursive formulation of the shortest-path problem, the cost of reaching the goal node R from any node at level l $(0 < l < r - 1)$ is

$$\begin{aligned}
C_0^l &= \min\{(c_{0,0}^l + C_0^{l+1}), (c_{0,1}^l + C_1^{l+1}), \ldots, (c_{0,n-1}^l + C_{n-1}^{l+1})\},\\
C_1^l &= \min\{(c_{1,0}^l + C_0^{l+1}), (c_{1,1}^l + C_1^{l+1}), \ldots, (c_{1,n-1}^l + C_{n-1}^{l+1})\},\\
&\vdots\\
C_{n-1}^l &= \min\{(c_{n-1,0}^l + C_0^{l+1}), (c_{n-1,1}^l + C_1^{l+1}), \ldots, (c_{n-1,n-1}^l + C_{n-1}^{l+1})\}.
\end{aligned}$$

Now consider the operation of multiplying a matrix with a vector. In the matrix-vector product, if the addition operation is replaced by minimization and the multiplication operation is replaced by addition, the preceding set of equations is equivalent to

$$\mathcal{C}^l = M_{l,l+1} \times \mathcal{C}^{l+1}, \tag{9.4}$$

where $\mathcal{C}^l$ and $\mathcal{C}^{l+1}$ are $n \times 1$ vectors representing the cost of reaching the goal node from each node at levels l and $l + 1$, and $M_{l,l+1}$ is an $n \times n$ matrix in which entry (i, j) stores the cost of the edge connecting node i at level l to node j at level $l + 1$. This matrix is

$$M_{l,l+1} = \begin{bmatrix} c_{0,0}^l & c_{0,1}^l & \cdots & c_{0,n-1}^l \\ c_{1,0}^l & c_{1,1}^l & \cdots & c_{1,n-1}^l \\ \vdots & \vdots & & \vdots \\ c_{n-1,0}^l & c_{n-1,1}^l & \cdots & c_{n-1,n-1}^l \end{bmatrix}.$$

The shortest-path problem has thus been reformulated as a sequence of matrix-vector multiplications. On a sequential computer, the DP formulation starts by computing $\mathcal{C}^{r-1}$ from Equation 9.3, and then computes $\mathcal{C}^{r-k-1}$ for $k = 1, 2, \ldots, r - 2$ using Equation 9.4. Finally, $\mathcal{C}^0$ is computed using Equation 9.2.

Since there are n nodes at each level, the cost of computing each vector $\mathcal{C}^l$ is $\Theta(n^2)$. The parallel algorithm for this problem can be derived using the parallel algorithms for the matrix-vector product discussed in Section 5.3. For example, on a mesh, $\Theta(n)$ processors can compute each vector $\mathcal{C}^l$ in $\Theta(n)$ time and solve the entire problem in $\Theta(rn)$ time.

Many serial monadic DP formulations with dependency graphs identical to the one considered here can be parallelized using a similar parallel algorithm. For certain dependency graphs, however, this formulation is unsuitable. Consider a graph in which each node at a level can be reached from only a small fraction of nodes at the previous level. Then matrix $M_{l,l+1}$ contains many elements with value ∞. In this case, matrix M is considered to be sparse matrix (a matrix containing many zeros) for the minimization and addition operations. This is because, for all x, $x + \infty = \infty$, and $\min\{x, \infty\} = x$. Therefore, the addition and minimization operations need not be performed for entries whose value is ∞. If we use a regular dense matrix-vector multiplication algorithm, the computational complexity of each matrix-vector multiplication becomes significantly higher than the corresponding sparse matrix-vector multiplication. Consequently, we must use a sparse matrix-vector multiplication algorithm to compute each vector. Parallel algorithms for sparse matrix-vector multiplication for certain types of sparse matrices are discussed in Chapter 11.

9.1.2 The 0/1 Knapsack Problem

A one-dimensional 0/1 knapsack problem is defined as follows. We are given a knapsack of capacity c and a set of n objects numbered $1, 2, \ldots, n$. Each object i has weight w_i and profit p_i. Object profits and weights are integers. Let $v = [v_1, v_2, \ldots, v_n]$ be a solution vector in which $v_i = 0$ if object i is not in the knapsack, and $v_i = 1$ if it is in the knapsack. The goal is to find a subset of objects to put into the knapsack so that

$$\sum_{i=1}^{n} w_i v_i \leq c$$

(that is, the objects fit into the knapsack) and

$$\sum_{i=1}^{n} p_i v_i$$

is maximized (that is, the profit is maximized).

A straightforward method to solve this problem is to consider all 2^n possible subsets of the n objects and choose the one that fits into the knapsack and maximizes the profit. Here we provide a DP formulation that is faster than the simple method when $c = O(2^n/n)$. Let $F[i, x]$ be the maximum profit for a knapsack of capacity x using only objects $\{1, 2, \ldots, i\}$. Then $F[n, c]$ is the solution to the problem. The DP formulation for this problem is as follows:

$$F[i, x] = \begin{cases} 0 & x \geq 0, i = 0 \\ -\infty & x < 0, i = 0 \\ \max\limits_{1 \leq i \leq n} \{F[i-1, x], (F[i-1, x - w_i] + p_i)\} & 1 \leq i \leq n \end{cases}$$

This recursive equation yields a knapsack of maximum profit. When the current capacity of the knapsack is x, the decision to include object i can lead to one of two situations: (1) the object is not included, knapsack capacity remains x, and profit is unchanged; (2) the object is included, knapsack capacity becomes $x - w_i$, and profit increases by p_i. The DP algorithm decides whether or not to include an object based on which choice leads to maximum profit.

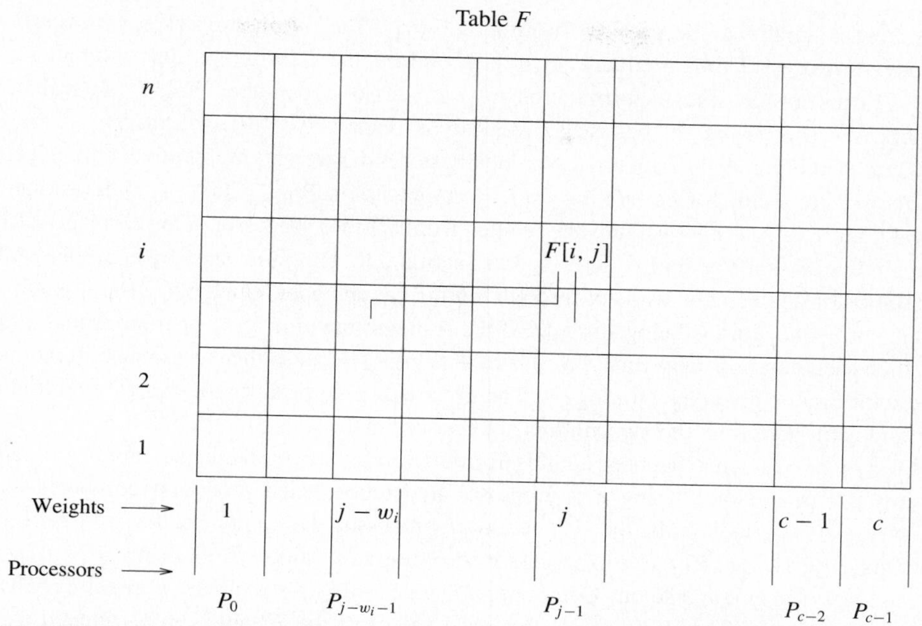

Figure 9.4 Computing entries of table F for the 0/1 knapsack problem. The computation of entry $F[i, j]$ requires communication with processors containing entries $F[i-1, j]$ and $F[i-1, j-w_i]$.

The sequential algorithm for this DP formulation maintains a table F of size $n \times c$. The table is constructed in row-major order. The algorithm first determines the maximum profit by using only the first object with knapsacks of different capacities. This corresponds to filling the first row of the table. Filling entries in subsequent rows requires two entries from the previous row: one from the same column and one from the column offset by the weight of the object. Thus, the computation of an arbitrary entry $F[i, j]$ requires $F[i-1, j]$ and $F[i-1, j-w_i]$. This is depicted in Figure 9.4. Computing each entry takes constant time; the sequential run time of this algorithm is $\Theta(nc)$.

This formulation is a serial monadic formulation. The subproblems $F[i, x]$ are organized into n levels for $i = 1, 2, \ldots, n$. Computation of problems in level i depends only on the subproblems at level $i - 1$. Hence the formulation is serial. The formulation is monadic because each of the two alternate solutions of $F[i, x]$ depend on only one subproblem. Furthermore, dependencies between levels are sparse because a problem at one level depends only on two subproblems from previous levels.

Consider a parallel formulation of this algorithm on a CREW PRAM with c processors labeled P_0 to P_{c-1}. Processor P_{r-1} computes the rth column of matrix F. When computing $F[j, r]$ during iteration j, processor P_{r-1} requires the values $F[j-1, r]$ and $F[j-1, r-w_j]$. Processor P_{r-1} can read any element of matrix F in constant time, so computing $F[j, r]$ also requires constant time. Therefore, each iteration takes constant time. Since there are n iterations, the parallel run time is $\Theta(n)$. The formulation uses c processors, hence, its processor-time product is $\Theta(nc)$. Therefore, the algorithm is cost-optimal.

Let us now consider its formulation on a c-processor hypercube. Table F is distributed among the processors so that each processor is responsible for one column. This is illustrated in Figure 9.4. Each processor locally stores the weights and profits of all objects. In the jth iteration, for computing $F[j, r]$ at processor P_{r-1}, $F[j-1, r]$ is available locally but $F[j-1, r-w_j]$ must be fetched from another processor. This corresponds to the circular w_j-shift operation described in Section 3.6. The time taken by a circular shift operation on a hypercube with cut-through routing has an upper bound of $(t_s + t_w + t_h \log c)$ (since only one word is being shifted). If the sum and maximization operations take time t_c, then each iteration takes time $t_c + t_s + t_w + t_h \log c$. Because there are n such iterations, the total time is given by $O(n \log c)$. The processor-time product for this formulation is $O(nc \log c)$; therefore, the algorithm is not cost-optimal.

Let us see what happens to this formulation as we increase the number of elements per processor. Using a p-processor hypercube, each processor computes c/p elements of the table. In the jth iteration, processor P_0 computes the values of elements $F[j, 1], \ldots, F[j, c/p]$, processor P_1 computes values of elements $F[j, c/p + 1], \ldots, F[j, 2c/p]$, and so on. Computing the value of $F[j, k]$, for any k, requires values $F[j-1, k]$ and $F[j-1, k-w_j]$. Required values of the F table can be fetched from remote processors by performing a circular shift. Depending on the values of w_j and p, the required nonlocal values may be available from one or two processors. The time for this operation is at most $(2t_s + t_w c/p + 2t_h \log p)$ (Section 3.6). Since each processor computes c/p such elements, the total time taken by a processor for each iteration is $t_c c/p + 2t_s + t_w c/p + 2t_h \log p$. Therefore, the parallel run time of the algorithm for n iterations is $n(t_c c/p + 2t_s + t_w c/p + 2t_h \log p)$. In asymptotic terms, this algorithm's parallel run time is $O(nc/p + n \log p)$. Its processor-time product is $O(nc + np \log p)$, which cost-optimal for $c = \Omega(p \log p)$.

There is an upper bound on the efficiency of this formulation. The reason is that the amount of data that needs to be communicated is of the same order as the amount of computation at each processor. This upper bound is determined by the values of t_w and t_c (Problem 9.1). Mapping this parallel algorithm onto a mesh results in a non-cost-optimal formulation (Problem 9.3). However, if all the weights are less than a certain constant, then the communication becomes localized for larger instances of the problems. For this case, the formulation becomes cost-optimal on a mesh (Problem 9.4).

9.2 Nonserial Monadic DP Formulations

The DP algorithm for determining the longest common subsequence of two given sequences can be formulated as a nonserial monadic DP formulation.

9.2.1 The Longest-Common-Subsequence Problem

Given a sequence $A = \langle a_1, a_2, \ldots, a_n \rangle$, a subsequence of A can be formed by deleting some entries from A. For example, $\langle a, b, z \rangle$ is a subsequence of $\langle c, a, d, b, r, z \rangle$, but $\langle a, c, z \rangle$ and $\langle a, d, l \rangle$ are not. The ***longest-common-subsequence*** (LCS) problem can be stated as follows. Given two sequences $A = \langle a_1, a_2, \ldots, a_n \rangle$ and $B = \langle b_1, b_2, \ldots, b_m \rangle$, find the longest sequence that is a subsequence of both A and B. For example, if $A = \langle c, a, d, b, r, z \rangle$ and $B = \langle a, s, b, z \rangle$, the longest common subsequence of A and B is $\langle a, b, z \rangle$.

Let $F[i, j]$ denote the length of the longest common subsequence of the first i elements of A and the first j elements of B. The objective of the LCS problem is to determine $F[n, m]$. The DP formulation for this problem expresses $F[i, j]$ in terms of $F[i-1, j-1]$, $F[i, j-1]$, and $F[i-1, j]$ as follows:

$$F[i, j] = \begin{cases} 0 & \text{if } i = 0 \text{ or } j = 0 \\ F[i-1, j-1] + 1 & \text{if } i, j > 0 \text{ and } x_i = y_j \\ \max\{F[i, j-1], F[i-1, j]\} & \text{if } i, j > 0 \text{ and } x_i \neq y_j \end{cases}$$

Given sequences A and B, consider two pointers pointing to the start of the sequences. If the entries pointed to by the two pointers are identical, then they form components of the longest common subsequence. Therefore, both pointers can be advanced to the next entry of the respective sequences and the length of the longest common subsequence can be incremented by one. If the entries are not identical then two situations arise: the longest common subsequence may be obtained from the longest subsequence of A and the sequence obtained by advancing the pointer to the next entry of B; or, the longest subsequence may be obtained from the longest subsequence of B and the sequence obtained by advancing the pointer to the next entry of A. Since we want to determine the longest subsequence, the maximum of these two must be selected.

The sequential implementation of this DP formulation computes the values in table F in row-major order. Since there is a constant amount of computation at each entry in the table, the overall complexity of this algorithm is $\Theta(nm)$. This DP formulation is nonserial monadic, as illustrated in Figure 9.5(a). Treating nodes along a diagonal as belonging to one level, each node depends on two subproblems at the preceding level and one subproblem two levels earlier. The formulation is monadic because a solution to any subproblem at a level is a function of only one of the solutions at preceding levels. (Note that, for the third case in Equation 9.5, both $F[i, j-1]$ and $F[i-1, j]$ are possible solutions to $F[i, j]$, and the optimal solution to $F[i, j]$ is the maximum of the two.) Figure 9.5 shows that this problem has a very regular structure.

To simplify the discussion, we discuss parallel formulation only for the case in which $n = m$. Consider a parallel formulation of this algorithm on a CREW PRAM with n processors. Each processor P_i computes the ith column of table F. Table entries are computed in a diagonal sweep from the top-left to the bottom-right corner. Since there

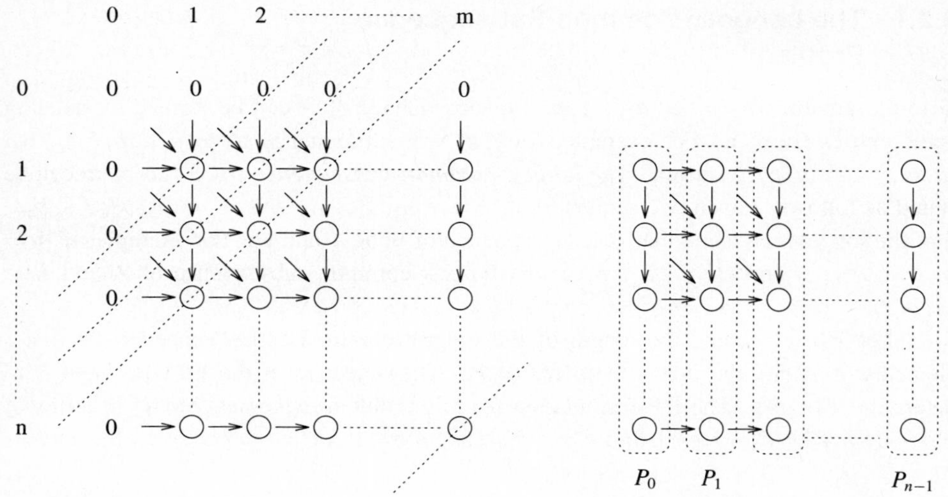

(a) (b)

Figure 9.5 (a) Computing entries of table F for the longest-common-subsequence problem. Computation proceeds along the dotted diagonal lines. (b) Mapping elements of the table to processors.

are n processors, and each processor can access any entry in table F, the elements of each diagonal are computed in constant time (the diagonal can contain at most n elements). Since there are $2n - 1$ such diagonals, the algorithm requires $\Theta(n)$ iterations. Thus, the parallel run time is $\Theta(n)$. The algorithm is cost-optimal, since its $\Theta(n^2)$ processor-time product equals the sequential complexity.

This algorithm can be adapted to run on a linear array of n processors by distributing table F among different processors. Processor P_i stores the $(i + 1)^{\text{st}}$ column of the table. Entries in table F are assigned to processors as illustrated in Figure 9.5(b). When computing the value of $F[i, j]$, processor P_{j-1} may need either the value of $F[i-1, j-1]$ or the value of $F[i, j-1]$ from the processor to its left. It takes time $t_s + t_w$ to communicate a single word from a neighboring processor. To compute each entry in the table, a processor needs a single value from its immediate neighbor, followed by the actual computation, which takes time t_c. Since each processor computes a single entry on the diagonal, each iteration takes time $(t_s + t_w + t_c)$. The algorithm makes $(2n - 1)$ diagonal sweeps (iterations) across the table; thus, the total parallel run time is

$$T_P = (2n - 1)(t_s + t_w + t_c).$$

Since the sequential run time is $n^2 t_c$, the efficiency of this algorithm is

$$E = \frac{n^2 t_c}{n(2n - 1)(t_s + t_w + t_c)}.$$

A careful examination of this expression reveals that it is not possible to obtain efficiencies above a certain threshold. To compute this threshold, assume it is possible to communicate values between processors instantaneously; that is, $t_s = t_w = 0$. In this case, the efficiency of the parallel algorithm is

$$E_{max} = \frac{1}{2 - 1/n}. \tag{9.5}$$

Thus, the efficiency is bounded above by 0.5. This upper bound holds even if multiple columns are mapped to a processor. Higher efficiencies are possible using alternate mappings (Problem 9.5). Parallel formulations for architectures such as the mesh and hypercube only require embedding the ring into the target architecture (Section 2.5).

Note that the basic characteristic that allows efficient parallel formulations of this algorithm is that table F can be partitioned so computing each element requires data only from neighboring processors. In other words, the algorithm exhibits locality of data access.

9.3 Serial Polyadic DP Formulations

Floyd's algorithm for determining the shortest paths between all pairs of nodes in a graph can be reformulated as a serial polyadic DP formulation.

9.3.1 Floyd's All-Pairs Shortest-Paths Algorithm

Consider a weighted graph G, which consists of a set of nodes V and a set of edges E. An edge from node i to node j in E has a weight $c_{i,j}$. Floyd's algorithm determines the cost $d_{i,j}$ of the shortest path between each pair of nodes (i, j) in V (Section 7.4.3). The cost of a path is the sum of the weights of the edges in the path.

Let $d_{i,j}^k$ be the minimum cost of a path from node i to node j, using only nodes $v_0, v_1, \ldots, v_{k-1}$. The functional equation of the DP formulation for this problem is

$$d_{i,j}^k = \begin{cases} c_{i,j} & k = 0 \\ \min\{d_{i,j}^{k-1}, (d_{i,k}^{k-1} + d_{k,j}^{k-1})\} & 0 \le k \le n-1 \end{cases}. \tag{9.6}$$

Since $d_{i,j}^n$ is the shortest path from node i to node j using all n nodes, it is also the cost of the overall shortest path between nodes i and j. The sequential formulation of this algorithm requires n iterations, and each iteration requires $\Theta(n^2)$ time. Thus, the overall run time of the sequential algorithm is $\Theta(n^3)$.

Equation 9.6 is a serial polyadic formulation. Nodes $d_{i,j}^k$ can be partitioned into n levels, one for each value of k. Elements at level $k + 1$ depend only on elements at level k. Hence, the formulation is serial. The formulation is polyadic since one of the solutions to $d_{i,j}^k$ requires a composition of solutions to two subproblems $d_{i,k}^{k-1}$ and $d_{k,j}^{k-1}$ from the previous level. Furthermore, the dependencies between levels are sparse because the computation of each element in $d_{i,j}^{k+1}$ requires only three results from the preceding level (out of n^2).

A simple CREW PRAM formulation of this algorithm uses n^2 processors. Processors are organized into a two-dimensional array in which processor $P_{i,j}$ computes the value of $d_{i,j}^{k}$ for $k = 1, 2, \ldots, n$. In each iteration k, processor $P_{i,j}$ requires the values $d_{i,j}^{k-1}$, $d_{i,k}^{k-1}$, and $d_{k,j}^{k-1}$. Given these values, it computes the value of $d_{i,j}^{k}$ in constant time. Therefore, the PRAM formulation has a parallel run time of $\Theta(n)$. This formulation is cost-optimal because its processor-time product is the same as the sequential run time of $\Theta(n^3)$. This algorithm can be adapted to practical architectures like the hypercube to yield efficient parallel formulations (Section 7.4.3).

As with serial monadic formulations, data locality is of prime importance in serial polyadic formulations since many such formulations have sparse connectivity between levels.

9.4 Nonserial Polyadic DP Formulations

In nonserial polyadic DP formulations, in addition to processing subproblems at a level in parallel, computation can also be pipelined to increase efficiency. We illustrate this with the optimal matrix-parenthesization problem.

9.4.1 The Optimal Matrix-Parenthesization Problem

Consider the problem of multiplying n matrices, $A_1, A_2, \ldots, A_n$, where each A_i is a matrix with r_{i-1} rows and r_i columns. The order in which the matrices are multiplied has a significant impact on the total number of operations required to evaluate the product. For example, consider three matrices A_1, A_2, and A_3 of dimensions 10×20, 20×30, and 30×40, respectively. The product of these matrices can be computed as $(A_1 \times A_2) \times A_3$ or as $A_1 \times (A_2 \times A_3)$. In $(A_1 \times A_2) \times A_3$, computing $(A_1 \times A_2)$ requires $10 \times 20 \times 30$ operations and yields a matrix of dimensions 10×30. Multiplying this by A_3 requires $10 \times 30 \times 40$ additional operations. Therefore the total number of operations is $10 \times 20 \times 30 + 10 \times 30 \times 40 = 18,000$. Similarly, computing $A_1 \times (A_2 \times A_3)$ requires $20 \times 30 \times 40 + 10 \times 20 \times 40 = 32,000$ operations. Clearly, the first parenthesization is desirable. The objective of the parenthesization problem is to determine a parenthesization that minimizes the number of operations. Enumerating all possible parenthesizations is not feasible since there are exponentially many of them.

Let $C[i, j]$ be the optimal cost of multiplying the matrices $A_i, \ldots, A_j$. This chain of matrices can be expressed as a product of two smaller chains, $A_i, A_{i+1}, \ldots, A_k$ and $A_{k+1}, \ldots, A_j$. The chain $A_i, A_{i+1}, \ldots, A_k$ results in a matrix of dimension $r_{i-1} \times r_k$, and the chain $A_{k+1}, \ldots, A_j$ results in a matrix of dimension $r_k \times r_j$. The cost of multiplying these two matrices is $r_{i-1} r_k r_j$. Hence, the cost of the parenthesization

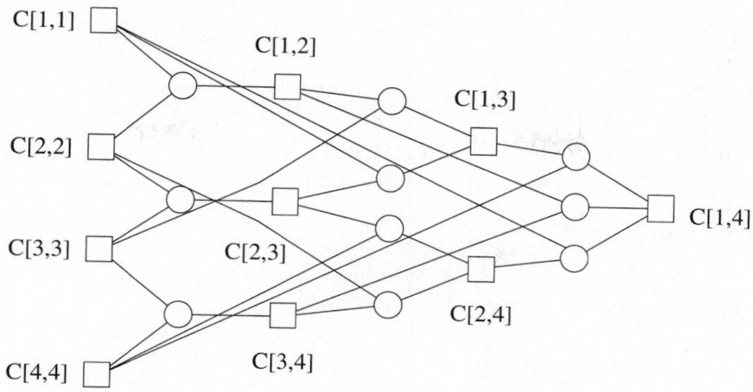

Figure 9.6 A nonserial polyadic DP formulation for finding an optimal matrix parenthesization for a chain of four matrices. A square node represents the optimal cost of multiplying a matrix chain. A circle node represents a possible parenthesization.

$(A_i, A_{i+1}, \ldots, A_k)(A_{k+1}, \ldots, A_j)$ is given by $C[i,k] + C[k+1, j] + r_{i-1}r_k r_j$. This gives rise to the following recurrence relation for the parenthesization problem:

$$C[i, j] = \begin{cases} \min_{i \le k < j} \{C[i,k] + C[k+1, j] + r_{i-1}r_k r_j\} & 1 \le i < j \le n \\ 0 & j = i, 0 < i \le n \end{cases} \tag{9.7}$$

Given Equation 9.7, the problem reduces to finding the value of $C[1, n]$. The composition of costs of matrix chains is shown in Figure 9.6.

Equation 9.7 can be solved if we use a bottom-up approach for constructing the table C that stores the values $C[i, j]$. The algorithm fills table C in an order corresponding to solving the parenthesization problem on matrix chains of increasing length. Visualize this by thinking of filling in the table diagonally (Figure 9.7). Entries in diagonal l corresponds to the cost of multiplying matrix chains of length $l + 1$. From Equation 9.7, we can see that the value of $C[i, j]$ is computed as $\min\{C[i,k] + C[k+1, j] + r_{i-1}r_k r_j\}$, where k can take values from i to $j - 1$. Therefore, computing $C[i, j]$ requires that we evaluate $(j - i)$ terms and select their minimum. The computation of each term takes time t_c, and the computation of $C[i, j]$ takes time $(j - i)t_c$. Thus, each entry in diagonal l can be computed in time lt_c.

In computing the cost of the optimal parenthesization sequence, the algorithm computes $(n - 1)$ chains of length two. This takes time $(n - 1)t_c$. Similarly, computing $(n - 2)$ chains of length three takes time $(n - 2)2t_c$. In the final step, the algorithm computes one chain of length n. This takes time $(n - 1)t_c$. Thus, the sequential run time of this algorithm is

$$T_S = (n-1)t_c + (n-2)2t_c + \cdots + 1(n-1)t_c,$$

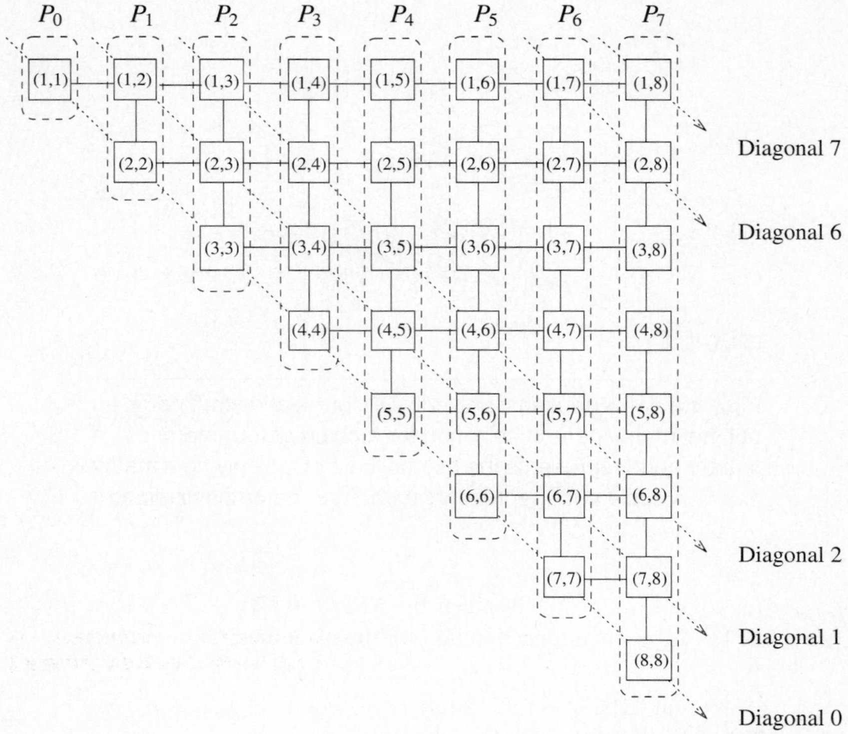

Figure 9.7 The diagonal order of computation for the optimal matrix-parenthesization problem.

$$
\begin{aligned}
&= \sum_{i=1}^{n-1} (n-i)it_c, \\
&\simeq (n^3/6)t_c. \qquad (9.8)
\end{aligned}
$$

The sequential complexity of the algorithm is $\Theta(n^3)$.

Consider the parallel formulation of this algorithm on a ring of n processors. In step l, each processor computes a single element belonging to the lth diagonal. Processor P_i computes the $(i+1)^{\text{st}}$ column of Table C. Figure 9.7 illustrates the partitioning of the table among different processors. After computing the assigned value of the element in table C, each processor sends its value to all other processors using an all-to-all broadcast (Section 3.3). Therefore, the assigned value in the next iteration can be computed locally. Computing an entry in table C during iteration l takes time lt_c because it corresponds to the cost of multiplying a chain of length $l+1$. An all-to-all broadcast of a single word on a ring of n processors takes time $(t_s + t_w)(n-1)$ (Section 3.3). The total time required to compute the entries along diagonal l is $(lt_c + (t_s + t_w)(n-1))$. The parallel run time is the sum of time taken over computation of $n - 1$ diagonals.

$$\begin{aligned} T_P &= \sum_{l=1}^{n-1} (lt_c + (t_s + t_w)(n-1)), \\ &= \frac{(n-1)(n)}{2} t_c + (t_s + t_w)(n-1)^2. \end{aligned}$$

The parallel run time of this algorithm is $\Theta(n^2)$. Since the processor-time product is $\Theta(n^3)$, which is the same as the sequential complexity, this algorithm is cost-optimal.

It is also possible to use a ring of p processors ($1 \le p \le n$). If there are n nodes in a diagonal, each processor stores n/p nodes. Each processor computes the cost $C[i, j]$ of the entries assigned to it. After computation, an all-to-all broadcast sends the solution costs of the subproblems for the just-finished diagonal to all the other processors. Because each processor has complete information about subproblem costs at preceding diagonals, no other communication is required. The time taken for all-to-all broadcast of n/p words is $(t_s + t_w n/p)(p-1)$. The time to compute n/p entries of the table in the lth diagonal is $lt_c n/p$. The parallel run time is

$$\begin{aligned} T_P &= \sum_{l=1}^{n-1} (lt_c n/p + (t_s + t_w n/p)(p-1)), \\ &= \frac{n^2(n-1)}{2p} t_c + t_s(n-1)(p-1) + \frac{t_w n(n-1)(p-1)}{p}. \end{aligned}$$

In order terms, $T_P = \Theta(n^3/p) + \Theta(n^2)$. Here, $\Theta(n^3/p)$ is the computation time, and $\Theta(n^2)$ the communication time. If n is sufficiently large with respect to p, communication time can be made an arbitrarily small fraction of computation time, yielding linear speedup.

This formulation can use at most $\Theta(n)$ processors to accomplish the task in $\Theta(n^2)$ time. This time can be improved by pipelining the computation of the cost $C[i, j]$ on $n(n+1)/2$ processors. Each processor computes a single entry $c(i, j)$ of matrix C. Pipelining works due to the nonserial nature of the problem. Computation of an entry on a diagonal t does not depend only on the entries on diagonal $t - 1$ but also on all the earlier diagonals. Hence work on diagonal t can start even before work on diagonal $t - 1$ is completed. This algorithm is discussed in detail in Section 12.1.4.

9.5 Summary and Discussion

This chapter provides a framework for deriving parallel algorithms that use dynamic programming. It identifies possible sources of parallelism, and indicates under what conditions they can be utilized effectively.

By representing computation as a graph, we identify three sources of parallelism. First, the computation of the cost of a single subproblem (a node in a level) can be parallelized. For example, for computing the shortest path in the multistage graph shown in

Figure 9.3, node computation can be parallelized because the complexity of node computation is itself $\Theta(n)$. For many problems, however, node computation complexity is lower, limiting available parallelism.

Second, subproblems at each level can be solved in parallel. This provides a viable method for extracting parallelism from a large class of problems (including all the problems in this chapter).

The first two sources of parallelism are available to both serial and nonserial formulations. Nonserial formulations allow a third source of parallelism: pipelining of computations among different levels. Pipelining makes it possible to start solving a problem as soon as the subproblems it depends on are solved. This form of parallelism is used in the parenthesization problem.

Note that pipelining was also applied to the parallel formulation of Floyd's all-pairs shortest-paths algorithm in Section 7.4.3. As discussed in Section 9.3, this algorithm corresponds to a serial DP formulation. The nature of pipelining in this algorithm is different than the one in nonserial DP formulation. In the pipelined version of Floyd's algorithm, computation in a stage is pipelined with the communication among earlier stages. If communication cost is zero (as in a PRAM), then Floyd's algorithm does not benefit from pipelining.

Throughout the chapter, we have seen the importance of data locality. If the solution to a problem requires results from other subproblems, the cost of communicating those results must be less than the cost of solving the problem. In some problems (the 0/1 knapsack problem, for example) the degree of locality is much smaller than that in other problems such as the longest-common-subsequence problem and Floyd's all-pairs shortest-paths algorithm.

9.6 Bibliographic Remarks

Dynamic programming was originally presented by Bellman [Bel57] for solving multistage decision problems. Various formal models have since been developed for DP [KH67, MM73, KK88]. Several textbooks and articles present sequential DP formulations of the longest-common-subsequence problem, the matrix chain multiplication problem, the 0/1 knapsack problem, and the shortest-path problem. [CLR90, HS78, PS82, Bro79].

Li and Wah [LW85, WL88] show that monadic serial DP formulations can be solved in parallel on systolic arrays as matrix-vector products. They further present a more concurrent but non-cost-optimal formulation by formulating the problem as a matrix-matrix product. Ranka and Sahni [RS90] present a polyadic serial formulation for the string editing problem and derive a SIMD parallel formulation based on a checkerboard partitioning.

The DP formulation of a large class of optimization problems is similar to that of the optimal matrix-parenthesization problem. Some examples of these problems are optimal triangularization of polygons, optimal binary search trees [CLR90], and CYK parsing [AU72]. The serial complexity of the standard DP formulation for all these problems is $\Theta(n^3)$. Several parallel formulations have been proposed by Ibarra et al. [IPS91] that use

$\Theta(n)$ processors on a hypercube and that solve the problem in $\Theta(n^2)$ time. Guibas, Kung, and Thompson [GKT79] present a systolic algorithm that uses $\Theta(n^2)$ processing cells and solves the problem in $\Theta(n)$ time. Karypis and Kumar [KK92] analyze three distinct mappings of the systolic algorithm presented by Guibas et al. [GKT79] and experimentally evaluate them by using the matrix-multiplication parenthesization problem on the nCUBE 2 multicomputer. They show that a straightforward mapping of this algorithm to a mesh architecture has an upper bound on efficiency of $1/12$. They also present a better mapping without this drawback, and show near-linear speedup on a mesh embedded into a 256-processor nCUBE 2 for the optimal matrix-parenthesization problem.

Many faster parallel algorithms for solving the parenthesization problem have been proposed, but they are not cost-optimal and are applicable only to theoretical models such as the PRAM. For example, the generalized method for parallelizing such programs is described by Valiant et al. [VSBR83] that leads directly to formulations that run in $O(\log^2 n)$ time on $O(n^9)$ processors. Rytter [Ryt88] uses the parallel pebble game on trees to reduce the number of processors to $O(n^6/\log n)$ for a CREW PRAM and $O(n^6)$ for a hypercube, yet solves this problem in $O(\log^2 n)$ time. Huang et al. [HLV90] present a similar algorithm for CREW PRAM models that run in $O(\sqrt{n}\log n)$ time on $O(n^{3.5}\log n)$ processors. DeMello et al. [DCG90] use vectorized formulations of DP for the Cray to solve optimal control problems.

As we have seen, the serial polyadic formulation of the 0/1 knapsack problem is difficult to parallelize due to lack of communication locality. Lee et al. [LSS88] use specific characteristics of the knapsack problem and derive a divide-and-conquer strategy for parallelizing the DP algorithm for the 0/1 knapsack problem on a MIMD message-passing computer (Problem 9.2). Lee et al. demonstrate experimentally that it is possible to obtain linear speedup for large instances of the problem on the nCUBE multicomputer.

Problems

9.1 Consider the parallel algorithm for solving the 0/1 knapsack problem on a hypercube in Section 9.1.2. The algorithm is cost optimal if $c = \Omega(p \log p)$. Derive the speedup and efficiency for this algorithm. Show that the efficiency of this algorithm cannot be increased beyond a certain value by increasing the problem size for a fixed number of processors. What is the upper bound on efficiency for this formulation as a function of t_w and t_c?

9.2 **[LSS88]** In the parallel formulation of the 0/1 knapsack problem presented in Section 9.1.2, the degree of concurrency is proportional to c, the knapsack capacity. Also this algorithm has limited data locality, as the amount of data to be communicated is of the same order of magnitude as the computation at each processor. Lee et al. present another formulation in which the degree of concurrency is proportional to n, the number of weights. This formulation also has much more data locality. In this formulation, the set of weights is partitioned among processors. Each processor computes the maximum profit it can achieve from its local weights

for knapsacks of various sizes up to c. This information is expressed as lists that are merged to yield the global solution.
Compute the parallel run time, speedup, and efficiency of this formulation on a hypercube- and a mesh- connected parallel computer. Compare the performance of this algorithm with that in Section 9.1.2.

9.3 Consider the parallel algorithm for solving the 0/1 knapsack problem on a hypercube in Section 9.1.2. Map this algorithm onto a mesh of $\sqrt{p} \times \sqrt{p}$ processors. During iteration i, a processor computes c/p elements of row i of table F. Derive the parallel run time, speedup, and efficiency for this algorithm. Show that the algorithm is not cost-optimal.

9.4 Consider the parallel algorithm for solving the 0/1 knapsack problem on a mesh (Problem 9.3). Assume that the weights of all the objects are below a certain value k. Compute the parallel run time, speedup, and efficiency in this case. Show that, under this assumption, the algorithm is cost-optimal.

9.5 We saw that the parallel formulation of the longest-common-subsequence problem has an upper bound of 0.5 on its efficiency. It is possible to use an alternate mapping to achieve higher efficiency for this problem. Derive a formulation that does not suffer from this upper bound, and give the run time of this formulation for a hypercube.
Hint: Consider the block-cyclic mapping discussed in Section 5.1.1.

9.6 **[HS78]** The traveling salesman problem (TSP) is defined as follows: Given a set of cities and the distance between each pair of cities, determine a tour through all cities of minimum length. A tour of all cities is a trip visiting each city once and returning to the starting point. The length of such a tour is the sum of distances traveled.
This problem can be solved using a DP formulation. View the cities as vertices in a graph $G(V, E)$. Let the set of cities V be represented by $\{v_1, v_2, \ldots, v_n\}$ and let $S \subseteq \{v_2, v_3, \ldots, v_n\}$. Furthermore, let $c_{i,j}$ be the distance between cities i and j. If $f(S, k)$ represents the cost of starting at city v_1, passing through all the cities in set S, and terminating in city k, then the following recursive equations can be used to compute $f(S, k)$:

$$f(S,k) = \begin{cases} c_{1,k} & S = \{k\} \\ \min_{m \in S - \{k\}} \{f(S - \{k\}), m\} + c_{m,k}\} & S \neq \{k\} \end{cases} \tag{9.9}$$

Based on equation 9.9, derive parallel formulations of the TSP for a PRAM, a mesh, and a hypercube. For each case, compute the parallel run time and the speedup. Are your parallel formulations cost-optimal?

9.7 **[HS78]** Consider the problem of merging two sorted files containing $O(n)$ and $O(m)$ records. These files can be merged into a sorted file in time $O(m + n)$. Given r such files, the problem of merging them into a single file can be formulated

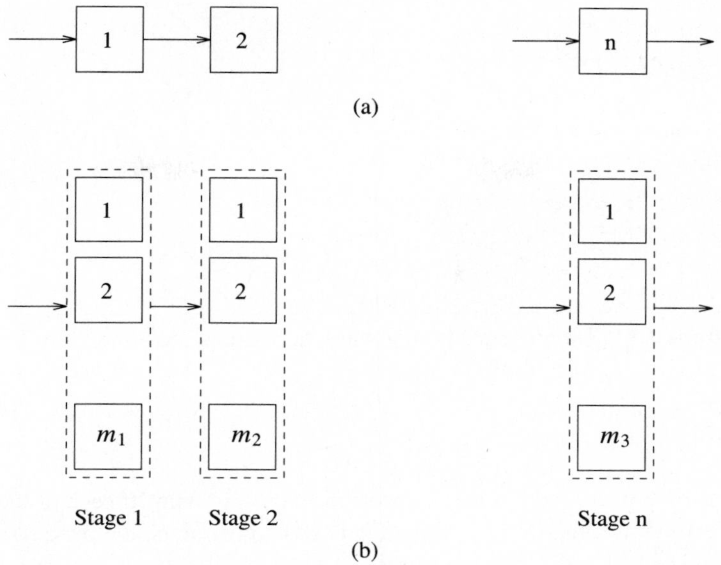

Figure 9.8 (a) n devices connected in a series within a circuit. (b) Each stage in the circuit now has m_i functional units. There are n such stages connected in the series.

as a sequence of merge operations performed on pairs of files. The overall cost of the merge operation is a function of the sequence in which they are merged. The optimal merge order can be formulated as a greedy algorithm.

Derive the recursive equations for this problem. Present parallel formulations for merging on the PRAM, the mesh, and the hypercube architectures. For each case, compute the parallel run time and the speedup. Are your parallel formulations cost-optimal? Comment on their similarity to other DP formulations.

9.8 **[HS78]** Consider the problem of designing a fault-tolerant circuit containing n devices connected in a series, as shown in Figure 9.8(a). If the probability of failure of each of these devices is given by f_i, the overall probability of failure of the circuit is given by $1 - \prod(1 - f_i)$. Here, $\prod$ represents a product of specified terms. The reliability of this circuit can be improved by connecting multiple functional devices in parallel at each stage, as shown in Figure 9.8(b). If stage i in the circuit has r_i duplicate functional units, each with a probability of failure given by f_i, then the overall probability of failure of this stage is reduced to $r_i^{m_i}$ and the overall probability of failure of the circuit is given by $1 - \prod(1 - r_i^{m_i})$. In general, due to physical reasons, the probability of failure at a particular level may not be $r_i^{m_i}$, but some function $\phi_i(r_i, m_i)$. The objective of the problem is to minimize the overall probability of failure of the circuit, $1 - \prod(1 - \phi_i(r_i, m_i))$.

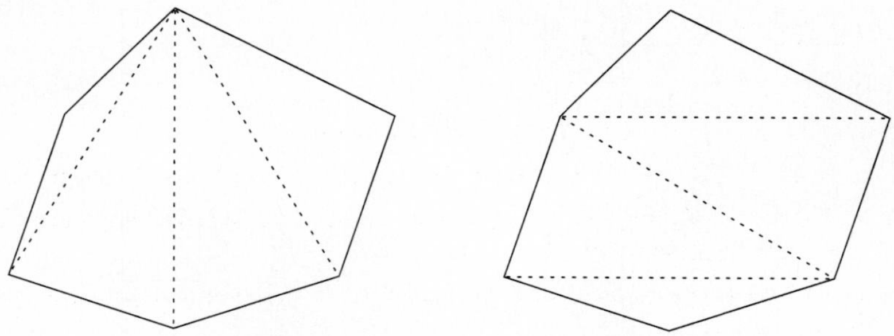

Figure 9.9 Two possible triangulation of a regular polygon.

Construction cost adds a new dimension to this problem. If each of the functional units used at stage i cost c_i then due to cost constraints, the overall cost $\sum c_i m_i$ should be less than a fixed quantity c.

The problem can be formally defined as

$$\text{Minimize } 1 - \prod(1 - \phi_i(r_i, m_i)), \text{ such that } \sum c_i m_i < c$$

where $m_i > 0$ and $0 < i \leq n$.

Let $f_i(x)$ represent the reliability of a system with i stages of cost x. The optimal solution is given by $f_n(c)$. The recursive equation for $f_i(x)$ is as follows:

$$f_i(x) = \begin{cases} 1 & i = 0 \\ \max\limits_{i \leq m_i \leq u_i} \{\phi_i(m_i) f_{i-1}(c - c_i m_i)\} & i \geq 1 \end{cases} \tag{9.10}$$

Classify this formulation into one of the four DP categories, and derive parallel formulations for a PRAM, a mesh, and a hypercube. For each formulation, determine its parallel run time, speedup, and isoefficiency function.

9.9 **[CLR90]** Consider the simplified optimal polygon-triangulation problem. This problem can be defined as follows. Given a simple polygon, break the polygon into a set of triangles by connecting nodes of the polygon with chords. This process is illustrated in Figure 9.9. The cost of constructing a triangle with nodes v_i, v_j, and v_k is defined by a function $f(v_i, v_j, v_k)$. For this problem, let the cost be the total length of the edges of the triangle (using Euclidean distance). The optimal polygon-triangulation problem breaks up a polygon into a set of triangles such that the total length of each triangle (the sum of the individual lengths) is minimized. Give a DP formulation for this problem. Classify it into one of the four categories and derive parallel formulations for a PRAM, a mesh, and a hypercube. For each formulation, determine its parallel run time, speedup, and isoefficiency function. ***Hint:*** This problem is similar to the optimal matrix-parenthesization problem.

References

[AU72] A. V. Aho and J. D. Ullman. *The Theory of Parsing, Translation and Compiling: Volume 1, Parsing*. Prentice-Hall, Englewood Cliffs, NJ, 1972.

[Bel57] R. Bellman. *Dynamic Programming*. Princeton University Press, Princeton, NJ, 1957.

[Bro79] K. Brown. Dynamic programming in computer science. Technical Report CMU-CS-79-106, Carnegie Mellon University, Pittsburgh, PA, 1979.

[CLR90] T. H. Cormen, C. E. Leiserson, and R. L. Rivest. *Introduction to Algorithms*. MIT Press, McGraw-Hill, New York, NY, 1990.

[DCG90] J. D. DeMello, J. L. Calvet, and J. M. Garcia. Vectorization and multitasking of dynamic programming in control: experiments on a CRAY-2. *Parallel Computing*, 13:261–269, 1990.

[GKT79] L. J. Guibas, H. T. Kung, and C. D. Thompson. Direct VLSI Implementation of Combinatorial Algorithms. In *Proceedings of Conference on Very Large Scale Integration, California Institute of Technology*, 509–525, 1979.

[HLV90] S. H. S. Huang, H. Liu, and V. Vishwanathan. A sub-linear parallel algorithm for some dynamic programming problems. In *Proceedings of 1990 International Conference on Parallel Processing*, III–261–III–264, 1990.

[HS78] E. Horowitz and S. Sahni. *Fundamentals of Computer Algorithms*. Computer Science Press, Rockville, MD, 1978.

[IPS91] O. H. Ibarra, T. C. Pong, and S. M. Sohn. Parallel recognition and parsing on the hypercube. *IEEE Transactions on Computers*, 40(6):764–770, June 1991.

[KH67] R. M. Karp and M. H. Held. Finite state processes and dynamic programming. *SIAM Journal of Applied Math*, 15:693–718, 1967.

[KK88] V. Kumar and L. N. Kanal. The CDP: A unifying formulation for heuristic search, dynamic programming, and branch-and-bound. In L. N. Kanal and V. Kumar, editors, *Search in Artificial Intelligence*, 1–27. Springer-Verlag, New York, NY, 1988.

[KK92] G. Karypis and V. Kumar. Efficient Parallel Mappings of a Dynamic Programming Algorithm. Technical Report TR 92-59, Computer Science Department, University of Minnesota, Minneapolis, MN, 1992.

[LSS88] J. Lee, E. Shragowitz, and S. Sahni. A hypercube algorithm for the 0/1 knapsack problem. *Journal of Parallel and Distributed Computing*, (5):438–456, 1988.

[LW85] G.-J. Li and B. W. Wah. Parallel processing of serial dynamic programming problems. In *Proceedings of COMPSAC 85*, 81–89, 1985.

[MM73] A. Martelli and U. Montanari. From dynamic programming to search algorithms with functional costs. In *Proceedings of the International Joint Conference on Artifi cial Intelligence*, 345–349, 1973.

[PS82] C. H. Papadimitriou and K. Steiglitz. *Combinatorial Optimization: Algorithms and Complexity*. Prentice-Hall, Englewood Cliffs, NJ, 1982.

[RS90] S. Ranka and S. Sahni. *Hypercube Algorithms for Image Processing and Pattern Recognition*. Springer-Verlag, New York, NY, 1990.

[Ryt88] W. Rytter. Efficient parallel computations for dynamic programming. *Theoretical Computer Science*, 59:297–307, 1988.

[VSBR83] L. G. Valiant, S. Skyum, S. Berkowitz, and C. Rackoff. Fast parallel computation of polynomials using few processors. *SIAM Journal of Computing*, 12(4):641–644, 1983.

[WL88] B. W. Wah and G.-J. Li. Systolic processing for dynamic programming problems. *Circuits, Systems, and Signal Processing*, 7(2):119–149, 1988.

CHAPTER **10**

Fast Fourier Transform

The discrete Fourier transform (DFT) plays an important role in many scientific and technical applications, including time series and wave analysis, solutions to linear partial differential equations, convolution, digital signal processing, and image filtering. The DFT is a linear transformation that maps n regularly sampled points from a cycle of a periodic signal, like a sine wave, onto an equal number of points representing the frequency spectrum of the signal. In 1965, Cooley and Tukey devised an algorithm to compute the DFT of an n-point series in $\Theta(n \log n)$ operations. Their new algorithm was a significant improvement over previously known methods for computing the DFT, which required $\Theta(n^2)$ operations. The revolutionary algorithm by Cooley and Tukey and its variations are referred to as the ***fast Fourier transform*** (FFT). Due to its wide application in scientific and engineering fields, there has been a lot of interest in implementing FFT on parallel computers.

Several different forms of the FFT algorithm exist. This chapter discusses its simplest form, the one-dimensional, unordered, radix-2 FFT. Parallel formulations of higher-radix and multidimensional FFTs are similar to the simple algorithm discussed in this chapter because the underlying ideas behind all sequential FFT algorithms are the same. An ordered FFT is obtained by performing bit reversal (Section 10.5) on the output sequence of an unordered FFT. Bit reversal does not affect the overall complexity of a parallel implementation of FFT.

In this chapter we discuss two parallel formulations of the basic algorithm: the ***binary-exchange algorithm*** and the ***transpose algorithm***. Depending on the size of the input n and the number of processors p, one of these may run faster than the other.

10.1 The Serial Algorithm

Consider a sequence $X = \langle X[0], X[1], \ldots, X[n-1] \rangle$ of length n. The discrete Fourier transform of the sequence X is the sequence $Y = \langle Y[0], Y[1], \ldots, Y[n-1] \rangle$, where

$$Y[i] = \sum_{k=0}^{n-1} X[k]\omega^{ki}, \quad 0 \le i < n. \tag{10.1}$$

In Equation 10.1, ω is the primitive n^{th} root of unity in the complex plane; that is, $\omega = e^{2\pi\sqrt{-1}/n}$, where e is the base of the natural logarithm. More generally, the powers of ω in the equation can be thought of as elements of the finite commutative ring of integers modulo n. The powers of ω used in an FFT computation are also known as ***twiddle factors***.

The computation of each $Y[i]$ according to Equation 10.1 requires n complex multiplications. Therefore, the sequential complexity of computing the entire sequence Y of length n is $\Theta(n^2)$. The fast Fourier transform algorithm described below reduces this complexity to $\Theta(n \log n)$.

Assume that n is a power of two. The FFT algorithm is based on the following step that permits an n-point DFT computation to be split into two $(n/2)$-point DFT computations:

$$\begin{aligned} Y[i] &= \sum_{k=0}^{(n/2)-1} X[2k]\omega^{2ki} + \sum_{k=0}^{(n/2)-1} X[2k+1]\omega^{(2k+1)i} \\ &= \sum_{k=0}^{(n/2)-1} X[2k]e^{2(2\pi\sqrt{-1}/n)ki} + \sum_{k=0}^{(n/2)-1} X[2k+1]\omega^{i} e^{2(2\pi\sqrt{-1}/n)ki} \\ &= \sum_{k=0}^{(n/2)-1} X[2k]e^{2\pi\sqrt{-1}ki/(n/2)} + \omega^{i} \sum_{k=0}^{(n/2)-1} X[2k+1]e^{2\pi\sqrt{-1}ki/(n/2)} \end{aligned} \tag{10.2}$$

Let $\tilde{\omega} = e^{2\pi\sqrt{-1}/(n/2)} = \omega^2$; that is, $\tilde{\omega}$ is the primitive $(n/2)^{\text{nd}}$ root of unity. Then, we can rewrite Equation 10.2 as follows:

$$Y[i] = \sum_{k=0}^{(n/2)-1} X[2k]\tilde{\omega}^{ki} + \omega^{i} \sum_{k=0}^{(n/2)-1} X[2k+1]\tilde{\omega}^{ki} \tag{10.3}$$

```
procedure R_FFT(X, Y, n, ω)
if (n = 1) then Y[0] := X[0] else
begin
    R_FFT(⟨X[0], X[2], ..., X[n − 2]⟩, ⟨Q[0], Q[1], ..., Q[n/2]⟩, n/2, ω²);
    R_FFT(⟨X[1], X[3], ..., X[n − 1]⟩, ⟨T[0], T[1], ..., T[n/2]⟩, n/2, ω²);
    for i := 0 to n − 1 do
        Y[i] := Q[i mod (n/2)] + ω^i T[i mod (n/2)];
end R_FFT
```

Program 10.1 The recursive, one-dimensional, unordered, radix-2 FFT algorithm. Here $\omega = e^{2\pi\sqrt{-1}/n}$.

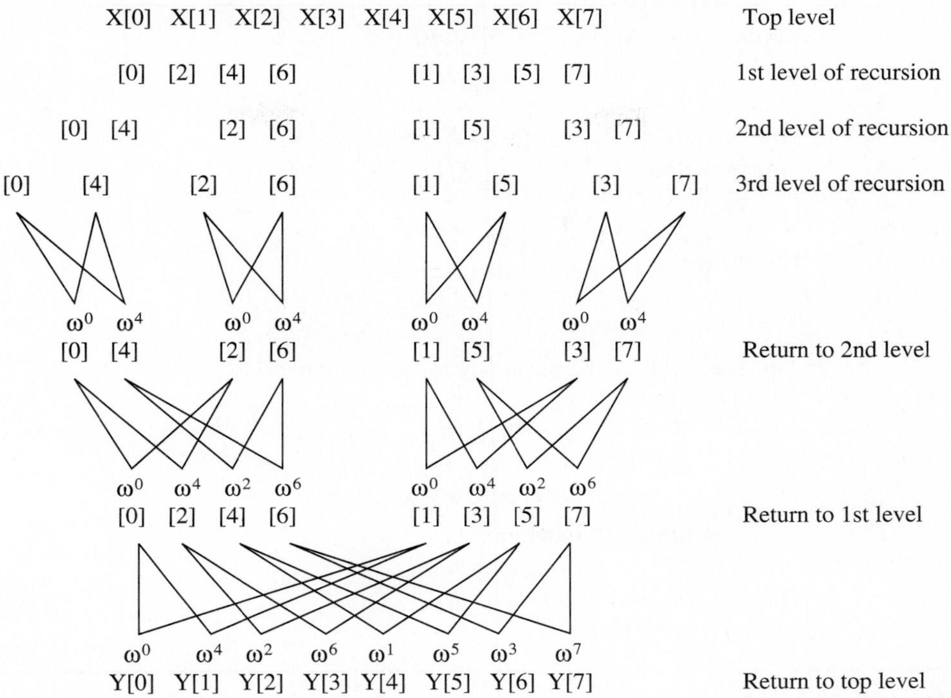

Figure 10.1 A recursive 8-point unordered FFT computation.

In Equation 10.3, each of the two summations on the right-hand side is an $(n/2)$-point DFT computation. If n is a power of two, each of these DFT computations can be divided similarly into smaller computations in a recursive manner. This leads to the recursive FFT algorithm given in Program 10.1. This FFT algorithm is called the radix-2 algorithm because at each level of recursion, the input sequence is split into two equal halves.

Figure 10.1 illustrates how the recursive algorithm works on an 8-point sequence. As the figure shows, the first set of computations corresponding to line 7 of Program 10.1 takes place at the deepest level of recursion. At this level, the elements of the sequence whose indices differ by $n/2$ are used in the computation. In each subsequent level, the difference between the indices of the elements used together in a computation decreases by a factor of two. The figure also shows the powers of ω used in each computation.

The size of the input sequence over which an FFT is computed recursively decreases by a factor of two at each level of recursion (lines 4 and 5 of Program 10.1). Hence, the maximum number of levels of recursion is $\log n$ for an initial sequence of length n. At the mth level of recursion, 2^m FFTs of size $n/2^m$ each are computed. Thus, the total number of arithmetic operations (line 7) at each level is $\Theta(n)$ and the overall sequential complexity of Program 10.1 is $\Theta(n \log n)$.

```
1.  procedure ITERATIVE_FFT(X, Y, n)
2.  begin
3.      r := log n;
4.      for i := 0 to n - 1 do R[i] := X[i];
5.      for m := 0 to r - 1 do          /* Outer loop */
6.          begin
7.              for i := 0 to n - 1 do S[i] := R[i];
8.              for i := 0 to n - 1 do   /* Inner loop */
9.                  begin

    /* Let (b_0 b_1 ··· b_{r-1}) be the binary representation of i */

10.                     j := (b_0 ... b_{m-1} 0 b_{m+1} ··· b_{r-1});
11.                     k := (b_0 ... b_{m-1} 1 b_{m+1} ··· b_{r-1});
12.                     R[i] := S[j] + S[k] × ω^(b_m b_{m-1} ··· b_0 0 ··· 0);
13.             endfor;   /* Inner loop */
14.     endfor;            /* Outer loop */
15.     for i := 0 to n - 1 do Y[i] := R[i];
16. end ITERATIVE_FFT
```

Program 10.2 The Cooley-Tukey algorithm for one-dimensional, unordered, radix-2 FFT. Here $\omega = e^{2\pi\sqrt{-1}/n}$.

The serial FFT algorithm can also be cast in an iterative form. The parallel implementations of the iterative form are easier to illustrate. Therefore, before describing parallel FFT algorithms, we give the iterative form of the serial algorithm. An iterative FFT algorithm is derived by casting each level of recursion, starting with the deepest level, as an iteration. Program 10.2 gives the classic iterative Cooley-Tukey algorithm for an n-point, one-dimensional, unordered, radix-2 FFT. The program performs $\log n$ iterations of the outer loop starting on line 5. The value of the loop index m in the iterative version of the algorithm corresponds to the $(\log n - m)^{\text{th}}$ level of recursion in the recursive version (Figure 10.1). Just as in each level of recursion, each iteration performs n complex multiplications and additions.

Program 10.2 has two main loops. The outer loop starting at line 5 is executed $\log n$ times for an n-point FFT, and the inner loop starting at line 8 is executed n times during each iteration of the outer loop. All operations of the inner loop are constant-time arithmetic operations. Thus, the sequential time complexity of the algorithm is $\Theta(n \log n)$. In every iteration of the outer loop, the sequence R is updated using the elements that were stored in the sequence S during the previous iteration. For the first iteration, the input sequence X serves as the initial sequence R. The updated sequence X from the final iteration is the desired Fourier transform and is copied to the output sequence Y.

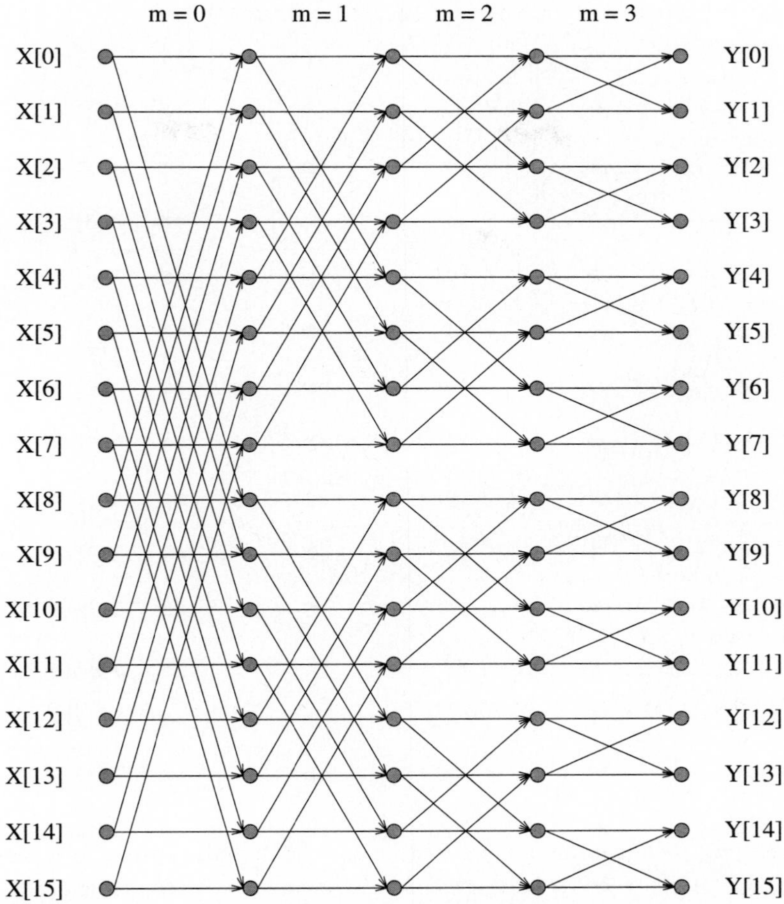

Figure 10.2 The pattern of combination of elements of the input and the intermediate sequences during a 16-point unordered FFT computation.

Line 12 in Program 10.2 performs a crucial step in the FFT algorithm. This step updates $R[i]$ by using $S[j]$ and $S[k]$. The indices j and k are derived from the index i as follows. Assume that $n = 2^r$. Since $0 \leq i < n$, the binary representation of i contains r bits. Let $(b_0 b_1 \cdots b_{r-1})$ be the binary representation of index i. In the mth iteration of the outer loop $(0 \leq m < r)$, index j is derived by forcing the mth most significant bit of i (that is, b_m) to zero. Index k is derived by forcing b_m to 1. Thus, the binary representations of j and k differ only in their m^{th} most significant bits. In the binary representation of i, b_m is either 0 or 1. Hence, of the two indices j and k, one is the same as index i, depending on whether $b_m = 0$ or $b_m = 1$. In the mth iteration of the outer loop, for each i between 0 and $n - 1$, $R[i]$ is generated by executing line 12 of Program 10.2 on $S[i]$ and on another

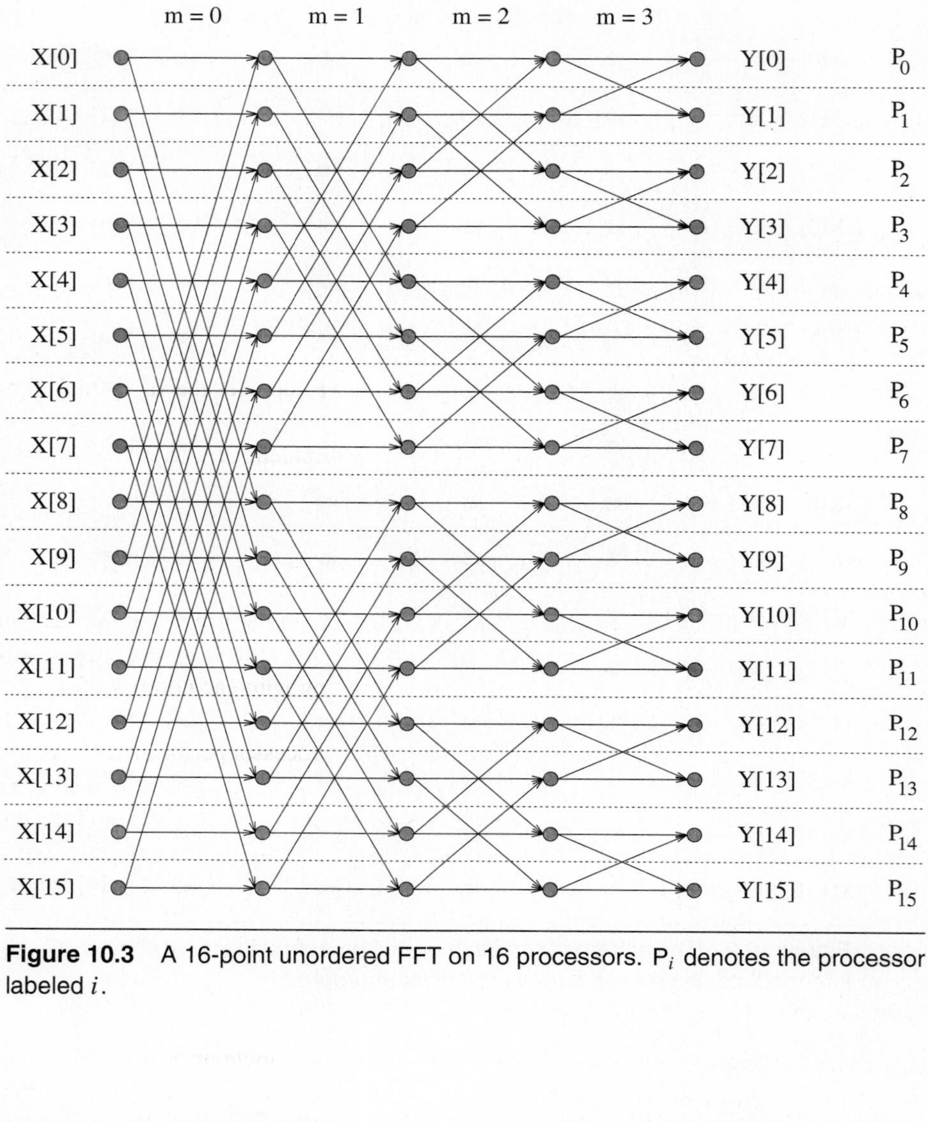

Figure 10.3 A 16-point unordered FFT on 16 processors. P_i denotes the processor labeled i.

element of S whose index differs from i only in the mth most significant bit. Figure 10.2 shows the pattern in which these elements are paired for the case in which $n = 16$.

10.2 The Binary-Exchange Algorithm

This section discusses the ***binary-exchange algorithm*** to perform FFT on a parallel computer. In this parallel formulation of FFT, exchange of data takes place between all pairs of processors with labels differing in one bit position.

10.2.1 Hypercube

In this subsection, we describe the implementation of the binary-exchange algorithm on a hypercube-connected parallel computer. We first consider the simple case in which each processor stores a single element of the input and generates a single element of the output.

One Element Per Processor

Consider an n-processor hypercube that computes an n-point FFT. Figure 10.3 illustrates the communication pattern of the binary-exchange algorithm for $n = 16$. As the figure shows, hypercube processor i $(0 \leq i < n)$ initially stores $X[i]$ and finally generates $Y[i]$. In each of the $\log n$ iterations of the outer loop, processor P_i updates the value of $R[i]$ by executing line 12 of Program 10.2. All n updates are performed in parallel.

To perform the updates, processor P_i requires an element of S from a processor whose label differs from i in only one bit. Recall that in a hypercube, a processor is connected to all those processors whose labels differ from its own in only one bit position. Thus, the parallel FFT computation maps naturally onto a hypercube because every pair of communicating processors is directly connected. In the first iteration of the outer loop, the labels of each pair of communicating processors differ only in their most significant bits. For instance, processors P_0 to P_7 communicate with P_8 to P_{15}, respectively. Similarly, in the second iteration, the labels of processors communicating with each other differ in the second most significant bit, and so on.

In each of the $\log n$ iterations of this algorithm, every processor performs one complex multiplication and addition, and exchanges one complex number with a directly-connected processor. Thus, there is a constant amount of work per iteration. Hence, it takes $\Theta(\log n)$ time to execute the algorithm in parallel by using a hypercube with n processors. This hypercube formulation of FFT is cost-optimal because its processor-time product is $\Theta(n \log n)$, the same as the complexity of a serial n-point FFT.

Multiple Elements Per Processor

Consider implementing the binary-exchange algorithm to compute an n-point FFT on a hypercube with p processors, where $n > p$. Assume that both n and p are powers of two. As Figure 10.4 shows, we partition the sequences into blocks of n/p contiguous elements and assign one block to each processor. Assume that the hypercube is d-dimensional (that is, $p = 2^d$) and $n = 2^r$.

An interesting property of the mapping shown in Figure 10.4 is that, if $(b_0 b_1 \cdots b_{r-1})$ is the binary representation of any i, such that $0 \leq i < n$, then $R[i]$ and $S[i]$ are mapped onto the processor labeled $(b_0 \cdots b_{d-1})$. That is, the d most significant bits of the index of any element of the sequence are the binary representation of the label of the processor that the element resides on. This property of the mapping plays a significant role in determining the amount of communication performed during the parallel execution of the FFT algorithm on a hypercube.

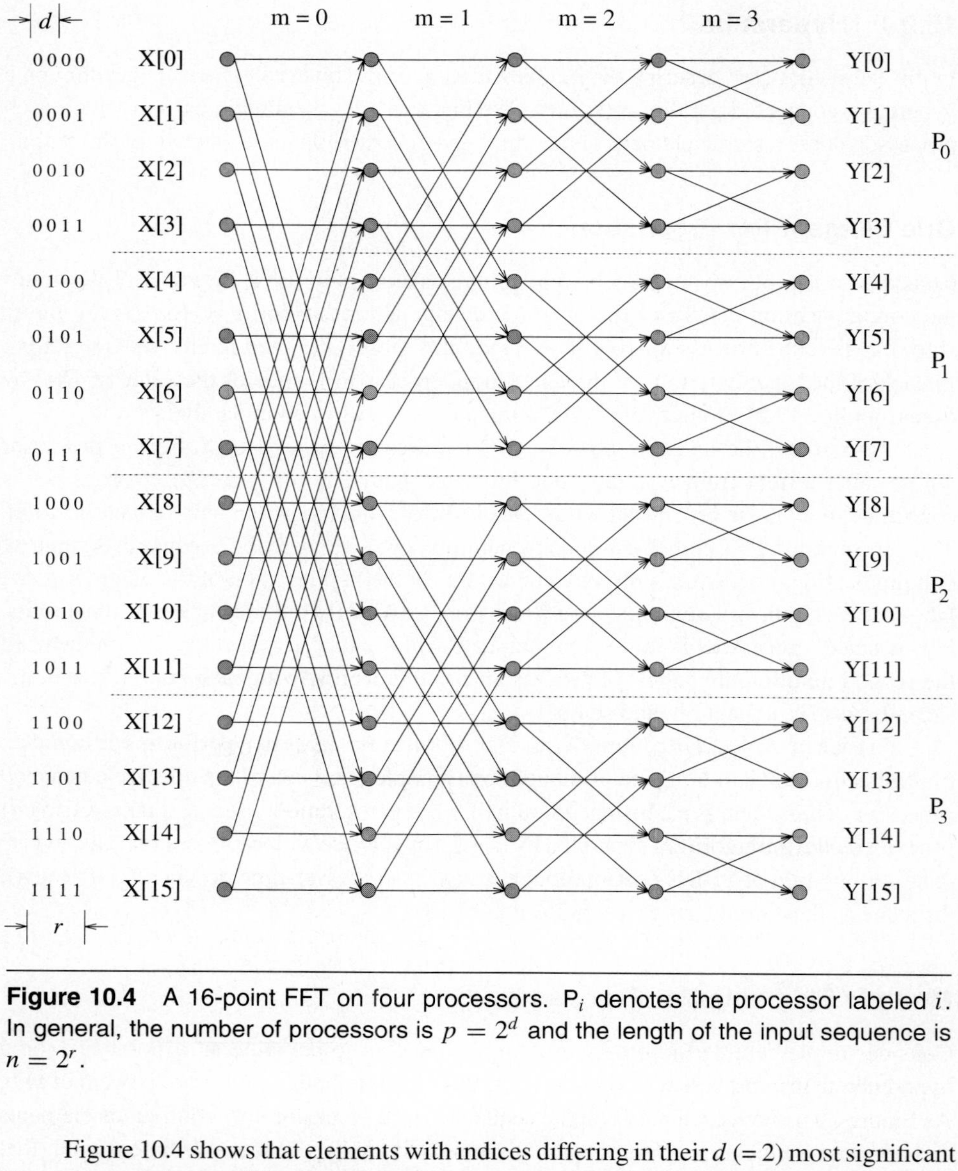

Figure 10.4 A 16-point FFT on four processors. P_i denotes the processor labeled i. In general, the number of processors is $p = 2^d$ and the length of the input sequence is $n = 2^r$.

Figure 10.4 shows that elements with indices differing in their d (= 2) most significant bits are mapped onto different processors. However, all elements with indices having the same d most significant bits are mapped onto the same processor. Recall from the previous section that an n-point FFT requires $r = \log n$ iterations of the outer loop. In the mth iteration of the loop, elements with indices differing in the mth most significant bit are combined. As a result, elements combined during the first d iterations reside on different processors, and pairs of elements combined during the last $(r - d)$ iterations reside on the same processors. Hence, this parallel FFT algorithm performs interprocessor communication only during the first $d = \log p$ of the $\log n$ iterations. There is no communication during the last $r - d$ iterations. Furthermore, in i^{th} of the first d iterations, all the elements that a processor requires come from exactly one other processor—the one whose label is different in the ith most significant bit.

Each communication operation exchanges n/p words of data. Since all communication takes place between directly-connected processors, the total communication time does not depend on the type of routing. Thus, the time spent in communication in the entire algorithm is $t_s \log p + t_w(n/p)\log p$. A processor updates n/p elements of R during each of the $\log n$ iterations. If a complex multiplication and addition pair takes time t_c, then the parallel run time of the binary-exchange algorithm for n-point FFT on a p-processor hypercube is

$$T_P = t_c \frac{n}{p} \log n + t_s \log p + t_w \frac{n}{p} \log p. \tag{10.4}$$

The processor-time product is $t_c n \log n + t_s p \log p + t_w n \log p$. For the parallel system to be cost-optimal, this product should be $O(n \log n)$—the sequential time complexity of the FFT algorithm. This happens when $p = O(n)$.

The expressions for speedup and efficiency are given by the following equations:

$$\begin{aligned} S &= \frac{t_c n \log n}{T_P} \\ &= \frac{pn \log n}{n \log n + (t_s/t_c) p \log p + (t_w/t_c) n \log p} \\ E &= \frac{1}{1 + (t_s p \log p)/(t_c n \log n) + (t_w \log p)/(t_c \log n)} \end{aligned} \tag{10.5}$$

Scalability Analysis

From Section 10.1, we know that the problem size W for an n-point FFT is

$$W = n \log n. \tag{10.6}$$

Since an n-point FFT can use a maximum of n processors with the mapping of Figure 10.3, $n \geq p$ or $n \log n \geq p \log p$ to keep p processors busy. Thus, the isoefficiency function of this parallel FFT algorithm is $\Omega(p \log p)$ due to concurrency. We now derive the isoefficiency function for the binary exchange algorithm due to the different communication-related terms. We can rewrite Equation 10.5 as

$$\frac{t_s p \log p}{t_c n \log n} + \frac{t_w \log p}{t_c \log n} = \frac{1 - E}{E}.$$

In order to maintain a fixed efficiency E, the expression $(t_s p \log p)/(t_c n \log n) + (t_w \log p)/(t_c \log n)$ should be equal to a constant $1/K$, where $K = E/(1 - E)$. We have defined the constant K in this manner to keep the terminology consistent with Chapter 4. As proposed in Section 4.4.3, we use an approximation to obtain closed expressions for the isoefficiency function. We first determine the rate of growth of the problem size with respect to p that would keep the terms due to t_s constant. To do that, we assume $t_w = 0$. Now the condition for maintaining constant efficiency E is as follows:

$$\begin{aligned}\frac{t_s p \log p}{t_c n \log n} &= \frac{1}{K}\\ n \log n &= K \frac{t_s}{t_c} p \log p\\ W &= K \frac{t_s}{t_c} p \log p \qquad (10.7)\end{aligned}$$

Equation 10.7 gives the isoefficiency function due to the overhead resulting from message startup time.

Similarly, we derive the isoefficiency function due to the overhead resulting from t_w. We assume that $t_s = 0$; hence, a fixed efficiency E requires that the following relation be maintained:

$$\begin{aligned}\frac{t_w \log p}{t_c \log n} &= \frac{1}{K}\\ \log n &= K \frac{t_w}{t_c} \log p\\ n &= p^{K t_w / t_c}\\ n \log n &= K \frac{t_w}{t_c} p^{K t_w / t_c} \log p\\ W &= K \frac{t_w}{t_c} p^{K t_w / t_c} \log p \qquad (10.8)\end{aligned}$$

If the term $K t_w / t_c$ is less than one, then the rate of growth of the problem size required by Equation 10.8 is less than $\Theta(p \log p)$. In this case, Equation 10.7 determines the overall isoefficiency function of this parallel system. However, if $K t_w / t_c$ exceeds one, then Equation 10.8 determines the overall isoefficiency function, which is now greater than the isoefficiency function of $\Theta(p \log p)$ given by Equation 10.7.

For this algorithm, the asymptotic isoefficiency function depends on the relative values of K, t_w, and t_c. Here, K is an increasing function of the efficiency E to be maintained, t_w depends on the bandwidth of the communication channels of the hypercube, and t_c depends on the speed of the processors being used. The FFT algorithm is unique in that the order of the isoefficiency function depends on the desired efficiency and hardware-dependent parameters. In fact, the efficiency corresponding to $K t_w / t_c = 1$ (that is, $1/(1 - E) = t_c / t_w$, or $E = t_c / (t_c + t_w)$) acts as a threshold. For a given hypercube with fixed t_c and t_w, efficiencies up to the threshold can be obtained easily. For $E \le t_c / (t_c + t_w)$, the asymptotic isoefficiency function is $\Theta(p \log p)$. Efficiencies much higher than the threshold $t_c / (t_c + t_w)$ can be obtained only if the problem size is extremely large. The reason is that for these efficiencies, the asymptotic isoefficiency function is $\Theta(p^{K t_w / t_c} \log p)$. The following examples illustrate the effect of the value of $K t_w / t_c$ on the isoefficiency function.

Example 10.1 Threshold Effect in the Binary-Exchange Algorithm

Consider a hypothetical hypercube for which the relative values of the hardware

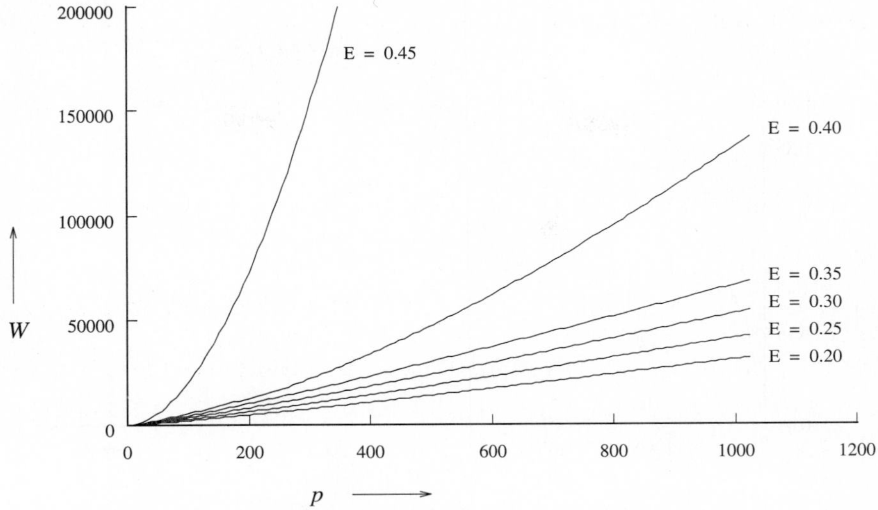

Figure 10.5 Isoefficiency functions of the binary-exchange algorithm on a hypercube with $t_c = 2$, $t_w = 4$, and $t_s = 25$ for various values of E.

parameters are given by $t_c = 2$, $t_w = 4$, and $t_s = 25$. With these values, the threshold efficiency $t_c/(t_c + t_w)$ is 0.33.

Now we study the isoefficiency functions of the binary-exchange algorithm on a hypercube for maintaining efficiencies below and above the threshold. The isoefficiency function of this algorithm due to concurrency is $p \log p$. From Equations 10.7 and 10.8, the isoefficiency function due to the t_s and t_w terms in the overhead function are $K(t_s/t_c)p \log p$ and $K(t_w/t_c)p^{Kt_w/t_c} \log p$, respectively. To maintain a given efficiency E (that is, for a given K), the overall isoefficiency function is given by:

$$W = \max\{p \log p, K\frac{t_s}{t_c} p \log p, K\frac{t_w}{t_c} p^{Kt_w/t_c} \log p\}$$

Figure 10.5 shows the isoefficiency curves given by this function for $E = 0.20$, 0.25, 0.30, 0.35, 0.40, and 0.45. Notice that the various isoefficiency curves are regularly spaced for efficiencies up to the threshold. However, the problem sizes required to maintain efficiencies above the threshold are much larger. The asymptotic isoefficiency functions for $E = 0.20$, 0.25, and 0.30 are $\Theta(p \log p)$. The isoefficiency function for $E = 0.40$ is $\Theta(p^{1.33} \log p)$, and that for $E = 0.45$ is $\Theta(p^{1.64} \log p)$.

Figure 10.6 shows the efficiency curve of n-point FFTs on a 256-processor hypercube with the same hardware parameters. The efficiency E is computed by using Equation 10.5 for various values of n, when p is equal to 256. The figure shows that the efficiency initially increases rapidly with the problem size, but the efficiency curve flattens out beyond the threshold. ■

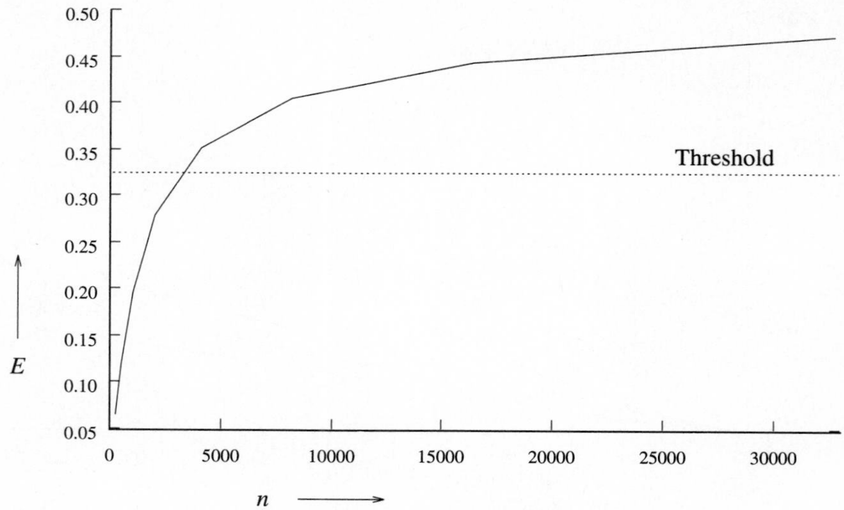

Figure 10.6 The efficiency of the binary-exchange algorithm as a function of n on a 256-processor hypercube with $t_c = 2$, $t_w = 4$, and $t_s = 25$.

Example 10.1 shows that there is a limit on the efficiency that can be obtained for reasonable problem sizes, and that the limit is determined by the ratio between the CPU speed and the bandwidth of the communication channels of the hypercube. This limit can be raised by increasing the bandwidth of the communication channels. However, making the CPUs faster without increasing the communication bandwidth lowers the limit. Hence, the binary-exchange algorithm performs poorly on a hypercube whose communication and computation speeds are not balanced. If the hardware is balanced with respect to its communication and computation speeds, then the binary-exchange algorithm is fairly scalable on a hypercube, and reasonable efficiencies can be maintained while increasing the problem size at the rate of $\Theta(p \log p)$.

10.2.2 Mesh

Assume that an n-point FFT is computed on a p-processor mesh with $\sqrt{p}$ rows and $\sqrt{p}$ columns, and that $\sqrt{p}$ is a power of two. Let $n = 2^r$ and $p = 2^d$. Also assume that the processors are labeled in a row-major fashion and that the data are distributed in the same manner as for the hypercube; that is, an element with index $(b_0 b_1 \cdots b_{r-1})$ is mapped onto the processor labeled $(b_0 \cdots b_{d-1})$.

As in case of the hypercube, communication takes place only during the first $\log p$ iterations between processors whose labels differ in one bit. However, unlike the hypercube, the communicating processors are not directly connected in a mesh. Consequently, messages travel over multiple links. Figure 10.7 shows the messages sent and received by processors 0 and 37 during an FFT computation on a 64-processor mesh. As the figure

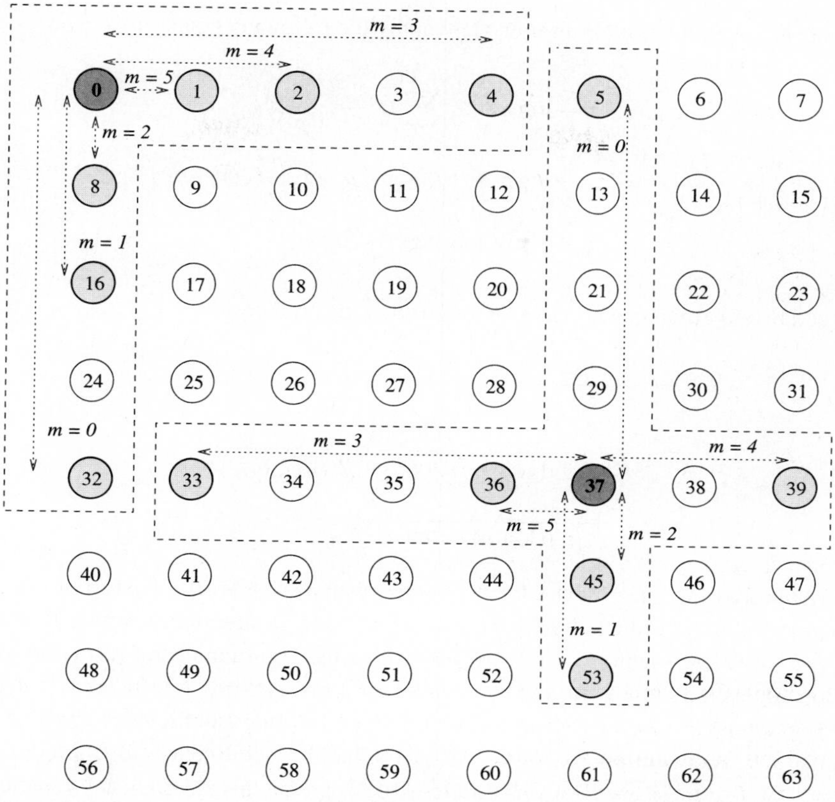

Figure 10.7 Data communication during an FFT computation on a square mesh of 64 processors. The figure shows all the processors with which the processors labeled 0 and 37 exchange data.

shows, processor 0 communicates with processors 1, 2, 4, 8, 16, and 32. Note that all these processors lie in the same row or column of the mesh as that of processor 0. Processors 1, 2, and 4 lie in the same row as processor 0 at distances of 1, 2, and 4 links, respectively. Processors 8, 16, and 32 lie in the same column, again at distances of 1, 2, and 4 links. More precisely, in $\log \sqrt{p}$ of the $\log p$ steps that require communication, the communicating processors are in the same row, and in the remaining $\log \sqrt{p}$ steps, they are in the same column. The distance between the communicating processors in a row or a column grows from one link to $\sqrt{p}/2$ links, doubling in each of the $\log \sqrt{p}$ steps. The same relationship holds for any processor in the mesh, such as processor 37 shown in Figure 10.7. Thus, the total time spent in performing rowwise communication is $\Sigma_{m=0}^{d/2-1}(t_s + t_w(n/p)2^m)$ for a mesh with store-and-forward routing. An equal amount of time is spent in columnwise communication. Recall that we assumed that a complex multiplication and addition pair takes time t_c. Since a processor performs n/p such calculations in each of the $\log n$

iterations, the overall parallel run time is given by the following equation:

$$\begin{aligned} T_P &= t_c \frac{n}{p} \log n + 2 \sum_{m=0}^{d/2-1} (t_s + t_w \frac{n}{p} 2^m) \\ &= t_c \frac{n}{p} \log n + 2(t_s \log \sqrt{p} + t_w \frac{n}{p} (\sqrt{p} - 1)) \\ &\approx t_c \frac{n}{p} \log n + t_s \log p + 2 t_w \frac{n}{\sqrt{p}} \end{aligned} \tag{10.9}$$

The speedup and efficiency are given by the following equations:

$$\begin{aligned} S &= \frac{t_c n \log n}{T_P} \\ &= \frac{pn \log n}{n \log n + (t_s/t_c) p \log p + 2(t_w/t_c) n \sqrt{p}} \\ E &= \frac{1}{1 + (t_s p \log p)/(t_c n \log n) + 2(t_w \sqrt{p})/(t_c \log n)} \end{aligned} \tag{10.10}$$

The processor-time product of this parallel system is $t_c n \log n + t_s p \log p + 2 t_w n \sqrt{p}$. The processor-time product should be $O(n \log n)$ for cost-optimality, which is obtained when $\sqrt{p} = O(\log n)$, or $p = O(\log^2 n)$. Since the communication term due to t_s in Equation 10.9 is the same as for the hypercube, the corresponding isoefficiency function is again $\Theta(p \log p)$ as given by Equation 10.7. By performing isoefficiency analysis along the same lines as in Section 10.2.1, we can show that the isoefficiency function due to the t_w term is $2K(t_w/t_c) 2^{2K(t_w/t_c)\sqrt{p}} \sqrt{p}$ (Problem 10.5). Given this isoefficiency function, the problem size must grow exponentially with the number of processors to maintain constant efficiency. Hence, this FFT algorithm is not very scalable on a mesh.

The communication overhead of the binary-exchange algorithm on a mesh cannot be reduced by using a different mapping of the sequences onto the processors. In any mapping, there is at least one iteration in which pairs of processors that communicate with each other are at least $\sqrt{p}/2$ links apart (Problem 10.2). Hence, the communication cost in this parallel system cannot be improved asymptotically. Even cut-through routing does not offer any performance improvement for the FFT algorithm on a mesh. The communication pattern of parallel FFT on a mesh is such that if the distance between two communicating processors is x links, then at least one link on the path is shared by x messages (Problem 10.3). Therefore, due to the overhead resulting from contention for communication channels, the overall parallel run time is the same as that given by Equation 10.9.

10.2.3 Extra Computations in Parallel FFT

So far, we have described a parallel formulation of the FFT algorithm on a hypercube and a mesh, and have discussed its performance and scalability in the presence of communication overhead on both architectures. In this section, we discuss another source of overhead that can be present in a parallel FFT implementation.

Table 10.1 The binary representation of the various powers of ω calculated in different iterations of an 8-point FFT (also see Figure 10.1). The value of m refers to the iteration number of the outer loop, and i is the index of the inner loop of Program 10.2.

	i							
	0	1	2	3	4	5	6	7
$m = 0$	000	000	000	000	100	100	100	100
$m = 1$	000	000	100	100	010	010	110	110
$m = 2$	000	100	010	110	001	101	011	111

Recall from Program 10.2 that the computation step of line 12 multiplies a power of ω (a twiddle factor) with an element of S. For an n-point FFT, line 12 executes $n \log n$ times in the sequential algorithm. However, only n distinct powers of ω (that is, ω^0, ω^1, ω^2, ..., ω^{n-1}) are used in the entire algorithm. So some of the twiddle factors are used repeatedly. In a serial implementation, it is useful to precompute and store all n twiddle factors before starting the main algorithm. That way, the computation of twiddle factors requires only $\Theta(n)$ complex operations rather than the $\Theta(n \log n)$ operations needed to compute all twiddle factors in each iteration of line 12.

In a parallel implementation, the total work required to compute the twiddle factors cannot be reduced to $\Theta(n)$. The reason is that, even if a certain twiddle factor is used more than once, it might be used on different processors at different times. If FFTs of the same size are computed on the same number of processors, every processor needs the same set of twiddle factors for each computation. In this case, the twiddle factors can be precomputed and stored, and the cost of their computation can be amortized over the execution of all instances of FFTs of the same size. However, if we consider only one instance of FFT, then twiddle factor computation gives rise to additional overhead in a parallel implementation, because it performs more overall operations than the sequential implementation.

As an example, consider the various powers of ω used in the three iterations of an 8-point FFT. In the mth iteration of the loop starting on line 5 of the algorithm, ω^l is computed for all i ($0 \le i < n$), such that l is the integer obtained by reversing the order of the $m + 1$ most significant bits of i and then padding them by $n - m - 1$ zeros to the right (refer to Figure 10.1 and Program 10.2 to see how l is derived). Table 10.1 shows the binary representation of the powers of ω required for all values of i and m for an 8-point FFT.

If eight processors are used, then each processor computes and uses one column of Table 10.1. Processor 0 computes just one twiddle factor for all its iterations, but some processors (in this case, all other processors 2–7) compute a new twiddle factor in each of the three iterations. If $p = n/2 = 4$, then each processor computes two consecutive columns of the table. In this case, the last processor computes the twiddle factors in the last two columns of the table. Hence, the last processor computes a total of four different

Table 10.2 The maximum number of new powers of ω used by any processor in each iteration of an 8-point FFT computation.

	$p = 1$	$p = 2$	$p = 4$	$p = 8$
$m = 0$	2	1	1	1
$m = 1$	2	2	1	1
$m = 2$	4	4	2	1
Total = $h(8,p)$	8	7	4	3

powers—one each for $m = 0$ (100) and $m = 1$ (110), and two for $m = 2$ (011 and 111). Although different processors may compute a different number of twiddle factors, the total overhead due to the extra work is proportional to p times the maximum number of twiddle factors that any single processor computes. Let $h(n, p)$ be the maximum number of twiddle factors that any of the p processors computes during an n-point FFT. Table 10.2 shows the values of $h(8,p)$ for $p = 1, 2, 4$, and 8. The table also shows the maximum number of new twiddle factors that any single processor computes in each iteration.

The function h is defined by the following recurrence relation (Problem 10.6):

$$\begin{aligned} h(n, 1) &= n \\ h(p, p) &= \log p && (p \neq 1) \\ h(n, p) &= h(n, 2p) + n/p - 1 && (p \neq 1, n > p) \end{aligned}$$

The solution to this recurrence relation for $p > 1$ and $n \geq p$ is

$$h(n, p) = 2(\frac{n}{p} - 1) + \log p.$$

Thus, if it takes time t_c' to compute one twiddle factor, then at least one processor spends $t_c' 2(n/p - 1) + t_c' \log p$ time computing twiddle factors. The total cost of twiddle factor computation, summed over all processors, is $2t_c'(n - p) + t_c' p \log p$. Since even a serial implementation incurs a cost of $t_c' n$ in computing twiddle factors, the total parallel overhead due to extra work ($T_o^{extra\_work}$) is given by the following equation:

$$\begin{aligned} T_o^{extra\_work} &= (2t_c'(n - p) + t_c' p \log p) - t_c' n \\ &= t_c'(n + p(\log p - 2)) \\ &= \Theta(n) + \Theta(p \log p) \end{aligned}$$

This overhead is independent of the architecture of the parallel computer used for the FFT computation. The isoefficiency function due to $T_o^{extra\_work}$ is $\Theta(p \log p)$. Since this term is of the same order as the isoefficiency terms due to message startup time and concurrency, the extra computations do not affect the overall scalability of parallel FFT.

10.3 The Transpose Algorithm

The binary-exchange algorithm yields good performance on a hypercube provided that the communication bandwidth and the processing speed of the CPUs are balanced. Efficiencies below a certain threshold can be maintained while increasing the problem size at a moderate rate with an increasing number of processors. However, this threshold is very low if the communication bandwidth of the hypercube is low compared to the speed of its processors. In this section, we describe a different parallel formulation of FFT for a hypercube interconnection network with cut-through routing. This parallel algorithm involves matrix transposition, and hence, is called the ***transpose algorithm***.

The performance of the transpose algorithm is worse than that of the binary-exchange algorithm for efficiencies below the threshold. However, it is much easier to obtain efficiencies above the binary-exchange algorithm's threshold using the transpose algorithm. Thus, the transpose algorithm is particularly useful when the ratio of communication bandwidth to CPU speed is low and high efficiencies are desired. On a hypercube with cut-through routing, the transpose algorithm has a fixed asymptotical isoefficiency function of $\Theta(p^2 \log p)$. That is, the order of this isoefficiency function is independent of the ratio between communication and computation speeds.

10.3.1 Two-Dimensional Transpose Algorithm

The simplest transpose algorithm requires a single transpose operation over a two-dimensional array; hence, we call this algorithm the ***two-dimensional transpose algorithm***.

Assume that $\sqrt{n}$ is a power of 2, and that the sequences of size n used in Program 10.2 are arranged in an $\sqrt{n} \times \sqrt{n}$ two-dimensional square array, as shown in Figure 10.8 for $n = 16$. Recall that computing the FFT of a sequence of n points requires $\log n$ iterations of the outer loop of Program 10.2. If the data are arranged as shown in Figure 10.8, then the FFT computation in each column can proceed independently for $\log \sqrt{n}$ iterations without any column requiring data from any other column. Similarly, in the remaining $\log \sqrt{n}$ iterations, computation proceeds independently in each row without any row requiring data from any other row. Figure 10.8 shows the pattern of combination of the elements for a 16-point FFT. The figure illustrates that if data of size n are arranged in an $\sqrt{n} \times \sqrt{n}$ array, then an n-point FFT computation is equivalent to independent $\sqrt{n}$-point FFT computations in the columns of the array, followed by independent $\sqrt{n}$-point FFT computations in the rows.

If the $\sqrt{n} \times \sqrt{n}$ array of data is transposed after computing the $\sqrt{n}$-point column FFTs, then the remaining part of the problem is to compute the $\sqrt{n}$-point columnwise FFTs of the transposed matrix. The transpose algorithm uses this property to compute the FFT in parallel by using a columnwise striped partitioning to distribute the $\sqrt{n} \times \sqrt{n}$ array of data among the processors. For instance, consider the computation of the 16-point FFT shown in Figure 10.9, where the 4×4 array of data is distributed among four processors such that each processor stores one column of the array. In general, the two-dimensional transpose algorithm works in three phases. In the first phase, a $\sqrt{n}$-point FFT is computed

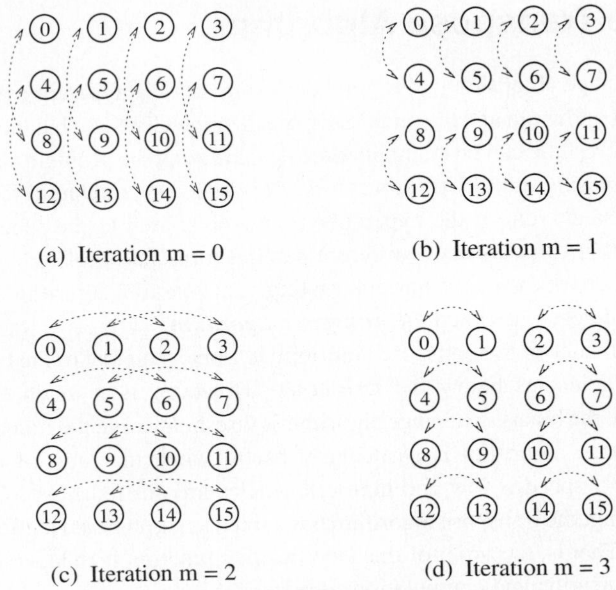

Figure 10.8 The pattern of combination of elements in a 16-point FFT when the data are arranged in a 4×4 two-dimensional square array.

for each column. In the second phase, the array of data is transposed. The third and final phase is identical to the first phase, and involves the computation of $\sqrt{n}$-point FFTs for each column of the transposed array. Figure 10.9 shows that the first and third phases of the algorithm do not require any interprocessor communication. In both these phases, all $\sqrt{n}$ points for each columnwise FFT computation are available on the same processor. Only the second phase requires communication for transposing the $\sqrt{n} \times \sqrt{n}$ matrix.

In the transpose algorithm shown in the Figure 10.9, one column of the data array is assigned to one processor. Before analyzing the transpose algorithm further, consider the more general case in which p processors are used and $1 \leq p \leq \sqrt{n}$. The $\sqrt{n} \times \sqrt{n}$ array of data is striped into blocks, and one block of $\sqrt{n}/p$ rows is assigned to each processor. In the first and third phases of the algorithm, each processor computes $\sqrt{n}/p$ FFTs of size $\sqrt{n}$ each. The second phase transposes the $\sqrt{n} \times \sqrt{n}$ matrix, which is striped columnwise among p processors. Recall from Section 5.2.2 that transposing a stripe-partitioned matrix requires an all-to-all personalized communication. The details of the all-to-all personalized communication operation, and its communication time expressions are given in Section 3.5.2.

Now we derive an expression for the parallel run time of the two-dimensional transpose algorithm on a hypercube with cut-through routing. The transpose algorithm performs no better than the binary-exchange algorithm on a mesh or on a hypercube with store-and-forward routing (Problem 10.7). Equation 5.3 gives the time required to transpose an $n \times n$

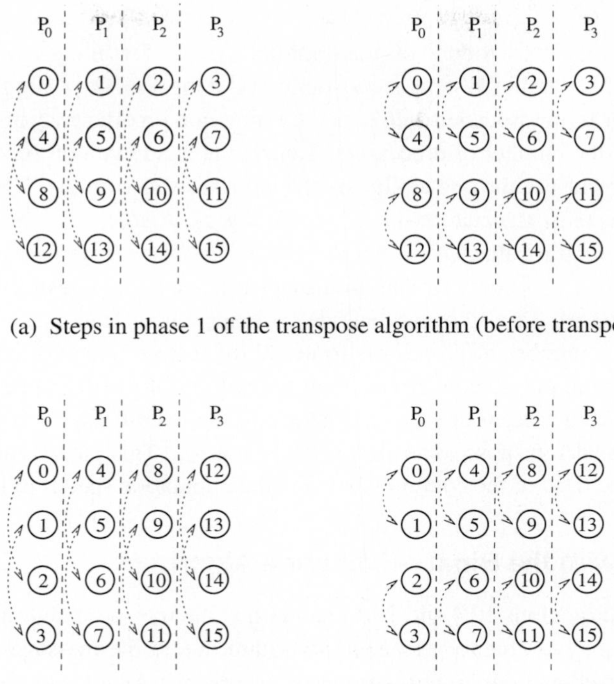

(a) Steps in phase 1 of the transpose algorithm (before transpose)

(b) Steps in phase 3 of the transpose algorithm (after transpose)

Figure 10.9 The two-dimensional transpose algorithm for a 16-point FFT on four processors.

matrix striped among p processors. Modifying this equation for an $\sqrt{n} \times \sqrt{n}$ matrix and ignoring the time for the local rearrangement of elements on each processor, the time spent in the second phase is $t_s(p-1) + t_w n/p + (t_h p/2) \log p$. The first and the third phase each take $t_c \times \sqrt{n}/p \times \sqrt{n} \log \sqrt{n}$ time. Thus, the parallel run time of the transpose algorithm on a hypercube with cut-through routing is given by the following equation:

$$\begin{aligned} T_P &= 2t_c \frac{\sqrt{n}}{p} \sqrt{n} \log \sqrt{n} + t_s(p-1) + t_w \frac{n}{p} + \frac{1}{2} t_h p \log p \\ &= t_c \frac{n}{p} \log n + t_s(p-1) + t_w \frac{n}{p} + \frac{1}{2} t_h p \log p \end{aligned} \quad (10.11)$$

The expressions for speedup and efficiency are as follows:

$$\begin{aligned} S &\approx \frac{pn \log n}{n \log n + (t_s/t_c)p^2 + (t_w/t_c)n + (t_h/2t_c)p^2 \log p} \\ E &\approx \frac{1}{1 + (t_s p^2)/(t_c n \log n) + t_w/(t_c \log n) + (t_h p^2 \log p)/(2t_c n \log n)} \end{aligned} \quad (10.12)$$

The processor-time product of this parallel system is $t_c n \log n + t_s p^2 + t_w n + (t_h p^2/2) \log p$. This parallel system is cost-optimal if $n \log n = \Omega(p^2 \log p)$.

Note that the term associated with t_w in the expression for efficiency in Equation 10.12 is independent of the number of processors. Hence, the bandwidth of the communication channels does not affect the scalability of the transpose algorithm. The isoefficiency function due to the term associated with t_h is $\Theta(p^2 \log p)$. Also, the degree of concurrency of this algorithm requires that $\sqrt{n} = \Omega(p)$ because at most $\sqrt{n}$ processors can be used to partition the $\sqrt{n} \times \sqrt{n}$ array of data in a striped manner. As a result, $n = \Omega(p^2)$, or $n \log n = \Omega(p^2 \log p)$. Thus, the problem size has to increase at least as fast as $\Theta(p^2 \log p)$ with respect to the number of processors to use all of them efficiently. The $\Theta(p^2 \log p)$ isoefficiency function due to concurrency and the t_h term of the overhead is greater than the $\Theta(p^2)$ isoefficiency term due to t_s. Therefore, the overall isoefficiency function of the two-dimensional transpose algorithm is $\Theta(p^2 \log p)$. This isoefficiency function is independent of the ratio of the communication and computation speeds of the hypercube.

Comparison with the Binary-Exchange Algorithm

A comparison of Equations 10.4 and 10.11 shows that the transpose algorithm has a much higher overhead than the binary-exchange algorithm due to the message startup time t_s, but has a lower overhead due to per-word transfer time t_w. As a result, either of the two algorithms may be faster depending on the relative values of t_s, t_w and t_h. For SIMD and shared-memory computers, in which t_s is very low, the transpose algorithm may be the algorithm of choice. On the other hand, the binary-exchange algorithm may perform better on a typical MIMD computer with a high communication bandwidth but a significant message startup time.

Recall from Section 10.2.1 that an overall isoefficiency function of $\Theta(p \log p)$ can be realized by using the binary-exchange algorithm if the efficiency is such that $Kt_w/t_c \leq 1$, where $K = E/(1-E)$. If the desired efficiency is such that $Kt_w/t_c = 2$, then the overall isoefficiency function of both the binary-exchange and the two-dimensional transpose schemes is $\Theta(p^2 \log p)$. When $Kt_w/t_c > 2$, the two-dimensional transpose algorithm is more scalable than the binary-exchange algorithm; hence, the former should be the algorithm of choice, provided that $n \geq p^2$. Note, however, that the transpose algorithm yields a performance benefit over the binary-exchange algorithm only if the target architecture is a hypercube with cut-through routing (Problem 10.7).

★ 10.3.2 The Generalized Transpose Algorithm

In the two-dimensional transpose algorithm, the input of size n is arranged in a $\sqrt{n} \times \sqrt{n}$ two-dimensional array that is stripe-partitioned among p processors. These processors, although physically connected in a hypercube network, can be regarded as arranged in a logical one-dimensional linear array. As an extension of this scheme, consider the n data points to be arranged in an $n^{1/3} \times n^{1/3} \times n^{1/3}$ three-dimensional array mapped onto a logical

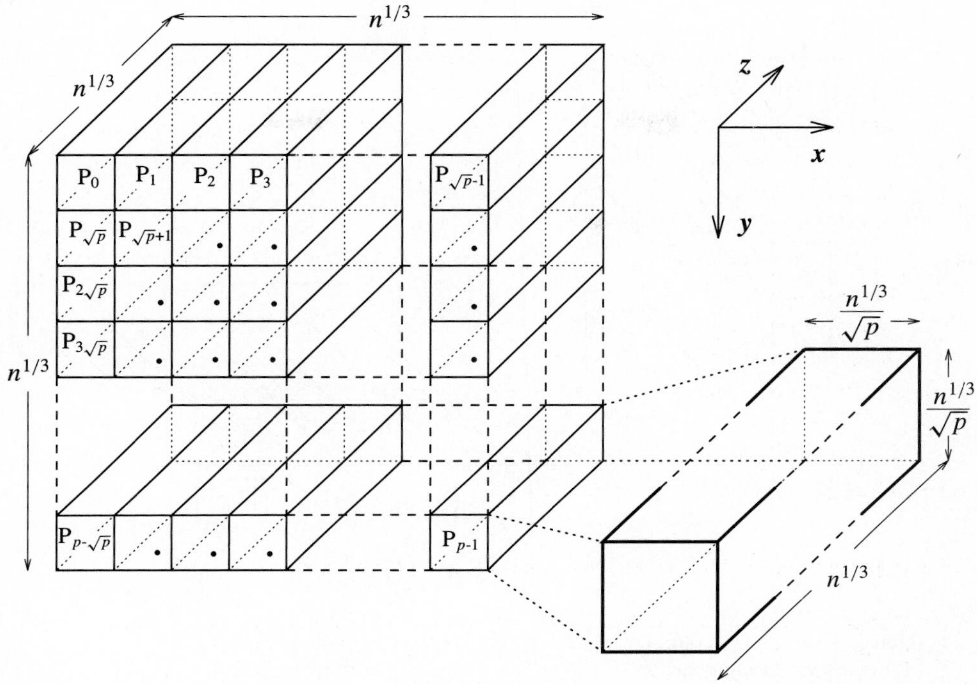

Figure 10.10 Data distribution in the three-dimensional transpose algorithm for an n-point FFT on p processors ($\sqrt{p} \leq n^{1/3}$).

$\sqrt{p} \times \sqrt{p}$ two-dimensional mesh of processors. Figure 10.10 illustrates this mapping. To simplify the algorithm description, we label the three axes of the three-dimensional array of data as x, y, and z. In this mapping, the x-y plane of the array is checkerboarded into $\sqrt{p} \times \sqrt{p}$ parts. As the figure shows, each processor stores $(n^{1/3}/\sqrt{p}) \times (n^{1/3}/\sqrt{p})$ columns of data, and the length of each column (along the z-axis) is $n^{1/3}$. Thus, each processor has $(n^{1/3}/\sqrt{p}) \times (n^{1/3}/\sqrt{p}) \times n^{1/3} = n/p$ elements of data.

Recall from Section 10.3.1 that the FFT of a two-dimensionally arranged input of size $\sqrt{n} \times \sqrt{n}$ can be computed by first computing the $\sqrt{n}$-point one-dimensional FFTs of all the columns of the data and then computing the $\sqrt{n}$-point one-dimensional FFTs of all the rows. If the data are arranged in an $n^{1/3} \times n^{1/3} \times n^{1/3}$ three-dimensional array, the entire n-point FFT can be computed similarly. In this case, $n^{1/3}$-point FFTs are computed over the elements of the columns of the array in all three dimensions, choosing one dimension at a time. We call this algorithm the ***three-dimensional transpose algorithm***. This algorithm can be divided into the following five phases:

(1) In the first phase, $n^{1/3}$-point FFTs are computed on all the rows along the z-axis.

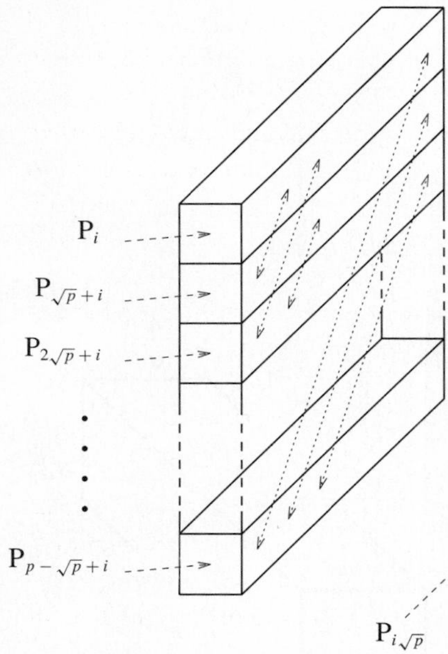

(a) Transpose in the ith column of processors during phase 2

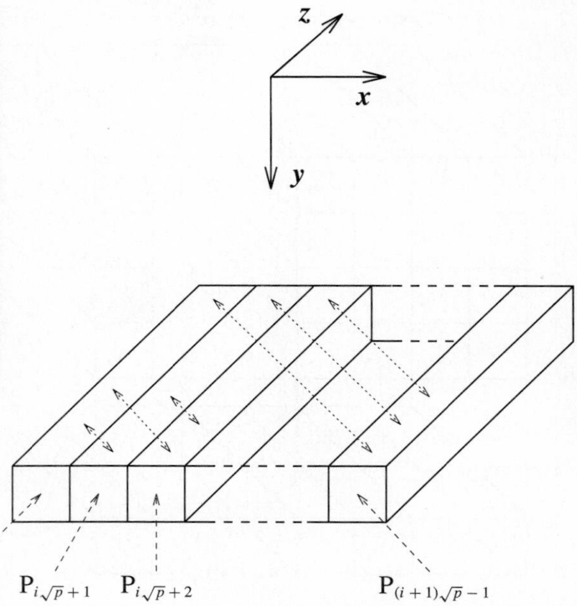

(b) Transpose in the ith row of processors during phase 4

Figure 10.11 The communication (transposition) phases in the three-dimensional transpose algorithm for an n-point FFT on p processors.

(2) In the second phase, all the $n^{1/3}$ cross sections of size $n^{1/3} \times n^{1/3}$ along the y-z plane are transposed.
(3) In the third phase, $n^{1/3}$-point FFTs are computed on all the rows of the modified array along the z-axis.
(4) In the fourth phase, each of the $n^{1/3} \times n^{1/3}$ cross sections along the x-z plane is transposed.
(5) In the fifth and final phase, $n^{1/3}$-point FFTs of all the rows along the z-axis are computed again.

For the data distribution shown in Figure 10.10, in the first, third, and fifth phases of the algorithm, all processors perform $(n^{1/3}/\sqrt{p}) \times (n^{1/3}/\sqrt{p})$ FFT computations, each of size $n^{1/3}$. Since all the data for performing these computations are locally available on each processor, no interprocessor communication is involved in these three odd-numbered phases. The time spent by a processor in each of these phases is $t_c n^{1/3} \log(n^{1/3}) \times (n^{1/3}/\sqrt{p}) \times (n^{1/3}/\sqrt{p})$. Thus, the total time that a processor spends in computation is $t_c(n/p)\log n$.

Figure 10.11 illustrates the second and the fourth phases of the three-dimensional transpose algorithm. As Figure 10.11(a) shows, the second phase of the algorithm requires transposing square cross sections of size $n^{1/3} \times n^{1/3}$ along the y-z plane. Each column of $\sqrt{p}$ processors performs the transposition of $(n^{1/3}/\sqrt{p})$ such cross sections. This transposition involves all-to-all personalized communications among groups of $\sqrt{p}$ processors with individual messages of size $n/p^{3/2}$. If a hypercube with cut-through routing is used, this phase takes time $t_s(\sqrt{p}-1) + t_w n/p + (t_h\sqrt{p}/4)\log p$. The fourth phase, shown in Figure 10.11(b), is similar. Here each row of $\sqrt{p}$ processors performs the transpose of $(n^{1/3}/\sqrt{p})$ cross sections along the x-z plane. Again, each cross section consists of $n^{1/3} \times n^{1/3}$ data elements. The communication time of this phase is the same as that of the second phase. The total parallel run time of the three-dimensional transpose algorithm for an n-point FFT on a p-processor hypercube with cut-through routing is

$$T_P = t_c\frac{n}{p}\log n + 2t_s(\sqrt{p}-1) + 2t_w\frac{n}{p} + \frac{1}{2}t_h\sqrt{p}\log p. \quad (10.13)$$

Having studied the two- and three-dimensional transpose algorithms, we can derive a more general q-dimensional transpose algorithm similarly. Let the n-point input be arranged in a logical q-dimensional array of size $n^{1/q} \times n^{1/q} \times \cdots \times n^{1/q}$ (a total of q terms). Now the entire n-point FFT computation can be viewed as q subcomputations. Each of the q subcomputations along a different dimension consists of $n^{(q-1)/q}$ FFTs over $n^{1/q}$ data points.

To execute the q-dimensional transpose algorithm on a hypercube with cut-through routing, we map the array of data onto a logical $(q-1)$-dimensional array of processors. These processors physically form a p-processor hypercube where $p \le n^{(q-1)/q}$, and $p = 2^{(q-1)s}$ for some integer s. The FFT of the entire data is now computed in $(2q-1)$ phases (recall that there are three phases in the two-dimensional transpose algorithm and five phases in the three-dimensional transpose algorithm). In the q odd-numbered phases, each processor performs $n^{(q-1)/q}/p$ of the required $n^{1/q}$-point FFTs. The total computation time for each processor over all q computation phases is the product of: q (the number of computation phases), $n^{(q-1)/q}/p$ (the number of $n^{1/q}$-point FFTs computed by each processor in each computation phase), and $t_c n^{1/q}\log(n^{1/q})$ (the time to compute a single $n^{1/q}$-point FFT). Multiplying these terms gives a total computation time of $t_c(n/p)\log n$.

In each of the $(q-1)$ even-numbered phases, sub-arrays of size $n^{1/q} \times n^{1/q}$ are transposed on rows of the q-dimensional logical array of processors. Each such row contains $p^{1/(q-1)}$ processors. One such transpose is performed along every dimension of the $(q-1)$-dimensional processor array in each of the $(q-1)$ communication phases. The time spent in communication in each transposition is $t_s(p^{1/(q-1)}-1) + t_w n/p + (t_h p^{1/(q-1)}\log p)/(2(q-1))$. Thus, the total parallel run time of the q-dimensional transpose algorithm for an n-point FFT on a p-processor hypercube with cut-through routing is

$$T_P = t_c\frac{n}{p}\log n + (q-1)t_s(p^{1/(q-1)}-1) + (q-1)t_w\frac{n}{p} + \frac{1}{2(q-1)}t_h p^{1/(q-1)}\log p. \quad (10.14)$$

Equation 10.14 can be verified by replacing q with 2 and 3, and comparing the result with Equations 10.11 and 10.13, respectively.

A comparison of Equations 10.11, 10.13, 10.14, and 10.4 shows an interesting trend. As the dimension q of the transpose algorithm increases, the communication overhead due to t_w increases, but that due to t_s decreases. The binary-exchange algorithm and the two-dimensional transpose algorithms can be regarded as two extremes. The former minimizes the overhead due to t_s but has the largest overhead due to t_w. The latter minimizes the overhead due to t_w but has the largest overhead due to t_s. The variations of the transpose algorithm for $2 < q < \log p$ lie between these two extremes. For a given hypercube, the specific values of t_c, t_s, and t_w determine which of these algorithms has the optimal parallel run time (Problem 10.10).

Note that, from a practical point of view, only the binary-exchange algorithm and the two- and three-dimensional transpose algorithms are feasible. Higher-dimensional transpose algorithms are very complicated to code. Moreover, restrictions on n and p limit their applicability. These restrictions for a q-dimensional transpose algorithm are that n must be a power of two that is a multiple of q, and that p must be a power of 2 that is a multiple of $(q-1)$. In other words, $n = 2^{qr}$, and $p = 2^{(q-1)s}$, where q, r, and s are integers.

Example 10.2 A Comparison of Binary-Exchange, 2-D Transpose, and 3-D Transpose Algorithms

This example shows that either the binary-exchange algorithm or any of the transpose algorithms may be the algorithm of choice for a given parallel computer, depending on the size of the FFT. Consider a 64-processor version of the hypercube described in Example 10.1 with $t_c = 2$, $t_s = 25$, and $t_w = 4$. Assume that the hypercube supports cut-through routing, and $t_h = 2$. Figure 10.12 shows speedups attained by the binary-exchange algorithm, the 2-D transpose algorithm, and the 3-D transpose algorithm for different problem sizes. The speedups are based on the parallel run times given by Equations 10.4, 10.11, and 10.13, respectively. The figure shows that for different ranges of n, a different algorithm provides the highest speedup for an n-point FFT. For the given values of the hardware parameters, the binary-exchange algorithm is best suited for very low granularity FFT computations, the 2-D transpose algorithm is best for very high granularity computations, and the 3-D transpose algorithm's speedup is the maximum for intermediate granularities. ■

10.4 Cost-Effectiveness of Meshes and Hypercubes for FFT

The scalability of an algorithm-architecture combination determines its capability to use an increasing number of processors effectively. Many algorithms are more scalable on costlier architectures than on some less expensive architectures. In such cases, the costlier architecture delivers better efficiency than a cheaper architecture for the same problem size and the same number of processors. If the same parallel algorithm is executed on two parallel computers with the same number of identical processors but different architectures, each computer spends the same amount of time performing useful computation. Any difference in efficiency can then be attributed to a difference in communication overhead.

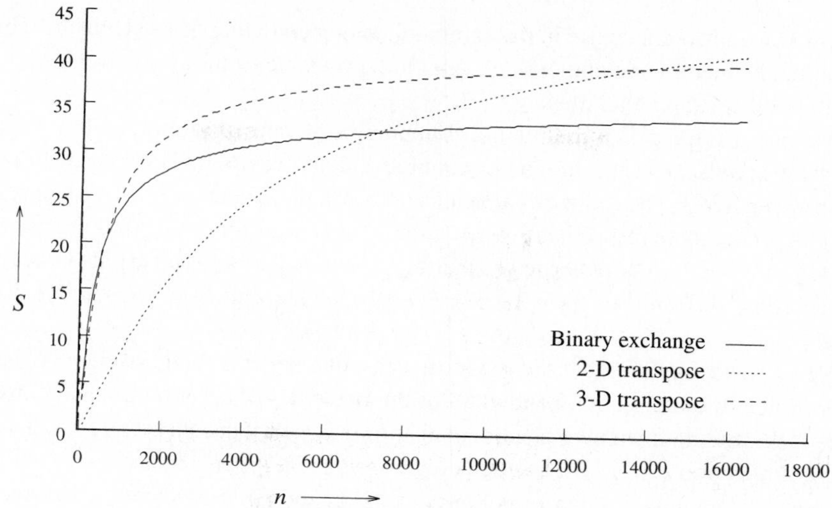

Figure 10.12 A comparison of the speedups obtained by the binary-exchange, 2-D transpose, and 3-D transpose algorithms on a 64-processor hypercube with $t_c = 2$, $t_w = 4$, $t_s = 25$, and $t_h = 2$. The hypercube is assumed to support cut-through routing.

The throughput of the cheaper architecture can be increased to match that of the costlier architecture by enhancing the channel bandwidth of the former so that the communication overhead of the algorithm becomes identical on each architecture. However, the extra communication hardware required to increase the channel bandwidth also raises the cost of the cheaper architecture. If the efficiency of an algorithm is matched on the two architectures, then the less expensive of the two is considered more cost-effective for the algorithm.

From the scalability analysis of Section 10.2, we see that the FFT algorithm performs much more poorly on a mesh than on a hypercube. However, constructing a mesh multicomputer is cheaper than constructing a hypercube with the same number of processors. This section analyzes the cost-effectiveness of the mesh and hypercube architectures with respect to two different criteria for the cost of a network.

Binary-Exchange Algorithm

If we neglect the message startup time (that is, $t_s = 0$), then the efficiency of an n-point FFT using the binary-exchange algorithm is approximately $(t_c \log n)/(t_c \log n + t_w \log p)$ on a p-processor hypercube, and $(t_c \log n)/(t_c \log n + 2t_w\sqrt{p})$ on a p-processor mesh (Equations 10.5 and 10.10). Assume that t_w and t_c are the same for both computers. Now for the same value of p, both computers will yield identical efficiencies if we reduce the per-word communication time on the mesh to t_w/w, where the factor w is chosen so that $2\sqrt{p}/w = \log p$ or $w = 2\sqrt{p}/\log p$. The reduction in t_w by a factor of w on the mesh can be realized by a w-fold increase in the communication bandwidth of its channels. This, in turn, can be attained by making each channel fatter by a factor of w or by replacing each link with w identical parallel links.

Assume that the cost of building a communication network for a parallel computer is directly proportional to the number of communication links in it. For this case, the cost of constructing hypercube and mesh networks delivering identical performance on parallel FFT is $p \log p$ and $4wp$, respectively, where $w = 2\sqrt{p}/\log p$. Since $8p\sqrt{p}/\log p$ is greater than $p \log p$ for all p (it is easier to see that $8\sqrt{p}/(\log p)^2 > 1$ for all p), it is cheaper to obtain the same performance from the binary-exchange algorithm on a hypercube than on a mesh.

Now consider a different criterion for the cost of a network, and assume that the cost is proportional to the bisection bandwidth of the network. The bisection bandwidth of a network is the minimum number of communication channels that connect any two halves of the network (Section 2.4.2). The bisection bandwidths of a hypercube and a mesh (without wraparound) containing p processors each, are $p/2$ and $\sqrt{p}$, respectively. To match the performance of the mesh with that of the hypercube for the binary-exchange algorithm, each of the channels of the mesh must be made wider by a factor of $w = 2\sqrt{p}/\log p$. With this modification, the bisection bandwidth of the mesh network becomes $2p/\log p$. Thus, the costs of the hypercube and mesh networks with p processors each, such that they yield similar performance for FFT, is proportional to $p/2$ and $2p/\log p$, respectively. For $p > 256$, such a mesh network is cheaper to build than a hypercube.

The preceding analysis shows that the performance of the FFT algorithm on a mesh can be improved considerably if its communication bandwidth is increased by replacing each link with $\sqrt{p}/2$ parallel links. However, the enhanced bandwidth can be fully utilized only if there are at least $\sqrt{p}/2$ data items to be transferred during each communication step. Consequently, the input data size n should be such that $n/p \geq \sqrt{p}/2$, or $n \geq p\sqrt{p}/2$. This yields an isoefficiency term of $\Theta(p^{1.5} \log p)$ due to concurrency, which is worse than that for the hypercube if $Kt_w/tc < 1.5$. Thus, for the mesh with wider channels to be more cost-effective than the hypercube, the problem size should be large enough to utilize the full bandwidth of the additional channels. The isoefficiency function of $\Theta(p^{1.5} \log p)$ is still a significant improvement over the mesh with channels of constant bandwidth, which has an exponential isoefficiency function for the FFT algorithm. In fact, $\Theta(p^{1.5} \log p)$ is the best possible isoefficiency for FFT on a mesh, even if the channel bandwidth is increased arbitrarily with the number of processors (Problem 10.11).

Two-Dimensional Transpose Algorithm

We can perform an analysis similar to the preceding one for the transpose algorithm. If the comparison is based on the two-dimensional transpose algorithm, and the cost of a network is proportional to the total number of links in it, then the hypercube proves to be more cost effective. That is because the factor w by which the bandwidth of the mesh channels must be increased in order to match the hypercube's performance is $\sqrt{p}/2$ (Problem 10.8). Thus, the relative costs of building a mesh and a hypercube that deliver identical performance for the FFT computation are $4p\sqrt{p}$ and $p \log p$, respectively. If the cost of the network is proportional to its bisection bandwidth, then for the two-dimensional transpose algorithm, the relative costs of the mesh and the hypercube that yield the same throughput is the same (Problem 10.9).

10.5 Bibliographic Remarks

Due to the important role of Fourier transform in scientific and technical computations, there has been great interest in implementing FFT on parallel computers and on studying its performance. Swarztrauber [Swa87] describes many implementations of the FFT algorithm on vector and parallel computers. Cvetanovic [Cve87] and Norton and Silberger [NS87] give a comprehensive performance analysis of the FFT algorithm on pseudo-shared-memory architectures such as the IBM RP-3. They consider various partitionings of data among memory blocks and, in each case, obtain expressions for communication overhead and speedup in terms of problem size, number of processors, memory latency, CPU speed, and speed of communication. Aggarwal, Chandra, and Snir [ACS89] analyze the performance of FFT and other algorithms on LPRAM—a new model for parallel computation. This model differs from the standard PRAM model in that remote accesses are more expensive than local accesses in an LPRAM. Parallel FFT algorithms and their implementation and experimental evaluation on various architectures have been pursued by many other researchers [AGGM90, Bai90, BCJ90, BKH89, DT89, GK93, JKFM89, KA88, Loa92]. Parts of the discussion of the transpose algorithm in this chapter are due to Rao [Rao92].

The basic FFT algorithm whose parallel formulations are discussed in this chapter is called the unordered FFT because the elements of the output sequence are stored in bit-reversed index order. In other words, the frequency spectrum of the input signal is obtained by reordering the elements of the output sequence Y produced by Program 10.2 in such a way that for all i, $Y[i]$ is replaced by $Y[j]$, where j is obtained by reversing the bits in the binary representation of i. This is a permutation operation (Section 3.6) and is known as ***bit reversal***. Norton and Silberger [NS87] show that an ordered transform can be obtained with at most $2d + 1$ communication steps, where $d = \log p$. Since the unordered FFT computation requires only d communication steps, the total communication overhead in the case of ordered FFT is roughly double of that for unordered FFT. Clearly, an unordered transform is preferred where applicable. The output sequence need not be ordered when the transform is used as a part of a larger computation and as such remains invisible to the user [Swa87]. In many practical applications of FFT, such as convolution and solution of the discrete Poisson equation, bit reversal can be avoided [Loa92]. If required, bit reversal can be performed by using an algorithm described by Van Loan [Loa92] for a distributed-memory parallel computer. The asymptotic communication complexity of this algorithm is the same as that of the binary-exchange algorithm on a hypercube.

Several variations of the simple FFT algorithm presented here have been suggested in the literature. Gupta and Kumar [GK93] show that the total communication overhead for mesh and hypercube architectures is the same for the one- and two-dimensional

FFTs. Certain schemes for computing the DFT have been suggested that involve fewer arithmetic operations on a serial computer than the simple Cooley-Tukey FFT algorithm requires [Nus82, RB76, Win77]. Notable among these are computing one-dimensional FFTs with radix greater than two and computing multidimensional FFTs by transforming them into a set of one-dimensional FFTs by using the polynomial transform method. A radix-q FFT is computed by splitting the input sequence of size n into q sequences of size n/q each, computing the q smaller FFTs, and then combining the result. For example, in a radix-4 FFT, each step computes four outputs from four inputs, and the total number of iterations is $\log_4 n$ rather than $\log_2 n$. The input length should, of course, be a power of four. Despite the reduction in the number of iterations, the aggregate communication time for a radix-q FFT remains the same as that for radix-2. For example, for a radix-4 algorithm on a hypercube, each communication step now involves four processors distributed in two dimensions rather than two processors in one dimension. In contrast, the number of multiplications in a radix-4 FFT is 25 percent fewer than in a radix-2 FFT [Nus82]. This number can be marginally improved by using higher radices, but the amount of communication remains unchanged.

Problems

10.1 Let the serial run time of an n-point FFT computation be $T_S = t_c n \log n$. When implemented on a p-processor hypercube, the parallel run time T_P is $t_c n \log n/p + t_w n \log n/p + t_h n \log p/p$. Assume that $t_c = 1$, $t_w = 0.2$, and $t_h = 1$.

(a) Write expressions for the speedup and efficiency.

(b) What is the isoefficiency function if an efficiency of 0.6 is desired?

(c) How will the isoefficiency function change (if at all) if an efficiency of 0.4 is desired?

(d) Repeat parts (b) and (c) for the case in which $t_w = 1$ and everything else is the same.

10.2 **[Tho83]** Show that, while performing FFT on a square mesh of p processors by using any mapping of data onto the processors, there is at least one iteration in which the pairs of processors that need to communicate are at least $\sqrt{p}/2$ links apart.

10.3 **[GK93]** Show that the parallel run time of an n-point FFT on a p-processor mesh is the same for both store-and-forward and cut-through routing schemes.

10.4 Describe the communication pattern of the binary-exchange algorithm on a linear array of p processors. What are the parallel run time, speedup, efficiency, and isoefficiency function of the binary-exchange algorithm on a linear array?

10.5 Show that, if $t_s = 0$, the isoefficiency function of the binary-exchange algorithm on a mesh is given by $W = 2K(t_w/t_c)2^{2K(t_w/t_c)\sqrt{p}}\sqrt{p}$.
Hint: Use Equation 10.10.

10.6 Prove that the maximum number of twiddle factors computed by any processor in the parallel implementation of an n-point FFT on p processors is given by the recurrence relation given in Section 10.2.3.

10.7 Derive expressions for the parallel run time, speedup, and efficiency of the two-dimensional transpose algorithm described in Section 10.3.1 for an n-point FFT on (a) a p-processor hypercube with store-and-forward routing, (b) a p-processor 2-D mesh with store-and-forward routing, (c) a p-processor mesh with cut-through routing, and (d) a linear array of p processors with cut-through routing.
Hint: Use Table 3.1 for the communication time expressions for all-to-all personalized communication on different architectures.

10.8 Ignoring t_s and t_h, by what factor should the communication bandwidth of a p-processor mesh with cut-through routing be increased so that it yields the same performance on the two-dimensional transpose algorithm for an n-point FFT on a p-processor hypercube with cut-through routing?
Hint: Compare the expression for efficiency derived in part (c) of Problem 10.7 with that in Equation 10.12.

10.9 Assume that the cost of building a network is proportional to its bisection bandwidth. What are the relative costs of mesh and hypercube networks employing the same number of processors that yield identical performance on the two-dimensional transpose algorithm for FFT? Assume cut-through routing on both the mesh and the hypercube.

10.10 You are given the following sets of communication-related constants (assume $t_h = 0$) for a hypercube network with cut-through routing: (i) $t_s = 250$, $t_w = 1$, (ii) $t_s = 50$, $t_w = 1$, (iii) $t_s = 10$, $t_w = 1$, (iv) $t_s = 2$, $t_w = 1$, and (v) $t_s = 0$, $t_w = 1$.

(a) Given a choice among the binary-exchange algorithm and the two-, three-, four-, and five-dimensional transpose algorithms, which one would you use for $n = 2^{15}$ and $p = 2^{12}$ for each of the preceding sets of values of t_s and t_w?

(b) Repeat part (a) for (1) $n = 2^{12}$, $p = 2^6$, and (2) $n = 2^{20}$, $p = 2^{12}$.

10.11 **[GK93]** Consider computing an n-point FFT on a $\sqrt{p} \times \sqrt{p}$ mesh. If the channel bandwidth grows at a rate of $\Theta(p^x)$ $(x > 0)$ with the number of processors p in the mesh, show that the isoefficiency function due to communication overhead is $\Theta(p^{0.5-x} 2^{2(t_w/t_c)p^{0.5-x}})$ and that due to concurrency is $\Theta(p^{1+x} \log p)$. Also show that the best possible isoefficiency for FFT on a mesh is $\Theta(p^{1.5} \log p)$, even if the channel bandwidth increases arbitrarily with the number of processors.

References

[ACS89] A. Aggarwal, A. K. Chandra, and M. Snir. Communication complexity of PRAMs. Technical Report RC 14998 (No. 64644), IBM T. J. Watson Research Center, Yorktown Heights, NY, Yorktown Heights, NY, 1989.

[AGGM90] A. Averbuch, E. Gabber, B. Gordissky, and Y. Medan. A parallel FFT on an MIMD machine. *Parallel Computing*, 15:61–74, 1990.

[Bai90] D. H. Bailey. FFTs in external or hierarchical memory. *The Journal of Supercomputing*, 4:23–35, 1990.

[BCJ90] E. C. Bronson, T. L. Casavant, and L. H. Jamieson. Experimental application-driven architecture analysis of an SIMD/MIMD parallel processing system. *IEEE Transactions on Parallel and Distributed Systems*, 1(2):195–205, 1990.

[BKH89] S. Bershader, T. Kraay, and J. Holland. The giant-Fourier-transform. In *Proceedings of the Fourth Conference on Hypercubes, Concurrent Computers, and Applications: Volume I*, 387–389, 1989.

[Cve87] Z. Cvetanovic. Performance analysis of the FFT algorithm on a shared-memory parallel architecture. *IBM Journal of Research and Development*, 31(4):435–451, 1987.

[DT89] L. Desbat and D. Trystram. Implementing the discrete Fourier transform on a hypercube vector-parallel computer. In *Proceedings of the Fourth Conference on Hypercubes, Concurrent Computers, and Applications: Volume I*, 407–410, 1989.

[GK93] A. Gupta and V. Kumar. The scalability of FFT on parallel computers. *IEEE Transactions on Parallel and Distributed Systems*, 4(8):922–932, August 1993. A detailed version available as Technical Report TR 90-53, Department of Computer Science, University of Minnesota, Minneapolis, MN.

[JKFM89] S. L. Johnsson, R. Krawitz, R. Frye, and D. McDonald. A radix-2 FFT on the connection machine. Technical report, Thinking Machines Corporation, Cambridge, MA, 1989.

[KA88] R. A. Kamin and G. B. Adams. Fast Fourier transform algorithm design and tradeoffs. Technical Report RIACS TR 88.18, NASA Ames Research Center, Moffet Field, CA, 1988.

[Loa92] C. V. Loan. *Computational Frameworks for the Fast Fourier Transform*. SIAM, Philadelphia, PA, 1992.

[NS87] A. Norton and A. J. Silberger. Parallelization and performance analysis of the Cooley-Tukey FFT algorithm for shared memory architectures. *IEEE Transactions on Computers*, C-36(5):581–591, 1987.

[Nus82] H. J. Nussbaumer. *Fast Fourier Transform and Convolution Algorithms*. Springer-Verlag, New York, NY, 1982.

[Rao92] V. N. Rao. *Personal Communication*. University of Central Florida, Orlando, FL, 1992.

[RB76] C. M. Rader and N. M. Brenner. A new principle for Fast fourier transform. *IEEE Transactions on Acoustics, Speech and Signal Processing*, 24:264–265, 1976.

[Swa87] P. N. Swarztrauber. Multiprocessor FFTs. *Parallel Computing*, 5:197–210, 1987.

[Tho83] C. D. Thompson. Fourier transforms in VLSI. *IBM Journal of Research and Development*, C-32(11):1047–1057, 1983.

[Win77] S. Winograd. A new method for computing DFT. In *IEEE International Conference on Acoustics, Speech and Signal Processing*, 366–368, 1977.

CHAPTER 11

Solving Sparse Systems of Linear Equations

Solving systems of linear equations is at the core of many problems in engineering and scientific computing. In Chapter 5 we addressed the problem of solving dense systems of linear equations—that is, solving a system of linear equations in which most coefficients are not zero. In this chapter we focus our attention on solving large sparse systems of equations in which a majority of the coefficients are zero. It is important to study sparse systems not only because we encounter them frequently in scientific computing problems, but also because they involve more complex algorithms and data structures than their dense counterparts.

Most scientific computing problems represent a physical system by a mathematical model. To make it suitable for computer solution, the continuous physical domain of the system being modeled is discretized by imposing a grid or a mesh over the domain. Either the grid points or the partitions of the domain dictated by the grid are then regarded as discrete elements. Solving the mathematical model over this discretized domain involves obtaining the values of certain physical quantities at every grid point. For example, Figure 11.1 shows a grid imposed over a sheet of metal insulated on two opposite sides and exposed to temperatures U_0 and U_1 on the other two sides. The steady-state temperature of the entire surface of the sheet is modeled by computing the temperature at each grid point. The same basic approach is used in modeling much more complex systems, such as weather patterns in the atmosphere, ocean currents, and stress on mechanical parts, just to name a few.

Each grid point of a discretized physical domain is simulated based on the influence of the neighboring elements and the surroundings of the domain. For example, in Figure 11.1, the temperature at point 24 is influenced by the temperature at points 16, 17, 18, 23, 32, 31, 30, and 25, and the temperature at point 0 is influenced by the value of U_0 as well as

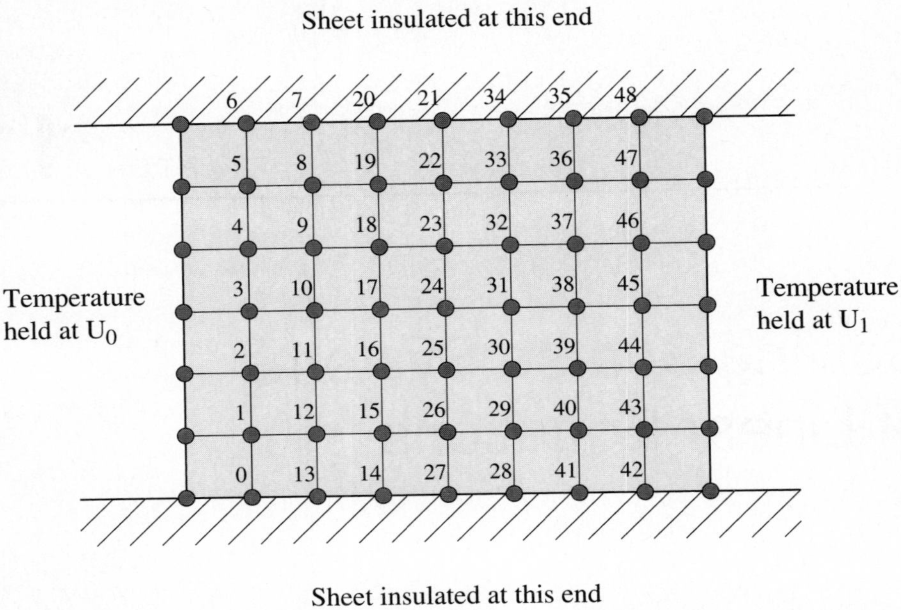

Figure 11.1 Example of a grid imposed over a physical domain consisting of a metal sheet. The temperature of the surface is modeled by computing its value at points 0 through 48.

the temperature at points 1, 12, and 13. Typically, the simulation of a single grid point yields a linear equation that relates the value of a desired physical quantity at the grid point to the values at its neighbors. Since there many grid points in the discretized domain, the task of solving the mathematical model is equivalent to that of solving the set of linear equations associated with all these points. The value of the physical quantity being modeled is represented by a variable at each grid point. The value of a variable in the system of equations depends on only a few other variables—those that correspond to neighboring grid points. As a result, only the coefficients of these variables are nonzero in a typical equation. Most of the coefficients in the system of equations are zero; hence the system is sparse.

As discussed in Section 5.5, a system of n linear equations can be represented in matrix form by $Ax = b$, where A is the $n \times n$ matrix of coefficients, b is an $n \times 1$ vector, and x is the $n \times 1$ solution vector. However, as discussed in Sections 11.3 and 11.5, solving the mathematical model does not always require that the coefficients be explicitly assembled in matrix form. In this chapter, we deal with systems for which, if explicitly assembled, the coefficient matrix A is a sparse matrix; that is, a majority of its elements are zero. More precisely, the matrix A is considered sparse if a computation involving it can utilize the number and location of its nonzero elements to reduce the run time over the same computation on a dense matrix of the same size.

$$\begin{pmatrix} 1 & 0 & 0 & 2 & 0 & 3 \\ 4 & 5 & 0 & 0 & 0 & 0 \\ 0 & 6 & 7 & 0 & 0 & 8 \\ 9 & 0 & 0 & 10 & 11 & 12 \\ 0 & 13 & 0 & 0 & 14 & 0 \\ 0 & 0 & 0 & 0 & 0 & 15 \end{pmatrix}$$

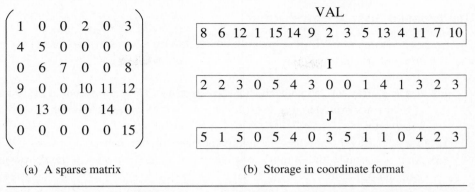

(a) A sparse matrix

VAL

8	6	12	1	15	14	9	2	3	5	13	4	11	7	10

I

2	2	3	0	5	4	3	0	0	1	4	1	3	2	3

J

5	1	5	0	5	4	0	3	5	1	1	0	4	2	3

(b) Storage in coordinate format

Figure 11.2 A 6×6 sparse matrix and its representation in the coordinate storage format.

11.1 Basic Operations

Since this chapter deals primarily with sparse matrices, we first introduce efficient storage schemes for sparse matrices and some simple linear algebra operations using them.

11.1.1 Storage Schemes for Sparse Matrices

It is customary to store an $n \times n$ dense matrix in an $n \times n$ array. However, if the matrix is sparse, storage is wasted because a majority of the elements of the matrix are zero and need not be stored explicitly. For sparse matrices, it is a common practice to store only the nonzero entries and to keep track of their locations in the matrix. A variety of storage schemes are used to store and manipulate sparse matrices. These specialized schemes not only save storage but also yield computational savings. Since the locations of the nonzero elements (and hence, the zero elements) in the matrix are known explicitly, unnecessary multiplications and additions with zero can be avoided. There is no single best data structure for storing sparse matrices. Different data structures are suitable for different operations. Also, some data structures are more suitable for a parallel implementation than others. In the following subsections we briefly describe some common sparse-matrix storage schemes.

Coordinate Format

Given a sparse matrix with q nonzero entries, the ***coordinate format*** stores these entries in a $q \times 1$ array *VAL* in any order. Two additional $q \times 1$ arrays I and J store the i and j coordinates (row and column numbers) of the entries. A 6×6 square matrix and the corresponding coordinate storage format are shown in Figure 11.2. In this figure, as in the remainder of the chapter, we number the rows and columns starting from 0.

Compressed Sparse Row Format

The ***compressed sparse row*** (CSR) format uses the following three arrays to store an $n \times n$ sparse matrix with q nonzero entries:

(1) A $q \times 1$ array *VAL* contains the nonzero elements. These are stored in the order of their rows from 0 to $n - 1$; however, elements of the same row can be stored in any order.
(2) A $q \times 1$ array J that stores the column numbers of each nonzero element.
(3) An $n \times 1$ array I, the ith entry of which points to the first entry of the ith row in *VAL* and J.

Figure 11.3 shows the sparse matrix of Figure 11.2(a) in CSR format. A related scheme is the ***compressed sparse column*** format (CSC), in which the roles of rows and columns are reversed. Another variation of CSR is the ***modified sparse row*** (MSR) format, in which the principal diagonal (which is often fully nonzero) is stored separately and the remaining elements are stored in the regular CSR format.

Diagonal Storage Format

The ***diagonal storage format*** is suited to sparse matrices whose nonzero entries are arranged in a few diagonals. Consider an $n \times n$ matrix consisting of d diagonals with nonzero elements (all other entries are zero). These nonzero diagonals are stored in an $n \times d$ array *VAL*. A $d \times 1$ array *OFFSET* stores the offset of each diagonal with respect to the principal diagonal. The order in which the diagonals are stored is not important. Figure 11.4 shows a sparse matrix stored in this fashion. Since all diagonals other than the principal diagonal have fewer than n elements, there will be unused locations in the array *VAL*. Any zeros within the d diagonals are stored explicitly.

Sometimes all the nonzero diagonals of a sparse matrix form a band around the principal diagonal. In this case, a variation of the diagonal format called ***banded format*** can be used. An $n \times n$ matrix with a band of u diagonals above the principal diagonal and

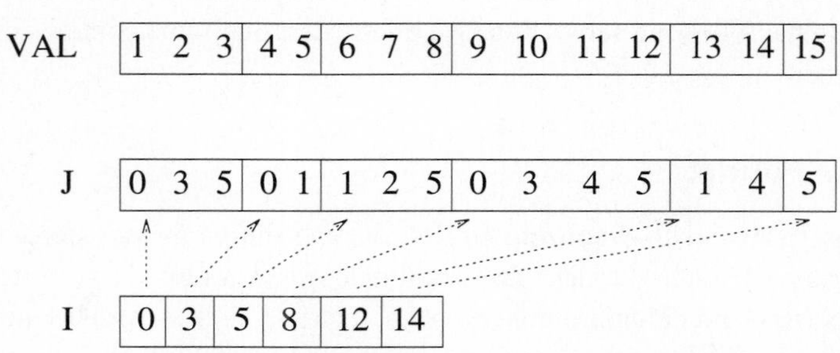

Figure 11.3 CSR storage of the 6×6 sparse matrix of Figure 11.2(a).

$$\begin{pmatrix} 1 & 2 & 0 & 0 & 0 & 0 \\ 3 & 4 & 5 & 0 & 0 & 0 \\ 0 & 6 & 7 & 0 & 0 & 0 \\ 8 & 0 & 9 & 10 & 11 & 0 \\ 0 & 13 & 0 & 0 & 14 & 15 \\ 0 & 0 & 16 & 0 & 17 & 18 \end{pmatrix}$$

(a) A sparse matrix

VAL

-	-	1	2
-	3	4	5
-	6	7	0
8	9	10	11
13	0	14	15
16	17	18	-

OFFSET

-3	-1	0	1

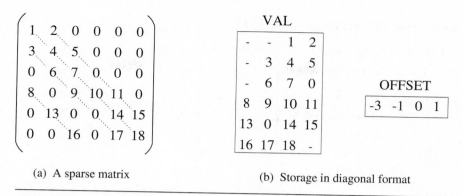

(b) Storage in diagonal format

Figure 11.4 A sparse matrix stored in the diagonal format.

l diagonals below it is stored in an $n \times (u + l + 1)$ array. Instead of the *OFFSET* array, banded format uses two parameters to indicate the thickness of the band and its lower or upper limit.

Ellpack-Itpack Format

The ***Ellpack-Itpack format*** is suitable for general sparse matrices in which the maximum number of nonzero elements in any row is not much larger than the average number of nonzero elements per row. In this scheme, an $n \times n$ sparse matrix in which the maximum number of nonzero elements in any row is m, is stored using two $n \times m$ arrays *VAL* and J. Each row of *VAL* contains the nonzero entries of the corresponding row of the sparse matrix, and the array J stores the column numbers of the corresponding entries in *VAL*. Figure 11.5 shows a sparse matrix stored in the Ellpack-Itpack format. All rows of *VAL* and J that have fewer than m nonzero elements in the original matrix have empty spaces. These empty spaces store some sentinel value (-1 in Figure 11.5(b)) that denotes the end of a row.

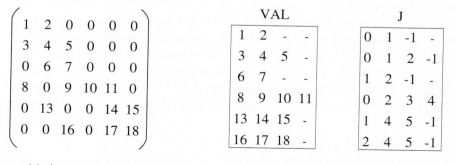

$$\begin{pmatrix} 1 & 2 & 0 & 0 & 0 & 0 \\ 3 & 4 & 5 & 0 & 0 & 0 \\ 0 & 6 & 7 & 0 & 0 & 0 \\ 8 & 0 & 9 & 10 & 11 & 0 \\ 0 & 13 & 0 & 0 & 14 & 15 \\ 0 & 0 & 16 & 0 & 17 & 18 \end{pmatrix}$$

(a) A sparse matrix

VAL

1	2	-	-
3	4	5	-
6	7	-	-
8	9	10	11
13	14	15	-
16	17	18	-

J

0	1	-1	-
0	1	2	-1
1	2	-1	-
0	2	3	4
1	4	5	-1
2	4	5	-1

(b) Storage in Ellpack-Itpack format

Figure 11.5 A sparse matrix stored in Ellpack-Itpack format.

$$\begin{pmatrix} 1 & 0 & 0 & 2 & 0 & 3 \\ 4 & 5 & 0 & 0 & 0 & 0 \\ 0 & 6 & 7 & 0 & 0 & 8 \\ 9 & 0 & 0 & 10 & 11 & 12 \\ 0 & 13 & 0 & 0 & 14 & 0 \\ 0 & 0 & 0 & 0 & 0 & 15 \end{pmatrix}$$

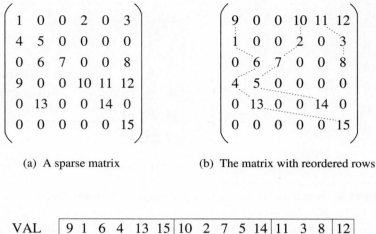

(a) A sparse matrix

$$\begin{pmatrix} 9 & 0 & 0 & 10 & 11 & 12 \\ 1 & 0 & 0 & 2 & 0 & 3 \\ 0 & 6 & 7 & 0 & 0 & 8 \\ 4 & 5 & 0 & 0 & 0 & 0 \\ 0 & 13 & 0 & 0 & 14 & 0 \\ 0 & 0 & 0 & 0 & 0 & 15 \end{pmatrix}$$

(b) The matrix with reordered rows

VAL	9 1 6 4 13 15	10 2 7 5 14	11 3 8	12
J	0 0 1 0 1 5	3 3 2 1 4	4 5 5	5

I	0	6	11	14

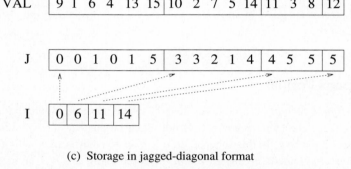

(c) Storage in jagged-diagonal format

Figure 11.6 The jagged-diagonal storage scheme.

Jagged-Diagonal Format

To store a sparse matrix in the ***jagged-diagonal format***, the rows of the matrix are ordered in the decreasing number of nonzero entries. The first nonzero entry of each row is stored in contiguous locations of a $q \times 1$ array *VAL*, where q is the total number of nonzero elements in the sparse matrix. These entries constitute the first jagged diagonal. Then the second nonzero entry of each row is stored in *VAL* (that is, the second jagged diagonal is assembled), and so on. Another $q \times 1$ array J stores the column numbers of the corresponding entries in *VAL*. A third array I of size $m \times 1$ contains pointers to the beginning of each jagged diagonal; m is the maximum number of nonzero entries in any row, which gives the total number of jagged diagonals. Figure 11.6 illustrates the jagged-diagonal storage scheme.

11.1.2 Vector Inner Product

Although not a sparse matrix operation, the inner product of two dense vectors is commonly used in iterative methods for solving systems of linear equations (Section 11.2). The inner product often determines the overall communication complexity and scalability of the

```
procedure INNER_PRODUCT (x, y, a, n)
begin
    a := 0;
    for i := 0 to n − 1 do
        a := a + x[i] × y[i];
end INNER_PRODUCT
```

Program 11.1 An algorithm for computing the inner product of two dense $n \times 1$ vectors x and y.

entire algorithm of which it is a part. As Program 11.1 shows, the inner product is a simple operation in which the corresponding elements of two vectors are multiplied and the resulting products are added together.

If the two $n \times 1$ vectors to be multiplied are uniformly partitioned among p processors, each processor performs n/p multiplications and $(n/p) - 1$ additions. The sums of the n/p products at each processor must be accumulated to obtain the inner product. Assume that the underlying architecture is a hypercube and that it takes time $t_s + t_w \approx t_s$ (assuming t_w to be small compared to t_s) to communicate one word of data between two directly-connected (by bidirectional links) processors. Whether the final inner product must be distributed to all processors (Example 3.7) or is required at only one processor (Example 4.1), the total communication time on a p-processor hypercube is approximately $t_s \log p$. If the underlying architecture is a square mesh with cut-through routing, the communication time is approximately $t_s \log p + 2t_h\sqrt{p}$ (Section 3.2.2).

Recall from Section 3.7.3 that, in addition to the standard data network, some parallel computers have a fast control network that can perform certain global operations in a small, almost constant, time. One such operation is reduction, which starts with a different value on every processor and ends with a single value in each processor that is the result of applying an associative operator (such as logical OR, logical AND, addition, maximum, or minimum) on all the initial values. Section 3.7.3 shows how this operation can be used to accumulate the partial sums and to distribute the value of the inner product to all the processors in the ensemble. As shown in Section 11.2, the presence of a fast reduction operation has a significant effect on the efficiency of iterative algorithms for solving sparse systems of equations.

11.1.3 Sparse Matrix-Vector Multiplication

The multiplication of a sparse matrix with a dense vector is one of the key operations in solving systems of linear equations using iterative methods (Section 11.2). It is, therefore, important to perform this operation efficiently in parallel. The sparse matrices resulting from linear systems of equations often have their nonzero elements distributed according to some pattern. Whenever possible, the parallel implementation of sparse matrix-vector multiplication is tuned according this pattern to attain maximum efficiency. In this sec-

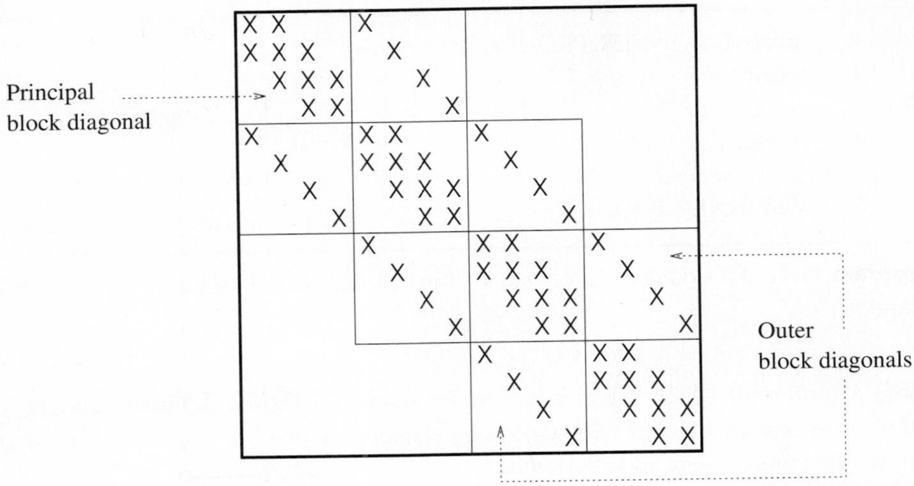

Figure 11.7 A 16×16 block-tridiagonal matrix. The nonzero elements are represented by the symbol $\times$. Zeros are not shown.

tion, we discuss matrix-vector multiplication for three types of sparse matrices that occur commonly in the context of linear systems of equations: (1) matrices in which all nonzero elements are arranged in a few diagonals parallel to and including the principal diagonal; (2) unstructured sparse matrices, in which the location of nonzero elements does not conform to any well-defined structure; and (3) banded sparse matrices, in which the nonzero elements are confined within a band around the principal diagonal; however, inside the band the nonzero elements are distributed in an unstructured manner.

Block-Tridiagonal Matrices

This subsection discusses multiplication of a vector by a sparse matrix that has all its nonzero elements distributed along five diagonals. Furthermore, the diagonals have very specific locations, as illustrated in Figure 11.7 for a 16×16 matrix. One of the five diagonals of the $n \times n$ matrix is the principal diagonal. There are two diagonals immediately adjacent to the principal diagonal on each side. Finally, there are two diagonals at a distance of $\sqrt{n}$ from the principal diagonal on each side. Systems of linear equations with a coefficient matrix of the type shown in Figure 11.7 occasionally arise in scientific computing. Such systems are also pedagogically popular, as they facilitate the exposition of certain key concepts without too many intricacies. Before we discuss matrix-vector multiplication involving this matrix, we will briefly describe how such a matrix originates.

As mentioned earlier, sparse systems of equation often arise from models of physical systems. The ***finite difference method*** is one of the techniques used to obtain an approximate solution to a partial differential equation governing the behavior of a physical system. The finite difference method imposes a regular grid on the physical domain. It

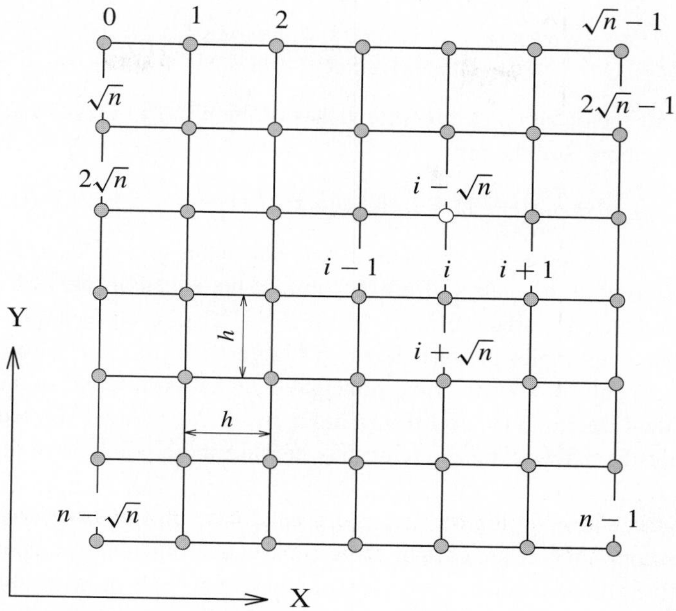

Figure 11.8 A $\sqrt{n} \times \sqrt{n}$ grid with natural ordering of grid points.

then approximates the derivative of an unknown quantity u at a grid point by the ratio of the difference in u at two adjacent grid points to the distance between the grid points. For example, consider a square domain discretized by $\sqrt{n} \times \sqrt{n}$ grid points, as shown in Figure 11.8. Assume that the grid points are numbered in a row-major fashion from left to right and from top to bottom, as shown in the figure. This ordering is called ***natural ordering***. Given a total of n points in the $\sqrt{n} \times \sqrt{n}$ grid, this numbering scheme labels the immediate neighbors of point i on the top, left, right, and bottom points as $i - \sqrt{n}$, $i - 1$, $i + 1$ and $i + \sqrt{n}$, respectively.

Assume that the partial differential equation governing the value of u over the domain is

$$\frac{\delta^2 u}{\delta X^2} + \frac{\delta^2 u}{\delta Y^2} = f. \tag{11.1}$$

Further assume that the values of u at the n grid points are stored in an $n \times 1$ vector x and that $x[i]$ is the value of u at point i. Let h be the distance between any two neighboring grid points. The finite difference approximation of Equation 11.1 yields the following:

$$\frac{1}{h}\left(\frac{x[i+1]-x[i]}{h} - \frac{x[i]-x[i-1]}{h}\right) +$$
$$\frac{1}{h}\left(\frac{x[i+\sqrt{n}]-x[i]}{h} - \frac{x[i]-x[i-\sqrt{n}]}{h}\right) = f$$

$$x[i-\sqrt{n}]+x[i-1]-4x[i]+x[i+1]+x[i+\sqrt{n}] \quad = \quad h^2 f$$

In general, the equation relating the values of the physical quantity at point i to its value at i's neighbors is of the form

$$a_i x[i-\sqrt{n}]+b_i x[i-1]+c_i x[i]+d_i x[i+1]+e_i x[i+\sqrt{n}] \quad = \quad f_i, \qquad (11.2)$$

where a_i, b_i, c_i, d_i, e_i, and f_i are constants. Each point on the grid yields one such equation, and hence, one row in the matrix of coefficients. If the equations are ordered from 0 to $n-1$, and variables are ordered from $x[0]$ to $x[n-1]$ in each equation, the resulting coefficient matrix resembles the one shown in Figure 11.7. In the ith row of the matrix, the four nonzero entries other than the principal diagonal correspond to the four nearest neighbors of the ith point in the grid shown in Figure 11.8. The rows corresponding to the boundary points have fewer nonzero elements because these points have fewer than four neighbors.

The matrix shown in Figure 11.7 is a special case of a ***block-tridiagonal matrix***. A block-tridiagonal matrix consists of three consecutive diagonals composed of matrix blocks along the principal diagonal. We refer to these diagonals of matrix blocks as ***block diagonals***. The block diagonals of the block-tridiagonal matrix we are considering here are composed of blocks of size $\sqrt{n} \times \sqrt{n}$. The blocks of the principal block diagonal are tridiagonal matrices with three consecutive diagonals in the center. The two outer block diagonals are composed of blocks that are simple diagonal matrices with only a nonzero principal diagonal. The principal block diagonal contains $\sqrt{n}$ blocks and each of the outer block diagonals consists of $\sqrt{n}-1$ blocks.

We will use the type of matrix shown in Figure 11.7 as the model block-tridiagonal matrix in the remainder of this chapter. However, all algorithms using a matrix with this structure are valid for a somewhat more general block-tridiagonal structure. In general, the size of the matrix is $l_1 l_2 \times l_1 l_2$ for some integers l_1 and l_2 (Problem 11.7). It consists of a principal block diagonal composed of $l_2 \times l_2$ tridiagonal matrices, and two adjacent block diagonals on either side composed of $l_2 \times l_2$ diagonal matrices. The principal block diagonal consists of l_1 blocks and the outer block diagonals contain $l_1 - 1$ blocks each. Such a matrix results if the underlying finite difference grid is an $l_1 \times l_2$ rectangle.

Parallel Implementation with Striped Partitioning of the Block-Tridiagonal Matrix Consider the multiplication of an $n \times n$ matrix of the type shown in Figure 11.7 with an $n \times 1$ vector using p processors. Figure 11.9 shows that the matrix and the vector are partitioned among p processors so that every processor gets n/p elements of the vector and each diagonal of the matrix. The diagonal storage scheme is the natural choice for this case. The array *VAL* is distributed among the processors by using block-striped partitioning, and the array *OFFSET* is not required because the offsets $-\sqrt{n}$, -1, 0, 1 and $\sqrt{n}$ are implicit.

Each row of the matrix requires five vector elements for multiplication. The vector element with which the principal diagonal entry of a row is multiplied has the same index as the number of the row, and is available at the same processor as the row. The vector

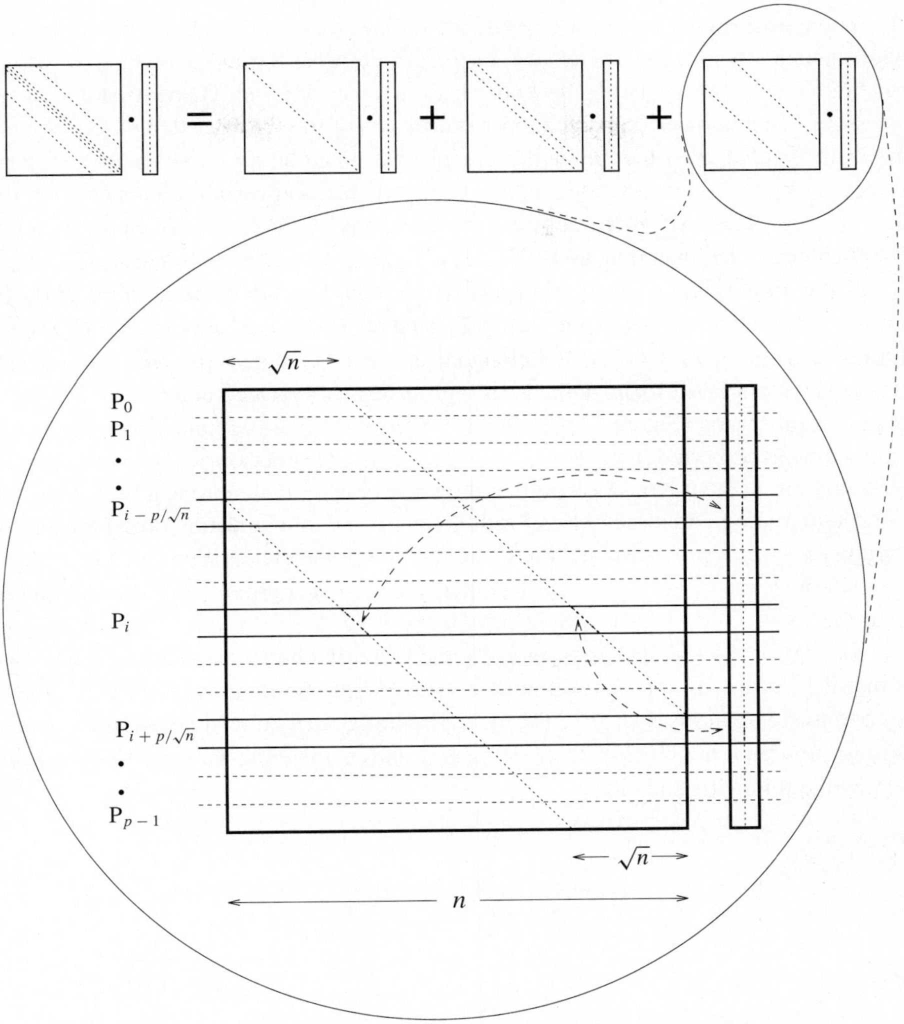

Figure 11.9 Data communication in matrix-vector multiplication with block-striped partitioning of a block-tridiagonal matrix.

elements with which the two inner diagonal entries are multiplied are also available on the same processor, except for the rows that lie on processor boundaries (for example, row number $(n/p) - 1$ is the last row on processor P_0 and needs vector elements $(n/p) - 2$ and n/p; the latter resides on processor P_1). Each processor exchanges its boundary elements with its neighboring processors, and thus, all vector elements required for multiplication with the inner diagonals are now available at each processor. This communication takes $2(t_s + t_w)$ time at each processor.

The entries in each row belonging to the outer diagonals must be multiplied with vector elements whose indices are greater or smaller than the index of the row by $\sqrt{n}$. The communication for this step depends on the number of vector elements stored in each processor. If the number of elements per processor (n/p) is greater than or equal to $\sqrt{n}$ (that is, $p \le \sqrt{n}$), then the required communication can be accomplished by each pair of neighboring processors exchanging $\sqrt{n}$ vector elements at partition boundaries in time $2(t_s + t_w\sqrt{n})$. This exchange subsumes the exchange of the boundary elements for the multiplication of the inner diagonals. Thus, the total communication time is $2(t_s + t_w\sqrt{n})$.

If the number of elements per processor is less than $\sqrt{n}$ (that is, $p > \sqrt{n}$), then processor P_j needs portions of the vector located at processors numbered $j \pm p/\sqrt{n}$ to multiply with the matrix elements belonging to the outer diagonals. As a result, each processor exchanges all its n/p elements with processors located at a distance of $p/\sqrt{n}$ from it on either side (Figure 11.9). This is a shift operation (without circulation) of the vector elements in both directions by a distance of $p/\sqrt{n}$ processors. The shift operation is described in Section 3.6. Assume that the underlying architecture is a hypercube with cut-through routing. As discussed in Section 3.6.2, the communication time for each shift is at most $t_s + t_w n/p + t_h \log p$. Thus, the total communication time (for the exchange of boundary elements and for the shifts) when $p > \sqrt{n}$ is approximately $4t_s + 2t_w n/p + 2t_h \log p$.

Except for the first and last $\sqrt{n}$ rows, there are five nonzero entries in each row of the matrix. Assuming that it takes time t_c to perform one multiplication and addition, the computation time is $5t_c n/p$. The overall parallel execution time for matrix-vector multiplication with the block-tridiagonal matrix and its mapping shown in Figure 11.9 is given by the following equations:

Case 1: $p \le \sqrt{n}$

$$T_P = \overbrace{5t_c n/p}^{\text{computation}} + \overbrace{2(t_s + t_w\sqrt{n})}^{\text{exchange with neighboring processors}} \tag{11.3}$$

Case 2: $p > \sqrt{n}$

$$T_P = \overbrace{5t_c n/p}^{\text{computation}} + \overbrace{2(t_s + t_w)}^{\text{exchange of boundary elements}} + \overbrace{2t_s + 2t_w n/p + 2t_h \log p}^{\text{shift operations}} \tag{11.4}$$

From Equation 11.4 it follows that the isoefficiency function of this parallel implementation of sparse matrix-vector multiplication is $\Theta(p \log p)$. Although this parallel formulation appears quite scalable, there is an upper limit on the efficiency for $p > \sqrt{n}$. The efficiency expression for this case is

$$E = \frac{5t_c}{5t_c + 4t_s p/n + 4t_w + (2t_h p \log p)/n}. \tag{11.5}$$

Equation 11.5 shows that efficiency cannot exceed $5t_c/(4t_w + 5t_c)$. This upper bound on efficiency depends only on the ratio of computation speed to communication bandwidth.

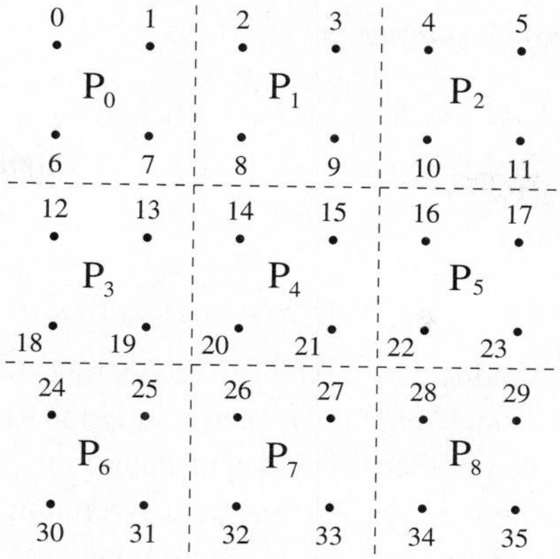

Figure 11.10 Partitioning a 6 × 6 grid on nine processors.

Therefore, higher efficiency cannot be obtained unless the problem size is increased so that $p \leq \sqrt{n}$, in which case the efficiency and isoefficiency function are determined by Equation 11.3. If fewer than $\sqrt{n}$ processors are used, the isoefficiency function due to both concurrency and communication is $\Theta(p^2)$ (Problem 11.12).

If the communication and computation speeds are not balanced, the performance of this parallel formulation of matrix-vector multiplication can be poor. However, we can overcome this upper bound on efficiency by using a better mapping of the matrix onto the processors. We discuss this mapping in the following subsection.

A Faster Parallel Implementation for Matrices Arising from Finite Difference Grids While multiplying the block-tridiagonal matrix of the type shown in Figure 11.7 with a vector, the ith row of the matrix requires an element $x[j]$ of the vector if and only if $A[i, j] \neq 0$. The element $A[i, j]$ is nonzero if and only if points i and j are neighbors in the grid. Thus, the processor storing the ith row of the matrix requires only those elements of the vector whose indices are the same as the indices of the grid points neighboring the ith point.

Now consider the mapping shown in Figure 11.10, which partitions the grid in a block-checkerboard fashion. This partitioning allocates rows of the matrix corresponding to the grid points within a partition to a single processor. The vector is partitioned similarly; the elements with indices corresponding to the grid points in a partition are allocated to a single processor. Using this partitioning, each processor stores $\sqrt{n/p}$ clusters of $\sqrt{n/p}$ matrix rows each (as well as vector elements with the same indices). The starting points of successive clusters are $\sqrt{n}$ rows apart.

To perform matrix-vector multiplication, each processor exchanges the vector elements corresponding to its $\sqrt{n/p}$ boundary points with each of its four neighboring processors. The communication time is $4t_s + 4t_w\sqrt{n/p}$ for both the mesh and hypercube architectures. The total parallel run time is

$$T_P = 5t_c\frac{n}{p} + 4t_s + 4t_w\sqrt{n/p}. \tag{11.6}$$

The expression for efficiency is

$$E = \frac{5t_c}{5t_c + 4t_s p/n + 4t_w\sqrt{p/n}}. \tag{11.7}$$

A comparison of Equations 11.4 and 11.6 shows that the second data distribution scheme for the block-tridiagonal matrix is strictly superior to the first when $p > \sqrt{n}$. Moreover, in the second scheme, there is no upper bound on efficiency. Thus, efficiency can be increased by increasing the problem size for a given number of processors.

Note that the way the grid points are numbered does not affect the communication overhead in this parallel implementation of matrix-vector multiplication. For a given grid and parallel computer, the communication overhead depends only on the way the grid is partitioned among the processors. If the grid is partitioned as shown in Figure 11.10 and vector elements and matrix rows with identical indices are mapped onto the same processor, then Equation 11.6 holds for any square grid whose points have four neighbors each. Hence, the partitioning illustrated in Figure 11.10 is useful not only for natural ordering and the resulting block-tridiagonal matrix, but also for other ordering schemes such as red-black and multicolored orderings (Section 11.2.2). In general, any $l_1l_2 \times l_1l_2$ matrix arising out of an rectangular $l_1 \times l_2$ finite difference grid can use the partitioning illustrated in Figure 11.10 to minimize communication in matrix-vector multiplication.

Unstructured Sparse Matrices

Consider the multiplication of an $n \times n$ unstructured sparse matrix A with an $n \times 1$ vector x. Assume that the average number of nonzero elements per row in A is m, and hence, the total number of nonzero elements in the entire matrix is mn. Recall that if A is a matrix of coefficients resulting from the model of a physical system, then each row of A contains the coefficients of a linear equation corresponding to one grid point. The number of nonzero coefficients in this equation is equal to the number of neighbors of this grid point. Thus, m is the average number of neighbors that a grid point has. As a result, m is essentially a constant independent of the size of the domain (or the size of the array A) and depends only on the nature of the grid imposed on the domain. The Ellpack-Itpack format is an appropriate storage scheme for A because the number of nonzero elements in different rows of A is not expected to vary over a wide range.

A Simple Parallel Implementation Since the Ellpack-Itpack format is row oriented, we partition the arrays *VAL* and J among p processors such that each processor receives n/p rows, or mn/p nonzero elements of matrix A. The vector x is partitioned uniformly so that each processor initially stores n/p elements.

Recall from Section 5.3 that for dense matrix-vector multiplication, each row of the matrix must be multiplied with the vector. Hence, the vector must be aligned with the rows

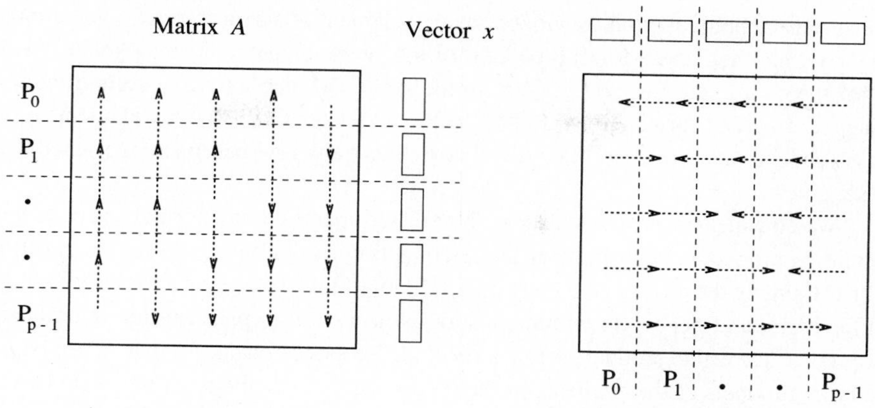

Figure 11.11 Data communication in matrix-vector multiplication with block-striped partitioning of an unstructured sparse matrix.

of the matrix in all the processors. Even in the sparse case, if the distribution of nonzero elements is random, then a row can have a nonzero entry in any column. The entire vector must be accessible to each row so that any of its nonzero entries can be multiplied with the corresponding element of the vector. Thus, matrix-vector multiplication requires an all-to-all broadcast among the processors as shown in Figure 11.11(a). The broadcast is followed by the computation phase, in which each processor performs an average of mn/p multiplications and additions. Since each processor is responsible for n/p rows of the matrix, after the computation step, every processor has n/p elements of the result vector, which is distributed among the processors in the same mapping as the starting vector x.

Assuming that the underlying architecture is a hypercube, the all-to-all broadcast of messages containing n/p vector elements among p processors takes $t_s \log p + t_w n$ time. If each multiplication and addition takes time t_c, then the parallel run time is

$$T_P = t_c m \frac{n}{p} + t_s \log p + t_w n. \qquad (11.8)$$

Equation 11.8 shows that the communication time, and hence the overall parallel run time, for this implementation of matrix-vector multiplication is $\Theta(n)$. Assuming that m, the average number of nonzero elements per row, is constant, the sequential time complexity of multiplying a sparse $n \times n$ matrix with a vector is also $\Theta(n)$. Thus, this parallel implementation does not lead to any asymptotic reduction in run time. Hence, the parallel implementation is non-cost-optimal and unscalable.

The only way to reduce the parallel run time of this algorithm is to reduce communication time. However, this is not possible if the matrix is partioned into stripes—either along the rows or along the columns. If the vector is distributed among all the processors, and a storage scheme is used in which a matrix element at a processor can potentially be in any column, then an all-to-all broadcast of the vector elements is unavoidable. This is true for the coordinate format (an entry in the array *VAL* can have any column number), the jagged-diagonal format (for instance, in Figure 11.6(c), the first six elements of *VAL* span columns 0 to 5 while storing a 6×6 array), and any row-based storage scheme such as CSR.

Now consider storing the matrix in compressed sparse column format and partitioning it among the processors such that each processor gets n/p columns. The vector is partitioned uniformly among the processors. As shown in Figure 11.11(b), the vector is already aligned with the rows, and hence, no communication is necessary to perform the multiplication. However, to have the product vector stored in the same format as that of the starting vector, the products of the elements of the ith row with the elements of the vector must be accumulated on the processor that stores the ith column (Problem 5.6). Thus, as shown in Figure 11.11(b), a multinode accumulation operation has to be performed with messages of size n/p. Recall from Chapter 3 that the communication time for this operation is $t_s \log p + t_w n$, which is the same as the communication time for rowwise striping.

A Faster Parallel Formulation for Unstructured Sparse Matrices First consider the parallel formulation independent of the storage scheme. Assume that the $n \times n$ sparse matrix is block-checkerboarded onto a logical $\sqrt{p} \times \sqrt{p}$ mesh of processors embedded in a physical hypercube. Also assume that the vector is partitioned uniformly among the $\sqrt{p}$ processors of the last column. This is the same scenario as in Figure 5.9, except that the matrix is now sparse. Regardless of the type of matrix, communication is the same as in Figure 5.9, and the total communication time on a hypercube with cut-through routing is approximately $t_s \log p + (t_w n \log p)/(\sqrt{p})$ (Problem 5.7).

Assume that nonzero elements are uniformly distributed over the sparse matrix. Checkerboard partitioning divides the matrix into blocks of size $n/\sqrt{p} \times n/\sqrt{p}$. If each row contains an average of m nonzero elements, then the average number of such elements in each block is $m/\sqrt{p} \times n/\sqrt{p}$ (a block has the $(1/p)^{\text{th}}$ portion of n/p rows). Thus, on an average, every processor performs approximately mn/p multiplications and additions. Assuming that it takes time t_c to perform a single addition and multiplication, the average time that a processor spends in computation is $mt_c n/p$. Note that this is only the average computation time per processor, and the actual time varies depending on the number of nonzero elements that fall in the block stored in the processor. For simplicity, we ignore this fact and assume a uniform computation time $(mt_c n/p)$ on each processor. The more realistic case, in which the processor containing the maximum number of nonzero elements determines the effective computation time, is discussed in Problem 11.4. Under this uniform workload assumption, the expressions for parallel run time, speedup, and efficiency are as follows:

$$T_P = mt_c \frac{n}{p} + t_s \log p + \frac{3}{2} t_w \frac{n}{\sqrt{p}} \log p \qquad (11.9)$$

$$S = \frac{mt_c pn}{mt_c n + t_s p \log p + (3t_w n\sqrt{p}/2) \log p} \qquad (11.10)$$

$$E = \frac{mt_c}{mt_c + (t_s p \log p)/n + (3\sqrt{p}\log p)/2} \tag{11.11}$$

From the preceding equations, we see that even this parallel formulation of matrix-vector multiplication is non-cost-optimal and unscalable, but its parallel run time is $\Theta(\log p) + \Theta((n/\sqrt{p})\log p)$, which is asymptotically smaller than the sequential run time.

A convenient format for storing the sparse matrix for this formulation is to store each block in a separate data structure. For example, if the Ellpack-Itpack format is used, then p separate sets of VAL and J arrays need to be maintained—one for each block residing on a separate processor.

A Scalable Parallel Implementation for Unstructured Sparse Matrices We now briefly discuss a scalable formulation of matrix-vector multiplication for a special class of unstructured sparse matrices. Let A be an $n \times n$ unstructured sparse matrix that has a symmetric structure. Let $G(A)$ be a graph with n nodes such that there is an edge between the ith and the jth nodes of $G(A)$ if and only if $A[i, j] \neq 0$ (or $A[j, i] \neq 0$). The matrix A is thus a weighted adjacency matrix of graph $G(A)$ in which each node corresponds to a row of A. A scalable parallel implementation of matrix-vector multiplication exists for a sparse matrix A provided that it is the adjacency matrix of a planar graph $G(A)$. A graph is planar if and only if it can be drawn in a plane such that no edges cross each other. Note that planarity of $G(A)$ is a sufficient, but not a necessary condition for the multiplication of matrix A with a vector to be scalable.

If the graph $G(A)$ is planar, it is possible to partition its nodes (and hence, the rows of A) among processors to yield a scalable parallel formulation for sparse matrix-vector multiplication. The amount of computation that a processors performs is proportional to the total number of nodes in that processor's partition. If $G(A)$ is planar, the total number of words that a processor communicates is proportional to the number of nodes lying along the periphery of that processor's partition. Furthermore, if $G(A)$ is planar, the number of processors with whom a given processor communicates is equal to the number of partitions with whom that processor's partition shares its boundaries. Hence, by reducing the number of partitions (thus, increasing the size of the partitions) it possible to increase the computation to communication ratio of the processors.

Figure 11.12 shows a structurally symmetric randomly sparse matrix and its associated graph. The vector is partitioned among the processors such that its ith element resides on the same processor that stores the ith row of the matrix. Figure 11.12 also shows the partitioning of the graph among processors and the corresponding assignment of the matrix rows to processors. While performing matrix-vector multiplication with this partitioning, the ith row of A requires only those elements of the vector whose indices correspond to the neighbors of the ith node in $G(A)$. The reason is that by the construction of $G(A)$, the ith row has a nonzero element in the jth column if and only if j is connected to i by an edge in $G(A)$. As a result, a processor performs communication for only those rows of A that correspond to the nodes of $G(A)$ lying at the boundary of the processor's partition. If the graph is partitioned properly, the communication cost can be reduced significantly

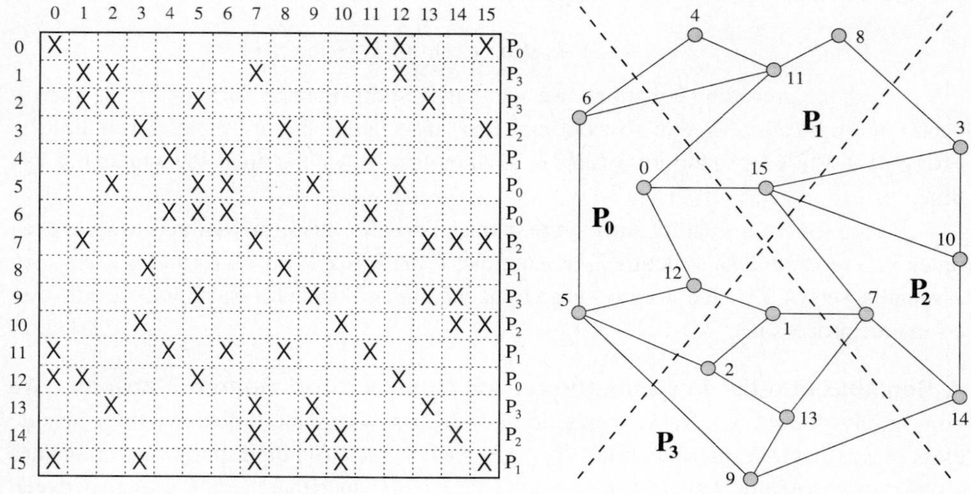

(a) A 16 x 16 symmetric random sparse matrix (b) The associated graph and its four partitions

Figure 11.12 A 16×16 unstructured sparse matrix with symmetric structure and its associated graph partitioned among four processors.

both in terms of the number of messages and the volume of communication (Problems 11.8 and 11.9).

Partitioning an arbitrary graph $G(A)$ to minimize interprocessor communication is a hard combinatorial problem. However, there are several good heuristics for graph partitioning. These partitioning techniques are described in detail in Section 11.3. Often, the origin of the unstructured sparse matrix A lies in a finite element problem. In such a case, the graph $G(A)$ can be derived from the finite element graph directly.

The technique described here can also be adapted for randomly sparse matrices that are non-symmetric in structure. In such cases, a directed graph results, and the communication takes place in the direction opposite to the direction of an edge crossing a partition boundary. For example, if $A[i, j] \neq 0$, then there is a directed edge from node i to node j in $G(A)$. If nodes i and j belong to different partitions, then the jth element of the vector must be sent to the processor storing the ith row of matrix A.

Banded Unstructured Sparse Matrices

We often encounter linear systems in which the nonzero elements of the sparse matrix of coefficients occur only within a band parallel to the principal diagonal. Even if the nonzero elements are scattered throughout the matrix, it is often possible to restrict them to a band by using certain reordering techniques. In this subsection we discuss matrix-vector multiplication for banded unstructured sparse matrices.

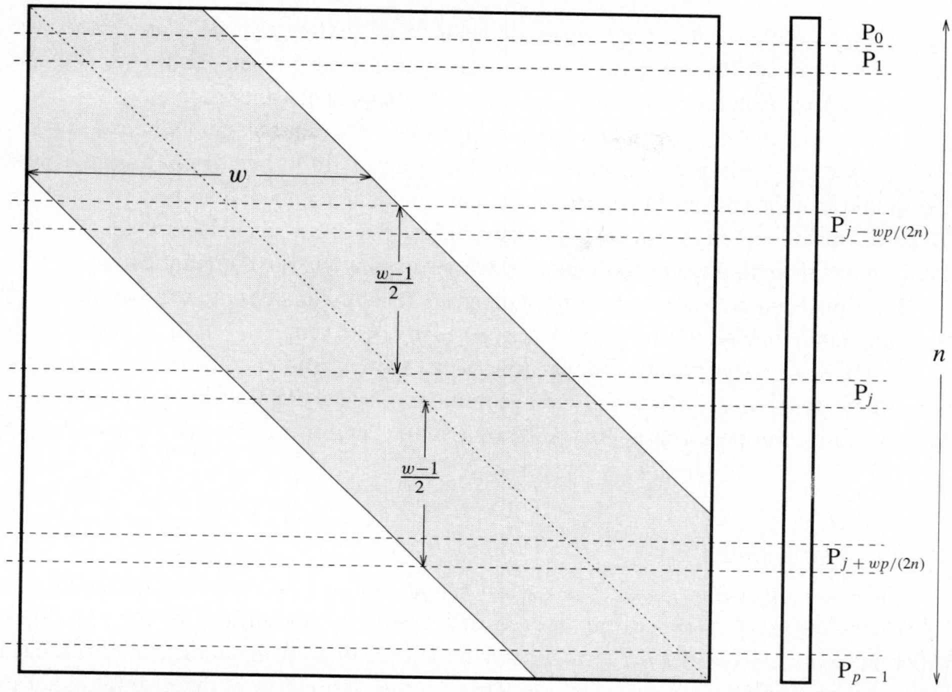

Figure 11.13 Matrix-vector multiplication with a block-striped partitioning of a banded unstructured sparse matrix.

For simplicity of analysis, we assume that the width of the band is w and that it spreads evenly to a width of $(w - 1)/2$ on both sides of the principal diagonal. The $n \times n$ matrix is stored in Ellpack-Itpack format, and the average number of nonzero elements per row is m. The matrix and the vector are distributed among the processors as shown in Figure 11.13. Each of the p processors initially stores the nonzero entries of n/p rows of the matrix and n/p elements of the vector. We consider only the case in which neither the width of the band nor the number of processors is trivially small. Hence, we assume that $n/p \ll w$.

Given the distribution of nonzero elements just described, the maximum column index of a nonzero element in the ith row of the matrix is $i + (w - 1)/2$, and its minimum column index is $i - (w - 1)/2$. Thus, the ith row requires those elements of the vector that have indices between $i - (w - 1)/2$ and $i + (w - 1)/2$. Furthermore, the indices of the rows that require the ith vector element lie between $i - (w - 1)/2$ and $i + (w - 1)/2$. Since each processor stores n/p matrix rows, the half band of $(w - 1)/2$ rows is spread among $\lceil (w - 1)p/2n \rceil$ processors. Hence, a processor needs to send all its n/p vector elements to $\lceil (w - 1)p/2n \rceil$ processors on either side. A typical processor P_j communicates with all the processors with labels between $j - \lceil (w - 1)p/2n \rceil$ and $j + \lceil (w - 1)p/2n \rceil$. From now on, we will assume that $wp/2n$ is a whole number and $\lceil w(p - 1)/2n \rceil$ is rounded off to $wp/2n$.

Thus, each processor sends all its vector elements to approximately wp/n processors (see Figure 11.13 for an illustration). Contrast this with the case of an unstructured sparse matrix, in which each processor sends its vector elements to all other processors.

Assuming that the processors are connected in a linear array, communication takes wp/n steps, $wp/2n$ in each direction in the linear array. In the first step, all processors (except those at the ends of the linear array) send vector elements to their neighbors in one direction. In subsequent steps, each processor stores the data received from one neighbor and forwards them to the other neighbor. After performing $wp/2n$ communication steps in one direction, each processor performs another $wp/2n$ similar steps in the other direction. The total communication time is $(t_s + t_w n/p) \times wp/n = t_s wp/n + t_w w$. Since there is an average of m nonzero elements per row of the matrix, and each processor stores the nonzero elements of n/p rows, the average number of scalar multiplication-addition pairs that each processor performs is mn/p. If we assume a uniform workload, the parallel run time is

$$T_P = t_c \frac{mn}{p} + t_s \frac{wp}{n} + t_w w. \tag{11.12}$$

The processor-time product is $t_c mn + t_s wp^2/n + t_w wp$. For cost-optimality, the processor-time product should not exceed the serial time complexity of the algorithm, which is $\Theta(mn)$. Consider the term associated with t_s first. If this term is not to exceed $\Theta(mn)$, then $p^2 w/n = O(mn)$, or $p = O(n\sqrt{m/w})$. Similarly, if the t_w term is not to exceed $\Theta(mn)$, then $wp = O(mn)$, or $p = O(mn/w)$. Since $m < w$, we have $m/w < 1$ and $m/w < \sqrt{m/w}$. Therefore, the overall (most restrictive) condition for cost-optimality is $p = O(mn/w)$.

Thus, matrix-vector multiplication with unstructured sparse matrices is cost-optimal and scalable if the nonzero elements are confined to a band rather than scattered over the entire matrix (Problems 11.10 and 11.11). The number of processors that can be used cost-optimally is directly proportional to the number of nonzero elements in each row of the sparse matrix, and inversely proportional to the width of the band in which the nonzero elements are distributed.

11.2 Iterative Methods for Sparse Linear Systems

Iterative methods are techniques to solve systems of equations of the form $Ax = b$ that generate a sequence of approximations to the solution vector x. In each iteration, the coefficient matrix A is used to perform a matrix-vector multiplication. The number of iterations required to solve a system of equations with a desired precision is usually data dependent; hence, the number of iterations is not known prior to executing the algorithm. Therefore, in this section we analyze the performance and scalability of a single iteration of an iterative method. Iterative methods do not guarantee a solution for all systems of equations. However, when they do yield a solution, they are usually less expensive than direct methods for matrix factorization. In the following section, we study some commonly used iterative methods for solving large sparse systems of linear equations.

11.2.1 Jacobi Iterative Method

The Jacobi iterative method is one of the simplest iterative techniques. The ith equation of a system of linear equations $Ax = b$ is

$$\sum_{j=0}^{n-1} A[i, j]x[j] \quad = \quad b[i]. \tag{11.13}$$

If all the diagonal elements of A are nonzero (or are made nonzero by permuting the rows and columns of A), we can rewrite Equation 11.13 as

$$x[i] \quad = \quad \frac{1}{A[i,i]}\left(b[i] - \sum_{j \neq i} A[i, j]x[j]\right). \tag{11.14}$$

The Jacobi method starts with an initial guess x_0 for the solution vector x. This initial vector x_0 is used in the right-hand side of Equation 11.14 to arrive at the next approximation x_1 to the solution vector. The vector x_1 is then used in the right hand side of Equation 11.14, and the process continues until a close enough approximation to the actual solution is found. A typical iteration step in the Jacobi method is

$$x_k[i] = \frac{1}{A[i,i]}\left(b[i] - \sum_{j \neq i} A[i, j]x_{k-1}[j]\right). \tag{11.15}$$

The process is said to have converged after k iterations of Equation 11.15 if the magnitude of the vector $(b - Ax_k)$ becomes reasonably small. The vector $(b - Ax)$ is zero for the exact solution x. Hence, $(b - Ax_k)$, denoted by r_k, represents the error in the approximation of x and is referred to as the ***residual*** after k iterations. The square root of the inner product $r_k^T r_k$ (that is, $\sqrt{r_k^T r_k}$, which is also called the ***two-norm*** of r_k and is denoted by $\|r_k\|_2$) is commonly used to represent the magnitude of the error at the end of the kth iteration. The procedure terminates when $\|r_k\|_2$ falls below a predetermined threshold, which is usually a very small fraction $\epsilon\|r_0\|_2$ (where, $0 < \epsilon \ll 1$) of the two-norm of the initial residual r_0.

We now express the iteration step of Equation 11.15 in terms of the residual r_k. Equation 11.15 can be rewritten as

$$x_k[i] = \frac{1}{A[i,i]}\left(b[i] - \sum_{j=0}^{n-1} A[i, j]x_{k-1}[j]\right) + x_{k-1}[i]. \tag{11.16}$$

By the definition of the residual, $r_{k-1} = b - Ax_{k-1}$. Therefore, $b[i] - \Sigma_{j=0}^{n-1} A[i, j]x_{k-1}[j]$ in Equation 11.16 can be replaced by $r_{k-1}[i]$. Hence, a Jacobi iteration is given by the following equation:

$$x_k[i] = \frac{r_{k-1}[i]}{A[i,i]} + x_{k-1}[i] \tag{11.17}$$

```
1.  procedure JACOBI_METHOD (A,b,x,ε)
2.  begin
3.      k := 0;
4.      Select initial solution vector x_0;
5.      r_0 := b − Ax_0;
6.      while (||r_k||_2 > ε||r_0||_2) do
7.      begin
8.          k := k + 1;
9.          for i := 0 to n − 1 do
10.             x_k[i] := r_{k−1}[i]/A[i, i] + x_{k−1}[i];  /* Equation 11.17 */
11.         r_k := b − Ax_k;
12.     endwhile;
13.     x := x_k;
14. end JACOBI_METHOD
```

Program 11.2 The serial Jacobi iterative method for solving a system of linear equations.

The resulting algorithm is given in Program 11.2. The Jacobi algorithm given in Program 11.2 is not guaranteed to converge for all types of matrices. One class of matrices for which it always converges is that of diagonally-dominant matrices. An $n \times n$ matrix A is ***diagonally dominant*** if and only if $|A[i, i]| > \Sigma_{j \neq i} |A[i, j]|, 0 \leq i < n$.

Parallel Implementation

Each iteration of the Jacobi method given in Program 11.2 performs three main computations: the inner product on line 6, the loop of lines 9 and 10, and the matrix-vector multiplication on line 11. If the matrix and the vector are mapped onto the processors of a parallel computer such that $A[i, i]$, $r_k[i]$, and $x_k[i]$ are assigned to the same processor for $0 \leq i < n$, then the loop of lines 9 and 10 does not require any communication. The mappings shown in Figures 11.9–11.13 all satisfy this condition. Sometimes, for the purpose of load balancing, a mapping like the one shown in Figure 11.29(a) (Problem 11.1) may be desirable. In this mapping, each processor performs the same number of scalar multiplications and additions while multiplying the matrix with a vector; however, $A[i, i]$ and $x[i]$ may not be assigned to the same processor. This situation can be remedied by modifying the mapping slightly. The principal diagonal of the $n \times n$ coefficient matrix A is treated as an $n \times 1$ vector and is stored separately from the rest of the matrix. Now the elements of the principal diagonal are mapped onto the same processors as those of the vectors r_k and x_k, and the rest of the matrix is mapped as shown in Figure 11.29(a).

Thus, the loop on lines 9 and 10 can be executed in parallel without any communication. The two steps that require communication in each iteration are the computation of the norm of the residual r_k (line 6), which is a vector inner product, and matrix-vector multiplication (line 11). Vector inner product and sparse matrix-vector multiplication are discussed in Sections 11.1.2 and 11.1.3, respectively. Of these, the operation with the larger communication overhead determines the overall performance and scalability of the Jacobi algorithm on a parallel architecture.

As discussed in Section 11.1.2, if no special hardware is available to add p numbers distributed on p processors, the communication time for an inner-product computation is $\Theta(\log p)$ on a hypercube and $\Theta(\sqrt{p})$ on a square mesh. This translates to a total overhead of $\Theta(p \log p)$ and $\Theta(p^{3/2})$ for each iteration on a hypercube and a mesh, respectively. Therefore, the isoefficiency function of an iteration of the Jacobi method is at least $\Theta(p \log p)$ on a hypercube and $\Theta(p^{3/2})$ on a mesh. As discussed in Section 11.1.3, the communication overhead in parallel sparse matrix-vector multiplication depends on the sparsity pattern on the matrix. If the structure of the sparse matrix is such that the isoefficiency function due to matrix-vector multiplication is less than that due to inner-product computation, then it is possible to reduce the overall isoefficiency function of an iteration of the Jacobi algorithm. Recall from Program 11.2 that the inner-product is computed in each iteration only to test for convergence (line 6). If the convergence test is performed once every $\log p$ iterations on a hypercube, then the total number of iterations may increase by at most $\log p$, but the overhead of each inner-product calculation is amortized over $\log p$ iterations. Thus, the total overhead due to the inner product calculations is reduced to $\Theta(p)$. The isoefficiency function due to the inner-product calculation is then also reduced to $\Theta(p)$. Similar results can be obtained by performing the convergence check once every $\Theta(\sqrt{p})$ iterations on a mesh.

11.2.2 Gauss-Seidel and SOR Methods

As we mentioned earlier, the Jacobi algorithm does not always converge. Even if it does, the rate of its convergence is often very slow. The Gauss-Seidel method improves on the convergence properties of the Jacobi method. However, like the Jacobi method, the Gauss-Seidel method is not always guaranteed to converge.

An iteration of the Jacobi method is based on Equation 11.15. During the kth iteration of Jacobi algorithm to solve an $n \times n$ system, the step of Equation 11.15 is performed to compute each $x_k[i]$ for $0 \le i < n$. The computation of $x_k[i]$ uses the values of $x_{k-1}[0], \ldots, x_{k-1}[i-1], x_{k-1}[i+1], \ldots, x_{k-1}[n-1]$. Assuming that the $x_k[i]$ values are computed in increasing order of i, the values of $x_k[0], \ldots, x_k[i-1]$ have already been computed before Equation 11.15 is used to compute $x_k[i]$. However, the Jacobi algorithm uses $x_{k-1}[0], \ldots, x_{k-1}[i-1]$ from the previous iteration. The Gauss-Seidel algorithm uses the most recent value of each variable, and as a result, often achieves faster convergence than the Jacobi algorithm. The basic Gauss-Seidel iteration is given by

$$x_k[i] = \frac{1}{A[i,i]}\left(b[i] - \sum_{j=0}^{i-1} x_k[j]A[i,j] - \sum_{j=i+1}^{n-1} x_{k-1}[j]A[i,j]\right). \qquad (11.18)$$

Parallel Implementation

The Gauss-Seidel algorithm performs the basic iteration given by Equation 11.18 until satisfactory convergence is achieved. As in Jacobi method, the test for convergence requires an inner-product computation that involves global communication. However, a convergence check need not be performed after each iteration. Given a parallel architecture, the frequency of the convergence check can be chosen to optimize the overall performance on that architecture (Section 11.2.1). The issues in parallelizing the inner-product computation are discussed in Section 11.1.2. In this section we concentrate on performing the iteration step of Equation 11.18 in parallel.

From a preliminary glance at Equation 11.18 it might appear that computing $x_k[0]$, $x_k[1], \ldots, x_k[n-1]$ in the kth iteration is completely sequential because $x_k[i]$ cannot be computed until $x_k[i-1]$ has been computed for $0 \le i < n$. This is indeed the case if the coefficient matrix A is dense. However, if A is sparse, the computation of $x_k[i]$ need not wait until $x_k[0], \ldots, x_k[i-1]$ have *all* been computed. A majority of elements in the sparse matrix A are zero. If $A[i, j]$ is zero, then $x_k[i]$ on the left-hand side of Equation 11.18 does not depend upon $x_k[j]$. Thus, $x_k[i]$ can be computed as soon as all $x_k[j]$ have been computed such that $j < i$ and $A[i, j] \neq 0$. At any time, all $x_k[i]$ for which this condition is true can be computed in parallel.

Since the computation of $x_k[i]$ depends only on the nonzero elements $A[i, j]$ (with $j < i$) in the coefficient matrix, the degree of parallelism in Gauss-Seidel method is a function of the sparsity pattern of the lower-triangular part of A. For example, consider the block-tridiagonal matrix of the form shown in Figure 11.7. Such a matrix results from a finite difference discretization with a natural ordering of grid points, as shown in Figure 11.8. In the $\sqrt{n} \times \sqrt{n}$ grid in Figure 11.8, except for the points on the left periphery, every point i has point $i-1$ as its neighbor. Therefore, except in the rows corresponding to the grid points on the left periphery, $A[i, i-1]$ is not equal to zero. As a result, for all but $\sqrt{n}$ values of i, the computation of $x_k[i]$ has to wait until $x_k[i-1]$ has been computed. Hence, natural ordering is not suitable for a parallel implementation of Gauss-Seidel algorithm. It can be shown that each Gauss-Seidel iteration on an $n \times n$ block-tridiagonal matrix of the form shown in Figure 11.7 takes at least $\Theta(\sqrt{n})$ time regardless of the number of processors used (Problem 11.13).

The order in which the grid points in a discretized domain are numbered determines the order of the rows and columns in the coefficient matrix, and hence, the location of its nonzero elements. The degree of parallelism in the Gauss-Seidel algorithm depends heavily on this ordering. The rate of convergence of the Gauss-Seidel algorithm for a given grid is also sensitive to this ordering. However, given enough processors, an ordering more amenable to parallelization is likely to yield a better overall performance, unless it results in much worse convergence.

Red-Black Ordering We now introduce a numbering scheme for a finite difference grid so that the resulting coefficient matrix permits a high degree of parallelism in a Gauss-Seidel iteration. We will later extend this scheme to deal with sparse matrices other than those

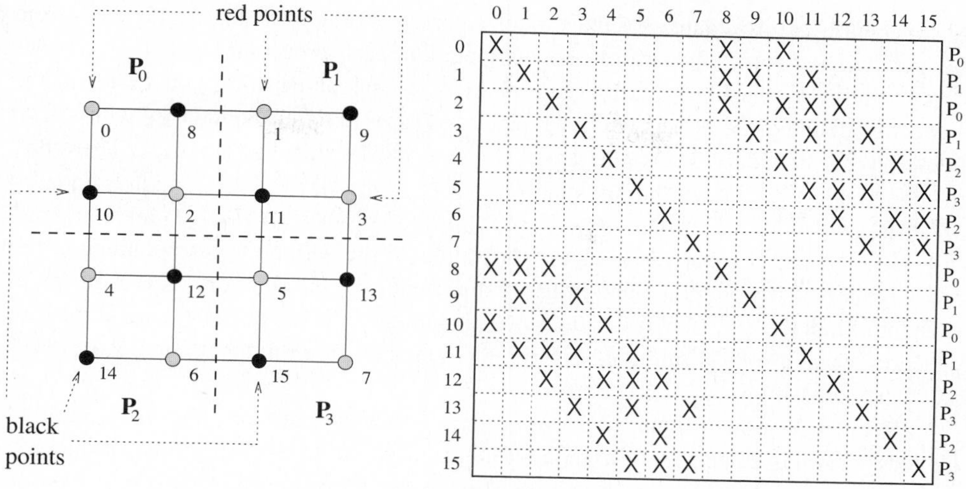

(a) A 4 X 4 grid with red-black ordering

(b) Corresponding coefficient matrix

Figure 11.14 A partitioning among four processors of a 4×4 finite difference grid with red-black ordering.

resulting from a finite difference discretization. Figure 11.14(a) illustrates this ordering, which is known as ***red-black ordering***. In red-black ordering, alternate grid points in each row and column are colored red, and the remaining points are colored black. For a uniform two-dimensional grid in which each point has a maximum of four neighbors, this ensures that no two directly-connected grid points have the same color. After assigning colors to the grid points, all red points are numbered first in natural order, leaving out the black points. This is followed by numbering all the black points in natural order. If the grid has a total of n points and n is even, the red points are numbered from 0 to $(n/2) - 1$ and the black points are numbered from $n/2$ to $n - 1$.

Figure 11.14(b) shows the sparse matrix resulting from the 4×4 grid of Figure 11.14(a). In the coefficient matrix, the first $n/2$ rows correspond to the red points, and the last $n/2$ rows correspond to the black points in the grid. Since red points have only black neighbors and vice versa, the first $n/2$ rows have nondiagonal nonzero elements in only the last $n/2$ columns, and the last $n/2$ rows have nondiagonal nonzero elements in only the first $n/2$ columns.

Consider a parallel implementation of the Gauss-Seidel method on a two-dimensional mesh of processors. The grid is partitioned among the processors of the mesh in a block-checkerboard fashion. Figure 11.14 shows the allocation of grid points and the rows of the coefficient matrix among four processors. With red-black ordering, each iteration of the Gauss-Seidel algorithm is performed in two phases. In the kth iteration, first, $x_k[0], x_k[1], \ldots, x_k[n/2-1]$ are computed in parallel. Each of these variables corresponds to red points, and uses values of the variables corresponding to its black neighbors from the previous iteration. To perform this computation, each processor sends the variables corresponding to the black points lying at each of its four partition boundaries to the respective neighboring processors. A typical processor has four boundaries with $\sqrt{n/p}$ points on each boundary. Half of these points are red and the other half are black. Therefore, the communication time of the first phase is $4 \times (t_s + t_w\sqrt{n/p} \times 1/2)$, which is equal to $4t_s + 2t_w\sqrt{n/p}$. In the second phase, $x_k[n/2], x_k[n/2+1], \ldots, x_k[n-1]$ are computed in parallel. Each of these variables use the values of the variables corresponding to the red neighbors that were computed in the first phase of the kth iteration. This requires an exchange of all the $\sqrt{n}/(2\sqrt{p})$ variables corresponding to the red points at each of the four partition boundaries. As in the first phase, the communication in the second phase takes $4t_s + 2t_w\sqrt{n/p}$ time.

Each evaluation of Equation 11.18 for the coefficient matrix resulting from a grid of the form shown in Figure 11.14(a) requires at most four multiplications, four subtractions, and one division. The number of multiplications and subtractions is at most four because there are at most four nondiagonal nonzero elements in each row of A—one corresponding to each of the four neighbors of a point in the grid. These operations are performed once for each variable in every iteration. Assuming that this constant amount of computation per grid point (or per row of the coefficient matrix) takes time t_c, the total execution time per iteration is

$$T_P = t_c n/p + 8t_s + 4t_w\sqrt{n/p}. \tag{11.19}$$

Equation 11.19 does not include the time spent in testing for convergence, which depends on how and with what frequency the convergence test is performed.

Multicolored Ordering for General Matrices Recall from Figure 11.12 that a matrix A can be regarded as the adjacency matrix of a graph $G(A)$. We now extend the idea behind red-black ordering to devise an ordering scheme for sparse matrices that arise from finite element problems (Section 11.3).

Multicolored ordering is an ordering scheme in which the nodes of graph $G(A)$ associated with a matrix A are colored such that no two neighboring nodes have the same color. Although coloring the graph in such a way is a combinatorial problem of exponential complexity, usually simple heuristics are sufficient to color most graphs arising out of practical problems by using a small number of colors. The nodes of each color are assigned labels one after the other, and all nodes of the same color have consecutive labels. The system of equations is rewritten such that the ith equation and the variable x_i correspond to the node labeled i in $G(A)$. Figure 11.15 shows the multicolored ordering of a graph with four colors. The coefficient matrix of the system of linear equations resulting from the grid of Figure 11.15 is of size 32×32. An iteration of parallel Gauss-Seidel algorithm to solve this system is performed in four phases. In the first phase of the kth iteration, $x_k[0], \ldots, x_k[7]$ are computed in parallel using $x_{k-1}[8], \ldots, x_{k-1}[31]$. In the second phase, $x_k[8], \ldots, x_k[15]$ are computed in parallel using $x_k[0], \ldots, x_k[7]$ and $x_{k-1}[16], \ldots, x_{k-1}[31]$. In the third phase, $x_k[16], \ldots, x_k[23]$ are computed in par-

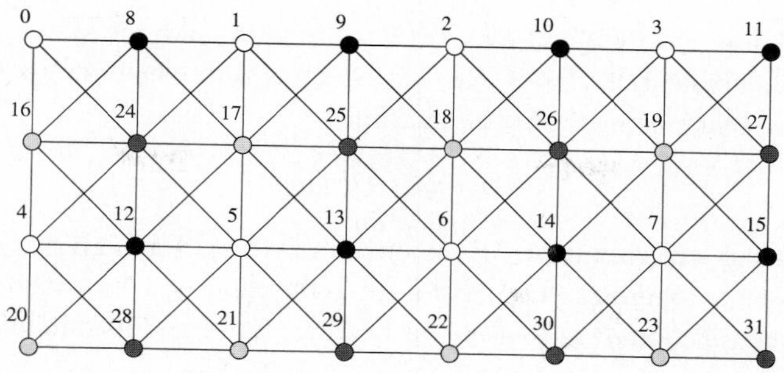

Figure 11.15 Multicolored ordering of a finite element graph using four colors.

allel using $x_k[0], \ldots, x_k[15]$ and $x_{k-1}[24], \ldots, x_{k-1}[31]$, and finally, in the fourth phase, $x_k[24], \ldots, x_k[31]$ are computed in parallel using $x_k[0], \ldots, x_k[24]$.

In general, if the coefficient matrix is ordered using multicolored ordering, the number of phases in a Gauss-Seidel iteration is equal to the number of colors used in the ordering. In any iteration, all variables corresponding to the grid points of the same color can be updated in parallel.

The SOR Method

Often, we can obtain a significant improvement in convergence speed by modifying the iteration step of Equation 11.18. The ***successive overrelaxation (SOR)*** method is such an extension of the Gauss-Seidel method. The SOR method computes $x_k[i]$ in the kth iteration as a weighted average of $x_{k-1}[i]$ and the $x_k[i]$ given by Equation 11.18. In the SOR algorithm, a parameter ω (typically, $0 < \omega \leq 2$) is appropriately chosen, and the following iteration step is used:

$$x_k[i] = (i - \omega)x_{k-1}[i] + \frac{\omega}{A[i,i]}\left(b[i] - \sum_{j=0}^{i-1} x_k[j]A[i,j] - \sum_{j=i+1}^{n-1} x_{k-1}[j]A[i,j]\right) \tag{11.20}$$

The parallelization issues and the communication costs in a parallel implementation of the SOR algorithm are the same as those for the Gauss-Seidel algorithm.

★ 11.2.3 The Conjugate Gradient Method

The ***conjugate gradient (CG) method*** is one of the most powerful and widely used iterative methods for solving large sparse systems of linear equations of the form $Ax = b$, where A is a symmetric positive definite matrix. A real $n \times n$ matrix A is ***positive definite*** if $x^T Ax > 0$ for any $n \times 1$ real, nonzero vector x.

The CG method belongs to a class of iterative methods known as ***minimization methods***. For a symmetric positive definite matrix A, the unique x that minimizes the quadratic function $q(x) = (1/2)x^T Ax - x^T b$ is the solution to the system $Ax = b$. The reason is that the gradient of $q(x)$ is $Ax - b$, which is zero when $q(x)$ is minimum. An iteration of a minimization method is of the form

$$x_k = x_{k-1} + \alpha_k p_k, \tag{11.21}$$

where α_k is a scalar step size and p_k is the direction vector. For a given x_{k-1} and p_k, the scalar α_k is chosen to minimize $q(x_k)$; that is, α_k is the value of α for which $q(x_{k-1} + \alpha p_k)$ is minimum. The function $q(x_{k-1} + \alpha p_k)$ is quadratic in α, and its minimization leads to the condition

$$\alpha_k = \frac{p_k^T r_{k-1}}{p_k^T A p_k}, \tag{11.22}$$

where $r_{k-1} = b - Ax_{k-1}$ is the residual vector after $k-1$ iterations. The residual need not be computed explicitly in each iteration because it can be computed incrementally by using its value from the previous iteration. In the kth iteration, the residual r_k can be expressed as follows:

$$\begin{aligned} r_k &= b - Ax_k \\ &= b - A(x_{k-1} + \alpha_k p_k) \\ &= b - Ax_{k-1} - \alpha_k A p_k \\ &= r_{k-1} - \alpha_k A p_k \end{aligned} \tag{11.23}$$

Thus, the only matrix-vector product computed in each iteration is Ap_k, which is already required to compute α_k (Equation 11.22).

If A is a symmetric positive definite matrix and $p_1, p_2, \ldots, p_n$ are direction vectors that are conjugate with respect to A (that is, $p_i^T A p_j = 0$ for all $0 < i, j \leq n, i \neq j$), then x_k in Equation 11.21 converges to the solution of $Ax = b$ in at most n iterations, assuming no rounding errors. In practice, however, the number of iterations that yields an acceptable approximation to the solution is much smaller than n. In the CG algorithm, the set of A-conjugate direction vectors is chosen as follows:

$$\begin{aligned} p_1 &= r_0 = b \\ p_{k+1} &= r_k + \frac{\|r_k\|_2^2 p_k}{\|r_{k-1}\|_2^2} \end{aligned} \tag{11.24}$$

With the preceding choice of direction vectors, the ratio $(p_k^T r_{k-1})/(p_k^T A p_k)$ is equal to $\|r_{k-1}\|_2^2/(p_k^T A p_k)$. Thus, Equation 11.22 can be rewritten as follows:

$$\alpha_k = \frac{\|r_{k-1}\|_2^2}{p_k^T A p_k} \tag{11.25}$$

Equations 11.21, 11.23, 11.24, and 11.25 lead to the conjugate gradient algorithm given in Program 11.3. The algorithm terminates when the two-norm of the current residual falls below a predetermined fraction of the two-norm of the initial residual r_0.

procedure CG (A, b, x, ϵ)
begin
$k := 0$; $x_0 := 0$; $r_0 := b$; $\rho_0 := \|r_0\|_2^2$;
while $(\sqrt{\rho_i} > \epsilon \|r_0\|_2)$ **do**
begin
if $(k = 0)$ **then** $p_1 := r_0$
else $p_{k+1} := r_k + \rho_k p_k / \rho_{k-1}$; /* Equation 11.24 */
$k := k + 1$;
$w_k := A p_k$;
$\alpha_k := \rho_{k-1} / p_k^T w_k$; /* Equation 11.25 */
$x_k := x_{k-1} + \alpha_k p_k$; /* Equation 11.21 */
$r_k := r_{k-1} - \alpha_k w_k$; /* Equation 11.23 */
$\rho_k := \|r_k\|_2^2$;
endwhile;
$x := x_k$;
end CG

Program 11.3 The conjugate gradient (CG) algorithm.

The Preconditioned Conjugate Gradient Algorithm

If the coefficient matrix A has l distinct eigenvalues, the conjugate gradient algorithm given in Program 11.3 converges to the solution of the system $Ax = b$ in at most l iterations (assuming no rounding errors). Therefore, if A has many distinct eigenvalues that vary widely in magnitude, the CG algorithm may require a large number of iterations to converge to an acceptable approximation to the solution. The speed of convergence of the CG algorithm can be increased by preconditioning A with the congruence transformation $\tilde{A} = RAR^T$, where R is a nonsingular matrix. R is chosen such that $\tilde{A}$ has fewer distinct eigenvalues than A. The CG algorithm is then used to solve $\tilde{A}\tilde{x} = \tilde{b}$, where $\tilde{x} = (R^T)^{-1}x$ and $\tilde{b} = Rb$. The resulting algorithm is called the ***preconditioned conjugate gradient (PCG) algorithm***.

There are certain problems with applying the CG algorithm directly to the system $\tilde{A}\tilde{x} = \tilde{b}$. Unless R is a diagonal matrix, the sparsity pattern of A is not preserved in $\tilde{A}$. Moreover, the matrix multiplications involved in computing $\tilde{A}$ can be expensive. Fortunately, it is possible to formulate the PCG algorithm so that the explicit computation of $\tilde{A}$ is avoided. A practical PCG algorithm works with the original matrix A; however, it maintains the same convergence rate as that for the system $\tilde{A}\tilde{x} = \tilde{b}$. Such a practical PCG algorithm is given in Program 11.4. The matrix M in the program is referred to as the ***preconditioner*** matrix and is given by $M = (R^T R)^{-1}$. If M is an identity matrix, then the PCG algorithm reduces to the unpreconditioned algorithm of Program 11.3.

In practical implementations of the PCG algorithm, the preconditioner M is directly chosen as a symmetric positive definite matrix, and computing it by using $M = (R^T R)^{-1}$

1. **procedure** PCG (A, b, M, x, ϵ)
2. **begin**
3. $k := 0$; $x_0 := 0$; $r_0 := b$; $\rho_0 := \|r_0\|_2^2$;
4. **while** $(\sqrt{\rho_i} > \epsilon \|r_0\|_2)$ **do**
5. **begin**
6. Solve the system $M z_k = r_k$;
7. $\gamma_k := r_k^T z_k$;
8. **if** $(k = 0)$ **then** $p_1 := z_0$
9. **else** $p_{k+1} := z_k + \gamma_k p_k / \gamma_{k-1}$;
10. $k := k + 1$;
11. $w_k := A p_k$;
12. $\alpha_k := \gamma_{k-1} / p_k^T w_k$;
13. $x_k := x_{k-1} + \alpha_k p_k$;
14. $r_k := r_{k-1} - \alpha_k w_k$;
15. $\rho_k := \|r_k\|_2^2$;
16. **endwhile**;
17. $x := x_k$;
18. **end** PCG

Program 11.4 The preconditioned conjugate gradient (PCG) algorithm.

is not required. For obvious reasons, M is chosen such that solving the system $M z_k = r_k$ on line 6 in each iteration of Program 11.4 is not too costly.

Parallel Implementations of the PCG Algorithm

As Program 11.4 shows, the PCG algorithm involves the following four types of computations in each iteration:

(1) **SAXPY operations:** The operations on lines 9, 13, and 14 of Program 11.4 are known as ***simple ax plus y (SAXPY)*** operations, where a is a scalar, and x and y are vectors. Each of these operations can be performed sequentially in time $\Theta(n)$, regardless of the preconditioner and the type of coefficient matrix. If all vectors are distributed identically among the processors, these steps require no communication in a parallel implementation. The reason is that the vector elements with the same indices are involved in a given arithmetic operation, and thus are locally available on each processor. Using p processors, each of these steps is performed in time $\Theta(n/p)$ on any architecture.

(2) **Vector inner products:** Lines 7, 12, and 15 in Program 11.4 involve vector inner-product computation. In a serial implementation, each of these steps is performed in $\Theta(n)$ time. As discussed in Section 11.1.2, a parallel implementation with p processors takes $\Theta(n/p) + t_s \log p$ time on the hypercube architecture and

$\Theta(n/p) + t_s \log p + 2t_h\sqrt{p}$ time on a mesh. If the parallel computer supports fast reduction operations, the communication time for the inner-product calculations can be ignored.

(3) **Matrix-vector multiplication:** The computation and the communication cost of the matrix-vector multiplication step of line 11 depends on the structure of the sparse matrix A. We study parallel implementations of the PCG algorithm for two cases—one in which A is a block-tridiagonal matrix of the type shown in Figure 11.7, and the other in which it is a banded unstructured sparse matrix.

(4) **Solving the system $Mz_k = r_k$:** The PCG algorithm solves a system of linear equations $Mz_k = r_k$ in each iteration (line 6). The preconditioner M is chosen so that solving the system $Mz_k = r_k$ is inexpensive compared to solving the original system of equations $Ax = b$. Nevertheless, preconditioning increases the amount of computation in each iteration. For good preconditioners, however, the increase is compensated by a reduction in the number of iterations required to achieve acceptable convergence.

The computation and the communication requirements of this step depend on the type of preconditioner used. In this chapter we study parallel implementations of the PCG algorithm for two types of preconditioning methods: (1) diagonal preconditioning, in which the preconditioner matrix M has nonzero elements only along the principal diagonal, and (2) incomplete Cholesky (IC) preconditioning, in which M is based on an incomplete Cholesky factorization of A. There are several variants of the IC preconditioner. We describe a few variants for which solving the system $Mz_k = r_k$ is an easily parallelizable operation. A PCG algorithm using IC preconditioning is also referred to as an ICCG algorithm.

Note that, among the four types of computations that we just described, an unpreconditioned conjugate gradient algorithm performs only the first three. In the remainder of this section, we consider parallel implementations of the PCG algorithm for different combinations of preconditioners and coefficient matrix types. As we will see, if M is a diagonal preconditioner, then solving the system $Mz_k = r_k$ does not require any interprocessor communication. Hence, the communication time in a CG iteration with diagonal preconditioning is the same as that in an iteration of the unpreconditioned algorithm.

A Diagonal Preconditioner and a Matrix Resulting from a Finite Difference Discretization Assume that the $n \times n$ coefficient matrix A arises from a $\sqrt{n} \times \sqrt{n}$ finite difference grid, and that the grid points (and hence, the matrix rows) are partitioned among the processors as shown in Figure 11.10. Let the preconditioner matrix M be a simple diagonal matrix with nonzero elements only along its principal diagonal, which is usually derived from (or is the same as) the principal diagonal of A. Solving the system $Mz_k = r_k$ on line 6 of Program 11.4 is equivalent to dividing each element of r by the diagonal entry of the corresponding row of M. No communication is required because elements with identical indices reside on the same processor. Hence, in a p-processor implementation, each processor performs this operation in $\Theta(n/p)$ time. The matrix-vector multiplication operation requires $\Theta(n/p)$ time for computation and $4t_s + 4t_w\sqrt{n/p}$ time for communication (Equation 11.6). Each of the three inner products takes $\Theta(n/p)$ for computation. Additionally, it takes approximately $t_s \log p$ time for communication on a hypercube and $t_s \log p + 2t_h\sqrt{p}$ time on a mesh with cut-through routing (Section 11.1.2).

The total time spent in performing all the computation in each iteration is $\Theta(n/p)$. If t_c' is the constant associated with the computation, then the parallel run time for a single iteration of the PCG algorithm on hypercube and mesh architectures is given by the following equations:

Hypercube:

$$T_P = \overbrace{t_c' \frac{n}{p}}^{\text{computation}} + \overbrace{3t_s \log p}^{\text{inner products}} + \overbrace{4t_s + 4t_w\sqrt{n/p}}^{\text{matrix-vector multiplication}} \qquad (11.26)$$

Mesh with cut-through routing:

$$T_P = \overbrace{t_c' \frac{n}{p}}^{\text{computation}} + \overbrace{3t_s \log p + 6t_h\sqrt{p}}^{\text{inner products}} + \overbrace{4t_s + 4t_w\sqrt{n/p}}^{\text{matrix-vector multiplication}} \qquad (11.27)$$

The isoefficiency functions of this implementation of the PCG algorithm for the hypercube and mesh architectures can be derived using the expressions in Equations 11.26 and 11.27, respectively. Since the total useful computation performed in each iteration is $\Theta(n)$, the isoefficiency function for the hypercube is $\Theta(p \log p)$, and that for the mesh is $\Theta(p\sqrt{p})$ for an iteration of the algorithm. Both isoefficiency functions result from the communication due to vector inner-product computations. If the algorithm is executed on a machine with a fast built-in reduction operation, this overhead can be ignored. In that case, the only time spent in communication in each iteration is $4t_s + 4t_w\sqrt{n/p}$ on both the mesh and hypercube architectures. The resulting expression for parallel run time is

$$T_P = t_c' \frac{n}{p} + 4t_s + 4t_w\sqrt{n/p}. \qquad (11.28)$$

An isoefficiency function of $\Theta(p)$ follows from Equation 11.28, which means that the parallel system is ideally scalable (Problem 11.17). Thus, for this algorithm, the availability of a fast reduction operation proves to be very useful.

An IC Preconditioner and a Matrix Obtained from Red-Black Ordering Program 5.6 gives a row-oriented Cholesky factorization algorithm for dense matrices. If the same algorithm is used to factorize a sparse matrix A as the product $L \times L^T$, where L is a lower-triangular matrix, then the factors L and L^T are much less sparse than A. A ***no-fill incomplete Cholesky factorization*** is a procedure that performs the computation of line 10 of Program 5.6 only if $A[i, j]$ is nonzero. Replacing line 10 of Program 5.6 by

if $A[i, j] \neq 0$ **then** $A[i, j] := A[i, j] - A[k, i] \times A[k, j];$

and executing the resulting algorithm on a sparse matrix A yields a sparse upper-triangular matrix L'^T. The locations of the nonzero elements in L'^T coincide exactly with the locations of the nonzero elements in the upper-triangular portion of A. Since A is symmetric, the locations of nonzero elements in L' coincide with those in the lower-triangular part of A.

We use the matrix $M = L'L'^T$ as the preconditioner on line 6 of the PCG algorithm given in Program 11.4. With this choice of M, the system $Mz_k = r_k$ is solved by solving the following two triangular systems:

(1) solve $L'u = r_k$
(2) solve $L'^T z_k = u$

We can adapt the back-substitution algorithm described in Section 5.5.3 to solve both of the preceding triangular systems (for the lower-triangular system, the outer loop of the back-substitution algorithm in Program 5.5 must be reversed). In the worst case, this process can be almost completely sequential; that is, it may require the variables of the triangular system to be solved one after the other. Therefore, it is important that the coefficient matrix A, and hence the triangular matrices L' and L'^T, is ordered so that the solution to $Mz_k = r_k$ in each iteration of the PCG algorithm can be parallelized effectively.

Consider an $n \times n$ matrix A of the form shown in Figure 11.14(b), which results from a red-black ordering of the points in a $\sqrt{n} \times \sqrt{n}$ finite difference grid. The matrices L' and L'^T have nonzero elements in the same locations as the nonzero elements in A's lower- and upper-triangular parts, respectively. While solving $L'u = r_k$, first, $u[0], u[1], \ldots, u[(n/2) - 1]$ are computed in parallel. The absence of nondiagonal nonzeros in the upper half of L' permits the values of these variables to be computed in parallel. Next, the values of these variables are substituted in the lower half of the system $L'u = r_k$ and the remaining variables $u[n/2], u[(n/2) + 1], \ldots, u[n - 1]$ are computed in parallel. Similarly, the upper-triangular system $L'^T z_k = u$ is solved in two phases—each computing half of the elements of z_k in parallel. Thus, the entire system $Mz_k = r_k$ is solved in four phases.

It is interesting to observe that there is a close similarity between performing a Gauss-Seidel iteration (Equation 11.18) on a matrix A and solving triangular systems with the same sparsity pattern as the corresponding triangular halves of A. If the coefficient matrix is derived from a red-black ordering of the points of a finite difference grid, then just like a Gauss-Seidel iteration, a triangular system is solved in two phases. In general, an ordering scheme that allows parallelization of a Gauss-Seidel iteration also allows parallelization of the solution of $Mz_k = r_k$ in the PCG algorithm.

Assume that the $\sqrt{n} \times \sqrt{n}$ finite difference grid from which the coefficient matrix A is derived is mapped onto a p-processor mesh by using a block-checkerboard partitioning as shown in Figure 11.10. A processor that stores the information related to the ith point in the grid also stores the ith rows of the factors L' and L'^T of the preconditioner matrix M. With this mapping of matrix rows onto the processors, the communication and computation times for solving $Mz_k = r_k$ in a PCG iteration are identical to the communication and computation times for performing the step given by Equation 11.18 in a Gauss-Seidel iteration (Problem 11.18). The other operations (that is, SAXPY, inner products, and matrix-vector multiplication) in an iteration of the parallel PCG algorithm take the same amount of time as in the case of diagonal preconditioning discussed earlier.

A Truncated IC Preconditioner and a Block-Tridiagonal Matrix It is usually observed that natural ordering of grid points leads to faster convergence of the conjugate gradient algorithm than do the red-black or multicolored orderings. In the IC preconditioning technique previously described, the step of solving the system $Mz_k = r_k$ is parallelizable to only a limited extent for block-tridiagonal matrices (Problems 11.13 and 11.18), which arise from the natural ordering of points in a finite difference grid. We now describe another variant of the IC preconditioner that permits a highly parallel solution to the system $Mz_k = r_k$ for a block-tridiagonal matrix of coefficients.

If A is a symmetric positive definite matrix, it can be expressed as

$$A = D + L + L^T,$$

where D is the diagonal matrix consisting of the diagonal entries of A, and L is the strictly lower-triangular matrix consisting of the two lower diagonals of A. The preconditioner matrix M is chosen as

$$M = (I + L\tilde{D}^{-1})\tilde{D}(I + \tilde{D}^{-1}L^T), \tag{11.29}$$

where the diagonal matrix $\tilde{D}$ is chosen such that the principal diagonals of A and M are the same. Hence, the relationship between D and $\tilde{D}$ is as follows:

$$\begin{aligned} D &= \text{diag}(M) \\ &= \text{diag}((I + L\tilde{D}^{-1})\tilde{D}(I + \tilde{D}^{-1}L^T)) \\ &= \text{diag}(\tilde{D} + L^T + L + L\tilde{D}^{-1}L^T) \\ &= \tilde{D} + \text{diag}(L\tilde{D}^{-1}L^T) \end{aligned} \tag{11.30}$$

Since D and L are known from A, the diagonal $\tilde{D}$ can be determined using Equation 11.30 (Problem 11.16). This $\tilde{D}$, substituted in Equation 11.29, determines the preconditioner M. However, the matrix M is not assembled explicitly. Only the triangular matrix $L\tilde{D}^{-1}$ needs to computed.

Let us refer to $L\tilde{D}^{-1}$ by the strictly lower-triangular matrix $-L'$. From Equation 11.29, the matrix M can be expressed as $M = (I - L')\tilde{D}(I - L'^T)$. Now the system $Mz_k = r_k$ is solved by the following steps:

(1)	solve	$(I - L')u = r_k$
(2)	solve	$\tilde{D}v = u$
(3)	solve	$(I - L'^T)z_k = v$

Since L' is a strictly lower-triangular $n \times n$ matrix, $L'^i = 0$ for $i \geq n$. Therefore, $(I - L')^{-1}$ can be expressed as $(I + L' + L'^2 + \cdots + L'^{n-1})$. A similar expansion also holds for L'^T. These series can be truncated to τ powers of L' and L'^T because M is a diagonally-dominant matrix, and the contribution of L'^{τ} and $(L'^{T})^{\tau}$ to $(I - L')^{-1}$ and $(I - L'^{T})^{-1}$, respectively, becomes smaller as τ increases. If $\tilde{L} = (I + L' + \cdots + L'^{\tau})$, then solving the system $Mz_k = r_k$ is equivalent to performing the following matrix-vector multiplications:

$$
\begin{array}{ll}
(1) & u \approx \tilde{L} r_k \\
(2) & v \approx \tilde{D}^{-1} u \\
(3) & z_k \approx \tilde{L}^T v
\end{array}
$$

Usually $\tau = 2, 3$, or 4 is chosen, depending on the degree of diagonal dominance of M and the degree of precision desired. We discuss each of these three cases of practical importance separately.

Assume that, in the parallel formulation of this algorithm, the communication overhead due to vector inner-product computations is eliminated by special hardware that provides a fast reduction operation. Hence, communication overhead is incurred only in matrix-vector multiplication on line 11, and in solving the system $Mz_k = r_k$ on line 6 of Program 11.4. This assumption allows us to concentrate on the impact of varying τ on the computation and communication requirements of the algorithm. We assume that the components of the preconditioner (such as $\tilde{D}$ and $\tilde{L}$) are precomputed. Therefore, the rest of the analysis in this section pertains only to the computation and communication that is performed in each iteration in a parallel implementation of the PCG algorithm.

If $\tau = 2$ is used, then $\tilde{L} = I + L' + L'^2$. The matrix $\tilde{L}$ has six diagonals—the principal diagonal and diagonals with offsets 1, 2, $\sqrt{n}$, $\sqrt{n} + 1$, and $2\sqrt{n}$ in the lower-triangular part. Similarly, $\tilde{L}^T$ has six diagonals in the upper triangular part. Let the time taken by an addition and a multiplication be t_c. Step (2) of the process of solving the system $Mz_k = r_k$ is similar to that for the diagonal preconditioner. Besides this step, the truncated IC preconditioner requires the multiplication of a vector with 12 diagonals—six in step (1), and six in step (3). As a result, in addition to the $t_c n/p$ computation time in each iteration (as for the diagonal preconditioner), each processor spends an extra $12 t_c n/p$ time solving the system $Mz_k = r_k$.

Recall from the discussion of matrix-vector multiplication for the block-tridiagonal matrix (Section 11.1.3) that to multiply a vector with the diagonals at offsets 1 and $\sqrt{n}$ in the upper- and lower-triangular parts of the coefficient matrix, a grid point requires information from all four of its neighboring points. As a result, each processor exchanges the vector elements for its $\sqrt{n/p}$ boundary points with each of its four neighbors. If the vector is multiplied by the diagonals with offsets 1, 2, $\sqrt{n}$, $\sqrt{n} + 1$, and $2\sqrt{n}$ in each half of the matrix, then each grid point needs information corresponding to the 12 neighboring points shown in Figure 11.16. Thus, matrix-vector multiplication involving the matrix $\tilde{L}$ requires each processor to exchange the vector elements for two layers of boundary points (that is, $2\sqrt{n/p}$ points) with each of its four neighbors. The total communication time for steps (1) and (3) is thus $4t_s + 8t_w\sqrt{n/p}$. Accounting for the $4t_s + 4t_w\sqrt{n/p}$ communication time for matrix-vector multiplication in line 11 of Program 11.4, the total communication time in each iteration is $8t_s + 12t_w\sqrt{n/p}$. The overall parallel run time of an iteration is given

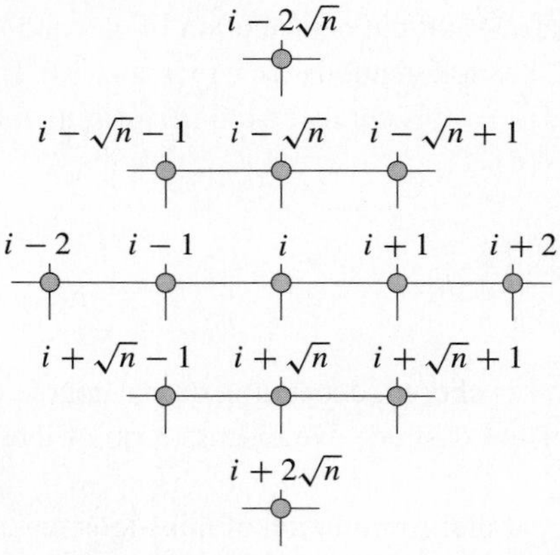

Figure 11.16 The 12 grid points from which point i receives vector elements.

by the following equations:

$$\begin{aligned} T_P &= \overbrace{12t_c n/p}^{\text{matrix-vector multiplications for solving } Mz_k = r_k} \\ &+ \overbrace{t_c' n/p}^{\text{other computations}} \\ &+ \overbrace{4t_s + 8t_w\sqrt{n/p}}^{\text{communication in solving } Mz_k = r_k} \\ &+ \overbrace{4t_s + 4t_w\sqrt{n/p}}^{\text{communication in matrix-vector multiplication}} \end{aligned}$$

$$T_P = (t_c' + 12t_c)\frac{n}{p} + 8t_s + 12t_w\sqrt{\frac{n}{p}} \qquad (11.31)$$

If $\tau = 3$ is chosen, then $\tilde{L} = I + L' + L'^2 + L'^3$, which can be rewritten as $(I+L')(I+L'^2)$. Here there are two methods to perform steps (1) and (3) of solving $Mz_k = r_k$. The first method constructs the matrices $I + L' + L'^2 + L'^3$ $I + L'^T + (L'^T)^2 + (L'^T)^3$ explicitly. Each of these matrices contains ten diagonals with offsets 0, 1, 2, 3, $\sqrt{n}$, $\sqrt{n}+1$, $\sqrt{n}+2$, $2\sqrt{n}$, $2\sqrt{n}+1$, and $3\sqrt{n}$. The total computation time for steps (1) and (3) is $20t_c n/p$ for each processor. Extending the case of $\tau = 2$ to $\tau = 3$, each processor exchanges the vector elements corresponding to the three layers of boundary points (that is, $3\sqrt{n/p}$ points) with each of its four neighbors before the two matrix-vector multiplications. This requires a total communication time of $4t_s + 12\sqrt{n/p}$. Thus, the parallel run time of an iteration is given by the following equations:

$$
\begin{aligned}
T_P &= \overbrace{20t_c n/p}^{\text{matrix-vector multiplications for solving } Mz_k = r_k} \\
&+ \overbrace{t_c^{'} n/p}^{\text{other computations}} \\
&+ \overbrace{4t_s + 12t_w\sqrt{n/p}}^{\text{communication in solving } Mz_k = r_k} \\
&+ \overbrace{4t_s + 4t_w\sqrt{n/p}}^{\text{communication in matrix-vector multiplication}}
\end{aligned}
$$

$$
T_P = (t_c^{'} + 20t_c)\frac{n}{p} + 8t_s + 16t_w\sqrt{\frac{n}{p}} \qquad (11.32)
$$

The second method for $\tau = 3$ uses the fact that $\tilde{L} = (I + L^{'})(I + L^{'2})$. This method performs step (1) in two stages. The first stage involves the multiplication of the vector r with $(I + L^{'2})$, which has four diagonals at offsets of 0, 2, $\sqrt{n} + 1$, and $2\sqrt{n}$. The product is then multiplied with $(I + L^{'})$, which has three diagonals with offsets 0, 1, and $\sqrt{n}$. Step (3) is performed similarly. Thus, the total computation time is $(2 \times 4 + 2 \times 3)t_c n/p$ $= 14t_c n/p$ per processor, per iteration. This time is less than the computation time for the case in which $\tilde{L} = I + L^{'} + L^{'2} + L^{'3}$ is used in unfactorized form. However, the communication time is now higher than in the previous case. Each processor exchanges vector elements for two layers of boundary points (that is, $2\sqrt{n/p}$ points) with each of its four neighbors. These vector elements are required for matrix-vector multiplication involving $(I + L^{'2})$ and $(I + (L^{'T})^2)$. In addition to this, each processor needs to exchange vector elements corresponding to its $\sqrt{n/p}$ boundary points with its four neighbors for multiplication with $(I + L^{'})$ and $(I + L^{'T})$. Thus, the total communication time (including that of the matrix-vector multiplication in line 11) per iteration is $12t_s + 16t_w\sqrt{n/p}$. The parallel run time for each iteration is as follows:

$$
\begin{aligned}
T_P &= \overbrace{14t_c n/p}^{\text{matrix-vector multiplications for solving } Mz_k = r_k} \\
&+ \overbrace{t_c^{'} n/p}^{\text{other computations}} \\
&+ \overbrace{8t_s + 12t_w\sqrt{n/p}}^{\text{communication in solving } Mz_k = r_k} \\
&+ \overbrace{4t_s + 4t_w\sqrt{n/p}}^{\text{communication in matrix-vector multiplication}}
\end{aligned}
$$

$$
T_P = (t_c^{'} + 14t_c)\frac{n}{p} + 12t_s + 16t_w\sqrt{\frac{n}{p}} \qquad (11.33)
$$

A comparison of Equations 11.32 and 11.33 shows that, although the term associated with t_c is smaller in Equation 11.33, the term associated with t_s is smaller in Equation 11.32. Hence, the choice of the method to be used in practice depends on the relative values of the machine-dependent constants t_c and t_s and on the values of n and p. Note that, whenever τ is odd, the series $(I + L' + \cdots + L'^{\tau})$ can be factorized as shown here for $\tau = 3$.

An analysis similar to that for $\tau = 2$ and $\tau = 3$ shows that, for $\tau = 4$, the computation time for solving the system $Mz_k = r_k$ is $30t_c n/p$. The total communication time per iteration is $8t_s + 20t_w\sqrt{n/p}$. For general τ, if $\tilde{L}$ is not factorized, the number of diagonals in $\tilde{L}$ is $(\tau+1)(\tau+2)/2$. These diagonals are distributed in $\tau + 1$ clusters at distances of $\sqrt{n}$ from each other. The first cluster, which includes the principal diagonal, has $\tau + 1$ diagonals, and then the number of diagonals in each cluster decreases by one. The last cluster has only one diagonal at a distance of $\tau\sqrt{n}$ from the principal diagonal. For $\sqrt{n/p} > \tau$, solving the system $Mz_k = r_k$ requires each processor to exchange vector elements corresponding to τ layers of boundary points (that is, $\tau\sqrt{n/p}$ points) with each of its four neighboring processors. The expression for parallel run time for the general case is given by the following equations:

$$
\begin{aligned}
T_P &= \overbrace{(\tau+1)(\tau+2)t_c n/p}^{\text{matrix-vector multiplications for solving } Mz_k = r_k} \\
&+ \overbrace{t_c' n/p}^{\text{other computations}} \\
&+ \overbrace{4t_s + 4\tau t_w\sqrt{n/p}}^{\text{communication in solving } Mz_k = r_k} \\
&+ \overbrace{4t_s + 4t_w\sqrt{n/p}}^{\text{communication in matrix-vector multiplication}}
\end{aligned}
$$

$$
T_P = (t_c' + (\tau^2 + 3\tau + 2)t_c)\frac{n}{p} + 8t_s + 4(\tau+1)t_w\sqrt{\frac{n}{p}} \qquad (11.34)
$$

Disregarding the communication in computing the inner products, a comparison of Equations 11.26 and 11.34 shows that the use of a truncated IC preconditioner involves more computation per iteration of the PCG algorithm over a simple diagonal preconditioner. On the other hand, an IC preconditioner significantly reduces the number of iterations required to achieve a given level of precision over a diagonal preconditioner. The truncated IC preconditioning also results in an efficiency higher than that in the case of diagonal preconditioning (Problem 11.19), assuming that the efficiency of a parallel implementation is computed with respect to an identical algorithm running on a single processor. The overall performance of the PCG algorithm is governed by the amount of computation per iteration, the number of iterations, and the efficiency of the parallel implementation. Therefore, IC preconditioning may yield a better overall parallel run time by virtue of a better efficiency than diagonal preconditioning, even if the latter is faster in a serial implementation. A comparison of truncated IC preconditioners with different values of

τ presents similar tradeoffs. Equation 11.34 shows that the amount of computation in each iteration is proportional to τ^2, and the volume of communication in each iteration is proportional to τ. Therefore, for the same values of n and p, both parallel run time and efficiency increase as τ increases. For a given problem, different values of τ may lead to optimal implementations for different values of p; a higher p favors a higher τ (Problem 11.19).

A Diagonal Preconditioner and a Banded Unstructured Sparse Matrix Consider a symmetric positive definite matrix of coefficients in which the nonzero elements are uniformly distributed in a band of width w along the principal diagonal. If there is an average of m nonzero elements per row, then as shown in Section 11.1.3, the parallel run time for matrix-vector multiplication is $t_c mn/p + t_s wp/n + t_w w$ (Equation 11.12). When we disregard the communication cost of vector inner product computation, the parallel run time of an iteration of the PCG algorithm using the diagonal preconditioner is

$$T_P = (t_c^{'} + t_c m)\frac{n}{p} + t_s\frac{wp}{n} + t_w w. \tag{11.35}$$

A Truncated IC Preconditioner and a Banded Unstructured Sparse Matrix Consider the use of the IC preconditioner for banded sparse matrices. The preconditioner matrix M is of the form $(I - L^{'})\tilde{D}(I - L^{'T})$, where $\tilde{D}$ is a diagonal matrix and $L^{'}$ is a strictly lower-triangular sparse matrix whose nonzero elements are located in exactly the same positions as in the lower-triangular part of the coefficient matrix A. The system $Mz_k = r_k$ is solved in the same manner as in the case of the block-tridiagonal matrix discussed earlier. Consider the general case in which $\tilde{L} = (I + L^{'} + \cdots + L^{'\tau})$ is used as an approximation of $(I - L^{'})^{-1}$. If $L^{'}$ has a bandwidth of $w/2$, then the bandwidth of $L^{'\tau}$ has an upper bound of $\tau w/2$ (Problem 11.20). As a result, $\tilde{L}$ also has a bandwidth of less than $\tau w/2$. The same holds true for $\tilde{L}^T$ as well. According to Equation 11.12, the total communication time to multiply both $\tilde{L}$ and $\tilde{L}^T$ with the vectors is, at most, $t_s \tau wp/n + t_w \tau w$.

The matrices $L^{'}$ and $L^{'T}$ consist of bands of width approximately $w/2$ along the principal diagonal in the lower and the upper-triangular halves, respectively. Since the sparsity pattern of $L^{'}$ and $L^{'T}$ in their respective halves is identical to that of A, they have an average of approximately $m/2$ nonzero elements per row (A has an average of m nonzero elements per row). If A is large and $m \ll w$, then the average number of nonzero elements per row in $L^{'\tau}$ and $(L^{'T})^\tau$ is $(m/2)^\tau$ (Problem 11.21). Since $1 + a + a^2 + \cdots + a^\tau < a^{\tau+1}$ for $a > 1$, the number of nonzero elements in $\tilde{L}$ and $\tilde{L}^T$ each has upper bound of $(m/2)^{\tau+1}$. Hence, the computation time per processor for solving the system $Mz_k = r_k$ on a p-processor ensemble is $2t_c(n/p)(m/2)^{\tau+1}$ in each iteration. The total time spent in solving $Mz_k = r_k$ in each iteration is $2t_c(n/p)(m/2)^{\tau+1} + t_s \tau wp/n + t_w \tau w$.

From Equation 11.12, the time required to perform matrix-vector multiplication is $t_c mn/p + t_s wp/n + t_w w$. Thus, the overall parallel run time per iteration of the PCG algorithm with a banded unstructured sparse matrix and truncated IC preconditioner is

$$T_P = \left(t_c^{'} + t_c(2(\frac{m}{2})^{\tau+1} + m)\right)\frac{n}{p} + t_s(\tau + 1)\frac{wp}{n} + t_w(\tau + 1)w. \tag{11.36}$$

11.3 Finite Element Method

The ***finite element method*** (FEM) is an active application area of massively parallel computing. FEM is a computational tool for deriving approximate numerical solutions to partial differential equations over a discretized domain.

To introduce the finite element method for solving differential equations, we use the simple example of modeling the steady-state temperature at various points on a metal sheet. As Figure 11.17 shows, the domain is a two-dimensional rectangular sheet of metal on which a regular grid of square elements is imposed. The domain is bounded by the coordinates $(0, 0)$, $(1, 0)$, $(1, 1)$, and $(0, 1)$. As the figure shows, the grid divides the domain into small areas called ***elements***. There are 48 elements in the discretized domain shown in Figure 11.17. The internal nodes or grid points at which the coefficients must be determined are labeled 0 through 48. Unlike the finite difference grid shown in Figure 11.8, a grid point exchanges information with all the other grid points with which it shares an element. Hence, each point has nine neighbors (including itself), and each row of the resulting sparse matrix of coefficients has nine nonzero entries.

The steady-state temperature u at any point (X, Y) on the metal sheet is governed by the Laplace equation

$$\frac{\delta^2 u}{\delta X^2} + \frac{\delta^2 u}{\delta Y^2} = 0. \tag{11.37}$$

The values of the physical quantity being modeled (in this case, temperature) at the boundary of the physical domain are governed by what are referred to as ***boundary conditions***. Since the sheet is insulated at the top and bottom, the following boundary conditions result:

$$\frac{\delta u}{\delta Y} = 0, \quad Y = 0, \quad 0 \leq X \leq 1 \tag{11.38}$$

$$\frac{\delta u}{\delta Y} = 0, \quad Y = 1, \quad 0 \leq X \leq 1 \tag{11.39}$$

Furthermore, assume that the temperatures at the other two ends of the sheet are U_0 and U_1, respectively. The corresponding boundary conditions are as follows:

$$u = U_0, \quad X = 0, \quad 0 \leq Y \leq 1 \tag{11.40}$$

$$u = U_1, \quad X = 1, \quad 0 \leq Y \leq 1 \tag{11.41}$$

The boundary conditions involving derivatives of the solution, such as those given by Equations 11.38 and 11.39, are referred to as ***Neumann boundary conditions***. Boundary

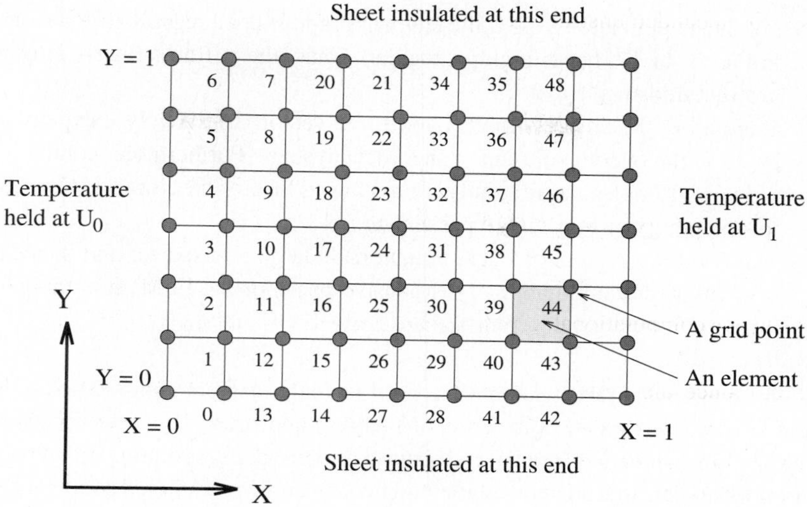

Figure 11.17 A grid dividing a sheet of metal into a finite element mesh of 48 elements. The internal nodes or grid points at which the coefficients must be determined are labeled 0 through 48. The nodes at the periphery are not labeled because the temperature at these points is determined by boundary conditions.

conditions involving only the solution, such as those given by Equations 11.40 and 11.41, are known as ***Dirichlet boundary conditions***.

The temperature on the surface of the sheet is a continuous function of X and Y governed by Equation 11.37. The FEM derives an approximation of this function by dividing the domain into elements. The value of the function is typically expressed as a simple polynomial that is a linear combination of a set of functions of X and Y called ***basis functions***. The coefficients of the basis functions at each node are derived from a system of linear equations. This system arises from the minimization of error between the approximate and exact solutions of the partial differential equation. Thus, the FEM transforms the Laplace equation into a set of linear equations of the form $Ax = b$. In the context of FEM, the coefficient matrix A is called the ***stiffness matrix*** and b the ***force vector***. This system is solved for the vector x, which gives the value of the coefficients of the basis functions at different node points in the discretized domain. The stiffness matrix A for the FEM can be derived by computing a set of definite integrals over the elements of the finite element graph. If nodes i and j in the finite element mesh share elements, then $A[i, j]$ is given by the summation of the integrals calculated over all the elements shared by points i and j. Thus, the only nonzero entries in the matrix are $A[i, j]$ such that grid points i and j share an element.

The following are some important properties of the stiffness matrix and the force vector:

(1) For most applications, the finite element graph is not a regular structure as shown in Figure 11.17, but is highly irregular. Thus, the stiffness matrix is usually an unstructured sparse matrix.
(2) Computing the stiffness matrix and force vector is relatively inexpensive compared to the overall solution of the linear system. Furthermore, computing individual entries of A requires only computations local to the element. Consequently, this computation is trivial to parallelize.
(3) The resulting system of linear equations is large and sparse, and hence solving it is the most computationally expensive phase of the FEM. It is this phase for which efficient parallel solutions are critical.

Both iterative and direct solvers are used in finite element computations. Iterative solvers are often less expensive in terms of memory and time. However, in some cases, iterative solvers are not guaranteed to converge to a solution, necessitating direct solvers. In this section we assume that an iterative method like the unpreconditioned conjugate gradient method (Program 11.3) is used, which performs SAXPY operations, vector inner-product computations, and a matrix-vector multiplication in each iteration.

The SAXPY operations do not involve any communication overhead. The communication time per iteration for vector inner products depends only on the number of processors in use. This time is $\Theta(\log p)$ on a hypercube and $\Theta(\sqrt{p})$ on a mesh. In the presence of a fast, hardware-supported reduction operation, we can assume that it is a small constant. The communication requirements of matrix-vector multiplication are critically dependent on the spatial decomposition of the domain and the assignment of its partitions to the processors. If the domain is partitioned among processors, then information corresponding to the elements at the partition boundaries is exchanged among neighboring processors during matrix-vector multiplication (Figure 11.12). In each iteration, the time spent in computation by a processor is proportional to the number of elements assigned to it. If a partition shares boundaries with α other partitions and has β boundary elements, the per-iteration communication time of the processor holding this partition is proportional to $\alpha t_s + \beta t_w$.

The principal issues in efficient parallel implementations of FEM are minimizing load imbalance among processors and maximizing the ratio of computation to communication on the processors. The former is achieved by assigning a nearly equal number of elements to each partition. The latter requires that the number of elements along a partition boundary be small compared to the total number of elements within the partition.

In the remainder of this section, we discuss some commonly used techniques for partitioning the finite element domain among processors. Although we chose examples with quadrilateral elements, triangular elements are also commonly used.

Partitioning Methods for Finite Element Graphs

The communication pattern, and hence the overall efficiency, of a parallel implementation of an FEM computation is a function of the partitioning of the domain among processors.

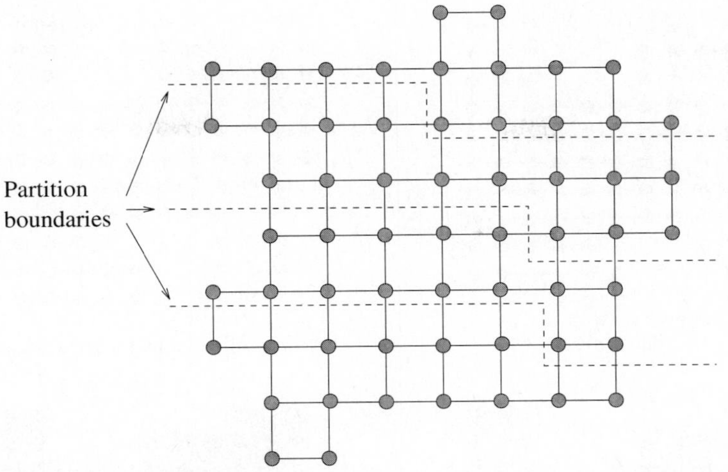

Figure 11.18 One-dimensional striped partitioning of a finite element mesh among four processors.

Deriving an optimal partitioning that balances the load and minimizes communication and idling costs is an NP-hard problem. Therefore, several heuristic schemes have been devised to derive reasonable partitions for finite element meshes in polynomial time.

One-Dimensional Striped Partitioning for Mesh Graphs A finite element graph is called a ***mesh graph*** or a finite element mesh if it is composed of quadrilateral elements and it can be embedded into a uniform two-dimensional grid such that each element boundary maps onto exactly one edge in the grid. For example, the finite element graph shown in Figure 11.18 is a mesh graph. A one-dimensional ***striped partitioning*** divides a finite element mesh into p stripes such that each stripe runs the length (or width) of the mesh. If the mesh has n nodes, striped partitioning assigns either $\lceil n/p \rceil$ or $\lfloor n/p \rfloor$ nodes to each processor. Figure 11.18 illustrates a one-dimensional striped partitioning of a finite element mesh among four processors.

One-dimensional striped partitioning generates stripes that adjoin only one stripe on either side. Consequently, even on weak architectures such as a linear array, the partitioning yields a nearest-neighbor mapping. To enforce the nearest neighbor constraint, a sufficient condition is that n/p (the number of elements assigned to a processor) is greater than the smaller dimension of the mesh. Striped partitioning affords good load balance and locality of communication. However, it may communicate large amounts of data among processors.

Two-Dimensional Striped Partitioning for Mesh Graphs The two-dimensional striped partitioning scheme maps a finite element mesh onto a two-dimensional mesh of processors. Figure 11.19 illustrates this process for a 2×2 mesh of processors. As shown in the figure, the two-dimensional striped partitioning uses two orthogonal one-dimensional

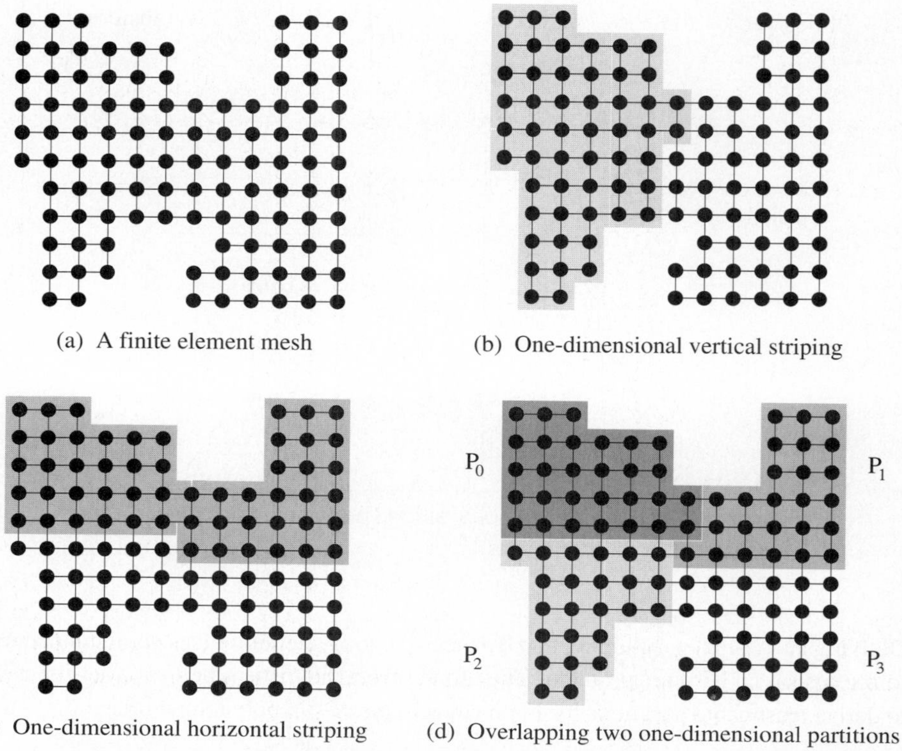

Figure 11.19 Two-dimensional striping of a mesh graph for a 2×2 mesh of processors.

striped partitions. First, the finite element graph is partitioned into vertical stripes (Figure 11.19(b)). Then the graph is striped horizontally (Figure 11.19(c)). Finally, the two partitionings are overlapped (Figure 11.19(d)), and the resulting partitions (whose number is equal to the product of vertical and horizontal partitions) are assigned to processors.

As Figure 11.19 illustrates, two-dimensional striping may not yield partitions with identical numbers of nodes. Consequently, the partitioning phase must be followed by another phase that balances the load between partitions. This load-balancing phase is called ***boundary refinement***. Boundary refinement balances the load by transferring nodes from heavily loaded to lightly loaded processors. At the same time, it maintains the nearest-neighbor relationships between partitions.

Assume that the total number of nodes (grid points) in the finite element mesh is n and that the number of nodes assigned to processor i in the initial partitioning is n_i. Also assume that there are p processors and that n is divisible by p. Boundary refinement uses a $p \times p$ ***load transfer matrix***. Entry (i, j) of this matrix specifies the number of nodes that must be transferred from the partition assigned to processor i to that assigned to processor j. For a perfect load balance, the net change in the load (the number of nodes) of processor

i should be $n_i - n/p$ (this can be positive or negative). This load is transferred from one of the four neighbors of processor i, which are referred to by $u(i)$ (up), $d(i)$ (down), $l(i)$ (left), and $r(i)$ (right). We ignore minor boundary overlaps between diagonally located processors (for example, P_1 and P_2 in Figure 11.19). Let U_i, D_i, L_i, and R_i represent the number of elements transferred to processor i from processors $u(i)$, $d(i)$, $l(i)$, and $r(i)$, respectively (these numbers can be negative). The entries in the load transfer matrix must satisfy the following conditions:

$$\begin{aligned} L_i + R_i + D_i + U_i &= n_i - n/p \\ L_i &= -R_{l(i)} \\ U_i &= -D_{u(i)} \end{aligned}$$

In addition to these, there are conditions corresponding to the partitions that lie on the boundary of the domain. The solution of the system of equations arising from the complete set of conditions yields the load transfer matrix. Note that the number of variables in this system of equations is $\Theta(p)$, whereas the number of variables in the original system of equations being solved by the FEM is n. In practice, n is much greater than p.

Having constructed the load transfer matrix, the load transfer (or boundary refinement) procedure proceeds iteratively. In each step, nodes on the boundary of partitions between two processors are identified and placed in a queue. The required number of nodes are transferred from this queue. If the number of nodes that need to be transferred is more than the number of nodes in the queue, the process is repeated.

Striped Partitioning Schemes for Generalized Graphs In the preceding sections, we studied striped partitioning for mesh graphs. A finite element graph that is not a mesh graph is referred to as a generalized graph. The elements of a ***generalized graph*** may not be squares or rectangles of a uniform size. Figure 11.20 shows a generalized finite element graph. The striping process described for mesh graphs does not extend naturally to generalized graphs, in which the elements are not organized into explicit rows and columns. For a generalized graph, a process called ***levelization*** organizes the graph into stripes.

Levelization begins by identifying a peripheral node or a set of connected peripheral nodes. A peripheral node is characterized by a peripheral edge, which belongs to a single element, unlike a non-peripheral edge, which belongs to two elements. Connected peripheral nodes on one boundary of the domain are assigned the label 1. All unlabeled nodes that share an element with a node labeled 1 are labeled 2. This process continues, and all unlabeled nodes sharing an element with a node labeled l are labeled $l+1$. Figure 11.20 illustrates a one-dimensional levelization of a finite element graph.

Striped partitioning of generalized graphs counts off nodes at a given level and proceeds to the next higher level when all the nodes at a level are exhausted. Let n be the total number of nodes and p be the number of processors. Let m be the total number of levels (labeled from 1 to m) and r_i be the sum of number of nodes in the two contiguous levels i and $i+1$. If $r = \max\{r_1, r_2, \ldots, r_{m-1}\}$, then a sufficient condition to ensure nearest-neighbor communication is that $n/p > r$.

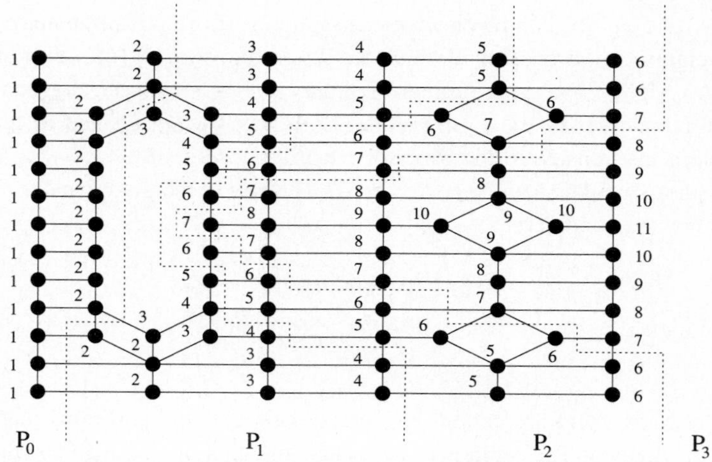

Figure 11.20 The levelization process for a generalized finite element graph. The levels partition the graph into four one-dimensional stripes that are assigned to four processors.

Two-dimensional striping partitions the graph similarly. Again, nodes are counted by levels, rather than along dimensions as in the case of mesh graphs.

Scattered Decomposition ***Scattered decomposition*** (also referred to as ***modular mapping***) is an extensively applied technique for decomposing highly irregular domains. This method balances the load by partitioning the domain into a large number r of rectangular clusters such that $r \gg p$. Each processor handles a disjoint set of r/p such clusters. For irregular problems, increasing r (and consequently decreasing the area of each partition) yields a better load balance. However, load balance is achieved at the cost of increased communication overhead between partitions that are not on the same processor.

Recursive Bisection Techniques ***Recursive bisection*** techniques partition the domain by recursively subdividing it into two parts at each step. For $p = 2^k$ processors, recursively subdividing the domain k times yields p partitions. Bisection techniques differ in the manner in which the domain is subdivided. These techniques are based on the assumption that it is possible to derive near-optimal partitions by subdividing the domain into two parts, maintaining optimality at each step.

In this section, we discuss three recursive bisection techniques based on different criteria for subdividing the domain.

(1) **Recursive Coordinate Bisection:** ***Recursive coordinate bisection*** is the most intuitive of the recursive bisection techniques. The domain is subdivided at each step, based on the physical coordinates of the nodes. Consider a finite element graph with the set of nodes $\{v_0, v_1, \ldots, v_{n-1}\}$. Assume that the spatial coordinates

of the nodes are available. Recursive coordinate bisection subdivides the domain into two parts along the longer dimension (assume that this is along the X axis). Nodes in the set $\{v_0, v_1, \ldots, v_{n-1}\}$ are sorted by their X coordinate. The first half of the sorted list of nodes is assigned to the first subdivision and the other half to the second subdivision. Each subdivision is then recursively divided, and the process continues until it generates p partitions.

This algorithm has two drawbacks. First, the partitions often have many edges of the grid that cross partition boundaries. Second, the partitions may be disconnected. Both properties are highly undesirable. They occur because recursive coordinate bisection uses no connectivity information. However, some recent coordinate bisection schemes do overcome these limitations (Section 11.6).

(2) **Recursive Graph Bisection:** Since recursive coordinate bisection ignores connectivity information, it is unable to minimize the number of grid edges crossing partition boundaries. ***Recursive graph bisection*** remedies this problem by using graph distance rather than coordinate distance to partition the domain.

Let $d_{i,j}$ be the number of edges on the shortest path from node v_i to node v_j. The recursive graph bisection technique first determines the two nodes in the graph that are farthest in terms of graph distance. Two nodes v_i and v_j are farthest if $d_{i,j} \geq d_{p,q}$ for every pair of nodes (v_p, v_q) in the graph. These nodes are called the ***extremities*** of the graph. All the other nodes are organized according to their distance from nodes v_i and v_j. A node is assigned to the partition containing the closer extremity.

It is computationally expensive to find the exact extremities of a graph. However, algorithms are available that yield good approximations of the extremities. An algorithm known as the ***reverse Cuthill-McKee*** algorithm is commonly used for this purpose. This algorithm determines the approximate extremities and uses one of them as the root for establishing a level structure. This process is identical to levelization for striped partitioning. Vertices are counted off as they are organized into the level structure, and the partitioning is complete when half of the nodes have been assigned. Note that this partitioning strategy ensures that at least one of the two partitions is connected.

(3) **Recursive Spectral Bisection:** Given a graph G, ***recursive spectral bisection*** uses the discrete ***Laplacian*** L_G of the graph to divide the domain into two parts. The matrix L_G is equal to $A - D$, where A is the adjacency matrix of graph G and D is a diagonal matrix in which element $D[i, i]$ is the degree $g(v_i)$ of node v_i. Therefore,

$$L_G[i, j] = \begin{cases} -g(v_i) & \text{if } i = j, \\ 1 & \text{if edge } (v_i, v_j) \text{ exists in the graph,} \\ 0 & \text{otherwise.} \end{cases} \tag{11.42}$$

The discrete Laplacian L_G is a negative semidefinite matrix. Furthermore, its largest eigenvalue is zero and the corresponding eigenvector consists of all ones.

Assuming that the graph is connected, the magnitude of the second largest eigenvalue gives a measure of the connectivity of the graph. The eigenvector corresponding to this eigenvalue, when associated with the nodes, gives a measure of the distances between the nodes. Consequently, it can be used to divide the domain into two parts. This vector is referred to as the ***Fiedler vector***. The partitioning is done by sorting nodes according to their weights in the eigenvector and dividing the sorted list of nodes into two equal parts.

The computationally intensive part of this algorithm is the computation of the Fiedler vector. One common algorithm used for computing this is the ***Lanczos algorithm***. The details of this algorithm are beyond the scope of this book. Readers are referred to Section 11.6 for related bibliographic remarks.

We have seen that recursive coordinate bisection may create partitions with shapes that have poor communication properties. Recursive graph partitioning yields more compact partitions but they may be disconnected. Recursive spectral bisection, on the other hand, yields connected partitions that are well balanced. Although a comprehensive performance analysis does not exist for these schemes, some experimental results tend to favor recursive spectral bisection over the other two schemes on a variety of problems.

11.4 Direct Methods for Sparse Linear Systems

Despite their high computational cost, direct methods are useful for solving sparse linear systems because they are general and robust. Although there is substantial parallelism inherent in sparse direct methods, only limited success has been achieved to date in developing efficient general-purpose parallel formulations for them. The reasons for this are twofold. First, the amount of computation relative to the size of the system to be solved is very small. For example, Gaussian elimination involving a dense $n \times n$ matrix has a sequential time complexity of $\Theta(n^3)$. In contrast to a dense matrix, consider the block-tridiagonal matrix of coefficients arising from a natural ordering of points on a $\sqrt{n} \times \sqrt{n}$ regular grid (Figure 11.7). Since the outermost diagonals are at a distance of $\sqrt{n}$ rows or columns from the principal diagonal, the two inner loops of Gaussian elimination are executed only $\sqrt{n}$ times, resulting in a sequential complexity of $\Theta(n^2)$. If the nested-dissection ordering described in Section 11.4.1 is used instead of a natural ordering, this complexity can be further reduced to $\Theta(n^{3/2})$. Since there are few computations in the overall problem, poor efficiencies result because even a modest amount of communication can create a serious imbalance in the relative amounts of time that processors spend in communication and computation.

The second reason for the inefficiency of parallel sparse direct solvers is that most attempts made to date to implement sparse direct methods on parallel computers are based on good serial formulations. The goals of a serial formulation, such as minimizing memory use and operation count, may be inappropriate in a parallel setting. Besides, these goals may seriously conflict with the goals of a parallel formulation, such as maximizing the number of independent tasks, minimizing communication, and balancing load among processors.

Developing efficient general-purpose parallel formulations of direct methods for unstructured or random sparse matrices is currently an active area of research. Although all of these methods are based on Gaussian elimination (for general matrices) and Cholesky factorization (for symmetric positive definite matrices), their parallel formulations can be quite complicated. In this section we only outline some general techniques used in parallel sparse direct solvers. We assume row-oriented Gaussian elimination (Program 5.4) and row-oriented Cholesky factorization (Program 5.6) as the base algorithms to adapt for sparse linear systems. Parallel implementations with column-oriented versions are very similar, and may be numerically superior for the reasons discussed in Section 5.5.4.

The process of obtaining a direct solution to a general sparse system of linear equations of the form $Ax = b$ consists of four distinct phases: ordering, symbolic factorization, numerical factorization, and solving a triangular system. In the following subsections, we discuss each of these phases.

11.4.1 Ordering

Ordering is an important phase of solving a sparse linear system because it determines the overall efficiency of the remaining steps. The aim of ***ordering*** is to generate a permutation of the original coefficient matrix so that the permuted matrix leads to a faster and more stable solution. The numerical stability of the solution is increased by ensuring that the diagonal elements or pivots are large compared to the remaining elements of their respective rows. The ordering criteria for obtaining a faster parallel solution are more complex.

During factorization, when a row of a sparse matrix A is subtracted from another row, some of the zeros in the latter row may become nonzero. When the kth row is the pivot, then a zero in position $A[i, j]$ becomes nonzero for all $i, j > k$ such that $A[i, k] \neq 0$ and $A[k, j] \neq 0$. In this case, the nonzero element at $A[i, j]$ is said to be generated as a result of ***fill-in***. For example, consider the sparse matrix shown in Figure 11.21(a), in which the nonzero elements are denoted by the symbol $\times$. In the first step of factorization, a multiple of row 0 is subtracted from rows 1, 4, and 7. This step changes the zeros at locations $A[1, 4]$, $A[1, 7]$, $A[4, 1]$, and $A[7, 1]$ to nonzero values. Each such fill-in is denoted by the symbol $\Box$. Now a multiple of row 1 is subtracted from rows 2, 4, and 7, introducing nonzero elements in positions $A[2, 4]$, $A[2, 7]$, $A[4, 2]$, and $A[7, 2]$. Figure 11.21(b) shows all the fill-in resulting from the complete factorization of the matrix.

It is possible to reorder the rows and columns of the matrix shown in Figure 11.21(a) so that factorization does not generate any nonzero elements in the positions occupied by zeros in the unfactorized matrix. Figure 11.21(c) shows one such permutation of this matrix. In this figure, the label of each row is of the form i (j). The label denotes that the ith row and column of the reordered matrix correspond to the jth row and column of the original matrix. Factorization of the reordered matrix does not result in any fill-in. In general, reordering may not completely eliminate fill-in, but in most cases it can significantly reduce it.

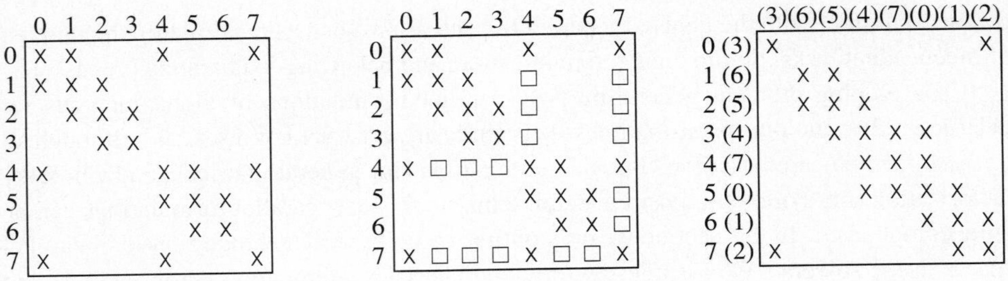

(a) A random sparse matrix (b) Fill-in on factorization (c) A no-fill-in reordering

Figure 11.21 Fill-in during the factorization of a sparse matrix and its reordering to eliminate fill-in. The nonzero elements in the original sparse matrix are denoted by ×, and the nonzero elements introduced due to fill-in are denoted by □. In part (c), the old row and column numbers before reordering are shown in parentheses.

In addition to providing numerical stability and reducing fill-in, another goal of ordering in a parallel sparse direct solver is to increase the number of independent tasks. For example, for the matrix shown in Figure 11.21(c), a multiple of row 0 can be subtracted from row 7 in parallel with the subtraction of a multiple of row 1 from row 2. In other words, both rows 0 and 1 can be used as pivots simultaneously. This kind of parallelism in Gaussian elimination is available only for sparse matrices. During the factorization of the original matrix in Figure 11.21(a), all pivots from 0 to 7 must be used sequentially. Thus, reordering the coefficient matrix can not only reduce the fill-in, but can also increase the parallelism in the factorization process.

Ordering the rows and columns of a matrix to minimize fill-in is a very expensive combinatorial problem with an exponential complexity. Therefore, heuristics are used for ordering. For a given sparse matrix, the best heuristic for reducing fill-in is not necessarily the one that results in maximum parallelism or minimum interprocessor communication. On current and future generation of message-passing parallel computers, the availability of memory may not be a major concern. Hence, reducing fill-in to restrict memory use is relatively less important in the parallel context.

In addition to increasing the memory requirement, fill-in also increases computation. However, even some increase in computation can be compensated, provided that the ordering scheme increases the number of parallel tasks and/or lowers communication during the factorization phase. This is because two important causes of inefficiency of parallel sparse direct methods are a low computation-to-communication ratio and insufficient parallelism. Hence, a parallel sparse direct solver may benefit from an ordering that reduces communication and increases parallelism, even at the cost of increasing the fill-in to some extent.

Although several good heuristics for ordering are known, in this section we describe two schemes that show promise for adaptation to parallel sparse direct solvers.

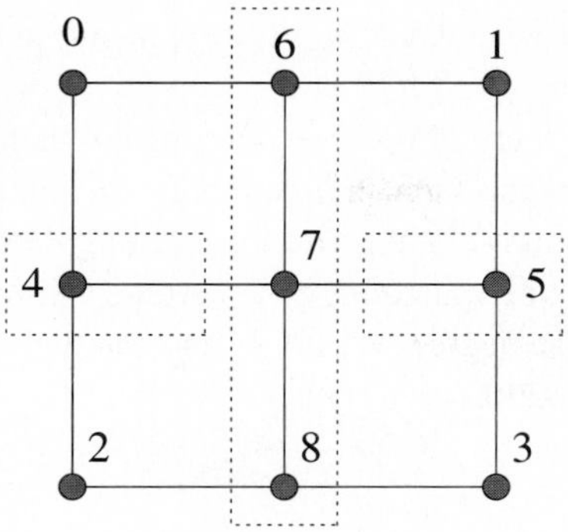

(a) A 3X 3 finite difference grid with nested dissection numbering

	0	1	2	3	4	5	6	7	8
0	X				X		X		
1		X				X	X		
2			X		X				X
3				X		X			X
4	X		X		X		□	X	□
5		X		X		X	□	X	□
6	X	X			□	□	X	X	□
7					X	X	X	X	X
8			X	X	□	□	□	X	X

(b) The resulting sparse matrix with fill-in on factorization

Figure 11.22 The nested-dissection ordering of a 3×3 finite difference grid.

Nested-Dissection Ordering

Nested-dissection ordering is best explained in terms of finite difference grids, as shown in Figure 11.22. Part (a) of this figure shows a small square grid of points. To obtain a nested-dissection ordering of the coefficient matrix resulting from this grid, we assign numbers to the grid points by following the nested-dissection algorithm. First, a set of points is chosen whose removal divides the domain into two disconnected subdomains of equal (or almost equal) size. The points that are chosen are numbered after all the points in both subdomains have been numbered. The points in the subdomains are recursively numbered by using the same strategy. After all grid points are numbered, the ordered matrix of coefficients is obtained by making the ith point correspond to the ith variable and the ith equation. The sparse matrix resulting from the nested-dissection ordering of the points in the grid of Figure 11.22(a) is shown in Figure 11.22(b).

Nested dissection can even be used for irregular grids and for sparse matrices that do not arise from finite element problems. An n-node graph can be constructed from the $n \times n$ matrix of coefficients A by placing an edge between points i and j if and only if $A[i, j] \neq 0$ or $A[j, i] \neq 0$, as shown in Figure 11.12. The nodes of the graph are renumbered as previously described. The matrix is then reordered according to the new numbering, subject to numerical stability.

Minimum-Degree Ordering

After k steps of Gaussian elimination, let c_i be the number of nonzero elements in the ith column of the $(n - k) \times (n - k)$ active matrix, and let r_i be the number of nonzero elements in its ith row. We define a cost function $C(i)$ as the product $(c_i - 1) \times (r_i - 1)$. In ***minimum-degree ordering***, The ith column is chosen as the pivot in the $(k + 1)^{\text{st}}$ iteration (that is, the ith row and column become the $(k+1)^{\text{st}}$ row and column) if $C(i)$ is minimum and $A[i, i]$ satisfies some numerical stability criterion.

The sparsity pattern of the matrix resulting from minimum-degree ordering is sensitive to tie-breaking between candidate pivots whose cost is the same. For example, the matrix shown in Figure 11.22(b) happens to satisfy the minimum-degree criterion, although other minimum-degree permutations are possible. Different permutations of a matrix satisfying the minimum-degree criterion may result in different degrees of fill-in and parallelism during the factorization phase (Problems 11.23 and 11.29).

11.4.2 Symbolic Factorization

The symbolic factorization phase determines the structure of the triangular matrices that would result from factorizing the ordered coefficient matrix. ***Symbolic factorization*** sets up the data structures for storing the resulting matrices, and allocates an appropriate amount of memory for these data structures. The information on the structure of the factors is also used by the algorithms for numerical factorization, which is the next phase of solving the system.

Symbolic factorization is quite complicated if numerical pivoting is required. In such cases, it is usually merged with the next phase, which is numerical factorization. If numerical pivoting is not required, then determining the sparsity pattern of the factors is straightforward. In this case, symbolic factorization simply determines the fill-in caused by the elimination of each row of the matrix in sequence. When the kth row of the coefficient matrix A is used as the pivot, a fill-in is created for every $A[i, j] \neq 0$ if $i, j > k$, $A[i, k] \neq 0$, and $A[k, j] \neq 0$.

For performing symbolic factorization on matrices that do not require numerical pivoting, serial algorithms are available whose run time is proportional to the number of nonzero elements in the matrix (Section 11.6). Due to the availability of very fast serial algorithms, and the high data-distribution cost involved in parallelizing them, implementations of parallel symbolic factorization on message-passing computers tend to be inefficient. Moreover, symbolic factorization is often performed once and then several systems with the same sparsity pattern are solved, amortizing the cost of symbolic factorization over all the systems.

11.4.3 Numerical Factorization

Numerical factorization refers to performing arithmetic operations on the coefficient matrix A to produce a lower-triangular matrix L and an upper triangular matrix U. Usually, the basic algorithm used for numerical factorization is either Gaussian elimination (for general systems) or Cholesky factorization (for symmetric positive definite systems). In this section we choose the row-oriented versions of these algorithms given in Programs 3.1 and 5.6, respectively.

In Gaussian elimination for dense matrices, pivots are chosen sequentially because a pivot modifies all the rows of the unfactorized part of the matrix. A row can be chosen

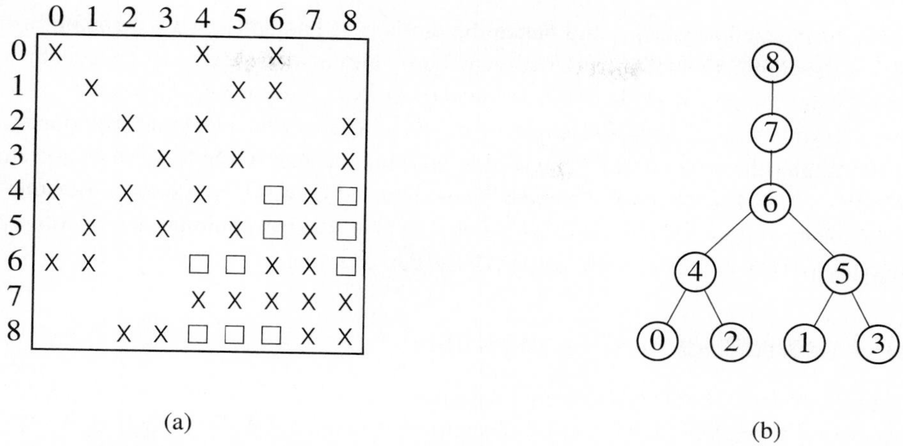

Figure 11.23 A sparse matrix and the corresponding elimination tree.

as a pivot row only after it has been modified by the previous pivot. In the sparse case, however, two or more rows can be completely independent. In a sparse matrix A, row k directly modifies row i if $i > k$ and $A[i, k] \neq 0$. Row k indirectly modifies row i if a row j modified (directly or indirectly) by row k modifies row i. Rows k and i are independent if row k does not modify row i directly or indirectly.

The mutually independent rows of a sparse matrix can be used as pivots in any order, or even simultaneously in a parallel implementation. This is a very important source of parallelism in sparse matrix factorization. For example, in Figure 11.22(b), rows 0, 1, 2, or 3 can be used as pivots in any order, or in parallel. The remaining four rows are modified by one or more of these rows. For example, row 4 cannot be used as a pivot until rows 0 and 2 have been used as pivots to modify row 4. Similarly, row 5 can be used as a pivot only after it has been modified by rows 1 and 3. Thus, a partial ordering exists among the rows of the sparse matrix that determines when a certain row can be used as a pivot.

A useful concept that yields this partial order and helps abstract this form of parallelism in sparse matrix factorization is that of ***elimination trees***. Assume that the matrix of coefficients A has been ordered such that the numerical stability criteria are satisfied and choosing pivots in the order 0 to $n - 1$ yields a stable solution. The elimination tree corresponding to this matrix has one node for each row. Node j is the parent of node i if $j > i$ and j is smallest among all k such that $A[k, i]$ is nonzero in the $(n-i) \times (n-i)$ active (unfactorized) part of the matrix remaining after the first $(i - 1)$ rows have been used as pivots. For instance, the sparse matrix of Figure 11.22(b) is reproduced in Figure 11.23(a), and the corresponding elimination tree is shown in Figure 11.23(b). In a parallel implementation, rows whose entire set of descendants has been eliminated can be eliminated in parallel.

Since each level of an elimination tree must be processed one after the other from the leaves to the root, the parallel run time is a function of the height of the tree. The average number of independent tasks, and hence the amount of parallelism, is a function of the width of the elimination tree. Thus, short and bushy elimination trees are more suitable for parallel sparse direct solvers than tall and lean trees.

The ordering of rows and columns of the sparse matrix plays an important role in determining the structure of the resulting elimination tree. Usually, nested-dissection ordering results in short, well-balanced trees, and minimum-degree ordering results in tall, unbalanced trees. However, it is observed in practice that minimum-degree ordering generates less fill-in than does the nested-dissection ordering.

Serial Sparse Factorization Algorithms

In the row-oriented serial Gaussian elimination algorithm for dense matrices (Program 5.4), during the kth iteration, the kth row of the matrix is used to update all remaining $n - k - 1$ rows. However, in the sparse case, the kth row is used to update only those rows in the active part of A that have a nonzero element in the kth column. Therefore, the serial algorithm for the sparse case is more complex since it must keep track of the sparsity pattern of the active part of the matrix to determine the rows that require modification by a pivot. To describe the sparse algorithm, we introduce the following two operations:

(1) *divide*(k), which divides every nonzero element of the kth row in the upper-triangular part of the matrix by $A[k, k]$; and

(2) *modify*$(i, A[k, *])$, which subtracts a multiple of the sparse vector $A[k, *]$ from the ith row of the matrix A. This multiple is the product of $A[i, k]$ and the kth row of A.

The *divide* operation corresponds to lines 5 and 6 of the dense algorithm given in Program 5.4, and the *modify* operation corresponds to lines 11 and 12. To keep track of the rows that each pivot should modify, we define a data structure S_i as the set of all the rows of A with indices smaller than i that modify the ith row during the factorization of A.

Program 11.5 outlines a serial sparse Gaussian elimination algorithm. This algorithm is fairly straightforward. It assumes that the numerical stability criteria have been taken into account in the ordering phase and that pivots can be chosen in order from 0 to $n - 1$. When the kth row is chosen as the pivot, all the *modify* (modify_gauss) operations are performed on this row (line 7). Then the pivot row is ready for the *divide* (divide_gauss) operation (line 8). The *divide* operation is followed by incorporating the pivot row (that is, the kth row) in S_i for all i such that the ith row needs to be modified by the kth row (line 9). Program 11.5 generates the data structures S_i during the course of factorization. Often, the data structures S_i are generated during the symbolic factorization phase. Note that, in practice, the steps on lines 6 and 7 do not require that the condition $j \in S_k$ be checked serially for all j from 0 to $k - 1$. The data structures of the sparse storage scheme being used maintain the relevant rows in the correct order. Similarly, all $A[i, k]$ $(k < i < n)$ on line 9 and all $A[k, j]$ $(k < j < n)$ on lines 15 and 21 in Program 11.5 are not explicitly checked for nonzero entries. If that was the case, then each execution of lines 9, 15 and

```
1.  procedure SERIAL_SPARSE_GAUSS (A)
2.  begin
3.      for i := 0 to n − 1 do S_i := Ø;
4.      for k := 0 to n − 1 do
5.      begin
6.          for j := 0 to k − 1 do
7.              if j ∈ S_k then modify_gauss (k, A[j, *]);
8.          divide_gauss (k);
9.          for all i such that ((i > k) and (A[i, k] ≠ 0)) do S_i := S_i ∪ {k};
10.     endfor;
11. end SERIAL_SPARSE_GAUSS
12.
13. procedure modify_gauss (i, A[k, *])
14. begin
15.     for all j such that ((j > k) and (A[k, j] ≠ 0)) do
16.         A[i, j] := A[i, j] − A[i, k] × A[k, j];
17. end modify_gauss
18.
19. procedure divide_gauss (k)
20. begin
21.     for all j such that ((j > k) and (A[k, j] ≠ 0)) do
22.         A[k, j] := A[k, j]/A[k, k];
23. end divide_gauss
```

Program 11.5 A serial sparse Gaussian elimination algorithm and the corresponding *modify* (modify_gauss) and *divide* (divide_gauss) operations.

21 would take $\Theta(n)$ time—the same as that for a dense matrix. The use of sparse storage schemes described in Section 11.1.1 helps keep track of the nonzero entries in a row or column of A. Thus, these operations can be performed in $\Theta(m)$ time, where m is the number of nonzero entries in the kth column (line 9) or the kth row (lines 15 and 21) of the active part of the matrix during the kth iteration of the outer loop of Gaussian elimination.

An algorithm similar to procedure SERIAL_SPARSE_GAUSS in Program 11.5 can be used to perform Cholesky factorization on a sparse symmetric positive definite matrix A. The *modify* and *divide* operations to be used in the case of Cholesky factorization are given by procedures modify_chol and divide_chol in Program 11.6. Note that, in the case of Cholesky factorization, the rows in S_k can be chosen in any order to modify the kth row. This is in contrast to Gaussian elimination, in which the rows in S_k must be applied in an increasing order while modifying the kth row.

```
procedure modify_chol (i, Vector)
begin
    for all j such that ((j ≥ i) and (Vector[j] ≠ 0)) do
        A[i, j] := A[i, j] − Vector[j];
end modify_chol

procedure divide_chol (k)
begin
    A[k, k] := √A[k, k];
    for all j such that ((j > k) and (A[k, j] ≠ 0)) do
        A[k, j] := A[k, j]/A[k, k];
end divide_chol
```

Program 11.6 The *modify* (modify_chol) and *divide* (divide_chol) operations for use with a sparse row-oriented Cholesky factorization.

A Parallel Implementation of Sparse Gaussian Elimination

There are three levels of parallelism available in sparse factorization:

(1) ***Fine-grain*** parallelism at the level of individual scalar floating-point operations.
(2) ***Medium-grain*** parallelism at the level of performing floating-point operations over nonzero elements of entire rows or columns of the coefficient matrix (such as *divide* and *modify* operations).
(3) ***Coarse-grain*** parallelism at the level of updating groups of rows or columns that can be solved independently of other such groups. If the factorization process is viewed as a collection of subtasks whose partial ordering is defined by an elimination tree, then coarse-grain parallelism refers to processing entire subtrees of the elimination tree.

Fine-grain parallelism is not suitable for message-passing computers, even with state-of-the-art hardware technology. We first describe a parallel implementation of sparse Gaussian elimination that exploits only medium-grain parallelism. In the next two subsections, we will describe parallel algorithms for sparse matrix factorization that exploit both medium- and coarse-grain parallelism.

Program 11.7 shows a parallel sparse Gaussian elimination algorithm for a message-passing parallel computer, in which each processor stores one row of the coefficient matrix. This algorithm uses n processors to factorize the $n \times n$ matrix A whose k^{th} row is initially assigned to the kth processor. Thus, the kth processor performs all the *modify*$(k, A[i, *])$ operations (for any i such that the ith row modifies the kth row; that is, $i \in S_k$) and the *divide*(k) operation. In the loop that starts at line 3, a processor receives the information

```
1.  procedure PARALLEL_SPARSE_GAUSS (my_id, A[my_id, *])
2.  begin
3.      for i := 0 to my_id − 1 do
4.          if i ∈ S_my_id then
5.          begin
6.              receive (A[i, *]) from the processor labeled i;
7.              modify_gauss (my_id, A[i, *]);
8.          endif;                /* Line 4 */
9.      divide_gauss (my_id);
10.     for all j such that ((j > my_id) and (A[j, my_id] ≠ 0)) do
11.         send (A[my_id, *]) to the processor labeled j;
12. end PARALLEL_SPARSE_GAUSS
```

Program 11.7 A parallel sparse Gaussian elimination algorithm for the case in which each processor stores one row of the matrix of coefficients. Data is mapped such that the processor labeled my_id stores row number my_id. The algorithm assumes that S_{my_id} has been generated during symbolic factorization, and is available before numerical factorization starts.

required to *modify* the row it stores. Note that a processor is blocked on the **receive** on line 6 until the *divide*(i) operation has been performed at processor i. When the entire subtree rooted at node k of the elimination tree has been processed and the *modify*$(k, A[i, *])$ operations have been performed for all $i \in S_k$, the *divide*(k) operation is performed. After performing the *divide* operation, a processor sends its row to all the processors that need this row to modify the rows assigned to them.

Program 11.7 is of academic interest only, as it would be too inefficient on any practical parallel computer. In practice, the number of processors used is much less than n, the dimension of the coefficient matrix A. An algorithm similar to Program 11.7 can be used to perform sparse Cholesky factorization as well. Unlike Gaussian elimination, for Cholesky factorization the modifying rows need not be received in order; a processor labeled k receives a sparse vector of the form $A[i, *]$ as soon as it arrives, and performs the *modify*$(k, A[i, *])$ operation. Finally, when *modify*$(k, A[i, *])$ has been performed for all $i \in S_k$, processor k performs *divide*(k).

Parallel Fan-Out Algorithm

We now describe a parallel algorithm (Program 11.8), known as the ***fan-out*** algorithm, for sparse matrix factorization. This algorithm uses fewer than n processors for an $n \times n$ matrix, and each processor stores more than one row of the sparse matrix of coefficients A. The set of rows belonging to the ith processor is stored in *List*(i). The algorithm performs a *divide* operation (line 10) on any of its rows after the subtree rooted at the node corresponding to that row has been processed and all the *modify* operations on that row have

```
1.  procedure PARALLEL_FAN_OUT (my_id, List(my_id))
2.  begin
3.     while (List(my_id) ≠ ∅) do
4.     begin
5.        if (∃i ∈ List(my_id) such that
              vectors A[k, *] have been received for all k ∈ S_i) then
6.        begin
7.           for k := 0 to i − 1 do
8.              if k ∈ S_i then modify_gauss (i, A[k, *]);
9.           List(my_id) := List(my_id) − {i};
10.          divide_gauss (i);
11.          for all j such that ((j > i) and(A[j, i] ≠ 0)) do
12.             send (j, A[i, *]) to processor storing the j^th row;
13.       endif;                 /* Line 5 */
14.       if (there is an incoming message) then
15.          receive and store the message;
16.    endwhile;                 /* Line 3 */
17. end PARALLEL_FAN_OUT
```

Program 11.8 A parallel fan-out algorithm for Gaussian elimination. Processor my_id stores the set of rows assigned to it in a list called *List*(my_id). The algorithm assumes that S_{my_id} has been generated during symbolic factorization, and is available before numerical factorization starts.

been performed. The algorithm then sends the divided row to the processors responsible for the rows that must be modified by the divided row.

Program 11.8 can be easily modified for sparse Cholesky factorization. In Cholesky factorization, the *modify* operations (line 8) can be performed in any order. Hence, it is not necessary to store a message. As soon as a message is received, the corresponding *modify* operation can be performed.

Note that, in the fan-out algorithm, the processor storing the ith row receives a message for every *modify*(i, $A[k, *]$) operation if the ith and k^{th} rows reside on different processors. The total number of messages sent can be reduced by concatenating all outgoing messages from a processor that modify the same row. If $k \in S_i \cap$ *List*(my_id) (that is, $A[k, *]$ belongs to those rows in S_i that reside on processor my_id), then a single message containing all such rows $A[k, *]$ is sent from processor my_id to the processor storing the ith row. This message is sent after the *divide*(k) operations for all $k \in S_i \cap$ *List*(my_id) have been performed on processor my_id. This strategy does not reduce the total volume of communication in sparse Gaussian elimination, but it reduces the overhead due to message startup time, which may otherwise dominate the communication time.

Parallel Fan-In Algorithm for Cholesky Factorization

This subsection describes a parallel algorithm for the row-oriented Cholesky factorization of sparse symmetric positive definite matrices. This algorithm, known as the ***fan-in*** algorithm, is an improvement over the fan-out algorithm. Recall from Program 11.5 that the *modify*$(i, A[k, *])$ operation in Gaussian elimination subtracts a multiple of a part of the kth row of the coefficient matrix from the corresponding part of the ith row. The factor by which the modifying row (that is, the kth row) is multiplied is the element $A[i, k]$ of the row to be modified (that is, the ith row). Unlike Gaussian elimination, in a row-oriented Cholesky factorization algorithm (Program 5.6), the factor by which the modifying row (that is, the kth row) is multiplied is the element $A[k, i]$ of the modifying row itself. This means that the multiple of the kth row that needs to be subtracted from the ith row can be computed at the processor that stores the kth row.

Recall that the number of messages passed in the fan-out algorithm can be reduced by concatenating all the outgoing messages from a processor that modify the same row. In the case of Cholesky factorization, the appropriate multiples of these outgoing rows can be added together and sent to the destination processor as a single vector, which is then subtracted from the row to be modified. Thus, not only the number of messages, but also the total volume of communication, is reduced. The fan-in algorithm is based on this strategy.

Program 11.9 gives the fan-in algorithm for the row-oriented Cholesky factorization of an $n \times n$ sparse symmetric positive definite matrix A. A significant difference between Programs 11.8 and 11.9 is that, after performing the *divide*(i) operation, a processor does not send the ith row to all the processors storing the rows that must be modified by the ith row. Instead, each processor stores sparse vectors $Update_j$ for $0 \leq j < n$. Initially, all the elements in these vectors are zeros. If the ith row modifies the jth row, then after *divide*(i) has been performed, the appropriate multiple of the former is computed by multiplying it with $A[i, j]$. The product $A[i, *] \times A[i, j]$ is then added to $Update_j$. After the *divide* operation has been performed on all rows stored at processor my_id that modify the jth row, processor my_id sends $Update_j$ to the processor storing the jth row. Thus, instead of sending one message for each component of $Update_j$, each processor with a nonzero $Update_j$ sends only one message to the processor storing the jth row. The processor storing the jth row, upon receiving an $Update_j$, subtracts it from the jth row.

Mapping Matrix Rows onto Processors

As mentioned earlier, fine-grain parallelism in sparse matrix factorization is not suitable for message-passing computers. However, exploiting only coarse-grain parallelism is unlikely to yield highly scalable parallel formulations. The reason is that, despite reducing communication costs, using only coarse-grain parallelism limits the degree of concurrency, which decreases further as the computation progresses toward the root of the elimination tree.

```
1.  procedure PARALLEL_FAN_IN (my_id, List(my_id))
2.  begin
3.      for i := 0 to n − 1 do Update^i := 0;
4.      while (List(my_id) ≠ ∅) do
5.      begin
6.          if (∃i ∈ List(my_id) such that divide_chol(j)
                        has been performed for all j ∈ S_i) then
7.          begin
8.              while (messages of the form (i, Vector) have not been received
                        from all processors that store rows belonging to S_i) do
9.              begin
10.                 receive (i, Vector);
11.                 modify_chol (i, Vector);
12.             endwhile;           /* Line 8 */
13.             List(my_id) := List(my_id) − {i};
14.             divide_chol(i);
15.             for all j such that ((j > i) and(A[j, i] ≠ 0)) do
16.             begin
17.                 Update_j := Update_j + A[i, j] × A[i, *];
18.                 if (divide_chol(k) has been performed
                        for all k ∈ (S_j ∩ List(my_id))) then
19.                     send (j, Update_j) to the processor storing the j^th row;
20.             endfor;             /* Line 15 */
21.         endif;                  /* Line 6 */
22.     endwhile;                   /* Line 4 */
23. end PARALLEL_FAN_IN
```

Program 11.9 A parallel fan-in algorithm for sparse direct row-oriented Cholesky factorization of symmetric positive definite matrices. The algorithm assumes that S_{my_id} has been generated during symbolic factorization, and is available before numerical factorization starts.

An ideal parallel formulation exploits both coarse-grain and medium-grain parallelism. As the computation progresses up the elimination tree, the availability of coarse-grain parallelism diminishes because the number of independent subtrees of the elimination tree decreases. However, medium-grain parallelism becomes more viable as the fill-in in the unfactorized part of the coefficient matrix increases, and hence, a typical *divide* or *modify* operation encounters more nonzero elements in a row. Therefore, it is advantageous to shift the emphasis systematically from coarse-grain to medium-grain parallelism as the computation progresses. Figure 11.24 shows a distribution of the rows of the matrix among the processors based on this approach.

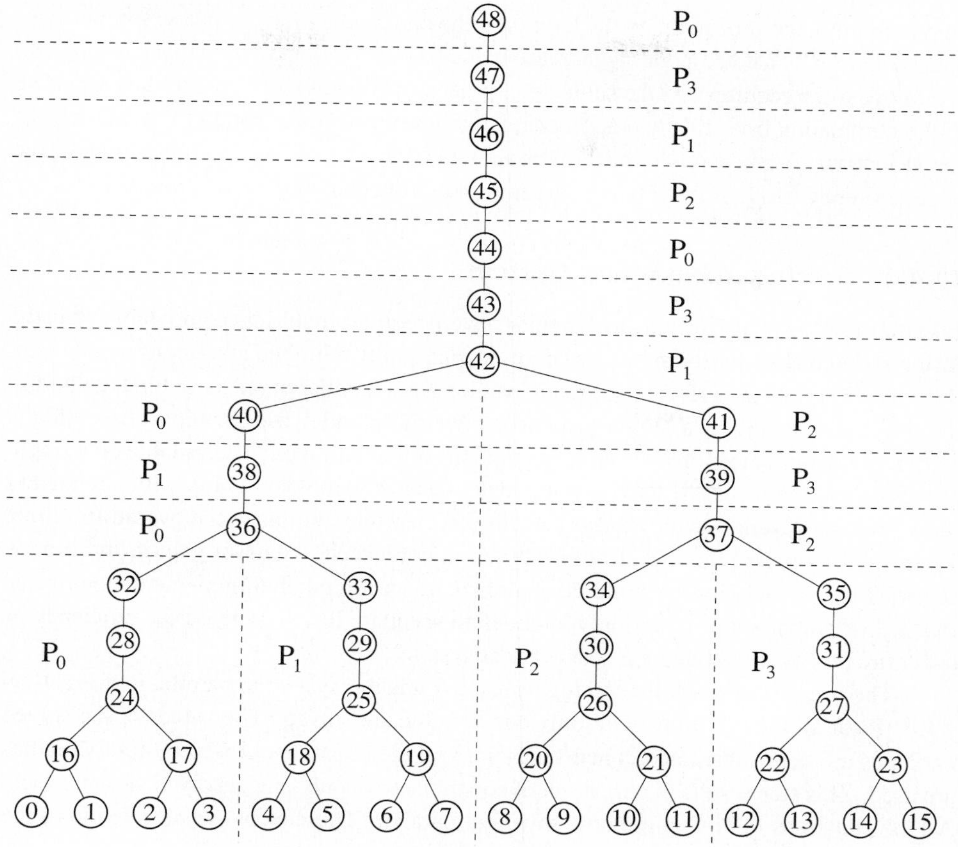

Figure 11.24 An example of a good strategy for using four processors to partition the elimination tree that corresponds to a matrix of coefficients resulting from the nested-dissection numbering of a 7×7 finite difference grid in which each processor has four neighbors.

Figure 11.24 shows the elimination tree corresponding to a matrix resulting from a nested-dissection numbering of a 7×7 finite difference grid of the form shown in Figure 11.8 (Problem 11.28). The lower, wider part of the elimination tree is partitioned vertically. In this part, independent subtrees are assigned to individual processors that perform complete updates on their respective sets of sparse rows. This assignment of subtrees to processors exploits coarse-grain parallelism. The upper, narrower part of the elimination tree is partitioned horizontally among the processors so that medium-grain parallelism is exploited. In this part of the elimination tree, individual rows are assigned to processors, and each processor performs *modify* and *divide* on its respective rows.

The partitioning strategy illustrated in Figure 11.24 keeps communication low in the initial stage of parallel factorization because the modifying and the modified rows mostly belong to the same processor. In the later part, the communication per processor increases but is balanced by a corresponding increase in the amount of computation that a *modify* or a *divide* operation requires. At the same time, processors do not starve due to the narrowing of the elimination tree. Such an approach is likely to yield better parallel formulations of sparse factorization because it limits the communication cost while providing a high degree of concurrency. Both of these factors are important for achieving good scalability.

11.4.4 Solving a Triangular System

Like the ordering phase, solving a triangular system requires much less computation than the factorization phase. Furthermore, often this step has only a limited amount of parallelism. Still, it is desirable to perform this step in parallel for a number of reasons. First, gathering the triangular factors at a single processor after the parallel factorization phase entails substantial communication overhead. Second, the amount of memory available on a single processor may be insufficient to accommodate the entire problem. Third, with a relatively more efficient parallel factorization method, this step may dominate the overall run time. Therefore, to prevent this step from becoming a bottleneck, whatever gain in run time is achieved by parallelizing it should be exploited. Even if a parallel implementation of this step is inefficient and provides only a moderate speedup, it will increase the efficiency of the entire process of solving the sparse linear system.

The overall approach for solving a sparse triangular system in parallel is straightforward. First, all the equations with only one variable are solved. The values of the solved variables are then substituted concurrently into all the equations in which these variables are used. This step results in a fresh set of equations with only one unsolved variable each. All the equations in this set are now solved in parallel. These steps are repeated until the entire system is solved.

11.5 Multigrid Methods

Multigrid methods are iterative algorithms for solving partial differential equations by using multiple grids of varying degrees of fineness over the same domain. An approximate solution obtained by a coarse discretization is used as the initial approximation for obtaining a more precise solution by a finer discretization, and so on.

Consider a domain D and a sequence of successively finer discretizations G_0, G_1, ..., G_m. Discretization G_0 is the coarsest, and G_m is the finest. Figure 11.25 illustrates such discretizations for a square domain with $m = 3$. As the figure shows, the grid points in G_i are a subset of the grid points in G_{i+1}. The linear system of equations arising from discretization G_0 is the smallest and, consequently, the easiest to solve. After a solution or an approximation to the solution of this system has been obtained, the values of the physical quantity being modeled (say, u) at the grid points in $G_1 - G_0$ are approximated by interpolation from the values of u at the grid points in G_0. The values of u at the grid points in G_1 thus obtained serve as the initial approximation for an iterative method to solve the

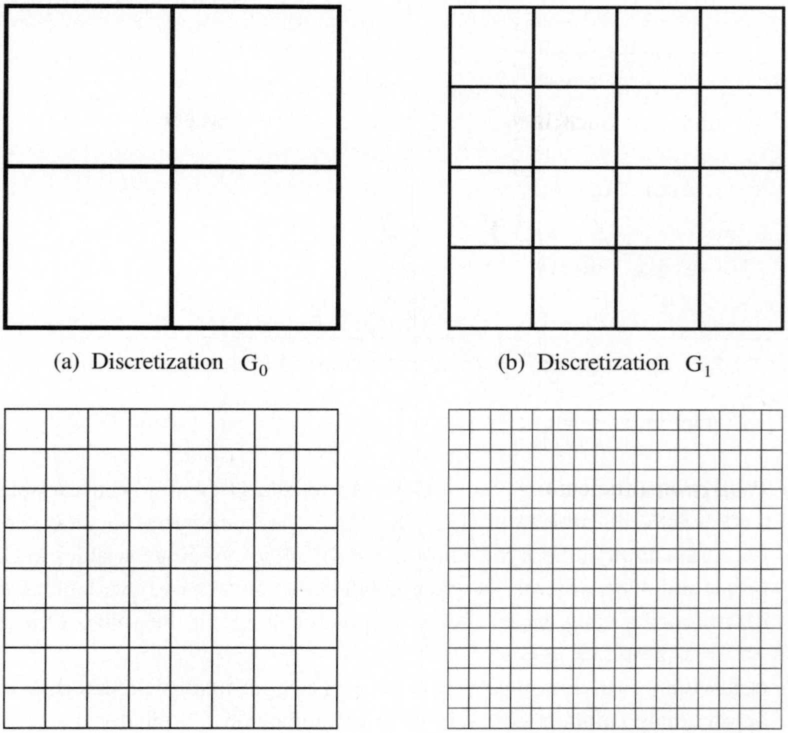

(a) Discretization G_0 (b) Discretization G_1

(c) Discretization G_2 (d) Discretization G_3

Figure 11.25 Successively finer discretizations of a domain.

system of linear equations arising out of G_1. This procedure is continued for successively finer discretizations.

The process that we just described is only a part of the multigrid method. In this method, which has several variations, information is exchanged bidirectionally between grids of varying granularity. The information from coarser discretizations is used to derive approximate starting points for finer grids. Information is also projected onto the coarser grids from the finer grids. In general, iterations over a certain discretization G_i are used to refine the solution at its grid points. This improved solution is either projected onto the next coarser grid G_{i-1} or interpolated onto the next finer grid G_{i+1}. Different variations of the multigrid method use different cycles of interpolation and projection, some of which are shown in Figure 11.26.

In summary, a typical multigrid algorithm involves three types of computations:

(1) ***Interpolation*** of values of variables in discretization G_i to approximate the values of variables in the next finer discretization G_{i+1}.

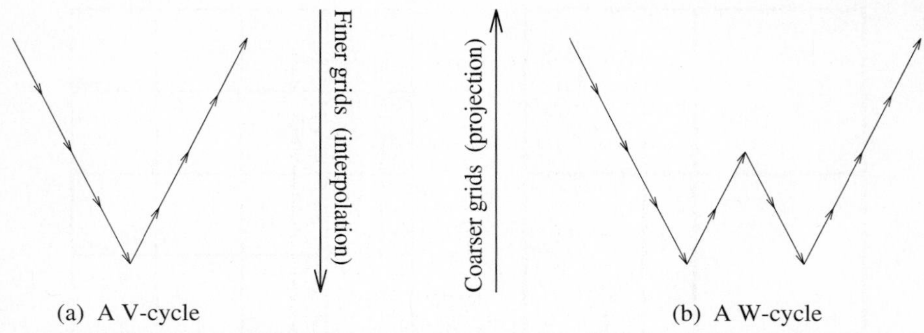

Figure 11.26 Some typical cycles of interpolation and projection used in multigrid methods.

(2) ***Projection*** of values of variables in discretization G_i onto the variables in the next coarser discretization G_{i-1}. Since G_{i-1} is a subset of G_i, the variables in G_{i-1} can simply inherit the values from the corresponding variables in G_i during projection. This process is known as ***injection***. Otherwise, a variable in G_{i-1} can be assigned a value based on the weighted average of the values of a cluster of variables around it in G_i.

(3) ***Relaxation***, which is the process of applying an iterative method to refine the approximate solution at any level of discretization. Typically, Jacobi, damped or weighted Jacobi, or Gauss-Seidel methods are used to perform relaxation in multigrid algorithms.

The advantages of using the multigrid technique are manifold. Usually, iterative methods converge faster on coarse grids than on fine grids. Furthermore, since the number of variables in the systems corresponding to coarse grids is very small, it is often possible to obtain exact solutions for these systems by using direct methods. Therefore, it is possible to obtain good starting points for iterations on fine grids at a relatively low computational cost. Iterative methods also converge faster with good initial approximations. In addition, the convergence rate of an iterative method is usually higher during the initial iterations. By iterating only a few times at each step of a cycle, we always work in the region of a high convergence rate. Thus, multigrid methods arrive at an acceptable solution to a system of linear equations arising out of a fine grid at a much faster rate than a typical iterative method applied directly on the same grid. Multigrid methods can be used for finite difference, finite element, or finite volume problems.

Parallel Implementation

We now consider a parallel implementation of a simple multigrid computation on a mesh-connected computer with cut-through routing. Since a mesh can be embedded into a hypercube, adapting this implementation for a hypercube is straightforward (Problem 11.31).

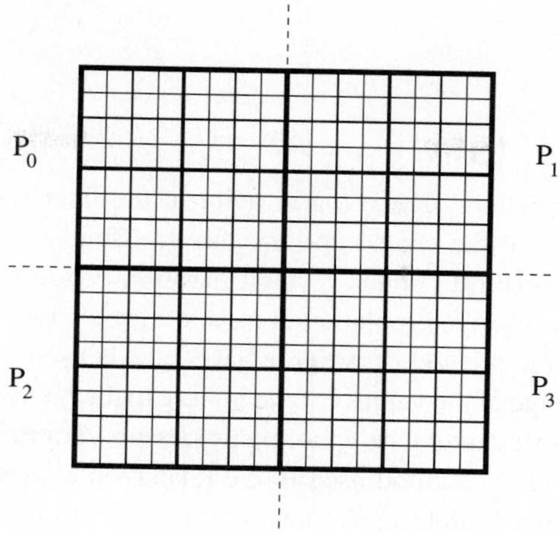

Figure 11.27 The domain of Figure 11.25 mapped onto four processors.

We assume that the domain is partitioned among the processors in a block-checkerboard fashion. Parallel implementations with the domain stripe-partitioned in one dimension are less efficient and less scalable (Problem 11.33).

First, we describe a parallel implementation of the multigrid technique for the simple case, in which the number of processors is less than or equal to the number of elements in the coarsest discretization of the domain. In this case there is no processor idling, and the only overhead is due to communication. Figure 11.27 shows such a partitioning of the domain and its discretizations G_0, G_1, G_2, and G_3, shown in Figure 11.25. Assume that $m+1$ is the total number of discretizations used ($G_0, G_1, \ldots, G_m$), the number of elements in the finest discretization G_m is n, and the number of elements in every successively coarser discretization reduces by a factor of c (in Figure 11.27, $m = 3$, $n = 256$, and $c = 4$). Hence, the number of elements in the coarsest discretization G_0 is n/c^m (for the case under consideration, $p \leq n/c^m$). Also assume that the total number of interpolations, projections, and relaxation iterations is the same for each discretization. Let this number be η.

While working with discretization G_i, the amount of computation that a processor performs during an interpolation, projection, or relaxation iteration is proportional to the number of elements in a partition in G_i. Let the combined constant of proportionality for all three types of computations be t_c. Since the number of elements per partition in G_m is n/p, the total time t_{comp} spent in computation by each processor during the execution of the entire multigrid procedure is given by the following equation:

$$t_{comp} = \eta t_c \sum_{i=0}^{m} \frac{n}{pc^i}$$

$$
\begin{aligned}
&= \eta t_c \frac{n(c - 1/c^m)}{p(c-1)} \\
&\approx \frac{t_c \eta c n}{p(c-1)}
\end{aligned}
\tag{11.43}
$$

During the interpolation phases, a grid point of the finer grid requires values corresponding to the points of the coarse grid around it. Thus, an exchange of the values corresponding to the coarse-grid points lying at partition boundaries among neighboring processors suffices to perform interpolation in parallel. Projection using injection requires no communication. If the method of weighted averages is used for projection, then this phase requires an exchange of the values corresponding to the points on the finer grid points lying at partition boundaries among neighboring processors. For the partitioning illustrated in Figure 11.27, the iterative method used in the relaxation phases also requires nearest-neighbor communication of values corresponding to the points along partition boundaries to compute the matrix-vector product in each iteration (Section 11.1.3 and Figure 11.10). We disregard the communication penalty in computing vector inner products during relaxation. This assumption is valid if either hardware-supported fast reduction operations render the cost of computing a global sum insignificant, or a relaxation method like the Jacobi method is used so that an inner product is not computed in every iteration (Section 11.2.1). Thus, in each interpolation and projection step, as well as in each relaxation iteration, a processor exchanges four messages—one with each neighbor. The size of each message is proportional to the number of grid points along an edge of the square partition assigned to the processor. The number of such boundary elements in discretization G_i is equal to the square root of the number of elements in each partition in G_i. Hence, the total time t_{comm} spent in communication by each processor during the entire multigrid procedure is given by the following equation:

$$
\begin{aligned}
t_{comm} &= 4\eta \sum_{i=0}^{m} \left(t_s + t_w \sqrt{\frac{n}{pc^i}} \right) \\
&= 4(m+1)t_s\eta + 4t_w\eta \frac{\sqrt{c} - 1/c^{m/2}}{\sqrt{c} - 1} \sqrt{\frac{n}{p}} \\
&\approx 4(m+1)t_s\eta + 4t_w\eta \frac{\sqrt{cn}}{(\sqrt{c} - 1)\sqrt{p}}
\end{aligned}
\tag{11.44}
$$

From Equations 11.43 and 11.44, the total parallel run time $t_{comp} + t_{comm}$ is

$$
T_P = \eta \left(t_c \frac{cn}{p(c-1)} + 4(m+1)t_s + 4t_w \frac{\sqrt{cn}}{(\sqrt{c}-1)\sqrt{p}} \right). \tag{11.45}
$$

We now consider the case in which the number of processors is greater than the number of elements in the coarsest discretization. Assume that $p = n/c^r$, where $0 \le r < m$; that is, the number of processors is equal to the number of elements in G_{m-r}. This case is illustrated in Figure 11.28 for $n = 256$, $m = 3$, $r = 1$, $c = 4$, and $p = 64$. As shown in the figure, some processors remain idle during the computations corresponding

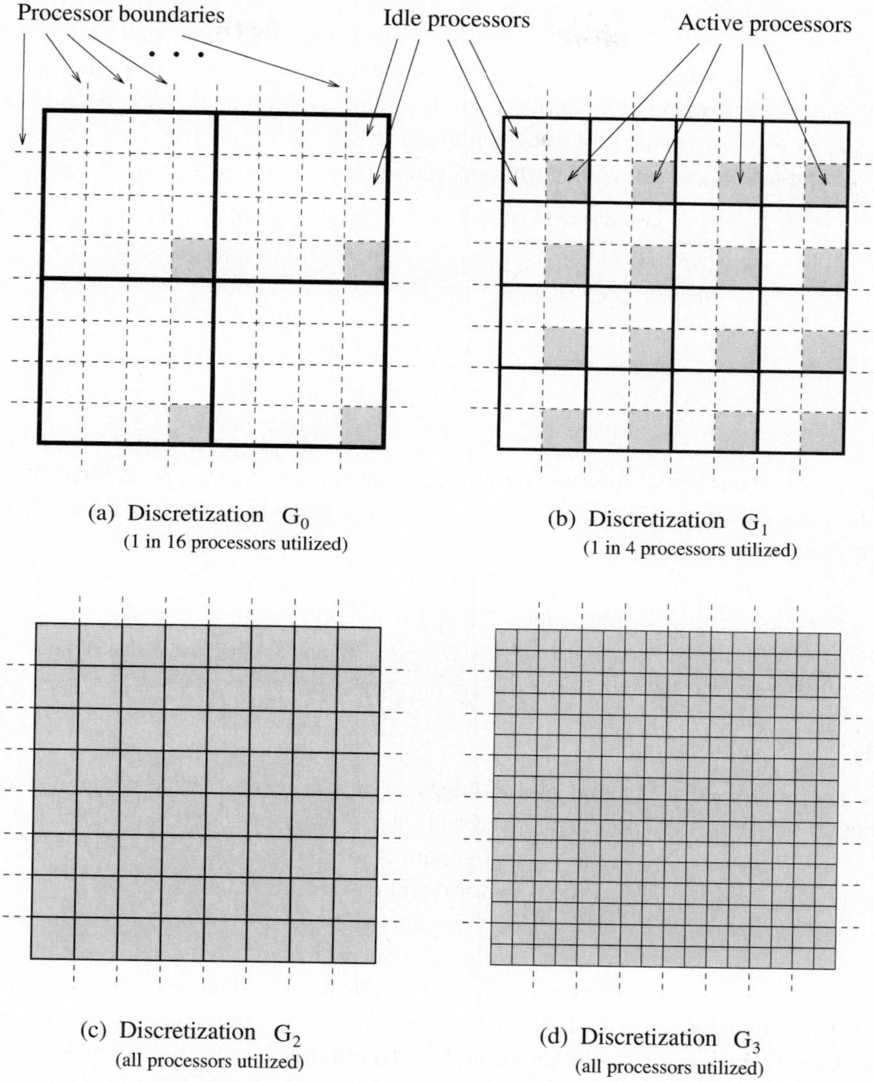

Figure 11.28 The domain of Figure 11.25 partitioned among 64 processors. In discretizations G_0 and G_1 there are multiple processors for a single element. Therefore, some processors remain idle and only the shaded processors are active. In discretization G_2, one element is assigned to each processor, and in G_3, four elements are assigned to each processor.

to $G_0, G_1, \ldots, G_{m-r-1}$. During the interpolations, projections, and relaxation iterations corresponding to these discretizations, the active processors perform only one computation and one communication in every iteration. However, on a two-dimensional mesh, the active processors are no longer directly-connected (Figures 11.28(a) and (b)). In the remaining discretizations $G_{m-r}, \ldots, G_m$, the computation per processor is proportional to the number of elements in each partition, and the volume of communication per processor is proportional to the square root of the number of elements in each partition. The overall parallel run time on a mesh with cut-through routing is given by the following equation:

$$
\begin{aligned}
T_P \quad &= \quad \overbrace{\eta\left((m-r)t_c + t_c \sum_{i=0}^{r} \frac{n}{pc^i}\right)}^{\text{computation or idling}} \\
&\quad + \overbrace{\eta\left(4(m+1)t_s + 4(m-r)t_w + 4t_w \sum_{i=0}^{r} \sqrt{\frac{n}{pc^i}} + 4t_h \sum_{i=1}^{m-r} \sqrt{c^i}\right)}^{\text{communication}}
\end{aligned}
$$

In practice, the number of processors p is much smaller than the number of elements n in the finest discretization. Hence, $(m-r) \ll \sqrt{n/p}$, and the expression for parallel run time can be approximated by

$$
\begin{aligned}
T_P \quad &\approx \quad \eta\left((m-r)t_c + t_c \frac{cn}{p(c-1)}\right) \\
&\quad + \eta\left(4(m+1)t_s + 4t_w \frac{\sqrt{cn}}{(\sqrt{c}-1)\sqrt{p}} + 4t_h \frac{\sqrt{c}}{\sqrt{c}-1}(c^{(m-r)/2}-1)\right).
\end{aligned}
\tag{11.46}
$$

The isoefficiency function of a multigrid computation on a mesh with cut-through routing is $\Theta(p)$ in the absence of overhead due to inner-product computations (Problem 11.30). In other words, the parallel system is ideally scalable and requires that n be proportional to p for cost optimality or for maintaining constant efficiency. However, the constant of proportionality depends on the values of m, r, and c (besides the hardware-related constants). Even if the number of processors is greater than the number of elements in the coarsest discretization, the isoefficiency function remains linear in p (Problem 11.32). The idling time of processors during the computation of coarse discretizations is only a small fraction of the total parallel run time. The reason is that the complexity of the interpolation, projection, and relaxation steps increases rapidly as the grid is made finer. Therefore, a large fraction of the run time is spent working with fine discretizations, which do not involve any idling.

11.6 Bibliographic Remarks

Due to the importance of sparse matrices in scientific and engineering applications, the amount of literature on parallel algorithms for sparse matrix computations is immense.

There are a number of good references for storage schemes and basic operations on sparse matrices [DER90, FWPS92, GL81, Pet91, Saa90, Wij89]. Ferng et al. [FPW93] discuss implementations of some basic sparse matrix-vector computations on SIMD computers. Parallel sparse matrix-vector multiplication is discussed by several authors [BEP93, CS93a, CS93b, Ham92].

Iterative methods for solving large sparse systems are very popular on parallel computers because they can be parallelized more easily than direct methods. Parallel iterative methods in general are discussed by Bertsekas and Tsitsiklis [BT89], Dongarra et al. [DDSvdV91], Golub and Ortega [GO93], and Petiton [Pet91]. Among iterative methods, parallelization of the conjugate gradient (CG) algorithm (and its variants) has received the most attention [And88, AOES88, DM91, GKS92, HS92, JP92, KC91, KS84a, LR88, MG87, PWD91, SS85, vdV82, vdV87a]. The description of the serial unpreconditioned and preconditioned CG algorithms in this chapter is based on the description by Golub and Van Loan [GL89b] and Golub and Ortega [GO93]. The truncated incomplete Cholesky preconditioner for block-tridiagonal matrices described in this chapter was first used by van der Vorst [vdV82] and subsequently studied by Kamath and Sameh [KS84b], and Gupta, Kumar, and Sameh [GKS92]. Variations of the CG algorithm for reducing the overall communication cost of synchronization and vector inner-product computation have been presented by some authors [AAIT89, CG89, DER93, DR92]. Parallel relaxation methods such as Jacobi, Gauss-Seidel, and SOR are described by Adams and Ortega [AO82], Bertsekas and Tsitsiklis [BT89], and Golub and Ortega [GO93]. In addition to the red-black and multicolored orderings for Gauss-Seidel and SOR methods presented in this chapter, Golub and Ortega [GO93] describe a ***diagonal ordering*** that facilitates pipelined implementations of these methods. In this chapter, we have not covered a class of iterative solvers known as ***projection methods***. Parallel projection methods have been discussed by Bramley and Sameh [BS89] and Kamath and Weeratunga [KW91]. Parallel implementations of the finite element method (FEM) based on unpreconditioned CG methods without explicitly assembling the stiffness matrix are discussed in detail by Fox et al. [FJL+88]. The performance of these techniques depends on the partitioning of the domain. A number of heuristic approaches have been presented to derive reasonable suboptimal partitions [AOES88, CR92, MO87, PCF+91, SE87].

A number of techniques have been developed for partitioning finite element graphs. Striped partitioning is described by Morrison and Otto [MO87] and Schwan et al. [SBB+87]. The use of scattered decomposition in FEM is described by Fox et al. [FJL+88], Morrison and Otto [MO87], and Williams [Wil87]. A detailed discussion on scattered decomposition along with several interesting analytical results is presented by Nicol and Saltz [NS90]. Berger and Bokhari [BB87] describe the use of binary decomposition. Sadayappan and Ercal [SE87] proposed the two-dimensional decomposition scheme with boundary refinement. Chung and Ranka [CR92] describe the two-way striping and greedy assignment schemes for partitioning FEM graphs and give the details of the load balancing algorithm for use in conjunction with two-dimensional striped partitioning. Heath and Raghavan [HR92] give a fully parallel algorithm for computing graph separators based on coordinate bisection. This scheme uses connectivity information to limit cross edges. Raghavan [Rag93b] extends this scheme to the three-dimensional case. Our discussion of recursive bisection is based on its description by Simon [Sim91]. Pothen et al. [PSL90] discuss the use of eigenvectors of the adjacency matrix to partition finite element graphs. A discussion of the Lanczos algorithm for computing the Fiedler vector can be found in the book by Parlett [Par80]. Pothen et al. [PSWB92] describe a new partitioning scheme for FEM graphs called ***spectral nested dissection***. The scalability of some of these partitioning techniques has been analyzed by Grama and Kumar [GK92].

Various ordering schemes for sparse matrices, and their suitability for parallel factorization have been studied by a number of researchers [GL89a, JK82, Liu89a, Liu89b, LL87, LPP89, PSWB92]. The work in developing efficient parallel ordering algorithms is fairly rudimentary to date, and only a few references are available on this topic [Con90, HR92, Liu85, Pet84].

Parallel symbolic factorization is treated by Alaghband [Ala89], Gilbert and Hafsteinsson [GH90], George et al. [GHLN87], Heath et al. [HNP91], Heath and Raghavan [HR93], and Zmijewski and Gilbert [ZG88].

The most computationally expensive phase of obtaining a direct solution to a sparse system of linear equations is numerical factorization. As a result, parallel numerical factorization has received much attention [AEL90a, AEL^+90b, AJ85, BDK^+89, CGLN84, Con86, DDSvdV91, GHLN89, GHLN88, GLN89, GN89, GS92, HNP91, HR93, Leu89, Rag93a, SR89, Zmi87]. A class of algorithms called ***multifrontal methods*** [DR83, Liu90a] is becoming increasingly popular for solving sparse linear systems on parallel computers. Multifrontal methods are generalizations of frontal methods, which keep a relatively small portion of the matrix in main memory at a time and use a full matrix representation for this active portion of the matrix. Multifrontal methods use multiple active portions, and this is the basic source of parallelism in a multifrontal algorithm. Parallel formulations of multifrontal methods have been described by Duff [Duf86], Geist [Gei87], Lucas [Luc87], Pothen and Sun [PS91], and Pozo and Smith [PS93]. Ashcraft et al. [AELS90] compare the fan-out, fan-in, and multifrontal approaches for sparse numerical factorization. The discussion on fine, medium, and coarse levels of granularity in sparse numerical factorization is due to Liu [Liu86]. Liu [Liu90b] discusses the role of elimination trees in sparse factorization in detail.

Solving triangular systems involves very few computations compared to factorization. Moreover, the process has limited parallelism. Therefore, the prospects for developing efficient parallel implementations of this phase are bleak. Solving sparse triangular systems of linear equations is discussed by Alvarado, Pothen, and Schreiber [APS92], Anderson and Saad [AS89], and Alvarado and Pothen [AS93].

In Section 11.4, we concentrated mainly on direct methods for solving sparse linear systems involving unstructured sparse matrices of coefficients. There are systems of practical importance in which the matrix of coefficients has a special structure. Notable among such systems are tridiagonal, block-tridiagonal, and banded systems. Parallel algorithms for solving tridiagonal systems have been described by Stone [Sto73,

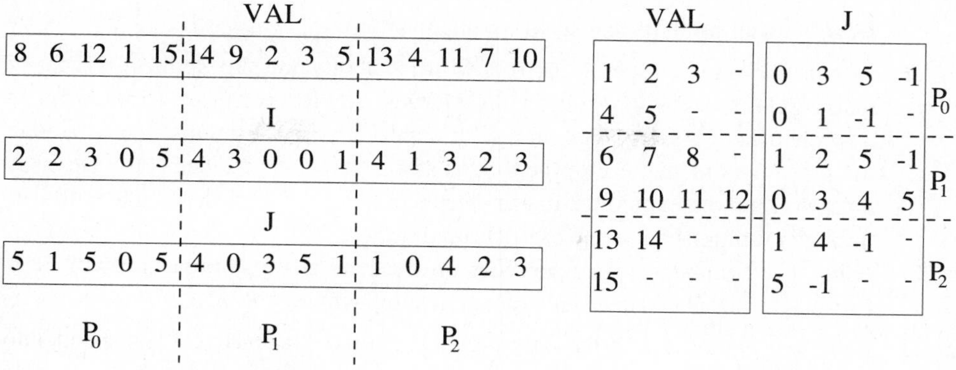

(a) A sparse matrix in coordinate format

(b) The matrix in Ellpack-Itpack format

Figure 11.29 A 6×6 sparse matrix stored in the coordinate format and the Ellpack-Itpack format.

Sto75], van der Vorst [vdV87b], and Wang [Wan81]. Parallel banded systems are discussed by Cleary [Cle89], Dongarra and Johnsson [DJ87], Johnsson [Joh85], Lawrie and Sameh [LS84], and Meier [Mei85].

Despite the best research efforts, there are still gaps in the current understanding of parallel sparse factorization. Most of the research up to the time of this writing has been empirical, and very few efforts to theoretically analyze the scalability and available parallelism of sparse direct methods have been made [Sch92, Wor91].

Multigrid techniques are gaining some popularity for solving linear systems. A few texts, such as those by Briggs [Bri87] and Hackbrush [Hac85], provide excellent discussions on multigrid methods. Bertsekas and Tsitsiklis [BT89], Fox et al. [FJL$^+$88], and Golub and Ortega [GO93] present parallelization techniques for the multigrid method. Chan and Saad [CS86], and Chan and Tuminaro [CT87] describe parallel implementations of multigrid algorithms on hypercubes. Chan and Schreiber [CS85] also address some issues in parallel multigrid algorithms.

Problems

11.1 Consider an unstructured sparse matrix stored in the coordinate format and partitioned uniformly among p processors as shown in Figure 11.29(a). Assuming that the underlying architecture is a hypercube with cut-though routing, give an expression for the time spent in communication to have the original matrix uniformly distributed among the processors in Ellpack-Itpack format as shown in Figure 11.29(b). Assume that the size of the matrix is $n \times n$, the total number of nonzero elements is q, and the number of processors is p. Describe algorithms for conversion between the two forms shown in Figures 11.29(a) and (b).

Hint: Use all-to-all personalized communication.

11.2 Assume that an $n \times n$ sparse matrix A with a total of q nonzero elements is mapped onto p processors as shown in Figure 11.29(a), so that each processor is assigned q/p elements. Assume that an $n \times 1$ vector x is uniformly distributed among the processors so that each processor is assigned n/p of its elements. Describe an algorithm to compute the matrix-vector product Ax on a hypercube with cut-through routing. What is the parallel run time?
Hint: The communication operations involved are all-to-all broadcast with $m \leq n/p$ and all-to-all personalized communication with $m \leq n/p^2$.

11.3 Refer to Problem 11.2. What is the parallel run time if the matrix A is mapped onto the processors as shown in Figure 11.29(b), so that each processor is responsible for n/p rows of the matrix? Compare this time with that obtained in Problem 11.2. What could be a possible advantage of using the coordinate format over the Ellpack-Itpack format?

11.4 Derive an expression for the parallel execution time of matrix-vector multiplication involving an $n \times n$ unstructured sparse matrix uniformly block-checkerboarded on a p-processor hypercube. Use the expected value of the maximum computation time as the effective computation time of all the processors. This time accounts for the idle time of all the processors other than the one that has the maximum amount of work. Assume a random distribution of nonzero elements among the rows of the matrix such that the average number of nonzeros per row is m.
Hint: **[KW85]** If there are r independent tasks with a mean completion time of μ and a standard deviation of σ, and if they are assigned to p processors such that each processor gets r/p tasks, then the expected completion time for the processor with the maximum load is $r\mu/p + \sigma\sqrt{2(r/p)\log p}$, provided that r is large compared to $p \log p$. In the problem at hand, $r = n^2$. The values of μ and σ can be computed as follows: Each of the elements of the $n \times n$ matrix can be considered equivalent to a task that takes zero time if the element is zero and t_c time if the element is nonzero. Since the fraction of the elements that are nonzero is $mn/n^2 = m/n$, the expected value of the completion time of any task is

$$\mu = t_c m/n.$$

The standard deviation is

$$\sigma = \sqrt{\frac{\Sigma_{i=1}^{n^2}(t_c x_i - \mu)^2}{n^2}},$$

where $x_i = 0$ if the ith (out of n^2) element of the matrix is zero, and $x_i = 1$ if the ith element is nonzero. Since the number of nonzero elements is mn and the number of zeros is $n^2 - mn$, we have

$$\sigma = t_c\sqrt{\frac{mn(1 - \frac{m}{n})^2 + (n^2 - mn)(\frac{m}{n})^2}{n^2}}$$

$$= t_c \sqrt{\frac{m(1 + (\frac{m}{n})^2 - 2\frac{m}{n}) + (n - m)(\frac{m}{n})^2}{n}}$$

$$= t_c \sqrt{\frac{m}{n} - (\frac{m}{n})^2}.$$

11.5 Repeat Problem 11.4 for the case in which the matrix is mapped onto a p-processor hypercube by using block-striped partitioning.

11.6 Assuming that $q = mn$, compare the parallel execution times obtained in Problems 11.2 and 11.5. Use the comparison to determine the situations in which the coordinate format (Figure 11.29(a)) is preferable over the Ellpack-Itpack format (Figure 11.29(b)) and vice versa.

11.7 Rewrite Equation 11.2 for an $l_1 \times l_2$ finite difference grid. Describe the structure of the block-tridiagonal coefficient matrix corresponding to the system of equations resulting from this finite difference grid.

11.8 Consider the multiplication of the matrix shown in Figure 11.12(a) with a 16×1 vector using four processors. For the mapping of rows onto processors as shown in the figure, what is the parallel run time of an optimal algorithm in terms of t_c (time to perform one multiplication and one addition), t_s, and t_w? How does this time compare with the run times of the other two mappings given in Section 11.1.3 (Equations 11.8 and 11.9).

11.9 Consider a parallel implementation of unstructured sparse matrix-vector multiplication based on partitioning the graph associated with the matrix as shown in Figure 11.12. Assume that (1) the $n \times n$ matrix has an average of m nonzero elements in each row and that the graph associated with the matrix is a planar graph partitioned uniformly among p processors; (2) in a typical partition of the graph, the number of nodes lying along the partition boundary (that is, the nodes with incident edges that cross the partition boundary) is of the order of the square root of the total number of nodes in the partition; and (3) each partition shares its boundaries with at most c other partitions, where c is a small constant. Derive an expression for the parallel run time of matrix-vector multiplication in order terms. Is the algorithm scalable? If so, derive an expression for the isoefficiency function in order terms.

11.10 Derive an expression for the isoefficiency function for multiplying a banded sparse $n \times n$ matrix with an $n \times 1$ vector by using the mapping shown in Figure 11.13. Assume that a row of the matrix has an average of m nonzero elements distributed uniformly in a band of width w around the principal diagonal of the matrix.

11.11 Derive an expression for the parallel run time on p processors for multiplying a banded unstructured sparse $n \times n$ matrix with an $n \times 1$ vector such that a row of the matrix has an average of m nonzero elements distributed uniformly in a band of width w around the principal diagonal of the matrix. Assume that $m = \alpha n^s$ ($\alpha > 0, 0 \leq s \leq 1$) and $w = \beta n^t$ ($\beta > 0, 0 \leq t \leq 1$). Derive expressions in terms of p, E, t_c, t_s, and t_w for the rate at which n has to increase with p to maintain the efficiency fixed at a value E for the following sets of values for α, β, s, and t:

(a) $\alpha = 5.0, s = 0.0, \beta = 1.0, t = 0.5$
(b) $\alpha = 0.001, s = 0.5, \beta = 1.0, t = 0.5$
(c) $\alpha = 0.001, s = 0.5, \beta = 1.0, t = 1.0$
(d) $\alpha = 0.001, s = 1.0, \beta = 1.0, t = 1.0$
(e) $\alpha = 0.001, s = 1.0, \beta = 1.0, t = 0.5$

11.12 Derive an expression for the isoefficiency function for the multiplication of an $n \times n$ block-tridiagonal matrix of the form shown in Figure 11.7 with an $n \times 1$ vector on a p-processor hypercube with the data mapping shown in Figure 11.9. Treat the cases $p > \sqrt{n}$ and $p \leq \sqrt{n}$ separately.

11.13 Show that a Gauss-Seidel iteration requires at least $2\sqrt{n} - 1$ sequential steps for a block-tridiagonal matrix derived from a $\sqrt{n} \times \sqrt{n}$ finite difference grid of the form shown in Figure 11.8. Show that, in the kth iteration, the computation of Equation 11.18 can be used to compute $x_k[i]$ for at most $\sqrt{n}$ values of i in parallel.

11.14 Give optimal partitionings of the grid shown in Figure 11.15 for the Gauss-Seidel algorithm on a four- and a 16-processor mesh with store-and-forward routing. Do any of the mappings change if the architecture is a hypercube or a mesh with cut-through routing?

11.15 Consider an $\sqrt{n} \times \sqrt{n}$ finite element graph of the type shown in Figure 11.15. Given an $\sqrt{p} \times \sqrt{p}$ mesh of processors, give an optimal partitioning for Gauss-Seidel algorithm. Disregarding the time spent in testing for convergence, what is the parallel run time of each iteration?

11.16 **[KS84b]** Consider the relationship $D = \tilde{D} + \text{diag}(L\tilde{D}^{-1}L^T)$, where the diagonal matrix D and the strictly lower-triangular matrix L are known. Derive a recurrence relation to determine the nonzero entries $\tilde{D}[i, i]$ of the unknown diagonal matrix $\tilde{D}$.

11.17 Derive the isoefficiency functions for an iteration of the PCG algorithm with a diagonal preconditioner for the hypercube and mesh architectures. Take the expressions for parallel run times for these architectures from Equations 11.26 and 11.27, respectively. Do the asymptotic isoefficiency functions change if the overhead due to vector inner-product computation is ignored (that is, if the expression for the parallel run time is taken from Equation 11.28)?

11.18 Show that, for an $n \times n$ matrix A derived from a finite difference grid partitioned among the processors as shown in Figure 11.10, the time to perform the step of Equation 11.18 in parallel is exactly equal to the parallel run time for solving $Mz_k = r_k$, where M is the preconditioner matrix derived from a no-fill incomplete Cholesky factorization of A.

11.19 Assume that $n = 65536$, $t_c^{'} = 10$, $t_c = t_w = 1$, and $t_s = 40$. Disregarding the $3t_s \log p$ term in Equation 11.26, plot T_P versus p curves for Equations 11.26, 11.31, 11.32, and 11.33. How does the value of τ effect the parallel run time, speedup, and isoefficiency function of an iteration of the PCG algorithm with a truncated IC preconditioner?

11.20 Show that a banded unstructured sparse matrix of bandwidth $w_1 + w_2 - 1$ results from the multiplication of two $n \times n$ banded unstructured sparse matrices with their nonzero elements distributed within bands of width w_1 and w_2 along their respective principal diagonals.

11.21 In Problem 11.20, assume that the average number of nonzero elements per row in the two matrices to be multiplied is m_1 and m_2, respectively. Show that the average number of nonzero elements per row in the product matrix is approximately $m_1 m_2$. Assume that n is large, $m_1 \ll w_1$, and $m_2 \ll w_2$.

11.22 Show that the sparse matrix of Figure 11.22(b) satisfies the criterion of minimum-degree ordering.

11.23 Reorder the sparse matrix shown in Figure 11.22(b) according to a different minimum-degree tie-breaking criterion. If, at any stage, there are multiple rows with the same cost, choose the one with the highest index. Which matrix has a higher fill-in, the one shown in Figure 11.22(b), or the one derived in this problem?

11.24 Plot the sparsity pattern of the coefficient matrix resulting from the nested-dissection ordering of a 7×7 finite difference grid of the form shown in Figure 11.8.

11.25 Reorder the sparse matrix of Problem 11.24 using minimum-degree ordering. To break ties, choose a row with the smallest index.

11.26 Reorder the sparse matrix of Problem 11.24 using a natural ordering and a red-black ordering of grid points.

11.27 Plot the locations of fill-in upon factorization in all the four sparse matrices in Problems 11.24–11.26. Which of these leads to maximum fill-in?

11.28 Draw the elimination trees for the four sparse matrices of Problems 11.24–11.26. Which of these results in maximum parallelism?

11.29 Reorder the sparse matrix of Problem 11.24 using minimum-degree ordering. To break ties, choose the row with the highest index. Plot the locations of fill-in upon factorization of the resulting matrix. Also draw the corresponding elimination tree. Does the tie-breaking strategy of minimum-degree ordering affect fill-in? Does it affect the degree of parallelism in numerical factorization?

11.30 Derive an expression for the isoefficiency function of the multigrid computation described in Section 11.5 for a mesh-connected parallel computer with cut-through routing. Assume that there is no overhead due to global sum computations and that the number of processors is equal to the number of elements in the coarsest discretization. What is the isoefficiency function in the absence of this assumption?

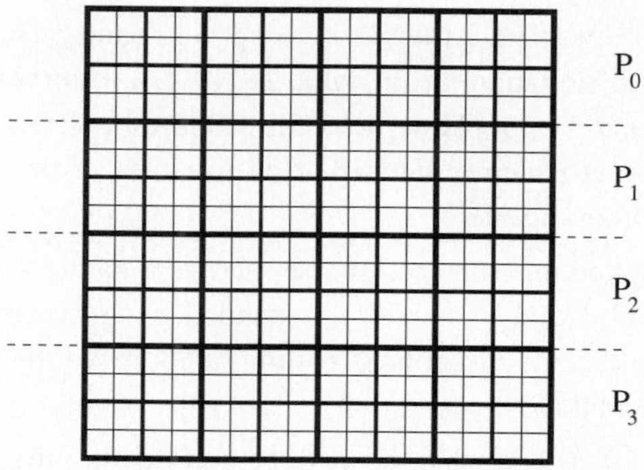

Figure 11.30 A domain with three levels of discretization stripe-partitioned among four processors of a linear array.

11.31 Derive an expression for the parallel run time and the isoefficiency function for performing the multigrid computation described in Section 11.5 on a hypercube. Assume that there is no overhead due to global sum computations, and the number of processors is equal to the number of elements in the coarsest discretization.

11.32 Show that the isoefficiency function of a multigrid computation on a mesh with cut-through routing in the absence of any overhead due to inner-product computations is linear in p, even if the number of processors is greater than the number of elements in the coarsest discretization.

Hint: Show that the total overhead due to processor idling is $\Theta(p)$.

11.33 Consider the multigrid algorithm for a square domain with discretizations G_0, G_1, ..., G_m. The finest discretization G_m has n elements, and the number of elements reduces by a factor of four in each successively coarser discretization. The domain is partitioned into stripes and distributed on a p-processor linear array as illustrated in Figure 11.30 for $m = 2$, $n = 256$, and $p = 4$. Derive expressions for the parallel run time and the isoefficiency function for this parallel implementation of the multigrid method under the assumptions of Section 11.5. For simplicity, assume that the number of processors is less than or equal to $\sqrt{n}/2^m$, so that there is no idling and so that communication always takes place among directly-connected processors in the linear array.

References

[AAIT89] D. Amitai, A. Averbuch, S. Itzikowitz, and E. Turkel. Asynchronous numerical solution of PDEs on parallel computers. In *Proceedings of the Fourth SIAM Conference on Parallel Processing for Scientific Computing*, 131–136, 1989.

[AEL90a] C. Ashcraft, S. C. Eisenstat, and J. W.-H. Liu. A fan-in algorithm for distributed sparse numerical factorization. *SIAM Journal on Scientific and Statistical Computing*, 11:593–599, 1990.

[AEL+90b] C. Ashcraft, S. C. Eisenstat, J. W.-H. Liu, B. W. Peyton, and A. H. Sherman. A compute-ahead implementation of the fan-in sparse distributed factorization scheme. Technical Report ORNL/TM-11496, Oak Ridge National Laboratory, Oak Ridge, TN, 1990.

[AELS90] C. Ashcraft, S. C. Eisenstat, J. W.-H. Liu, and A. H. Sherman. A comparison of three column based distributed sparse factorization schemes. Technical Report YALEU/DCS/RR-810, Yale University, New Haven, CT, 1990. Also appears in *Proceedings of the Fifth SIAM Conference on Parallel Processing for Scientific Computing*, 1991.

[AJ85] G. Alaghband and H. Jordan. Multiprocessor sparse L/U decomposition with controlled fill-in. Technical Report 85-48, ICASE, NASA Langley Research Center, Hampton, VA, 1985.

[Ala89] G. Alaghband. Parallel pivoting combined with parallel reduction and fill-in control. *Parallel Computing*, 11:201–221, 1989.

[And88] E. Anderson. Parallel implementation of preconditioned conjugate gradient methods for solving sparse systems of linear equations. Technical Report 805, CSRD, University of Illinois at Urbana, Urbana, IL, 1988.

[AO82] L. M. Adams and J. M. Ortega. A multi-color SOR method for parallel computation. In *Proceedings of the 1982 International Conference on Parallel Processing*, 53–56, 1982.

[AOES88] C. Aykanat, F. Ozguner, F. Ercal, and P. Sadayappan. Iterative algorithms for solution of large sparse systems of linear equations on hypercubes. *IEEE Transactions on Computers*, 37(12):1554–1567, 1988.

[APS92] F. L. Alvarado, A. Pothen, and R. Schreiber. Highly parallel sparse triangular solution. Technical Report RIACS TR 92.11, NASA Ames Research Center, Moffet Field, CA, May 1992. Also appears in J. A. George, John R. Gilbert, and J. W.-H. Liu, editors, *Sparse Matrix Computations: Graph Theory Issues and Algorithms* (An IMA Workshop Volume). Springer-Verlag, New York, NY, 1992.

[AS89] E. Anderson and Y. Saad. Solving sparse triangular linear systems on parallel computers. *International Journal of High Speed Computing*, 1:73–96, 1989.

[AS93] F. L. Alvarado and R. Schreiber. Optimal parallel solution of sparse triangular systems. *SIAM Journal on Scientific and Statistical Computing*, 14:446–460, 1993.

[BB87] M. J. Berger and S. H. Bokhari. Partitioning strategy for nonuniform problems on multiprocessors. *IEEE Transactions on Computers*, C-36(5):570–580, 1987.

[BDK+89] J. Browne, J. J. Dongarra, A. H. Karp, K. Kennedy, and D. J. Kuck. 1988 Gordon Bell prize (special report). *IEEE Software*, May 1989.

[BEP93] F. Bodin, J. Erthel, and T. Priol. Parallel sparse matrix by vector multiplication using a shared virtual memory environment. In *Proceedings of the Sixth SIAM Conference on Parallel Processing for Scientific Computing*, 421–428, 1993.

[Bri87] W. L. Briggs. *A Multigrid Tutorial*. SIAM, Philadelphia, PA, 1987.

[BS89] R. Bramley and A. H. Sameh. Parallel row projection algorithms for nonsymmetric systems. In *Proceedings of the Fourth SIAM Conference on Parallel Processing for Scientific Computing*, 60–62, 1989.

[BT89] D. P. Bertsekas and J. N. Tsitsiklis. *Parallel and Distributed Computation: Numerical Methods*. Prentice-Hall, Englewood Cliffs, NJ, 1989.

[CG89] A. T. Chronopoulos and C. W. Gear. On the efficient implementation of preconditioned s-step conjugate gradient methods on multiprocessors with memory hierarchy. *Parallel Computing*, 11:37–53, 1989.

[CGLN84] E. Chu, J. A. George, J. W.-H. Liu, and E. G.-Y. Ng. Users guide for SPARSPAK–A: Waterloo sparse linear equations package. Technical Report CS-84-36, University of Waterloo, Waterloo, IA, 1984.

[Cle89] A. Cleary. *Algorithms for solving narrowly banded linear systems on parallel computers by direct methods*. Ph.D. thesis, Applied Mathematics, University of Virginia, Charlottesville, VA, 1989.

[Con86] J. M. Conroy. Parallel direct solution of sparse linear system of equations. Technical Report TR1714, University of Maryland, College Park, MD, 1986.

[Con90] J. M. Conroy. Parallel nested dissection. *Parallel Computing*, 16:139–156, 1990.

[CR92] Y.-C. Chung and S. Ranka. Mapping finite element graphs on hypercubes. *Journal of Supercomputing*, 6:257–282, 1992.

[CS85] T. F. Chan and R. Schreiber. Parallel networks for multigrid algorithms: Architecture and complexity. *SIAM Journal on Scientific and Statistical Computing*, 6:698–711, 1985.

[CS86] T. F. Chan and Y. Saad. Multigrid algorithms on the hypercube multiprocessor. *IEEE Transactions on Computers*, C-35:969–977, 1986.

[CS93a] R. Cook and J. Sadecki. Sparse matrix vector multiplication. Technical report, Center for Mathematical Software Research, University of Liverpool, UK, 1993.

[CS93b] R. Cook and J. Sadecki. Sparse matrix vector product on distributed-memory MIMD architectures. In *Proceedings of the Sixth SIAM Conference on Parallel Processing for Scientific Computing*, 429–436, 1993.

[CT87] T. F. Chan and R. S. Tuminaro. Implementation of multigrid algorithms on hypercubes. In M. T. Heath, editor, *Hypercube Multiprocessors 1987*. SIAM, Philadelphia, PA, 1987.

[DDSvdV91] J. J. Dongarra, I. S. Duff, D. C. Sorensen, and H. A. van der Vorst. *Solving Linear Systems on Vector and Shared Memory Computers*. SIAM, Philadelphia, PA, 1991.

[DER90] I. S. Duff, M. Erisman, and J. K. Reid. *Direct Methods for Sparse Matrices*. Oxford University Press, Oxford, UK, 1990.

[DER93] E. D'Azevedo, V. Eijkhout, and C. H. Romine. A matrix framework for conjugate gradient methods and some variants of CG with less synchronization overhead. In *Proceedings of the Sixth SIAM Conference on Parallel Processing for Scientific Computing*, 644–646, 1993.

[DJ87] J. J. Dongarra and S. L. Johnsson. Solving banded systems on a parallel processor. *Parallel Computing*, 5:219–246, 1987.

[DM91] E. M. Daoudi and P. Manneback. Parallel ICCG algorithm on distributed-memory architecture. In *Proceedings of the Fifth SIAM Conference on Parallel Processing for Scientific Computing*, 78–83, 1991.

[DR83] I. S. Duff and J. K. Reid. The multifrontal solution of indefinite sparse symmetric linear equations. *ACM Transactions on Mathematical Software*, 9:302–325, 1983.

[DR92] E. D'Azevedo and C. H. Romine. Reducing communication costs in the conjugate gradient algorithm on distributed-memory multiprocessors. Technical Report ORNL/TM-12192, Oak Ridge National Laboratory, Oak Ridge, TN, 1992.

[Duf86] I. S. Duff. Parallel implementation of multifrontal schemes. *Parallel Computing*, 3:193–204, 1986.

[FJL+88] G. C. Fox, M. Johnson, G. Lyzenga, S. W. Otto, J. Salmon, and D. Walker. *Solving Problems on Concurrent Processors: Volume 1*. Prentice-Hall, Englewood Cliffs, NJ, 1988.

[FPW93] W. Ferng, S. G. Petiton, and K. Wu. Basic sparse matrix computations on data parallel computers. In *Proceedings of the Sixth SIAM Conference on Parallel Processing for Scientific Computing*, 462–466, 1993.

[FWPS92] W. Ferng, K. Wu, S. G. Petiton, and Y. Saad. Basic sparse matrix computations on massively parallel computers. Technical Report 92-084, Army High Performance Computing Research Center, University of Minnesota, Minneapolis, MN, 1992.

[Gei87] G. A. Geist. Solving finite element problems with parallel multifrontal schemes. In M. T. Heath, editor, *Hypercube Multiprocessors, 1987*, 656–661. SIAM, Philadelphia, PA, 1987.

[GH90] J. R. Gilbert and H. Hafsteinsson. Parallel symbolic factorization of sparse linear systems. *Parallel Computing*, 14:151–162, 1990.

[GHLN87] J. A. George, M. T. Heath, J. W.-H. Liu, and E. G.-Y. Ng. Symbolic Cholesky factorization on a local memory multiprocessor. *Parallel Computing*, 5:85–95, 1987.

[GHLN88] J. A. George, M. T. Heath, J. W.-H. Liu, and E. G.-Y. Ng. Sparse Cholesky factorization on a local memory multiprocessor. *SIAM Journal on Scientific and Statistical Computing*, 9:327–340, 1988.

[GHLN89] J. A. George, M. T. Heath, J. W.-H. Liu, and E. G.-Y. Ng. Solution of sparse positive definite systems on a hypercube. *Journal of Computational and Applied Mathematics*, 27:129–156, 1989. Also available as Technical Report ORNL/TM-10865, Oak Ridge National Laboratory, Oak Ridge, TN, 1988.

[GK92] A. Grama and V. Kumar. Scalability analysis of partitioning strategies for finite element graphs. In *Supercomputing '92 Proceedings*, 83–92, 1992.

[GKS92] A. Gupta, V. Kumar, and A. H. Sameh. Performance and scalability of preconditioned conjugate gradient methods on parallel computers. Technical Report TR 92-64, Department of Computer Science, University of Minnesota, Minneapolis, MN, 1992. A short version appears in *Proceedings of the Sixth SIAM Conference on Parallel Processing for Scientific Computing*, pages 664–674, 1993.

[GL81] J. A. George and J. W.-H. Liu. *Computer Solution of Large Sparse Positive Definite Systems*. Prentice-Hall, Englewood Cliffs, NJ, 1981.

[GL89a] J. A. George and J. W.-H. Liu. The evolution of the minimum degree ordering algorithm. *SIAM Review*, 31(1):1–19, March 1989.

[GL89b] G. H. Golub and C. V. Loan. *Matrix Computations: Second Edition*. The Johns Hopkins University Press, Baltimore, MD, 1989.

[GLN89] J. A. George, J. W.-H. Liu, and E. G.-Y. Ng. Communication results for parallel sparse Cholesky factorization on a hypercube. *Parallel Computing*, 10(3):287–298, May 1989.

[GN89] G. A. Geist and E. G.-Y. Ng. Task scheduling for parallel sparse Cholesky factorization. *International Journal of Parallel Programming*, 18(4):291–314, 1989.

[GO93] G. H. Golub and J. M. Ortega. *Scientific Computing: An Introduction with Parallel Computing*. Academic Press, Boston, MA, 1993.

[GS92] J. R. Gilbert and R. Schreiber. Highly parallel sparse Cholesky factorization. *SIAM Journal on Scientific and Statistical Computing*, 13:1151–1172, 1992.

[Hac85] W. Hackbrush. *Multigrid Methods with Applications*. Springer-Verlag, New York, NY, 1985.

[Ham92] S. W. Hammond. Mapping unstructured grid computations to massively parallel computers. Technical Report RIACS TR 92.14, NASA Ames Research Center, Moffet Field, CA, 1992.

[HNP91] M. T. Heath, E. G.-Y. Ng, and B. W. Peyton. Parallel algorithms for sparse linear systems. *SIAM Review*, 33:420–460, 1991. Also appears in K. A. Gallivan et al. *Parallel Algorithms for Matrix Computations*. SIAM, Philadelphia, PA, 1990.

[HR92] M. T. Heath and P. Raghavan. A Cartesian nested dissection algorithm. Technical Report 92-1772, Department of Computer Science, University of Illinois, Urbana, IL, 1992. To appear in *SIAM Journal on Matrix Analysis and Applications*, 1994.

[HR93] M. T. Heath and P. Raghavan. Distributed solution of sparse linear systems. Technical Report 93-1793, Department of Computer Science, University of Illinois, Urbana, IL, 1993.

[HS92] S. W. Hammond and R. Schreiber. Efficient ICCG on a shared-memory multiprocessor. *International Journal of High Speed Computing*, 4(1):1–22, March 1992.

[JK82] J. Jess and H. Kees. A data structure for parallel L/U decomposition. *IEEE Transactions on Computers*, C-31:231–239, 1982.

[Joh85] S. L. Johnsson. Solving narrow banded systems on ensemble architectures. *ACM Transactions on Mathematical Software*, 11:271–288, 1985.

[JP92] M. T. Jones and P. E. Plassmann. Scalable iterative solution of sparse linear systems. Technical report, Argonne National Laboratory, Argonne, IL, 1992.

[KC91] S. K. Kim and A. T. Chronopoulos. A class of Lanczos-like algorithms implemented on parallel computers. *Parallel Computing*, 17:763–777, 1991.

[KS84a] C. Kamath and A. H. Sameh. The preconditioned conjugate gradient algorithm on a multiprocessor. In R. Vichnevetsky and R. S. Stepleman, editors, *Advances in Computer Methods for Partial Differential Equations*. IMACS, 1984.

[KS84b] C. Kamath and A. H. Sameh. The preconditioned conjugate gradient algorithm on a multiprocessor. Technical Report ANL/MCS-TM-28, Argonne National Labs, Mathematics and Computer Science Division, Argonne, IL, 1984.

[KW85] C. P. Kruskal and A. Weiss. Allocating independent subtasks on parallel processors. *IEEE Transactions on Software Engineering*, SE-11(10):1001–1016, October 1985.

[KW91] C. Kamath and S. Weeratunga. Projection methods on a distributed-memory MIMD multiprocessor. In *Proceedings of the Fifth SIAM Conference on Parallel Processing for Scientific Computing*, 92–97, 1991.

[Leu89] M. R. Leuze. Independent set orderings for parallel matrix factorization by Gaussian elimination. *Parallel Computing*, 10:177–191, 1989.

[Liu85] J. W.-H. Liu. Modification of the minimum degree algorithm by multiple elimination. *ACM Transactions on Mathematical Software*, 11:141–153, 1985.

[Liu86] J. W.-H. Liu. Computational models and task scheduling for parallel sparse Cholesky factorization. *Parallel Computing*, 3:327–342, 1986.

[Liu89a] J. W.-H. Liu. A linear reordering algorithm for parallel pivoting of chordal graphs. *SIAM Journal on Discrete Mathematics*, 2:100–107, 1989.

[Liu89b] J. W.-H. Liu. Reordering sparse matrices for parallel elimination. *Parallel Computing*, 11:73–91, 1989.

[Liu90a] J. W.-H. Liu. The multifrontal method for sparse matrix solution: Theory and practice. Technical Report CS-90-04, York University, Ontario, Canada, 1990. Also appears in *SIAM Review*, 34:82–109, 1992.

[Liu90b] J. W.-H. Liu. The role of elimination trees in sparse factorization. *SIAM Journal on Matrix Analysis and Applications*, 11:134–172, 1990.

[LL87] C. E. Leiserson and T. G. Lewis. Orderings for parallel sparse symmetric factorization. In *Proceedings of the Third SIAM Conference on Parallel Processing for Scientific Computing*, 27–32, 1987.

[LPP89] T. G. Lewis, B. W. Peyton, and A. Pothen. A fast algorithm for reordering sparse matrices for parallel factorization. *SIAM Journal on Scientific and Statistical Computing*, 10:1146–1173, 1989.

[LR88] R. W. Leland and J. S. Rolett. Evaluation of parallel conjugate gradient algorithm. In K. W. Morton and M. J. Baines, editors, *Numerical Methods in Fluid Dynamics III*, 478–483. Oxford University Press, Oxford, UK, 1988.

[LS84] D. H. Lawrie and A. H. Sameh. The computation and communication complexity of a parallel banded system solver. *ACM Transactions on Mathematical Software*, 10:185–195, 1984.

[Luc87] R. Lucas. *Solving planar systems of equations on distributed-memory multiprocessors*. Ph.D. thesis, Department of Electrical Engineering, Stanford University, Palo Alto, CA, 1987. Also see *IEEE Transactions on Computer Aided Design*, 6:981–991, 1987.

[Mei85] U. Meier. A parallel partition method for solving banded systems of linear equations. *Parallel Computing*, 2:33–43, 1985.

[MG87] R. Melhem and D. B. Gannon. Toward efficient implementation of preconditioned conjugate gradient methods on vector supercomputers. *International Journal of Supercomputing Applications*, I(1):70–97, 1987.

[MO87] R. Morrison and S. W. Otto. The scattered decomposition for finite elements. *Journal of Scientific Computing*, 2(1), March 1987.

[NS90] D. M. Nicol and J. H. Saltz. An analysis of scatter decomposition. *IEEE Transactions on Computers*, 39:1337–1345, November 1990.

[Par80] B. N. Parlett. *The Symmetric Eigenvalue Problem*. Prentice-Hall, Englewood Cliffs, NJ, 1980.

[PCF+91] J. W. Parker, T. Cwik, R. Ferraro, P. Liewer, P. Lyster, and J. Patterson. Helmholtz finite elements performance on Mark III and Intel iPSC/860 hypercubes. In *The Sixth Distributed Memory Computing Conference Proceedings*, 1991.

[Pet84] F. Peters. Parallel pivoting algorithms for sparse symmetric matrices. *Parallel Computing*, 1:99–110, 1984.

[Pet91] S. G. Petiton. Massively parallel sparse matrix computation for iterative methods. Technical Report YALEU/DCS/878, Yale University, Department of Computer Science, New Haven, CT, 1991.

[PS91] A. Pothen and C. Sun. Distributed multifrontal factorization using clique trees. In *Proceedings of the Fifth SIAM Conference on Parallel Processing for Scientific Computing*, 34–40, 1991.

[PS93] R. Pozo and S. L. Smith. Performance evaluation of the parallel multifrontal method in a distributed-memory environment. In *Proceedings of the Sixth SIAM Conference on Parallel Processing for Scientific Computing*, 453–456, 1993.

[PSL90] A. Pothen, H. D. Simon, and K.-P. Liou. Partioning sparce matrices with eigenvectors of graphs. *SIAM Journal of Mathematical Analysis and Applications*, 11(3):430–452, 1990.

[PSWB92] A. Pothen, H. D. Simon, L. Wang, and S. T. Bernard. Towards a fast implementation of spectral nested dissection. In *Supercomputing '92 Proceedings*, 42–51, 1992.

[PWD91] S. G. Petiton and C. Weill-Duflos. Very sparse preconditioned conjugate gradient on massively parallel architectures. In *Proceedings of the 13th World Congress on Computation and Applied Mathematics*, 1991.

[Rag93a] P. Raghavan. Distributed sparse Gaussian elimination and orthogonal factorization. Technical Report 93-1818, Department of Computer Science, University of Illinois, Urbana, IL, 1993.

[Rag93b] P. Raghavan. Line and plane separators. Technical Report 93-1794, Department of Computer Science, University of Illinois, Urbana, IL, 1993.

[Saa90] Y. Saad. SPARSKIT: A basic tool kit for sparse matrix computations. Technical Report 90-20, Research Institute for Advanced Computer Science, NASA Ames Research Center, Moffet Field, CA, 1990.

[SBB+87] K. Schwan, W. Bo, N. Bauman, P. Sadayappan, and F. Ercal. Mapping parallel applications to a hypercube. In M. T. Heath, editor, *Hypercube Multiprocessors 1987*, 141–151. SIAM, Philadelphia, PA, 1987.

[Sch92] R. Schreiber. Scalability of sparse direct solvers. Technical Report RIACS TR 92.13, NASA Ames Research Center, Moffet Field, CA, May 1992. Also appears in J. A. George, John R. Gilbert, and J. W.-H. Liu, editors, *Sparse Matrix Computations: Graph Theory Issues and Algorithms* (An IMA Workshop Volume). Springer-Verlag, New York, NY, 1992.

[SE87] P. Sadayappan and F. Ercal. Mapping of finite element graphs onto processor meshes. *IEEE Transactions on Computers*, C-36:1408–1424, 1987.

[Sim91] H. D. Simon. Partitioning of unstructured problems for parallel processing. *Computing Systems in Engineering*, 2(2/3):135–148, 1991.

[SR89] P. Sadayappan and S. K. Rao. Communication reduction for distributed sparse matrix factorization on a processors mesh. In *Supercomputing '89 Proceedings*, 371–379, 1989.

[SS85] Y. Saad and M. H. Schultz. Parallel implementations of preconditioned conjugate gradient methods. Technical Report YALEU/DCS/RR-425, Yale University, Department of Computer Science, New Haven, CT, 1985.

[Sto73] H. S. Stone. An efficient parallel algorithm for the solution of a tridiagonal linear system of equations. *Journal of the ACM*, 20:27–38, 1973.

[Sto75] H. S. Stone. Parallel tridiagonal equation solvers. *ACM Transactions on Mathematical Software*, 1:289–307, 1975.

[vdV82] H. A. van der Vorst. A vectorizable variant of some ICCG methods. *SIAM Journal on Scientific and Statistical Computing*, III(3):350–356, 1982.

[vdV87a] H. A. van der Vorst. Large tridiagonal and block tridiagonal linear systems on vector and parallel computers. *Parallel Computing*, 5:45–54, 1987.

[vdV87b] H. A. van der Vorst. Large tridiagonal and block tridiagonal linear systems on vector and parallel computers. *Parallel Computing*, 5:45–54, 1987.

[Wan81] H. H. Wang. A parallel method for tridiagonal equations. *ACM Transactions on Mathematical Software*, 7:170–183, 1981.

[Wij89] H. A. G. Wijshoff. Implementing sparse BLAS primitives on concurrent/vector processors: a case study. Technical Report 843, Center for Supercomputing Research and Development, University of Illinois, Urbana, IL, 1989.

[Wil87] W. I. Williams. Load balancing on hypercubes: A preliminary look. In M. T. Heath, editor, *Hypercube Multiprocessors 1987*, 108–113. SIAM, Philadelphia, PA, 1987.

[Wor91] P. H. Worley. Limits on parallelism in the numerical solution of linear PDEs. *SIAM Journal on Scientific and Statistical Computing*, 12:1–35, January 1991.

[ZG88] E. Zmijewski and J. R. Gilbert. A parallel algorithm for sparse symbolic factorization on a multiprocessor. *Parallel Computing*, 7:199–210, 1988.

[Zmi87] E. Zmijewski. *Sparse Cholesky factorization on a multiprocessor*. Ph.D. thesis, Department of Computer Science, Cornell University, Ithaca, NY, 1987.

CHAPTER 12

Systolic Algorithms and their Mapping onto Parallel Computers

Advances in semiconductor technology have made it possible to put a large number of transistors on a single silicon lattice. These Very Large Scale Integrated (VLSI) circuits can be used to implement algorithms directly in hardware. This approach usually yields good performance because the VLSI circuit is customized to a particular algorithm.

A ***systolic system*** is such a combination of an algorithm and an integrated circuit that implements it. A systolic system has a simple and regular design. It consists of a set of interconnected ***cells*** that operate in parallel. This collection of cells is called a ***systolic array***. Each cell performs some operations and contains a small number of registers. These registers are used as temporary memory locations for intermediate computations. The cells of a systolic array are either all of the same type or a mixture of a few different types. Cells can be interconnected in a number of ways. Figure 12.1 illustrates some commonly used systolic interconnection networks. Each cell is connected to a small number of neighboring cells (independent of the total number of cells) in a regular fashion. Because of the regularity of the interconnection patterns, systolic systems are easy to design and manufacture. The algorithm implemented by a systolic system is referred to as a ***systolic algorithm***.

A systolic array is connected to an external memory that stores both input data and results. Figure 12.2 shows a schematic diagram of how a systolic array is connected to external memory. Only the cells at the boundaries of the systolic array are connected to external memory. In a systolic system, data elements flow from external memory in a rhythmic fashion, passing through many cells before the results return to external memory. Upon receiving data elements, each cell performs some computations and transmits the

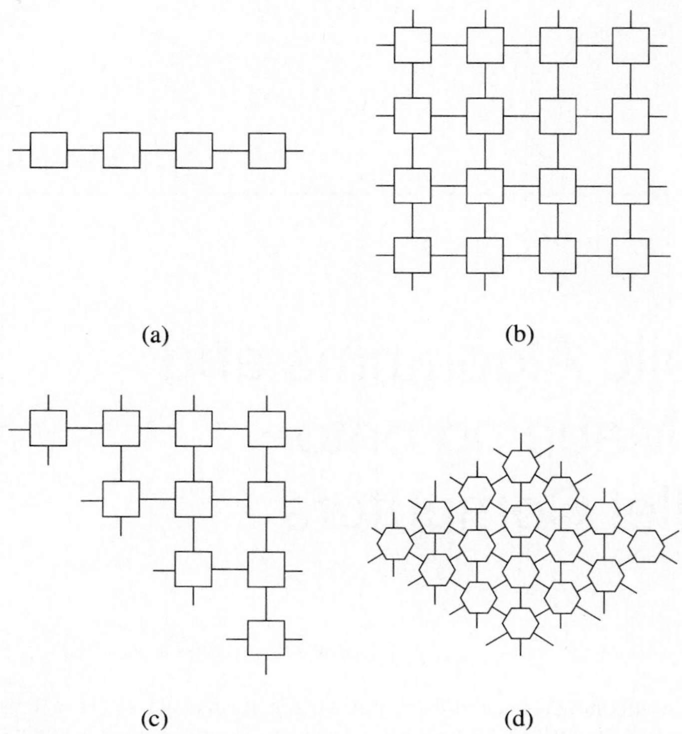

Figure 12.1 Various cell interconnection patterns in systolic arrays: (a) one-dimensional (linear), (b) two-dimensional (rectangular), (c) triangular, and (d) hexagonal.

data to adjacent processors. Intermediate results and data may flow in a systolic system at different speeds and in multiple directions.

Computations in a systolic system are performed synchronously. That is, every systolic algorithm consists of a well-defined sequence of time steps during which specific computations and data transfers are performed. These time steps are called ***systolic clock cycles*** or ***systolic cycles*** for short. If we treat a systolic system as a parallel computer, we can analyze its performance by using the metrics developed in Chapter 4. The number of cells in a systolic array is the number of processors. The ***cell-time product*** is equivalent to the processor-time product for systolic systems.

Systolic systems have been designed for a wide range of applications including signal and image filtering, matrix computations, graph algorithms, language recognition, dynamic programming, and relational database operations. Since systolic algorithms require regular interconnections and nearest-neighbor communication, it is possible to map them onto general-purpose parallel computers. Studying the mapping of systolic algorithms onto general-purpose parallel computers is important because systolic algorithms may be the

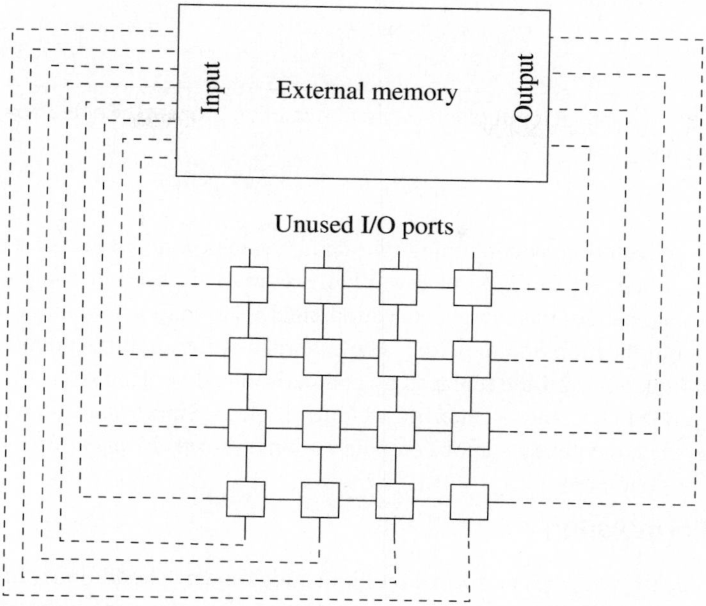

Figure 12.2 Connecting a systolic array to the external memory.

only known, or the best-known way to solve some problems in parallel. By mapping them onto general-purpose parallel computers, we can avoid designing new parallel algorithms. In fact, some of the algorithms presented earlier in this book are mappings of systolic algorithms onto parallel computers. For example, the pipelined version of Floyd's all-pairs shortest-path algorithm (Section 7.4.3) is an adaptation of a systolic algorithm.

This chapter briefly introduces systolic systems and presents a number of ways for mapping these systems onto general-purpose parallel computers.

12.1 Examples of Systolic Systems

This section presents examples of representative systolic systems to illustrate the flavor of systolic algorithms.

12.1.1 Convolution

The first problem we consider is that of computing the convolution of a sequence of numbers. One form of the ***convolution*** problem is defined as follows: Given a sequence of weights $w = \langle w_1, w_2, \ldots, w_n \rangle$ and a sequence of numbers $x = \langle x_1, x_2, \ldots, x_m \rangle$, where $m > n$, compute the sequence $y = \langle y_1, y_2, \ldots, y_{m-n+1} \rangle$, such that

$$y_j = x_j w_1 + x_{j+1} w_2 + \ldots + x_{j+n-1} w_n. \tag{12.1}$$

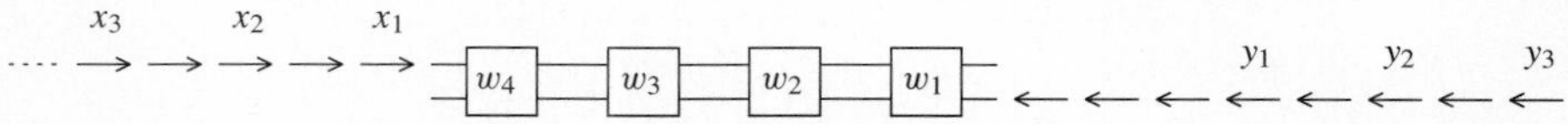

Figure 12.3 A systolic formulation of the convolution problem. Each arrow denotes a single systolic cycle.

We can view convolution as combining two data streams (w and x) in a certain manner to form a single data stream (y). Convolution is commonly used in computations such as signal filtering, pattern matching, correlation, interpolation, polynomial evaluation, and polynomial multiplication and division. For example, if the multiplication and addition operations in Equation 12.1 are replaced by comparison and boolean AND operations, the convolution problem becomes a pattern-matching problem. Since each y_j can be computed in $\Theta(n)$ time, the convolution can be computed in time $\Theta(nm)$ by using Equation 12.1.

Systolic Formulation

To compute each y_j, we must perform n multiplications and $n-1$ additions. In one systolic formulation, each cell in the systolic array computes a product term for different y_j values in each systolic cycle. Consider a sequence of four weights $\langle w_1, w_2, w_3, w_4\rangle$ and a sequence of six numbers $\langle x_1, x_2, \ldots, x_6\rangle$. The systolic array must compute the following:

$$\begin{aligned} y_1 &= x_1w_1 + x_2w_2 + x_3w_3 + x_4w_4 \\ y_2 &= x_2w_1 + x_3w_2 + x_4w_3 + x_5w_4 \\ y_3 &= x_3w_1 + x_4w_2 + x_5w_3 + x_6w_4 \end{aligned}$$

Consider a one-dimensional systolic array that has four cells, c_1, c_2, c_3, and c_4, in which cell c_i stores weight w_i. As the elements of sequence x move along the systolic array, they are multiplied by the elements of w stored in the cells and the results are added to the appropriate elements of y. Since each y_j contains four distinct product terms (involving elements of sequence w) that are computed by different cells, each y_j must move along the systolic array, accumulating these terms. Note that not all possible x_iw_k values are needed. For example, x_1w_1 is the only product term involving x_1.

Since the memory available in each cell is fixed (that is, independent of the input size), the algorithm must ensure that when a cell computes a particular product term $x_{i+j-1}w_i$ the corresponding y_j value also resides in the same cell. This is because $x_{i+j-1}w_i$ must be added to the current value of y_j. If y_j does not reside on the same cell, the $x_{i+j-1}w_i$ term has to be stored in cell c_i. Figure 12.3 illustrates this systolic formulation.

The input sequence x and the output sequence y enter the systolic array at opposite ends. The elements of sequence x are fed into the systolic array at every other systolic cycle, and the elements of sequence y wait three systolic cycles before they start entering the systolic array. Subsequent elements of sequence y enter the systolic array at every other systolic cycle. The elements of y are not read from the external memory but are initialized

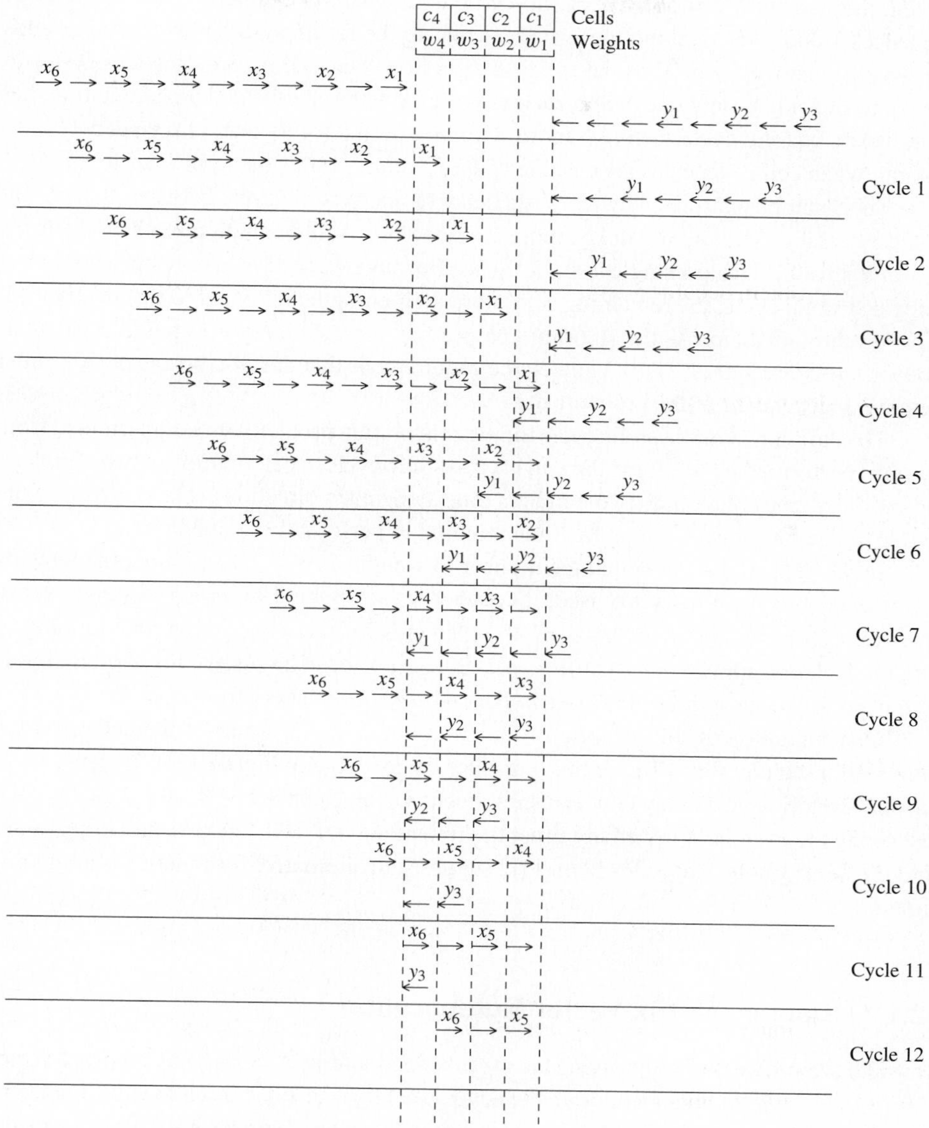

Figure 12.4 The systolic cycles of the systolic formulation of the convolution problem.

to zero. Figure 12.4 shows the computations performed by the systolic system for this example.

Initially, the weights are loaded into the four cells in the order shown in Figure 12.4. During the first three systolic cycles, no computations are performed as the elements of sequences x and y move along the systolic array. In the fourth systolic cycle, cell c_1 adds the term $x_1 w_1$ to y_1. Similarly, in the fifth systolic cycle, cell c_2 adds the term $x_2 w_2$ to y_1. Up to this point, only one cell in each systolic cycle has performed a computation, but in the sixth systolic cycle, cells c_1 and c_3 compute terms for y_2 and y_1, respectively. In general, when cell c_k receives an x_i value and a y_j value, it adds the term $x_i w_k$ to y_j.

This example clarifies why there is a delay of one systolic cycle between subsequent x_i and y_j values. Without the delay, more than one cell would compute product terms for the same y_j value during a single systolic cycle. But since y_j resides in only one cell during a single systolic cycle, the remaining cells store their computed product terms locally until y_j passes through them. As the algorithm progresses, more memory is required since more product terms are stored. This violates the requirement that systolic arrays have limited memory, independent of the problem size.

The duration of one systolic cycle for the convolution problem can be determined from the steps performed by the algorithm. In each systolic cycle, a cell multiplies two numbers, adds two numbers, and sends two numbers (one along each direction). The duration of the systolic cycle must be as long as the time required to perform these operations.

In the general case in which the number of weights is n and the number of elements in sequence x is m, n cells are used. Sequence y lags behind by $n - 1$ systolic cycles. Since the algorithm computes $(m - n + 1)$ elements for sequence y, the total number of systolic cycles is approximately $2(m - n)$. Because n cells are used, this formulation is asymptotically cost-optimal. For $n \ll m$ the cell-time product is $\Theta(nm)$.

One limitation of this systolic formulation is that at most half of the cells perform computations at any time. To see this, consider the example in Figure 12.4. Because there is a one–systolic-cycle delay between subsequent y_j values, no more than $n/2$ such values pass along the systolic array at any time; the remaining $n/2$ cells do not contain y_j values until the next systolic cycle. Problem 12.2 suggests an alternative formulation without this limitation.

12.1.2 Banded Matrix-Vector Multiplication

Consider the problem of multiplying an $n \times n$ banded matrix $A = (a_{i,j})$ by an $n \times 1$ vector $x = [x_1, \ldots, x_n]^T$ to obtain the product vector $y = [y_1, \ldots, y_n]^T$. Recall from Chapter 11 that the nonzero terms of a banded matrix form a band of diagonals on both sides of the main diagonal. The problem of performing the matrix-vector multiplication is illustrated in Figure 12.5.

The ***width*** of the banded matrix A is defined to be $w = r + q - 1$, where r and q are as shown in Figure 12.5. Since computing each y_i element requires at most w multiplications and additions, the overall complexity of the matrix-vector product is $\Theta(nw)$.

$$
\begin{bmatrix}
a_{1,1} & a_{1,2} & \cdots & a_{1,r} & 0 & 0 & 0 \\
a_{2,1} & a_{2,2} & \ddots & \ddots & \ddots & 0 & 0 \\
\vdots & \ddots & \ddots & \ddots & \ddots & \ddots & 0 \\
a_{q,1} & \ddots & \ddots & \ddots & \ddots & \ddots & \ddots \\
0 & \ddots & \ddots & \ddots & \ddots & \ddots & \ddots \\
0 & 0 & \ddots & \ddots & \ddots & \ddots & \ddots
\end{bmatrix}
\begin{bmatrix} x_1 \\ x_2 \\ \vdots \\ x_q \\ \vdots \\ x_n \end{bmatrix}
=
\begin{bmatrix} y_1 \\ y_2 \\ \vdots \\ y_q \\ \vdots \\ y_n \end{bmatrix}
$$

Figure 12.5 Banded matrix-vector multiplication.

Systolic Formulation

Computing each element of the product vector y requires computing and adding at most w product terms of the form $a_{i,j}x_j$. One systolic formulation uses w cells, each of which computes a product term of a different y_i element. Notice the similarity of this approach to the systolic system for the convolution problem described in Section 12.1.1. In fact, we can formulate the convolution problem as a special case of banded matrix-vector multiplication. For example, if the number of weights n is equal to four, and the number of elements m in the sequence x is equal to six, the convolution problem can be formulated as the following banded matrix-vector multiplication:

$$
\begin{bmatrix}
w_1 & w_2 & w_3 & w_4 & 0 & 0 \\
0 & w_1 & w_2 & w_3 & w_4 & 0 \\
0 & 0 & w_1 & w_2 & w_3 & w_4
\end{bmatrix}
\begin{bmatrix} x_1 \\ x_2 \\ x_3 \\ x_4 \\ x_5 \\ x_6 \end{bmatrix}
=
\begin{bmatrix} y_1 \\ y_2 \\ y_3 \end{bmatrix}
$$

The main difference between these two problems is that the weights are the same for all y_i values in the convolution problem; that is, the rows of matrix A contain identical nonzero entries. Entries in two consecutive rows are skewed by a single column. However, the rows of matrix A are different in the general banded matrix-vector multiplication problem. Thus, the systolic formulation for the banded matrix-vector multiplication problem must be able to accommodate different $a_{i,j}$ values.

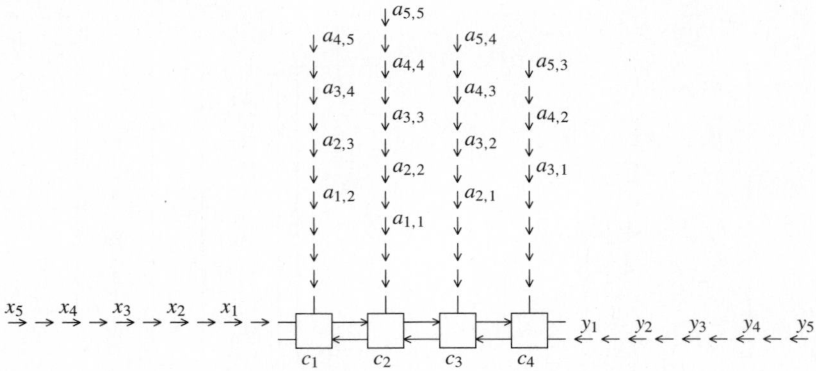

Figure 12.6 The one-dimensional systolic array that computes the banded matrix-vector multiplication for $r = 2$, $q = 3$, and $n = 5$.

Consider the case in which $r = 2$, $q = 3$, and $n = 5$. The banded matrix-vector formulation for this configuration is:

$$\begin{bmatrix} a_{1,1} & a_{1,2} & 0 & 0 & 0 \\ a_{2,1} & a_{2,2} & a_{2,3} & 0 & 0 \\ a_{3,1} & a_{3,2} & a_{3,3} & a_{3,4} & 0 \\ 0 & a_{4,2} & a_{4,3} & a_{4,4} & a_{4,5} \\ 0 & 0 & a_{5,3} & a_{5,4} & a_{5,5} \end{bmatrix} \begin{bmatrix} x_1 \\ x_2 \\ x_3 \\ x_4 \\ x_5 \end{bmatrix} = \begin{bmatrix} y_1 \\ y_2 \\ y_3 \\ y_4 \\ y_5 \end{bmatrix} \tag{12.2}$$

The width of this banded matrix is $w = r + q - 1 = 4$. A systolic system that performs this banded matrix-vector multiplication is shown in Figure 12.6.

The elements of vector y (which are initially zero) move to the left, the elements of vector x move to the right, and the elements of matrix A move down. When a cell contains a y_i, an x_j, and an $a_{i,j}$, it multiplies x_j with $a_{i,j}$ and adds the product to y_i. Each y_i accumulates all its terms—namely $a_{i,i-2}x_{i-2}$, $a_{i,i-1}x_{i-1}$, $a_{i,i}x_i$, and $a_{i,i+1}x_{i+1}$—before it leaves the systolic array. Figure 12.7 illustrates the first seven systolic cycles of the execution of the systolic formulation. Observe that, at any time, alternating cells are idle because there is one systolic cycle delay between successive elements of vectors x and y.

In the general case in which the width of the band is $w = r + q - 1$, w cells are used for banded matrix-vector multiplication. Elements of vector x enter the systolic array after $\max\{q - r, 0\}$ systolic cycles, and elements vector y enter the systolic array after $\max\{r - q, 0\}$ systolic cycles. The elements of matrix A's main diagonal enter cell c_r after $\max\{q - 1, r - 1\}$ systolic cycles. Each adjacent diagonal enters the corresponding cell at subsequent systolic cycles as shown in Figure 12.6. The algorithm terminates when y_n exits the systolic array after approximately $2n$ systolic cycles. Since the cell-time product is $\Theta(nw)$, this systolic formulation is asymptotically cost-optimal.

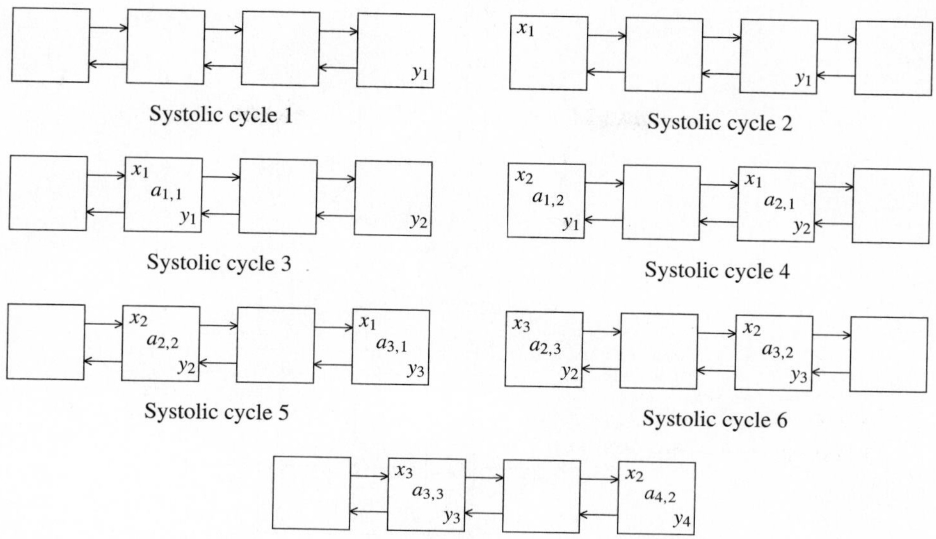

Figure 12.7 The first seven systolic cycles of the systolic formulation of banded matrix-vector multiplication for $r = 2$, $q = 3$, and $n = 5$.

12.1.3 Matrix Multiplication

In the previous two sections we discussed systolic formulations of problems that required one-dimensional systolic arrays. In this and the following section we consider problems that use two-dimensional systolic arrays. Consider the problem of multiplying two $n \times n$ matrices. The product of an $n \times n$ matrix $A = (a_{i,j})$ and an $n \times n$ matrix $B = (b_{i,j})$ is an $n \times n$ matrix $R = (r_{i,j})$ whose elements are given by

$$r_{i,j} = \sum_{k=1}^{n} a_{i,k} b_{k,j}. \tag{12.3}$$

We can compute the product of the two matrices from Equation 12.3 by using Program 5.2. The complexity of multiplying two $n \times n$ matrices is $\Theta(n^3)$.

Systolic Formulation

As mentioned, we use a two-dimensional systolic array to perform matrix multiplication. In particular, we use n^2 cells arranged as an $n \times n$ mesh. Cell $c_{i,j}$ is responsible for computing entry $r_{i,j}$ of the product matrix. To see how this approach works, consider the following recurrences:

$$\begin{aligned} r_{i,j}^{(0)} &= 0 \\ r_{i,j}^{(k)} &= r_{i,j}^{(k-1)} + a_{i,k} b_{k,j} \end{aligned}$$

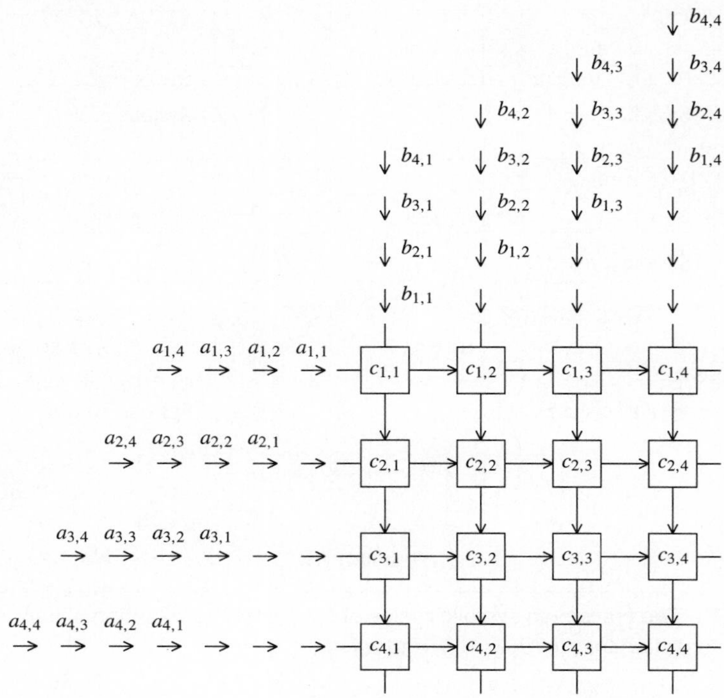

Figure 12.8 The systolic system used for computing the multiplication of two 4×4 matrices A and B.

$$r_{i,j} = r_{i,j}^{(n)}$$

By expressing $r_{i,j}$ as a recurrence relation involving $r_{i,j}^{(k)}$, we see that each cell $c_{i,j}$ must compute $r_{i,j}^{(k)}$ for all values of k. Each cell adds a new product term $a_{i,k}b_{k,j}$ to the previous $r_{i,j}^{(k-1)}$ value. Thus, every cell $c_{i,j}$ initializes $r_{i,j}$ to zero, and every time it receives corresponding $a_{i,k}$ and $b_{k,j}$ elements, it adds their product to $r_{i,j}$. The systolic formulation for $n = 4$ is shown in Figure 12.8. Matrices A and B are fed into the boundary cells in column 1 and row 1. Each row i of A lags one systolic cycle behind row $i - 1$ of A for $2 \leq i \leq n$. Similarly, column j of matrix B lags one systolic cycle behind column $j - 1$ of B for $2 \leq j \leq n$. These delays ensure that element $a_{i,k}$ meets element $b_{k,j}$ in cell $c_{i,j}$ at the right time. When cell $c_{i,j}$ finishes computing $r_{i,j}$, it sends $r_{i,j}$ along the rows so that matrix R leaves the systolic array. The first six systolic cycles of this systolic formulation are shown in Figure 12.9.

The computations performed by each cell $c_{i,j}$ are shown in Program 12.1. The run time of this formulation is determined by the time required by cell $c_{n,n}$ to compute element $r_{n,n}$. Since the nth row of A lags $n - 1$ systolic cycles behind the first row of A, the first element of this row enters the systolic array after n systolic cycles. Once it is in the systolic

Upon receiving $a_{i,k}$ and $b_{k,j}$ from cells $c_{i-1,j}$ and $c_{i,j-1}$,
cell $c_{i,j}$ performs the following operations during each systolic cycle:

1. multiply $a_{i,k}$ by $b_{k,j}$
2. add the result to $r_{i,j}$
3. send $a_{i,k}$ to cell $c_{i+1,j}$
4. send $b_{k,j}$ to cell $c_{i,j+1}$

Program 12.1 The operations performed in each systolic cycle by each cell. If $k = n$ (that is, if cell $c_{i,j}$ has received the last pair of elements), cell $c_{i,j}$ then also sends $r_{i,j}$ to cell $c_{i+1.j}$. Also, if $c_{i,j}$ is a cell on the boundary of the systolic array, it receives (sends) elements from (to) the input (output) ports.

array, the first element reaches cell $c_{n,n}$ after n additional systolic cycles. Similarly, after $2n$ systolic cycles, the first element of the nth column of B reaches cell $c_{n,n}$. Since computing each $r_{i,j}$ requires n systolic cycles (n multiplications and additions), the overall run time of this systolic formulation is $3n$ systolic cycles. Therefore, the cell-time product of this formulation is $\Theta(n^3)$, which is cost-optimal.

12.1.4 Optimal Matrix Parenthesization

Consider the evaluation of the product of n matrices, $A_1, A_2, \ldots, A_n$, where each A_i is a matrix with r_{i-1} rows and r_i columns. Recall from Chapter 9 that the optimal matrix-parenthesization problem is to find the order of multiplying the matrices that minimizes the total number of operations. This problem can be solved by using dynamic programming. Let $d_{i,j}$ be the cost of multiplying the matrices $A_i, A_{i+1}, \ldots, A_j$. The dynamic programming paradigm constructs the solution to this problem based on solutions of its subproblems. This approach yields the following recurrence relation for the parenthesization problem:

$$d_{i,j} = \begin{cases} \min\limits_{i \le k < j} \{d_{i,k} + d_{k+1,j} + r_{i-1} r_k r_j\} & 1 \le i < j \le n \\ 0 & i = j, 1 \le i \le n \end{cases} \tag{12.4}$$

Given Equation 12.4, the problem reduces to finding the value of $d_{1,n}$.

The solution to Equation 12.4 is obtained by using a bottom-up approach. Computing $d_{i,j}$ requires computing the cost of $(j - i)$ possible parenthesizations and taking their minimum. The sequential complexity of the algorithm is approximately $n^3/6$ for sufficiently large n. Figure 12.10 shows the first four steps of the sequential algorithm. Chapter 9 provides further details on the sequential algorithm.

Systolic Formulation

A careful investigation of the sequential algorithm for solving the optimal matrix-parenthesization problem suggests a systolic formulation. Figure 12.10 shows that the

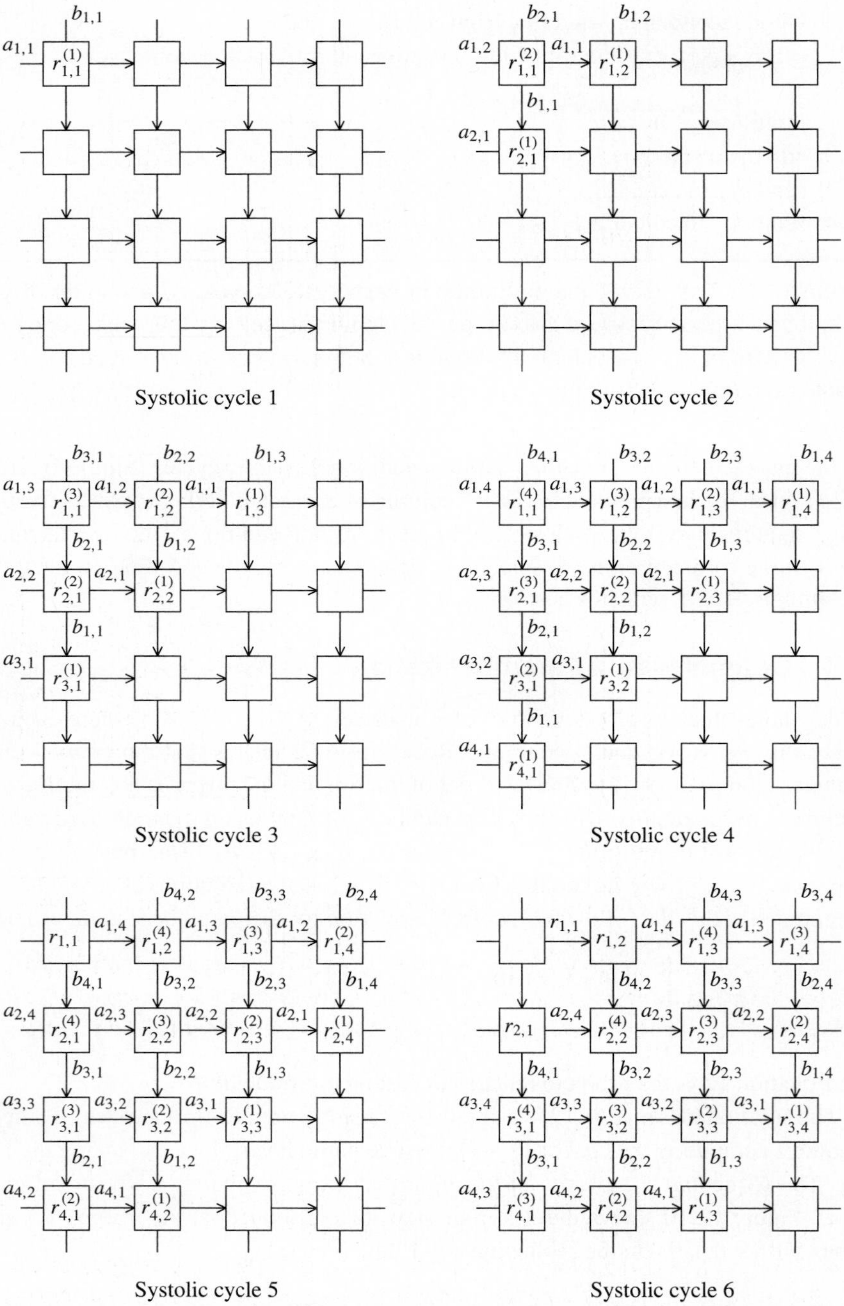

Figure 12.9 The first six systolic cycles of a systolic formulation of matrix multiplication for $n = 4$.

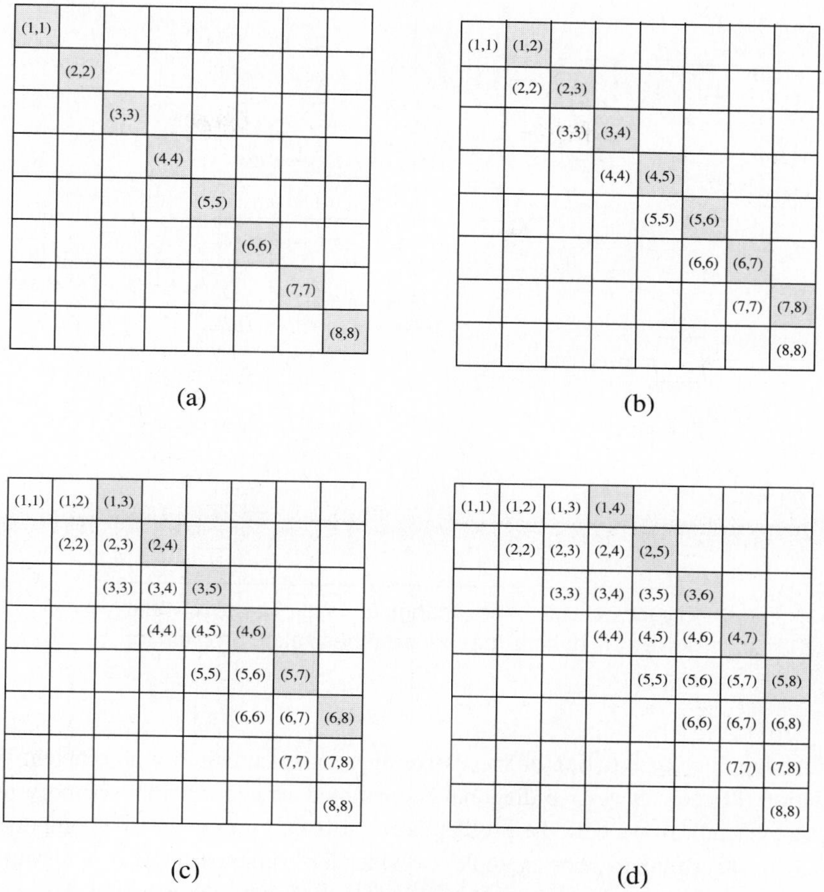

Figure 12.10 The optimal matrix-parenthesization problem is solved bottom-up by solving subproblems of increasing length. A two-dimensional array D is used to store the values of $d_{i,j}$. Parts (a) through (d) show the entries of matrix D being computed that correspond to solving subproblems of length one through four. Note that this process is similar to filling matrix D diagonally.

entries of matrix D are computed in a diagonal order that corresponds to matrix chains of increasing length. Each entry $D[i, j]$ (corresponding to $d_{i,j}$) depends only on entries $D[i, k]$ and $D[k+1, j]$ for $k = i, i+1, \ldots, j-1$, which belong to shorter chains. Thus, to compute $D[i, j]$, only the values from the ith row and j^{th} column of array D are needed.

This suggests that a systolic formulation can be derived by using $n(n+1)/2$ cells in a triangular interconnection pattern. This systolic array is illustrated in Figure 12.11 for $n = 6$. Cell $c_{i,j}$ computes value $d_{i,j}$. After computing $d_{i,j}$, each cell sends its value to those cells that need it to compute their own value.

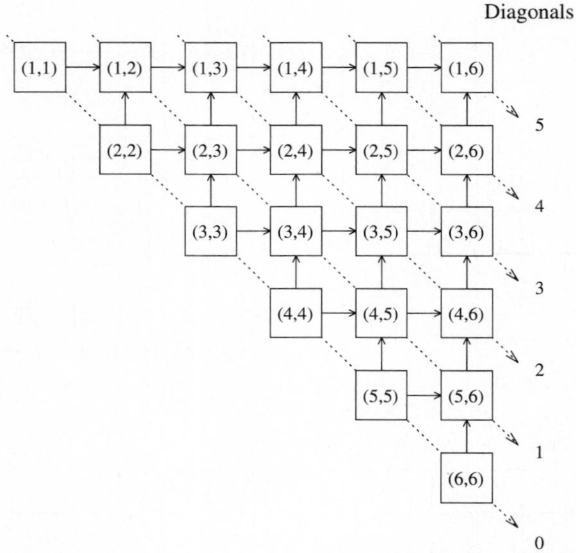

Figure 12.11 The triangular systolic array that solves the optimal matrix-parenthesization problem for $n = 6$.

Overlapping computation of successive diagonals is crucial for an efficient systolic formulation. If each successive diagonal is computed sequentially, the memory requirements of each cell grows with the problem size. It is easy to overlap the computation of diagonals in this problem. For example, consider the computation of $d_{1,6}$. From Equation 12.4 we see that $d_{1,6}$ depends on the following parenthesizations:

(1)	(1,5) — (6,6), of diagonal 4 and diagonal 0
(2)	(1,4) — (5,6), of diagonal 3 and diagonal 1
(3)	(1,3) — (4,6), of diagonal 2 and diagonal 2
(4)	(1,2) — (3,6), of diagonal 1 and diagonal 3
(5)	(1,1) — (2,6), of diagonal 0 and diagonal 4

When the $d_{i,j}$ costs of the second diagonal have been computed, the values of $d_{1,3}$ and $d_{4,6}$ are known; thus, part of the computation for $d_{1,6}$ can be performed (corresponding to part 3 in the list). Similarly, when the $d_{i,j}$ costs of the third diagonal have been computed, the values of $d_{1,4}$, $d_{3,6}$, $d_{5,6}$ and $d_{1,2}$ are known; thus, the computations corresponding to parts 2 and 4 can be performed. This example illustrates that computations of different diagonals can be overlapped. In general, after diagonal t is finished, some computation for the subsequent t diagonals can be performed (Problem 12.4). Specifically, the cost of two possible parenthesizations can be computed for each subsequent t diagonals, and one for the $(2t + 1)^{\text{th}}$ diagonal.

For each cell to perform its computations, the $d_{i,j}$ values must travel along the systolic array to the appropriate cells. If all the $d_{i,j}$ values are passed on as they are arrive, then some values will accumulate at processors before they can be used. For example, at cell $c_{1,6}$, values $d_{1,1}$ and $d_{1,2}$ arrive before $d_{2,6}$ and $d_{3,6}$. Ideally, a value should arrive at a cell when the cell is ready to use it. The systolic system achieves this by imposing the following communication protocol. When a cell $c_{i,j}$ belonging to diagonal t computes $d_{i,j}$, it sends $d_{i,j}$ up and to the right. The value $d_{i,j}$ travels in both directions, moving one cell every systolic cycle for the first t systolic cycles. In subsequent systolic cycles, $d_{i,j}$ continues along both directions, moving one cell every two systolic cycles. Data movement stops when $d_{i,j}$ reaches a boundary cell. This difference in transmission speeds guarantees that $d_{i,j}$ values arrive at a cell when the cell is ready to use them.

The work in diagonal t can start only after diagonal $t/2$ has been computed. The elements of diagonal $t/2$ reach the processors of diagonal t after $t/2$ systolic cycles. After that, every cell of the tth diagonal receives elements in every other systolic cycle. An element of the tth diagonal needs the costs of two pairs of subproblems: one pair of the form (diagonal k, diagonal $t-k$) and one pair of the form (diagonal $t-k$, diagonal k). In each alternate systolic cycle, every cell of the tth diagonal receives two of these pairs. Hence, elements of the tth diagonal are computed t systolic cycles after the elements of the $(t/2)^{\text{th}}$ diagonal have been computed. Thus, the overall run time of this systolic formulation is

$$n + \frac{n}{2} + \frac{n}{4} + \cdots 1 = 2n - 1 = \Theta(n).$$

Since the cell-time product is $\Theta(n^3)$, the formulation is cost-optimal.

12.2 General Issues in Mapping Systolic Systems onto Parallel Computers

Efficient mapping of a systolic system onto a general-purpose parallel computer poses two problems: (1) architectural differences between systolic arrays and parallel computers and (2) the low absolute efficiency of systolic systems.

12.2.1 Architectural Differences between Systolic Arrays and Parallel Computers

In all the systolic systems presented in Section 12.1, the duration of the systolic cycle ensures that the computation and communications performed in each step finishes during the systolic cycle. For example, the systolic cycle for the matrix multiplication systolic system is long enough to compute the operations in Program 12.1: a product, an addition, and two communications. Let t_c be the time to multiply and add two numbers, and t_d be the time to send a number to an adjacent cell. If we assume that data can be transferred through separate communication links simultaneously, then the systolic cycle of this systolic system is at least $(t_c + t_d)$. Since the systolic system requires $3n$ systolic cycles to multiply two $n \times n$ matrices, the overall run time of the systolic system is

$$T_P = 3n(t_c + t_d). \tag{12.5}$$

Because a systolic array is constructed as a special purpose VLSI circuit, t_d is quite small. Therefore, the length of the systolic cycle is dominated by the computation time t_c.

Consider what happens if we map the systolic system for the matrix multiplication problem onto a general-purpose mesh-connected parallel computer with $n \times n$ processors. The operations performed by each processor are the same as those performed by each cell of the systolic array. However, the time for each iteration (analogous to the systolic cycle) is $(t_c + 2t_s + 2t_w)$, where t_s is the message startup time, and t_w is the per-word transfer time. In this case the duration of an iteration is no longer dominated by t_c. If the parallel computer is MIMD, then the startup cost t_s is substantially higher than either t_c or t_w. The per-word transfer time t_w is also usually higher than t_c (recall that t_c is the time to multiply and add two numbers). In typical MIMD parallel computers, $2t_s + 2t_w$ is several orders of magnitude greater than t_c. Therefore, each iteration is dominated by communication cost, leading to a parallel formulation with poor performance. For example, if $2t_s + 2t_w$ is ten times greater than t_c, then the efficiency of the matrix multiplication algorithm on a mesh is one eleventh of the efficiency of a systolic array. A good mapping of a systolic system onto a parallel computer must eliminate such inefficiencies.

Another architectural difference between systolic arrays and parallel computers is the interconnection networks they use. Since systolic arrays are custom designed to facilitate a particular systolic algorithm, many interconnection networks have been proposed. Some of these interconnection networks are similar to those available in general-purpose parallel computers, but others are not. For example, the interconnection network for the systolic system that solves the convolution problem (Section 12.1.1) is similar to a ring. However, the hexagonal interconnection network shown in Figure 12.1(d) does not correspond to any widely available interconnection network for general-purpose parallel computers. The hexagonal systolic array can be mapped onto a mesh-connected parallel computer, but some of the systolic array links will be mapped onto two mesh links, as shown in Figure 12.12.

12.2.2 Absolute Efficiency of Systolic Systems

Consider again the systolic system for the problem of multiplying two $n \times n$ matrices. As discussed in Section 12.2.1, the systolic cycle for the systolic system is dominated by t_c, so we can safely ignore the other terms of Equation 12.5. Therefore, multiplying two $n \times n$ matrices takes approximately $3nt_c$ time on the systolic system. As mentioned in Section 12.1.3, this formulation is cost-optimal. However, the systolic formulation does three times more work than the sequential algorithm, since the cell-time product is $3n^3t_c$. Therefore, the efficiency of this formulation cannot be more than $1/3$. A straightforward mapping of this systolic system onto a mesh-connected parallel computer with n^2 processors yields an algorithm that also requires $3n$ iterations. Thus, the inefficiencies of the systolic

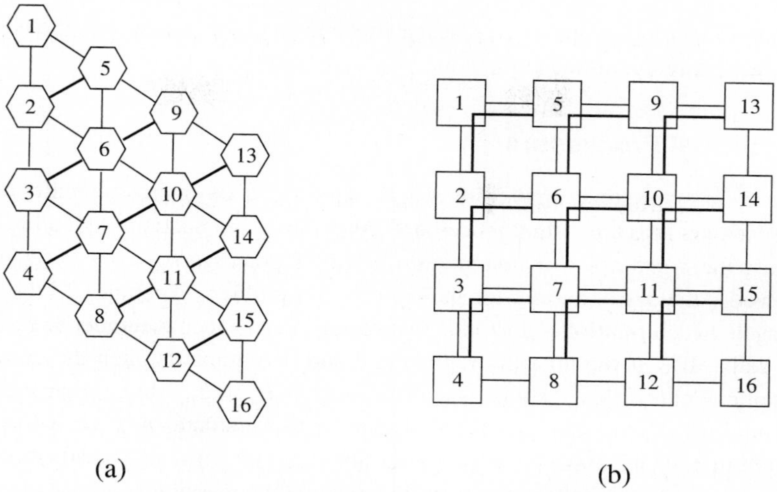

Figure 12.12 A mapping of a hexagonal systolic array (a) onto a mesh-connected parallel computer (b).

system are inherited by the mesh formulation. However, better efficiency can usually be obtained by using fewer than n^2 processors and a better mapping.

12.3 Mapping One-Dimensional Systolic Arrays

This section presents mappings for systolic systems having a one-dimensional interconnection network similar to the one shown in Figure 12.1(a). The systolic arrays for the convolution problem (Section 12.1.1) and the banded matrix-vector multiplication problem (Section 12.1.2) fall into this category. A linear systolic array is similar to a ring-connected parallel computer; we therefore assume that the target parallel computer is a ring. Since a ring network can be embedded in other interconnection networks such as the mesh and hypercube (Section 2.5), the mappings discussed here also apply to them.

Consider a one-dimensional systolic array with n cells. A straightforward mapping requires a ring with n processors and assigns the computations performed by each cell to a corresponding processor. This mapping does not yield efficient parallel formulations. As discussed in the previous sections, it inherits the inefficiencies of the systolic system, and its performance is further reduced by the higher values of t_s and t_w associated with general-purpose parallel computers. To eliminate these problems, we use fewer processors than the number of cells in the systolic array. Since the number of cells in a systolic array depends on the size of the problem being solved, the use of fewer processors than cells also enables us to develop a parallel formulation that is independent of problem size.

In the following sections we present various techniques to map systolic algorithms onto fixed-size ring-connected computers.

12.3.1 Virtual Processors

One way to map a systolic array with n cells onto a general-purpose parallel computer with p processors is to use virtual processors. As discussed in Sections 4.2 and 6.2.2, each processor in the p-processor ring emulates n/p virtual processors.

Consider the systolic array for the convolution problem (Section 12.1.1). In each systolic cycle, a cell multiplies and adds two numbers and sends a number to each of two adjacent cells. If t_c is the time to multiply and add two numbers, then the execution of each systolic cycle of this systolic system takes $t_c + 2t_s + 2t_w$ time on an n-processor ring. Using virtual processors, each physical processor emulates n/p virtual processors in each iteration. If we make no assumptions about the mapping of virtual onto physical processors, then adjacent cells of the systolic array might correspond to processors that are up to $p/2$ communication links away. Therefore, each iteration of the systolic algorithm might require up to $(n/p)(t_c + 2t_s + pt_w)$ time.

However, for most systolic arrays, it is possible to find a mapping of virtual to physical processors that preserves the characteristics of the interconnection network; that is, adjacent virtual processors are mapped onto adjacent physical processors. In this case, each iteration could still require $(t_c + 2t_s + 2t_w)$ time, and because each physical processor emulates n/p virtual processors, the complete iteration takes $(n/p)(t_c + 2t_s + 2t_w)$ time. Assuming that m (that is, the length of sequence x) is sufficiently large with respect to n, the overall run time of the convolution problem is

$$T_P = 2m\frac{n}{p}(t_c + 2t_s + 2t_w)$$

and the processor-time product is $2mn(t_c + 2t_s + 2t_w)$, which is greater than the sequential run time mnt_c, leading to an efficiency substantially less than one.

12.3.2 Block-Striped Mapping

Another way to map the cells of a one-dimensional systolic array onto a ring-connected parallel computer is to use the block-striped mapping (Section 5.1.1). It maps the n cells of a systolic array to a p-processor ring by assigning consecutive blocks of n/p cells to consecutive processors. Since adjacent cells of the systolic array are mapped onto either the same or an adjacent processor, this mapping preserves the nearest-neighbor communication pattern of the systolic system. We now illustrate this mapping for the convolution problem.

Let n be the number of weights and m be the size of the sequence x. Let $P_0, P_1, \ldots, P_{p-1}$ be the p processors of a ring-connected parallel computer. Each processor of the ring stores n/p weights. Since each processor has its own memory and there is no external memory, the sequences x and y must be distributed with care. From Figure 12.3 we see that the elements of sequences x and y enter the systolic array at cells

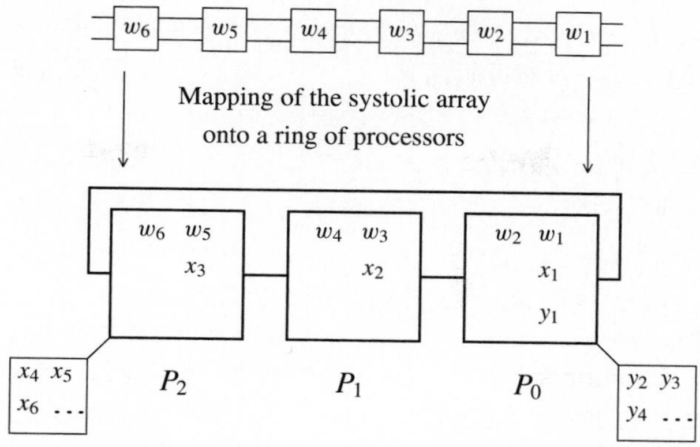

Figure 12.13 A mapping of the systolic array for the convolution problem onto a ring-connected parallel computer. The number of cells is $n = 6$, and the number of processors is $p = 3$.

c_n and c_1, respectively. A simple mapping stores the entire sequence x in processor P_{p-1} and the entire sequence y in processor P_0. However, since during the first $n - 1$ systolic cycles the input sequences simply move along the systolic array to align themselves (see cycles 1–3 in Figure 12.4), a better mapping stores the elements of sequence x already aligned. This mapping is illustrated in Figure 12.13 for a convolution problem with six weights.

The first six steps of the ring mapping for a convolution problem with nine weights are shown in Figure 12.14. In each step (or systolic cycle) of the ring algorithm, each processor computes some $x_i w_k$ terms, shifts the sequence x one position to the right, and shifts the sequence y one position to the left. Since there is a one–systolic-cycle delay between subsequent x_i and y_j values, each processor stores at most $\lceil n/(2p) \rceil$ elements of y during each systolic cycle. Therefore, it spends at most $\lceil n/(2p) \rceil t_c$ time performing computations. Each processor also sends at most two numbers in each systolic cycle (an x_i to the right and a y_j to the left), which takes $(2t_s + 2t_w)$ time. The number of systolic cycles required to compute y_1 is n, since it has to align with weight w_n in processor P_{p-1}. After this, each of the $m - n$ subsequent y_j values is computed every two systolic cycles. The total number of systolic cycles is $2(m - n) + n$. The approximate parallel run time of this formulation is

$$
\begin{aligned}
T_P &= (2(m-n)+n)\left(\frac{n}{2p}t_c + 2t_s + 2t_w\right), \\
&= \left(m - \frac{n}{2}\right)\left(\frac{n}{p}t_c + 4t_s + 4t_w\right).
\end{aligned}
$$

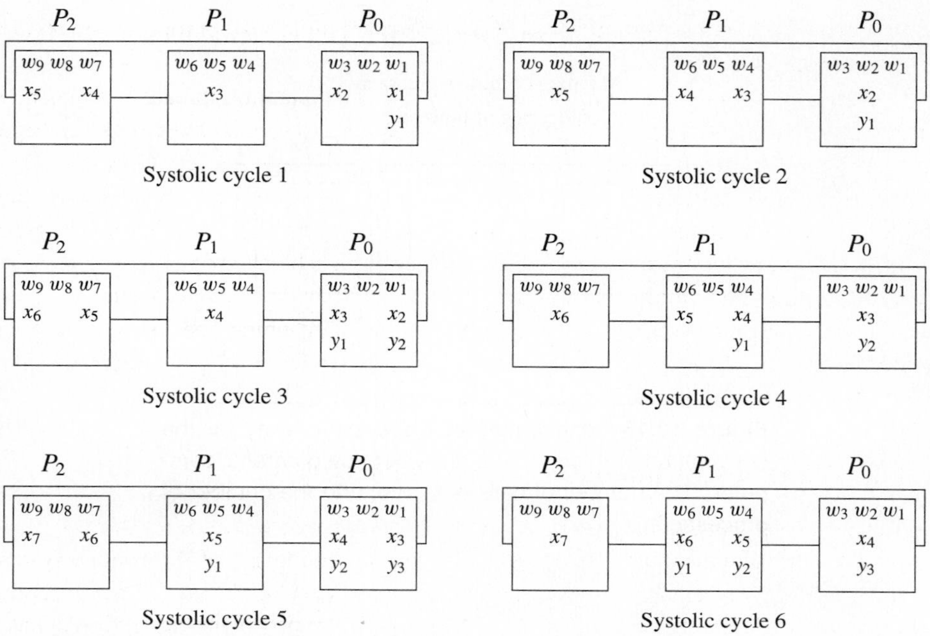

Figure 12.14 The first six systolic cycles of the ring formulation for the convolution problem.

Since the time required to solve the convolution problem on a serial computer is approximately $(m-n)nt_c$, the efficiency of this mapping is

$$E = \frac{(m-n)nt_c}{(m-n/2)(nt_c+4pt_s+4pt_w)}. \quad (12.6)$$

If we assume that m is substantially larger than n (that is, $m-n \approx m$ and $m-n/2 \approx m$), then Equation 12.6 simplifies to

$$E = \frac{1}{1+(4pt_s)/(nt_c)+(4pt_w)/(nt_c)}.$$

Since p is smaller than n, the efficiency approaches one for sufficiently large problem sizes. Thus, the block-striped mapping efficiently maps the systolic system for the convolution problem onto a ring-connected parallel computer.

However, if m is not significantly large with respect to n, the efficiency of block-striped mapping is lower. For example, if m is only twice as large as n, then from Equation 12.6, the largest efficiency that can be obtained is 0.67. To explain why, we introduce the concept of ***computational startup latency*** or ***latency***. Latency is defined as the time elapsed from the beginning of the computation until all processors (or cells of a systolic array) have begun performing computation. For instance, in the systolic system for matrix multiplication, it takes $\Theta(n)$ time from the time when cell $c_{1,1}$ starts computing until cell $c_{n,n}$ starts computing. Similarly, the latency of the systolic system for the convolution problem is $\Theta(n)$.

Latency is a good indication of the speed at which computation spreads in the parallel computer. A small latency means that it does not take long before all the processors begin computing, and it usually implies good load balancing. A large latency, however, might result in a poor load balance. When a block-striped mapping is used to map the convolution problem onto a ring-connected computer, it takes roughly $n - (n/p)$ systolic cycles before the input stream arrives at the last processor. Therefore, a block-striped mapping yields a parallel formulation whose latency is $\Theta(n)$. Notice that this latency is similar to the latency of the systolic system. Therefore, a block-striped mapping does not decrease the inherent latency of the systolic system for this problem, which is why its efficiency has a non-cost-optimal upper bound for small values of m.

12.3.3 Other One-Dimensional Mappings

The block-striped mapping in the previous section does not reduce the latency of the systolic system. An alternate mapping is to assign cells from different parts of the systolic system to each processor by using the cyclic-striped mapping (Section 5.1.1). This mapping is illustrated in Figure 12.15(b). The latency of cyclic-striped mapping is significantly smaller than that of block-striped mapping. It takes only p systolic cycles before the input stream arrives at the last processor. Therefore, the cyclic-striped mapping yields a parallel formulation whose latency is $\Theta(p)$. Besides improving latency, cyclic-striped mapping has the advantage of better distributing the load among the processors. Notice that each processor gets cells from separate areas of the systolic array. If separate cells perform different amounts of computation, then cyclic-striped mapping balances the load better than block-striped mapping. This is illustrated in the two-dimensional mappings presented in the next section.

Although cyclic-striped mapping has a better latency and does a better job of balancing work, it may incur higher communication overhead than does block-striped mapping. Consider the systolic system for the convolution problem. Using block-striped mapping, in any systolic cycle each processor sends only one input or output element to its neighbors. If cyclic-striped mapping is used, in any systolic cycle each processor sends n/p input or output elements to its neighbors. This may lead to a significantly higher communication overhead. However, in some cases, communication overhead is not as bad. Consider the sequence x in the convolution problem. For cyclic-striped mapping, each x_i circulates in the ring n/p times. If we assume that each processor has an adequate amount of memory (which is true for general-purpose parallel computers), then after each x_i has circulated in the ring once, each processor stores the value of x_i and it does not need to be communicated again. Although this works for the sequence x, it does not work for the sequence y. Since the value of each y_j changes as it moves in the ring, its value cannot be stored but must be communicated during each systolic cycle. However, the communication overhead of cyclic-striped mapping is not always higher than that of block-striped mapping. For example, another systolic formulation can be developed (Problem 12.3), that instead of

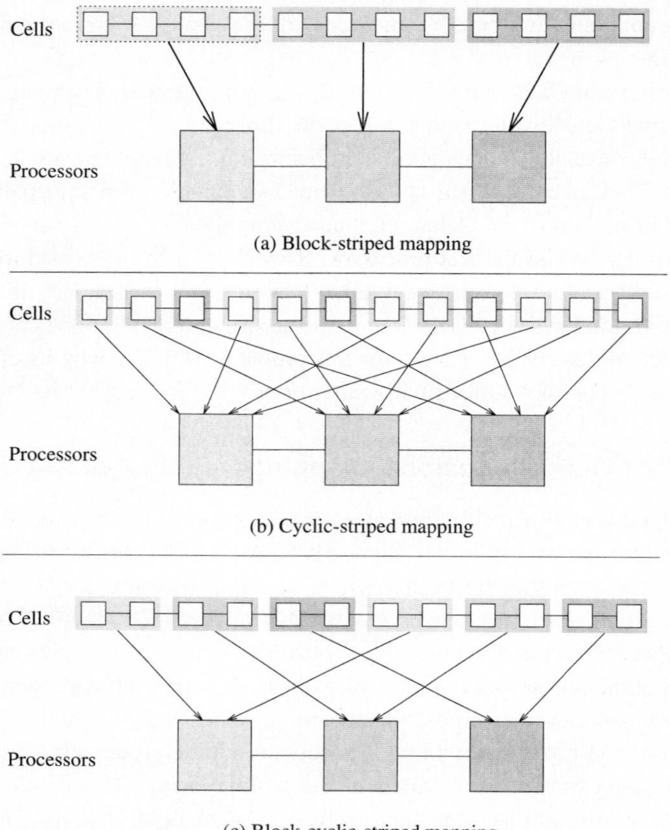

Figure 12.15 Three possible mappings of a one-dimensional systolic array onto a ring-connected parallel computer.

storing the weights in each cell, stores the y_j values and communicates only the x_i and w_k values. For this systolic formulation, the communication requirements of cyclic-striped mapping and block-striped mapping are similar.

A mapping that combines the low latency of cyclic-striped mapping and the low communication overhead of block-striped mapping is the block-cyclic-striped mapping (Section 5.1.1). This mapping is illustrated in Figure 12.15(c). Recall that this mapping groups blocks of consecutive cells and maps them onto the ring by using the cyclic-striped mapping. In order for this to work, the size of each block must be significantly smaller than n/p. If the size of each block is one, block-cyclic-striped mapping reduces to cyclic-striped mapping; if the size of each block is n/p, the block-cyclic-striped mapping reduces to block-striped mapping. If b is the size of each block, the latency of block-cyclic-striped mapping is $\Theta(bp)$, which is between that of block-striped and cyclic-striped mappings. The communication requirement of block-cyclic-striped mapping is also between that of block-striped and cyclic-striped mappings. In each systolic cycle, block-cyclic-striped mapping sends at most $n/(bp)$ elements to its neighbors. By adjusting b, we achieve a balance between latency and communication overhead.

12.4 Mapping Two-Dimensional Systolic Arrays

This section presents mappings for the systolic systems that have two-dimensional interconnection networks similar to the ones shown in Figure 12.1(b) and (c). The systolic arrays for the matrix multiplication problem (Section 12.1.3) and the optimal matrix-parenthesization problem (Section 12.1.4) fall into this category. We assume that the target parallel computer has a mesh interconnection network. Since a mesh network can easily be embedded into other interconnection networks such as the hypercube (Section 2.5), the mappings discussed here also apply to them. The remaining sections concentrate on mapping the systolic system for the optimal matrix-parenthesization problem. Mapping the systolic system for the matrix-multiplication problem is left as an exercise (Problem 12.10).

Recall that in the systolic system for the optimal matrix-parenthesization problem (Section 12.1.4), $d_{i,j}$ values are communicated at two speeds so that values arrive at a cell when the cell is ready to use them. This is important for systolic algorithms, since each cell has only a small amount of memory. However, a general-purpose processor has enough memory to store values that arrive earlier. Our mappings communicate values with no delays; processors store received values in their local memory until needed.

Despite this simplification, mapping the systolic algorithm for the optimal matrix-parenthesization problem onto a mesh-connected parallel computer poses several problems. For the reasons discussed in Section 12.3, direct implementation of the systolic algorithm (using $n(n+1)/2$ processors) leads to an inefficient algorithm and poor utilization of a parallel computer. Therefore, we map more than one cell onto a single mesh processor. The computation per systolic cycle associated with each processor is usually proportional to the number of cells assigned to it. The total amount of communication performed by a processor is usually proportional to the number of cells whose neighbors in the systolic array are mapped onto other mesh processors. For example, if we map $n/\sqrt{p} \times n/\sqrt{p}$ cells to each processor, then the computation is proportional to n^2/p and the communication is proportional to $n/\sqrt{p}$. By varying the number of processors, we can adjust the ratio of communication to computation.

Furthermore, an efficient mapping must keep as many processors as possible doing useful work. Due to the nature of the systolic algorithm, the computations move in a wave front in the systolic array. At any time, only a diagonal band of cells is performing computation, while the remaining cells either have finished their share of the work or are waiting to receive results for subproblems being computed. This computational pattern leads to idle cells during the execution of the algorithm and, depending on the mapping, might also lead to idle processors in the target parallel computer.

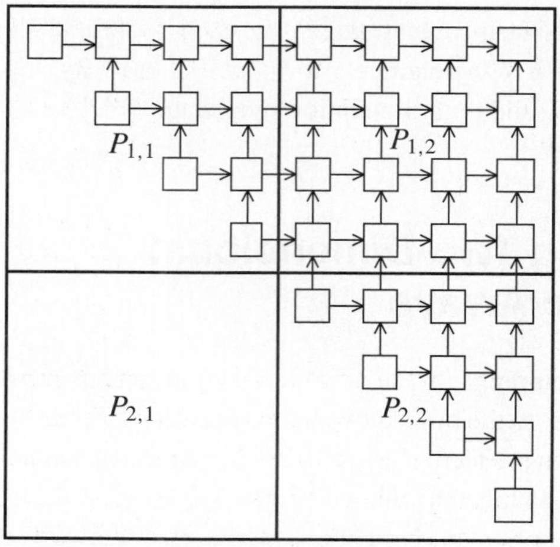

Figure 12.16 Block-checkerboard mapping onto a 2 × 2 mesh. Mesh processors are shown as large squares, systolic cells as small squares.

Finally, the amount of computation performed by cells in the systolic algorithm differs from cell to cell. Each cell computes a value $d_{i,j}$. The amount of computation required is related to the diagonal to which $d_{i,j}$ belongs and is proportional to $(j - i)$. Hence, even though we may be able to map the same number of cells onto each processor, the amount of computation may still vary significantly.

Given these criteria for efficient mappings of the optimal matrix-parenthesization algorithm to a mesh-connected parallel computer, we present and analyze two distinct mappings that address these issues to varying degrees. We assume that the mesh has $\sqrt{p} \times \sqrt{p}$ processors and that n is a multiple of $\sqrt{p}$.

12.4.1 Block-Checkerboard Mapping

A straightforward mapping is to use the block-checkerboard mapping (Section 5.1.2). Recall that block-checkerboard mapping groups together blocks of $n/\sqrt{p} \times n/\sqrt{p}$ cells and maps them onto a single processor. Because of the triangular shape of the systolic array, processors $P_{i,j}$ for $i > j$ are not assigned any cells, and processors $P_{i,i}$ are assigned only $(n/(2\sqrt{p}))(n/\sqrt{p} + 1)$ cells. Figure 12.16 illustrates this mapping. Each processor stores $d_{i,j}$ values for cells in at most $n/\sqrt{p}$ rows and $n/\sqrt{p}$ columns; hence, the memory requirement at each processor is $\Theta(n^2/\sqrt{p})$. Notice that this memory requirement is a direct consequence of eliminating the two speeds for data transfer used in the systolic algorithm.

The only cells that need to communicate with the surrounding processors are those along the periphery of the block, where for every diagonal element received or computed each processor can perform computations on some of the diagonals residing on it.

Block-checkerboard mapping has several limitations. It maps cells onto only $\sqrt{p}(\sqrt{p}+1)/2$ processors; thus, the remaining $\sqrt{p}(\sqrt{p}-1)/2$ processors are always idle. Also, due to the nature of the algorithm, the band of diagonal entries being computed resides on a small number of diagonally adjacent mesh processors. For example, after entries on diagonal t have been computed, the algorithm performs computations on the following $\min\{t, n-t\}$ diagonals. While processors containing these diagonals perform computations, the remaining processors either have finished their work or are waiting to receive diagonal elements that are currently being computed. Finally, because computations associated with a cell increase for successive diagonals, processors have different work loads even though they have the same number of cells.

While analyzing the performance of the block-checkerboard mapping, we concentrate on the amount of computation $T_{calc}^{P_{1,\sqrt{p}}}$, performed by processor $P_{1,\sqrt{p}}$ because this processor performs more computation than any other. Thus, $T_{calc}^{P_{1,\sqrt{p}}}$ is a lower bound on the parallel run time T_P.

Processor $P_{1,\sqrt{p}}$ computes elements from the last $(2n/\sqrt{p}-1)$ diagonals that is, diagonal numbers $n-2n/\sqrt{p}+1, n-2n/\sqrt{p}+2, \ldots, n-1$. Note that each cell along the ith diagonal requires i computations, but cells below this diagonal require less work, and cells above this diagonal require more work. The sum of the work at any two cells that are symmetrically located across this diagonal is equal to twice the work of a cell on diagonal i. The number of the middle diagonal at processor $P_{1,\sqrt{p}}$ is $(\sqrt{p}-1)(n/\sqrt{p})$. Because there are n^2/p cells on processor $P_{1,\sqrt{p}}$, the total amount of computation performed by this processor is

$$\begin{aligned} T_{calc}^{P_{1,\sqrt{p}}} &= \frac{n^2}{p}\left((\sqrt{p}-1)\frac{n}{\sqrt{p}}\right)t_c, \\ &= \frac{n^3}{p}t_c - \frac{n^3}{p\sqrt{p}}t_c. \end{aligned} \qquad (12.7)$$

Ignoring the low-order term, processor $P_{1,\sqrt{p}}$ spends $(n^3/p)t_c$ time performing computation. Thus, the processor-time product is at least $n^3 t_c$, which is six times more than the work performed by the serial algorithm (Equation 9.8). Due to this excess computation, the efficiency of the parallel formulation is bounded by

$$E < \frac{(n^3 t_c)/6}{n^3 t_c} = \frac{1}{6} \approx 0.167. \qquad (12.8)$$

The parallel run time of the algorithm is actually much greater than $T_{calc}^{P_{1,\sqrt{p}}}$ due to processor idling. In fact, a more precise upper bound on efficiency is $1/12$. The actual efficiency of the algorithm is even smaller than that due to communication costs not accounted for in the preceding analysis. Problem 12.7 discusses a variation of the block-checkerboard

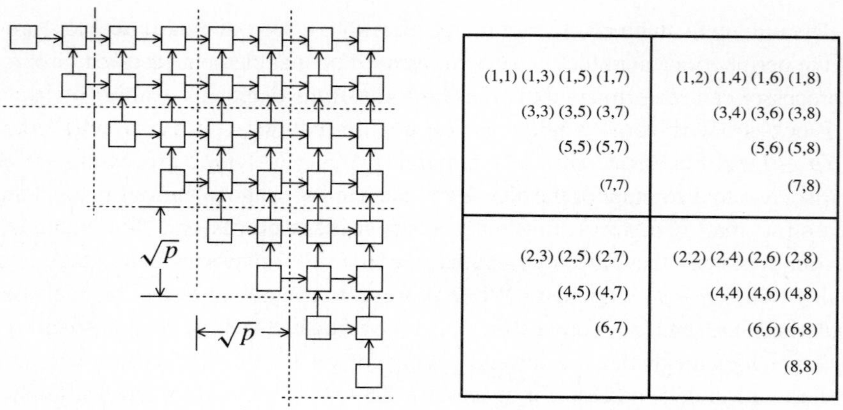

Figure 12.17 Cyclic-checkerboard mapping of an 8×8 systolic array to a 2×2 mesh.

mapping in which each processor has a roughly equal number of cells. The upper bound on the efficiency of that scheme is still much less than one.

★ 12.4.2 Cyclic-Checkerboard Mapping

The block-checkerboard mapping fails to fully address the issues involved in efficiently mapping the systolic array algorithm onto a mesh-connected parallel computer. Although the block-checkerboard mapping maintained communication locality, the work load was unevenly distributed among the processors. Here we present a formulation that uses the cyclic-checkerboard mapping (Section 5.1.2). This mapping not only preserves the communication characteristics of the block-checkerboard mapping but also evenly distributes the work among the processors.

Recall from Section 5.1.2 that the cyclic-checkerboard mapping assigns successive rows and columns of cells to successive rows and columns of a wraparound mesh. Specifically, cell $c_{i,j}$ of the systolic array is mapped onto processor $(((i-1) \bmod \sqrt{p}) + 1, ((j-1) \bmod \sqrt{p}) + 1))$ of the mesh. Although adjacent rows and columns of the systolic array are mapped onto adjacent rows and columns of the mesh, the amount of communication is similar to the block-checkerboard mapping. That is because when cell $c_{i,j}$ sends its results to cell $c_{i,j+1}$, the result is also received by cells $c_{i,j+1+k\sqrt{p}}$ for $k = 1, 2, 3, \ldots$. This mapping is illustrated in Figure 12.17. The memory requirement for each processor is $\Theta(n^2/\sqrt{p})$.

In block-checkerboard mapping, each processor is assigned portions of consecutive diagonals; in cyclic-checkerboard mapping, each processor is assigned portions of diagonals that are $\sqrt{p}$ apart. The amount of work required to compute a diagonal element increases as the diagonal number increases; thus, in block-checkerboard mapping the processors having higher-numbered diagonals do more work than those having lower-numbered ones. In cyclic-checkerboard mapping, however, each processor is assigned an equal number of low- and high-numbered diagonals, balancing the work allocated to each processor. Furthermore, because consecutive systolic array rows and columns reside on consecutive mesh rows and columns, the latency of cyclic-checkerboard mapping is smaller than that of block-checkerboard; that is, processors start working earlier than with block-checkerboard mapping.

As in the performance analysis of block-checkerboard mapping, we concentrate on processor $P_{1,\sqrt{p}}$. It performs computation for cells that belong in the diagonals $\sqrt{p}-1, 2\sqrt{p}-1, \ldots, n-1$. The computation performed by this processor is

$$\begin{aligned} T_{calc}^{P_{1,\sqrt{p}}} &= t_c \sum_{i=1}^{n/\sqrt{p}} \left(\frac{n}{\sqrt{p}} + 1 - i\right)(i\sqrt{p}-1), \\ &= \frac{n^3}{6p}t_c + \frac{n^2}{2\sqrt{p}}t_c + \frac{3n^2}{2p}t_c + \frac{3n}{2\sqrt{p}}t_c + \frac{n}{3}t_c. \end{aligned} \tag{12.9}$$

The computations performed by any processor $P_{i,j}$ (Problem 12.8) is

$$T_{calc}^{P_{i,j}} = T_{calc}^{P_{1,\sqrt{p}}} - (i - 1 + \sqrt{p} - j)\frac{n^2}{p}. \tag{12.10}$$

Thus, in the worst case, the computations performed by any other processor will be smaller only by $O(n^2/\sqrt{p})$. As n increases, this imbalance becomes insignificant compared to the work done by each processor. Therefore, if we ignore low-order terms in Equation 12.9 the computation performed by $P_{1,\sqrt{p}}$ is

$$T_{calc}^{P_{1,\sqrt{p}}} = \frac{n^3}{6p}t_c. \tag{12.11}$$

In order to prove that cyclic-checkerboard mapping yields a cost-optimal parallel formulation, we must compute the amount of time spent performing communication (including idling) by processor $P_{1,\sqrt{p}}$. An upper bound on this communication time $T_{comm}^{P_{1,\sqrt{p}}}$ for processor $P_{1,\sqrt{p}}$ (Problem 12.9) is

$$T_{comm}^{P_{1,\sqrt{p}}} < \left(\frac{n^2}{\sqrt{p}} + n\right)t_c + \left(\frac{n^2}{\sqrt{p}} + n\right)t_w + 2nt_s. \tag{12.12}$$

If we ignore low-order terms Equation 12.12 is simplified to

$$T_{comm}^{P_{1,\sqrt{p}}} < \frac{n^2}{\sqrt{p}}t_c + \frac{n^2}{\sqrt{p}}t_w + 2nt_s. \tag{12.13}$$

An upper bound on the parallel run time of the algorithm is $T_{comm}^{P_{1,\sqrt{p}}} + T_{calc}^{P_{1,\sqrt{p}}}$. Ignoring low-order terms, from Equations 12.11 and 12.13, the parallel run time of the algorithm is

$$T_P < \frac{n^3}{6p}t_c + \frac{n^2}{\sqrt{p}}t_w + 2nt_s. \tag{12.14}$$

Thus, the efficiency of the algorithm is

$$E = \frac{\frac{n^3}{6}t_c}{(n^3 t_c)/6 + n^2\sqrt{p}t_w + 2npt_s},$$
$$= \frac{1}{1 + 6\sqrt{p}t_w/n + 12pt_s/n^2}. \quad (12.15)$$

From Equation 12.15 we see that, as n increases, the efficiency of the algorithm increases and approaches one. Hence, cyclic-checkerboard mapping yields a cost-optimal parallel formulation. Also from this equation we see that the isoefficiency function is $\Theta(p^{1.5})$. This isoefficiency function is the same for both the overhead due to extra work and the overhead due to communication. Thus, cyclic-checkerboard mapping can effectively utilize $O(n^2)$ processors.

12.4.3 Summary of Two-Dimensional Mappings

Besides block-checkerboard and cyclic-checkerboard mapping, there are a variety of other mappings. An alternative mapping reduces the two-dimensional topology to a one-dimensional topology by using the block-striped mapping. Block-striped mapping may be a good candidate when the number of processors is small compared to the size of the problem. We can also use block-cyclic-checkerboard mapping in much the same way as it is used for the one-dimensional case. Cyclic-checkerboard mapping usually has smaller latency compared to block-checkerboard mapping. It usually takes $\Theta(n)$ time for computations to spread out in block-checkerboard mapping and $\Theta(\sqrt{p})$ in cyclic-checkerboard mapping.

Comparing the various mappings presented, we see that block-checkerboard mapping preserves communication locality, and cyclic-checkerboard mapping achieves good load balance. In many problems these two goals are interrelated; satisfying one satisfies the other. However, there are problems in which these goals are at odds. Achieving communication locality leads to load imbalance, and achieving load balance leads to non-local communication. In such cases, block-cyclic-checkerboard mapping can yield a better overall performance (Problem 12.12).

12.5 Bibliographic Remarks

Kung et al. [FK80, KL78, Kun79, KL80, Kun82] introduced the concept of systolic systems. Several books [Kun88, MC80, Ull84] provide a good introduction to systolic systems, the VLSI model of computations, and methodologies for designing systolic systems. Kung [Kun87] offers a comprehensive listing of systolic systems. The Warp machine [AAG+87] is a general-purpose one-dimensional systolic array. Kung [Kun80, Kun82] describes systolic systems for the convolution problem including the one presented in Section 12.1.1. The convolution algorithm can be easily modified to solve problems such as the discrete Fourier transform, polynomial multiplication, and pattern matching [LW85a]. The systolic system for the banded matrix-vector multiplication problem described in Section 12.1.2 was presented by Kung and Leiserson [KL78, KL80]. Our discussion in Section 12.1.2 is influenced by [KL78, KL80]. Kung and Leiserson [KL78, KL80] also presented systolic systems for LU-decomposition of sparse matrices and triangular linear systems. The systolic system for the matrix multiplication problem described in Section 12.1.3 is similar to the one presented in Akl [Akl89] and Kung [Kun88]. Finally, the systolic system for the optimal matrix-parenthesization problem presented in Section 12.1.4 is due to Guibas, Kung, and Thompson [GKT79], who also present a systolic system for computing the transitive closure of a graph.

Methodologies for synthesizing systolic algorithms from problem specifications have been derived. Lamport [Lam74] and Moldovan and Fortes [MF86] consider a broad class of problems solvable sequentially by nested loop programs. Chen [Che85], Shang [SF88], and Quinton [Qui84] also provide methodologies for synthesizing systolic algorithms from nested loops. A parametric approach using design characteristics is presented by Li and Wah [LW85b]. Li and Wah [LW85a] provide a systematic methodology for the design of optimal pure systolic arrays for algorithms that are representable as linear recurrence processes. This methodology was used in developing the systolic system for the matrix multiplication problem described in Section 12.1.3. Various projection strategies for mapping a design graph to a fixed-size systolic architecture can be found in the book by Kung [Kun88]. Prasanna and Tsai [PT89] present a unified framework to design linear systolic arrays. Ibarra, Kim, and Palis [IKP86] present methods for designing systolic algorithms using sequential machines. Prasanna and Tsai [PT90] present methods for mapping dynamic programming algorithms onto one-dimensional systolic arrays. Systolic arrays are classified into semisystolic arrays and pure systolic arrays. Semisystolic arrays have global data communication, pure systolic arrays do not. In this chapter we considered only pure systolic arrays. Semisystolic arrays have the advantage of making the initial algorithm design phase easier. Leiserson, Rose, and Saxe [LRS83] introduce the technique of retiming that converts a semisystolic array into a pure systolic array. Fortes, Fu, and Wah [FFW88] provide a critical review of various methodologies for designing systolic systems.

The efficiency of systolic systems is usually analyzed with respect to the lower bound on the area of the VLSI chip and the time it takes to solve the problem. The area A of a VLSI chip reflects its cost, and the time T reflects how fast the problem is solved. A suitable metric should be a function of A and T such as $A^x T^y$ [Ull84]. Some popular metrics are A, AT, and AT^2. AT is identical to the processor-time product for systolic arrays. For VLSI systems other than systolic arrays, AT is not necessarily identical to the processor-time product, as the area may not proportional to the number of processors.

Despite the large number of systolic systems, little work has been done in developing methods of efficiently mapping systolic systems onto general-purpose parallel computers. Most of the mappings presented so far were mapped on a case-by-case basis. Moldovan and Fortes [MF86] present algorithms of mapping systolic algorithms to fixed-size systolic arrays. Their mappings are based on dividing the algorithm index set into bands and then mapping these bands into the processor space. Ibarra and Sohn [IS90] consider mappings of systolic algorithms to hypercube-connected parallel computers. They consider one- and two-dimensional systolic systems and present mappings that reduce communication overhead and latency. Among the mappings they consider are block-striped mapping for both one- and two-dimensional systolic arrays and block-checkerboard mapping for two-dimensional systolic arrays. Karypis and Kumar [KK93] present efficient mappings for two-dimensional systolic systems. For the optimal matrix-parenthesization problem, they show that cyclic-checkerboard and block-cyclic-checkerboard mappings lead to a parallel formulation whose efficiency approaches one for a sufficiently large number of processors. Sections 12.4.1 and 12.4.2 are based upon the paper by Karypis and Kumar [KK93].

Problems

12.1 Consider the convolution problem described in Section 12.1.1. Derive a parallel formulation for a hypercube-connected computer that uses $m \times n$ processors and that solves the problem in $\Theta(\log m)$ time. Is your formulation cost-optimal? If not, modify your algorithm so that it becomes cost-optimal. Can you convert your algorithm into a systolic system? If yes, explain how; otherwise explain why not.

12.2 **[Kun82]** Consider the following systolic formulation of the convolution problem. The weights are loaded into the cells as in the formulation presented in Section 12.1.1. However, the sequences x and y move in the same direction but at different speeds. The sequence x moves at twice the speed of the sequence y. Describe the systolic formulation, and provide an example with four weights and six x values. What is the run time of your systolic formulation?

12.3 **[Kun82]** Develop a systolic formulation for the convolution problem in which each cell stores one y value and the elements of sequences x and w move in the systolic array. Analyze the run time of your systolic system. Map the systolic system onto a ring by using block-striped and cyclic-striped mapping. Which mapping yields better performance?

12.4 Consider the optimal matrix-parenthesization problem described in Section 12.1.4. Show that after $d_{i,j}$ values of diagonal $0, 1, \ldots, t$ have been computed, these values can be used to

(a) compute two possible parenthesizations for each element in the subsequent t diagonals.

(b) compute one possible parenthesization for the $(2t + 1)^{\text{th}}$ diagonal.

12.5 Consider the mapping of the systolic system that solves the convolution problem described in Section 12.3.1. In this mapping, virtual processors are used for each cell of the systolic array. Assume that the mapping of virtual onto physical processors is done in such a way that communication locality is preserved. Analyze the run time of your mapping. Is there an upper bound on the efficiency of this mapping? How does this mapping compare with the block-striped mapping?

12.6 Consider the block-striped mapping of the convolution problem described in Section 12.3.2. In this formulation, both sequences x and y are stored in the boundary processors. Describe an alternative method of distributing the sequences among the processors to insure that all processors have roughly the same number of elements. Note that your distribution should preserve the systolic cycle delays in the sequences. Modify the block-striped mapping formulation to take advantage of the new data distribution. Analyze the performance of your formulation (that is, derive the parallel run time, efficiency, and the isoefficiency function).

12.7 Consider the mapping of the systolic system that solves the optimal matrix-parenthesization problem (Section 12.4.1). One of the limitations of the block-checkerboard mapping is that it does not use almost half of the processors of the mesh. Derive a mapping that is similar to block-checkerboard mapping but that utilizes all the processors. Note that the number of cells mapped onto each processor should be roughly the same. Analyze the performance of your mapping. Derive an upper bound on the efficiency by using an analysis similar to that for the block-checkerboard mapping.

12.8 For the cyclic-checkerboard mapping of the systolic system for the optimal matrix-parenthesization problem (Section 12.4.1), derive Equation 12.10.

12.9 For the cyclic-checkerboard mapping of the systolic system for the optimal matrix-parenthesization problem (Section 12.4.1), derive Equation 12.12.

12.10 Consider the systolic system for the matrix multiplication problem presented in Section 12.1.3. Show how to map this algorithm onto a mesh of processors by using the block-checkerboard mapping. Analyze the exact run time of your mapping. Is there any way to premap the input matrices onto the processors so that to improve the performance? What is the exact run time of your mapping?

12.11 Perform an analysis similar to that of Problem 12.10 but use cyclic-checkerboard mapping instead of block-checkerboard mapping. Which mapping is better, and why?

12.12 An alternative to both the block-checkerboard and the cyclic-checkerboard mappings is the block-cyclic-checkerboard mapping described in Chapter 5. Does the block-cyclic-checkerboard mapping improve the performance of either the matrix multiplication or the optimal matrix-parenthesization algorithm? Explain your answer.

12.13 Identify the characteristics that a systolic algorithm should have to insure that the block-cyclic-checkerboard mapping is superior to both the block-checkerboard and cyclic-checkerboard mapping.

References

[AAG+87] M. Annaratone, E. Arnould, T. Gross, H. T. Kung, M. Lam, O. Menzilcioglu, and J. A. Webb. The Warp computer: Architecture, implementation, and performance. *IEEE*

Transactions on Computers, C-36(12), December 1987.

[Akl89] S. G. Akl. *The Design and Analysis of Parallel Algorithms*, 179–181. Prentice-Hall, Englewood Cliffs, NJ, 1989.

[Che85] M. C. Chen. Synthesizing systolic design. In *Proceedings of International Symposium on VLSI Technology*, 1985.

[FFW88] J. A. B. Fortes, K. S. Fu, and B. W. Wah. *Systematic Approaches to the Design of Algorithmically specified Systolic Arrays*, 454–494. Elsevier, New York, NY, 1988.

[FK80] M. J. Foster and H. T. Kung. The design of special-purpose VLSI chips. *Computer*, 13(1):26–40, January 1980.

[GKT79] L. J. Guibas, H. T. Kung, and C. D. Thompson. Direct VLSI implementation of combinatorial algorithms. In *Proceedings of Conference on Very Large Scale Integration, California Institute of Technology*, 509–525, 1979.

[IKP86] O. H. Ibarra, S. M. Kim, and M. A. Palis. Designing systolic algorithms using sequential machines. *IEEE Transactions on Computers*, C-36(6):531–542, June 1986.

[IS90] O. H. Ibarra and S. M. Sohn. On mapping systolic algorithms onto the hypercube. *IEEE Transactions on Parallel and Distributed Systems*, 1(1):48–63, January 1990.

[KK93] G. Karypis and V. Kumar. Efficient parallel mappings of a dynamic programming algorithm: A summary of results. In *7th International Parallel Processing Symposium*, 563–568, 1993.

[KL78] H. T. Kung and C. E. Leiserson. Systolic arrays for VLSI. In *Sparse Matrix Proceedings*, 256–282. Society of Industrial and Applied Mathematics, 1978.

[KL80] H. T. Kung and C. E. Leiserson. *Algorithms for VLSI Processor Arrays*, chapter 8.3. Introduction to VLSI Systems. Addison-Wesley, Reading, MA, 1980.

[Kun79] H. T. Kung. Let's design algorithms for VLSI systems. In *Proceedings of Caltech Conference on Very Large Scale Intergration*, 65–90, 1979.

[Kun80] H. T. Kung. Special-purpose devices for signal and image processing. In *Proceedings of SPIE*, 76–84. Society of Photo-Optical Instrumentation Engineers, 1980.

[Kun82] H. T. Kung. Why systolic architectures? *Computer*, 15(1):37–46, January 1982.

[Kun87] H. T. Kung. A listing of systolic papers. Technical report, Computer Science Department, Carnegie-Mellon University, Pittsburgh, PA, 1987.

[Kun88] S. Y. Kung. *VLSI Array Processors*. Prentice-Hall, Englewood Cliffs, NJ, 1988.

[Lam74] L. Lamport. The parallel execution of DO loops. *Communication of the ACM*, 83–93, February 1974.

[LRS83] C. E. Leiserson, F. M. Rose, and J. B. Saxe. Optimizing synchronous circuitry by retiming. In R. Bryant, editor, *Proceedings of 3rd Caltech Conference on Very Large Scale Intergration*, 87–116, 1983.

[LW85a] G.-J. Li and B. W. Wah. The design of optimal systolic arrays. *IEEE Transactions on Computers*, C–34(1):66–77, January 1985.

[LW85b] G.-J. Li and B. W. Wah. Parallel processing of serial dynamic programming problems. In *Proceedings of COMPSAC 85*, 81–89, 1985.

[MC80] C. Mead and L. Conway. *Introduction to VLSI systems*. Addison-Wesley, Reading, MA, 1980.

[MF86] D. I. Moldovan and J. A. B. Fortes. Partitioning and mapping algorithms into fixed size systolic arrays. *IEEE Transactions on Computers*, C-35:1–12, January 1986.

[PT89] V. K. Prasanna and Y.-C. Tsai. Designing linear systolic arrays. *Journal of Parallel and Distributed Computing*, 7:441–463, 1989.

[PT90] V. K. Prasanna and Y.-C. Tsai. Mapping dynamic programming onto linear array. *Journal of VLSI Signal Processing*, 335–343, 1990.

[Qui84] P. Quinton. Automatic synthesis of systolic arrays from uniform recurrent equations. In *Proceedings 11th Symposium of Computer Architecture*, 208–214, 1984.

[SF88] W. Shang and J. A. B. Fortes. Independent partitioning of algorithms with uniform dependencies. In *Proceedings of 1988 International Conference of Parallel Processing*, 26–33, 1988.

[Ull84] J. D. Ullman. *Computational Aspects of VLSI*. Computer Science Press, Rockville, Maryland, 1984.

CHAPTER 13

Parallel Programming

We have presented parallel algorithms for many problems in this book. To run these algorithms on a parallel computer, we need to implement them in a programming language. In addition to providing all the functionality of a sequential language, a language for programming parallel computers must provide mechanisms for sharing information among processors. It must do so in a way that is clear, concise, and readily accessible to the programmer. A variety of parallel programming paradigms have been developed. This chapter discusses the strengths and weaknesses of some of these paradigms, and illustrates them with examples.

13.1 Parallel Programming Paradigms

Different parallel programming languages enforce different programming paradigms. The variations among paradigms are motivated by several factors. First, there is a difference in the amount of effort invested in writing parallel programs. Some languages require more work from the programmer, while others require less work but yield less efficient code. Second, one programming paradigm may be more efficient than others for programming on certain parallel computer architectures. Third, various applications have different types of parallelism, so different programming languages have been developed to exploit them. This section discusses these factors in greater detail.

13.1.1 Explicit versus Implicit Parallel Programming

One way to develop a parallel program is to code an explicitly parallel algorithm. This approach, called ***explicit parallel programming***, requires a parallel algorithm to explicitly specify how the processors will cooperate in order to solve a specific problem. The compiler's task is straightforward. It simply generates code for the instructions specified by the programmer. The programmer's task, however, is quite difficult.

Another way to develop parallel programs is to use a sequential programming language and have the compiler insert the constructs necessary to run the program on a parallel computer. This approach, called ***implicit parallel programming***, is easier for the programmer because it places a majority of the burden of parallelization on the compiler.

Unfortunately, the automatic conversion of sequential programs to efficient parallel ones is very difficult because the compiler must analyze and understand the dependencies in different parts of the sequential code to ensure an efficient mapping onto a parallel computer. The compiler must partition the sequential program into blocks and analyze dependencies between the blocks. The blocks are then converted into independent tasks that are executed on separate processors. Dependency analysis is complicated by control structures such as loops, branches, and procedure calls. Furthermore, there are often many ways to write a sequential program for a given application. Some sequential programs make it easier than others for the compiler to generate efficient parallel code. Therefore, the success of automatic parallelization also depends on the structure of the sequential code. Some recent languages, such as Fortran D, allow the programmer to specify the decomposition and placement of data among processors. This makes the job performed by parallelizing compilers somewhat simpler.

13.1.2 Shared-Address-Space versus Message-Passing

In the shared-address-space programming paradigm, programmers view their programs as a collection of processes accessing a central pool of shared variables. The shared-address-space programming style is naturally suited to shared-address-space computers. A parallel program on a shared-address-space computer shares data by storing it in globally accessible memory. Each processor accesses the shared data by reading from or writing to shared variables. However, more than one processor might access the same shared variable at a time, leading to unpredictable and undesirable results. For example, assume that x initially contains the value 5 and that processor P_1 increases the value of x by one while processor P_2 decreases it by one. Depending on the sequence in which the instructions are executed, the value of x can become 4, 5, or 6. For example, if P_1 reads the value of x before P_2 decreases it, and stores the increased value after P_2 stores the decreased value, x will become 6. We can correct the situation by preventing the second processor from decreasing x while it is being increased by the first processor. Shared-address-space programming languages must provide primitives to resolve such mutual-exclusion problems.

In the ***message-passing*** programming paradigm, programmers view their programs as a collection of processes with private local variables and the ability to send and receive data between processes by passing messages. In this paradigm, there are no shared variables among processors. Each processor uses its local variables, and occasionally sends or receives data from other processors. The message-passing programming style is naturally suited to message-passing computers.

Shared-address-space computers can also be programmed using the message-passing paradigm. Since most practical shared-address-space computers are nonuniform memory access architectures, such emulation exploits data locality better and leads to improved performance for many applications. On shared-address-space computers, in which the local memory of each processor is globally accessible to all other processors (Figure 2.5(a)), this emulation is done as follows. Part of the local memory of each processor is designated as a communication buffer, and the processors read from or write to it when they exchange data. On shared-address-space computers in which each processor has local memory in addition to global memory (Figure 2.5(b)), message passing can be done as follows. The local memory becomes the logical local memory, and a designated area of the global memory becomes the communication buffer for message passing.

Many parallel programming languages for shared-address-space or message-passing MIMD computers are essentially sequential languages augmented by a set of special system calls. These calls provide low-level primitives for message passing, process synchronization, process creation, mutual exclusion, and other necessary functions. Extensions to C, Fortran, and C++ have been developed for various parallel computers including nCUBE 2, iPSC 860, Paragon XP/S CM-5, TC 2000, KSR-1, and Sequent Symmetry. In order for these programming languages to be used on a parallel computer, information stored on different processors must be explicitly shared using these primitives. As a result, programs may be efficient, but tend to be difficult to understand, debug, and maintain. Moreover, the lack of standards in many of the languages makes programs difficult to port between architectures. Parallel programming libraries, such as PVM, Parasoft EXPRESS, P4, and PICL, try to address some of these problems by offering vendor-independent low-level primitives. These libraries offer better code portability compared to earlier vendor-supplied programming languages. However, programs are usually still difficult to understand, debug, and maintain.

13.1.3 Data Parallelism versus Control Parallelism

In some problems, many data items are subject to identical processing. Such problems can be parallelized by assigning data elements to various processors, each of which performs identical computations on its data. This type of parallelism is called ***data parallelism***. An example of a problem that exhibits data parallelism is matrix multiplication (Section 5.4.1). When multiplying two $n \times n$ matrices A and B to obtain matrix $C = (c_{i,j})$, each element $c_{i,j}$ is computed by performing a dot product of the ith row of A with the jth column of B. Therefore, each element $c_{i,j}$ is computed by performing identical operations on different data, which is data parallel.

Several programming languages have been developed that make it easy to exploit data parallelism. Such languages are called ***data-parallel programming languages*** and programs written in these languages are called ***data-parallel programs***. A data-parallel program contains a single sequence of instructions, each of which is applied to the data elements in lockstep. Data-parallel programs are naturally suited to SIMD computers.

A global control unit broadcasts the instructions to the processors, which contain the data. Processors execute the instruction stream synchronously. Data-parallel programs can also be executed on MIMD computers. However, the strict synchronous execution of a data-parallel program on an MIMD computer results in inefficient code since it requires global synchronization after each instructions. One solution to this problem is to relax the synchronous execution of instructions. In this programming model, called ***single program, multiple data*** or SPMD, each processor executes the same program asynchronously. Synchronization takes place only when processors need to exchange data. Thus, data parallelism can be exploited on an MIMD computer even without using an explicit data-parallel programming language.

Control parallelism refers to the simultaneous execution of different instruction streams. Instructions can be applied to the same data stream, but more typically they are applied to different data streams. An example of control parallelism is ***pipelining.*** In pipelining, computation is parallelized by executing a different program at each processor and sending intermediate results to the next processor. The result is a pipeline of data flowing between processors. Algorithms for problems requiring control parallelism usually map well onto MIMD parallel computers because control parallelism requires multiple instruction streams. In contrast, SIMD computers support only a single instruction stream and are not able to exploit control parallelism efficiently (Section 2.1.1).

Many problems exhibit a certain amount of both data parallelism and control parallelism. The amount of control parallelism available in a problem is usually independent of the size of the problem and is thus limited. In contrast, the amount of data parallelism in a problem increases with the size of the problem. Therefore, in order to use a large number of processors efficiently, it is necessary to exploit the data parallelism inherent in an application.

Note that not all data-parallel applications can be implemented using data-parallel programming languages nor can all data-parallel applications be executed on SIMD computers. In fact, many of them are more suited for MIMD computers. For example, the tree search problem discussed in Chapter 8 has data parallelism, since successors must eventually be generated for all the nodes in the tree. However, the actual code for generating successor nodes contains many conditional statements. Thus, depending upon the node being generated, different instructions are executed. As shown in Figure 2.3, such programs perform poorly on SIMD computers. In some data-parallel applications, the data elements are generated dynamically in an unstructured manner, and distribution of data to processors must be done dynamically. For example, in the tree-search problem (Chapter 8) the nodes in the tree are generated during the execution of the search algorithm, and the tree grows unpredictably. To obtain a good load balance, the search space must be divided dynamically among processors. Data-parallel programs can perform data redistribution only on a global scale; that is, they do not allow some processors to continue working while other processors redistribute data among themselves. Hence, problems requiring dynamic distribution are harder to program in the data-parallel paradigm.

Data-parallel languages offer the programmer high-level constructs for sharing information and managing concurrency. Programs using these high-level constructs are easier to write and understand. Some examples of languages in this category are Dataparallel C and C*. However, code generated by these high-level constructs is generally not as efficient as handcrafted code that uses low-level primitives. In general, if the communication patterns required by the parallel algorithm are not supported by the data-parallel language, then the data-parallel program will be less efficient.

13.2 Primitives for the Message-Passing Programming Paradigm

Existing sequential languages can easily be augmented with library calls to provide message-passing services. This section presents the basic extensions that a sequential language must have in order to support the message-passing programming paradigm.

Message passing is often associated with MIMD computers, but SIMD computers can be programmed using explicit message passing as well. However, due to the synchronous execution of a single instruction stream by SIMD computers, the explicit use of message passing sometimes results in inefficient programs.

13.2.1 Basic Extensions

The message-passing paradigm is based on just two primitives: `SEND` and `RECEIVE`. `SEND` transmits a message from one processor to another, and `RECEIVE` reads a message from another processor.

The general form of the `SEND` primitive is

```
SEND(message, messagesize, target, type, flag)
```

`Message` contains the data to be sent, and `messagesize` is its size in bytes. `Target` is the label of the destination processor. Sometimes, `target` can also specify a set of processors as the recipient of the message. For example, in a hypercube-connected computer, `target` may specify certain subcubes, and in a mesh-connected computer it may specify certain submeshes, rows, or columns of processors.

The parameter `type` is a user-specified constant that distinguishes various types of messages. For example, in the matrix multiplication algorithm described in Section 5.4.1 there are at least two distinct types of messages. The first type contains data from the rows of the matrix, and the second contains data from the columns of the matrix.

Usually there are two forms of `SEND`. One allows processing to continue immediately after a message is dispatched, whereas the other suspends processing until the message is received by the target processor. The latter is called a ***blocking*** `SEND`, and the former a ***nonblocking*** `SEND`. The `flag` parameter is sometimes used to indicate whether the `SEND` operation is blocking or nonblocking.

When a `SEND` operation is executed, the operating system performs the following steps. It copies the data stored in `message` to a separate area in the memory, called the ***communication buffer***. It adds an operating-system-specific header to the message that includes `type`, `flag`, and possibly some routing information. Finally, it sends the message. In newer parallel computers, these operations are performed by specialized routing hardware. When the message arrives at the destination processor, it is copied into this processor's communication buffer and a system variable is set indicating that a message has arrived. In some systems, however, the actual transfer of data does not occur until the receiving processor executes the corresponding `RECEIVE` operation.

The `RECEIVE` operation reads a message from the communication buffer into user memory. The general form of the `RECEIVE` primitive is

```
RECEIVE(message, messagesize, source, type, flag)
```

There is a great deal of similarity between the `RECEIVE` and `SEND` operations because they perform complementary operations. The `message` parameter specifies the location at which the data will be stored and `messagesize` indicates the maximum number of bytes to be put into `message`. At any time, more than one message may be stored in the communication buffer. These messages may be from the same processor or different processors. The `source` parameter specifies the label of the processor whose message is to be read. The `source` parameter can also be set to special values, indicating that a message can be read from any processor or a set of processors. After successfully completing the `RECEIVE` operation, `source` holds the actual label of the processor that sent the message.

The `type` parameter specifies the type of the message to be received. There may be more than one message in the communication buffer from the `source` processor(s). The `type` parameter selects a particular message to read. It can also take on a special value to indicate that any type of message can be read. After the successful completion of the `RECEIVE` operation, `type` will store the actual type of the message read.

As with `SEND`, the `RECEIVE` operation can be either blocking or nonblocking. In a blocking `RECEIVE`, the processor suspends execution until a desired message arrives and is read from the communication buffer. In contrast, nonblocking `RECEIVE` returns control to the program even if the requested message is not in the communication buffer. The `flag` parameter can be used to specify the type of `RECEIVE` operation desired.

Both blocking and nonblocking `RECEIVE` operations are useful. If a specific piece of data from a specific processor is needed before the computation can proceed, a blocking `RECEIVE` is used. Otherwise, it is preferable to use a nonblocking receive. For example, if a processor must receive data from several processors, and the order in which these data arrive is not predetermined, nonblocking `RECEIVE` is usually better.

Most message-passing extensions provide other functions in addition to `SEND` and `RECEIVE`. These functions include system status querying, global synchronization, and setting mode for communication. Another important function is `WHOAMI`. The `WHOAMI` function returns information about the system and the processor itself. The general form of the `WHOAMI` function is:

```
WHOAMI(processorid, numofprocessors).
```

`Processorid` returns the label of the processor, and `numofprocessors` returns the total number of processors in the parallel computer. The `processorid` is the value used for the `target` and `source` parameters of the `RECEIVE` and `SEND` operations. The total number of processors helps determine certain characteristics of the topology of the parallel computer (such as the number of dimensions in a hypercube or the number of rows and columns in a mesh).

Most message-passing parallel computers are programmed using either a ***host-node*** model or a ***hostless*** model. In the host-node model, the host is a dedicated processor in charge of loading the program onto the remaining processors (the nodes). The host also performs housekeeping tasks such as interactive input and output, termination detection, and process termination. In contrast, the hostless model has no processor designated for such housekeeping tasks. However, the programmer can program one of the processors to perform these tasks as required.

The following sections present the actual functions used by message passing for some commercially-available parallel computers.

13.2.2 nCUBE 2

The nCUBE 2 is an MIMD parallel computer developed by nCUBE Corporation. Its processors are connected by a hypercube interconnection network. A fully configured nCUBE 2 can have up to 8192 processors. Each processor is a 32-bit RISC processor with up to 64MB of local memory. Early versions of the nCUBE 2's system software supported the host-node programming model. A recent release of the system software primarily supports the hostless model.

The nCUBE 2's message-passing primitives are available for both the C and Fortran languages. The nCUBE 2 provides nonblocking `SEND` with the use of the `nwrite` function.

C

```
int nwrite(char *message, int messagesize, int target, int type,
                int *flag)
```

Fortran

```
integer function nwrite(message, messagesize, target, type, flag)
dimension message (*)
integer messagesize, target, type, flag
```

The functions of `nwrite`'s parameters are similar to those of the `SEND` operation discussed in Section 13.2.1. The main difference is that the `flag` parameter is unused. The nCUBE 2 does not provide a blocking `SEND` operation.

The blocking `RECEIVE` operation is performed by the `nread` function.

C

```
int nread(char *message, int messagesize, int *source, int *type,
    int *flag)
```

Fortran

```
integer function nread(message, messagesize, source, type, flag)
dimension message (*)
integer messagesize, source, type, flag
```

The `nread` function's parameters are similar to those of `RECEIVE` with the exception of the `flag` parameter, which is unused. The nCUBE 2 emulates a nonblocking `RECEIVE` by calling a function to test for the existence of a message in the communication buffer. If the message is present, `nread` can be called to read it. The `ntest` function tests for the presence of messages in the communication buffer.

C
```
int ntest(int *source, int *type)
```

Fortran
```
integer function ntest(source, type)
integer source, type
```

The `ntest` function checks to see if there is a message in the communication buffer from processor `source` of type `type`. If such a message is present, `ntest` returns a positive value, indicating success; otherwise it returns a negative value. When the value of `source` or `type` (or both) is set to -1, `ntest` checks for the presence of a message from any processor or of any type. After the function is executed, `type` and `source` contain the actual source and type of the message in the communication buffer.

The functions `npid` and `ncubesize` implement the `WHOAMI` function.

C
```
int npid()
int ncubesize()
```

Fortran
```
integer function npid()
integer function ncubesize()
```

The `npid` function returns the processor's label, and `ncubesize` returns the number of processors in the hypercube.

13.2.3 iPSC 860

Intel's iPSC 860 is an MIMD message-passing computer with a hypercube interconnection network. A fully configured iPSC 860 can have up to 128 processors. Each processor is a 32-bit i860 RISC processor with up to 16MB of local memory. One can program the iPSC using either the host-node or the hostless programming model. The iPSC provides message-passing extensions for the C and Fortran languages. The same message-passing extensions are also available for Intel Paragon XP/S, which is a mesh-connected computer.

The iPSC's nonblocking `SEND` operation is called `csend`.

C
```
csend(long type, char *message, long messagesize, long target,
      long flag)
```

Fortran
```
subroutine csend(type, message, messagesize, target, flag)
integer type
integer message (*)
integer messagesize, target, flag
```

The parameters of `csend` are similar to those of `SEND` (Section 13.2.1). The `flag` parameter holds the process identification number of the process receiving the message.

This is useful when there are multiple processes running on the `target` processor. The iPSC does not provide a blocking `SEND` operation. We can perform blocking `RECEIVE` by using the `crecv` function.

C
```
crecv(long type, char *message, long messagesize)
```

Fortran
```
subroutine crecv(type, message, messagesize)
integer type
integer message (*)
integer messagesize
```

Comparing the `crecv` function with the `RECEIVE` operation, we see that the `source` and `flag` parameters are not available in `crecv`. However, `crecv` allows information about the source processor to be encoded in the `type` parameter. The iPSC provides nonblocking `RECEIVE` by using a function called `irecv`. The arguments of `irecv` are similar to `crecv`, with the exception that `irecv` returns a number that is used to check the status of the receive operation. The program can wait for a nonblocking receive to complete by calling the `msgwait` function. It takes the number returned by `irecv` as its argument and waits until the nonblocking `RECEIVE` operation has completed.

The iPSC functions `mynode` and `numnodes` are similar to `WHOAMI`. They return the label of the calling processor and the number of processors in the hypercube, respectively.

C
```
long mynode()
long numnodes()
```

Fortran
```
integer function mynode()
integer function numnodes()
```

13.2.4 CM-5

The CM-5, developed by Thinking Machines Corporation, supports both the MIMD and SIMD models of computation. A fully configured CM-5 can have up to 16384 processors connected by a fat tree interconnection network (Section 2.4). The CM-5 also has a control network, used for operations involving many or all processors. Each CM-5 node has a SPARC RISC processor and four vector units with up to 32MB of local memory. One can program the CM-5 using either the host-node or hostless programming models.

When the CM-5 is used in MIMD mode, it is programmed with the use of message-passing primitives that are available for the C, Fortran, and C++ languages.

The CM-5's blocking `SEND` function is `CMMD_send_block`.

C
```
int CMMD_send_block(int target, int type, void *message,
    int messagesize)
```

Fortran
```
integer function CMMD_send_block(target, type, message,
          messagesize)
integer target, type
integer message (*)
integer messagesize
```

The parameters of CMMD_send_block are similar to those for the generic SEND primitive. The CM-5's nonblocking SEND operation is CMMD_send_async.

C

```
CMMD_mcb CMMD_send_async(int target, int type, void *message,
         int messagesize, void (*handler)(CMMD_mcb))
```

Fortran

```
integer function CMMD_send_async(target, type, message,
         messagesize, handler)
integer target, type
integer message (*)
integer messagesize, handler
```

Most of the parameters required by CMMD_send_async are similar to those required by the SEND operation. The CMMD_send_async function returns a pointer to a message control block (CMMD_mcb) after it has queued the message for transmission. The programmer is responsible for preserving the data in the buffer pointed to by message, and for freeing the CMMD_mcb when the message has been sent. The parameter handler allows the programmer to define a handler routine that is invoked automatically when the message has been sent.

The CM-5 provides blocking RECEIVE with the CMMD_receive_block function.

C

```
int CMMD_receive_block(int source, int type, void *message,
    int messagesize)
```

Fortran

```
integer function CMMD_receive_block(source, type, message,
         messagesize)
integer source, type
integer message (*)
integer messagesize
```

A nonblocking RECEIVE operation is provided by the function CMMD_receive_async.

C

```
CMMD_mcb CMMD_receive_async(int source, int type, void *message,
         int messagesize, void (*handler)(CMMD_mcb))
```

Fortran

```
integer function CMMD_receive_async(source, type, message,
         messagesize, handler)
integer source, type
integer message (*)
integer messagesize, handler
```

The parameters of the CMMD_receive_block and CMMD_receive_async operations are similar to those for the corresponding CMMD_send_block and CMMD_send_async operations.

On the CM-5, the send function does not actually send the message until the destination node invokes a receive function, indicating that it is ready to receive a message. Furthermore, the CMMD send functions send no more data than the receiver has signaled it can accept. Thus, the number of bytes sent is the smaller of the number of bytes requested (that is, the messagesize of the send function) and the number of bytes the receive function allows (that is, the messagesize of the receive function).

The CM-5 provides the functionality of `WHOAMI` with the functions `CMMD_self_address` and `CMMD_partition_size`. These functions return the label of the calling processor and the total number of processors.

C
```
int CMMD_self_address()
int CMMD_partition_size()
```

Fortran
```
int function CMMD_self_address
int function CMMD_partition_size
```

13.2.5 Example Program

Consider the simple matrix multiplication algorithm presented in Section 5.4.1. An implementation of this algorithm in C for the nCUBE 2 is given below.

```
/*
 * This program implements key components of matrix multiplication on
 * nCUBE 2.
 * This programm is for illustrative purposes only.
 */

#include <stdio.h>
#include <stdlib.h>
#include <memory.h>
#include <string.h>
#include <math.h>

/* Message types */
#define ROWSEND  10 /* indicates that the message contains row parts */
#define COLSEND  11 /* indicates that the message contains column parts */

/* Global Variables */
int **a, **b, **c;  /* compute c = ab, for matrices a, b, c */
int n;              /* size of the matrices */
int sqrtp;          /* square root of the number of processors */
int *buffer;        /* communication buffer */
int pid;            /* processor label */
int up,down;        /* up and down neighbors of pid */
int left,right;     /* left and right neighbors of pid */
int x,y;            /* x and y coordinates of pid in the mesh */

/***************************************************************************
* Usage mmult <n>
***************************************************************************/
main(int argc, char *argv[])
{
  /* Find who I am */
  pid = npid();
  sqrtp = sqrt(ncubesize());

  if (argc != 2) {
    if (pid == 0)  /* messages are printed only by processor 0 */
      printf("\nUsage: mmult <n>\n");
    exit(0);  /* all the processors exit */
```

```
  }

  n = atoi(argv[1]);  /* get n */
  if (n % sqrtp != 0)  /* if n is not a multiple of sqrtp */
    n -= n % sqrtp; /* make it */

  if (pid == 0) {
    printf("\nYou are using %a dx%d mesh of processors,",sqrtp,sqrtp);
    printf("\nand you want to multiply two %dx%d matrices.", n, n);
  }

  if (n <= 0)
    exit(0);  /* exit if you got a funny n */

  /* Initialization */
  initmesh();      /* Initialize the mesh to hypercube embedding */
  allocatevars(); /* Allocate variables */
  initvars();      /* Initialize variables */

  /* Communication */
  rowshifts();  /* send along the rows */
  colshifts();  /* send along the columns */

  /* Finally, perform some computation */
  mmult();
}

/**************************************************************************
* This function initializes variables to accommodate the embedding of a
* mesh onto a hypercube by computing the gray codes. This function returns
* values for left, right, up, down. The code is omitted.
**************************************************************************/
initmesh() {}

/**************************************************************************
* This function allocates space for a, b, c, and buffer. Code is omitted.
**************************************************************************/
allocatevars() {}

/**************************************************************************
* This function initializes the matrices. Code is omitted.
**************************************************************************/
initvars() {}

/**************************************************************************
* This function performs the row shift of the blocks of matrix a.
**************************************************************************/
rowshifts()
{
  int i,j,k;  /* index variables */
  int type;   /* the type of the message being sent/received */
  int source; /* from where the message was sent */

  /* Copy the local block in the communication buffer */
  for (i=0; i<n/sqrtp; i++)
```

```
    for (j=0; j<n/sqrtp; j++)
      buffer[i*(n/sqrtp)+j] = a[i][x*(n/sqrtp)+j];

  type = ROWSEND;
  source = right;

  for (k=1; k<sqrtp; k++) {
    /* Send the block to the processor to the left */
    nwrite(buffer, sizeof(int)*(n/sqrtp)*(n/sqrtp), left, type, NULL);

    /* Read the block from the processor on the right */
    nread(buffer, sizeof(int)*(n/sqrtp)*(n/sqrtp), &source, &type, NULL);

    /* Copy the block received into the appropriate place */
    for (i=0; i<n/sqrtp; i++)
      for (j=0; j<n/sqrtp; j++)
        a[i][((x+k)%sqrtp)*(n/sqrtp)+j] = buffer[i*(n/sqrtp)+j];
  }
}

/***************************************************************************
* This function performs the column shift of the blocks of matrix b.
***************************************************************************/
colshifts()
{
  int i,j,k;  /* index variables */
  int type;   /* the type of the message being sent/received */
  int source; /* from where the message was sent */

  /* Copy the local block in the communication buffer */
  for (i=0; i<n/sqrtp; i++)
    for (j=0; j<n/sqrtp; j++)
      buffer[i*(n/sqrtp)+j] = b[y*(n/sqrtp)+i][j];

  type = COLSEND;
  source = down;

  for (k=1; k<sqrtp; k++) {
    /* Send the block to the processor to the up */
    nwrite(buffer, sizeof(int)*(n/sqrtp)*(n/sqrtp), up, type, NULL);

    /* Read the block from the processor to the down */
    nread(buffer, sizeof(int)*(n/sqrtp)*(n/sqrtp), &source, &type, NULL);

    /* Copy the block received into the appropriate place */
    for (i=0; i<n/sqrtp; i++)
      for (j=0; j<n/sqrtp; j++)
        b[((y+k)%sqrtp)*(n/sqrtp)+i][j] = buffer[i*(n/sqrtp)+j];
  }
}

/***************************************************************************
* This function performs the matrix multiplication.
***************************************************************************/
mmult()
```

```
{
  int i,j,k; /* index variables */

  for (i=0; i<n/sqrtp; i++)
    for (j=0; j<n/sqrtp; j++) {
      c[i][j] = 0;
      for (k=0; k<n; k++)
        c[i][j] += a[i][k]*b[k][j];
    }
}
```

This program multiplies two $n \times n$ matrices by using p processors arranged as a $\sqrt{p} \times \sqrt{p}$ logical mesh. The program first determines the label of the processor and the total number of processors available in the system. It does this with the `npid` and `ncubesize` functions. Next, the program gets the size of the matrices from the user and proceeds to set up parameters for embedding a mesh into the hypercube. The mesh-to-hypercube embedding is done by using the Gray code mapping discussed in Section 2.5. For this problem each processor needs to know only its four neighbors and its own coordinates in the mesh. This information is returned by the function `initmesh`.

After embedding a mesh into the hypercube, the program acquires the necessary parts of matrices `a` and `b` in order to compute the block of the product matrix `c` assigned to it. It does this by a sequence of circular shifts, one along the rows and one along the columns. The functions `rowshifts` and `colshifts` perform this operation. Function `rowshifts` performs $\sqrt{p} - 1$ send and receive operations to and from the processors to the right and the left. Function `colshifts` is similar to `rowshifts` but communicates along the other dimension of the mesh. Note that two message types are defined: `ROWSEND` for rows and `COLSEND` for columns. These message types ensure that the appropriate messages are read. Finally, after finishing the circular shifts, the program performs the matrix multiplication. It does this by using function `mmult`, which computes the block of matrix `c` local to each processor.

The iPSC 860 and the CM-5 versions of the matrix multiplication program can be derived from the nCUBE 2 version if we replace the message-passing and system-query functions with the appropriate calls for each parallel computer.

13.3 Data-Parallel Languages

The main emphasis of data-parallel languages is to make it easier for the programmer to express the data parallelism available within a program in a manner that is independent of the architectural characteristics of a given parallel computer. A data-parallel language has the following characteristics:

(1) It generates only a single instruction stream.
(2) It implies the synchronous execution of instructions. Hence, it is much easier to write and debug data-parallel programs, since race conditions and deadlocks are impossible.

(3) It requires the programmer to develop code that explicitly specifies parallelism.

(4) It associates a virtual processor with the fundamental unit of parallelism. The programmer expresses computation in terms of operations performed by virtual processors. The advantage of virtual processors is that programmers need not be concerned with the number of physical processors available on a parallel computer. They simply specify how many processors they need. However, using virtual processors inappropriately may result in inefficient parallel programs (Sections 4.2 and 13.3.1).

(5) It allows each processor to access memory locations in any other processor. This characteristic creates the illusion of a shared address-space and simplifies programming since programmers do not have to perform explicit message passing.

Since data-parallel languages hide many architectural characteristics from the programmer, writing data-parallel programs is generally easier than writing programs for explicit message passing. However, the ease of programming comes at the expense of increased compiler complexity. Compilers for data-parallel languages must map virtual processors onto physical processors, generate code to communicate data, and enforce synchronous instruction execution.

13.3.1 Data Partitioning and Virtual Processors

In a data-parallel language, data are distributed among virtual processors. The virtual processors must be mapped onto the physical processors at some point. If the number of virtual processors is greater than the number of physical processors, then several virtual processors are emulated by each physical processor. In that case, each physical processor partitions its memory into blocks—one for each virtual processor it emulates—and executes each instruction in the program once for each of the virtual processors. For example, assume that an instruction increments the value of a variable by one and that three virtual processors are emulated by each physical processor. The physical processors execute the instruction by performing three consecutive increment operations, one for each virtual processor. These operations affect the memory blocks of each virtual processor.

The amount of work done by each physical processor depends on the number of virtual processors it emulates. If *VPR* is the ratio of virtual to physical processors, then the work performed by each physical processor for each program instruction is greater by a factor of *VPR*. This is because each physical processor has to execute *VPR* instructions for each program instruction. However, the amount of communication performed may be smaller or larger than *VPR*. For instance, if the virtual processors are mapped so that neighboring virtual processors reside on physical processors that are farther away, the communication requirements will be higher than *VPR* (Problem 4.4). In most cases, however, it is possible to map virtual processors onto physical processors so that nearest-neighbor communication is preserved. If this is the case, some virtual processors may need to communicate with virtual processors mapped onto the same physical processor. Depending on how smart the emulation is, this may lead to lower communication requirements.

Some data-parallel languages contain primitives that allow the programmer to specify the desired mapping of virtual processors onto physical processors. As Section 12.3.1 shows, this is essential in developing efficient parallel programs. The efficiency of a mapping depends on both the data communication patterns of the algorithm, and the interconnection network of the target computer. For example, a mapping suited to a hypercube-connected parallel computer may not be suited to a mesh-connected parallel computer. In the following sections we present examples of some of todays data-parallel languages.

13.3.2 C*

C* is a data-parallel programming language that is an extension of the C programming language. C* was designed by Thinking Machines Corporation for the CM-2 parallel computer. The CM-2 is a fine-grain SIMD computer with up to 65,536 processors. Each CM-2 processor is one bit wide, and supports up to 1Mbit of memory. C* is also available for the CM-5.

C* adheres to the ANSI standard for C, so programs written in ANSI C compile and run correctly under C*. In addition, C* provides new features for specifying data parallelism. The features of C* include the following

(1) A method to describe the size and the shape of parallel data and to create parallel variables.
(2) Operators and expressions for parallel data that provide functionality such as data broadcasting and reduction. Some of these operators require communication.
(3) Methods to specify data points within selected parallel variables on which C* code is to operate.

Parallel Variables C* has two types of variables. A ***scalar*** variable is identical to an ordinary C variable; scalar variables are allocated in the host processor. A ***parallel*** variable is allocated on all node processors. A parallel variable has as many elements as the number of processors.

A parallel variable has a ***shape*** in addition to a type. A shape is a template for parallel data—a way to configure data logically. It defines how many parallel elements exist and how they are organized. A shape has a specific number of dimensions, referred to as its ***rank***, with a given number of processors or ***positions*** in each dimension. A dimension is called an ***axis***. For example, the following statement declares a shape called `mesh`, of rank two and having 1,048,576 positions:

```
shape [1024][1024]mesh;
```

Similarly, the following statement declares a shape of rank four with two positions along each axis:

```
shape [2][2][2][2]fourcube;
```

The `fourcube` shape declaration declares a template containing a total of $2 \times 2 \times 2 \times 2 = 16$ positions. A shape should reflect the most logical organization of the problem's data. For example, a graphics program might use the `mesh` shape to represent the two-dimensional images that it is going to process. However, not all possible configurations can be declared using the `shape` primitive. For example, `shape` does not allow us to declare a triangular-shaped or a diamond-shaped mesh. However, we can do this by declaring a larger shape and using only a portion of it. For example, we can obtain a triangular shape by declaring a square shape and using only half of it.

C* does not allow the programmer to specify virtual-to-physical processor mappings explicitly. C* maps virtual processors onto physical processors so that neighboring virtual processors are mapped onto neighboring physical processors. However, C* allows us to specify across which dimensions of the shape communication will be performed more frequently. The compiler uses this information to reduce communication cost.

After a shape is specified, parallel variables of that shape can be declared. Parallel variables have a type, a storage class, and a shape. The following statement declares the parallel variable `count` of type `int` and shape `ring`:

```
shape [8192]ring;
int:ring count;
```

This declaration creates a parallel variable `count` with 8192 positions each of which is allocated to a different processor. We can access individual elements of the parallel variable `count` by using ***left indexing***. For example, `[1]count` accesses the value of the `count` that resides on the second processor (numbering is from 0 to 8191). Figure 13.1 illustrates the differences between scalar and parallel variables.

Any standard or user-defined data type can be used with parallel variables. For example, an entire C structure can be a parallel variable. As another example, `int:fourcube a[1000]` declares the 16-position parallel variable `a`, in which each element is an array of 1000 integers.

Parallel Operations C* supports all standard C operations and a few new operations for data-parallel programming. In addition, C* defines additional semantics for standard C operations when they are used with parallel variables.

If the operands of an operation are scalar, then C* code behaves exactly like standard C code and the operation is performed on the host computer. The situation is different when one or more operands are parallel variables. For example, consider a simple assignment statement of the form `x += y`, where both `x` and `y` are parallel variables. This assignment adds the value of `y` at each shape position to the value of `x` at the corresponding shape position. All additions take place in parallel. Note that an expression that evaluates to a parallel variable must contain parallel variables of the same shape as the resulting parallel variable. Hence, in this example, `x` and `y` must be of the same shape. In a statement of the

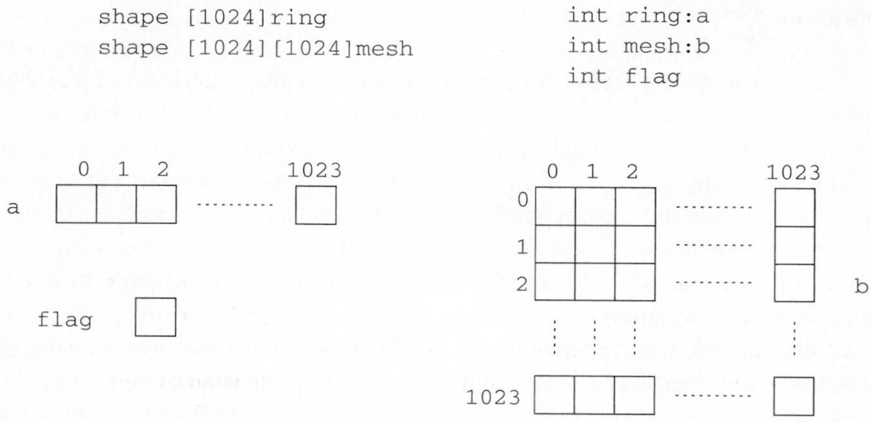

Figure 13.1 Examples of parallel and scalar variables. a and b are parallel variables of different shapes, and flag is a scalar variable. Courtesy of Thinking Machines Corporation.

form x = a, where a is a scalar variable, the value of a is stored in each position of x. This is similar to a broadcast operation.

A more interesting situation arises when the left side of an assignment operation is a scalar variable and the right side is a parallel variable. There are two cases in which this assignment makes sense. In the first case, the parallel variable is fully left indexed. For instance, if a is a scalar variable and x is a parallel variable of rank one, then a = [4]x is a valid statement and assigns to a the value of x at the fifth position of the shape. In the second case, the operation is one of those shown in Table 13.1. The result of these operations is a reduction. For instance, a += x sums all the values of x and stores the result in a.

Table 13.1 C* reduction operations.

Operator	Meaning
+=	Sum of values of parallel variable elements
-=	Negative of the sum of values
&=	Bitwise AND of values
^=	Bitwise XOR of values
|=	Bitwise OR of values
<?=	Minimum of values
>?=	Maximum of values

Choosing a Shape The `with` statement enables operations on parallel data by setting the current shape. Operations are performed on parallel variables of the current shape. In the following example, the `with` statement is required for performing the parallel addition:

```
shape [8192] ring;
int:ring x, y, z;
with (ring)
  x = y+z;
```

Setting the Context C* has a `where` statement that restricts the positions of a parallel variable on which operations are performed. The positions to be operated on are called ***active positions***. Selecting the active positions of a shape is called setting the ***context***. For example, the `where` statement in the following code avoids division by zero:

```
with (ring) {
  where (z != 0)
    x = y / z;
}
```

The `where` statement can include an `else` clause. The `else` clause complements the set of active positions. Specifically, the positions that were active when the `where` statement was executed are deactivated, and the inactive positions are activated. For example,

```
with (ring) {
  where (z != 0)
    x = y / z;
  else
    x = y;
}
```

On the CM-2 (since it is an SIMD machine) the `where` and `else` clauses are executed serially. One should limit the use of the `where-else` clause because multiple context settings degrade performance substantially.

Communication C* supports two methods of interprocessor communication. The first is called ***grid communication***, in which parallel variables of the same type can communicate in regular patterns. The second method is called ***general communication***, in which the value of any element of a parallel variable can be sent to any other element, whether or not the parallel variables are of the same shape. The regularity of grid communication makes it considerably faster than general communication on many architectures. In particular, on CM-2, grid communication can be mapped onto the underlying interconnection network quite efficiently.

Data communication in C* uses left indexing, but instead of using a scalar value to left-index a parallel variable, a parallel variable is used. This operation is called ***parallel left indexing***. A parallel left index rearranges the elements of the parallel variable based on the values stored in the elements of the parallel index. The index must be of the current shape.

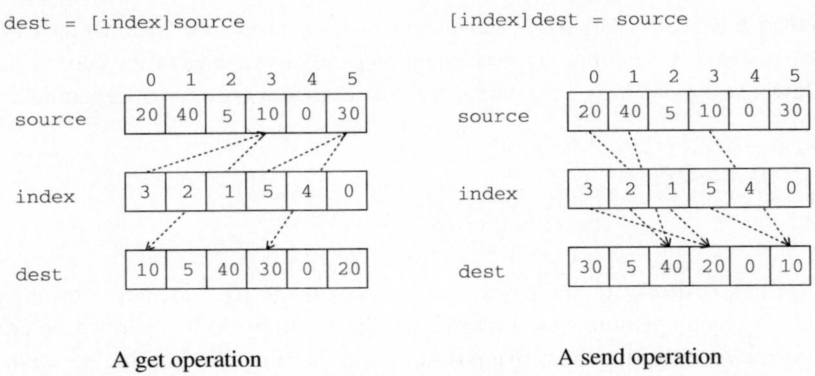

Figure 13.2 Examples of the *send* and *get* general communication operations. Courtesy of Thinking Machines Corporation.

C* allows both *send* and *get* operations. If `index`, `dest`, and `source` are parallel variables of rank one, the general form of the send operation is

```
[index]dest = source;
```

and the general form of the get operation is

```
dest = [index]source;
```

These operations are illustrated in Figure 13.2.

For general communication, the values of the `index` variable can be arbitrary. For grid communication, C* uses a new function called `pcoord` to provide a self-index for a parallel variable along a specified axis. In grid communication, data can be sent only a fixed distance along each dimension. For example,

```
dest1d = [pcoord(0)+1]source1d;
```

shifts the elements stored in `source1d` by one to the right,

```
dest1d = [pcoord(0)-2]source1d;
```

shifts the elements by two to the left, and

```
dest2d = [pcoord(0)+1][pcoord(1)+1]source2d;
```

shifts the elements of `source2d` by one to the left and up. Note that `dest1d` and `source1d` are one-dimensional shapes, whereas `dest2d` and `source2d` are two-dimensional shapes. Wraparound shifts are achieved by using the modulus operation. For example,

```
dest2d = [(pcoord(0)+1)%%4][(pcoord(1)+1)%%3]source2d;
```

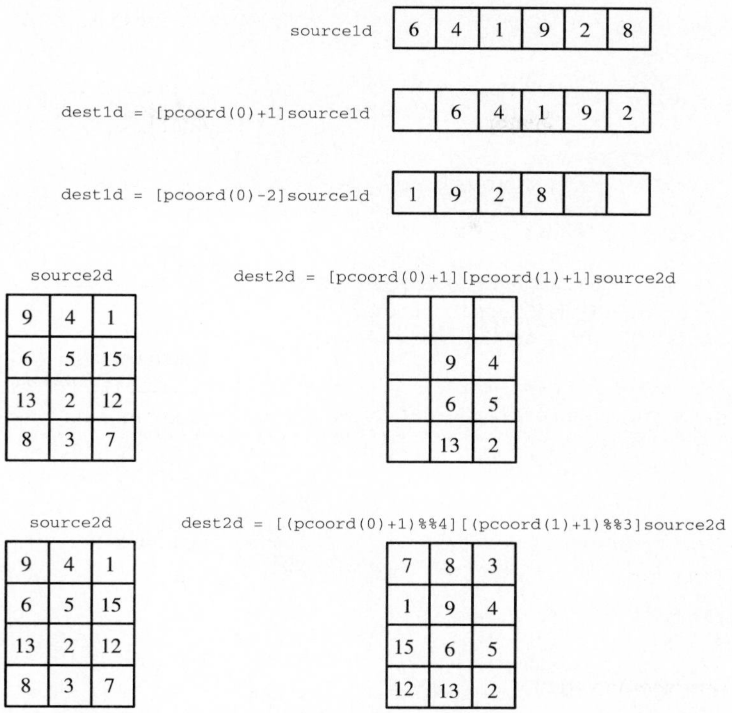

Figure 13.3 Examples of grid communication.

shifts the elements by one to the right and down. The elements that fall off the two-dimensional shape are wrapped around. Note that the numbers 4 and 3 used in the modulus operation, are the number of positions along the corresponding axis. The operator '%%' is similar to C's '%' operator but works with negative values as well. Figure 13.3 shows examples of grid communication.

Example Programs The example we consider is the matrix multiplication algorithm used in Section 13.2.5. We consider two implementations of the same algorithm. The first uses virtual processors, and the second explicitly maps elements onto the physical processors. The first implementation is the following:

```
/*
 * This program implements key components of matrix multiplication
 * in C* using n*n virtual processors.
 * This program is for illustrative purposes only.
 */

#include <stdlib.h>
#include <stdio.h>
#include <ctype.h>
#include <cscomm.h>
```

```
/* Some constants */
#define N      256  /* the size n of the matrices */


/* Declare the shape that the program is using */
shape [N][N]mesh;  /* a 2-dimensional mesh */

/* Global variables */
int:mesh a[N];      /* holds the row of a */
int:mesh b[N];      /* holds the column of b */
int:mesh c;         /* holds the product */
int:mesh buffer;    /* used during communication */

/***********************************************************************
* The program that performs the matrix multiplication
***********************************************************************/
main()
{
  int i;

  with (mesh) { /* choose the appropriate shape */

    /* Perform the shift first along the rows */
    buffer = a[pcoord(1)];
    for (i=1; i<N; i++)
      /* Get the buffer from the adjacent processor */
      buffer = [pcoord(0)][(pcoord(1)+1)%%N]buffer;
      a[(pcoord(1)+i)%N] = buffer;

    /* Perform the shift first along the columns */
    buffer = b[pcoord(0)];
    for (i=1; i<N; i++)
      /* Get the buffer from the adjacent processor */
      buffer = [(pcoord(0)+1)%%N][pcoord(1)]buffer;
      b[(pcoord(0)+i)%N] = buffer;

    /* perform the matrix multiplication */
    c = 0;
    for (i=0; i<N; i++)
      c += a[i]*b[i];
  }
}
```

The program multiplies two $n \times n$ matrices (as shown, $n = 256$). The program defines a single shape called `mesh` that is a two-dimensional grid of size 256×256. This shape closely resembles the topology and data distribution of the matrix multiplication algorithm. Each shape position computes an element of the product matrix. Notice that the program does not specify how many processors are used. If there are 4,092 processors in the machine, each physical processor is assigned 16 shape positions.

The program starts by performing circular shifts of the elements of matrices `a` and `b`. At the end of these shifts, each processor has the required rows of matrix `a` and the

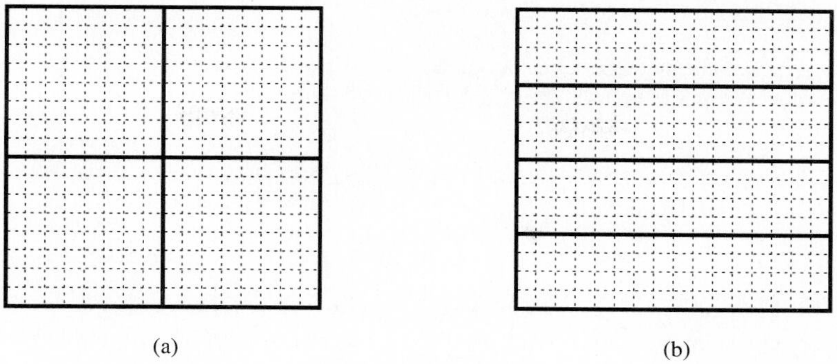

Figure 13.4 Mapping virtual processors onto physical processors. (a) The two-dimensional shape of virtual processors is mapped onto four processors using the block-checkerboard mapping. (b) The two-dimensional shape is mapped using the block-striped mapping.

required columns of matrix `b`. For the circular shifts, the left index of the variable `buffer` is computed modulo n to achieve wraparound communication. Finally, each processor computes one element of the product matrix.

As discussed earlier (Sections 4.2 and 12.3.1), using virtual processors does not always yield the best formulation. For this example, virtual processors may be mapped onto physical processors in many ways, two of which are shown in Figure 13.4. The first mapping leads to a better formulation, because the second yields poor performance. In many cases, we can obtain better performance by explicitly defining a partitioning that maps matrix elements onto processors. The matrix multiplication implementation with explicit mapping leads to the following implementation:

```
/*
 * This program implements key components of matrix multiplication
 * in C* with an explicit mapping.
 * This program is for illustrative purposes only.
 */

#include <stdlib.h>
#include <stdio.h>
#include <ctype.h>
#include <cscomm.h>

/* Some constants */
#define N        256   /* the size n of the matrices */
#define SQRTP     64   /* the square root of the number of processors used */

/* The following data structure holds a block of size
 * (N/SQRTP)*(N/SQRTP) */
struct submatrixdef {
  m[N/SQRTP][N/SQRTP];
};
```

```
typedef struct submatrixdef submatrixdef;

/* Declare the shape that the program is using */
shape [SQRTP][SQRTP]mesh;  /* a 2-dimensional mesh */

/* Global variables */
submatrixdef:mesh a[SQRTP];     /* the array that holds the rows of a */
submatrixdef:mesh b[SQRTP];     /* the array that holds the columns of a */
submatrixdef:mesh c;            /* the array that holds the product */
submatrixdef:mesh buffer;       /* used as a buffer during communication */

/*********************************************************************
 * The program that performs the matrix multiplication using p virtual
 * processors.
 *********************************************************************/
main()
{
  int i,j,k;  /* index variables */

  with (mesh) { /* choose the appropriate shape */

    /* Perform the shift along the rows */
    buffer = a[pcoord(1)];
    for (i=1; i<SQRTP; i++) {
      /* Get the buffer from the adjacent processor */
      buffer = [pcoord(0)][(pcoord(1)+1) %% SQRTP]buffer;
      a[(pcoord(1)+i)%SQRTP] = buffer;
    }

    /* Perform the shift along the columns */
    buffer = b[pcoord(0)];
    for (i=1; i<SQRTP; i++) {
      /* Get the buffer from the adjacent processor */
      buffer = [(pcoord(0)+1) %% SQRTP][pcoord(1)]buffer;
      b[(pcoord(0)+i)%SQRTP] = buffer;
    }

    /* Perform the matrix multiplication */
    for (i=0; i<N/SQRTP; i++)
      for (j=0; j<N/SQRTP; j++) {
        c.m[i][j] = 0;
        for (k=0; k<N; k++)
          /* The following assignment is complicated because of the way
           * the program stores the rows and columns of matrix a and b */
          c.m[i][j] += a[k/(N/SQRTP)].m[i][k%(N/SQRTP)]*
                       b[k/(N/SQRTP)].m[k%(N/SQRTP)][j];
      }
  }
}
```

The program uses a data structure called `submatrixdef` that stores a block of size $(n/\sqrt{p}) \times (n/\sqrt{p})$. Using this data structure, the $n/\sqrt{p}$ rows of matrix `a` assigned to each processor is defined as an array of $\sqrt{p}$ such blocks. This is necessary because of the communication operations. The columns of matrix `b` and the part of matrix `c` assigned to each processor are defined similarly. By explicitly mapping a block of a, b, and c to each processor, we control the amount of communication required.

The first implementation uses virtual processors and lets the compiler and the operating system map them to the physical processors. If a good mapping is chosen, its performance would be similar to that of the second implementation. On the other hand, we see that the first implementation requires more memory than the second. The virtual processor implementation requires each physical processor to store $\Theta(n^3/p)$ elements, and the implementation that uses explicit blocking requires only $\Theta(n^2/\sqrt{p})$ elements.

To summarize, in general we can say that data-parallel programs tend to be smaller than explicit message-passing programs. Furthermore, programs that use the virtual-processor paradigm tend to be simpler to implement.

13.3.3 CM Fortran

Thinking Machines Corporation has developed a Fortran-based data-parallel language that runs on both the CM-2 and CM-5 parallel computers. The CM Fortran language is an extension of Fortran 77 supplemented with array-processing extensions from Fortran 90. The array-processing features map easily onto the SIMD architecture of the CM-2, as well as the CM-5 running in SIMD mode.

The essence of the Fortran 90 array-processing features is that they treat arrays as first-class objects. An array can be referenced by name in an expression or assignment and passed as an argument to any Fortran intrinsic function; the operation is performed on every element of the array. For example,

```
REAL A(40,40,40)
....
A = 8.0           ! Sets all 64,000 elements to 8.0
A = A * 2.0       ! All 64,000 elements contain 16.0
A = SQRT(A)       ! All 64,000 elements contain 4.0
```

The serial implementation of Fortran 90 treats arrays as objects but generates serial code. The Connection Machine stores each array element in the memory of a separate virtual processor and operates on all elements simultaneously.

In contrast to C*, CM Fortran does not provide new data types to support parallelism; thus, we need not take any special action to use the processors of the CM-2 or the CM-5. The CM Fortran compiler allocates arrays on either the host or the processors, depending on how they are used. The rules are as follows:

(1) Arrays that are used only in Fortran 77 constructs in a program, as well as all scalar data, reside on the host. Essentially, the host executes all of the Fortran 77 code.

(2) Arrays that are used in array operations anywhere in a program reside on the processors. The processors execute all of the Fortran 90 code.

CM Fortran supplies a rich set of intrinsic functions for transforming arrays. The array transformations that can be performed are data movement, array reduction, array construction, and array multiplication.

Conformable Arrays When an expression or an assignment involves two or more arrays, the arrays must be ***conformable***; that is, they must be of the same size and shape. Scalars can be used freely in array assignments and array-valued expressions, since Fortran 90 defines a scalar as conformable with any array. Arrays of different sizes and shapes can coexist in the memory of the processors (in different sets of virtual processors), but conformable arrays are always stored in the same set of processors in the same order. For instance, if `A`, `B`, and `C` are one-dimensional arrays of size 10, then elements `A(1)`, `B(1)`, and `C(1)` all reside in the memory of the same processor, as do `A(2)`, `B(2)`, and `C(2)`, and so forth. Each processor executes operations on its own set of array elements; no data motion occurs between processors. If arrays are not conformable, then corresponding array elements do not reside in the memory of the same processor. This fact suggests one of the basic principles of CM Fortran programming: operations on corresponding elements of conformable arrays use the system the most efficiently.

Selecting Array Elements Data parallelism requires that some operations be performed only on certain data elements. An array assignment can be made conditional on an array's values by enclosing the assignment in a `WHERE` statement. `WHERE` is the array-processing extension of the Fortran `IF` statement and is similar to the `where` statement in C*. For example, the following statement prevents division by zero:

```
WHERE (A .NE. 0)  C = B/A
```

Communication Like C*, CM Fortran provides two types of communication: ***grid communication***, which moves data in a regular fashion, and ***general communication***, which allows arbitrary data movement.

Fortran 90 defines ***triplet subscripts***, a new construct for specifying a sequence of subscripts in an array reference. The subscript sequence indicates the subset, or section, of the array to be operated on. The triplet subscript has the following form:

```
array-name(first : last : stride)
```

A triplet indicates the first element, the last element, and an increment interval. The `first` and `last` subscripts default to the declared bounds of the array, and `stride` defaults to one. In CM Fortran, array sections are particularly useful for moving data in regular grid patterns. Data elements are moved by assigning one section of an array to another section of the same array or another array. As with all array operations, array sections must be conformable. For example, if `A` and `B` are one-dimensional arrays, then the statement

```
A(2:9:1) = B(3:10:1)
```

shifts the first eight elements of `B` after position two by one position to the left, and assigns them to `A`. Figure 13.5(a) illustrates this and other examples of this type of communication.

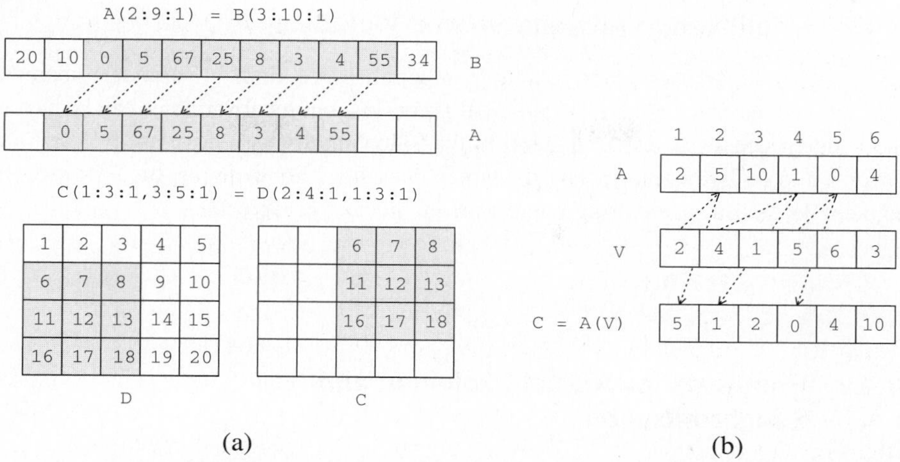

Figure 13.5 Examples of CM Fortran (a) grid communication and (b) vector (or general) communication. Courtesy of Thinking Machines Corporation.

A vector-valued subscript is a form of array section that uses a vector as a subscript. The values of the vector need not be ordered, and there is no fixed stride. This construct specifies an arbitrary selection of array values along a dimension. Vector-valued subscripts are useful for vector permutations and for indexing into a vector or an array. Figure 13.5(b) shows an example of this type of communication. Notice that this type of communication is similar to C*'s get operation.

Besides single-dimension communication, CM Fortran also provides general communication between dimensions by using the `FORALL` statement. A `FORALL` statement defines one or more index variables and uses them in an assignment, thus indicating an action that depends on the positions of the target array elements. `FORALL` is a powerful feature for expressing data motion. For example, `FORALL` can perform, in parallel, arbitrary permutations of multidimensional arrays. The following statement indexes into matrix `H`, using index arrays `X` and `Y`:

```
FORALL  (I=1:N,J=1:M)   G(I,J) = H(X(I,J), Y(I,J))
```

13.4 Primitives for the Shared-Address-Space Programming Paradigm

The primitives required for the shared-address-space programming paradigm fall into three categories: (1) primitives to allocate shared variables, (2) primitives for mutual exclusion and synchronization, and (3) primitives for creating processes.

13.4.1 Primitives to Allocate Shared Variables

The shared-address-space programming paradigm has two kinds of variables: shared and local. Shared variables are accessible to all processes, but local variables can be accessed only by the process that declared them. In the following discussion we use two keywords, `shared` and `private`, to specify the type of variables. For example, the following code fragment declares a shared array `b` and a private integer variable `i`:

```
shared int b[10000];
private int i;
```

13.4.2 Primitives for Mutual Exclusion and Synchronization

When separate processes access shared variables, it is important that the operations do not conflict with each other. A ***critical section*** contains code that must be executed by only one process at a time. Languages using the shared-address-space programming paradigm provide ***locks*** to help the programmer enforce mutual exclusion for critical section execution. These locks are usually implemented by using a special type of shared variable that can be manipulated only by ***atomic operations***. An operation is atomic if it cannot be interrupted by another process. Each lock can be owned by at most one process at any time. The process that owns the lock can execute the corresponding critical section. When a process leaves the critical section, it releases the lock. If a process tries to acquire a lock that is currently owned by another process, it enters a ***busy-wait*** cycle or suspends execution. In a busy-wait cycle, a processor continuously checks the lock, waiting for it to be released. When a process suspends execution, it joins a queue associated with the lock it tried to acquire. The process becomes active again when the lock has been released and the process is at the front of the queue.

Example 13.1 Solving a Mutual-Exclusion Problem
To solve the problem of increasing and decreasing the value of `x` in Section 13.1.2, we create a lock that determines which process has access to `x`. In our hypothetical language, `lock access_x` declares a lock called `access_x`. The function `get_lock(lock)` causes a process to enter a busy-wait cycle until it acquires the lock. The function `release_lock(lock)` releases a lock. The problem is solved by executing the following code by each process:

```
/* Code for one process */       /* Code for the other process */
get_lock(access_x);              get_lock(access_x)
x = x + 1;                       x = x - 1;
release_lock(access_x);          release_lock(access_x);
```

■

Besides locks, other mechanisms, such as semaphores and monitors, are also provided by languages using the shared-address-space programming paradigm to help the programmer enforce mutual exclusion in more complicated situations.

During the concurrent execution of processes, there are situations in which the processes need to synchronize before the end of the execution. Synchronization is achieved by a ***barrier synchronization*** primitive. This primitive is executed when the processes need to synchronize, and operates as follows. Each processes wait at the barrier for every other processes. After synchronization, all processes proceed with their execution.

13.4.3 Primitives for Creating Processes

In the shared-address-space programming paradigm, process creation is done by a system call that creates processes identical to the parent process. These processes share the variables declared `shared` by the parent process, as well as the locks declared and initialized by the parent process. Once created, subprocesses can perform independent computations. After the subprocesses have been created, the single execution thread is partitioned into several threads with access to shared data. Creating subprocesses is similar to spawning new processes in any multitasking operating system. On most shared-address-space computers, this operation is called ***fork*** (after a similar system call in the UNIX operating system). The parent process continues execution after creating its subprocesses. When the subprocesses terminate, they merge by using another primitive, typically called ***join***.

Instead of creating processes at the beginning of the execution, we can also have a single process, usually called the ***master process***. When the master process needs to perform a task in parallel it can create a predetermined number of other processes that work in parallel to perform the task. These processes are usually called ***slave processes***. When the task is complete, the slave processes terminate and control returns to the master process. Later, the master can create slave processes again. For example, consider a program that consists of a sequence of computationally intensive loops separated by some bookkeeping computations. Using the master-slave approach, the master performs the bookkeeping and creates slave processes to perform the computations required by each loop. We assume that there is a function called `slave-spawn(func)` that creates a predetermined number of slave processes, each executing the function `func`. Slave processes partition the work done by `func` in a predetermined way.

In the following sections we discuss an example of a parallel computer and language that implement the shared-address-space programming paradigm.

13.4.4 Sequent Symmetry

The Sequent Symmetry is a shared-address-space computer that runs the DYNIX operating system, a multiprocessor version of UNIX. The Symmetry is a bus-based system that can use up to thirty 32-bit processors. Even if no effort is made to parallelize a user application, all DYNIX processes potentially run in parallel. In addition, users can specify explicit parallelism. The entire main memory is equally accessible to all processors. Each processor also has some local cache memory.

The Symmetry is programmed in languages such as C and Fortran. These languages include extensions that allow programs to specify explicit parallelism. Shared variables are declared in C by using the `shared` data-type modifier. Shared variables are declared in Fortran by putting all the shared data into the same COMMON block, then giving compiler directives indicating that the COMMON block is to reside in shared memory. All other variables are private.

The Symmetry supports two different ways of creating processes. The first is called ***multitasking*** and the other is called ***microtasking***. We create multitasks by using the `fork` function and microtasks by using the `m_fork` function. `Fork` is the standard UNIX process creation function that creates an identical copy of the calling process. `M_fork` takes the function that will be executed by all the processes as an argument. For microtasking, the user specifies how many processes to create with the `m_set_procs` function. The processes take significantly less time to be created compared to the time required for the `fork` function. The number of processes that can be created is limited by the number of available physical processors in the system. However, this does not impose any limit on the computational granularity assigned to each process. Processes can be assigned small amounts of computation and request more work when they run out. This is illustrated in the example programs in the next section.

The Symmetry provides two new data types for C to allow locks and barrier synchronization. These data types are `slock_t` for locks and `sbarrier_t` for barrier synchronization. The operations defined on these types depend on whether microtasking or multitasking is used. The operations are shown in Table 13.2.

13.4.5 Example Programs

Consider again the simple matrix-multiplication algorithm. We present two different microtasking-based implementations of the algorithm. The main difference between these programs is the granularity of computation assigned to each process.

The matrices `a` and `b` to be multiplied and the result matrix `c` are declared as `shared`, so all processors can access them. In the first version, each process computes an element of the matrix `c`. If after finishing its computation, there are more elements of `c` not being computed by other processes, a process requests another element and computes it. This series of operations continues until `c` has been computed.

```
/*
 * This program implements key components for multiplying two matrices
 * a and b. The result is stored in matrix c. This is the first version.
 * This program is for illustrative purposes only.
 */

#include <stdio.h>
#include <parallel/microtask.h>
#include <parallel/parallel.h>
```

Table 13.2 Operations allowed by the Sequent Symmetry on `slock_t` and `sbarrier_t` variable types.

Multitasking	
Operations on `slock_t`:	
`s_init_lock()`	initialize a lock
`s_lock()`	set the lock
`s_unlock()`	clear the lock
Operations on `sbarrier_t`:	
`s_init_barrier()`	initialize the barrier variable
`s_wait_barrier()`	wait for all multitasks to reach the barrier
Microtasking	
Operations on `slock_t`:	
`m_lock()`	set the lock
`m_unlock()`	clear the lock
Operations on `sbarrier_t`:	
`m_sync()`	wait for all microtasks to arrive
`m_single()`	wait for master process to call `m_multi()`
`m_multi()`	resume all slaves in parallel

```
#define SIZE 100       /* The size of matrices */
#define MAXPROCS 25    /* The maximum number of processes to be spawned */

/* * Shared data */
shared float a[SIZE][SIZE];
shared float b[SIZE][SIZE];
shared float c[SIZE][SIZE];
shared next_c;         /* Holds the next element of c to be computed */

/*******************************************************************
* The program that manages the matrix multiplication
*******************************************************************/
main()
{
  init_matrix(a, b, c);      /* initialize matrices a, b, and c.
                                The code is omitted */
  next_c = MAXPROCS;         /* the first element not being assigned
                                to a processes */
  m_set_procs(MAXPROCS);     /* set number of processes to MAXPROCS */
  m_fork(matmul, a, b, c);   /* execute parallel loop */
  m_kill_procs();            /* kill child processes */
}
```

```
/**********************************************************************
* Matrix multiplication function. Each process computes elements of
* matrix c until all elements have been computed.
**********************************************************************/
matmul(a, b, c)
float a[][SIZE], b[][SIZE], c[][SIZE];
{
  int done;       /* flag to indicate no more work */
  int i, j, k;    /* index variables */

  /* get the initial element of c */
  i = m_get_myid()/SIZE;
  j = m_get_myid()%SIZE;

  done = 0;
  do {
    for (k=0; k<SIZE; k++)   /* compute c[i,j] */
      c[i][j] += a[i][k] + b[k][j];

    m_lock();  /* wait to read shared variable next_c */
    if (next_c >= SIZE*SIZE)
      done = 1;  /* no more work is left */
    /* get the next c[i,j] element */
    i = next_c/SIZE;
    j = next_c%SIZE;
    next_c++;  /* update the next available element of c */
    m_unlock();  /* release the lock */
  } while (!done);
}
```

In the second version, the program spawns 25 processes and assigns a block of 20×20 elements of matrix c to each of these processes. By doing this, the work is equally partitioned among the processes. This version implements the block-checkerboard partitioning discussed in Section 5.4.

```
/*
 * This program implements key components for multiplying two matrices
 * a and b. The result is stored in matrix c. This is the second version.
 * This program is for illustrative purposes only.
 */

#include <stdio.h>
#include <parallel/microtask.h>
#include <parallel/parallel.h>

#define SIZE 100          /* The size of matrices */
#define MAXPROCS 25       /* The maximum number of processes to be
  spawned */
#define SQRTMAXPROCS 5 /* The square root of MAXPROCS */

/* * Shared data */
shared float a[SIZE][SIZE];
shared float b[SIZE][SIZE];
shared float c[SIZE][SIZE];
```

```
/***********************************************************************
* The program that manages the matrix multiplication
***********************************************************************/
main()
{
  init_matrix(a, b, c);        /* initialize matrices a, b, and c.
                                  The code is omitted */
  m_set_procs(MAXPROCS);       /* set number of processes to MAXPROCS */
  m_fork(matmul, a, b, c);     /* execute parallel loop */
  m_kill_procs();              /* kill child processes */
}


/***********************************************************************
* Matrix multiplication function. Each process computes a block of
* elements of matrix c.
***********************************************************************/
matmul(a, b, c)
float a[][SIZE], b[][SIZE], c[][SIZE];
{
  int i, j, k;   /* index variables */
  int x, y;      /* which block the process is computing */

  /* get the initial element of c */
  x = m_get_myid()/SQRTMAXPROCS;
  y = m_get_myid()%SQRTMAXPROCS;

  for (i = x*SIZE/SQRTMAXPROCS; i < (x+1)*SIZE/SQRTMAXPROCS;; i++)
    for (j = y*SIZE/SQRTMAXPROCS; j < (y+1)*SIZE/SQRTMAXPROCS;; j++)
      for (k=0; k<SIZE; k++)   /* compute c[i,j] */
        c[i][j] += a[i][k] + b[k][j];
}
```

Several observations can be made about the two versions of the matrix-multiplication program. The first version is conceptually easier to program and understand since it partitions the work among the processes in a straightforward manner. The interprocess communication overhead, however, is significantly higher compared to the second version. Every time a process runs out of work it has to get the next element of c that has not been assigned to another process. This involves acquiring and releasing a lock. When many processes are trying to get an element to compute, this can take a significant amount of time. On the other hand, programs written to exploit fine-grain parallelism (as in the first version) have the potential of achieving better load balancing, because work is dynamically allocated to idle processes.

The major advantage of the second version over the first is that it exploits data locality. In the first version, each process computes elements that belong at various parts of matrix c. As a result, for each element it computes, a process might need different rows and columns of a and b. These columns will most likely not be in the local cache. In the second version, however, each process reuses the rows and columns of a and b it needs, increasing the possibility that these will be in the local cache. Preserving data locality becomes even more important in NUMA shared-address-space computers. For such machines, the second version only has to copy the rows and columns of `a` and `b` it requires from shared memory to local memory. It then proceeds with its computation by accessing only local memory. Thus, contention for shared memory decreases and the overall performance of the algorithm increases.

Note that this program is smaller than both the message-passing and the data-parallel implementations presented earlier.

13.5 Fortran D

Several parallel programming languages have been proposed that lie between explicit and implicit parallel languages. These languages provide facilities that enable the compiler to generate efficient parallel code. Fortran D is one such language.

Fortran D programs specify how the data (such as Fortran arrays) are assigned to processors. The compiler uses this information to generate parallel programs. Although Fortran D exploits data parallelism, it is not a data-parallel programming language. In pure data-parallel programming languages, the programmer specifies the code to be executed by each processor, and the code is replicated in all the processors. In Fortran D, the programmer describes the computation as a single program. The programmer does not specify how data elements are moved between processors; the compiler uses knowledge about how the data are distributed to generate code for each processor. The facilities provided by Fortran D for data decomposition and distribution are significantly richer than those provided by conventional data-parallel languages (such as the `shape` primitive of C*).

The problem of mapping arrays onto processors is approached at two levels: ***problem mapping*** and ***machine mapping***. Problem mapping determines the alignment of arrays with respect to each other. The problem mapping is influenced by the structure of the underlying computation. If a computation requires corresponding elements from two separate arrays, it is better to align the arrays. This ensures that, after the distribution of arrays on different processors, these elements will belong to the same processor. As an example, consider the problem of matrix addition. In order to avoid any communication, the matrices to be added must be aligned with each other.

Machine mapping determines the distribution of the data on the actual parallel machine. This distribution is influenced by hardware characteristics such as the topology and communication mechanism.

Fortran D supports problem mapping with the `DECOMPOSITION` and `ALIGN` statements, and machine mapping with the `DISTRIBUTE` statement. These capabilities are described in the following subsections. In addition to these statements, Fortran D also provides irregular data distribution and dynamic data decomposition (that is, the ability to change the alignment or distribution of a decomposition at any point in the program).

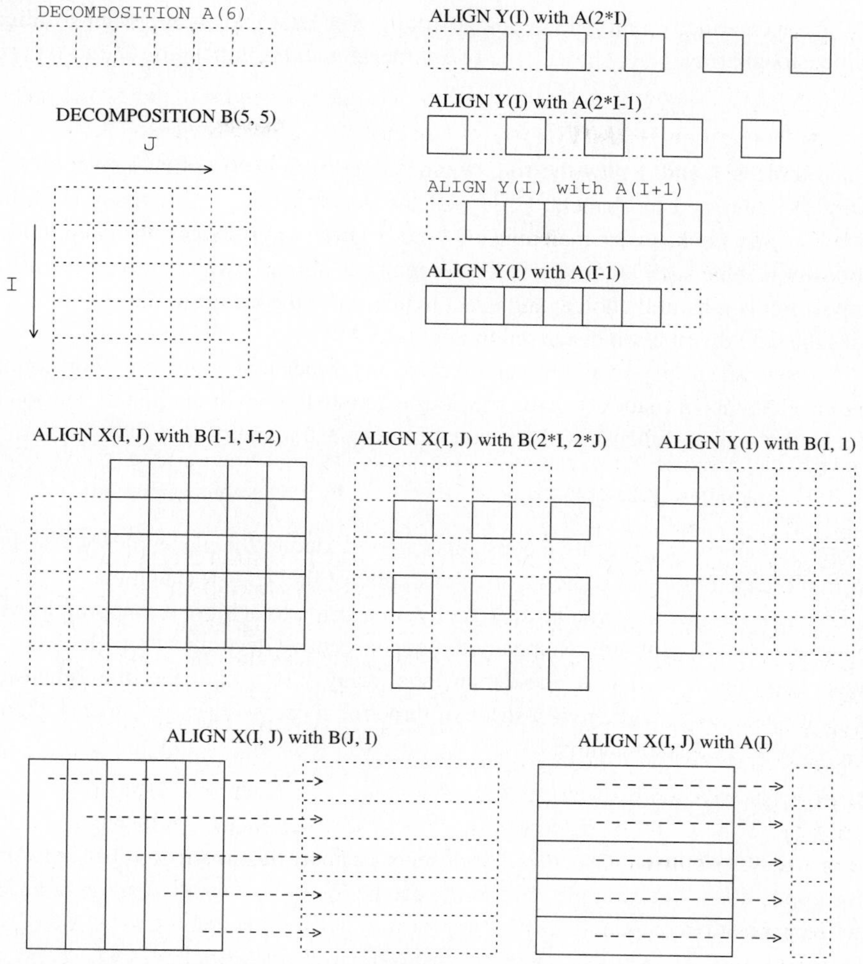

Figure 13.6 Examples of the ALIGN statement.

13.5.1 Problem Mapping

The DECOMPOSITION statement declares the name, dimensionality, and size of a decomposition. A decomposition is simply an abstract layout or index domain. For example, the following statements declare a one-dimensional decomposition of size N called A, and a two-dimensional decomposition of size N×N called B.

```
DECOMPOSITION A(N)
DECOMPOSITION B(N,N)
```

The ALIGN statement maps arrays with respect to a decomposition. There are a variety of possible alignments in Fortran D. The simplest alignment occurs when the array is mapped exactly onto the decomposition. For example, if we want to align a two-dimensional array X(N,N) with the two-dimensional decomposition B, the syntax is

```
ALIGN X(I,J) with B(I,J)
```

The indices I and J play the role of placeholders, indicating that element (I,J) of matrix X is mapped to element (I,J) of the decomposition. For many algorithms described in this book, exact matching may be a good way to align the data with the decomposition. One such algorithm is matrix multiplication, in which a two-dimensional decomposition is a natural choice, and exact matching of the arrays to the decomposition provides the data distribution discussed in Section 5.4.1.

The user can specify an alignment offset for any dimension of an array. For example, to shift the elements of matrix X in the previous example by two in the first dimension and by three in the second dimension, the syntax of the ALIGN statement is

```
ALIGN X(I,J) with B(I+2,J+3)
```

In general, any positive or negative constants can be added to the placeholders to indicate the desired offset. Figure 13.6 shows some examples of the ALIGN statement.

The ALIGN statement can be specified with a stride to achieve a mapping in which consecutive array elements are mapped onto nonconsecutive decomposition elements. For example, if we want to map a one-dimensional array Y(N) onto the one-dimensional decomposition A such that there is a stride of three for successive array elements, then the syntax of the ALIGN statement is

```
ALIGN Y(I) with A(3*I)
```

The ALIGN construct also allows the user to permute the dimensions between arrays and decompositions. For example, this ability can be used to map the transpose of an array onto a decomposition:

```
ALIGN X(I,J), with B(J,I)
```

It is sometimes convenient to ignore certain dimensions of the array when mapping an array onto a decomposition. All data elements in the unassigned dimensions are mapped onto the same location in the decomposition.

Conversely, it may be necessary to map arrays with fewer dimensions onto the decomposition. In this case, it is necessary to specify the mapping for each dimension of the array and the actual position of the array in the unmapped dimensions of the decomposition. One example is mapping a vector onto a two-dimensional decomposition in matrix-vector multiplication (Section 5.3). This can be done by using the following statement:

```
ALIGN Y(I) with B(I,N)
```

This statements aligns the vector Y with the last column of the decomposition.

In many of the ALIGN statements presented, some of the array elements do not fit within the decomposition. In this case, Fortran D allows the programmer to specify whether the elements should be truncated or wrapped around.

13.5.2 Machine Mapping

The DISTRIBUTE statement takes a decomposition and distributes it to available processors. Each dimension of a decomposition can be distributed differently. Three types of distributions are supported by Fortran D: BLOCK, CYCLIC, and BLOCK_CYCLIC. If p is the number of processors and n is the size of a dimension in the decomposition, the distributions are described as follows:

(1) BLOCK distribution divides the decomposition into contiguous chunks of size n/p, assigning one block to each processor. For example, if B(N,N) is a two-dimensional decomposition, then the statement DISTRIBUTE B(BLOCK, BLOCK) assigns blocks of $(N/\sqrt{p}) \times (N/\sqrt{p})$ elements to each processor. The BLOCK decomposition can be used to map elements onto processors in a blocked style. If the decomposition is one-dimensional, then this distribution corresponds to block-striped mapping (Section 5.1.1). If the decomposition is two-dimensional, then this distribution corresponds to block-checkerboard mapping (Section 5.1.2).

(2) CYCLIC distribution specifies a round-robin division of the decomposition, assigning every p^{th} element to the same processor. The statement DISTRIBUTE B(CYCLIC, CYCLIC) distributes the elements of the decomposition in a manner similar to the cyclic mapping. If the decomposition is one-dimensional, then this distribution corresponds to cyclic-striped mapping (Section 5.1.1). If the decomposition is two-dimensional, then this distribution corresponds to cyclic-checkerboard mapping (Section 5.1.2).

(3) BLOCK_CYCLIC is similar to CYCLIC but takes a parameter m. It first divides the dimension into contiguous chunks of size m and then assigns these chunks in the same fashion as CYCLIC. If the decomposition is one-dimensional, then this distribution corresponds to block-cyclic-striped mapping (Section 5.1.1). If the decomposition is two-dimensional, then this distribution corresponds to block-cyclic checkerboard mapping (Section 5.1.2). For example, DISTRIBUTE B(BLOCK_CYCLIC(2), BLOCK_CYCLIC(2)) distributes the elements in a block-cyclic-checkerboard mapping mapping with block size of two.

Any one of these three types of distributions can be assigned for each dimension of the decomposition. For multidimensional decompositions, different combinations of distribution patterns may be assigned to distinct dimensions. The asterisk (*) denotes dimensions that are assigned locally; these dimensions are not distributed. Figure 13.7 illustrates some of these distributions.

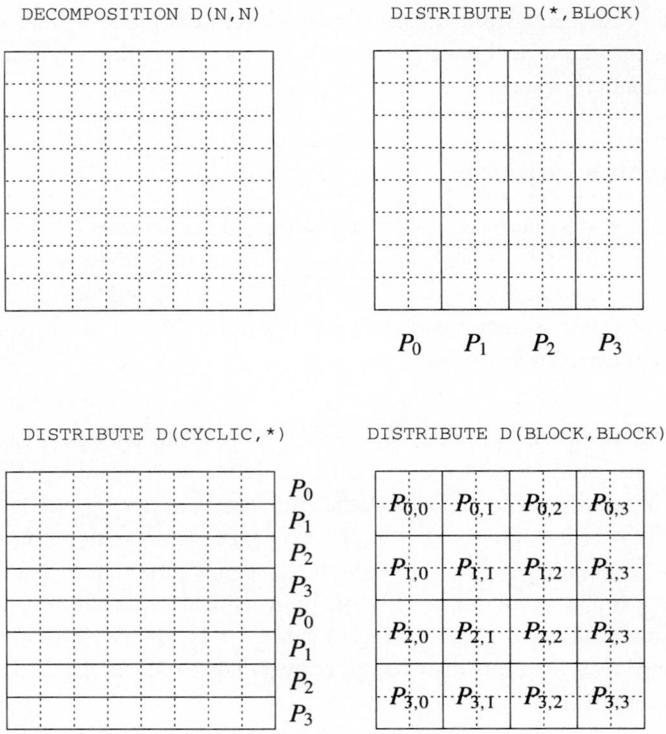

Figure 13.7 Various decomposition-to-processor distributions.

For example, to implement Dijkstra's single-source shortest-paths algorithm (Section 7.3), we must map the rows of the adjacency matrix onto the processors. If `X(N,N)` is the adjacency matrix and `A(N,N)` is the two-dimensional decomposition, this can be done by the following statements:

```
ALIGN X(I,J) with A(I,J)
DISTRIBUTE A(BLOCK,*)
```

Fortran D also allows us to specify processor allocations, where the allocation gives the number of processors assigned to each dimension of the decomposition. This allows the user to change the default assignment of the compiler, which is to assign an equal number of processors to each dimension.

13.5.3 Example Program

As for the previous programming paradigms, the example we consider is that of multiplying two matrices. The Fortran D version of matrix multiplication is the following:

```
C       This program is for illustrative purposes only.
C
        PROGRAM mmult
        INTEGER a(1000,1000), b(1000,1000), c(1000,1000)
C
C       ************************************************************
C       * Set the number of processors to be used
C       ************************************************************
C
        PARAMETER (n$proc = 100)
C
C       DECOMPOSITION mesh(1000,1000)
C       ALIGN a, b, c, WITH mesh
C       DISTRIBUTE mesh(BLOCK,BLOCK)
C
C       ************************************************************
C       * Perform the matrix multiplication
C       ************************************************************
C
        DO i = 1, 1000
          DO j = 1, 1000
            DO k = 1, 1000
              c(i,j) = c(i,j) + a(i,k)*b(k,j)
            ENDDO
          ENDDO
        ENDDO
C
      END
```

This program multiplies two 1000×1000 matrices, a and b, and stores the result in matrix c. Notice how similar this code is to the sequential implementation of matrix multiplication. In fact, the computation loops are the same for both the sequential and the parallel version. The only difference is the DECOMPOSITION, DISTRIBUTE, and ALIGN statements at the beginning of the program.

The program initially selects the number of processors to use with the parameter n$proc. It then declares a two-dimensional decomposition of size 1000×1000 and aligns the three matrices on the decomposition by mapping them exactly onto it. Next, it distributes the decomposition to the available processors by using blocks in each dimension. Each processor is responsible for a 100×100 block.

Having specified the data decomposition and distribution, the program proceeds to perform matrix multiplication by using the sequential algorithm. The efficiency of the generated code depends solely on the compiler's ability to analyze dependencies and perform the necessary interprocessor communication in such a way as to mimic the parallel formulations presented earlier. If the compiler uses the simple heuristic that a processor acquires all the data that it needs before performing computation, then the resulting program would have performance similar to the one described in Section 5.4.1. However, it appears much more difficult to arrive at the other matrix multiplication algorithms, such as Cannon's and DNS (Sections 5.4.2 and 5.4.4), even with a sophisticated compile-time analysis.

13.6 Bibliographic Remarks

Several books provide details on various programming paradigms and languages. Lewis and El-Rewini [LER92] and Lester [Les93] provide an introduction to parallel programming paradigms. Ben-Ari [BA82] and Brawer [Bra89b] cover programming aspects of shared-address-space parallel computers and concurrent programming in general. Hatcher and Quinn [HQ91] give a comprehensive introduction to the data-parallel programming paradigm. Hoare [Hoa85] discusses the concept of communicating sequential processes (CSP) as a means of programming for concurrency. Andrews [And91] covers basic concepts and practical examples for programming shared-address-space and message-passing computers.

Several surveys provide comparative studies of various parallel programming languages and paradigms. Karp [Kar87] surveys parallel programming languages with emphasis on languages for shared-address-space and message-passing computers. Bal, Steiner, and Tanenbaum [BST89] survey recent programming languages for distributed computing systems. In particular, they discuss languages based on synchronous and asynchronous message passing, the rendezvous mechanism, remote procedure calls, object-oriented programming, atomic transactions, functional programming, and logic programming. Shapiro [Sha89] surveys a family of concurrent logic programming languages. Carriero and Gelernter [CG89] present a framework for parallel programming. This framework is based on their classification of parallelism as result parallelism, agenda parallelism, and specialist parallelism. Cheng [Che93] provides brief summaries of many programming languages and tools.

Hillis and Steele [HS86] were the first to advocate the data parallel paradigm for programming on large-scale, fine-grain SIMD parallel computers such as the CM-2. The data-parallel languages that are available for CM-2 are C* [Thi90a], described in Section 13.3.2; CM Fortran [Thi91], described in Section 13.3.3; and *Lisp [Thi90b], which is a data-parallel version of Lisp. C* and CM Fortran are also available on CM-5. MP-2 [Mas92a] is another commercially-available SIMD parallel computer. The MP-2 is programmed by using data-parallel extensions to C and Fortran [Mas91, Mas92b]. Hatcher and Quinn [HQ91, HQA$^+$91, HQL$^+$91, QH90] describe a data-parallel variation of C called Dataparallel C. Dataparallel C is a variant of the original C* for the Connection Machine as described by Rose and Steele [RS87]. Note that the current version of C* is substantially different from the original one. Dataparallel C is available on various MIMD computers [HQ91]. Blelloch and Chatterjee [CBF91, BC90, Ble90] have also developed data-parallel programming languages for MIMD computers. DINO [RSW90] extends the C language for data-parallel programming. PC++ [BBG$^+$91] is a data-parallel extension to C++. Parallaxis [Bra89a] extends Modula-2 for data-parallel programming. X3H5 [ANS92] is an emerging ANSI standard for extensions to Fortran and C for the SPMD shared-address-space programming paradigm. Our discussion of data-parallel programming is influenced by Hatcher and Quinn [HQ91].

Message-passing computers are typically programmed in conventional sequential languages augmented with message-passing primitives. For additional information about such extensions for the nCUBE 2 parallel computer, refer to [nCU90]; for the CM-5, see [Thi92a, Thi92b, Thi92c]; and for the iPSC 860, refer to [Int92a, Int92b]. EXPRESS [Par90], PVM [DGMS91, Sun90], P4 [BL92], and PICL [GHPW90] are vendor independent sets of library routines that are available for a variety of commercial parallel computers. They can also be used to program a network of heterogeneous computers to function as a large parallel computer. The Message Passing Interface Forum [Mes93] is in the process of defining a set of library interface standards for message passing.

The Fortran D language and compiler were developed at Rice University [FHK$^+$90, HKK$^+$92, HKT92]. Fortran 90 [ISO91] extends Fortran 77 for parallel programming. High Performance Fortran (HPF) [Hig93] is an emerging standard that extends Fortran 90 for high-performance parallel programming. Fortran M [FC92] extends Fortran 77 for parallelism at the task level.

Significant work has been done in parallelizing sequential programs. The monographs by Banerjee [Ban88a], Wolfe [Wol89], and Zima and Chapman [ZC91] review the issues involved. Efforts to extract parallelism from sequential programs have concentrated mainly on loops. Loop parallelization has the potential of providing significant speedup, since loops perform most of the computation in many programs. This research has resulted in a variety of techniques for data dependency testing, loop restructuring for higher parallelism, and scheduling loop iterations onto processors [Ban88b, BC86, Cyt86, Cyt87, LYZ89, Pol87, Pol88a, Pol88b, WB87, Wol86]

Many tools have been developed that attempt to extract parallelism from sequential programs. These tools include Parafrase-2 [Pol90], SUPERB [ZBG88], PFC [AK82], and PTOOL [All86]. Numerous methods have been proposed for data dependency testing [Ken81]. FORGE 90 [App92] is a toolkit for interactively parallelizing Fortran loops. PARASCOPE [CCH$^+$87] is an environment for the development of parallel scientific programs written in a shared-address-space parallel dialect of Fortran 77.

SR [AO93] is a language for programming shared-address-space as well as message-passing computers. SR has two main concepts: resources and operations. By a novel integration of these ideas, it supports shared variables, semaphores, synchronous and asynchronous message passing, RPC and rendezvous. Concurrent C [GR88, TAAT84] extends the C language by adding support for distributed programming. SISAL [FCO90] is a general-purpose functional language for parallel numeric computation. Linda [CG90, GCCC85] is a coordination language that provides language extensions to C and Fortran for parallel programming by using the shared-address-space programming paradigm. OCCAM [Pou86] is a language based upon communicating sequential processes [Hoa85].

A number of debugging and visualization tools have been developed to aid in programming parallel computers [Che93]. ParaGraph [HE91, Hea93] helps the programmer graphically visualize the behavior and performance of parallel programs on message-passing computers. ParaGraph takes as input execution traces created by PICL [GHPW90] and produces an animated graphical depiction of the behavior of the parallel program. ParaGraph provides a wide range of graphical display formats. Users can select those formats that best visualize the behavior of their programs.

References

[AK82] J. R. Allen and K. Kennedy. PFC: A program to convert Fortran to parallel form. In *Proceedings of the IBM Conference on Parallel Computers and Scientific Computing*, 1982.

[All86] J. R. Allen. PTOOL: A semi-automatic parallel programming assistant. In *Proceedings of the 1986 International Conference on Parallel Processing*, 1986.

[And91] G. R. Andrews. *Concurrent Programming Principles and Practice*. Benjamin/Cummings, Redwood City, CA, 1991.

[ANS92] ANSI Technical Committee X3H5. *Parallel Processing Model for High Level Programming Languages*. 1992.

[AO93] G. R. Andrews and R. A. Olsson. *The SR Programming Language: Concurrency in Practice*. Benjamin/Cummings, Redwood City, CA, 1993.

[App92] Applied Parallel Research. *FORGE 90, Baseline System User's Guide*. Version 8.0 edition. 1992.

[BA82] M. Ben-Ari. *Principles of Concurrent Programming*. Prentice-Hall, Englewood Cliffs, NJ, 1982.

[Ban88a] U. Banerjee. *Dependence Analysis for Supercomputing*. Kluwer Academic Publishers, Boston, MA, 1988.

[Ban88b] U. Banerjee. An introduction to a formal theory of dependence analysis. *Journal of Supercomputing*, 2, 1988.

[BBG+91] F. Bodin, P. Beckman, D. B. Gannon, S. Narayana, and S. Yang. Distributed pC++: Basic ideas for an object parallel language. In *Supercomputing '91 Proceedings*, 273–282, 1991.

[BC86] M. Burke and R. Cytron. Interprocedural dependence analysis and parallelization. In *Proceedings of the SIGPLAN 86 Symposium on Compiler Construction*, 1986.

[BC90] G. E. Blelloch and S. Chatterjee. VCODE: A data-parallel intermediate language. In *Proceedings of the Third Symposium on the Frontiers of Massively Parallel Computation*, New York, NY, 1990. IEEE Press.

[BL92] R. Butler and E. Lusk. User's guide to the P4 parallel programming system. Technical Report ANL–92/17, Argonne National Laboratory, Argonne, IL, 1992.

[Ble90] G. E. Blelloch. *Vector Models for Data-Parallel Computing*. MIT Press, Cambridge, MA, 1990.

[Bra89a] T. Braunl. Structured SIMD programming in parallaxis. *Structured Programming Journal*, 10(3), 1989.

[Bra89b] S. Brawer. *Introduction to Parallel Programming*. Academic Press, Boston, MA, 1989.

[BST89] H. E. Bal, J. G. Steiner, and A. S. Tanenbaum. Programming languages for distributed computing systems. *ACM Computing Surveys*, 21(3):261–322, September 1989.

[CBF91] S. Chatterjee, G. E. Blelloch, and A. L. Fisher. Size and access inference for data-parallel programs. In *Proceedings of the 1991 ACM SIGPLAN Conference on Design and Implementation of Programming Languages*, 1991.

[CCH+87] A. Carle, K. D. Cooper, R. T. Hood, K. Kennedy, L. Torczon, and S. K. Warren. A practical environment for scientific programming. *IEEE Computer*, 20(11):75–89, November 1987.

[CG89] N. Carriero and D. Gelernter. How to write parallel programs: A guide to the perplexed. *ACM Computing Surveys*, 21(3):323–357, September 1989.

[CG90] N. Carriero and D. Gelernter. *How to Write Parallel Programs*. MIT Press, Cambridge, MA, 1990.

[Che93] D. Y. Cheng. A survey of parallel programming languages and tools. Technical Report RND–93–005, NASA Ames Research Center, Moffet Field, CA, 1993.

[Cyt86] R. Cytron. Doacross: Beyond vectorization for multiprocessors. In *Proceedings of the 1986 International Conference on Parallel Processing*, 1986.

[Cyt87] R. Cytron. Limited processor scheduling of Doacross loops. In *Proceedings of the 1987 International Conference on Parallel Processing*, 1987.

[DGMS91] J. J. Dongarra, G. A. Geist, R. Manchek, and V. S. Sunderam. A users' guide to PVM. Technical Report 37831–6367, Oak Ridge National Laboratory, Oak Ridge, TN, 1991.

[FC92] I. Foster and K. M. Chandy. Fortran M: A language for modular parallel programming. Preprint mcs-p327-0992, Argonne National Laboratory, Argonne, IL, 1992.

[FCO90] J. T. Feo, D. C. Cann, and R. R. Oldehoeft. A report on the SISAL language project. *Journal of Parallel and Distributed Computing*, 12(10):349–366, December 1990.

[FHK+90] G. C. Fox, S. Hiranandani, K. Kennedy, C. Koelbel, U. Kremer, C. Tseng, and M. Wu. Fortran D language specification. Technical Report TR 90-141, Department of Computer Science, Rice University, Houston, TX, 1990.

[GCCC85] D. Gelernter, N. Carriero, S. Chandran, and S. Chang. Parallel programming in Linda. In *Proceedings of the 1985 International Conference on Parallel Processing*, 255–263, 1985.

[GHPW90] G. A. Geist, M. T. Heath, B. W. Peyton, and P. H. Worley. PICL: A portable instrumented communication library, C reference manual. Technical Report ORNL/TM-11130, Oak Ridge National Laboratory, Oak Ridge, TN, 1990.

[GR88] N. H. Gehani and W. D. Roome. *The Concurrent C Programming Language*. Silicon Press, Summit, NJ, 1988.

[HE91] M. T. Heath and J. A. Etheridge. Visualizing the performance of parallel programs. *IEEE Software*, 5(9):29–39, September 1991.

[Hea93] M. T. Heath. Recent developments and case studies in performance visualization using ParaGraph. In G. Haring and G. Kotsis, editors, *Performance Measurement and Visualization of Parallel Systems*, 175–200. Elsevier Science Publishers B. V., New York, NY, 1993.

[Hig93] High Performance Fortran Forum. *High Performance Fortran Language Specification*. 1993.

[HKK+92] S. Hiranandani, K. Kennedy, C. Koelbel, U. Kremer, and C. Tseng. An overview of the Fortran D programming system. In *Languages and Compilers for Parallel Computing, Fourth International Workshop*. Springer-Verlag, Santa Clara, CA, 1992.

[HKT92] S. Hiranandani, K. Kennedy, and C. Tseng. Compiler support for machine-independent parallel programming in Fortran D. In J. H. Saltz and P. Mehrotra, editors, *Languages, Compilers, and Run-Time Environments for Distributed Memory Machines*. North-Holland, Amsterdam, The Netherlands, 1992.

[Hoa85] C. A. R. Hoare. *Communicating Sequential Processes*. Prentice-Hall, Cambridge, MA, 1985.

[HQ91] P. J. Hatcher and M. J. Quinn. *Data-Parallel Programming*. Scientific and Engineering Computation Series. MIT Press, Cambridge, MA, 1991.

[HQA+91] P. J. Hatcher, M. J. Quinn, R. J. Anderson, A. J. Lapadula, B. K. Seevers, and A. F. Bennett. Architecture-independent scientific programming in Dataparallel C: Three case studies. In *Supercomputing '91 Proceedings*, 1991.

[HQL+91] P. J. Hatcher, M. J. Quinn, A. J. Lapadula, B. K. Seevers, R. J. Anderson, and R. R. Jones. Data-parallel programming on MIMD computers. *IEEE Transactions on Parallel and Distributed Systems*, July 1991.

[HS86] W. D. Hillis and G. L. Steele. Data parallel algorithms. *Communication of the ACM*, 29(12):1170–1183, December 1986.

[Int92a] Intel Corporation. *iPSC/860 C Compiler User's Guide*. Order Number: 312130-002. 1992.

[Int92b] Intel Corporation. *iPSC/860 System User's Guide*. 1992.

[ISO91] ISO/ODE. *Information Technology—Programming Languages—Fortran*. Reference Number ISO/IEC 1539:1991 (E). 1991.

[Kar87] A. H. Karp. Programming for parallelism. *IEEE Computer*, 20(9):43–57, May 1987.

[Ken81] K. Kennedy. *A Survey of Data-Flow Analysis Techniques*. Prentice-Hall, Englewood Cliffs, NJ, 1981.

[LER92] T. G. Lewis and H. El-Rewini. *Introduction to Parallel Computing*. Prentice-Hall, Englewood Cliffs, NJ, 1992.

[Les93] B. P. Lester. *The Art of Parallel Programming*. Prentice-Hall, Englewood Cliffs, NJ, 1993.

[LYZ89] Z. Li, P. C. Yew, and C. Q. Zhu. Data dependence analysis on multidimensional array references. In *ACM International Conference on Supercomputing*, 1989.

[Mas91] MasPar Computer Corporation. *MasPar Parallel Application Language (MPL)*. Document Part Number: 9302-0100, Software Version 2.1. 1991.

[Mas92a] MasPar Computer Corporation. *MasPar MP-1 and MP-2 Architecture Specification*. Document Part Number: 9300-5001. 1992.

[Mas92b] MasPar Computer Corporation. *MasPar Programming Language (ANSI C compatible MPL)*. Document Part Number: 9302-0001, Software Version 3.0. 1992.

[Mes93] Message Passing Interface Forum. *Document for a Standard Message-Passing Paradigm (Draft)*. August 1993.

[nCU90] nCUBE Corporation. *nCUBE 2 Programmer's Guide*. Beaverton, OR. 1990.

[Par90] Parasoft Corporation. *Express C User's Guide*. Version 3.0 edition. 1990.

[Pol87] C. D. Polychronopoulos. Loop coalescing: A compiler transformation for parallel machine. In *Proceedings of the 1987 International Conference on Parallel Processing*, 1987.

[Pol88a] C. D. Polychronopoulos. *Parallel Programming and Compilers*. Kluwer Academic Publishers, Boston, MA, 1988.

[Pol88b] C. D. Polychronopoulos. Toward auto-scheduling compilers. *The Journal of Supercomputing*, 1988.

[Pol90] C. D. Polychronopoulos. The structure of Parafase-2: An advanced parallelizing compiler for C and Fortran. In *Languages and Compilers for Parallel Computing, Research Monographs in Parallel and Distributed Computing*. MIT Press, Cambridge, MA, 1990.

[Pou86] D. Pountain. *A Tutorial Introduction to OCCAM Programming*. INMOS Corporation. England. 1986.

[QH90] M. J. Quinn and P. J. Hatcher. Compiling SIMD programs for MIMD architectures. In *Proceedings of the 1990 International Conference on Computer Languages*, 291–296, 1990.

[RS87] J. R. Rose and G. L. Steele. C*: An extended C language for data parallel programming. Technical Report TR PL 87–5, Thinking Machines Corporation, Cambridge, MA, 1987.

[RSW90] M. Rosing, R. B. Schnabel, and R. P. Weaver. The DINO parallel programming language. Technical Report CU-CS-501-90, Computer Science Department, University of Colorado at Boulder, Boulder, CO, 1990.

[Sha89] E. Shapiro. The family of concurrent logic programming languages. *ACM Computing Surveys*, 21(3):413–510, September 1989.

[Sun90] V. S. Sunderam. PVM: A framework for parallel distributed computing. *Concurrency: Practice and Experience*, 2(4):315–339, December 1990.

[TAAT84] Y. Tsujino, M. Ando, T. Araki, and N. Tokura. Concurrent C: A programming language for distributed systems. *Software Practical Experience*, 14(11):1061–1078, November 1984.

[Thi90a] Thinking Machines Corporation. *C* Programming Guide, Version 6.0*. Cambridge, MA. 1990.

[Thi90b] Thinking Machines Corporation. **Lisp Programming Guide*. Cambridge, MA. 1990.

[Thi91] Thinking Machines Corporation. *CM Fortran Reference Manual*. Version 1.0 and 1.1. Cambridge, MA. 1991.

[Thi92a] Thinking Machines Corporation. *CMMD Reference Manual*. Version 2.0 Beta. Cambridge, MA. 1992.

[Thi92b] Thinking Machines Corporation. *CMMD User's Guide*. Version 2.0 Beta. Cambridge, MA. 1992.

[Thi92c] Thinking Machines Corporation. *The Connection Machine CM-5 Technical Summary*. Cambridge, MA. 1992.

[WB87] M. Wolfe and U. Banerjee. Data dependence and its application in parallel processing. *International Journal of Parallel Programming*, 16(2), April 1987.

[Wol86] M. Wolfe. Loop skewing: The wavefront method revisited. *International Journal of Parallel Programming*, 15(4), 1986.

[Wol89] M. Wolfe. Optimizing supercompilers for supercomputers. In *Research Monographs in Parallel and Distributed Computing*. MIT Press, Cambridge, MA, 1989.

[ZBG88] H. P. Zima, H. J. Bast, and M. Gerndt. SUPERB: A tool for semi-auto MIMD/SIMD parallelization. *Parallel Computing*, 6:1–18, 1988.

[ZC91] H. P. Zima and B. Chapman. *Supercompilers for Parallel and Vector Computers*. Frontier Series. ACM Press, New York, NY, 1991.

APPENDIX **A**

Complexity of Functions and Order Analysis

Order analysis and the asymptotic complexity of functions are used extensively in this book to analyze the performance of algorithms.

A.1 Complexity of Functions

When analyzing parallel algorithms in this book, we use the following three types of functions:

(1) **Exponential functions:** A function f from reals to reals is called an ***exponential*** function in x if it can be expressed in the form $f(x) = a^x$ for $x, a \in \Re$ (the set of real numbers) and $a > 1$. Examples of exponential functions are 2^x, 1.5^{x+2}, and $3^{1.5x}$.

(2) **Polynomial functions:** A function f from reals to reals is called a ***polynomial*** function of ***degree*** b in x if it can be expressed in the form $f(x) = x^b$ for $x, b \in \Re$ and $b > 0$. A ***linear*** function is a polynomial function of degree one and a ***quadratic*** function is a polynomial function of degree two. Examples of polynomial functions are 2, $5x$, and $5.5x^{2.3}$.
A function f that is a sum of two polynomial functions g and h is also a polynomial function whose degree is equal to the maximum of the degrees of g and h. For example, $2x + x^2$ is a polynomial function of degree two.

(3) **Logarithmic functions:** A function f from reals to reals that can be expressed in the form $f(x) = \log_b x$ for $b \in \Re$ and $b > 1$ is ***logarithmic*** in x. In this expression, b is called the ***base*** of the logarithm. Examples of logarithmic

functions are $\log_{1.5} x$ and $\log_2 x$. Unless stated otherwise, all logarithms in this book are of base two. We use $\log x$ to denote $\log_2 x$, and $\log^2 x$ to denote $(\log_2 x)^2$.

Most functions in this book can be expressed as sums of two or more functions. A function f is said to ***dominate*** a function g if $f(x)$ grows at a faster rate than $g(x)$. Thus, function f dominates function g if and only if $f(x)/g(x)$ is a monotonically increasing function in x. In other words, f dominates g if and only if for any constant $c > 0$, there exists a value x_0 such that $f(x) > cg(x)$ for $x > x_0$. An exponential function dominates a polynomial function and a polynomial function dominates a logarithmic function. The relation *dominates* is transitive. If function f dominates function g, and function g dominates function h, then function f also dominates function h. Thus, an exponential function also dominates a logarithmic function.

A.2 Order Analysis of Functions

In the analysis of algorithms, it is often cumbersome or impossible to derive exact expressions for parameters such as run time, speedup, and efficiency. In many cases, an approximation of the exact expression is adequate. The approximation may indeed be more illustrative of the behavior of the function because it focuses on the critical factors influencing the parameter.

Example A.1 Distances Traveled by Three Cars
Consider three cars A, B, and C. Assume that we start monitoring the cars at time $t = 0$. At $t = 0$, car A is moving at a velocity of 1000 feet per second and maintains a constant velocity. At $t = 0$, car B's velocity is 100 feet per second and it is accelerating at a rate of 20 feet per second per second. Car C starts from a standstill at $t = 0$ and accelerates at a rate of 25 feet per second per second. Let $D_A(t)$, $D_B(t)$, and $D_C(t)$ represent the distances traveled in t seconds by cars A, B, and C. From elementary physics, we know that

$$
\begin{aligned}
D_A(t) &= 1000t, \\
D_B(t) &= 100t + 20t^2, \\
D_C(t) &= 25t^2.
\end{aligned}
$$

Now, we compare the cars according to the distance they travel in a given time. For $t > 45$ seconds, car B outperforms car A. Similarly, for $t > 20$ seconds, car C outperforms car B, and for $t > 40$ seconds, car C outperforms car A. Furthermore, $D_C(t) < 1.25 D_B(t)$ and $D_B(t) < D_C(t)$ for $t > 20$, which implies that after a certain time, the difference in the performance of cars B and C is bounded by the other scaled by a constant multiplicative factor. All these facts can be captured by the order analysis of the expressions. ■

The Θ Notation: From Example A.1, $D_C(t) < 1.25D_B(t)$ and $D_B(t) < D_C(t)$ for $t > 20$; that is, the difference in the performance of cars B and C after $t = 0$ is bounded by the other scaled by a constant multiplicative factor. Such an equivalence in performance is often significant when analyzing performance. The Θ notation captures the relationship between these two functions. The functions $D_C(t)$ and $D_B(t)$ can be expressed by using the Θ notation as $D_C(t) = \Theta(D_B(t))$ and $D_B(t) = \Theta(D_C(t))$. Furthermore, both functions are equal to $\Theta(t^2)$.

Formally, the Θ notation is defined as follows: given a function $g(x)$, $f(x) = \Theta(g(x))$ if and only if for any constants $c_1, c_2 > 0$, there exists an $x_0 \geq 0$, such that $c_1 g(x) \leq f(x) \leq c_2 g(x)$ for all $x \geq x_0$.

The O Notation: Often, we would like to bound the growth of a particular parameter by a simpler functions. From Example A.1 we have seen that for $t > 45$, $D_B(t)$ is always greater than $D_A(t)$. This relation between $D_A(t)$ and $D_B(t)$ is expressed using the O (big-oh) notation as $D_A(t) = O(D_B(t))$.

Formally, the O notation is defined as follows: given a function $g(x)$, $f(x) = O(g(x))$ if and only if for any constant $c > 0$, their exists an $x_0 \geq 0$, such that $f(x) \leq cg(x)$ for all $x \geq x_0$. From this definition we deduce that $D_A(t) = O(t^2)$ and $D_B(t) = O(t^2)$. Furthermore, $D_A(t) = O(t)$ also satisfies the conditions of the O notation.

The Ω Notation: The O notation sets an upper bound on the rate of growth of a function. The Ω notation is the converse of O notation; that is, it sets a lower bound on the rate of growth of a function. From Example A.1, $D_A(t) < D_C(t)$ for $t > 40$. This relationship can be expressed using the Ω notation as $D_C(t) = \Omega(D_A(t))$.

Formally, given a function $g(x)$, $f(x) = \Omega(g(x))$ if and only if for any constant $c > 0$, there exists an $x_0 \geq 0$, such that $f(x) \geq cg(x)$ for all $x \geq x_0$.

Properties of Functions Expressed in Order Notation

The order notations for expressions have a number of properties that are useful when analyzing the performance of algorithms. Some of the important properties are as follows:

(1) $x^a = O(x^b)$ if and only if $a \leq b$.
(2) $\log_a(x) = \Theta(\log_b(x))$ for all a and b.
(3) $a^x = O(b^x)$ if and only if $a \leq b$.
(4) For any constant c, $c = O(1)$.
(5) If $f = O(g)$ then $f + g = O(g)$.
(6) If $f = \Theta(g)$ then $f + g = \Theta(g) = \Theta(f)$.
(7) $f = O(g)$ if and only if $g = \Omega(f)$.
(8) $f = \Theta(g)$ if and only if $f = \Omega(g)$ and $f = O(g)$.

Author Index

Subject Index

Copyright Permissions

Some figures and part of the text in Chapter 4 originally appeared in the article "Isoefficiency Function: A Scalability Metric for Parallel Algorithms and Architectures" in *IEEE Parallel and Distributed Technology*, August 1993. The material is reprinted here by permission of the publisher, IEEE.

Part of the text in Chapter 8 originally appeared in the article "Scalable Load Balancing Techniques for Parallel Computers" in the *Journal of Distributed and Parallel Computing*, 1994. The material is reprinted here by permission of the publisher, Academic Press, Inc.

Part of the text in Chapter 8 originally appeared in the article "Parallel Depth-First Search, Part II: Analysis" in the *International Journal of Parallel Programming*, December 1987, volume 16, number 6, pages 501–519. The material is reprinted here by permission of the publisher, Plenum Press.

Some figures and part of the text in Chapter 10 originally appeared in the article "Scalability of FFT on Parallel Computers" in *IEEE Transactions on Parallel and Distributed Systems*, July 1993, volume 4, number 7. The material is reprinted here by permission of the publisher, IEEE.

Part of the text in Chapter 11 originally appeared in the article "Performance and Scalability of Preconditioned Conjugate Gradient Method on the CM-5" in the *Proceedings of the Sixth SIAM Conference on Parallel Processing for Scientific Computing*, March 1993, pages 664–674. The material is reprinted here by permission of the publisher, SIAM.

Some figures and part of the text in Chapter 12 originally appeared in the article "Efficient Parallel Mappings of a Dynamic Programming Algorithm: A Summary of Results" in the *Proceedings of 7th International Parallel Processing Symposium*, 1993, pages 563–568. The material is reprinted here by permission of the publisher, IEEE.

Trademark Notices

CDC Cyberplus is a trademark of Control Data Corporation.
CM-2, CM-5, C*, *Lisp, and CM Fortran are trademarks of Thinking Machines Corporation.
DAP and DAP 610 are trademarks of Advanced Memory Technology.
Dash is a trademark of Stanford University.
DYNIX and Symmetry are trademarks of Sequent Computers Systems, Inc.
FX-8 and FX-2800 are trademarks of Alliant Corporation.
Illiac IV is a trademark of University of Illinois.
iPSC, iPSC-1, iPSC-2, iPSC-860, i860, and Paragon XP/S are trademarks of Intel Corporation.
J-Machine is a trademark of Massachusetts Institute of Technology.
KSR-1 is a trademark of Kendall Square Research.
MPP is a trademark of Goodyear Corporation.
MasPar MP-1 and MP-2 are trademarks of MasPar Computer Corporation.
Mosaic C and The Cosmic Cube are trademarks of California Institute of Technology.
Multimax is a trademark of Encore Computer Corporation.
NYU Ultracomputer is a trademark of New York University.
nCUBE 2 is a trademark of nCUBE Corporation.
ParaScope is a trademark of Rice University.
RP3 is a trademark of International Business Machines.
SPARC is a trademark of Sun Microsystems.
TC-2000 is a trademark of BBN Advanced Computers.
Tera is a trademark of Tera Computer Systems.
Unix is a trademark of AT&T Bell Labs.
VPP500 is a trademark of Fujitsu Ltd.
Y-MP and T3D are trademarks of Cray Research, Inc.